THE CHRONICLE OF THE ŁÓDŹ GHETTO, 1941–1944

THE CHRONICLE OF THE ŁÓDŹ GHETTO 1941-1944

EDITED BY LUCJAN DOBROSZYCKI

TRANSLATED BY RICHARD LOURIE, JOACHIM NEUGROSCHEL, AND OTHERS

YALE UNIVERSITY PRESS
NEW HAVEN AND LONDON

The English edition of *The Chronicle of the Łódź Ghetto*
has been prepared with the assistance and
cooperation of the Eastern European Jewish History
Translation and Publication Fund established by Lawrence Newman.

Designed by Sally Harris
and set in Zapf Book type by Composing Room of Michigan, Inc.
Printed in the United States of America by
Vail-Ballou Press, Binghamton, New York.

Library of Congress Cataloging in Publication Data

Main entry under title:

The Chronicle of the Łódź ghetto, 1941–1944.

   Includes index.
   1. Jews—Poland Łódź—Persecutions.   2. Holocaust,
Jewish (1939–1945)—Poland—Łódź—Personal narratives.
3. Łódź (Poland)—Ethnic relations.   I. Dobroszycki, Lucjan.
DS135.P62L627   1984   943.8'4   84-3614
ISBN 0-300-03208-0

10   9   8   7   6   5   4   3

CONTENTS

ACKNOWLEDGMENTS

Utterly cut off from the rest of the world, the authors of the *Chronicle* of the Łódź ghetto did not know when, or even if, their work would appear in print, although they made frequent reference to their "future reader." Today, exactly forty years after the chroniclers made their final entry, the *Chronicle* is appearing in English translation. This could not have come about without the help of many good people both here and in Europe, a few of whom I would like to mention by name.

My dear friend and fellow historian, Adam Kersten of Warsaw, who died suddenly and prematurely last year, begrudged me neither his time nor his energy when, before my departure from Poland for the United States, he spent many weeks micro-filming the archives I had amassed over the course of many years' labor. It is always with affection that I remember Władysław Bartoszewski, a professor at the Catholic University in Lublin and Jerzy Jedlicki of the Institute of History at the Polish Acade-my of Sciences, both friends of mine who aided in putting my papers in order when I was closing my apartment in Warsaw. Neither can I forget my Danish friend, Helge Tønnesen of the Royal Library of Copenhagen, who, during several trips to Warsaw, took the greater part of my notes on the Łódź ghetto with him for safekeeping.

I feel a special gratitude toward my American friend, Lawrence Newman, a New York City lawyer and professor of law. It was he who for many years, while attending my tutorial classes in the history of the Polish Jews at YIVO's Max Weinreich Center, assisted me in all aspects of the work on the *Chronicle* and who, by establishing the Translation and Publication Fund, created the conditions that made the English edition possible.

I carried out all the work on the English edition of the *Chronicle* at the YIVO Institute for Jewish Research, which, with its invaluable library and archives, has become a second home for me. And thus I am immeasurably grateful to all my colleagues at YIVO and particularly to Dina Abramowicz, the head of the library, and to Marek Web, the Chief Archivist, for their daily kindness and cooperation.

I owe special thanks to Nachman Zonabend for making available to me his collec-tion of documents and photographs on the Łódź ghetto.

I should also like to thank Richard Lourie, who, with his characteristic respect for his own language and that of the original, translated the Polish text of the *Chronicle* as well as the introduction and footnotes that I wrote for this edition.

vii

Here too is an opportunity to express my appreciation to the staff of Yale University Press and especially to Maura Shaw Tantillo, Charlotte Dihoff, and Tülin Duda, for their scrupulous attention to the editorial quality of this book.

Finally, allow me to thank my wife, Felicja, and my daughter, Joanna, for their constant support of my work and also for the patience they have always shown me, at times more than I deserved.

New York City, 1984   L. D.

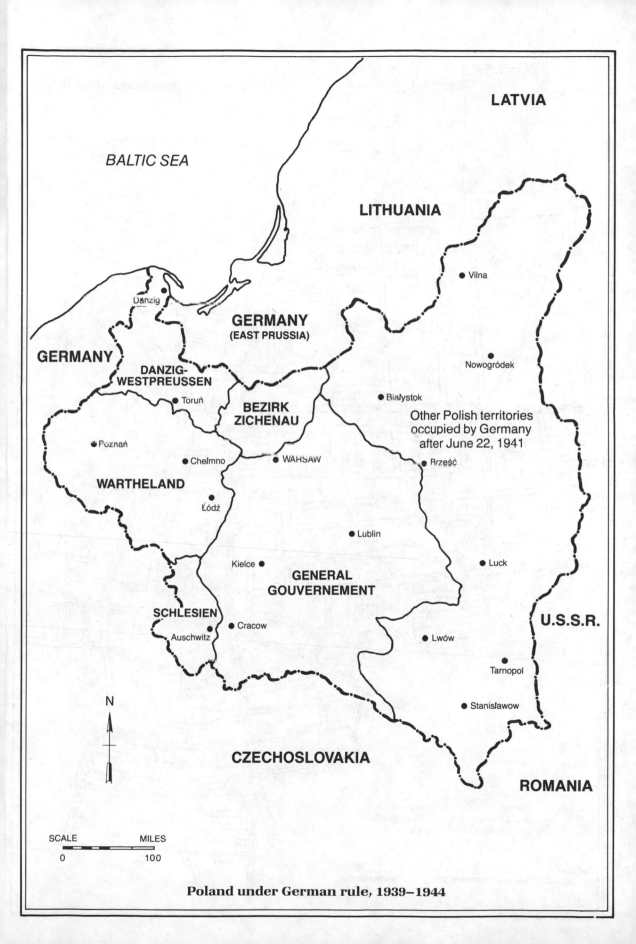

Poland under German rule, 1939–1944

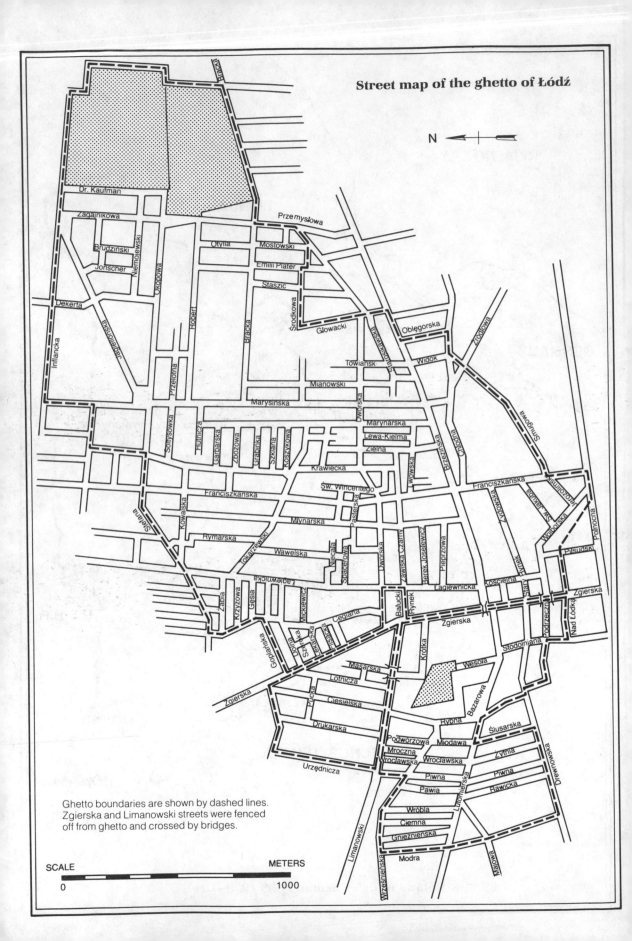

Street map of the ghetto of Łódź

N

Ghetto boundaries are shown by dashed lines.
Zgierska and Limanowski streets were fenced
off from ghetto and crossed by bridges.

SCALE   METERS

0   1000

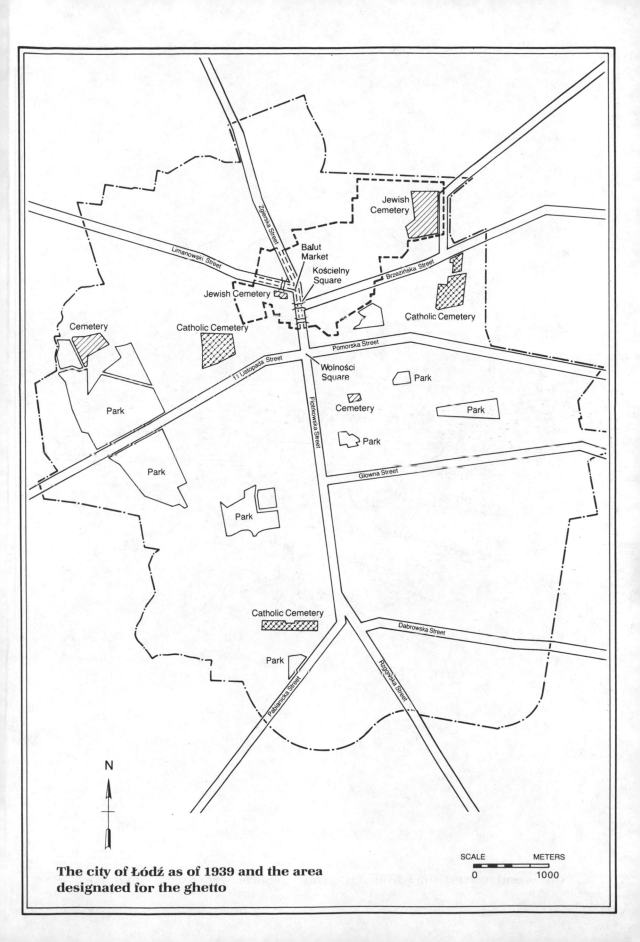

The city of Łódź as of 1939 and the area
designated for the ghetto

N

SCALE   METERS
0   1000

Jewish
Cemetery

Limanowski Street

Zgierska Street

Bałut
Market

Kościelny
Square

Jewish Cemetery

Brzezińska Street

Catholic Cemetery

Cemetery

Catholic Cemetery

Pomorska Street

11 Listopada Street

Wolności
Square

Fichtkowska Street

Park

Cemetery

Park

Park

Park

Park

Glowna Street

Park

Park

Catholic Cemetery

Park

Dabrowska Street

Pabianicka Street

Rzgowska Street

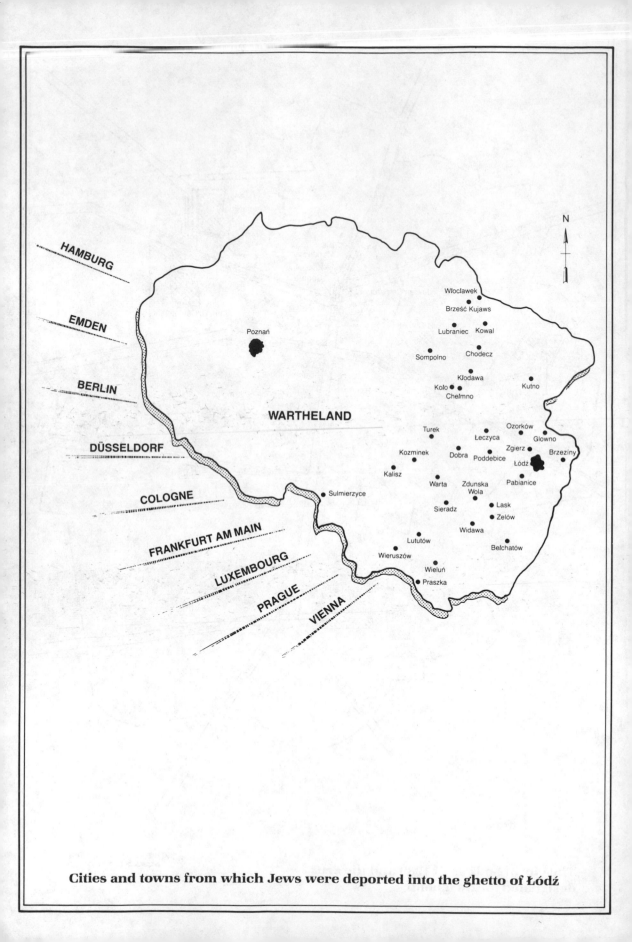

Cities and towns from which Jews were deported into the ghetto of Łódź

INTRODUCTION

THE CHRONICLE AND ITS AUTHORS

It was Monday, May 4, 1942. The chroniclers of the Łódź ghetto recorded the events of the day just as they had the previous day, a year ago that day, and even earlier. As usual, they began with the weather. The remaining information they treated point by point, assigning a heading to each news item. That day there were eleven items, ranging in significance from the crucial to what could, given the times, be considered minor. To take but examples of the former, on that day the *Chronicle* reported that, in the Łódź ghetto, 61 people died whereas there were no births; for reasons known only to itself, three days before, on May 1, a German medical commission stamped letters on the chests of 1,200 people; at 8 o'clock in the morning the first transport of 1,000 people, which included Western European Jews who had arrived in the Łódź ghetto scarcely six months before, departed from a sidetrack for a destination unknown to anyone in the ghetto. Baggage, knapsacks, and even hand-carried packages were being taken from the deportees; in fear of deportation, 60-year-old Julia Baum from Frankfurt am Main committed suicide by hanging herself. . . .

The *Chronicle* of the Łódź ghetto is moving in its simplicity and, at the same time, constitutes a document of immense historical significance. The wealth of information it contains, the accuracy of its record, and the systematic manner in which it was compiled make the *Chronicle* a source unparalleled among writings on the destruction of European Jews during the Second World War. Unlike many personal accounts of that time, the *Chronicle* was not only written on a day-to-day basis, but the facts and events it describes are based on first-hand information or on documents that also came into being from day to day. This was largely due to the fact that the *Chronicle* was composed by an institution which had official access, as it were, to nearly all of the ghetto's internal records, that institution being the Archives of the Eldest of the Jews in the Łódź ghetto.

The Archives—or the Department of Archives, to use its official name—was founded on the strength of a decision by Mordecai Chaim Rumkowski, the Eldest of the Jews, on November 17, 1940, as the fifth in a series of sections of the so-called departments of population records of the Łódź ghetto.[1] Aside from the Archives,

---

1. Archiwum Żydowskiego Instytutu Historycznego (The Archives of the Jewish Historical Institute), Warsaw (henceforth: AZIH [AJHI]), M. C. Rumkowski Records (henceforth: Rum. Records), no. 470.

these interconnected institutions included the Registration Bureau, the Department of Statistics, the Department of Vital Statistics, the Rabbinical Bureau, and a photography workshop, which was set up somewhat later.[2] All these sections were headed by Henryk Neftalin, an attorney who helped organize many of the ghetto's other administrative branches and who was a confidant of M. C. Rumkowski.[3]

Initially, the Archives was located at 4 Miodowa Street and then was transferred, along with all the other departments of population records, to 4 Kościelny Square. In its new location the Archives occupied a sequestered room with an entrance of its own. Of course the other departments of the ghetto's Jewish administration were aware that the Archives was one of the many offices and institutions of the Eldest of the Jews: correspondence from the Archives carried interoffice stamps and seals. The German Ghetto Administration also was obviously aware of the Archives.[4] There was, however, a tendency to keep the existence and especially the activities of the Archives hidden, particularly in order to screen its location from the German authorities and the various Nazi commissions that inspected the ghetto.[5]

The Archives was originally founded to preserve archival materials from both the former pre-war Jewish community and those offices that had arisen in the ghetto but that, for one reason or another, had ceased to function.[6] In the course of time, however, the Archives' range of activity expanded considerably: it began to amass information for a history of the Łódź ghetto. The guiding principle in this deliberate undertaking was, as defined by Henryk Neftalin, to create a basis of source materials "for future scholars studying the life of a Jewish society in one of its most difficult periods."[7]

2. Archives of the YIVO Institute for Jewish Research, New York (henceforth: YIVO Archives), Nachman Zonabend Collection (henceforth: Zon.), no. 733.

3. A young legal apprentice before the war, Henryk Neftalin was undoubtedly one of the most interesting figures among the high-ranking officials in the Jewish administration. A titan of work and a brilliant organizer, he was known to practically no one, apart, of course, from a sizable group of co-workers in the departments under his jurisdiction and some of the intellectuals in the Łódź ghetto, whom he attempted to help as much as he could, often by finding occupations for them or by providing them with financial aid. Jakub Szulman, a well-known figure in the Labor Zionist party in Poland before the war, described H. Neftalin in a memoir written in the ghetto: "He is a quiet, modest, industrious person. He attracted people's attention and their affection. Moreover, he was one of the few people in the ghetto whose head was not turned by high office. An honest man without pretension, he was concerned with the good of the ghetto and its people" (p. 41). The original memoir, written in Yiddish with notes in Russian, can be found in the Archives of the Ghetto Beit Lohamei Haghetaot Fighters' House, Israel (henceforth: Szulman, Memoir).

4. The Archives was included in the official scheme for the ghetto, which was known to the German authorities. It is also known that the circulars and orders amassed in the Archives were sometimes put to use by the ghetto's Jewish administration for purposes that included providing duplicates to the German Department of Statistics (*Statistisches Amt*) in Łódź, AZIH (AJHI), Rum. Records, no. 2118.

5. Bernard Ostrowski, one of the archivists, characterizes the Archives as semi-clandestine in his report to the Centralna Żydowska Komiscja Historyczna (The Central Jewish Historical Commission) in Łódź in 1947, AZIH (AJHI), Report no. 2841. Ostrowski spoke more fully about working conditions in the Archives when we met in the spring and summer of 1967 in Israel.

6. The degree of continuity in the Archives' activity is evidenced by, among others, a document dated July 19, 1944, that is, less than two weeks before the final liquidation of the ghetto. This document is a listing of the accounts of the quilt and pillow workshop (*Steppdecken u. Kissen Betrieb*) for the years 1942–44, which were submitted to the Archives (YIVO Archives, Zon. no. 733). The raw materials (down and feathers) used in the workshop had been confiscated from Jews during the liquidation of Jewish settlements in *Wartheland* or upon their arrival in the death camp in Chełmno.

7. From the speech delivered by Neftalin on the first anniversary of the founding of the Archives (AZIH

To that end, the workers in the Archives were granted full authority by Rumkowski to collect materials from all agencies of the Jewish administration. In a memorandum of November 18, 1940, he instructed the agencies to furnish them with all data and documents related to the activities within their purview.[8] The archivists also had the opportunity to conduct interviews with the Jewish administration's leading representatives, and preserved the information thus obtained in written form. Furthermore, valuable information was acquired at the conferences of the directors of the various departments, which were frequently attended by the head of the Archives, who kept the minutes of those meetings.[9]

In a little less than four years the Archives gathered materials from both the German and the Jewish ghetto administrations, including orders, proclamations, memorandums, the texts of speeches, official correspondence of every sort, statistical data, a variety of printed and mimeographed material, photographs, and other visual documentation. It also collected the more valuable books and manuscripts left behind in the ghetto by intellectuals, scholars, and rabbis (those who came from the West, as well as the local population) who had died or been resettled.[10] For example, after the Jews who had been resettled in the ghetto from Germany, Luxembourg, Austria, and Czechoslovakia were deported, the Archives set up a separate file of the documents they left behind. Comprising approximately 2,370 items, this file includes manuscripts, letters, ID's, registration cards, etc., which were cataloged by the Archives— every item was arranged alphabetically, and numbered, and an index of names was drawn up for the whole.[11]

Concurrent with the gathering and assembling of materials in the Archives, there were efforts to produce monographs. At that time the work of the Archives was divided into subjects, such as the history of the ghetto, economic problems, the life of children in the ghetto, questions of religion and culture, and Yiddish and Hebrew literature. Of the works still extant, two monographs deserve particular attention. The first, written in Polish, is concerned with the history of the Jews of Łódź from September, 1939, that is, from the outbreak of the German-Polish war, to the end of May, 1940, when the Łódź ghetto was hermetically sealed off. The second, written in German, contains a history of the ghetto from May, 1940, to the end of that year.[12] The value of these works is increased by the fact that they quote, *in extenso*, documents from the early period of the German occupation of Łódź, which have not been

---

[AJHI], Rum. Records, no. 2113]. This was stressed even earlier by Józef Klomontynowski, the first director of the Archives. In a letter he wrote to Rumkowski on November 16, 1940, on his acceptance for work in the Archives that was to be created, he stated: "I fully appreciate the far-reaching significance of this treasure house for historians of the future" (Ibid., no. 2118).

8. A certificate made out on November 25, 1940, in the name of J. Klementynowski, refers to this memorandum; see also the document of authorization, of April 15, 1941, for the other Archives workers, ibid., no. 2118.

9. The minutes and reports of Rumkowski's various meetings with representatives of the Jewish administration or from the sessions of specially created committees, ibid., no. 2115.

10. Cf., for example, the letter to Józef Zelkowicz authorizing him to safeguard the library of Rabbi Eliahu Treistman, June 16, 1942, YIVO Archives, Zon. no. 943.

11. AZIH (AJHI), Rum. Records, no. 2118.

12. "Historia getta Litzmannstadt [Łódź]. Cześć pierwsza: Z miasta do getta" (History of the Litzmannstadt [Łódź] ghetto. Part one: From the city to the ghetto), ibid., no. 2110, and, "Das Getto in Litzmannstadt" [Łódź], ibid., a copy of which is in the YIVO Archives.

preserved. Another item of value is the so-called Lexicon compiled by the Archives, which provides detailed biographical data on high-ranking officials in the Jewish administration and prominent personalities in the Łódź ghetto, as well as information about the administration's agencies.[13] Some of the Lexicon's entries contain information about various aspects of the ghetto's life, customs, and language, including the singular words that developed under the wartime conditions in a Jewish community. Of value too are articles about certain institutions and workshops, sketches and essays on selected problems of the day, such as hunger in the ghetto and the food distribution system, housing conditions, and the role of the courtyard in the closed Jewish quarter.[14] And, finally, the Archives gave rise to the *Chronicle*, undoubtedly its most comprehensive project.[15]

The *Chronicle*, like nearly all the other work performed in the Archives, was a group effort in which everyone employed there took part. Moreover, this group of people worked well and harmoniously together, despite differences in age, education, previous profession, country of origin, and language, not to mention differences in world view. What united them was their common fate and their awareness of a common goal. Brief biographical sketches of the leading authors of the *Chronicle* follow.[16]

Julian Cukier (1900–43), journalist and publicist, came of a prominent, well-known family of Polish Jews. His father, Ludwik Cukier, a Łódź industrialist, was a distinguished representative of the Jewish Community and on the boards of many institutions, including the oldest charitable organization in Łódź, Gemiluth Hasadim, and the Montefiore lodge of B'nai B'rith. Until the outbreak of the war, Julian Cukier, under the pen name of Stanisław Cerski, was a contributor to *Republika*, a liberal daily paper in Łódź which was also a syndicate that published many Polish periodicals with nation-wide circulation. In the ghetto, Cukier began working in the Archives as soon as it was founded in November, 1940. Called the Plutarch of the ghetto by colleagues, he initiated the writing of the *Chronicle* and guided the enterprise until lung disease forced him to cease working. He died on April 7, 1943.[17]

Szmul Hecht (1923–43) was a native of Wieluń, a town to the southwest of Łódź. He was resettled to the Łódź ghetto during the total liquidation of Jewish settlements in

---

13. Lexicon of the ghetto, AZIH (AJHI), Rum. Records, unnumbered.

14. Essays and reportage, ibid., nos. 2111–13.

15. The chronicle has been a well-known literary genre since Biblical times, but it is noteworthy that in Łódź, before the war, the *kehillah* (*Żydowska Gmina Wyznaniowa*), the Jewish institution of self-government, published a periodical in three languages (Polish, Yiddish, and Hebrew) entitled *Kronika Gminy Żydowskiej* (*Khronik fun der yidisher kehile in Lodzh, Khronika shel ha'kehila ha'ivrit*—The Chronicle of the Jewish Community), 1930–39.

16. Biographical data about the authors of the *Chronicle* is based on published sources, the records of the ghetto Registration Bureau and the Lexicon (AZIH [AJHI], Rum. Records), the private notes of Oskar Rosenfeld, Yad Vashem Archives, Jerusalem, 6/106 (henceforth: Rosenfeld, Private notes), and the *Chronicle* itself. One notes with embarrassment how the authors of the *Chronicle* are all but forgotten today. The names have vanished as have the people themselves. With the exception of Zelkowicz, they are not listed in any postwar encyclopedia, although a number of them—Oskar Rosenfeld, Abram Kamieniecki, Bernard Heilig, Oskar Singer—had many accomplishments to their names long before they were incarcerated in the ghetto of Łódź.

17. In that same year, archivists and *Chronicle* contributors S. Hecht, B. Heilig, and A. S. Kamieniecki also died. Obituaries written by their colleagues appear in the *Chronicle* on April 7, June 22 and 30, and October 12.

the provinces of Łódź, Poznań, and Bydgoszcz (Pomorze-Pomerania) in the summer of 1942.

Dr. Bernard Heilig (1902–43), an outstanding scholar, was a specialist in the economic history of the Jews and the author of many works in that field.[18] These included a comprehensive history of his native city of Prostějov (Prossnitz), one of the oldest Jewish settlements in Moravia, which, with the considerable participation of its Jewish population, became one of Europe's largest producers of textiles and ready-made clothing in the nineteenth and twentieth centuries. Heilig was deported from Prague to the Łódź ghetto in October, 1941.

Dr. Abram S. Kamieniecki (1874–1943) was born in Słonim, in the Jewish Pale of Settlement of the Russian section of partitioned Poland. In addition to the religious and secular education he received in his native city, he studied philosophy and philology at universities in Heidelberg, Berlin and Berne, where he specialized in Biblical studies. Kamieniecki is the author of many scholarly works that, for the most part, were published in the Berlin *Zeitschrift für die Alttestamentarische Wissenschaft*. He was also an author and one of the chief editors of the *Evreiskaia Entsiklopedia* (Jewish Encyclopedia) published in Russian by Brockhaus and Efron in St. Petersburg, in 1906–13. He was very active in the Łódź Jewish community in *interbellum* Poland. One of Kamieniecki's last projects before the outbreak of the war was the sponsorship of an encyclopedic publication in Yiddish entitled *Lodzher gezelshaftlekhkayt: Almanakh* (Almanac of Łódź Society), the first volume of which appeared in 1938, with a preface written by him.

Dr. Oskar Rosenfeld (1884–1944), born in Korycany, Moravia, a graduate of Vienna University, and a writer and publicist, was deported from Prague to the Łódź ghetto in October, 1941. As a youth Rosenfeld became associated with the Zionist movement, and later he worked with Theodor Herzl and Hugon Zuckermann, with whom he collaborated in establishing the first Jewish theater (*jüdische Künstlerspiele*) in Vienna. In the years 1928–38 he was the editor of the Zionist weekly in Vienna, *Die Neue Welt;* after the *Anschluss* he moved to Prague, where he was a correspondent for *The Jewish Chronicle* of London. Rosenfeld authored many books, including *Philipp Otto Runge in der Romantik, Die vierte Galerie* (Vienna, 1910), and *Mendl Ruhig* (Heidelberg, 1914). He also translated into German many classic and contemporary works of Yiddish literature from Mendele Moykher Sforim, Sholom Aleichem and Isaac Leib Peretz to Joseph Opatoshu, H. Leivik (Leyvik Halpern), and Israel Joshua Singer. Rosenfeld's literary activity remained creative and varied in the ghetto, as attested to by both the essays he wrote for the *Chronicle* and his private notes, which, fortunately, have been preserved.

Dr. Oskar Singer (1883–1944), publicist and writer, contributor to many general and Jewish periodicals (among others, *Prager Tagblatt Montag,* and the Zionist magazines *Selbswehr: Jüdisches Volksblatt* and *Jüdische Nachrichten*), he was the author of the anti-Nazi play *Herren der Welt: Zeitstück in 3 Akten* (Refta-Verlag, Prague-Vienna-

18. These include, in addition to those mentioned in the *Chronicle* (see pp. 350–51), the following: *Die tschechoslowakische Konfektionsindustrie* (n.p., 1932); *Eine mahrische Stadt und ihr Getto* (Brunn, 1932); *Aktuelles aus der Geschichte des Hauses Ehrenstamm, 1752–1852* (Brunn, 1934).

Zurich, 1935), the preface to which was written by Walter Tschuppik, a well-known publicist in the thirties. Like Heilig and Rosenfeld, Oskar Singer was deported from Prague to the Łódź ghetto.

Józef Zelkowicz (1897–1944), writer and ethnographer, was born in Konstantynów, a small town near Łódź. At the age of eighteen he was ordained a rabbi, by virtue of the education he had received in his very religious family home and after his graduation from a yeshivah. However, he was never a practicing rabbi. He enrolled in the Normal School, graduation from which enabled him to teach in state schools. But it was writing and the study of history and customs, not teaching, which came to constitute his central interest. At first he wrote in Polish, but from the mid-twenties on he wrote almost exclusively in Yiddish. His articles, essays, and research works were published in nearly all the newspapers and periodicals in Poland and also in the United States (including the *Jewish Daily Forward, Morgen zhurnal,* and the *Amerikaner*). He was also connected early on with the Jewish Research Institute, the Vilna YIVO, and served as a board member of its branch in Łódź. It was while he worked with YIVO that he wrote and published his two major scholarly works: *Der toyt un zayne baglayt-momentn in der yidisher etnografye un folklor* (Death and Its Accompanying Factors in Jewish Ethnography and Folklore)[19] and *A bild funem yidish-gezelshaftlekhn lebn in a poylish shtetl in der 2-ter helft fun 19-tn y'h* (The Image of Jewish Social Life in a Polish *Shtetl* in the Mid-nineteenth Century).[20] Aside from his share in compiling the *Chronicle,* and as part of his work at the Archives, Zelkowicz wrote a series of essays, a stirring account of the deportations in September, 1942, to mention but one, that are of monumental significance for a history of the closed Jewish quarter.[21]

The following people were also employed in the Archives: Alicja de Bunon, Jerachmil Bryman, H. Dumnow, Jaszuńska, M. Nowak, Dr. Halpern, Bernard Ostrowski (an engineer), and Dr. Peter Wertheimer. Thus, the staff of both the Archives and the *Chronicle* was not large, numbering barely ten to fifteen persons, including the assistants. The staff was initially directed by Dr. Józef Klementynowski, who, after assuming another position in the Jewish ghetto administration, was replaced by Dr. Oskar Singer as Head of Archives.

Like other office workers, the archivists were permanent employees whose salaries were determined by the Jewish ghetto administration. Although they received a supplementary food allocation, the hunger that reigned throughout the ghetto decimated the ranks of the Archives' workers as well. Three of them, Cukier, Hecht, and Heilig, died in the prime of life, like many other people in the ghetto. The others shared the fate of the Jewish quarter during the total liquidation of the ghetto in August, 1944. Only one of them, Bernard Ostrowski, survived the war.

On January 12, 1941, something less than two months after the Archives was founded, the first of the *Chronicle*'s bulletins was written. After that the *Chronicle* was

19. *Lodzher visnshaftlekhe shriftn* 1 (1938), pp. 149–90.

20. Ibid., pp. 191–215.

21. Fragments of Józef Zelkowicz's essays and reportage were published by Isaiah Trunk in *Lodzher geto* [The Łódź Ghetto] (New York: Yad Vashem—YIVO Institute for Jewish Research, 1962), pp. 139–41, 148–50, 195–200, 203–04, 314–27, 424–28, 440–44, 451–54; and by Lucy S. Dawidowicz in *A Holocaust Reader* (New York: Behrman House, 1976), pp. 298–316.

produced systematically with entries written nearly every day until the first half of 1944. The *Chronicle* would first be written out in longhand, then five or six carbon copies were typed on longer than standard-sized paper. All told, the *Chronicle* consists of about 1,000 bulletins ranging in size from half a page to ten or even more in length. Although, like the other material in the Archives, not all of the bulletins of the *Chronicle* have survived,[22] one may safely assume on the basis of the sequence of numbered bulletins, an analysis of their contents, and their chronological order that the gaps are not great and do not exceed five to ten percent of the whole.

From January 12, 1941, to September 1, 1942, the *Chronicle* was written in Polish and called *Biuletyn Kroniki Codziennej* (Daily Chronicle Bulletin), and then, from September, 1942, to July 30, 1944, it was written in German and called *Tageschronik* (the Daily Chronicle). For a short time—from September to December, 1942—the *Chronicle* was written simultaneously in both languages, Polish and German, the former by a team of writers from Łódź, the latter by deportees from the West.[23]

The principal author of the *Chronicle* in Polish was Julian Cukier, with the collaboration of Abram S. Kamieniecki and Bernard Ostrowski. This is basically a daily, though sometimes individual bulletins will describe a few days or even periods of two weeks or a month.[24] Every event is, however, noted under its proper date. Only in rare instances—when entries are included at significantly later dates—do the authors violate chronological order in the narrative, and those entries usually represent a continuation of some previously described incident.

As opposed to the Polish version, the German Tageschronik bulletins, written chiefly by Oskar Singer, with the aid of Alicja de Bunon, Bernard Heilig, Oskar Rosenfeld, and Peter Wertheimer, were strictly daily accounts: a given issue of the bulletin corresponded to a given day (with only a few exceptions, such as the entry covering December 1–19, 1942) and were consistently and consecutively numbered according to the calendar.

As a collective work, the *Chronicle* is, obviously, not uniform either in structure or style. The differences are especially apparent when the Polish and German texts are compared. The latter is more laconic and uniform and therefore more lucid, although at times, curiously enough, it also seems detached.

22. It will probably never be possible to determine what percentage of the Archives' materials is represented by those that have been found. Thus far, only two large finds are known to have survived. The first batch of materials was found and safeguarded according to instructions given by Bernard Ostrowski and passed along by Nachman Zonabend, who succeeded in evading deportation and remained on the grounds of the ghetto until its liberation in January, 1945. The second batch of materials was retrieved in October, 1946, from where it had been hidden underground in Łódź at 13 Lutomierska St., the site of the Fire Department in the ghetto. The work of unearthing the documents was performed by the Central Jewish Historical Commission of Łódź and supervised by Dr. Józef Kermisz, who at that time was the director of the archival section. It is also known that a third batch was buried at the Jewish cemetery in September, 1944, the same time that the materials were buried at 13 Lutomierska St. The Germans, however, succeeded in tracking down that batch and forced the director of the cemetery to reveal its hiding place, see Bernard Ostrowski, AZIH (AJHI), Report no. 2841; *Dos naye lebn* (Łódź), October 4, November 28, 1946. Recollections of Nachman Zonabend, with whom I had the opportunity to speak over the years in Warsaw, Stockholm, and New York.

23. The original typed text of the Biuletyn Kroniki Codziennej and Tageschronik is in the Jewish Historical Institute in Warsaw.

24. A typical *Chronicle* entry began with the words: "Today, at 5:30 A.M." . . ., "Yesterday, in the evening hours" . . ., "This morning" . . ., "Around 6:00 P.M." or "A few minutes after 8:00 A.M. . . ."

However, in both the Polish and German versions, the *Chronicle* is marked by a consistent formal and thematic structure. Individual bulletins which belong to nearly the same series relate the events of a given day and also whatever struck the chronicler as worthy of mention. Every fact and event is, as mentioned previously, entered under an appropriate title or heading. In time, those headings became fixed and were used repeatedly, their subjects necessarily recurrent. Such subjects include the weather, the temperature being noted in Celsius, births and deaths (the German version provides up-to-date and accurate population counts for the ghetto on a given day), shootings near the barbed wire fence surrounding the ghetto, suicides, the arrival of food supplies and their rationing to the inhabitants of the ghetto, prices on the black market and incidents of smuggling into the ghetto, matters of public health and disease levels in the ghetto, orders from the German authorities and inspections of the ghetto by various outside commissions, actions taken by the Jewish ghetto administration and its departments and workshops, cultural activities, Jewish holidays and customs in the ghetto, rumors, and, finally, the settling of local Jews and those from the West into the ghetto and their eventual deportation from it.

In addition to accounts of the day's events, the *Chronicle* occasionally contains more discursive articles and essays on topics unconnected to a given date, such as "Necessity is the Mother of Invention," which discusses Henryk Wosk's ideas on finding a use for frozen or rotten potatoes, or "Registration of Christians Residing in the Ghetto," which describes the reasons why this group, albeit a small one, did not leave the Jewish quarter, or, finally, a street scene entitled "*Es geyt a yeke mit a teke*" (There Goes a *Yeke* with a Briefcase), which depicts a local troubadour who formed a duet with a Jew resettled to the ghetto from Vienna and sang songs he himself had composed while the latter accompanied him on the zither or guitar.

While these supplementary articles and essays appeared sporadically at first and, in general, dealt with curiosities or rather incidental topics, later, during that most tragic time, the time of constant deportations to and from the ghetto, they changed character entirely and also began to appear more often. In the Polish version of the *Chronicle*, apart from a notation of place and date, these entries had no special title, while in the German version they came under the heading "Sketches of Ghetto Life" [*Kleine Getto Spiegel*] and were signed with the initials of Oskar Rosenfeld, Oskar Singer, Peter Wertheimer, or Alicja de Bunon. Both types of essay supplement each other and, along with the daily bulletins, make the *Chronicle* a more complete record of the facts, events, and moods of the ghetto.

A VIEW FROM THE INSIDE

The *Chronicle* of the Łódź ghetto, like the other works compiled in the Archives of the Eldest of the Jews, arose under singular circumstances which must be discussed if the document is to be fully understood.

The diaries, memoirs, and chronicles that were written by Jews in the German-occupied countries during World War II were single-handed efforts, usually prompted only by some inner need on the part of the authors,[25] or, needless to say, by the

---

25. I do not at all wish to belittle the significance of the appeals made by many people that the atrocities committed by the German occupier be recorded at once and that documents in that regard be

desire to transmit testimony from the age of extermination to posterity.[26] This type of writing, by nature highly subjective and intimate, was done in secret and would have been dangerous to the author and those around him if exposed. This very fact indicates a conscious choice and a stance by the writer toward the forces and events at work in his world. The deliberateness of the act freed the writer to express himself without constraint, although some instinctively used coded language. However, what did limit the diarist or memoirist during the German occupation was his relative lack of sources of information. Any source that was at all available was taken into account, whether it was official or clandestine in origin or derived from the secretly monitored Allied radio broadcasts.

This was not the case with the *Chronicle* of the Łódź ghetto. The fact that it was compiled in one of the offices of the Jewish ghetto administration had to entail certain limitations as far as both content and approach were concerned. There are at least three limiting factors to consider: first, the degree to which its authors were constrained by the caution dictated by the Germans' daily presence in the ghetto; second, the question of the chroniclers' actual range of knowledge concerning events in the ghetto itself and beyond its limits; third, the relations between the authors of the *Chronicle* and the Jewish ghetto administration in general and Chairman Rumkowski in particular.

The Germans were unaware that the *Chronicle* was being written—its contents leave no doubt in that regard and no document or any other evidence has been found

---

collected. The famous challenge hurled by Szymon Dubnow, the venerable Jewish historian, right before he was deported from the ghetto to a death camp in Riga, and the far-reaching project directed by Emanuel Ringelblum, the founder and head of *Oyneg shabes*, the clandestine archives in the Warsaw ghetto, are but two examples. The point, however, is that this was done nearly everywhere, in the ghettos and camps, by people in hiding, on the "Aryan" side, and in the forests, even without such appeals. The recording and preservation of testimony and the belief that it would some day be deciphered proved to be one of man's indestructible needs.

26. I cannot resist quoting one example here. In January, 1943, when the Jews were being deported from the Warsaw ghetto, Stefan Ernest succeeded in escaping to the "Aryan" side. It would seem that he would have then remained as aloof as possible from the concerns of the Jewish quarter. He did not, however, cease to be a hunted Jew on the other side of the wall. Because of his very Jewish features he was forced constantly to be in hiding, which is where he began his history of the Warsaw ghetto, concluding it with this entry:

It's the morning of May 28, 1943. Out of close to two hundred *black* ballots signifying *death*, there happens to be one *white* one signifying a hypothetical *life* . . . Fate, chance, have permitted me to draw the *white* ballot. . . . But even though I can clearly see that in my own personal situation I am hardly one of the stronger "candidates for survival" and that by virtue of my "features," means, and physical and mental strength, I have *no chance* in the final struggle on this side, I continue to write. I wish to repay fate for granting me a few weeks' extension of life and to give testimony as to how things really were. I want to believe and I do believe that my voice will not be alone in describing these events and that there are and will be others who will present evidence as well. Better, comprehensive, exact. And not only in writing but also in direct speech, when the time comes they will tell what all this was like . . . I am hiding in a cellar without any fresh air, without adequate or regular food, with no toilet facilities, with no prospect of any change in these conditions in which I vegetate and which enjoin me to value every hour I survive as if it were gold . . . I can clearly feel that I am losing strength, it's becoming harder and harder to breathe . . . The struggle to save myself is hopeless . . . Here, on this side of the wall . . . But—that's not important. Because I am able to bring my account to its end and trust that it will see the light of day when the time is right . . . And people will know what happened . . . And they will ask, is this the truth? I reply in advance: No, this is not the truth, this is only a small part, a tiny fraction of the truth . . . Even the mightiest pen could not depict the whole, real, essential *truth*. [AZIH (AJHI), Diaries and Memoirs (VII), p. 112]

that would indicate that the German Ghetto Administration had been informed or had by its own means learned of the *Chronicle*'s existence.[27] Nevertheless, the chroniclers, as employees of the Jewish administration, had to reckon with the possibility that their work could be uncovered at any moment. And that is the primary explanation for the very cautious tone and the absence of evaluation whenever the Germans are mentioned. Only bare facts are presented, with a certain inevitability about them. The chroniclers seemed to have adopted the following principle: since it is not possible to write about those who commit the crimes, we will speak of their victims, and in some detail. And in that manner, nearly every instance of the martyring of the ghetto's population is echoed by the *Chronicle*, even though things are not always called by name. The text is full of euphemisms and impersonal descriptions. All events seem to occur suspended in a void. The normal order of emphasis is reversed, causes and effects are transposed. The plundering of the ghetto is presented by the *Chronicle* as a "buy-up campaign" that operates "to the satisfaction of the interested parties"; people summoned to the German criminal police (*Kripo*) for unknown reasons inexplicably end up in the hospital or mortuary; the hunger rations supplied to the ghetto by the German Ghetto Administration arrive "in quantities which correspond to the quantities announced as needed"; and, finally, there are those constant resettlements of people into the ghetto and the deportations from it into the unknown. . . . It would appear that the Jews are limiting their rights themselves, persecuting and destroying each other. The occupier is imperceptible. The Germans and their policy toward the Jews are either mentioned tersely or not at all—just when the Germans are defining which ghetto dwellers will live and which ones will die! Vehicles arrive in the Jewish quarter from the city, go around to all the hospitals, load up the patients, and drive them away. Where, why? The chroniclers were not in the habit of asking too many questions. They never report what the victims think and feel about those who caused their tragedy, even when they are being sent to their deaths. There are only facts and the descriptions of events: how things really were, how the Jews lived and died in the ghetto until the Germans began deporting them one after the other to death camps.

The chroniclers knew as much as any ghetto dweller did about the nature of the resettlements and deportations—that is, next to nothing. There was a great deal of guesswork. There were efforts to puzzle out the routes the trains took and, on that basis, to establish the transports' destinations. They clutched at straws, seeking even the smallest sign that would indicate that the deportees had gone—as they had been told—to rural settlements where they would work the fields with the peasants and where they would have more to eat than in the overpopulated ghetto. People did not believe or wish to believe that all of this, from beginning to end, could be an unmitigated lie, even if things were not, in fact, as they had been presented. What could be done with that great mass of people, those hundreds of families, those people in the prime of life and their children? The belief that the Germans' plans for those people were not entirely evil was fortified, among other things, by the fact that people leaving

---

27. There is no way of knowing if there was a copy of the *Chronicle* among the Archives' materials uncovered by the Germans at the cemetery during the liquidation of the ghetto in 1944. (See also note 22, above, p. xv.)

the ghetto were able to exchange their ghetto money, worthless outside the ghetto, for a few German marks (*Reichsmark*) which, as a rule, Jews in the ghetto were not allowed to possess. And when that exchange was halted during the course of the deportation, it was explained by the belief that from then on the transports of deportees would not be sent to Germany or to that part of Poland that had been directly incorporated into the Third Reich after the fighting in September, 1939, but to the *Generalgouvernement*, where the Polish złoty, not the German mark, was the official means of exchange. Rumors circulated concerning postcards and letters supposedly sent by deportees to relatives and friends in the ghetto, from which it would appear that the deportees are "working under conditions that are bearable."[28] Practically no one, if anyone, knew at that time that the rumors about the cards and letters were circulated by the German Ghetto Administration and that the few pieces of mail that actually did arrive in the ghetto were either forged by the Gestapo or coerced from the victims before their execution.[29] Gestapo agents played a direct role in lulling people, especially when deportations were underway. Here is the *Chronicle*'s report in connection with this campaign of misinformation:

THE FIRST NEWS ABOUT THE DEPORTEES

On April 12, a high officer of the secret police [Gestapo], who is serving as commander of the camp where the people deported from this ghetto are now located, was briefly at Bałut Market. This is the first definite source of information concerning the deportees; for the record, it is worth adding that the story of their whereabouts that circulated with the most persistence has, this time, been confirmed. It has now been irrefutably established that the camp is located in the region bordering directly on the town of Koło, now called Warthbrücken. The camp houses about 100,000 Jews, indicating that besides the 44,000 resettled from this ghetto, Jews from other cities have been concentrated in that camp. This gigantic camp was formerly a living site for Germans from Volhynia. Apparently 30,000 people had been living there. They left the barracks in perfectly decent order, and even left their furniture for the Jews to use. The food supply at the camp is, apparently, exemplary. Those fit to work are employed on the camp grounds repairing roads and performing agricultural tasks. Workshops are to be set up in the very near future.[30]

In accordance with what seems to be their principle where Germans are concerned, the chroniclers do not comment on this information. They make no attempt even to speculate as to the reason why this least trustworthy of individuals had taken the trouble to convince the Jews in this matter. Moreover, the chroniclers refrain from drawing conclusions, even though the facts at their disposal are evidence enough

---

28. See below, p. 141.
29. Edward Serwański, *Obóz zagłady w Chełmnie nad Nerem* [The death camp in Chełmno on the Ner] (Poznań: Wydawnictwo Poznańskie, 1964), p. 41; (see also below, p. 349). At that time, postal cards that arrived from the workers who had been recruited and sent from the ghetto to perform forced labor in Germany and in territories incorporated into the Reich were sometimes confused with cards that were supposedly sent by people deported to the death camp in Chełmno.
30. Below, p. 145.

that the Germans spread lies about the fate of the deportees. Thus, without comment, but just for the sake of accuracy in chronicling, as they were in the habit of pointing out, they also write down this item of news:

LARGE SHIPMENTS OF BAGGAGE

have been sent to the ghetto since May 25. The people of the ghetto are tremendously puzzled by the arrival of these shipments, which contain clothes of all sorts and other things and which are transported here each day by trucks, including five-ton vehicles. The Department of Used Articles has been ordered to store all this material. The department has assigned some enormous warehouses for that purpose, namely those at 75 Brzezińska Street, 20 Marynarska Street, 93 Franciszkańska Street, and 32 Dolna Street. What is it that these large trucks are carrying? It would be difficult to enumerate the contents. One reason is the tonnage involved which, in every case, exceeds 100,000 kilograms and is perhaps even higher. Among their contents, the things most frequently encountered are improvised sacks made from rugs, blankets, sheets, and so on. This type of bundle indicates that they were not packed by their owners but by other hands. These bundles for the most part contain clothing, linen, and bedding. This latter has passed through disinfection. Among other frequently encountered items are shirts and slips rolled together, three or four at a time, and also two pairs of pants rolled up with a few pairs of unmentionables. Nearly all the jackets and coats bear traces of having been ripped along their seams . . . There are a lot of goods, for example, curtains, which are brand new. There are also a great many *taleysim* [prayer shawls]. There are no knapsacks or suitcases to be seen. Documents—letters, papers, ID cards, and so on, that had been issued in Western European cities—often fall out of the bundles, but there are also a great many from Włocławek, and often there are papers that were drawn up in this ghetto as well.

A very significant percentage of the items are brand new. For the time being, these things have been placed in storage; they will be distributed to the deportees from the surrounding areas, to the residents of the Old People's Home and orphanage, and perhaps even to the Clothing Department.[31]

Indeed, in the Łódź ghetto, nothing was known about the fate of the deportees, at least during the first phase of deportation, which, with a few short interruptions, ran from January 16 to May 15, 1942. During those four months, 54,979 people were deported in 54 transports from the ghetto to the death camp in Chełmno, on the river Ner. At the time, no one was aware of the existence of the camp. It is difficult to establish when and by what means the terrible news of its existence reached the ghetto. Summer, 1942, is nearly always mentioned as the time, for it was then that a letter dated January, 1942, was supposed to have arrived from the rabbi of Grabów, a small town to the northwest of Łódź. Based on the eyewitness account of someone

31. Below, pp. 190–91.

who had succeeded in escaping from the camp, the letter provided information that the Jews from Łódź and the surrounding area were being murdered in Chełmno.[32]

Grabów's letter and the means by which it reached the ghetto have never been thoroughly investigated. Our knowledge of it comes not from contemporaneous sources but from three mutually contradictory post-war accounts.[33] Without in the least denying its existence, one cannot be sure who in the ghetto had read the letter or even knew of it, much less what influence that letter might have had on the attitudes of ghetto dwellers. One thing does, however, seem certain: the real significance of the resettlements and deportations became clear to anyone with the strength and courage to face the truth only during the so-called *Gehsperre*, the daytime curfew between September 1 and 12, 1942. It was then that the Germans deported 15,685 people from the ghetto in an utterly barbaric fashion, openly conducting their roundup on the spot—in courtyards, squares, and on the street, going from house to house—selecting children, old people, the sick (or those who simply did not appear to be in good health) for the transport. The pages of the *Chronicle* for those dates leave no doubt that the ghetto had begun to realize the gravity of the situation, especially if, beside the daily bulletins, we also take into consideration Józef Zelkowicz's shocking reports on the September roundups and deportations, parts of which were incorporated into the *Chronicle* as soon as they were written.[34]

What was a long and well-kept secret in the Łódź ghetto had been known almost

32. The full text of the letter reads:

My Dearest Ones!

I had not yet replied to your letters since I had not known exactly what was being discussed. Now, to our great misfortune, we know everything. An eyewitness who by chance was able to escape from hell has been to see me . . . I learned everything from him. The place where everyone is being put to death is called Chełmno, not far from Dąbie; people are kept in the nearby forest of Łochów. People are killed in one of two ways: either by shooting or by poison gas. This is what happened to the towns of Dąbie, Izbica Kujawska, and others. Recently, thousands of gypsies have been brought there from the so-called Gypsy camp in Łódź and the same is done to them. Do not think that a madman is writing; unfortunately, it is the cruel and tragic truth (Good God!). O Man, throw off your rags, sprinkle your head with ashes, or run through the streets and dance in madness . . . I am so wearied by the sufferings of Israel, my pen can write no more. My heart is breaking. But perhaps the Almighty will take pity and save the "last remnants of our People."
Help us, O Creator of the World!
Grabów, 1/19/42   Jakub Szulman

Dokumenty i materialy z czasów okupacji niemieckiej w Polsce, vol. 1: *Obozy* (Documents and materials from the time of the German occupation in Poland, vol. 1, The camps), ed. N. Blumental, with an introduction by Filip [Philip] Friedman (Łódź: Wydawnictwo Centralnej Komisji Historycznej, 1946), p. 233.

33. A letter to the Central Jewish Historical Commission in Łódź by M. Szwarc, ibid., p. 233; I. Tabaksblat, *Khurbn Lodzh* (Buenos Aires: Union Central Israelita Polaca en la Argentina, 1946), pp. 103–4; J. Nirenberg, "Di geshikte fun lodzher geto," *In di yorn fun yidishn khurbn* (New York: *Unser tsayt*, 1949), pp. 261–62.

34. See below, pp. 248–55. I have deliberately used the words people *had begun to realize* in the text, but this does not mean in the least that people were able or willing to believe what they heard. Jakub Poznański wrote the following in his ghetto diary in an entry dated as late as September 27, 1943: ". . . persistent rumors circulate about the liquidation of the ghettos in various Polish cities. In my opinion, people are exaggerating, as usual. Even if certain excesses have taken place in some cities, that still does not incline one to believe that Jews are being mass-murdered. At least I consider that out of the question." *Pamiętnik z getta łódzkiego* [Memoir from the Łódź ghetto] (Łódź: Wydawnictwo Łódzkie, 1960), p. 102.

from the start in Warsaw. Since January, 1942, both the Polish and the Jewish resistance movements had gradually learned about the existence of the camp in
Chełmno and the fates of the Jews deported there. The first information was obtained
from Polish railroad workers, local residents, foresters; later, more detailed accounts
were to come from eyewitnesses—those few people who had succeeded in escaping
from the death camp.[35] After February of that year, the clandestine press, including
the newspapers published in Polish, Yiddish, and Hebrew in the Warsaw ghetto,
began writing about Chełmno. At first this information was presented with great
incredulity and skepticism and then, increasingly, as indisputable and supported by
a large number of facts. The truth about Chełmno was also transmitted to the free
world—for the most part, in reports passed on by Ringelblum's Warsaw-Ghetto Underground Archives through the Polish Resistance to the Polish government-in-exile
in London and its Jewish representatives, Artur Zygelbojm and Ignacy Schwarzbart.
The Allied governments and the press were thereupon informed.[36] The news that
had been sent out to the world returned by radio to occupied Poland, although not
everyone was able to listen, an act punishable by death. On June 26, 1942, Emanuel
Ringelblum noted in the diary he kept in the Warsaw ghetto: "This morning, the
English radio broadcast about the fate of Polish Jewry. They told about everything we
know so well: about Słonim and Vilna, Lemberg and Chełmno, and so forth. For long
months we have been suffering because the world was deaf and dumb to our unparalleled tragedy."[37] Two months later one of the most comprehensive reports
about Chełmno to come out of the Warsaw ghetto was available in English translation,
in a periodical published in New York entitled *The Ghetto Speaks*.[38]

The Łódź ghetto was far less-informed not only of Chełmno but of a great many
other events occurring in the world and on the fronts. There was practically no
communication between the ghetto and the city of Łódź, if one ignores, of course,
that which was under German control, although even that was minimal in comparison with other ghettos.[39] In the Łódź ghetto people were not allowed to possess
or even read the *Litzmannstädter Zeitung*, the official organ of the local occupying

35. Among them were Mordka Podchlebnik, Szymon Srebrny, and Jakób Grajowski (Blumental, *Doku-
menty i materiały*, vol. 1, pp. 239–42, 244–45); the account by Grajowski, who worked as a grave digger in
Chełmno in January, 1942, was on display in 1983 as part of an exhibit, Code Name *Oyneg shabes:* Emanuel
Ringelblum's Underground Archives in the Warsaw Ghetto, 1940–1943, at the YIVO Institute for Jewish
Research, New York.

36. What information did reach the West and what was done with it is another question entirely. The
subject has recently been treated by Walter Laquer in *The Terrible Secret: Suppression of the Truth About
Hitler's 'Final Solution'* (Boston: Little, Brown and Company, 1980), chaps. 4–5, and Deborah E. Lipstadt,
"*The New York Times* and the News about the Holocaust: A Quantified Study," *World Congress of Jewish
Studies, 7–14 August, 1977, Jerusalem. Proceedings* (Jerusalem, 1980), pp. 45–73.

37. *Notes from the Warsaw Ghetto: The Journal of Emmanuel* [sic] *Ringelblum*, ed. Jacob Sloan (New
York: Schocken Books, 1974), p. 295.

38. Published by the organization, American Representation of the General Jewish Workers' Union of
Poland, the special issue is entitled "The First Authentic Report Received from Poland about Gas-
executions of Jews" (1942), pp. 1–3; the report sent from Warsaw to London is entitled "Masowe
egzekucje Żydów w pow[iecie] kolskim" (Mass execution of Jews in Koło county). Copies of both are in
the YIVO Archives.

39. Unlike Jews in other ghettos, those of Łódź were not sent to work in the city. The few exceptions
are described by the *Chronicle*.

authorities.[40] The Polish clandestine press did not reach the ghetto either; in any case, in the city of Łódź that press was very small, poorly organized, and had a limited readership.[41] Also, the smuggling between the "Aryan" and the Jewish parts of the city, which was so well known in other ghettos and, besides supplying the starving populace with additional food, was an excellent means of communication, was rather incidental in Łódź and played neither of those two roles there.

The Łódź ghetto truly was hermetically sealed, cut off from other Jews and non-Jews alike. Aside from a few sporadic incidents, Jews could enter and leave the ghetto once, that is, when they were resettled into it or resettled out of it. That state of affairs had little to do with the barbed wire fences around the ghetto or the German sentries who guarded the boundaries of the ghetto and shot anyone, even without formal cause, who approached those boundaries, often without issuing a warning. The presence of the German criminal police and its network of informers within the ghetto itself was not crucial here either. All those physical obstacles could have been surmounted, even if at great effort, expense, and risk. What determined the ghetto's isolation is to be sought elsewhere, primarily in the situation that had existed in the city of Łódź since the first few weeks of the German occupation.

After the conclusion of hostilities in September, 1939, and the division of Polish territory under German occupation into two parts—territories directly incorporated into the Third Reich and the *Generalgouvernement*—Łódź found itself in the latter. What's more, it had already been designated as the capital of the so-called Generalgouvernement and the seat of its governor, Hans Frank. That situation did not continue for very long. Łódź, and the greater part of Łódź province, was, after deliberations on the highest level in Berlin and "in accordance with the wishes of the local German population," added to the *Reichsgau Wartheland (Warthegau)*, which, along with Reichsgau Danzig, West Prussia, and the former Polish Silesia constituted one of the three German administrative units incorporated into the Reich by an earlier decree issued by Hitler on October 8, 1939.

From that time on Łódź and its environs were subjected to intensive germanization. The name of the city was changed to *Litzmannstadt* in honor of Karl Litzmann, the German general who fell in battle near Łódź in 1915. All streets and squares were given German names. The Polish language had already been suppressed throughout

---

40. Interesting in this context is the extant correspondence among Rumkowski, the owners of newspaper kiosks in the ghetto, and *Amtsleiter* Hans Biebow, the head of the German Ghetto Administration. On June 7, shortly after the ghetto was closed, the *Litzmannstädter Zeitung* ceased delivery to the ghetto and the kiosk workers, having nothing to sell, lost their sole means of livelihood. On the 10th of the month, Rumkowski wrote to Biebow appealing for further delivery of newspapers because the populace was used to reading them and, moreover, because the lack of newspapers might provide an incentive for smuggling, especially among children. In his reply of June 14, Biebow informed Rumkowski that no newspapers could be delivered but that he was, incidentally, interested in knowing if newspapers were still making their way into the ghetto and how much a copy cost on the black market. He then ordered Rumkowski to issue a ruling concerning the punishment, not only for those guilty of possessing newspapers but for those who read them as well (AZIH [AJHI], Rum. Records, Applications; *Gettoverwaltung*, nos. 25, 382, 405). See also, Dobroszycki, *Die legale polnische Presse im Generalgouvernement, 1939–1945* (Munich: Institut für Zeitgeschichte, 1977), pp. 16–18, 28–32.

41. Dobroszycki, *Centralny katalog polskiej prasy konspiracyjnej* 1939–1945 [Comprehensive catalogue of the Polish clandestine press] (Warsaw: Instytut Historii Polskiej Akademii Nauk, 1962), p. 302.

the Wartheland.[42] There was not even a Nazi press in the Polish language as there was in the Generalgouvernement, which Hitler considered, at least, to be the "home" of the Poles. The Polish language was barred from schools, theatres, and cinemas. All levels of administration and municipal self-rule, even the lowest of them, passed into German hands, and German became the sole official language. The city of Łódź had neither a Polish police nor fire department, two uniformed organizations which continued to function in the Generalgouvernement throughout the war, under German control, of course. Litzmannstadt—as Nazi propaganda slogans declared—had become a great German industrial city in the "East."

The policy of germanizing Łódź substantially altered the city's demographic structure and the topographic distribution of the ethnic population. Whereas at the beginning of the war, in 1939, Łódź included about 60,000 local Germans, the so-called Volksdeutschen, at the end of the war, in 1944, the German population had increased to some 143,000.[43] This was the result of Germans from the Old Reich being settled there permanently or for a term of service; of ethnic Germans coming to Łódź from the Baltic republics, Volhynia, and eastern Galicia in accordance with the German pact with the Soviet Union, as part of the Ribbentrop-Molotov agreement of August 23, 1939, and the other decisions issuing from it; finally, the growth of Litzmannstadt occurred as a result of Nazi efforts to discover individuals with a so-called certain percentage of German blood among the people of the city. Those meeting the standards became members of the privileged class and their names were entered on the appropriate German lists (*Deutsche Volksliste*). Any member of Łódź's old German population or person of German descent who did not share the invaders' world-view and policies was not tolerated, no matter who he was. To name but three: Robert Geyer, the descendant of a pioneer in the textile industry and the owner of one of the largest industrial plants in Łódź; Dr. Juliusz Bursche, the bishop of the Evangelical-Augsburg Church; and Oskar Seidler, leader of the German Socialist Party in Łódź. Geyer was murdered by the Gestapo in October, 1939, Bursche, placed in the Sachsenhausen-Oranienburg concentration camp, where he died in February, 1942, and Seidler, incarcerated along with his son.[44]

Wartime Łódź was not only germanized but Nazified like no other large city in occupied Europe. The Polish population, whose number fluctuated from around 396,000 in 1940 to around 343,000 in 1944, was thrust into the role of pariah.[45] The city had been almost entirely pacified. This the occupiers achieved by means of terror, constant surveillance, and the expulsion of undesirable elements, and by depriving people of independent incomes and removing the Polish population from certain districts of the city, including those in close proximity to the ghetto. And thus there

---

42. According to the general census of 1931, in Łódź, 53,562 people indicated German as their native language and 51,159 indicated Protestant as their religion (see Alfons Krysiński, "Struktura narodowościowa miast polskich" (The national makeup of Polish cities), *Sprawy Narodowościowe* 3 (1937), pp. 268–69.

43. Some ethnic Germans were also added to the population of Łódź when the city's size was increased in 1940 by the incorporation of a few suburban communities and settlements.

44. Mirosław Cygański, *Z dziejów okupacji hitlerowskiej w Łodzi* [On the history of the Nazi occupation of Łódź] (Łódź: Wydawnictwo Łódzkie, 1967), pp. 63, 64; Bolesław Olszewski, *Lista strat kultury polskiej* [The casualty list of Polish culture] (Warsaw: S. Arct, 1947), p. 30.

45. Cygański, *Z dziejów okupacji*, p. 162.

arose a sort of no-man's-land between the Jewish quarter and the "Aryan" part of the city. Ultimately, a ghetto Jew could cross the fence but there would be no one waiting on the other side to serve him as a guide, supply him with the necessary papers, and provide him with initial accommodations, irrespective of motive or principle, for money or not. It is a fact that, apart from one very special and singular case, there is no record thus far of any Jewish family or individual surviving the war in Łódź by being on "Aryan" territory, as occurred in Warsaw, Cracow, Lwów, Lublin, and many other Polish cities.[46] The Jews in the Łódź ghetto were indeed cut off as nowhere else. Only scraps of news reached the ghetto directly from without, to be supplemented by reports derived from a few, scattered clandestine radios of varying quality.[47] Information thus obtained, real or—as is so movingly depicted by Jurek Becker in *Jacob the Liar*—imaginary, was people's only source of hope in those days. From Becker, to whom the Łódź ghetto has not been alien, I also take these words: "Well . . . it's evening. Don't ask me the exact time. Only the Germans know that. . . ."

Knowing very little of what was taking place outside the ghetto, and writing even less than they knew, the chroniclers concentrated all their efforts on the ghetto and its inhabitants, of which they were themselves an integral part. They swelled from hunger along with everyone else, even if one of them might chance upon an extra bowl of soup or a food coupon. The chroniclers always identified with the ghetto dwellers and seemed to be speaking on their behalf. But, as already mentioned elsewhere, the *Chronicle* was written in the Archives, which, in turn, was a part of the Jewish ghetto administration, which, naturally, could not be indifferent to the light in which its actions were presented by the chroniclers. When submitting a plan for the newly created Department of Archives to Rumkowski, Dr. Józef Klementynowski, its director, wrote that he would indeed make sure that the materials collected be as close to reality as possible, but hastened to add that he was willing to follow any advice from the Eldest.[48] In his account, Bernard Ostrowski said outright that the *Chronicle* could only record what had passed Rumkowski's censorship and that he, Rumkowski, received copies of the daily *Chronicle* bulletins.[49] Did he read them, did he voice any opinions on them? And if so, to whom? Who besides Rumkowski knew

---

46. The special case was a family I know well: Ryszard Gabriel (born in 1933) and Alfred Emanuel (born in 1934), the young sons of a mixed marriage between Henryk Olszer, an engineer, and Jadwiga Szadkowski, did not move to the ghetto in 1940 as did their parents. They remained with Jadwiga's parents, Maria and Leon Szadkowski, at 2 Centralna St. in the Marysin section of Łódź. Ryszard and Alfred hid there, never leaving the apartment, until the city was liberated in January, 1945. During the liquidation of the ghetto in 1944, Jadwiga escaped from the ghetto and joined her sons and parents. Jadwiga, her two sons, and their families emigrated to the United States and, at present, live in New York. In October, 1944, Henryk Olszer was deported with the final group of 500 Jews to Sachsenhausen-Oranienburg and from there to the work camp in Königswusterhausen. After being liberated, he returned to Poland where he was reunited with his family. He died in Łódź in 1958.

47. Even what did manage to penetrate the ghetto was only rarely noted by the *Chronicle*, and, then, casually and after some time had elapsed. For example, the news of the German attack on Russia was not mentioned until the bulletin of June 26–30, 1941, and then only to say that, "In connection with the war with the Soviets, in the last ten days of June there has been a sudden increase in the price of packaged goods, which the ghetto had received mostly from the USSR" (p. 62).

48. A letter of November 16, 1940, AZIH [AJHI], Rum. Records, no. 2118.

49. AZIH [AJHI], Report no. 2841.

that the *Chronicle* was being written in the Archives, who else had access to it?[50] Neither in the *Chronicle* itself nor in any other contemporaneous source is there any mention of this subject. As far as Rumkowski is concerned, it is known that he visited the Archives many times, acquainted himself with certain of its ongoing projects, and inquired about various matters, but never the *Chronicle.* So this question, not, at bottom, a crucial one, remains unanswered. The *Chronicle* itself, and many other sources as well, provide more than adequate evidence that working in the Archives limited the chroniclers' freedom to write and the scope of their inquiry, creating an intellectual barrier that was all but insurmountable. This is most evident when the *Chronicle* deals with Rumkowski, and it is completely immaterial here if what the *Chronicle* writes about him resulted from some sort of formal censorship or the self-control the authors themselves exercised.

M. C. Rumkowski, the Eldest of the Jews, has the place of prominence in the *Chronicle.* He, his program, and his actions are not subjected to criticism. He could be described only in superlatives and with the respect accorded a good and just man. Consequently, the *Chronicle* is full of homage to Rumkowski—a pronoun referring to him is always capitalized. He is also infallible; anyone who thought otherwise, and on the pages of the *Chronicle* rarely did one dare to think otherwise, was an enemy of peace in the ghetto. Thus, the protests and defiance shown by the people, whether they be demonstrations against hunger or strikes in the ghetto workshops, are presented outside their real context. For instance, the strike in the carpenters' workshop in January, 1941, the *Chronicle* notes, "was organized by irresponsible individuals intent on disturbing the law and public order created by the ghetto authorities who watch over the peace, safety, and food supplies of the ghetto dwellers."[51]

The *Chronicle* suffered hindrance in other areas besides that of evaluation. The chroniclers' lack of independence is evident even in their selection of facts, especially when the attitudes and actions of those who "rule" or thought they ruled were concerned. The achievements of the Jewish ghetto administration are scrupulously noted, whereas its negative or possibly unpardonable aspects remain in the shadows or are passed over in silence. The *Chronicle* is not able to tell us much about the administration's higher officials or about the privileged stratum, which was estranged from ghetto society until one , Salomon Hercberg, the commissioner of the Order Service and commandant of Central Prison, took a misstep and fell from power. Then they are able to write pejoratively even about his appearance and clothing. We learn that Hercberg had been living in clover in the ghetto, that he owned three apartments and had been "the lord and master of Marysin as if he were the governor of the most beautiful section of the ghetto," that he received special commissions "in connection with the rounding-up of the ghetto's undesirable elements," and that

50. Jakub Poznański, a man generally well informed about what was happening in the ghetto and whose wife worked in an office in one of the departments of population records, that is, in a room right beside the Archives, apparently knew little about the work actually being conducted there, and nothing of the existence of the *Chronicle.* He made the following entry in his diary, dated July 26, 1943: "I still have not mentioned that in the office of population records there exists a special chamber with the high-sounding name of the Archives. Apparently, documents concerning the history of the ghetto are compiled there. The average person has little chance of getting a glimpse of those confidential records. I've had a few chances to scan one fragment or another briefly. They contain nothing but panegyrics in honor of the Chairman and statistical data." *Pamiętnik z getta łódzkiego,* p. 85.

51. Below, pp. 5, 14, and n. 23.

many times, he had "personally organized and directed night raids on apartments, as well as the raids that were carried out in broad daylight on the streets."[52]

The chroniclers, so restrained and cautious where "their own" ghetto was concerned, were eloquent in revealing the disconcerting situations in "other peoples'" ghettos, under "foreign rule," such as the ghetto in Pabianice. Relying on accounts given by the Jews resettled to the Łódź ghetto from that in Pabianice, the authors of the *Chronicle* present an unretouched picture of the *Judenrat* and the conditions prevailing there. On the other hand, everything in the Łódź ghetto ran like clockwork, as Rumkowski once put it. Innumerable departments and workshops celebrate the anniversary of their founding in a festive mood. The Łódź ghetto is continually introducing new means for improving production. People are dying but the ghetto is developing, new and splendid buildings keep going up. When writing of such things, the chroniclers sometimes lose their sense of measure. The following example is horrendous but not isolated. In an entry dated December 14, 1941, and headed "Road to the Cemetery Under Construction," we read: "The construction of an excellent road to the cemetery has been in progress in Marysin for three weeks now. . . . The road is being built according to the latest in technical design; it will consist of three layers: a foundation of brick, an embankment, and a surface strewn with coal cinders. This road connects with the three-quarter kilometer road already built that runs along Robert Street. Moreover, Otylia Street, which leads to the factory on Mostowski Street, is also being paved. The building of exemplary roads under present conditions is a monument to the ghetto's vitality."[53] It should be added that more than 43,000 ghetto dwellers took that road to the cemetery.

The *Chronicle*'s near total lack of cognitive inquiry and critical analysis in the wake of events is particularly evident when the authors are writing about the mood of the populace and about its relations with Rumkowski. The image of Rumkowski presented by the chroniclers does not at all correspond to what people in the ghetto actually thought of him. In the diaries and memoirs known to have been written in the ghetto, and ignoring what was written about him after the war, Rumkowski is severely criticized, frankly hated, or simply ridiculed. The authors of these personal accounts no doubt represent, to some degree, an accurate cross-section of the ghetto, even if only of those who took to writing. They were: Dawid Sierakowiak,[54] a left-leaning gymnasium student; Jakub Poznański,[55] the manager of a ghetto workshop; Shlomo Frank Frenkel,[56] an Order Service man connected to the Zionist-Revisionists, a semi-clandestine group active in the ghetto; Leon Hurwitz, an engineer and, before the war, a member of the Folkists, a Jewish populist party in Poland; Jakub Szulman,[57] a co-

---

52. Below, p. 137.

53. Below, p. 94.

54. *Dziennik* . . . (Diary), ed. Dobroszycki, with an introduction by Adolf Rudnicki (Warsaw: Iskry, 1960), pp. 226.

55. *Pamiętnik z getta łódzkiego*, p. 285.

56. *Togbukh fun lodzher geto* (Buenos Aires: Union Central Israelita Polaca en la Argentina, 1958); see also, a review by Dobroszycki in *Biuletyn Żydowskiego Instytutu Historycznego* 30 (1959), pp. 152–57.

57. In his unpublished notes, Szulman coolly analyzes Rumkowski's policies during the ghetto's first year and a half, with a good many digressions about his activities in the Jewish community before the war. Without doubting that Rumkowski was, as he put it, "a man with clean hands," Szulman voices very critical views about the way he ran the ghetto, and especially about his autocratic behavior and megalomania. (Szulman, Memoir).

worker of Rumkowski, a leader of the Labor Zionist party, and, in the ghetto, chief of a hospital; and, finally, for even this memoir should not be overlooked, the anonymous author who took his notes along on the way to Auschwitz, where he had been deported during the liquidation of the ghetto in the summer of 1944.[58]

Probably the most critical remarks on and the greatest ridicule of Rumkowski and conditions in the ghetto are to be found in Leon Hurwitz's as yet unpublished notes, of which the following is a small fragment:

> The ghetto's internal life is reminiscent of the feudal system of the middle ages, for example, that of a rich Russian boyar. The peasants, the prince's private property, are only machines to perform work. They have come into the world and are alive exclusively so that the prince might derive profit and pleasure from them. But princes—and this holds true in our case as well—love to dazzle their subjects. In this our own prince is indefatigable. He hops from one workshop to another, from one office to another and everywhere—among office workers, managers, laborers, guards, and peasants—he sows fear and dread. Although those sudden, unmotivated "inspections" were rare events, they always caused someone suffering, which should come as no surprise. An office worker would have his face slapped or be deprived of work for a very long time, until the end of the Rumkowski dynasty, unless the barbed wire around the ghetto were to disappear first. And Rumkowski was glad to perform these sadistic and insane pranks in the presence of one "minister" or another. He should tremble for his own fate.[59]

It would be difficult to believe that the chroniclers were entirely uncritical in their attitudes toward Rumkowski and his administration. It can even be assumed that the panegyrics in Rumkowski's honor in the *Chronicle* were the price the chroniclers paid to be able to transmit what they wished to posterity, to history.[60] In this context, the personal notes of Dr. Oskar Rosenfeld, one of the principal coauthors of the *Chronicle*, are revelatory. Supplied with a clear warning, "Private diary, not to be read, a memoir for the future," Rosenfeld's notes suggest that Rumkowski had been subjected to the scrutiny of the workers of the Archives and that a critical view of him was not out of the question. Not many critical observations are to be found in Rosenfeld's text, but what there is is very pointed, even sarcastic, and written with great indigna-

---

58. "Papiery oświęcimskie" (Auschwitz papers), *Szukajcie w popiołach: Papiery znalezione w Oświęcimiu* (Search in the ashes: Papers found in Auschwitz), eds. Janusz Gumkowski and Adam Rutkowski (Łódź: Wydawnictwo Łódzkie, 1965), pp. 41–121.

59. The original diary is among Hurwitz's other papers in AZIH (AJHI), Rum. Records, no. 11; A. Wolf Jasny, the author of a monograph about the Łódź ghetto, is of the opinion, shared by others after him, that Leon Hurwitz and Józef Klementynowski, the first head of the Archives, are one and the same. The facts do not support this position. It suffices to compare the manuscripts by each man that have been preserved to confirm that they were written by two different people. Moreover, as far as Leon Hurwitz (who was supposed to have assumed the name Klementynowski in the ghetto) is concerned, there is copious extant documentation that allows one to determine his family background, place of work in the ghetto, residence, and so forth. Several of Klementynowski's documents have also been preserved. He always wrote under his own name, had a definite address, and signed his papers with his full name. See also, A. Wolf Jasny, *Geshikhte fun yidn in Lodzh in di yorn fun daytsher-oysrotung* (Tel-Aviv: I. L. Peretz Library, 1960), pp. 222, 325–26.

60. The expression "the reader of the future" is to be found more than once in the *Chronicle*.

tion. Such observations are made in the margin next to his remarks on the Jewish police in the ghetto and its brutal, Gestapo-like behavior, where he goes on to define the police as a group, and class apart, of the Eldest's followers which also served as his bodyguard, *"Schutzgarde für Chaim,"* to use Rosenfeld's own words.[61] Elsewhere, Rosenfeld characterizes Rumkowski as a man divided into two extreme and mutually contradictory parts: "a well-mannered man, tidy, peaceful, good, religious, a traditional Jew on the one hand and, on the other, sordid, ridiculous, ironic, slovenly, insidious, unpredictable, treacherous, murderous."[62] It would be difficult to assume that none of the other archivists shared Rosenfeld's views. Moreover, severely critical remarks, if not directly about Rumkowski then about the ghetto's bureaucracy and police, are to be found in the essays of Józef Zelkowicz, another coauthor of the *Chronicle,* essays which have been preserved in full. Around mid-1942, the *Chronicle* itself begins to reflect certain changes in the ghetto, not so much in its general assessments but in the tone of its entries. There are fewer apologetics for the administration, at least fewer than before, more understanding of the processes at work in ghetto society, and more reflections on the gravity or outright hopelessness of the situation.

It is not its interpretations or judgments, however, that render the *Chronicle* unique. Its value derives from the wealth of facts recorded in it day after day, when there were over 200,000 Jews living in the ghetto and when the ghetto was being emptied, also day by day, until the Jewish community had ceased to exist.

When the chroniclers sat down to record the events of the day they had no idea what tomorrow might bring. They could not have foreseen, therefore, that the ghetto's post office, literally created out of nothing at great effort, would not be able to send mail, and when, as they note, the ban on mail to the Generalgouvernement was lifted on May 10, 1944, there would no longer be any Jews in that area to receive mail. Neither were the chroniclers able to imagine that the ghetto's orphanages, homes for the aged, and hospitals, whose founding had required such effort, would soon be turned into workshops, and that their inhabitants would be evacuated, "resettled." The chroniclers also could not have known that the tramline whose construction they had so recently described in such detail, in the belief that it was a sign of some stabilization, would serve the Germans in their deportations by carrying ghetto dwellers to the railroad station in Marysin, from which they were sent to the death camps in Chełmno and Auschwitz. Indeed, as the Chroniclers themselves noted on July 15, 1944, "The ghetto [. . .] lost the habit of thinking more than a few hours ahead."[63]

The *Chronicle* of the Łódź ghetto is a document with universal significance. On the one hand, it is reminiscent of the medieval chronicles written in besieged towns that were doomed to destruction and, on the other, of a censored contemporary newspaper, not to be read by anyone except those who wrote it. The chroniclers worked with the facts: viewing people as individuals and as members of families and society in a closed Jewish quarter, where a loaf of bread, allocated for eight days, was often

---

61. Rosenfeld, Private notes: "Erinnerungen, Heft D," p. 8.
62. Ibid.: "Heft G, 26.X.1942, Aufzeichnungen zur Erinnerungen, bleibt Manuskript," p. 3.
63. Below, p. 526.

consumed the moment it was received, potato peels became a prized food item, to be issued by prescription and even then only to a few, and the only people who had the right to live were those still fit, or who had been judged fit, to work. Thus, the primary subjects of the *Chronicle* were the Jewish community, the form human relations took there, what determined whether one person went less hungry than another or was deported sooner or later than another, and how the ghetto was decimated over a period of four years. Almost everything is known about the perpetrators and their crimes, but very little about their victims. One might search in vain among the German documents, otherwise so abundant and precise, for evidence of the feelings, thoughts, and attitudes of the people who, before they were destroyed, had been marked, counted, photographed, and deliberately starved and tortured both physically and morally. It is in the contemporaneous accounts of the victims that one will find descriptions of the piling up of events, the evolution of experience, and the mechanism of change, as seen through their eyes in a given minute, hour, or day.

FORTY YEARS LATER

Viewed as a source for a history of the Jewish community in Łódź during the Nazi occupation, the *Chronicle* would appear to be without a beginning, for its writing commenced on January 12, 1941, that is, 492 days after the German Eighth Army, under the command of General Blaskowitz, seized the city. The *Chronicle* also lacks any final entries, for work on it ceased on July 30, 1944, when the Germans had ordered the ghetto liquidated and all its inhabitants vacated. Four days later, with the first transport, the total deportation of the Jews from the Łódź ghetto was underway, a process that would last until the end of August. Łódź, after Warsaw the second largest Jewish community in Europe, was destroyed.

Łódź had close to 250,000 Jews before the Second World War, one-third of the city's total population.[64] If there were any place in Poland where Jews could consider themselves at home and safe, no city had more of a claim to this than Łódź. They had been there since 1793, when Łódź, with a total population of 191, was an insignificant, scarcely perceptible dot on the map of Poland.[65] Like the other people who emigrated to Łódź, the Jews came from far and wide, until that little settlement had grown into one of the major centers of textile production in Europe. Thereafter, universally known as the Polish Manchester or the city of factory smokestacks, Łódź achieved its magnitude and international importance in the course of barely a century due to the considerable contributions of the Jews, who functioned as entrepreneurs, merchants, and managers, and as workers, artisans, and cottage industry laborers. Indeed, it is difficult to imagine the fact that Łódź's development as a textile city in the nineteenth century literally began from nothing, without any of the factories and large industrial plants that were to be built and owned by Dawid Lande, Abraham Prussak, Szaja Rosenblat, Moryc Zand, I. K. Poznański, Nachum Ejttingon, Uszer Kon,

64. *Concise Statistical Year-Book of Poland: September 1939–June 1941* (London: The Polish Ministry of Information, 1941), p. 17, Table 25.

65. Jan Wąsicki, *Opisy miast polskich z lat 1793–1794* [Descriptions of Polish cities, 1793–1794] (Poznań: Adam Mickiewicz University, 1962), pp. 1025–28.

and many others.[66] Thus, the city's economic life as a whole was from its very inception defined by and often dependent on its Jewish citizens. Both the Jews and the non-Jews were well aware of this fact, which, from time to time, produced antagonisms quite apart from the ethnic tensions that arose in a city inhabited by Poles, Jews, and Germans. Ethnic friction was especially pronounced in the second half of the 1930s, after Hitler had come to power in Germany and when anti-Semitic feelings had increased throughout Poland after the death of Marshal Józef Pilsudski. But even during that critical period the situation was more bearable in Łódź than anywhere else, despite the move toward Fascism by the local German population and increased activity by the parties of the Polish nationalist right. For several years the Polish socialists had gained a majority in elections to the Łódź City Council, in large measure because of the Jewish vote and a coalition with the Jewish labor parties, the Bund and the Poale Zion. As a result of that cooperation, the Council twice elected a socialist mayor, first Norbert Barlicki and then Jan Kwapiński.[67]

An integral part of the city's administrative and economic structure, the Jews of Łódź were also an organized national and religious minority with its own distinctive way of life and a variegated network of institutions—from the broadest, most inclusive, that is, from the kehillah, a self-governing institution of public law, of which all Jews were automatically members and whose basic characteristics were shaped by Talmudic tradition, to the *ad hoc* committees elected by a building's residents. Both within the context of the kehillah and apart from it, the Jews of Łódź had their own economic aid and free loan societies, their hospitals and clinics, homes for the elderly, orphanages, religious and secular schools, theaters and music clubs, public libraries and sports clubs, press and publishing houses, and political parties and youth organizations. All this lent Łódź a character all its own both during the work week, when the city was a beehive of activity, and on the Sabbath and holidays, when its normal big-city rhythm was much subdued. Although, like all Jews in Poland, those in Łódź had cause to be alarmed by the reports of a coming war, they nevertheless retained a considerable degree of optimism. Perhaps the war could be averted, Poland appeared very strong, and besides, England and France were on its side . . . The diary kept by Dawid Sierakowiak would seem to present an accurate reflection of the city's mood in the week before the Germans invaded Poland. What follow are excerpts from diary entries he made after radio broadcasts had announced the news of the Ribbentrop-Molotov Pact, concluded in Moscow on August 23, 1939:

Thursday, August 24, 1939

Mobilization! We don't know whether this is merely a scare or not; in any case, nearly all the recruits are reporting. Many of our neighbors have already gone. Terrible scenes of farewell are being played out on the city's streets, but in the

---

66. Filip [Philip] Friedman, *Dzieje Żydów w Łódźi od początków osadnictwa do roku 1863* [History of the Jews of Łódź from the Earliest Settlements to 1863] (Łódź: Łódzki Oddział Żydowskiego Towarzystwa Krajoznawczego w Polsce, 1938), pp. 189–266; Adam Ginsberg, *Łódź: Studium monograficzne* (Łódź: Wydawnictwo Łódzkie, 1962), pp. 18–22.

67. Janusz Zarnowski, *Polska Partia Socjalistyczna w latach 1935–1939* [The Polish Socialist Party, 1935–1939] (Warsaw: Książka i Wiedza, 1965), pp. 147–51, 328–34.

blocks around us there is a heroic calm . . . There is not the slightest trace of defeatism.

Saturday, August 26, 1939

Today, I read Mayor [Jan] Kwapiński's appeal for people to volunteer to dig anti-aircraft ditches. Having first obtained my parents' permission, I immediately signed up at the police station, as did all my schoolmates, and tomorrow morning I go to work. There are tens of thousands of volunteers. Even the lack of tools presents no obstacle to the mass of people reporting. Old Jews, the young, women, Hasids, all citizens (except for the Germans) are thronging to volunteer. The bloody Hun will not pass!

Monday, August 28, 1939

There is still no real information but, increasingly, it seems true that Hitler has withdrawn. He has called off the party congress in Nuremberg. Today, my bones ache like everyone else's from yesterday's work. Fifty thousand people were out digging in our city.

Wednesday, August 30, 1939

General mobilization! All reservists up to the age of 40 have been called to arms.

Thursday, August 31, 1939

Today, an alert was announced for 1 A.M. but was called off after awhile. At two o'clock we were told to go to sleep. . . . There was no alert. In the morning my mother brought some thick sheets of paper which we rolled into cylinders, glued, and stuffed with rags. As a defense against gas. The air force remains on constant alert.[68]

At daybreak on September 1, 1939, the German army attacked without having declared war. Thereafter, everything would move at an accelerated pace, though neither in Łódź nor anywhere else in Poland did many people assume that the invaders would penetrate to the center of the country so rapidly. That they, in fact, had, came as a complete shock in part because the system of informing the public was often misinformed about the course of events on the fronts. On the 6th, 7th, and 8th of September, the Polish press reported that Polish troops had entered German territory, that Berlin had been bombed by thirty Polish planes, and that French troops were having enormous success and had entered the Rhineland. Given such information, one can understand how stunned people were on September 8 when the tanks of General Reinhardt's Fourth Armored Division arrived outside Warsaw and the advance detachments of the German army appeared on the streets of Łódź.[69]

The occupying forces experienced no special difficulties in taking Łódź and firmly establishing themselves there. The invader's police forces, including *Einsatzgruppe III* of the Reich Security Main Office (*Reichssicherheitshauptamt—RSHA*), whose task

---

68. A copy of the typescript of the hitherto unpublished parts of the diary is in the YIVO Archives.
69. Dobroszycki, "Prasa polska w okresie kampanii wrześniowej" (The Polish press during the Polish-German campaign), *Rocznik Historii Czasopiśmiennictwa Polskiego*, 5/1 (1966), p. 162.

was to carry out special orders against the civilian population, were aided and abetted by very large and well-organized pro-Hitler elements among the local German population. These were primarily ethnic Germans grouped around two political parties: the *Deutsche Volksverband* and *Jung Deutsche Partei*. Those groups and their entire organizational and propaganda machines were at the disposal of the newly-created municipal administration and supplied personnel to all its agencies from the various police forces to the directors of nearly every city office.[70]

The occupying authorities, with personnel of this sort at their service, immediately had the city in pincers, keeping its inhabitants, principally the Jews, in a state of constant terror. The local Nazis were well aware of who was who among the Jews of the city and who owned what. In the days following the taking of Łódź, even before the new authorities had begun to define what was forbidden for the Jews, for what infractions they would be punished, and what the punishments would be, the Jews were subjected to harassment, persecution, and physical abuse. They were stopped on the streets and either roughed up or forced to perform the most outrageous jobs, some of which had a purpose while others were absolutely useless, they were dragged out of their apartments, dislodged from some buildings and even from entire blocks, and robbed whenever there were any valuables for the taking.[71] The first anti-Jewish ordinances came somewhat later. Between September 18 and the end of December, 1939, those ordinances concerned—in chronological order—the prohibition of religious ceremonies and prayers in synagogues during Rosh Hashana and Yom Kippur; the freezing of bank accounts; forced labor to be performed for the Germans; the disbanding of all pre-war Jewish organizations and institutions; the introduction of a curfew between 7:00 P.M. and 8:00 A.M.; deprivation of the right to trade in leather and leather products and textiles in any form; the establishment of a German trusteeship in all Jewish factories and enterprises; the order that all Jewish stores bear the marking *JUDE* in yellow letters; that all wireless radios be handed in; a ban on the possession of droshkys, wagons, pushcarts, and so forth; the wearing of Stars of David front and back, on the chest and shoulders; a prohibition against using municipal transportation—tramcars and buses.[72]

To obey German orders and prohibitions did not provide the slightest guarantee of peace. Just as they had before these announcements, savage terrorism and lawlessness continued to be employed throughout the city.[73] The fact of being a Jew was

---

70. Cygański, *Z dziejów okupacji*, pp. 25–37.

71. An account compiled in the Department of Archives of the Eldest of the Jews in the Łódź ghetto entitled "Wojna" (The War), AZIH (AJHI), Rum. Records, no. 2110. There is a copy in the YIVO Archives.

72. The occupying authorities' anti-Jewish ordinances were published in the German authorities' official newspaper, the *Deutsche Lodzer Zeitung. Mit den amtlichen Bekanntmachungen der deutschen Militär-und Zivilbehörden*, whose title was changed on November 12 to *Lodzer Zeitung, Lodscher Zeitung mit den amtlichen Bekanntmachungen der deutschen Militär-und Zivilbehörden*. Finally, on June 12, it assumed the name, *Litzmannstädter Zeitung mit dem amtlichen Bekanntmachungen für Stadt und Kreis Litzmannstadt*; cf. also, "Historia getta Litzmannstadt"; the Diary of Dawid Sierakowiak: September 8–December 31, 1939; *Dokumenty i materiały, III, Getto łódzkie* (Documents and materials, III, the Łódź Ghetto) ed. Artur Eisenbach (Łódź: Centralna Zydowska Komisja Historyczna, 1946), pp. 51, 59–61; Cygański, *Z dziejów okupacji*, p. 35.

73. The great police terrorism reigning in the city was remarked upon, and disapproved of, by the commander of the Eighth German Army, General Johannes Blaskowitz, in his memorandum to the Reich chancellory. Martin Broszat, *Nationalsozialistische Polenpolitik, 1939–1945* (Hamburg: Fischer Bucherei, 1965), pp. 44–45.

sufficient cause for attack. The first mass murder in Łódź took place on October 18, 1939. On the afternoon of that day a group of SS men drove over 100 people, men and women, out of the Astoria cafe, where the Jewish intellectuals used to meet. Some were murdered, others bought their release at high prices but were forced first to dig graves for those who had already been killed.[74] Less than a month later, on the night of November 11, the Nazis burned the synagogues of Łódź, including the two most magnificent ones—the Old Orthodox Synagogue on Wolborska Street and the Reformed Synagogue on Kościuszko Boulevard. On that same day, the monument to Tadeusz Kościuszko, famous for his role in the Polish Uprising and in the American Revolution, was demolished on Wolność (Freedom) Square, which had been renamed Deutschlandplatz.

The acts committed by the Nazis during their first two to three months of rule, no matter how barbaric they might have seemed, were only sporadic instances of violence, whereas their long-range plans for the Jewish population had only just been launched. When Łódź was incorporated into the Third Reich on November 7, 1939, the city automatically came under the general instructions for the entire Jewish population inhabiting territories that had been fully annexed. The initial document was the order of September 21, 1939, issued by Reinhard Heydrich, chief of the Reich Security Main Office, to all mobile units (Einsatzgruppen) of the security police in occupied Polish territories.[75] It will be necessary to return to this document more than once, but attention should be given here to its statement that the territories stipulated for annexation should be purged of Jews to *the degree possible*. More emphatic directives in this matter were issued by *SS-Reichsführer* Heinrich Himmler on October 30, that is, after Hitler's decree on annexation was announced.[76] It was demanded that all Jews as well as a still undetermined number of Poles particularly hostile to Germany be deported to the Generalgouvernement from all former Polish provinces that had been incorporated into the Reich. Pursuant to this, on November 12, *SS-Obergruppenführer* Wilhelm Koppe, the chief of police in Wartheland, cited Himmler's directives and announced that the resettlement action must be launched and carried out without "regard for any other interests," and that for the time being, between November 15, 1939, and February 28, 1940, 200,000 Poles and 100,000 Jews, including 30,000 from Łódź itself, had to be dislodged from Wartheland.[77] We know from another source that a few days before this, on the night of November 7, Koppe and his counterpart in Cracow, SS-Obergruppenführer Friedrich Krüger, signed an agreement concerning the receiving of resettled persons and their distribution in the Generalgouvernement.[78]

The order concerning resettlement was put into effect in Łódź immediately, and without any special preparation. By November, 1939, the German authorities de-

---

74. Tabaksblat, *Khurbn Lodzh*, pp. 21–24.
75. There is an English translation of the document in Dawidowicz, ed., *A Holocaust Reader*, pp. 59–64.
76. *Eksterminacja Żydów na ziemiach polskich w okresie okupacji hitlerowskiej: Zbiór dokumentów* [The extermination of the Jews on Polish territory during the Nazi occupation: A collection of documents], ed. T. Bernstein, A. Eisenbach, and A. Rutkowski (Warsaw: Żydowski Instytut Historyczny, 1957), p. 29.
77. Ibid., pp. 30–32.
78. Ibid., p. 32. (This information is from the court records of the trial of Artur Greiser at the Supreme Court in Poland, which ran between June 21 and July 9, 1946.)

manded that the Eldest of the Jews supply them with his plan for resettlement as well as a list of the 50,000 Jews who were to leave the city. At first, anyone who wished to leave voluntarily and, toward that end, anyone registered at the office of the Elders had the right to take hand luggage with him and, in addition, received a grant in the amount of 50 złotys from the Community. Later on, when volunteering was curtailed or stopped entirely, the German police intervened: brutal resettlements began, the worst and most dangerous phase of which ran from December 11 to 16, 1939. It was the people who lived on Zgierska and Łagiewnicka streets and on Kościuszko Boulevard who suffered the most at that time.[79] The people to be resettled were herded with only the clothes on their backs to the railroad station, where they were loaded onto waiting, unheated cattle cars that contained no sanitary facilities whatsoever. Thus they traveled, sometimes for two to three days, without food or water or any clear idea of where they were being taken, nor were the stations that would be their destinations informed of their coming.[80] Initially, the ruling circles of the General-gouvernement agreed to this, but, in the course of time, they reversed themselves and demanded a cessation to the resettlement of new Jews to their territory. Among the highest Nazi ranks in Berlin, voices were also heard questioning whether it was in the interest of the Reich to be resettling people at that very time or whether they should wait for a more suitable moment. It was chiefly Göring, the Plenipotentiary for the Four Year Plan, who had doubts about this matter. During a conference at Karinhall on February 12, 1940, he stated that "all orders concerning resettlement should be suspended for the time being so as not to reduce the amount of usable manpower and impede the country's economic development."[81] Somewhat later, on March 23, 1940, Göring returned to this problem again in a letter to Himmler, Wilhelm Frick, the Reich's minister of internal affairs, and Hans Frank, the Generalgouverneur of the occupied Polish territories. After ascertaining that Frank was in principle ready to receive further transports of Jews from the Reich, Göring demanded, however, that no resettlement action be undertaken without his permission and without Frank's prior agreement.[82] Least pleased by this turn of events were the central police authorities and the leaders of the Wartheland. The head of that province, Gauleiter Artur Greiser, appealed to Frank to accept Jews from Łódź, while Himmler had to win Göring's approval to exclude the Jews of Łódź from that ban so that the resettlements from that city could continue.[83] Yet, Göring's decision remained in force although no one denied that the evacuation of Łódź's Jews would take place, and specific deadlines for its conclusion were even set. The first was to commence on July 1, 1940, the

79. Ibid., pp. 36–37: "Historia getta Litzmannstadt", pp. 1–12.

80. For a letter from Gschlisser, a high-ranking official in the Labor Bureau of the Generalgouvernement to the governor of Cracow province concerning the inhuman conditions prevailing during the transfer of Jews and Poles from the Wartheland to Cracow province on December 29, 1939, as well as the account by Otto G. Wächter, the governor of the Cracow province, on the same subject, written in January, 1940, see T. Bernstein, et al., *Eksterminacja Żydów na ziemiach polskich*, pp. 38–39, 45–46.

81. *Nazi Conspiracy and Aggression* (Washington: United States Government Printing Office, 1945), vol. 8, p. 402.

82. A copy of Göring's letter is in the YIVO Archives.

83. A confidential note of April 3, 1940, by Dr. Wilhelm Stuckart, a deputy minister in the Reich's Ministry of Internal Affairs, concerns a conference of April 1, 1940, on the Łódź ghetto. A copy of the letter is in the YIVO Archives.

second on October 1, until, finally, in September of that year it was decided that the resettlement of Jews to the Generalgouvernement was, for the time being, out of the question.[84] This decision was based on reasons of a very general nature among the most important of which were, undoubtedly, the dropping of a project to create a reservation for Jews in the Lublin province of the Generalgouvernement and a reluctance to concentrate a great mass of Jews so near what was then the Russian-German border.[85] It is also very likely that the plan to exploit Łódź's large and highly skilled Jewish labor force right on the spot to serve the German war economy played a role in the decision to desist from resettlement. As we shall see, this factor would be taken into account at several points, though it was always treated as only a temporary solution.

The creation of the Łódź ghetto also was viewed by the occupiers as only a temporary solution. Preparations for the ghetto had begun early in the winter of 1939, that is, during the period of the largest forced resettlements to the Generalgouvernement, when there could not have been the slightest doubt in the Wartheland that the resettlements might be suspended on orders from above. Moreover, it was just at that time that a special section known as IV B4 was created in the Reich's Security Main Office in Berlin to provide overall coordination for the resettlement and transferral of populations in Germany and the occupied territories. A then little-known Gestapo expert on Jewish affairs, *SS-Sturmbannführer* Adolf Eichmann, was appointed to head this section.[86] And so, certain that the resettlement of Jews from Łódź was and would continue to be carried out but seeing that this could not be accomplished all at once, the local Nazi party and police authorities moved to isolate the Jews in a separate and closed quarter of the city from which it would also prove easier to evacuate them. The occupier's desires demanded haste: to exclude the Jews entirely from the body of the city, to liquidate Jewish assets and assume control of them as quickly as possible, and to vacate at once a large number of apartments for the ethnic Germans then arriving in Łódź from behind the demarcation line with the USSR, that is, from the Baltic countries, Volhynia, and eastern Galicia. Of course, in their internal correspondence, whose function was to help them convince themselves, and in their public pronouncements, which were chiefly for propaganda purposes, the Nazis put forward other reasons for isolating the Jews—that they represented a criminal element, were the bearers of contagious diseases, were unwilling to work, and so forth.[87]

Although a plan for separate Jewish quarters on occupied Polish territories had been postulated in the order by Heydrich on September 21, 1939, the first document in Łódź that mentions the creation of a ghetto is a secret memorandum from *SS-Brigadenführer* Friederich Übelhör, chief of police of one of the regions of the Warthe-

---

84. A. Eisenbach, *Hitlerowska polityka zagłady Żydów* [The Nazi policy of exterminating the Jews] (Warsaw: Książka i Wiedza, 1961), p. 231.

85. On the subject of the so-called Lublin reservation see Eisenbach, *Hitlerowska polityka zagłady Żydów*, pp. 165–82; Philip Friedman, *Roads to Extermination: Essays on the Holocaust*, ed. Ada June Friedman, with an introduction by Salo Wittmayer Baron (Philadelphia: 1980), pp. 34–58.

86. *Biuletyn Głównej Komisji Badania Zbrodni Hitlerowskich w Polsce* (The Bulletin of the Main Commission for the Investigation of Nazi Crimes in Poland) 12 (1960), p. 53.

87. These propaganda slogans are repeated nearly verbatim in the confidential letter written by Dr. Stuckart in connection with the conference in the Reich's Ministry of Internal Affairs.

land,[88] issued on December 10.[89] He too headed a staff composed of representatives of the city's police, municipal, and financial authorities whose task it was to work out all the details connected with the creation of the ghetto. Less than two months later, on February 8, 1940, the Łódź chief of police, SS-Brigadenführer Johannes Schäfer, ordered the establishment of the ghetto.[90] Accompanied by police terror, the process of concentrating Łódź's entire Jewish population into a predetermined part of the city thus commenced, and on April 30 Schäfer ordered the Jewish quarter to be definitively closed, thereby creating the first ghetto in the Wartheland and the first one in a large metropolitan area.[91] Despite its provisional character, it was to last, if not as a whole then in part, until the summer of 1944, when it was the only ghetto left on Polish territory.[92]

The Germans chose the most neglected, northern districts of the city, Stare Miasto (the Old Town) and Bałuty, for the ghetto. In the years 1822–61, Stare Miasto had been designated as the restricted area for Łódź's Jewish population in Congress Poland under Russian domination.[93] Bałuty, in turn, was a very poor and hastily constructed settlement that had only been incorporated into the greater city of Łódź during the First World War.[94] Both of those districts, along with the suburban areas of Marysin, constituted the ghetto, which initially measured four square kilometers and whose circumference, marked by a barbed wire fence, amounted to 11 kilometers.[95] Within the ghetto, housing conditions were critical, to say the very least. Out of a total number of 31,721 apartments, most of them one room, only 725 had running water. The majority of them did have electricity, but, in accordance with a police ruling, the ghetto was not allowed to use its lights, especially during the winter of 1940/41, from 8 P.M. to 6 A.M.[96]

There are practically no authoritative sources as to the number of Jews in occupied Łódź before the closing of the ghetto, and those derived from the German authorities have to be rejected *a priori* because, from the very beginning, they did not include Jews in the censuses they took.[97] On the other hand, both in secret documents and in propaganda literature, the Germans employed round figures that not only were

88. Wartheland was divided into three regions: Poznań, Inowrocław, and Kalisz (later: Łódź), or in German: *Posen, Hohensalza,* and *Litzmannstadt.*

89. Eisenbach, *Dokumenty i materiały, III,* pp. 26–31.

90. Ibid., pp. 35–50.

91. Ibid., pp. 74–75.

92. Übelhor concluded his memorandum with the words: "The creation of a ghetto is clearly only a temporary move. I reserve the right to decide the time frame and the means for clearing the ghetto, and the city, of Jews. In any case, the ultimate goal must be to burn out this pestilence entirely." Eisenbach, *Dokumenty i materiały, III,* p. 31.

93. Friedman, *Historia Żydów w Łódzi,* pp. 45–54.

94. Ginsberg, *Łódź: Studium monograficzne,* pp. 28–29, 42, 51, 98.

95. YIVO Archives, Zon. 855, no. 3.

96. Order of the day for November 14, 1940, signed by Schäfer's successor SS-Brigadenführer Dr. Karl-Wilhelm Albert; cf. the *Chronicle* entry dated March 3, 1941.

97. Tadeusz Olejnik, "Stan ludności na obszarze województwa łódzkiego włączonym do III Rzeszy: Na podstawie spisu przeprowadzonego w grudniu 1939" (The Population level in the area of Łódź province incorporated into the Third Reich: based on the count taken in December, 1939), *Rocznik Łódzki* 16 (1972), Table 6. Without explanation, this table also lists 64 persons of Jewish nationality, 84 of the Mosaic faith, and 286 whose language is listed as Yiddish. This probably reflects the presence of Jews who were citizens of foreign countries. The majority of them were later settled in the ghetto.

without basis but also purposely overestimated. Übelhör, for example, in his memorandum of December 10, 1939, mentions the figure of 320,000 Jews in Łódź,[98] while Karl Marder, the mayor of the city, claims, in a study sent to the Ministry of Internal Affairs in Berlin on October 27, 1941, that 200,000 people had entered the ghetto.[99] Both of the figures are incorrect and reveal how the Nazi bureaucracy reported Jewish matters, not only in Łódź but elsewhere as well.[100]

Any attempt to determine the number of Jews in Łódź after September 1, 1939, should take the *antebellum* status quo as its point of departure. Based on data from the last Polish census of 1931 and on estimates by the Łódź Department of Vital Statistics for the next eight years, there is general agreement that the number of Jews in Łódź in that period fluctuated between 230,000 and 250,000. The outbreak of the war brought abrupt changes: large numbers of people throughout Poland were immediately in migration. Those migrations were, of course, swift and chaotic and therefore not registered or included in any demographic records. On the basis of other sources one can, however, indicate at least the nature and direction of the wartime migrations, especially those that assumed mass proportions. As far as the Jews of Łódź were concerned, their movement was almost exclusively out of the city,[101] in particular in the following series of events: (1) the departure of a number of people on September 6 and 7, 1939, in response to an appeal issued by a Polish government spokesman over the radio for all men fit to bear arms to head east where a new line of defense was to be formed; (2) the flight of many thousands of Jews east of the Bug River to territory taken by the Red Army after September 17, 1939, flights that continued from October, 1939, until at least January, 1940; (3) voluntary departures to various cities and towns in the Generalgouvernement, which were possible until the closing of the ghetto; and finally, (4) the above-mentioned resettlements in the winter of 1939.[102] As a result of all these various forms of migration, the decrease in Łódź's Jewish population may, without fear of great error, be estimated at something between 65,000 and 85,000. There are also no fundamental reasons to question the data compiled by the ghetto's Department of Vital Statistics, which, based on the popula-

98. Eisenbach, *Dokumenty i materiały, III,* p. 26.

99. As far as the number of the ghetto's inhabitants is concerned, this work cites official data supplied by the German authorities in charge of the ghetto. Those authorities considered that the population count taken on June 16, 1941, by order of the German authorities, was incomplete. Copies of Marder's letter and study of the ghetto are in the YIVO Archives.

100. When in the summer of 1942 the Germans deported 300,000 Jews from the Warsaw ghetto to the death camp at Treblinka, that seemed too few to Dr. Ludwig Fischer, the governor of the Warsaw district, who boasted in his report to the higher authorities in Cracow: "Insgesamt sind etwa 400,000 Juden aus Warschau evakuiert worden," *Zweimonatsbericht des Gouverneurs des Distrikts Warschau von 12 Oktober 1942 für die Monate August und September 1942* (p. 7).

101. On May 1, 1940, when the ghetto was sealed off, about 4 percent of the population was from towns and cities other than Łódź, see Abraham Melezin, *Przyczynek do stosunków demograficznych wśród ludności żydowskiej w Łodzi, Krakowie i Lublinie podczas okupacji niemieckiej* [On the demographical structure of the Jewish population in Łódź, Cracow, and Lublin during the German occupation] (Łódź: Centralna Żydowska Komisja Historyczna, 1946), p. 10.

102. I. Lewin "Di geheyme evakuatsye komisye" (The Secret Evacuation Committee), *Lodzher yizker-bukh* [Łódź memorial book] (New York: United Emergency Relief Committee for the City of Łódź, 1943), pp. 77–80; Jasny, *Di geshikhte fun yidn in Lodzh,* pp. 83–87; Dobroszycki, "Restoring Jewish Life in Post-war Poland," *Soviet Jewish Affairs* 3/2 (1973), pp. 58–60; Władysław Bartoszewski, *1859 dni Warszawy* [Warsaw's 1,859 days] (Cracow: Wydawnictwo Znak, 1974), pp. 29–30.

tion count of June 16, 1940, and various later corrections, calculated that on May 1, the first day of the closed ghetto's existence, the population stood at 163,177.[103] From May 1 to February of the next year, when the *Chronicle*'s bulletins begin to report regularly on the level of population in the ghetto, the following changes in population had taken place:[104]

June 16, 1940–January 31, 1941

Increase		Decrease	
Births	702	Deaths	7,383
Arrivals from outside the ghetto	349	Left the ghetto	307
Returned to ghetto from forced labor	3	Sent to perform forced labor outside the ghetto	990
TOTAL	1,054	TOTAL	8,680

In accordance with the principles adopted even before the closing of the Jewish quarter, which remained in effect unchanged until its liquidation, the ghetto administration was concentrated in two branches of German local authority: the political/police and the administrative/economic. The former included the local police (*Schutzpolizei, Schupo* for short), the criminal police (*Kriminalpolizei,* Kripo) and the secret state police (*Geheime Staatspolizei,* Gestapo). The latter was chiefly concentrated in the municipality of Łódź.[105]

The Schutzpolizei, together with its auxiliary units, guarded the ghetto from the outside. According to its orders, the Schutzpolizei was supposed to shoot from the "Aryan" side at anyone who did not obey the cry, "HALT." On the Jewish side, however, it could shoot anyone approaching the barbed wire fence surrounding the ghetto without even a word of warning. The Schupo had also been instructed to allow no one into the ghetto, no matter who that person might be, without a valid pass signed by the chief of police and bearing the so-called Stamp No. 1.[106]

The German criminal police was headquartered within the ghetto, in its very center. Its seat was a parish building connected to the Church of the Most Blessed Virgin Mary, which it had taken over and which had undergone the necessary remodeling, especially in its cellars, assigned for use as prison cells. Kripo headquarters, known throughout the ghetto as the Red House, because of the color of the brick

---

103. According to the (uncorrected) count from June 16, 1940, there were 157,955 people in the ghetto of whom 72,530 were men (45.92 percent) and 85,425 (54.08 percent) were women. Out of the total number of the ghetto's inhabitants, 7,582 were children up to 3 years of age (3,856 boys and 3,726 girls) and 28,606 were children between the ages of 3 and 14 (14,431 boys and 14,175 girls). See the letters of M. C. Rumkowski to the German Ghetto Administration on June 16 and 20, 1940, AZIH (AJHI), Rum. Records, no. 66.

104. From the Department of Vital Statistics of the Eldest of the Jews (YIVO Archives, Zon. 877, no. 6).

105. A few days before the closing of the ghetto, these matters, among others, were discussed at a meeting held on April 27, 1940, by the head of the Kalisz region, the mayor of Łódź, the chief of police of the city, and officials from the Łódź department of the Main Trusteeship Office East (*Haupttreuhandstelle Ost*), a central organization concerned with assuming possession of Jewish property. Eisenbach, *Dokumenty i materiały, III,* pp. 73–75.

106. Ibid., pp. 81–87.

exterior, became a place of torture, sowing terror among the inhabitants of the closed quarter. Aside from its police-terror functions, the Kripo was concerned with collecting information about all articles of value located within the ghetto or hidden by Jews in the city and with conducting searches and arrests in that regard. The real or imagined owner of such valuables was subject to torture. The criminal police's duties also included a constant day-and-night patrol of the grounds of the ghetto, to check that its isolation was maintained and, in particular, to be on the lookout for smugglers.[107] Above all, however, the Kripo took an active part in all the deportations, whether people were being sent to perform forced labor outside the ghetto or to death and concentration camps.

The most important and, at the same time, the most dreaded police force was the Gestapo, all too well known everywhere for its cruelty. In Łódź, its core consisted of the police personnel who had arrived there with Einsatzgruppe III of the Reich Security Main Office in September, 1939. All the other police forces operating within the ghetto itself and around its boundaries were *de facto* subordinate to the Gestapo. It also kept political surveillance over the city municipality and all of its departments. Every head of the Gestapo was, by virtue of his office, the political superior of the president of the Łódź region, to whom the city was subordinate.[108] Thus, nothing of significance could occur in the ghetto without the knowledge and consent of the Gestapo. This primarily concerned the treatment of the Jewish population, establishing its living conditions, as well as all the settlement and resettlement actions, which were, after all, organized and directed by the municipal Gestapo on a signal from headquarters. Two individuals played a particularly sinister role here—*SS-Hauptsturmführer* Dr. Otto Bradfisch, the chief of the Łódź Gestapo, and its commissioner for Jewish affairs (Gruppe II B.4 Judenangelegenheiten), SS-Obersturmführer Günter Fuchs.

Bradfisch, born in 1903, a lawyer by training, with many years of membership in the Nazi party behind him, arrived in Łódź in January, 1942, to replace SS-Hauptsturmführer Robert Schefe. That was at the beginning of the first great deportation of about 70,000 ghetto inhabitants to the death camp in Chełmno on the Ner River. Bradfisch was not selected for that post by chance—he had acquired considerable experience in the mass murder of Jews before he was named head of the Gestapo in Łódź. As soon as the war between Germany and Russia broke out in June, 1941, Bradfisch, then chief of the Gestapo in Neustadt, in the Rhein palatinate, was assigned to the mobile killing units as commander of *Einsatzkommando* 8 in Einsatzgruppe B at the German Army Group Center. Apart from his original and principal Gestapo duties in Łódź, he soon had the entire city in his hands, becoming the police mayor of Łódź after Werner Ventzki's departure in August, 1943.[109]

Günter Fuchs, Bradfisch's subordinate, was born in 1911. He graduated from the humanist gymnasium in Breslau and attended the law department of the university there. He did not pass the state examinations, which did not, however, prevent him from making a career for himself. In 1932 he joined the Nazi party, and a year later, the

---

107. Ibid., pp. 92–98.
108. Cygański, *Z dziejów okupacji*, p. 105.
109. On Ventzki, see below, p. 190, n. 58.

SA, the uniformed, brown-shirt storm troops (*Sturmabteilung*). After completing the school for security police leaders in Berlin-Charlottenburg, Fuchs ended up in Łódź in January, 1940. As Gestapo commissioner for Jewish affairs, he was often on the grounds of the ghetto, among other reasons, personally to direct various police actions.[110]

The city municipality, as the second branch of authority over the Jewish quarter was, as opposed to the political and police branch, supposed to fulfill functions that the occupier defined as constructive and whose aim was to put all the ghetto's labor forces to work. To that end, a department possessing rather broad authority was created as part of the city's general administration. Initially, when the establishment of the ghetto was conceived only as a means for temporarily concentrating Łódź's Jewish population before resettling it to the Generalgouvernement, that department's principal function was to supply the ghetto with food in exchange for goods, valuables, and money (German marks and foreign currency), and ensuring that the Jews fulfilled their obligation to work. Hence, the name of that department—the Department of Food Supply and Economics (*Ernährungs Wirtschaftsamt*). However, after the liquidation of the ghetto was postponed and the occupation authorities began to display interest in the economic exploitation of the ghetto, the role and the task of the city in the organization of the Jewish quarter increased significantly. The Department of Food Supply and Economics was renamed the Ghetto Administration (*Gettoverwaltung*), and, from October, 1940, on that department increased to enormous proportions, with offices in both the city and the ghetto, administering all the Jewish quarter's economic and human resources. Among the Gettoverwaltung's specific tasks was to receive orders from interested parties, that is, from the Reich's war industry and from private companies, and to supply the ghetto with the necessary raw materials and machines. At the same time, the Gettoverwaltung supervised the ghetto's entire range of internal affairs on a daily basis. Hans Biebow headed this department throughout, both under its former name and as the Gettoverwaltung. He was directly subordinate to the mayor of the city of Łódź and administered the ghetto on his behalf.

Biebow, whose title was *Amtsleiter*, was undoubtedly a rather colorful figure, a sort of combination of good businessman and loyal Nazi whose behavior reflected both sides of his personality by turns. He was 38 years old when he assumed control of the ghetto. The son of the director of an insurance company, he was, like his father, a businessman operating on a large scale, independent, and even rather well-to-do. Just before the outbreak of the war his coffee business in Bremen employed about 250 workers and had monthly sales of one million German marks. It is difficult to be certain what impelled Biebow to join the Nazi party. It is a fact, however, that he became active only after Hitler had come to power, perhaps out of fear for his business's subsequent fate, but even then he preserved a certain caution, joining the party only toward the end of 1937. The post of head of the ghetto administration may have seemed very lucrative to him, and it also exempted him from military service and,

---

110. More on Bradfisch and Fuchs can be found in *Justiz und NS-Verbrechen. Sammlung deutscher Strafurteile wegen Nationalsozialistischer Tötungsverbrecher 1946–1966*, vol. 19 (Amsterdam: University Press, 1978).

later on, from going to the front. In any case, there is much evidence extant that he went to great lengths to secure that post and, to that end, sought support from many people.[111] He felt entirely at ease in the ghetto and personally profited greatly from it, as befitted the sybarite that he was. Moreover, he did not have 250 workers under him there, as he had had in Bremen, but tens of thousands of workmen whose needs required little attention, and he also had nearly unlimited power over all the inhabitants of the ghetto. Apart from Biebow, none of the Nazis realized so clearly how much the ghetto could benefit the Reich economically. Biebow was well acquainted with every workshop in the ghetto, its directors, engineers, and technical staff, and had a precise sense of what every factory was producing and at what low cost, or more precisely, in exchange for what paltry, even outright starvation rations. The initiative to liquidate the ghetto certainly did not originate with him, although he rarely displayed even the slightest sign that the fate of its inhabitants was of any concern to him. His sole interest was the ghetto's productivity and the profit to be derived from it. On that level, he was able to maintain businesslike relations with some of the Jewish workshop directors, though, naturally, he kept a proper distance, and his moods tended to vary. He never forgot, however, that he was a German, and he ruled the ghetto with a firm hand. And more than once he beat and bloodied one or another ghetto dweller, including even Rumkowski, the Eldest of the Jews.[112]

The fate of the ghetto obviously did not rest in the hands of the local authorities alone. The city authorities as well as all of the local police forces had their counterparts both on the provincial and the central levels to which they were subordinate. In the Wartheland these were the *Reichsstatthalter* and Gauleiter Artur Greiser, who was head of both the state and Nazi party territorial units, on the one hand and, on the other, SS-Obergruppenführer Wilhelm Koppe, the Higher SS and Police Leader.[113] In Berlin, at the very top, these were Göring, as Hitler's deputy and the Plenipotentiary for the Four Year Plan, Himmler, the SS-Reichsführer and Chief of the German Police, and Frick, the Reich's Minister of the Interior. Moreover, for one reason or another, a series of other Reich departments and ministries considered the ghetto's affairs, because of the goods produced there, to be of their direct concern—to mention but one example, the Armament Ministry headed by Albert Speer and the Armaments Inspection of the German Armed Forces in the Wartheland. Frequently, the jurisdictions of various departments on the city, provincial, or central levels were either at odds or overlapped with one another.[114] At times, quarrels would arise among them

111. "Z autobiografii i papierów osobistych H. Biebowa" (From the autobiography and personal papers of H. Biebow), Eisenbach, ed., *Dokumenty i materiały, III*, pp. 252–55.

112. See below, pp. 504–05.

113. A member of the Nazi party even before Hitler came to power, Greiser was chairman of the senate of the Free City of Danzig in the years 1934–39. He was sentenced to death as a war criminal in Poland by the National Supreme Court on July 9, 1946 (Krüger's successors were Theo Berkelmann and Heinz Reinefarth).

114. This is how Edward Crankshaw has described the confusion of authority that existed in the Third Reich:
"If the reader finds himself muddled by the strange overlappings and divisions of authority and executive power, he may be assured that he is in good company: the Germans themselves were also muddled. Even at Nuremberg, with its remarkable gathering of forensic talent, the court never succeeded in unravelling the tangle and laying bare the outlines of the hierarchy—for the very good reason that no rigid outline ever existed. In the light of accumulated knowledge we can get a clearer picture than was possible at Nuremberg; but it will only be to find out that behind the apparently iron front of Teutonic organisation there was a sort of willed chaos," *Gestapo: An Instrument of Tyranny* (London: Viking Press, 1959), p. 63.

over specific questions. In general, however, if one overlooks entirely the otherwise well-known animosities and personal quarrels that existed throughout the Nazi hierarchy, the differences of opinion concerning the Jewish quarter can be reduced to the following: should Jews from the Old Reich be resettled into the Łódź ghetto, to whom do the things confiscated from its inhabitants belong, is the ghetto sufficiently productive or wouldn't it be better to change the ghetto into a forced labor camp, at what moment should the ghetto as a whole cease to exist, and, finally, who is to take possession of the property after the ghetto is vacated?[115] As a rule, the final decision in fundamental questions belonged to the police and security service. The positions taken by others could to some degree modify the police's plans, postpone their execution somewhat, but it was rare that they could change them entirely. When, however, some decision had been made in regard to the ghetto, the police could count on the complete cooperation of the civilian authorities beginning with the Gettoverwaltung and Biebow himself.

By order of the German authorities, there also existed an internal Jewish administration within the ghetto. It arose considerably earlier than the ghetto itself and, moreover, under the threat of reprisals, was compelled to take part in the creation of the ghetto. It was burdened with the responsibility of transporting the Jewish population from all the districts of Łódź to the area assigned for the ghetto, and there, of necessity, had to find housing for them and, later on, to provide them with some form of social existence. The more important departments of the internal administration, along with the Jewish police, fire department, and the departments of economics and social welfare, had already begun to be organized, so that when the ghetto was closed permanently on May 1, 1940, the Jewish administration had already been formed in outline.[116]

In fact, the very beginnings of the Jewish administration should be ascribed to the time when, in letters on the 13th and 14th of October, 1939, the occupation commissioner of Łódź, on behalf of the Chief of Civil Administration of the German Eighth Army, appointed the Eldest of the Jews and ordered him to disband the old Jewish community institution of self-government (the kehillah) and to select a group of co-workers that would constitute a Council of Elders (*Ältestenrat*). Rumkowski was appointed the Eldest.[117] There are various and contradictory stories about why it was

---

115. Property left behind after the deportation of the Jews from Łódź and the surrounding towns and cities became the focal point of endless disputes and quarrels on all levels of the Nazi organization in Wartheland and elsewhere. Gauleiter Greiser tried to put some kind of "order" into the matter, and in an ordinance dated March 23, 1942, decided that the only beneficiary of Jewish property, including money, foreign currency, merchandise, and household items, should be the Gettoverwaltung of the city of Łódź. In turn, the Gettoverwaltung started to sell some items to various German offices and institutions to whom their origin was no secret. In the files of the Gettoverwaltung, letters have been found in which the office of the People's Welfare (*Amt für Volkswohlfart*) complained that the clothing they had received for the winter welfare campaign for the German people (*Winterhilfswerk des deutsches Volkes*) was in poor condition, that many of the garments were bloodstained while some 51 pieces were marked with Stars of David, and that, in the future, they should be cleaned. Letter from Poznań to Łódź, January 16, 1943, in *Dokumenty i materiały do dziejów okupacji niemieckiej w Polsce, II: "Akcje" i "Wysiedlenia,"* ed. Józef Kermisz (Łódź: Centralna Żydowska Komisja Historyczna, 1946), pp. 168–70.

116. Danuta Dąbrowska, "Administracja żydowska w Łódźi i jej agendy w okresie od początku okupacji do zamknięcie getta, 9/8/39–4/30/40," (The Jewish administration of Łódź and its departments from the beginning of the occupation until the closing of the ghetto), *Biuletyn Żydowskiego Instytutu Historycznego* 45–46 (1964), pp. 132–37.

117. AZIH [AJHI], Rum. Records, no. 2110.

Rumkowski specifically who was appointed to that post and under what circumstances the appointment occurred. One version has it that he was selected because of his noble appearance, while another claims that it resulted from a certain linguistic misunderstanding stemming from Rumkowski's inadequate knowledge of German,[118] and finally, a third, but by no means the last, version maintains that Rumkowski himself sought out the nomination and, to that end, even employed a certain subterfuge.[119] None of them, however, is supported by any documents—they either simply do not exist or no trace of them has as yet been found. On the other hand, what did take place during the first few weeks of the occupation of the city is rather well known and that, in turn, could be of help in establishing at least the general outline of the circumstances which led to Rumkowski's emergence as the Eldest of the Jews.

When the German army occupied the city, the organized social existence of the Jews of Łódź was immediately curbed if not entirely subdued. There was not a single Jewish institution represented in, nor any Jewish individual on, the civic committee whose task it was to maintain order in the city during the emergency. That committee was formed on the night of September 6, that is, when the Polish authorities had withdrawn from Łódź and the German army was about to occupy the city. No Jews had joined the committee since it did not wish to provoke the invader, with whom it would be in contact. It was also thought that this would be better for the Jews themselves. The committee, which was composed of well-known and, for the most part, respected citizens, both Poles and ethnic Germans, undoubtedly made some contribution to maintaining tranquility and order.[120] But in matters relating to the Jewish population the committee proved of no influence, although it did make some attempt to render the Jews aid, especially as far as provisions and sanitary conditions were concerned. The Jews were automatically excluded, so to speak, from the protection of the law and any of the city's institutions. The Jewish organizations themselves were at once thrown into a state of complete disorganization—their coffers were empty, their bank accounts frozen, the freedom of their personnel to move about the city was greatly curtailed, their premises were frequently visited by the police or simply by marauders, and the ranks of their executives had been decimated by the arrests that were the order of the day. Moreover, the leader of any Jewish institution or political party who felt endangered because of his former activity fled Łódź either before or immediately after the occupation of the city. There were many members of the kehillah among those refugees, including Jakub Lejb Mincberg, its chairman of many years who, at the same time, had been a member of the Polish parliament as a representative of the religious party Agudath Israel.[121]

In occupied Łódź, in an atmosphere of tension and anxiety about the future, a meeting of the incomplete kehillah council was hastily called on September 12, 1939.

---

118. According to this version, which can hardly be taken seriously, a Gestapo officer was supposed to have asked at a meeting of the kehillah's board: "Which of you is the Eldest," which Rumkowski took to mean: which of you is the oldest. Rumkowski rose and said that he was.

119. Tabaksblat, *Khurbn Lodzh*, p. 32; Nirenberg, *In di yorn fun yidishn khurbn*, pp. 235–36.

120. Wojewódzkie Archiwum Państwowe (The State Archive of Łódź Province), *Biuletyn* (Bulletin), nos. 1–3, 1015/3; Dobroszycki, *Die legale polnische Presse im Generalgouvernement*, pp. 28–32.

121. Marian Fuks, *Polski Słownik Biograficzny* (Polish Biographical Dictionary), vol. 21 (Wrocław: Zakład Narodowy imienia Ossolińskich, 1976), pp. 281–82.

During that session a new chairman was elected, Abram Lajzor Pł400ywacki, who was also from Agudath Israel and its former vice-chairman, and M. C. Rumkowski was unanimously elected his deputy.[122] It quickly became apparent, however, that it was not Pływacki but Rumkowski who had taken the helm of the community's affairs, for he was the more energetic, the more suited to work under any conditions, and also the readier to assume responsibilities without always realizing what consequences they might entail. In any case, exactly one month after the elections in the kehillah, Rumkowski was appointed the Eldest of the Jews. That had been enough time for the Germans to form some picture of the kehillah's affairs, especially since a secret police officer was constantly at its headquarters at 18 Pomorska Street. Rumkowski could not help but attract attention, and that seems to have been the deciding factor in naming him the Eldest. Besides, hardly any of Rumkowski's associates would have wanted to compete with him for that post, which was, officially at least, to be accepted under threat of repressive measures.[123]

Rumkowski was 62 years old when he became the Eldest of the Jews in Łódź and he was a person who had already experienced a good deal in life.[124] Moreover, he was entirely alone in the world: he had become a widower before the war, had no children, and the people who knew him best say that he never had any friends among his colleagues. Everything seemed to indicate that he had not succeeded in life. As a businessman and manufacturer he had twice lost everything, once just before the First World War and once after the Russian Revolution. Thus, after the war, he was without financial means or specific profession, and had only a minimal formal education. Apart from the traditional *kheyder* he had four or five years of elementary school in the village of Ilino in Tsarist Russia, where he had been born. He had tried his hand at a variety of occupations in independent Poland until finally becoming an insurance agent. It was not, however, in his livelihood that he sought the outlet for his energy and ambition, for at the beginning of the twenties he proposed a project for creating a new Jewish orphanage. Supported by an endowment from the American Joint Distribution Committee, but principally due to his contacts in the business world, Rumkowski succeeded in collecting sums of money, large for those times, that allowed him to build an orphanage on a farm in Helenówek, outside of Łódź. He became its director and held that position, undoubtedly a source of great prestige for him, without interruption for the entire period between the wars. Other of his important though less absorbing functions in the Jewish community included serving as a board member in the local Zionist party and on the kehillah board, to which he was elected in 1931 as Zionist party candidate. In each of the positions he held, Rumkowski had the reputation of a man who went his own way without taking anyone else

122. Dąbrowska, "Administracja żydowska w Łódźi," p. 11.

123. The view that Rumkowski had serious competition for the position of Eldest of the Jews from Rabbi Dr. Symcha Treistman is based on a misunderstanding, ibid., p. 119.

124. Brief biographical information on Rumkowski is recorded in the *Chronicle* on the occasion of his marriage to Regina Weinberger on December 23–25, 1941 (p. 99). The most reliable and at the same time the most objective information on Rumkowski was found in the memoirs of J. Szulman. Also used were *Lodzher gezelshaftlekhayt:Almanakh*, ed. M. Frankental (Łódź, 1939), and certain articles and reports in the Yiddish pre-war press in Łódź, which discuss Rumkowski's activities both in the Orphanage in Helenówek and on the kehillah board.

into consideration and who was frequently engaged in conflict, even with the party to which he had belonged for many years. When, for example, shortly before the war, differences of opinion within the kehillah board caused the Zionists to recall all their members, Rumkowski would not submit to that decision, for which he was disciplinarily dismissed from the party. Rumkowski, however, had the ability of stubbornly sticking to his own, and argued that both intelligence and conscience dictated that in such a difficult period the unity of that essential institution should not be broken. He remained in the kehillah and was still a member when the war broke out.[125]

To be sure, Rumkowski is far from exceptional in going directly from the kehillah board to the Jewish administration, which was generally known as the Jewish Council (Judenrat). Other candidates acted similarly nearly everywhere else in Poland, something that had figured in the invader's advance plans.[126] Heydrich's directives of September 21, 1939, had expressly ordered the creation of a Council of Elders in every Jewish community, to be formed, as much as possible, from the remaining important individuals and rabbis, who were to be burdened with the responsibility for carrying out all orders to the letter and on time. Although an identical role was assigned them everywhere, the Jewish Councils, depending on the area in which they were established, differed from one another in how they carried out the tasks imposed on them, in the principles used within the council for the division of labor, and in their responsibility to the German authorities. While in many communities the Jewish Councils constituted a collective body in terms of their organizational structure, it was a one-man institution in Łódź from the very beginning. The council was personified in Rumkowski and the title conferred on him, the Eldest of the Jews, was at the same time the official name of his administration. And, indeed, within the ghetto, his was the decisive voice. Everyone and everything was subordinate to him there, and his power ended only when German authority began. That principle was strictly observed, on both ends, though for different reasons and motives. As far as the Germans were concerned, they never even attempted to preserve an appearance of observing any norms in regard to the Jews of Łódź. The absence of decorum in their behavior was brought to a monstrous perfection right from the start. And thus, less than a month after Rumkowski had been ordered to select a Council of Elders, all but eight of its 30 members were arrested during a single day in November, 1939, taken away, and killed.[127] Rumkowski returned bruised from Gestapo headquarters after attempting to intervene in their case. But since there seemed to be no order against selecting a new Council of Elders, he did just that. The Germans, however, treated this as a mere formality, and the council, which never had any importance, soon ceased to exist of its own accord. One man was entirely sufficient for the Germans in Łódź, and it did not matter who he was as long as he was absolutely obedient, able to maintain order in the Jewish quarter, and knew how to mobilize people for work.

Rumkowski took his appointment as Eldest of the Jews very seriously, although it is

---

125. *Nayer togblat* (The New Daily), Łódź, February 14, 1938, p. 9; April 4, 1938, p. 7.

126. For more on this subject, see Isaiah Trunk, *Judenrat: The Jewish Councils in Eastern Europe under Nazi Occupation* (New York: Macmillan Co., 1972), pp. 14–35.

127. Dąbrowska, "Administracja żydowska w Łódźi," p. 120; a complete list of the 30 members of the first Council of the Elders was published in Eisenbach, ed., *Dokumenty i materiały, III*, p. 20.

difficult to assume that he considered it a step forward socially. It is also unlikely that he accepted the post in hopes of gaining material and/or personal advantage. To deal with the affairs of a community seemed to be his calling, and with the outbreak of the war, his activities in that field and his sense of his own importance grew considerably. He was well aware of what the German Nazis were capable of, but he believed that, with proper behavior, things could somehow be worked out. He was not alone in that opinion, especially in the beginning. Rumkowski, however, maintained that conviction until the very end. He deceived himself the most and was the least able to understand the truth even though he should have known better than anyone that the Nazis would disregard the inexhaustible benefits that could be derived from the work of the hands and minds of the Jews of Łódź, of whom he was in charge. At the same time, he thought that even if he failed to change their policy toward the Jews in any way, he could at least somewhat diminish its severity and render it less violent and brutal. That tactic became an obsession for him, and he saw in it a need to act at any cost, or that was how he explained the situation to himself and others. As events developed, his line of thought assumed the form of an outright imperative: since a given Nazi action against the Jews was irrevocable and since no help could be expected from any quarter, less blood would flow and there would be fewer victims if the Jews themselves carried out the action. During the first months of the occupation, decisions were made in that spirit concerning matters which, in light of later events, might seem entirely insignificant. For example, in order to eliminate roundups in the streets and buildings, the Jewish administration took it upon itself to deliver a number of Jewish workers, arranged in advance, to points indicated by the German authorities.[128] This is what happened in practice and Rumkowski was proud of the arrangement. The roundups, however, did not come to a complete halt. Frequently, people on the way to one job were grabbed and taken to another, as well as to places other than those officially agreed upon. Nevertheless, this was viewed as progress of a sort. Those were, however, only innocent beginnings. Terrible things, things neither foreseeable nor even conceivable, were to happen later in the closed ghetto.

The ghetto's first year was relatively calm, so much so that it could have appeared that the Germans had achieved their aim and would draw the line there. The Jews had been settled in a closed quarter of the city, where it was easier to supervise them, extract the last of their valuables, and make use of them as a nearly free labor force concentrated in various workshops. The entire Jewish quarter was also cut off from the network of municipal services, including electricity, fire department, and mail.

---

128. In the previously mentioned account, compiled in the ghetto's Department of the Archives, entitled "Wojna" (The war), there is, among other passages, the following on the subject of roundups for forced labor: "Immediately after the Germans had entered Łódź, forced labor for Jews began . . . It was not in the least a matter of performing tasks connected with the war effort or even of doing some useful work; the point was to humiliate them with any sort of dirty and difficult work, often of no use to anyone. Actions were conducted, people were rounded up on the streets, hunted down, dragged from tramcars and droshkys, and led off like criminals to the so-called work places. . . . It was a daily occurrence [for people to be forced] to clean toilets with their hands and scrape floors with their fingernails . . . [women were ordered] to remove their underclothing and use it to wash floors, windows, and toilets. . . . Based on the first order issued by the authorities on October 5, 1939, concerning forced labor for Jews, the kehillah demanded that the owners and managers of buildings furnish them with a list of male Jewish tenants between the ages of 18 and 45," AZIH [AJHI], Rum. Records, no. 2110, pp. 1–7.

The Germans handed over entirely the ghetto's administrative, peace-keeping, economic, and social affairs to the Eldest of the Jews, endowing him with broad powers, and this was what formed the basis for the ghetto's so-called internal autonomy.

Disregarding the fact that the term autonomy was being misused, Rumkowski treated it as seriously as he did his own title, and within that framework created an enormous network of various departments, offices, councils and special commissions, which at their peak employed some 10,000 people. Apart from the departments of food supply, soup kitchens, health, and social welfare, Rumkowski built a large enforcement apparatus consisting of the various forms of police, the courts, and prison. Concurrently, he established more and more new workshops and enterprises where, as he usually put it, "his" many-thousand-strong army of workers was employed. All told, this transformed the ghetto into a sort of Lilliputian quasi-centralized state where there was practically no place for private initiative or for any sort of unsupervised public activity. And a corresponding unique social structure was formed in the ghetto. The Eldest of the Jews was at the top and directly beneath him were the heads of the workshops, departments, police, and court. They were followed by instructors, skilled workers, and those who distinguished themselves by performing good work or heavy labor. Next came the majority of the ghetto dwellers, that is, the working people and, increasingly toward the end, persons unemployed or unfit for work. This hierarchy determined a person's privileges, meaning the quantity and quality of the rations allocated to a given stratum as a supplement to the general daily norm. The resulting inequality created a constant state of tension among the inhabitants of the ghetto. Undoubtedly, an equitable distribution of food would have contributed greatly to improving the ghetto's mood and morale but only to a negligible, even microscopic degree could it have altered the general situation of hunger. If one passes over the corruption that was indeed a factor in the ghetto and the relatively generous rations allocated to those at the top of the Jewish administration, most privileges came down to the number of additional grams of bread or sugar a person received or whether he had an additional workshop soup coupon on a given day.[129] This hierarchically ordered society was, however, entirely dependent on the Jewish administration's bureaucracy, which, for all its anomalies and absurdity, functioned rather efficiently and provided services that brought the people of the ghetto a certain amount of relief, aid, even order, in those difficult conditions. There was an apparent, even excessive, normality, and probably nowhere were mass deaths from hunger and a stopgap society so closely coupled as they were in the Łódź ghetto.

The Germans did not concern themselves with the ghetto's internal affairs as long as they had no reason to. Taking that into account, the Jewish administration reinstated many essential institutions for the public's welfare. Teaching was resumed in some of the elementary schools, both the secular and the religious, and in the gymnasiums and lyceums, where, among other subjects, Hebrew language and literature, Latin, and classical philosophy were taught. Although the Jewish holidays were, as a

---

129. Oskar Rosenfeld observed: "We live in a community. Of the 104,000 inhabitants of the ghetto, according to the count in July, 1942, about 100,000 are living on the same level. The other 4,000 are living in somewhat more favorable conditions due to their larger rations and better hygienic conditions" (Private notes, "Notizen als Erinnerungen, Heft E").

rule, compulsory workdays, they were observed both privately and in the few prayer houses that had been opened in the ghetto. The rabbinate, a part of the administration of the Eldest of the Jews, performed religious marriages; circumcision ceremonies also took place, and it was even possible to buy matzoth with a ration card during Passover. And, finally, the ghetto had a theater and concert hall, to mention but two of its many cultural institutions. All those forms of activity, regardless of whether they were for a select circle or not, played a very important role. They were organized not only to render the intolerable less so, or to alleviate the current situation to some degree, but also—with a mind to the future—to ensure that when liberation came people would have something with which to start life over again. Thus, the various ghetto activities were a sort of adhesive that maintained the old ties, customs, and loyalties, and seemed to keep people from forgetting what should and should not be done. To meet for common prayer, or in a school room, at a wedding in the presence of a rabbi, or at a literary evening or concert was, undoubtedly, proof that, despite everything, ghetto society had not given in and continued to resist, at least psychologically. The ghetto's overt institutions were at the same time meeting places for members of political organizations and parties, which led a semi-clandestine existence in the ghetto. In the absence of radios and newspapers these were good places for people to communicate, especially during difficult situations and times of conflict, of which there was never a shortage in the ghetto.

In the ghetto's internal affairs, conflicts and even mass street demonstrations, one of which took place right after the ghetto was sealed,[130] arose principally against Rumkowski's administration. The populace of the ghetto viewed the administration as directly culpable for their hunger, for the inequitable allocation of the rations arriving from outside, and for the rampant lawlessness. At that time it was the former workers' parties, chiefly the Bund, the *Poale Zion*, and the communists that took up the cry of struggle. In keeping with their traditions and also with a seemingly incomplete grasp of the radical changes that had resulted from the Nazi occupation of the country in general and Łódź in particular, those parties reverted to street demonstrations and strikes as their principal means of protest. They were, of course, doomed to failure; to maintain some sort of discipline in the ranks of demonstrators exhausted by hunger, for instance, was nearly impossible. Moreover, the demonstrators began increasingly to be led by elements not connected with any party, by random individuals, or by people from the criminal world and so-called strong men. During one such demonstration in the summer of 1940, brutally suppressed by the Eldest of the Jews' police, demands were voiced that the ghetto's authorities include Germans. Its bearings lost, the crowd could not imagine that things could be any worse. The illusions were dispelled when the German police entered the ghetto and opened fire on the crowds. That was the end of open street demonstrations in the ghetto, though labor strikes would erupt from time to time in various workshops, chiefly as a protest against management. Yet, Rumkowski was able to believe that he

---

130. For more on this and the many other mass demonstrations against Rumkowski and his administration see "Podziemne życie polityczne w getcie łódzkim: 1940–1944. Dokumenty i materiały" (Underground political activities in the Łódź ghetto: 1940–1944. Documents and materials), *Biuletyn Żydowskiego Instytutu Historycznego*, 54 (1965), p. 133.

was in control of the situation. To be on the safe side, however, he removed the potential organizers of disturbances, at first by arresting them or sending them out of the ghetto to do forced labor, and, later on, by including them on the lists of those to be deported. Chiefly affected by this were the "strong men," for he considered them irresponsible in their actions, capable of anything. On the other hand, Rumkowski rarely if ever penalized the leaders of the political parties, including the communists. He had too much faith in their prudence, intelligence, and sense of responsibility. At most, he refused to allow them to occupy certain posts or, "as a punishment," had them removed from one "good" job or another. At times he also conducted negotiations with them in an attempt to exploit, neutralize, or intimidate them, and once in a while he would make minor concessions. But he never retreated from his program of "work and peace" at any cost. As he constantly stressed in his private conversations and public speeches, he, the Eldest of the Jews, was responsible for the ghetto and only he knew how best to serve its inhabitants. In general, he only accepted other people's views and positions when they were presented to him as if they were his own or when they referred to something he was supposed to have said himself.

Rumkowski's speeches frequently give the impression that he spoke patronizingly to the people in the ghetto, the way he had to his helpless orphans in Helenówek. For its part, the ghetto bureaucracy responded by paying him the homage he had grown accustomed to in the orphanage where he had received congratulatory scrolls, poems, and verses on his birthday or other such occasions.[131] It is difficult to guess whether this was something he in fact sought or whether his associates thought it was what he wanted. In any case, he raised no objections and accepted it all as his due. His portraits were duly hung in every ghetto office, he was idolized in speeches, and his likeness graced the ghetto postage stamp, which had won first prize in a special competition. The stamp was never put into circulation—but this was not Rumkowski's fault.[132] One must also leave aside the question of why such homage prevailed in the ghetto when even potato peels were a rarity and helped many a person satisfy the hunger constantly gnawing at him.

Rumkowski rarely doubted that he was in the right. News from outside the ghetto, however scant it might have been, and especially his two trips to the Warsaw ghetto and what he saw there, only strengthened that belief in him. And, in turn, what the people in Warsaw heard from him and from others about the Łódź ghetto filled them with outright fear.[133] This is not the place for analogies between the two ghettos, different in so many respects. But to paraphrase what someone who traveled from the Warsaw ghetto to the one in Łódź said, people were dying of hunger in identical proportions in both places. The difference, however, was that while in Warsaw the dead lay on the streets for a long time before they were buried, in Łódź burial took place almost immediately.[134] A statistical picture of the mortality rate in both ghettos

131. A lengthy article by B. A. Gliksman on the festivities in Helenówek in connection with Rumkowski's fiftieth birthday was published in one of the larger daily newspapers in Łódź, *Lodzher togblat*, March 21, 1927, p. 2.

132. Cf. below, p. 464, n. 8.

133. Among others, A. Czerniakow and E. Ringelblum have written about this; see below, p. 58 and n. 70.

134. "Mama's cousin, who managed to make her way here from Warsaw, was at our house today. She told us various things, from which the following conclusions can be drawn: on the average, things are

is presented below:[135]

Year	Warsaw	Per 1,000 inhabitants	Łódź	Per 1,000 inhabitants
1940	8,991	23.5	6,197	39.2
1941	43,238	90.0	11,328	75.7
1942	39,719	140.0	18,134	159.8

Although the number of "natural" deaths was already horribly high in the ghetto of Łódź, this would soon prove not to be the greatest menace for its inhabitants. Beginning in the second half of 1941, it was not starvation that had become the principal means of exterminating the Jews but deportation to the camps. When this process first began, Rumkowski himself probably did not realize its true significance, so he repeated Biebow's words without hesitation: "the fate of the deportees would not be so tragic as generally anticipated in the ghetto. They won't be behind barbed wire, they will be doing agricultural work."[136] Convinced of this, Rumkowski submitted to the orders from the German authorities and supplied people for the transports. Then new demands came. He obeyed them all, as he used to say, so that they would "not be executed by others."[137] With each new demand he continued to delude himself that this was the last, that he would succeed in saving at least a part of the populace. The tragedy of Rumkowski's position lay in the fact that the Germans would have deported Jews with or without him, as they had during the Gehsperre in September, 1942, when the elderly, the sick, and children were sent from the ghetto. It was then that Rumkowski was on the verge of suicide.[138] For reasons known only to himself, Rumkowski did not follow the example of Adam Czerniakow of the Warsaw ghetto.

In the second half of 1941, as realized by few people at the time, the Nazis' "Final Solution of the Jewish Problem" entered an entirely new phase, one of direct genocide. This occurred at the moment when, after attacking Russia, the Germans were literally intoxicated with their initial victories and believed more than ever before, or after, that they were on the threshold of the Thousand Year Reich. The killing of human beings at once assumed forms and dimensions unprecedented in history. Mass executions by firing squads were carried out by the mobile killing units (Einsatzgruppen) at the rear of the German troops as they advanced deeply into the Soviet

---

much worse in Warsaw than here . . . thousands of people are dying on the streets and are not being buried while here burials are extremely well organized!" Dawid Sierakowiak, *Dziennik*, pp. 96–97. Here I would like to cite two other of the boy's unpublished diary entries, made nearly half a year after his mother was deported to the death camp in Chełmno on the Ner: (Saturday, March 6, 1943, Łódź) "My poor once-strong father died today at four o'clock in the afternoon"; (Monday, March 8) "Our father has left us 1 kilogram of bread, a little cheese, three teaspoons of sugar, and around twenty grams of oil. We will not sell any of it." Dawid Sierakowiak died at the age of 19 on August 8, 1943, of tuberculosis of the lungs, and his younger and only sister, Natalia, was deported to Auschwitz during the liquidation of the ghetto in August, 1944.

135. In the years 1929–38 the mortality rate in the Jewish community of Łódź was 9.6 per 1,000 inhabitants.

136. From a speech delivered by him on January 17, 1942.

137. Ibid.

138. Rosenfeld, Private notes (September 19, 1942).

Union. In the course of barely six months, from the middle of June to the end of December, 1941, they murdered about 1,000,000 Jews. The places of execution included, among others, Babi Yar, Minsk, and Ponary, which became symbols of the martyrdom of the Jews of the Ukraine, Byelorussia, and the Baltic countries—Lithuania, Latvia, and Estonia.

The executions had scarcely begun in the East when the question of the fate of the Jewish population throughout the province of Wartheland, but chiefly in the Łódź ghetto was reopened. Accordingly, the head of the resettlement office in Poznań, SS-Sturmbannführer Rolf Heinz Hoppner, sent the following memorandum, quoted here *in extenso*, to Eichmann, his superior in the RSHA:[139]

SO/S
Memorandum   Posen, July 16, 1941

RE: Solution of the Jewish Problem

During talks in the office of the Reich province, various departments broached the subject of the solution of the Jewish problem in Wartheland. The following solutions have been proposed:

1. That all Jews be taken from Wartheland to a camp for 300,000 Jews that will be set up barracks-style as close as possible to the coal basin, and where there will be a variety of barracks equipped for economic enterprises, tailor shops, shoemakers', and so forth.

2. All the Jews in Wartheland will be placed in this camp. Jews fit to work can, if need be, be grouped in labor crews and taken out of the camp.

3. A camp of this type, in the opinion of the Chief of Police in Łódź, SS-Brigadenführer Albert, could be supervised by significantly smaller forces than has thus far been the case. Moreover, the danger of an epidemic, which still exists for the adjacent population in Łódź and in the other ghettos, could be kept to a minimum.

4. There is a danger of not being able to feed all the Jews this winter. Serious consideration is required on the question of whether the most humanitarian solution would not be to finish off those Jews who are unfit for work by some expedient means. In any case, that would be less unpleasant than allowing them to die from hunger.

5. Moreover, it was also proposed that all Jewish women capable of bearing children be sterilized in that camp so that the Jewish problem would be fully solved to all intents and purposes with this generation.

6. The Reichsstatthalter [Greiser] has not yet voiced an opinion on this matter. There is a feeling that the president of the [Łódź region], Übelhör, does not wish the ghetto to cease to exist, for it seems that he is making quite a good profit off it.

---

139. Hoppner's memorandum, along with his personal letter to Eichmann, came to light during the trial of Artur Greiser in 1946. The complete text in Polish translation and a photocopy of the original are in *Biuletyn Głównej Komisji Badania Zbrodni Hitlerowskich w Polsce* 13 (1960), pp. 69–70 and 27F–29F; cf. also *Documents of Destruction: Germany and Jewry, 1933–1945*, ed. Raul Hilberg (Chicago: Quadrangle Books, 1971), pp. 87–88.

As an example of the money to be made off the Jews: I have been informed that the Reich Labor Ministry pays 6 RM from a special account for each Jew sent to work, whereas a Jew costs only 80 pfennigs.

In a personal letter ("Lieber Kamerad Eichmann") attached to this memorandum, Hoppner added, among other things: "These things do sound somewhat fantastic but, in my opinion, they are entirely feasible."

Hoppner's memorandum, in which, for the first time, we find an official statement proposing that "Jews who are unfit for work" be killed "by some expedient means," is a document of great importance both in light of later events in the Wartheland itself and because of the general decision that emerged in Berlin concerning the total liquidation of the Jews. A decision of such far-ranging significance could only have been made by Hitler himself or, at least, with his express approval. On the whole, all historians agree on this point though they differ as to the date of the decision, the form in which it was handed down, and to whom that decision was communicated directly. There are no easy answers to these and other questions, due to the lack of relevant documents, which have either not been preserved or, what is equally possible, never existed, since Hitler's decision might not have been communicated in writing but orally. For that reason, all attempts to establish the exact time of transition from one phase to another in the Nazi "Final Solution" are based on two other essential and well-known documents. They are Göring's letter of July 31, 1941, authorizing Heydrich "to execute all the necessary organizational, material, and financial preparations for the complete solution of the Jewish question in the German sphere of influence in Europe," and the minutes of a conference called by Heydrich (at the Reich Security Main Office in Berlin, at Am Grossen Wannsee No. 56–58, on January 20, 1942) and devoted to a discussion of the plan for exterminating the Jews.[140]

The exchange of opinions in Wartheland and Göring's letter to Heydrich, which came somewhat later, are without a doubt closely connected, although it is unlikely that Hoppner's memorandum might have marked the beginning of it all.[141] However, the discussions that took place in his province in the summer of 1941 are a good example of a certain initiative originating in the lower ranks, and it could even be viewed as pressure from the field on the central authorities. This is a phenomenon that is frequently overlooked when the period of Jewish extermination is examined. Of course, in a state such as the Third Reich, practically nothing could happen without an order from above; nevertheless, it is a mistaken opinion that the Nazis did not listen carefully to the voice of the "masses," especially when those masses were their own. In any case, Hoppner's letter was on Eichmann's desk when he was supposed to have passed on to Göring, ready for his signature, the letter to Heydrich

140. English translations of the two documents are published in *A Holocaust Reader*, ed. Dawidowicz, pp. 72–82.

141. Cf. the polemics on the subject of the memoranda that arose between Artur Eisenbach, "O należyte zrozumienie genezy zagłady Żydów" (On the proper understanding of the origin of the extermination of the Jews) and Julian Leszczyński, "Z dziejów zagłady Żydów w Kraju Warty: Szkice do genezy ludobójstwa hitlerowskiego" (From the history of the extermination of the Jews in the Wartheland: Essays on the origin of Nazi genocide) in *Biuletyn Żydowskiego Instytutu Historycznego* 104 (1977), pp. 55–69, and 82 (1972), pp. 57–72.

of July 31, 1941.[142] The memorandum was soon followed by deeds: the extermination of the Jews in Wartheland began long before the conference in Wannsee took place, granting even that it was initially planned for December 9, 1941.[143] It was in this province, recently incorporated into the Reich, that the first death camp in Nazi-occupied Europe was established.

At first, in October, 1941, there was an attempt in Wartheland to imitate the methods used by the Einsatzgruppen in the East. It began with the concentrating of 3,000 Jews from the surrounding villages and towns in a place known as Zagórze (Hintenberg in German), in Koło county, from which they were taken by truck to the nearby Kazimierz Forest and executed by firing squads.[144] This method of killing was, however, quickly abandoned. What was possible to do close to the front and under the cover of military operations proved very difficult in "peaceful" villages and towns. Moreover, the actions of the Einsatzgruppen occasionally caused protests from some of the leaders of the German Armed Forces, who were disturbed chiefly by the negative influence the sight and reports of mass executions might have on the morale of their soldiers.[145]

Gas began to be used instead of firearms for killing people.

In the fall of 1941 a special operational police and SS unit was formed whose task was to select a suitable place for a death camp and to carry out the first experimental actions. Fritz Lange was appointed the commanding officer of the unit, which took its name from him: Sonderkommando Lange.[146] Later on, when Chełmno had already been designated as the place of execution and when Lange had been replaced by SS-Hauptsturmführer Hans Johann Bothmann, the camp began to be called Sonderkommando Kulmhof, the germanized form of Chełmno, a small village on the banks of the river Ner, a tributary of the Warta. The distance between Łódź and Chełmno was some thirty-five miles; there

142. *Ich, Adolf Eichmann: Ein historischer Zeugenbericht*, ed. Rudolf Aschenauer (Leoni am Starnberger See: Druffel-Verlag, 1980), p. 479. For a discussion of the meaning and timing of the Nazi "Final Solution," see M. Broszat, "Hitler und die Genesis der 'Endlösung'," *Anlass der Thesen von David Irving*; and Christopher R. Browning, "Zur Genesis der 'Endlösung': Eine Antwort an Martin Broszat," *Vierteljahrshefte für Zeitgeschichte* 25 (1977), pp. 739–75; 29 (1981), pp. 97–109.

143. The invitations to the conference were sent out on October 23. The originally scheduled meeting date was postponed until January 20, 1942, due to the attack on Pearl Harbor.

144. *The Ghetto Speaks* 2 (1942), pp. 1–3.

145. As a rule, however, as Raul Hilberg has observed, the army cooperated with the Einsatzgruppen to an extent that far exceeded the minimum support functions guaranteed in the OKH–RSHA agreement signed at the end of May, 1941, as part of the preparations for invading Russia (*Plan Barbarossa*), Hilberg, *Destruction of European Jews*, pp. 187, 196; see also, ibid., "VII/Mobile Killing Operation," pp. 176–256, and *The Holocaust: Selected Documents in Eighteen Volumes*, vol. 10, ed. John Mendelsohn (New York: Garland Publishing Co., 1982).

146. The basic sources on the subject of Chełmno are: Władysław Bednarz, "Obóz zagłady Chełmno," *Biuletyn Głownej Komisji Badania Zbrodni Niemieckich w Polsce* 1 (1946), pp. 147–61, and his book entitled *Obóz straceń w Chełmnie nad Nerem* [The death camp in Chełmno on the Ner] (Warsaw: Państwowy Instytut Wydawniczy, 1946); Blumental, *Dokumenty i materiały*, vol. 1, pp. 227–66. A biography of Bothmann, including details of his career in the Nazi movement, is presented by Josef Wulf in *Lodz: Das Letzte Getto auf polnischen Boden*, Bundeszentrale für Heimatdienst (Bonn, 1962), pp. 83–84. For information on the Nazi death camps in general, see: Ino Arndt and Wolfgang Scheffler, "Organisierter Massenmord an Juden in nationalistischen Vernichtungslagern: Ein Beitrag zur Richtigstellung apologetischer Literatur," *Vierteljahrshefte für Zeitgeschichte* 24 (1976), pp. 105–35; and Konnelhim Feig, *Hitler's Death Camps: The Sanity of Madness* (New York: Holmes and Meier, 1981).

was direct access by road and by the Łódź-Kalisz-Koło rail line. From Koło to Chełmno was only eight-and-a-half miles, which were covered by narrow gauge railway to Powiercie, and from there the journey was completed by other means of transportation or on foot. The only buildings of any importance in Chełmno were a small two-story palace still in ruins from the First World War, a church, and the farm buildings on the palace property. Those buildings and the former homes of the village's residents, who had been forced to move, as well as a few newly constructed barracks, constituted the entire expanse of the camp, a total of no more than three hectares. From there, the bodies of the victims asphyxiated by exhaust fumes from the vans whose motors had been especially adapted to that purpose were taken the two-and-a-half miles to the Rzuwowski Forest in Precinct 77, where they were buried and then burned to cover the traces of the crime. This is recalled here by the Forest Inspector (*Forstmeister*) of Koło county, Heinz May:

In the Fall of 1941, I was informed by Forest Constable Stagemeir, whose seat was in the Ladorudź Forest district, that special commandoes had arrived in Chełmno and had demanded firewood from him. In saying this, Stagemeir was strangely serious, something I paid little attention to at first. Marshall Göring was supposed to come to Koło county to battue, so I assumed that the commandoes were there to protect Göring. I gave instructions that the official be issued firewood.

Somewhat later I was traveling from Chełmno to Koło accompanied by the *Landrat* and *Kreisleiter* Becht. As we were driving through the forest, Becht said, pointing in the direction of Precinct 77, "Your trees will be growing better soon." When I looked inquiringly at him, he replied that Jews make good fertilizer. I wanted more information but Becht was very mysterious and changed the subject.

I spent a long time puzzling over his enigmatic allusions but was unable to understand what he had meant.

I rejected *a priori* my growing suspicion that some sort of terrible action against the Jews was to be carried out here, for that would have violated common sense. I again recalled Forest Constable Stagemeir's behavior, but, having no explanations, I tried to forget the matter. I was not yet aware of the full brutality and cruelty of the National Socialist regime.

A few weeks later, my youngest son returned from school on vacation. I took him with me when traveling on official business through Koło-Chełmno. There was a closed truck in a ditch by Precinct 77 (the road runs right by the border). A second truck had been hitched to the front of the first and was attempting to pull it back onto the road. All this blocked the way. My son got out of our truck and walked over to a group of men in police uniforms who were bustling about the vehicle. I was soon to hear those officials rebuking my son; I too got out and walked over to those vehicles. The truck in the ditch was about four meters in length and about two meters high; its rear door was closed with an iron bolt from which a padlock hung. A definitely unpleasant smell came from the truck and from the men standing around it.

When I asked whether the road was soon to be clear, I was told impolitely that they would pull the truck a little to the side and that I should try to make it past.

My son was in Koło a few days later. On his return he told me that the police officials were assembling groups of Jews there and taking them away by truck. I immediately recalled what Becht had said and no longer had any doubt that a terrible thing was happening in the Ladorudź Forest, something that I had at first been unable to believe.

I immediately telephoned Forest Constable Stagemeir and asked him what was going on in his forest district. He replied that Precinct 77 had been entirely surrounded by military police. When during his official rounds he had approached the sentries, he was told to turn around and leave the area immediately, otherwise he could count on being shot.

The sentries had been ordered to shoot anyone approaching Precinct 77.

Stagemeir was not able to tell me any more than this by phone. I told him to remain at home and I drove in my truck to see him at once.

On the road I saw more closed trucks as they were turning off toward Precinct 77. That precinct was surrounded by a thick spruce forest and young 12- to 15-year-old trees.

Stagemeir explained to me that a large detachment of military police was stationed in Chełmno. The palace on the western side of Chełmno had been enclosed by a high wooden fence. Military police sentries armed with rifles were standing by the entrance. . . .

I passed by there on the way back to my forest district and confirmed that what Stagemeir had said concerning the wooden fence and the sentries was true. There were row upon row of trucks with improvised canvas tops in Chełmno. Women, men, and even children had been crammed into those trucks . . .

During the short time I was there I saw the first truck drive up to the wooden fence. The sentries opened the gates. The truck vanished into the palace courtyard, and immediately afterwards another closed truck came out of the courtyard and headed for the forest. And then both sentries closed the gates.

There was no longer the slightest doubt that terrible things, things never before known in human history, were being played out there.[147]

Early on, Chełmno was designated chiefly for Jews from the Old Reich and the newly incorporated territories, as well as those from the Protectorate of Bohemia and Moravia, even though Greiser personally solicited "special treatment" (*Sonderbehandlung*) from Himmler for only 100,000 Jews from his Wartheland.[148] Sonderbehandlung, *Sauberungsaktion* (purge actions), *Weiter nach Osten zu transportieren* (to send the Jews further east)—regardless of whether that was the actual direction,

---

147. *Die grosse Lüge—Chełmno, der Nationalsozialismus, wie ihn das deutsche Volk nicht kennt: Ein Erlebnisbericht von H. May* (The great lie—Chełmno, national socialism in a form unknown to the German people: a memoir by H. May). May's memoir, written in February, 1945, was turned over to the American military authorities, who in turn sent it to the Warsaw Main Commission for the Investigation of German Crimes, where it remains to this day. The third chapter of his memoir, "The Mass Murder of the Jews," was published in the original German and in a Polish translation by Karol Marian Pospieszalski in *Przegląd Zachodni* 3 (1962), pp. 87–105.

148. It has not been determined precisely when Greiser made this request; the information comes from his letter to Himmler on May 1, 1942, in which he states that the special action (Sonderbehandlung) approved by Himmler at one point in regard to the approximately 100,000 Jews in Wartheland will be concluded in the course of two or three months (Bernstein, et al., *Eksterminacja Żydów na ziemiach polskich*, pp. 288–90).

Evakuierung von Juden nach dem Osten (evacuation of Jews to the East)—those are only some randomly chosen examples of the many euphemisms used by the Nazis for purposes of camouflage. When Himmler, in turn, asked Greiser not to voice opposition to the resettlement of foreign Jews to the Łódź ghetto (because the Führer desired that the Old Reich and the Protectorate be "liberated from the Jews"), he assured Greiser that their stay in the ghetto would be temporary and that they would "be sent further east" in the spring of next year.[149] Himmler's letter to Greiser was dated September 18, 1941. Exactly one month later transports of Jews from Germany, Austria, Bohemia, and Luxembourg began arriving in the Łódź ghetto. By the end of the action in November, the total number of Jews resettled came to 19,953. The table below presents a fuller picture of the individual transports—their origins, their dates of arrival in the ghetto, and the number of persons they contained.[150]

Point of Origin	Number of Transports	Date of Arrival	Men	Women	Total
Berlin	4	10/18, 25, 30; 11/2	1,587	2,467	4,055 [?]
Frankfurt am Main	1	10/22	460	726	1,186
Cologne	2	10/23 (both)	795	1,219	2,014
Emden[a]	—	10/25	41	81	122
Hamburg	1	10/26	417	646	1,063
Düsseldorf	1	10/26	454	550	1,005 [?]
Vienna	5	10/16, 24, 28, 29; 11/3	1,733	3,266	4,999
Prague	5	10/19, 22, 27; 11/1, 3	2,546	2,453	4,999
Luxembourg	1	10/18	230	282	512
TOTAL			8,263	11,690	19,953

[a]The Jews from Emden arrived in the ghetto with the second transport from Berlin.

149. Here is the partial text of Himmler's letter to Greiser:

"Der Führer wünscht, dass möglichst bald das *Altreich* und das *Protektor at* vom *Westen nach dem Osten von Juden geleert* und befreit werden. Ich bin daher bestrebt, möglichst noch in diesem Jahr die Juden des Altreichs und des Protektorats zunächst einmal *als erste Stufe* in die vor zwei Jahren neu zum Reich gekommenen Ostgebiete zu transportieren, um sie im nächsten Frühjahr noch weiter nach dem Osten abzuschieben," Helmut Krausnik, "Judenverfolgung," in *Anatomie des SS-Staates*, vol. 2 (Olten and Freiberg: Walter Verlag, 1965), p. 374.

150. The table is based on accounts in the Department of Vital Statistics of the Eldest of the Jews entitled "Eingesiedelte im Jahre 1941 aus dem Altreich, Wien, Prag, Luxemburg und aus Leslau [Włocławek] und Umgebung, AZIH (AJHI) Rum. Records and YIVO Archives, Zon. nos. 878–880. The American Embassy in Berlin regularly and accurately briefed the Secretary of State in Washington about the ongoing deportation of Jews from Germany. In a cable dated October 20, 1941, we read:

"Authentic information has now been obtained that at least 20,000 Jews are to be deported from German cities mostly to the Ghetto of Lodz before the end of this month. The first group of 1,000 people left Berlin on October 18 after standing for between 24 and 48 hours in the Synagogue in Levetzowstrasse which can normally accommodate only 300 persons for overnight lodging. Another 2,000 leave Frankfurt-on-Main today and a further 2,000 leave Cologne tomorrow while a second

The deportation of Jews from Western Europe to the Łódź ghetto took place nearly everywhere according to one and the same pattern with only minor deviations. Though there were no ghettos in Germany, Austria, Bohemia, and Luxembourg, the Jews there had come under the Nuremberg law for quite some time, their names and addresses were well known and, beginning on September 19, 1941, they wore Stars of David. Thus, after determining the total number of Jews anticipated for deportation in a given period, the Gestapo would either round them up and escort them to designated assembly points or have the offices of imposed Jewish organizations (the *Reichsvereinigung* and *Zentralstelle für die jüdische Auswanderung*) send out notices to the Jewish residents to report there on their own. In Prague, for example, the assembly point was Messepalast, a long-idle exposition site containing buildings used for displaying merchandise, while in Berlin the synagogue on Levetzowstrasse, in the Moabit district, was used. All possessions had to be left intact in people's apartments; valuables, jewelry, money, and all documents and papers had to be handed over personally to the authorities. The deportees were allowed only to take 50 kilograms of baggage with them, which included five kilograms of food, and up to 100 German marks. All the activities pursuant to departure were accompanied by a great deal of paperwork, as if it were of special concern to the authorities to indicate that everything was proceeding in accordance with the law. It was not only a question of not arousing any suspicions among the Jews as to the purpose of their journey but, principally, of preserving appearances for their own local public, which, as opposed to that in the East, the Nazis took into some account. The deportees were thus given many forms to fill out and sign and were provided with documents of resettlement for their journey, even though few of them knew where they were going. After two or three days at the assembly point, they were taken to the railroad station, where normal passenger trains, guarded by police, were waiting for them. As soon as the passengers were aboard, the often studied politeness of the German personnel employed in deportation would come to an end.[151]

The Jews newly arrived in the Łódź ghetto had, for the most part, been recruited from all segments of Western European society. There were upper- and middle-class people among them, they included doctors and lawyers, painters and musicians, writers and journalists, former university professors and officers of the German, Austrian, and Czechoslovakian armies, and religious people and nonbelievers, in-

---

contingent is to depart on October 24. These groups consist almost entirely of elderly Jews but it is anticipated that under present plans all Jews in Germany will be deported within a few months."

(Mendelsohn, *The Holocaust: Selected Documents*, vol. 8: *Deportation of the Jews to the East: Stettin, 1940, to Hungary, 1944*, p. 23).

151. The instructions given to the storm troopers (SA-men) who were to round up the Jews even included an order to do it without mistreatment or abuse. For more about the deportation of the Jews from Germany, Austria, Czechoslovakia, and Luxembourg, see: Rosenfeld, Private notes ("Eintragungen, Heft A"), pp. 1–21; Berlin Gestapo Trial, Leo Baeck Institute Archives, Microfilm no. 239; Ruth Alton (Tauber) "Deportiert von den Nazis," ibid., no. 493; *Dokumente zur Geschichte der Frankfurter Juden, 1933–1945* (Frankfurt am Main: Verlag Waldemar Kramer, 1963), pp. 507–18; Dobroszycki, "Die Wiener Juden im Getto von Lodz," *Die Gemeinde* 9 (1965), pp. 13, 15; H. G. Adler, *Der verwaltete Mensch: Studien zur Deportation der Juden aus Deutschland* (Tübingen: J. C. B. Mohr, 1974), pp. 168–76, passim; *Jüdisches Leben in Deutschland: Selbstzeugnisse zur Sozialgeschichte 1918–1945*, vol. 3, ed. Monika Richarz (Stuttgart: Deutsche Verlag-Anstalt, 1982), pp. 346–412.

cluding Catholics and Protestants—Jews who had converted or partners in mixed marriages. What was immediately striking and at the same time anxiety-producing was the very high percentage of the middle-aged and elderly. In fact, more than half of the new arrivals were over 50 years old, a dangerous age for living in the ghetto, and 1,400 of those were 70 or over. Many of that latter group came to the ghetto directly from homes for the elderly or hospitals.

For the Jews of Western and Eastern Europe to meet on the grounds of the ghetto was a shock for both. The former, people largely assimilated into German life, had difficulty in finding a common language with the Jews of Łódź. The Western European Jews were also unable to understand why they had been sent such a great distance when the ghetto's starving population was in no condition to play host to them. Both groups were, however, bound by many ties, not the least of which was their now common fate. In that context, one of the newcomers from Western Europe, Dr. Oskar Rosenfeld, wrote the following in his private notes: "It is a good thing for me suddenly to be a part of all you East European Jews. We are all equally afraid of *Ashkenaz* [Germany], fate, our hard life, and what still awaits us."[152]

At nearly the same time as the Jews from Western Europe arrived in the ghetto, an intensive population movement began, one which comprised hundreds of thousands of Jews and was to continue, with some interruptions, until September, 1942. The population had two destinations, especially beginning at the end of 1941. Children, the elderly, and the sick were sent to the camp in Chełmno, which had been in operation since the first week of December. People classified as fit for work were deported to the Łódź ghetto, which the Germans thereafter gave the name *Gau-Getto des Reichsgaues Wartheland*. There, all inhabitants, that is both the local population and those from the countries of Western Europe, as well as those from the towns and villages in the environs, underwent a process of selection that resulted in some remaining in the ghetto while others were deported to Chełmno. In that manner, by the end of the first wave of extermination, the Nazis had put more than 250,000 Jews to death, liquidating in the process all the Jewish settlements that had existed outside of Łódź for centuries. These were: Kalisz, Sieradz, Główno, Wieruszów, Praszka, Pabianice, Włocławek, Zgierz, Zelów, Koźminek, Łask, Wieluń, Zduńska Wola, Warta, Sulmierzyce, Dąbie, Kowale Pańskie, Lututów, Sempolno, Kłodawa, Kutno, Brześć Kujawski, Chodecz, Kowal, Lubraniec, Ozorków, Bełchatów, Brzeziny, Stryków, and many others as well.[153]

After the deportations to the Wartheland there were about 89,500 Jews in the Łódź ghetto. Theoretically, they had all, with few exceptions, been designated as fit to work. In fact, the ghetto's demographic structure formed a highly misshapen pyramid: a truncated cone without a base. The absence of people even somewhat along in years or young children was all too evident. Children above the age of eight were consid-

152. Rosenfeld, Private notes, "Heft 11," p. 16/208. It should be noted, however, that the majority of the resettled Jews from the west never became integrated into the ghetto population.

153. Kermisz, ed., *Dokumenty i materiały do dziejów okupacji niemieckej w Polsce*, vol. 1; I. Trunk, "Studie tsu der geshikhte fun yidn in Wartheland in der tkufe fun umkum, 1939–1944, *Bleter far geshikhte*" II/1–2 (1949), pp. 147–66; D. Dąbrowska, "Zagłada skupisk żydowskich w okresie okupacji hitlerowskiej" (The destruction of Jewish settlements during the Nazi occupation), *Biuletyn Żydowskiego Instytutu Historycznego*, 13–14 (1955), pp. 157–84.

ered workers, and many of them were employed in the workshops. All institutions of social welfare and public service, such as the homes for the elderly, the orphanages, the hospitals, the schools, and the prayer houses, had been eliminated and their buildings or quarters turned into factories. The ghetto's so-called autonomy had in fact ceased to exist, giving way to increasing interference from the German authorities in matters thus far considered purely internal and the exclusive domain of the Eldest of the Jews. The deciding factor in all aspects of ghetto life was whether or not a given person was employed. Everyone, if not yet rendered helpless by hunger, realized that his life literally depended on his working. Even in 1943, a relatively peaceful year, when mass deportations to and from the ghetto had ceased, there were periods when people without working papers were grabbed on the streets and in their homes day and night and deported to a death camp. The ghetto had been turned into something like one great factory—toward the end of 1943 it contained more than 90 enterprises employing over 75,000 workers. The ghetto maintained itself exclusively on orders from the outside, primarily from the military. Uniforms and boots, underwear and bed linen were manufactured, goods were made of wood and metal, leather and fur, down and paper, and electrical and telecommunication devices were produced. The ghetto received orders from all the branches of the service, the army, air force, and navy, that is, from the *Heeresbekleidungsamt*, *Bekleidunsamt der Luftwafe*, *Marinebekleidungsamt*, and *Wehrmachtbeschaffungsamt*. The need for manpower in Germany increased daily, especially when the Allied air forces were carrying out mass bombing raids on the Reich's economic base and after the defeat of German armies at Stalingrad and El-Alamein. The military leaders were well aware of this and, for the moment, were indifferent to who worked for them as long as the orders were filled. As far as the Łódź ghetto was concerned, it was known that its workers were able to supply nearly full sets of uniforms for 5,000 soldiers in a week's time.[154] But the German armed forces never opposed extermination actions. At most, attempts were made to postpone them—as was to occur in Łódź, the last of more than 200 ghettos in occupied Poland. Among those most interested in war production, and a man responsible for supplying the German army, Albert Speer, the Reich's Minister of Armaments, was to write the following 35 years later, as if still not realizing that a word from him could have determined the lives and deaths of more than 80,000 people:

> I certainly could have helped at times, for instance in Łódź, when Greiser wanted to liquidate the ghetto. Perhaps I might even say that my considerations were not merely rational when I did a few things to enable the victims to survive. But I cannot claim that humane considerations stood above the interests of a wartime economy. If I was able to help, I had a feeling of satisfaction. If I was unable to help, I turned my back on the misery insofar as I perceived it. My motivation had gotten "out of plumb"; for me the question of efficiency was decisive. Even if it had been possible occasionally to secure better treatment, the fact remains that those people were ruthlessly exploited. Today, we recognize that even a simple relative humanity is far from adequate. We are dealing with a fundamental question that, back then, I generally perceived in terms of efficien-

154. Eisenbach, *Hitlerowska polityka zagłady Żydów*, pp. 560–61.

cy. Exploitation was in the foreground. We did not do what we might and could have done to keep those people alive![155]

Speer's comments refer to a period when the question of liquidating the Łódź ghetto had become current again. It began with Himmler's letters to Greiser in June and September, 1943, ordering that the ghetto be transformed into a labor camp with the stipulation, however, that it not be located in Łódź or any other part of Wartheland but in Lublin province. Before this relocation came to pass, the entire project collapsed, chiefly because, after the Soviet army's offensives in the summer and fall of 1943, and in the winter and spring of 1944, the front had moved quite close to Lublin province. Himmler, however, did not abandon his plan and, in December, 1943, again proposed that the Łódź ghetto be converted into a concentration camp. He placed Oswald Pohl, the head of the Economic/Administrative Main Office (*SS-Wirtschaft-Verwaltungshauptamt*—WVHA), in charge of carrying out the operation. Pohl, in turn, passed on the execution of that task to the *Ostindustrie GbmH (Osti)*, a company working with the WVHA whose concern was the exploitation of the Jewish labor force by setting up labor camps after the liquidation of ghettos in the Generalgouvernement. In connection with the new mission, the head of Osti, Dr. Max Horn, traveled to Łódź accompanied by Eichmann to examine the problem thoroughly on the spot, which resulted in their drawing up a long paper entitled: "Business Concerns in Litzmannstadt Ghetto and the Ostindustrie GmbH."[156] Selecting the facts that suited them and arranging these to fit their preconceived ideas, the authors of the paper were of the opinion that the ghetto was not profitable from the point of view of German interests, its productivity was too low, and it was improperly managed. The Jews there, they continued, were in constant possession of all materials related to the vital statistical data of the population of the ghetto, the factories were headed by Jewish personnel, there were still more than 5,000 children under the age of 10 in the ghetto, the ghetto's area was still too large, making the distance between one workshop and another too great, and—the point on which they end—too many people in the ghetto were working in areas not directly related to the war economy, such as in the factory producing carpets from rags. Only a concentration camp could, according to the authors, serve as a panacea to all that. The camp should be administered by Osti and should elicit the cooperation of the Gettoverwaltung, with the exception of its director and his deputy, and at least 200 German *Kapo*, to be brought in from the Reich.

The paper by Horn and Eichmann was sent to Pohl on January 24, 1944, and there it remained, for the reaction of the Wartheland authorities was immediate and negative. First and foremost, the very fact that the entire plan to change the ghetto into a camp had come from without could not have antagonized the local authorities more, especially since Greiser had not even been informed of the enterprise and Biebow had simply been shoved aside by the authors of the document. And besides, this was one of the many instances of strife typical of the Nazi administrative hierarchy. In the

155. Albert Speer, *Infiltration*, trans. Joachim Neugroschel (New York: Macmillan Co., 1981), p. 10.

156. This paper, as well as all the other documents cited here (the correspondence among Pohl, Himmler, and Greiser) on the subject of Ostindustrie and its attempts to take over the Łódź ghetto are among the Nuremberg Trial materials (Pohl case), NO.–519, National Archives, Washington, D.C.

quarrel that subsequently arose, the Jewish population of the ghetto was the least of factors and the ghetto's productivity or lack of it was not, strictly speaking, the point either. The causes lay, rather, in affronts to self-esteem, in people's sense of position, and in who was, in fact, to decide when the ghetto would be liquidated and who was to inherit the grounds of the ghetto along with its economic base—the province, the city, or the Berlin police and the SS. While Greiser was seeking aid from Himmler himself in the dispute, Biebow was soliciting support from military circles, primarily in the Armament Inspection divisions in Poznań and Łódź. The very choice of patrons was decisive in the outcome.

In February, 1944, when Himmler was visiting Poznań, Greiser obtained everything he wanted from him, which he then immediately listed point by point in a letter to Pohl as if to nail down the success he had achieved. Here is the complete text of Greiser's letter:

Posen, February 14, 1944

Top Secret!

Dear Party Comrade Pohl,
On the occasion of the Reichsführer's visit to Posen yesterday and today, I had the opportunity to discuss and clear up two issues concerning your sphere of activity. The first issue is this:
The ghetto in Litzmannstadt is not to be transformed into a concentration camp, as was pointed out by *SS-Oberführer* Beier and SS-Hauptsturmführer Dr. Volk, who were sent to my *Gau* by your office. Their discussions took place in my office, in the *Reichsstatthal* in Posen, on the 5th of February. The decree issued by the SS-Reichsführer on June 11, 1943, will therefore not be carried out. I have arranged the following with the Reichsführer:
(a) The ghetto's manpower will be reduced to a minimum and retain only as many Jews as are essential to the war economy.
(b) The ghetto therefore remains a Gau [a province] ghetto of the Wartheland.
(c) The reduction will be carried out by SS-Hauptsturmführer Bothmann's special Sonderkommando, which has already had prior experience in the Gau. The Reichsführer will give orders to withdraw SS-Hauptsturmführer Bothmann and his Sonderkommando from his mission in Croatia and again place him at the disposal of the Wartheland.
(d) The utilization and administration of the contents of the ghetto remains in the hands of the Wartheland.
(e) After all Jews are removed from the ghetto and it is liquidated, the entire grounds of the ghetto are to go to the town of Litzmannstadt. The Reichsführer will then give appropriate instructions to the Main Trustee Office East (Haupttreuhandstelle Ost).
May I ask you to send me your suggestions in this matter as soon as possible.
With comradely greetings and
Heil Hitler
Yours
signed Greiser

Slightly less than six months later Himmler returned to the question of the Łódź ghetto, again firmly deciding that it was to be liquidated at once. This time, however, he approached Greiser directly, who accepted this as an order without a word of discussion. When he heard the rumors that the Armament Ministry and the Armament Inspection division in Poznań were again making efforts, as he himself had six months before, to postpone the decision to put an end to the ghetto, Greiser hastened at once to inform Himmler of this development by telegram in the following words:

> Reichsführer: The Armaments Inspection division has undertaken considerable counterthrusts against your order to clear the ghetto in Litzmannstadt. On the night of June 5, Reich Minister Speer requested, through the officer on duty in the Armaments Inspection, the number of people employed in the various manufacturers in the ghetto, their weekly work time, as well as the weekly output in the various branches of production, allegedly in order to present these figures to the Führer. Since I have finished the preparations for clearing the ghetto and have undertaken the first evacuations of the same, I duly inform you of this thrust to thwart your orders. Heil Hitler, Greiser.[157]

Himmler's reply arrived the next day and was very brief: "Dear Greiser: Many thanks for your telegram of 6/9. I request that you carry out the matter as before."[158]

On June 16, by order of the German authorities, the Eldest of the Jews issued the proclamation concerning voluntary registration of people to perform manual labor outside the ghetto. When there were too few volunteers, or none at all, people were taken by force. The first transport left from a side track in the ghetto exactly one week later. All told, 7,196 people were sent from the ghetto between June 23 and July 14 via Kutno and Koło to Chełmno.

On Saturday, July 15, there was a public announcement that, also by order of the German authorities, the resettlement had been suspended. The entire ghetto rejoiced as it never had before. None of the Jews was aware that this interruption, only temporary, had been caused by the sudden dissolution of the death camp in Chełmno (Kulmhof) on July 14, 1944. That had been done out of fear that the camp would fall into the hands of the Red Army as a result of its rapid progress during the summer offensive, which was bringing its troops closer to the borders of the Generalgouvernement.

As always, knowing nothing of what was happening, the ghetto was filled with both anxiety and expectation. The news that reached it from the outside, no matter how skimpy and fragmentary it was, infused the ghetto with hope. People began counting the days, tracing maps in sand in their courtyards, peering through the fence to see which direction the military vehicles were taking. In retrospect, the sequence of events would appear as follows:

July 18—The troops of the First Byelorussian front of the Soviet Army went on the offensive, moving from Volhynia toward Lublin.

157. Speer, *Infiltration*, p. 287.
158. Ibid.

July 20—Anti-Nazi conspirators in German army uniforms made an attempt on Hitler's life at his headquarters that nearly succeeded.

July 23—The commander of the Warsaw German army garrison ordered that German women be evacuated from the city.

July 24—Lublin was taken by Soviet troops.

July 29—The Russians established a bridgehead on the Vistula in the vicinity of Baranów, near Sandomierz, and their armored advance guard reached the right bank of the Vistula, opposite Warsaw.

August 1—The armed uprising against the Germans (that was to last for 63 days) broke out in Warsaw. (The Russian offensive halted on the banks of the Vistula. The Soviet Army's new offensive began in January, 1945).

On August 2, the following proclamation appeared on the walls of the ghetto in German and in Yiddish:[159]

> By order of the *Oberbürgermeister von Litzmannstadt*, the ghetto must be moved to a new location.
>
> Factory workers will travel with their families to perform manual labor.
>
> The first transport will depart on August 3, 1944. Five thousand people must report each day.
>
> A person can bring no more than 15–20 kilograms with him.
>
> Leaving in the first transport are: Workshop No. 1, Tailors' Main Office, 45 Łagiewnicka Street and Workshop No. 2, Tailoring factory, 36 Łagiewnicka Street.
>
> Family members of factory workers should join their transport. In that way, separation of families will be avoided.
>
> There will be separate notices concerning the workshops that are to be moved in the next phase.
>
> Those departing should report to temporary housing in the barracks at the [side track railroad] station in Radogoszcz.
>
> The first transport will leave the ghetto at 8:00 A.M., and those affected should appear at the points indicated no later than 7:00 A.M.

Litzmannstadt-Getto   C. Rumkowski
August 2, 1944   Der Älteste der Juden
                                                    in Litzmannstadt

With the posting of this proclamation, the liquidation of the Jewish quarter immediately assumed a total character. At that time, according to the *Chronicle* of July 30, 1944, there were still 68,561 persons in the ghetto. The first proclamation was followed by others. They were all printed in German and in Yiddish and signed by Rumkowski. Only one, that of August 7, was signed jointly by Rumkowski and Biebow (besides one signed by the mayor of Łódź), something that had rarely, if ever, occurred before. The August 2nd proclamation, like all others, called on specific workshops to report voluntarily to their transports at the indicated time.[160] Moreover, Biebow, and Bradfisch as well, made personal appeals at specially called meetings of

159. YIVO Archives, Zon. no. 453.
160. Ibid.

workers for people to obey this ruling, since, due to the closeness of the front, the ghetto had to be moved well into Germany, where labor was needed. There were few people by then who believed those assurances and even fewer who wished to leave voluntarily. Everyone already knew that the Russians were only some 120 kilometers from Łódź,[161] a distance normally traveled in an hour or so by express train. People did their best to postpone their departure by hiding in cellars, attics, wherever they could. At first the Jewish police attempted to remove them from their homes by force, by depriving them of their food rations. The police, however, were in no condition to be very effective: fewer people were reporting voluntarily with each passing day and the number supplied by the police was also gradually decreasing. The Germans stepped in: on August 9, the fire department, armed with rifles, entered the ghetto from the city and was supplemented by Schutzpolizei detachments the next day. They surrounded one block after another, ordering the Jewish police to drag people out of hiding.[162] The first proclamation signed only by the Gestapo appeared on August 17. It ordered that the block mentioned therein be vacated, street by street, threatening anyone found there after August 18 with death. That proclamation was repeated on August 23, except that now it referred to a significantly smaller area of the ghetto, from which the last resisters began to be dragged.[163]

The next and final Gestapo proclamation bore the date August 28, 1944. The ghetto had already, in fact, ceased to exist. Among those on the transport that left that day from the side track were Rumkowski, his wife, the son they had adopted in the ghetto, and Rumkowski's brother Józef and his wife.[164] Like all the previous transports, the one that left the ghetto on August 28, 1944, was sent to Auschwitz-Birkenau.

The Jewish community of Łódź had been brought to an end.

At the critical moment the Łódź ghetto proved to be more defenseless than any of the others.[165] Entirely alone, with no possibility of contacting anyone on the other

161. On the day after Allied forces landed at Normandy (D-Day), there were large-scale arrests of those listening to radios clandestinely in the ghetto. The German police did not, however, succeed in eliminating them entirely. After a very short time, news received by radio again began circulating by word of mouth. A diary written by an unidentified boy is very interesting in this regard. His notes, begun on May 5, 1944, and running through the end of July, were written in several languages (Polish, English, Hebrew and Yiddish) in the margins and between the lines of a novel by François Coppée, *Les Vrais Riches*. These notes clearly indicate that he had access to information from radio sources. The original diary is in Yad Vashem, in Jerusalem. See also, the *Chronicle* entry for June 7, 1944, pp. 498–99.

162. Poznański, *Pamiętnik z getta łódzkiego*, pp. 200–02.

163. YIVO Archives, Zon. nos. 1379, 1394.

164. There are no reliable sources on Rumkowski's final days, both before his leaving the ghetto and after his arrival in Auschwitz, where he perished.

165. Even Daniel Weiskopf, M.D., had no weapons; he had made several futile efforts to establish contact with the resistance movement on the "Aryan" side and, for that purpose, had formed an underground group in the ghetto. He decided not to report to the transport when the ghetto was being liquidated, for he was well aware of where it was headed. His hiding place was discovered, however, and Biebow himself appeared on the spot with his deputy, Schwind. A fight broke out between them and Weiskopf, a man of Herculean strength. In the course of the fight Biebow reached for his weapon and opened fire on Weiskopf, who was already badly beaten and who would later be killed by a bullet to the heart. (The trial of Hans Biebow in Łódź: testimony by Mieczysław Reichman, whose specially constructed hiding place Dr. Weiskopf had been using, and testimony by Biebow, copies of which are in AZIH (AJHI); cf. *Ruch podziemny w gettach i obozach* (The underground movement in the ghettos and camps), ed. Betti Ajzensztajn, with a foreword by Michał M. Borwicz (Łódź: Centralna Żydowska Komisja Historyczna, 1946).

side of the barbed wire, possessing not even a single firearm, it had been at the mercy of its oppressors from start to finish.[166] It was not able to undertake the slightest act of armed self-defense, even though the young Jews of Łódź had been raised with the same traditions, gone to the same schools, and been active in the same political and social organizations as their peers in Warsaw, Białystok, and Wilna. The "Aryan" side, the forest as a place of refuge, and fighting in a partisan detachment, which elsewhere were at least possibilities, were entirely out of the question in Łódź.[167]

There are still open graves in the Jewish cemetery in Łódź, just past the main gate and to the left by the wall. The Nazis had prepared those graves for the last of the Jews, who had remained behind to clean up the ghetto after the deportation of its populace. The hasty flight of the Germans from the city on January 18, 1945, in the face of the swiftly advancing Russian troops prevented them from committing that particular crime. The next morning Łódź was liberated. On what had been the grounds of the ghetto, there were now, including those who had come out from the hiding places, 877 people.[168]

Among that miraculously saved group of people were the ones who found and safeguarded the first of the Archives' materials and documents, which included the *Chronicle* of the Łódź ghetto, written by Alicja de Bunon, Julian Cukier (Cerski), Szmul Hecht, Bernard Heilig, Abram S. Kamieniecki, Józef Klementynowski, Bernard Ostrowski, Oskar Rosenfeld, Oskar Singer, Peter Wertheimer, Józef Zelkowicz et al.

THE ENGLISH EDITION

The English edition of the *Chronicle* of the Łódź ghetto is abridged. While preparing it for print, I made every effort to safeguard its integrity as a document and to preserve the unity of its contents. The basic criterion for selection was to include those materials which would have been essential to the authors of the *Chronicle* while they were writing it and those that have not lost their value as information over the course of time. I have not, however, omitted entirely events of lesser importance or those elements that might be considered monotonously repetitive. Monotony was very much a part of the times. No individual entry has been cut, no matter how long. Also, if one entry is not fully comprehensible without another made at an earlier date, I have either included both or provided the necessary information in square brackets. Important changes and corrections made by the authors in the original text, whether typed in or entered by hand, have been indicated in footnotes. In addition, I have

---

166. M. Balberyszski, in Eisenbach, *Dokumenty i materiały*, vol. 6.

167. I deal with this problem at greater length in "Jewish Elites under German Rule," *The Holocaust: Ideology, Bureaucracy and Genocide*, eds. Henry Friedlander and Sybil Milton (Millwood: Kraus International Publications, 1980), pp. 221–30.

168. After the deportations in August, 1944, the Germans kept two groups of people behind in what had been the ghetto: one, about 700 people, was to clean up the evacuated area; the other, about 500 men and women, were mostly the managers and technical staff of former ghetto workshops and departments and their families. The latter group had been chosen by the Gettoverwaltung to work in a labor camp that was to be set up in Germany. Toward the end of October, 1944, all the men from this group were deported to Oranienburg-Sachsenhausen and from there transferred to Königswusterhausen, while the women were sent to Ravensbrück and later somewhere else. Bendet Hershkovitch, "The Ghetto in Litzmannstadt (Lodz)," *YIVO Annual of Jewish Social Science* 5 (1950), p. 121.

included a few complete bulletins for each year, often without regard to their contents, in order to present at least a sampling of the *Chronicle* in its original form.[169] These are the bulletins of January 12, March 1, and October 1–15, 1941; September 1–19, November 5, and December 28, 1942; January 19, July 1, and September 30, 1943; and finally, those of February 8 and July 30, 1944.

All told, the English edition contains a fourth of the original text of the *Chronicle*. Much of the material that has been omitted is from those parts of the *Chronicle* that consist of routine entries made on a daily or weekly basis—the weather, the food rations, prices on the black market, changes in the population, and so forth. Information about the daily functioning of specific departments in the Jewish administration and the workshops, as well as their reorganization and personnel changes, has also, to a significant degree, been left out. At times entire days have been excluded since it was the importance of the events recorded, and not the dates themselves, that was taken into consideration. Finally, the limitations of a one-volume edition compelled me to omit information or articles that are, in fact, of considerable interest. I did, however, try to make sure that an entire subject did not disappear along with an eliminated section, and I also tried to maintain the original's sense of proportion in regard to the frequency with which a given subject was treated.

Considering the conditions under which it was written, the original text of the *Chronicle* is lucid and precise. Compiled from one day to the next in haste by several authors who wrote in two different languages and could not know when and if their work would ever reach print, the *Chronicle* does have its linguistic and stylistic flaws, as well as errors and inconsistencies in naming departments and positions, the spelling of names and places, and units of weight and measure. Some superficial flaws were emended silently in the process of translation. However, most corrections and explanations are inserted into the text in square brackets or appended in footnotes. Slight changes have been made in punctuation and paragraphing only when necessary for comprehension. Nearly all of the italics in the original text have been omitted because they were haphazard, more typographic than meaningful. A separate and more difficult task was to standardize and find English equivalents for the numerous departments, sections, and offices, and the permanent and *ad hoc* commissions that were part of the Jewish administration. Without some attempt at making order out of the ghetto's chaotic and constantly changing bureaucratic structure, this edition of the *Chronicle* would have made difficult reading. Street names, which appear in the *Chronicle* under their old Polish names and then under the newly imposed German names, have also been made uniform. For the sake of clarity, a list of the ghetto's street names in both languages has been furnished in an appendix. Names of people, usually slightly Polonized Jewish names (e.g., Rojzla—Reyzl; Mojzesz—Moyshe, Moses), have been left unchanged, with the Polish spelling retained.

---

169. *Kronika getta łódzkiego*, 2 vols., eds. D. Dąbrowska and L. Dobroszycki (Łódź: Wydawnictwo Łódzkie, 1965–66), vol. 1–2, 632 and 607 pages, respectively. The *Chronicle* for the first two years (1941 and 1942) was published in its entirety in Poland. The following volumes, announced for publication, did not appear because, by order of the state authorities, the Łódź Publishing House broke its agreement with the editors. The banning of the *Chronicle* from print was just one part of the larger anti-Jewish and anti-Israel campaign unleashed in Poland immediately after the Six Day War in 1967.

This edition has been annotated with both the specialist and the general reader in mind.

The Polish text of the *Chronicle* was translated by Richard Lourie; the German, by Joachim Neugroschel, and, in part, by Jean Steinberg and Howard Stern.

This volume is illustrated with over 70 photographs, most of them not previously published. Their source, like the *Chronicle*'s, is the Łódź ghetto Archives, which, besides documents, also amassed a wide range of visual materials about the closed Jewish quarter.

Henryk Neftalin, the organizer of the ghetto Archives.

Abmeldung. *Rag II*

Familienname *Heilig* geb. *31 05 43*

Vornamen *Bernhard*

Vornamen der Eltern *Edmund u Jella*

Stand *verheir.* Geburtsort *Prostmir*

Geburtsdatum *21.9.1902* Religion *mos*

Beruf *Beamter* Karten Nr.

Der Obengenannte verliess am *29. 6 43*

die Wohn. Nr. *13* an der *A H*

Nr *21* Ursache *Tod Lungen + be:*

Neue Adresse

Anmerkungen :

Litzmannstadt-Getto, d. *30. 6* 194 *3*

Eigenhändve Unterschrift.
des verantwortlichen Hausverwalters.

Eigenhändige Unterschrift des
Abgemeldeten oder Wohnungsinhabers.

Eigenhändige Unterschrift des
verantwortlichen Hausverwalters.

Eigenhändige Unterschrift
des Angemeldeten

DER AELTESTE DER JUDEN IN LITZMANNSTADT.

Abmeldung ✓ 4066 / 43

Familienname _Hecht_ geb. _____

Vornamen _Szmul_

Vornamen der Eltern _Pinkus u Estera_

Stand _ledig_ Geburtsort _Kielce_

Geburtsdatum _17·2·1923_ Religion _mos_

Beruf _Büroangestellte_ Karten Nr. _____

Der Obengenannte verliess am _12·10 43_

die Wohn. Nr. _7_ an der _Gasse_

Nr _5_ Ursache _Tb Lungen t.b._

Neue Adresse _____

Anmerkungen:

Litzmannstadt-Getto, d. _14. VO_ 194_3_

Eigenhänd ge Unterschrift
des verantwortlichen Hausverwalters.

Eigenhändige Unterschrift des
Abgemeldeten oder Wohnungsinhabers

Litzmannstadt, d.

Eigenhändige Unterschrift des
verantwortlichen Hausverwalters.

Eigenhändige Unterschrift
des Angemeldeten

OPPOSITE AND ABOVE: From the files of the ghetto Registration Bureau: notices of the deaths from tuberculosis of Dr. Bernard Heilig and Szmul Hecht, authors of the *Chronicle.*

Engineer Bernard Ostrowski, an author of the *Chronicle*.

Dr. Oskar Rosenfeld (left) and Dr. Oskar Singer (right), authors of the *Chronicle*, with Weksler, clandestine radio listener in the ghetto. Photographer: Mendel Grossman.

Dr. Oskar Singer in his study in Prague.

WYDZIAŁ ARCHIWUM
BIULETYN KRONIKI CODZIENNEJ

STAN POGODY.
Najniższa temperatura dnia wyniosła 14 stopni poniżej zera.-Słonecznie.

KRYMINALISTYKA.
Za kradzieże aresztowano dziś s osób,z tytułu innych przekroczeń za-
trzymano II osób.

ZGONY I NARODZINY.
Zmarło dziś w Ghecie 37 osób,urodzin nie rejestrowano.

POGOTOWIE Straży Porządkowej w związku z uruchomieniem warsztatów
pracy trwa w dalszym ciągu.Zauważyć warto,iż uruchomienie nie pod-
lega wytwórnie pieszowy warsztatów/Trzenotskadeka 75/,w których to warsztatach
praca odbywa się normalnie.W ciągu dnia nie odnotowano żadnego wypadku

ZWYŻKA TENDENCJA A TAKŻE MOŻLIWYCH.
W handlu prywatnym przecidno dziś za chleb 12mk.,kaszę-11,00,Mąkę -10mk.,
kartofle 2.60.-Tendencja zwyżkowa.

OPAŁ STAŁYM.
W związku z przyciskiem opałowym cena węgla i drzewa w handlu prywatnym
uległa zniżce.Za najgrubszy węgiel żądano 1,50,miał 0,45,:: drzewo 0,50
za kilogram.Zaofiarowaniu materiałów opałowych znacznie wzrosło.

Z HURTOWNI TYTONIOWEJ.
Wydział Tytoniowy Przełożonego Starszeństwa Żydów mieści się przy ul.
Brzezińskiej 24.Został on powołany do życia w dniu 10 czerwca ub.r.
Jest to hurtowy punkt rozdzielczy,który obiorcami są izw.lidzi
wojenni w liczbi 120 osób.Po dwuch inwalidów posiada i kiosk z wyrobi
mi tytoniów mi.Łącznia więc liczba czy innych w Gecie kiosków inwalidzkich
wynosi 60.Pozatem hurtownie sprzedaje wyroby tytuniów poszczególnym
resortom dla urzędników i robotników.Warto zauważyć iż rabat ze sprzedaży
tytoniu i papierosów urzędnikom przypada do podziału dla inwalidów
ciągu ostatnich 6 tygodnia z kreku towaru hurtownia wstrzymała sprzedaż,
wznawiając ją w ostatnich 4 daiach w związku z przybyciem do Geta tru-
sporu "paliwa".Moraszie sprzedawane są jedynie papierosy /Ballerina,cena
a talicama 0e80 pudełka z 20 sztuk/przy ogromnej frekwencji obiorców.
Aby rozntownie nie wyczerpać posiadanego zapasu papierosów hurtownia dzien-
nie sprzedaje jedynie do 100 rys.papierosów.Nawiasem mówiąc zapotrzebo-
wanie Geta na papierosy wynosi dd 100 do 150 tys.mk.mies. przy popycie
prawie wyłącznie na najtańsze gatunki.Zależnie w przybl.1/3 tego zapotrze

The front page of the Biuletyn Kroniki Codziennej (Daily Chronicle Bulletin) of January 28, 1941.

Tagesbericht von Dienstag, den 11. Januar 1944, Tageschronik
Das Wetter: 5 Grad unter Null, trockene Kälte.
Sterbefälle: 5, Geburten: keine
Festnahmen: Verschiedene 1
Bevölkerungsstand: ca.pol.

Sonstiges: Am 11.1.44 verübte Sandberg Jesek,ca.10,...,wohnhaft Franzstr.3u,durch Sprung
"Stockwerke setnou Wohnhauses Selbstmord. Der Arzt der
Rettungswache stellte den eingetretenen Tod fest.-

Tagesnachrichten.

Antsleiter Biebow ist heute im Getto eingetroffen und hat die Führung
seines Amtes sofort wieder übernommen. Er hatte längere Unterredungen
mit dem Präses und Arni Jakubowicz und beauftragte den Leiter der
der sofortigen Lieferung, verschiedener statistischen Ueberzeichte. Der
Präses brachte mit der Durchführung dieser die Produktion betreffenden
Aufstellungen den FUKM.
Eine Kommission, bestehend aus zwei Herren, ist im Getto eingetroffen.
Ueber den Zweck und den Charakter dieser Kommission ist nichts in
Erfahrung zu bringen. Es ist lediglich festzustellen,dass auf dem
Baumter-ring eine gewisse Nervosität herrscht.-

Approvisation.

Die Lage ist nach wie vor schlecht. Kleine Zaubren ändern nichts an den
Bild. Die Leichenstizinwürden wickeln sich nur im Rahmen der normalen
Zuteilungen für das Getto ab und lediglich etwas können dürften der
Lichtblick der nächsten Tag sein.

Ressortnachrichten.

Die Tischlerei II hat die Produktion der Akkumulatorenkisten in vollem
Umfange aufgenommen. Die 4000 Kisten werden in zwei bis drei Tagen fer-
tiggestellt sein.
Die Arbeiter an Holzläger Nadertal und die bei den Winterkulisten
Beschäftigten erhielten eine einmalige Zuweisung von 500 g Mehl und
200 g Wurst.
Strassenreinigung: Die Ressorts müssen infolge Mangel an Gerätten an-
deren Arbeitskräften zur Reinigung der angrenzenden Strassen und Plätze
Arbeiter zur Verfügung stellen.

Sanitäts- und Gesundheitswesen.

Die Grippe-Epidemie dauert an. Bis in die späten Abendstunden stehen
lange Schlangen vor den Apotheken. Leider ist auch ein grosser Teil
des Personals der Sanitätsabteilung erkrankt, so dass nicht einmal die
Rönngenqualifikationen durchgeführt werden können.

The front page of the Tageschronik (Daily Chronicle) of January 12, 1944.

The front page of the Biuletyn Kroniki Codziennej (Daily Chronicle Bulletin) of January 28, 1941.

The front page of the Tageschronik (Daily Chronicle) of January 12, 1944.

Mendel Grossman photographed by Nachman Zonabend.

Nachman Zonabend's ID card.

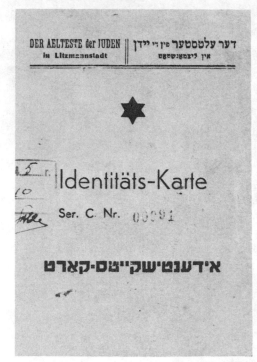

PART I: 1941

WEATHER

Ten degrees below zero.[2] No wind. Sunny.

THE CHAIRMAN AT AN INSPECTION OF THE REGISTRATION DEPARTMENT

This morning Chairman [Mordecai C.] Rumkowski, Eldest of the Jews, inspected the departments of population records, which are located in offices at 4 Miodowa Street. During his inspection, the Chairman took a lively interest in the work done by officials in specific departments, such as the Registration Bureau, the Department of Vital Statistics, and the Archives. After concluding his inspection, the Chairman held a protracted conference with [Henryk] Neftalin, the attorney who is the director of these departments.

DEATHS AND BIRTHS

Today 52 people died in the ghetto. The principal cause of death was heart disease, followed by exhaustion from hunger and cold, with tuberculosis in third place. Fourteen births were registered (seven boys and seven girls).

DEMANDS MADE BY MEMBERS OF THE ORDER SERVICE[3]

Today a delegation of Order Service employees appeared at their headquarters to petition for an improvement in conditions, the restoration of food and fuel supplements, wage increases, and so on. This petition was rejected by the authorities since the [ghetto's] own goal—the most uniform possible distribution of food among the population as a whole—ruled out the possibility of granting special privileges to certain categories even though they performed important public services. On the other hand, to ease the lot of the Order Service, the commandant promised to make an effort to enlarge the police mess halls so that they could serve the families of the policemen as well. Thus, the canteens will dispense meals three times a day to more than two thousand people.

CRIME

On the basis of reports from the Order Service precincts, 12 incidents of theft as well as 6 instances of various other offenses were recorded today.

---

1. The *Daily Chronicle Bulletin* for Sunday, January 12, 1941, is given in its entirety here.
2. All temperature readings in the *Chronicle* are given in centigrade.
3. *Służba Porządkowa* or *Straż Porządkowa* (Order Guard) in Polish, *Ordnungsdienst* in German—the Jewish police in the ghetto of Łódź, created on orders from the German authorities by M. C. Rumkowski, the Eldest of the Jews, on March 1, 1940. The Jewish police were neither armed nor in uniform. They did, however, wear distinctive caps, blue and white armbands with Stars of David, and carried rubber nightsticks. Throughout the ghetto's existence the chief of the Order Service was Leon Rozenblat (1894–1944), a bank director and an officer in the reserves before the war. In August, 1944, while the ghetto was being liquidated, he was deported to Auschwitz.

A SUICIDE ATTEMPT

Eighteen-year-old Abram Nożycki (of 21 Zgierska Street) threw himself to the pavement from the window of a fourth floor staircase at 2 Marynarska Street. The emergency physician arriving at the scene determined that Nożycki had suffered a number of injuries and, after applying first aid, brought him to Hospital No. 1 in critical condition.[4]

THE DEPARTMENT OF FOOD SUPPLY

The Department of Food Supply is in the process of reorganizing itself, a task which consists of decentralizing certain sections, such as those concerned with selling groceries, bread, fuel, vegetables, dairy products, etc. Begun on the first of this month, the work will be concluded at the end of the month. It will undoubtedly greatly increase efficiency in food distribution.

A SECOND FOOD RATION CARD

Today a proclamation[5] from the Eldest of the Jews concerning the implementation of a second ration card[6] was posted on the walls of the ghetto. The card will go on sale on the fourteenth of this month. Compared to the first ration cards, the new one is more substantial because its allocation includes a number of vegetables. A major improvement, subject to recall, is the possibility of continuing to buy rations with the first card. This proclamation was received very favorably by the populace.

NECESSITIES ON THE MARKET

Today the following items were on sale in private trade: bread at 6.50 marks[7] per kilogram, potatoes—2.50 marks, kasha—12 marks, coal dust—0.60 marks, coal—1–2 marks (depending on the type), wood—0.70 marks, matches—0.20 marks (per box), tobacco—2.90 marks (50 grams).

COMPLAINTS CONCERNING PROVISIONS

Most of the complaints concerning provisions this week had to do with shortages in the supply of kasha. It should be noted that this foodstuff, second in importance only

4. Initially there were five hospitals with a total of 1,225 beds, two first aid stations, four outpatient clinics, and six pharmacies in the ghetto. With the exception of one pharmacy owned by S. Kon and A. Fajneman (until September 1, 1941), all establishments related to health care in the ghetto were run by the Jewish administration.

5. Excepting the period from March 7 to September 21, 1941, when a newspaper with information and announcements was published in the ghetto, the proclamations posted on walls and fences were the only means by which the public was kept informed of regulations, food allocations, orders, prohibitions, etc. They were all signed by Rumkowski, except for a very few which were issued directly by the German authorities. These posters were of various colors depending on the kind of paper available at the time, and of varying shapes and sizes depending on the length of the text. The proclamations were printed in Yiddish, Polish, and German, or in combinations thereof.

6. That is, the second allocation in the month of January.

7. In all cases where the *Chronicle* speaks of marks, it is referring to so-called ghetto marks, that is, receipts (*Markquittungen*) for German marks or for other currencies which the people of the ghetto had to exchange by order of the German authorities. Beginning on July 8, 1940, ghetto marks became the sole official legal tender in the closed Jewish quarter and had no value outside of it. The bills were printed outside the ghetto, in Łódź, in denominations of 50 pfennigs, 1, 2, 5, 10, and 50 marks. They did, however, bear the signature of M[ordecai Chaim] Rumkowski and thus were known colloquially as *Rumki* or *Chaimki*.

to bread and potatoes, has thus far been supplied in relatively large quantities; however, this is the first week in which there has been any delay in the supply of kasha. Fifty thousand kilograms of kasha are requested per week to supply every resident of the ghetto with 50 grams per day. The private market has reacted by raising the price to 12 marks per kilogram. The price of sugar is now at 9 marks, whereas, until the present time, these prices had been reversed.

AN INCREASE IN THE BREAD RATION?

The rumors on this subject persist. And this most absorbing of questions to ghetto dwellers is on everybody's lips.

FIRST AID CHRONICLE

Today the First Aid Service was called out 59 times. In five cases the doctors recorded deaths, while in the other 54 they administered first aid. Three of the deaths occurred from exhaustion. Thirty-five cases of internal illnesses, seventeen of surgical trauma, one attack of madness, and one suicide were noted.

STREET DEMONSTRATIONS

Yesterday's mass demonstrations for an increase in food and fuel rations were repeated this afternoon. It is worth noting that, since the September incidents, there has not been a single instance of the peace being disturbed in the ghetto.[8] It has been determined beyond question that this action was organized by irresponsible individuals intent on disturbing the peace and public order created by the authorities who watch over the law, safety, and food supplies of the ghetto dwellers. A characteristic of this incident is the fact that the individuals inciting the crowd had been recruited from among the workers who enjoy supplemental food allowances and, meanwhile, sell those rations at black market prices. The demonstrations took place in front of the hospital on Łagiewnicka Street[9] as well as at several points along Brzezińska Street. Several times, the crowd attempted to steal food that was being transported by wagon, but was thwarted by the hard stance taken by the Order Service. Heavy police patrols have been keeping watch on the ghetto's streets for an entire day now. Peace was completely restored by the afternoon.

A SAD CASE OF SAVAGERY

A crowd consisting of a few hundred people has demolished a wooden shed on the property at 67 Brzezińska Street. While the wood was being stolen, the roof of the shed collapsed, crushing several people. In spite of their desperate cries, no one came to

8. The September incidents mentioned here refer to earlier, largely spontaneous mass demonstrations which took place in the ghetto in June, July, August, and September of 1940. They were directed against Rumkowski and his administration, for he was held to blame for hunger and lawlessness in the ghetto. The Jewish police were used against the demonstrators, but the street demonstrations ended only when the German police stepped in and opened fire on the crowd. People were killed and wounded.

If the summer demonstrations, especially those in the first days of June, were to some degree directed by the pre-war workers' parties, chiefly the Bund (*Algemeyner yidisher arbeter bund*), then the demonstrations in January, 1941, were headed by a variety of ad hoc committees, such as the Committee for the Defense of the Jewish Populace from Hunger in the Ghetto.

9. Rumkowski's private apartment was located in Hospital No. 1 at 34/36 Łagiewnicka Street.

their aid and the robbery continued unabated. Thirty-six-year-old Frania Szabnek died as a result of her injuries. Two other persons suffered serious injuries. This lamentable instance of moral savagery, a direct result of agitation by lawless elements, clearly illustrates the necessity for an all-out struggle against the parasites of the underworld.

PARADOXES OF GHETTO LIFE

An Eight-Year-Old Informer
Appearing at one of the precincts of the Order Service, an 8-year-old boy filed a report against his own parents, whom he charged with not giving him the bread ration due him. The boy demanded that an investigation be conducted and that the guilty parties be punished. No comment . . .

Stairs Stolen
The residents of a building found themselves in a very disconcerting situation when, after waking up, they discovered that in the course of the night unknown culprits had stolen . . . their stairs as well as the handrail and banister.

THE FUR BUY-UP DRIVE

The day before yesterday was the deadline for submitting furs for sale. In connection with the conclusion of this drive which was of unusually lively interest to thousands of ghetto residents, it is worthwhile to trace its entire course as well as to describe the results achieved. The obligation to submit furs of every sort for the buy-up was imposed on the [ghetto's] residents by the Chairman's Proclamation No. 179, dated December 17 of last year. The deadline, originally set for January 1 of this year, was extended because of the flood of applications to the 10th of this month, after which time, in accordance with the above-mentioned proclamation, "all furs found in the possession of private individuals will be confiscated."

The Bank of the Eldest of the Jews, located on Ciesielska Street, was charged with executing the fur buy-up campaign.[10] By the deadline of the 10th of this month, the bank had paid out the sum of 350,000 marks for the furs purchased and the number of sellers had reached approximately 3,500. On the 9th of this month the making of cash payments was partially suspended; however, with the aim of stepping up the drive, the bank has limited its functions solely to taking applications and paying out advances to the tenderers. Only the purchase of smaller articles has been completed. Typically in this drive, the more expensive furs were submitted in the first phase and the shabbier items predominated in the final stage. The items most frequently submitted for sale were fur overcoat linings, collars, and women's accessories. Over 5,000

10. All institutions, offices, and workshops in the ghetto had "The Eldest of the Jews" (*Der Älteste der Juden in Litzmannstadt-Getto*) appended to their titles and appearing on their letterheads, signs, seals, etc. Rumkowski's bank in the ghetto was founded on June 26, 1940, and, in the course of time, its more important functions came to include the exchange of *Reichsmark* for ghetto marks; the purchase of all types of valuables, currencies, and goods from the ghetto population; the role of intermediary in the collection of debts from outside the ghetto, and the receipt of all payments and money orders made from the outside to residents of the ghetto; and the regulation of the supply of ghetto marks in the Jewish quarter. All valuables exacted by the bank from the Jewish population were seized by the German Ghetto Administration (Gettoverwaltung). Only a negligible portion of the valuables acquired in this fashion was used to cover the cost of the food sent to the ghetto by the Germans.

items passed through the hands of specialists on the busiest days. On the average, the appraisal prices were 25 percent higher than pre-war prices (with 1 mark equaling 2 złotys).[11] As to the quality of the fur pieces sold, nearly 50 percent fell into the very shabby category, 30 percent were middling, and barely 20 percent were good. The number of new furs offered for sale was entirely insignificant. The appraisals were done by experts and then passed on to the committee that determined the amount of payment. If it possessed information about the seller's financial condition, the committee often made considerable allowances. In that respect, the drive, carried out in accord with the Chairman's intent, brought some financial relief to those people who were forced to sell their fur pieces. Considering that this drive was undertaken as a result of orders from the [German] authorities, it should be stated that it was conducted in the most remunerative manner possible for those concerned. This was due to the fact that the Chairman was able to gain full power to conduct the buy-up under his own official auspices. A second extremely positive factor was that furs in the possession of people whose work for the commonweal requires especially warm clothing were exempted from the buy-up. This affected doctors, nurses, police, and janitors. Similarly, within the limits of his authority, the Chairman also exempted the furs belonging to a certain number of sick people as well as those belonging to the elderly. Finally, it should be noted that furs of little value were exempted from the obligatory sale. In all such cases the parties involved received the appropriate documents and their furs were provided with an official seal.

Several thousand customers were accommodated in such a short period of time because of the uncommonly efficient technical organization and the selfless work of the entire team, which had a proper sense of the importance of this matter. Today, summing up the results of the drive now concluded, one must undoubtedly stress that this job was done strictly to satisfy the needs of the parties involved as much as possible and with a full awareness of its social nature. Unfortunately, it is highly typical that in many cases the parties concerned did not appreciate these good intentions, mistakenly assuming that this was a normal business transaction done for profit. The Chairman himself inaugurated the drive, working along with the committees on the first day and, several times, inspecting the bank to provide the committee members with precise information. The work was divided as follows: the administration was in the hands of J. Szkólnik and J. Izraelski. There were two committees, and three on the most active days. The committees were composed of members of the bank's administration, namely, the president, H. Szyfer, counselors P. Blaugrund and H. Fein, and A. Englard, who was a member of the appraisal committee. The work of the experts was performed by J. Opatowski and S. Brajsztajn.

NECESSITY IS THE MOTHER OF INVENTION

Mr. Wosk's Sensational Ideas

The incredibly difficult living conditions experienced by the inhabitants of the ghetto make it an arena exceptionally responsive to human ingenuity and to inventions that

---

11. The prices fixed in these compulsory transactions did not begin to approximate the free-market value of the furs surrendered for sale.

On September 11, 1939—that is, while hostilities were still going on between Germany and Poland—the German authorities arbitrarily set the rate of exchange at one German mark for two Polish złotys. At first money could be exchanged only in very limited amounts, and after November 27, 1939, the Polish złoty ceased to be legal tender in Łódź as well as in other Polish territories incorporated into the Reich.

can resolve the most varied problems arising from the lack of everyday necessities. Henryk Wosk, a known inventor and holder of a number of patents, has presented himself to the Community[12] authorities with a plan for the creation of a department of ideas, modeled after the former Bureau of Patents. Mr. Wosk's plan calls for ghetto residents to report any useful ideas to the above-mentioned department, which will remunerate them for the costs involved. On their part, the ghetto authorities would ask the department [of ideas] to suggest solutions to various problems and these would be brought to the public's attention. The department will award prizes to those persons who find the best solutions to the problems. Moreover, the inventors will have the opportunity to work while implementing their ideas. In this way, a series of benefits—employment opportunities for hitherto unemployed but productive individuals, for instance—will accrue. It will also encourage ideas whose realization will result in improved living conditions for the inhabitants of the ghetto. As to Mr. Wosk's current ideas, the following are worth mentioning: (1) the utilization of frozen or spoiled potatoes; (2) the full exploitation of coal dust; (3) the artificial production of ice using an inexpensive method that is possible under current conditions; (4) replacing glass with other suitable materials due to the present shortage. Mr. Wosk's proposals have caused great interest among the ghetto's higher circles.

The carrying out of Mr. Wosk's project will undoubtedly provide an inducement for other ideas of a productive nature. Thus far, exuberant ingenuity has flourished in only one specifically commercial area of ghetto life: the production of items whose sale is reckoned always and only for profit and which are devoid of any value for the consumer. We are thinking of the mass production of "confectionary" goods, for example, which are without value and even harmful to health, as well as of counterfeits of every sort, from gold to fuel.

TUESDAY, JANUARY 14, 1941

A SEARCH

A search was conducted today by the [German] authorities on the premises of the United Engravers firm located at 2 Brzezińska Street.[13] Gold objects were confiscated.

SUPPLYING THE GHETTO WITH FUEL

Apart from the question of food supply, the greatest plague for the inhabitants of the ghetto has been the shortage of fuel during the severe frosts that have been persisting

---

12. Here, and in other places in the *Chronicle*, the term *Community* (*[Zydowska] Gmina [Wyznaniowa]* in the original Polish text) refers to the ghetto's Jewish administration. Although the *Gmina* or *kehillah* (in Hebrew), the institution of Jewish self-government, was disbanded in Łódź by the German authorities in October, 1939, use of the term was continued from force of habit by both the ghetto's populace and the offices of the Nazi-imposed Jewish Council, the Jewish ghetto administration. The latter considered itself a continuation of the pre-war kehillah, though there was no basis in fact for this since the kehillah was always an autonomous institution of public law that derived its authority from Talmudic tradition, the legal status granted it by the state, and, in pre-war times, from the free elections held in the community.

13. This was one of the few private firms in the ghetto. All businesses, workshops, artisan shops, stores, restaurants, and so forth, with very few exceptions, were either closed down, liquidated, or taken over by the relevant divisions of the Jewish ghetto administration—if they had not already been confiscated by the German authorities.

for a few weeks now. It should be noted that this week brought some long and eagerly awaited improvement in the ghetto's fuel supply, namely, a 40 to 50 percent increase. The coal delivered was of the sort known as base coal. However, the distribution of the coal to the people of the ghetto is, unfortunately, still out of the question—even with amounts such as these. All that has been achieved is the possibility of completely satisfying the needs of the workshops[14] and the Community kitchens, as well as the departments and institutions of the Eldest of the Jews, the Department of Health chief among them. Demand fluctuates around 700 bushels (including the coke). Wood from demolished sheds, old, uninhabited, dilapidated houses, fences, etc., is also stored at the central fuel yard. This brings in about twenty thousand kilograms of wood per day. The demolition is performed by the Fuel Department's own work crews. Up to one hundred thousand kilos of wood are distributed per week for building alterations. Moreover, wood is sent to the soup kitchens and to plants that produce cured meat products. This week, the increase in the fuel shortage has still not been overcome, but there are already prospects for a resolution of the most urgent issue—the distribution of fuel to the populace. This will come in the very near future.

SAD BUT TRUE: "LINES" ARE ALSO OBLIGATORY FOR THE DECEASED

"You can't die either these days," complained a woman who had come to arrange formalities in the mortuary office in connection with the death of her mother. There is nothing exaggerated about such complaints if one considers that, with the current increase in the death rate, a minimum of three days' wait to bury the dead, sometimes even ten days, has become an everyday occurrence. The causes of this abnormal state of affairs are worth noting. There are scarcely three horses left in the ghetto to draw the hearses, a totally inadequate number in view of the current increase in the death rate. Several times, there was such a "backlog" in the transporting of bodies to the cemetery that, out of necessity, a sideless hauling wagon had to be pressed into service and loaded with several dozen bodies at the same time. Before the arrival of the current frosts, when the death rate in the ghetto did not exceed 25 to 30 cases per day (before the war the average death rate among the Jewish population of the city amounted to six per day),[15] there were 12 gravediggers employed at the cemetery. Today there are around 200. In spite of such a horrendously large number of gravediggers, no more than 50 graves can be dug per day. The reason: a lack of skilled labor, as well as problems connected with the ground being frozen. And this causes the macabre "line" to grow longer.

---

14. Workshops (*resorty pracy* in Polish, *Arbeitsressorts* in German) were factories of all kinds established and managed by the Jewish administration in the ghetto. These factories almost exclusively filled orders for German military and civilian authorities or for private German companies. The *Chronicle* will sometimes call a workshop a department or vice versa, which, on the one hand, corresponded to actual changed names and, on the other, was a result of insufficient correction of the daily entries.

15. That is, six deaths out of Łódź's overall pre-war Jewish population of 230,000–250,000, whereas the ghetto numbered only 154,261 inhabitants in January, 1941.

WEDNESDAY, JANUARY 15, 1941

A TRAGIC DEATH

A tragic accident occurred this afternoon on Łagiewnicka Street near [Bałut] Market. A large crowd of people attacked a wagon loaded with rutabaga with the aim of robbing it. During the incident, 80-year-old Rywka Fajga Zejdeman (of 15 Pieprzowa Street) was pushed under the wheels of the wagon. Besieged by the crowd, the driver was unable to halt his horse at once, as a result of which the old woman was killed on the spot.

DEATH ON A BRIDGE[16]

While crossing the bridge over Zgierska Street between Kościelny Square and Luto-mierska Street, 66-year-old Kurz Mendel (of 25 Oficerska Street) suffered a heart attack. The victim was taken to a first aid station. Kurz died in the ambulance without recovering consciousness.[17] His body was taken to the mortuary at Hospital No. 3.

THURSDAY, JANUARY 16, 1941

DEATH FROM EXHAUSTION

Thirty-six-year-old Abe Abram Baumarc died on the night of January 16. He had lived alone at 10 Pieprzowa Street. The first aid physician summoned determined the cause of death to be complete exhaustion resulting from hunger.

BREAD RATION INCREASED BY HALF A KILOGRAM

Today, the Chairman's decision was announced concerning a supplemental alloca-tion of bread on next Sunday, the 19th, in the amount of 500 grams per person, apart from the normal daily ration of 300 grams. This supplement will be sold for bread

16. Two main arteries leading to Poznań and Warsaw crossed the territory of the ghetto—one, Lima-nowski St., went to Aleksandrów, a town located to the northwest of Łódź, and the other, Zgierska, went to Zgierz, another town, situated to the north of the city. For that reason, the roadways of both streets were not part of the ghetto, whereas the sidewalks and the buildings on those streets did fall within the limits of the ghetto. The isolated roadways of Limanowski and Zgierska streets thus divided the ghetto into three parts. Foot traffic by ghetto residents took place via three wooden bridges that joined the ghetto's sidewalks and were especially constructed for that purpose. Points and gates in the enclosure around the ghetto, guarded by German police from outside and by Jewish police from within, were designated for vehicular traffic. In addition, there were gates at a few other points designated for pedestrians.

17. Automobiles, trucks, motorcycles, and even bicycles belonging to Jews were confiscated by the German authorities practically at the beginning of the occupation of Łódź in 1939. The "legal" sanction for this act was an order by the chief of the German police on December 2, 1939, forbidding Jews to possess vehicles of any sort. Consequently, all vehicles in the ghetto, with the exception of two or three tram cars for transporting people to their places of work and the Fire Department's two old cars and a motorcycle, were horse-drawn, or, more commonly, were drawn by people. The First Aid Service used either a horse-drawn ambulance or a droshky (a four-wheeled, horse-drawn cab for up to six passengers).

ration coupon 19. Workshop and factory workers will, on that day, receive the above-mentioned 800 grams like the rest of the populace. As is generally known, manual laborers are receiving a double bread ration, that is, 600 grams.

FRIDAY, JANUARY 17, 1941

AN INCREASE IN RELIEF ALLOWANCES[18]

Today Proclamation No. 197 was posted on the ghetto's walls informing the populace of the Chairman's decision to increase relief allowances for the month of January, undertaken "in spite of the severe financial situation." Children up to the age of 14 will receive seven marks for the month of January, adults from 15 to 60—10 marks, elderly people up to 70—12 marks, those from 71 to 79—14 marks, and people over 80—16 marks. The post office will forward the relief allowances, as it has so far. The increase in relief allowances occasioned intense satisfaction among the populace.

SATURDAY, JANUARY 18, 1941

DEATH ON THE STREET

Thirty-four-year-old Icek Mendel Korona (of 21 Tokarzewski Street) died on Marysińska Street. The cause of death was exhaustion caused by hunger. En route from confinement in Precinct II to the hospital, Abram Goldap, a prisoner, died.

A CONCERT BY MISS BRONISŁAWA ROTSZTAT

As usual, the concert by Miss Bronisława Rotsztat, the talented violinist, played to a full house and enjoyed great success in the ghetto. Her rendition of Wieniawski's concerto, executed with verve, was especially noteworthy. Professor Teodor Ryder accompanied.[19]

18. On September 20, 1940, that is, not long after the hunger demonstrations, the Eldest of the Jews established a relief system for the unemployed, the poorly paid workers in the Jewish administration and the workshops, children up to 14 years of age, and people over 60.

19. Bronisława Rotsztat, violinist, before the war a soloist in the Łódź Symphony Orchestra. In the ghetto she performed at private gatherings, in some of the soup kitchens, and at the House of Culture, established by the Jewish ghetto administration on March 1, 1941. When the ghetto was being liquidated in August, 1944, she was deported to Auschwitz. After her liberation, she returned to Łódź and became concertmistress of the newly formed philharmonic orchestra.

Teodor Ryder (1881–1944), pianist, conductor, and educator born in Piotrków, Poland. After studying music abroad, he performed in Germany, France, and Switzerland. In 1916 he returned to Poland, where he at first performed with the Warsaw Opera and then moved to Łódź, where he conducted the Symphony Orchestra, headed the Opera Department, and was also the symphony music conductor for Radio Poland. In the ghetto he was one of the founders of the House of Culture, where he performed regularly. He was deported to Auschwitz in 1944.

SUNDAY, JANUARY 19, 1941

A SUICIDE

Today at 5:30, 27-year-old Frajda Ejber, originally from Lublin, hung herself in her apartment at 43 Hohensteiner (Zgierska Street).[20] The young woman took her own life from depression related to her tuberculosis.

THE FOOD SUPPLY SITUATION

Before the Bakeries Are Put into Operation
An event characteristic of the food supply situation last week was the resumption, after a long interruption, of flour delivery to the ghetto. Such sizable shipments have started arriving that it has become feasible to put the ghetto's own bakeries into operation. The first bakeries, five in number, will commence work on the night of the 20th of this month. Several hundred sacks of flour are arriving in the course of a day.

Moreover, there has been an improvement in the delivery of potato flour, oatmeal, straw, and hay. The shortage of straw has become a major complaint in the hospitals. At present, 1,650 kilograms of straw are earmarked for filling straw pallets. The remaining quantity of straw has been designated for use as fodder.[21]

The shortage of potatoes is also felt, but to a somewhat lesser degree than last week. The supply of milk fluctuates around 1,000 liters a day, which makes it possible to dispense portions of 200 grams to children up to the age of three and to the sick who have certificates from a physician. The delivery of onions remains completely suspended. The supply of rapeseed oil is adequate. Bread has been brought in at a daily rate of between 43 and 75 thousand kilograms. The delivery of bread in these amounts, in addition to the flour supply, now enables the Department of Food Supply to store this most important foodstuff, which in turn makes it possible to raise the current bread ration to 400 and perhaps even 450 grams per day.

MONDAY, JANUARY 20, 1941

PEOPLE ARE DYING FROM HUNGER AND COLD

As determined by physicians of the Department of Health today, there were three cases of death as the result of complete physical exhaustion brought on by hunger

---

20. Even before the creation of the ghetto, the occupying authorities were renaming streets in Łódź, changing the Polish names to German ones. (In searching for names the German authorities recalled a previous period when Łódź had been under German control, i.e., 1915–18 during the First World War.) Consequently, at times both names appear in the *Chronicle* simultaneously; the Polish text, however, uses the Polish names most frequently, whereas the German text uses the German. Here and elsewhere in the present edition of the *Chronicle*, if only the German name of a street was used, its Polish name has been restored.

21. Fodder was provided for a rather small number of cows, oxen, horses, goats, and other domestic animals, some of which belonged to various departments of the ghetto Jewish administration and some to private parties. At some point, pasture land was set aside in Marysin for the Gettoverwaltung's animals and horses.

and cold: Icek Brona, aged 34, Abram Szmulewicz, aged 69, and 57-year-old Ita Kinster.

FROM THE COURT:[22] THEY STOLE WHAT THEY GUARDED

Today the Court of the Eldest of the Jews examined the case of a policeman and a watchman accused of stealing wood that had been entrusted to their care. The watchman received a sentence of five months in prison, the policeman was condemned to four months at hard labor.

TUESDAY, JANUARY 21, 1941

BREAD RATION INCREASED TO 400 GRAMS

Today, Proclamation No. 200 of the Eldest of the Jews was posted to inform the ghetto that beginning Friday, the 24th of January, 1941, every resident of the ghetto will receive 400 grams of bread. Supplemental bread rations will stop on that day. The increase in the bread ration, by relieving the greatest complaint of the population at large, caused universal and intense satisfaction among the starving masses who inhabit the ghetto.

THE PRIVATE MARKET NOTES

a sharp decrease in the price of bread, to 11 marks per kilogram, because of the increase in the bread ration (it is worth noting that the price of bread had already reached 15 marks). Potatoes are holding at 13 marks, coal of the best sort, at 1.80 marks with a slight tendency to drop, and coal dust, at 0.45 marks.

A STRANGE ROBBERY

Yesterday evening, Brzezińska Street was the scene of a chase, that of a thief who literally buckled under the weight of the loot he had stolen: the entry door from Epsztajn's grocery located on the same street, at No. 43. The thief was seized, and the door was returned to its rightful owner. Today the perpetrator of the theft was summarily sentenced by the court to three months in prison. The thief in question is Frajluś Kiwe, known in the criminal world by the nickname *Mogn* ("Stomach").

WEDNESDAY, JANUARY 22, 1941

DEATHS AND BIRTHS

Thirty-eight people died. Two babies were born, one male and one female.

---

22. The court convened by Rumkowski in the ghetto on September 18, 1940, was an institution of very limited range and dubious independence. It dealt with both civil and criminal cases. The court's sentences included fines, imprisonment, and hard labor in the ghetto—for example, the cleaning of cesspools in buildings without plumbing or the removal of excrement in wagons drawn by people. The chairman of the court was Szaja-Stanisław Jakobson (1906–44), a doctor of law and a graduate of Jagellonian University. During the liquidation of the ghetto, he was deported to Auschwitz.

THE STRUGGLE FOR FUEL

A crowd has wantonly demolished a wooden shed on the property at 11/13 Kielma [Marysińska] Street. At one point the roof of the shed collapsed, crushing several of those committing the theft. The first aid physician summoned to the scene administered first aid to the victims.

THURSDAY, JANUARY 23, 1941

DEATHS AND BIRTHS

Today, 45 people died in the ghetto. No births were registered.

THE CARPENTERS' STRIKE

Today a strike broke out among the carpenters employed in the Community workshops. Three hundred and fifty workers joined the strike and occupied the premises on Drukarska Street, where the carpenters' shop is located. The strike was undertaken as a protest against the revocation of the supplemental bread rations now that the bread ration distributed uniformly among the population has been increased to 400 grams. Moreover, the strikers put forward a series of demands including one for an increase in pay (actually that demand had been met even before the strike action, although, thus far, the extent of the increase has not been determined). In addition, the strikers demanded that they receive afternoon meals without having to use ration coupons. Approximately half of the workers employed in the carpenters' shop took part in the sit-in strike. At one o'clock P.M. a detachment of the Order Service numbering 70 policemen was summoned to the premises where the workshops are located. The Order Service called for the strikers to vacate the premises. That attempt achieved no results and, accordingly, they began to remove the strikers by force. After vacating the hall on the first floor, the strikers massed on the second floor, having barricaded the door. After breaking in the door, the Order Service managed to expel all the workers in the course of about one hour. During the action, several workers and policemen were injured, some more severely than others. One of the victims required first aid. The workers continued to gather in the street in front of the carpenters' shop. They were dispersed by the police within a quarter of an hour and peace was restored.[23]

23. In the papers of Józef Zelkowicz, a more extensive and detailed account of the carpenters' strike is to be found. The papers are dated 24 and 26 January and 2 February. For information, Zelkowicz relied on the leaflets issued by the strikers and on conversations with participants in the events; he was in contact with both sides, that is, with representatives of the Jewish administration, who suppressed the strike, and with the workers. Among other things, his account includes, *in extenso*, the following demands put forward by the carpenters, the rejection of which was the direct cause of the strike:
"(1) A pay raise of 20 pfennigs per hour for workers in the first two categories and 10 pfennigs per hour for workers in the last two categories; (2) In view of the prevailing high cost of living, the carpenters, even with a raise, will not be able to support themselves, so half of their wages should be paid them in the form of food products; (3) Because of the present food supply system, the carpenters are unable to perform the heavy physical labor required by the profession, and so should be given—as was done previously—a supplemental daily soup (not on the food ration card); (4) That the supplements they have thus far been receiving in the form of special bread cards not be eliminated." (Published in Yiddish in Isaiah Trunk, *Lodzer geto*, pp. 440–44; in Polish translation in *Biuletyn Żydowskiego Instytutu Historycznego* (*Bulletin of the Jewish Historical Institute*), 54 (1965), pp. 16–19.

A CASE OF SMUGGLING

Yesterday the court received a case involving a smuggling charge for adjudication from the [German] authorities. It is worth noting that this is the first instance of such a case being directed here by the authorities with instructions that it be adjudicated under the aegis of the court of the Eldest of the Jews.

SLIPPERY ICE

Now, to the daily afflictions of the ghetto dwellers, a new one has been added: the slippery ice and the thawing snow on the streets are creating incredible difficulties in foot traffic. Pedestrians are performing sheer acrobatics at every step on the sidewalk or roadway. In the evening, especially when darkness covers the majority of the unlighted streets and when (after eight o'clock) the light filtering out from apartment windows is shut off, walking presents difficulties that are utterly insurmountable. The First Aid Service was summoned several times for cases in which legs had been broken on the street. Under these conditions, the campaign for snow removal in the ghetto, so energetically undertaken by our Chairman, is enjoying universal approval.

FRIDAY, JANUARY 24, 1941

WORKSHOPS CEASE OPERATIONS TEMPORARILY

Today all workshops were closed on orders from the Chairman. The Chairman's proclamation was posted in front of the premises in which the enterprises affected are located, explaining the motives for the above-mentioned decision. This notice made it clear that, due to agitation by irresponsible individuals, regrettable incidents have been incited whose intent was to disrupt the normal course of work. As a result of these incidents, it was necessary to resort to the forcible expulsion of workers from the workshop building they had occupied. According to information in the Chairman's possession, similar incidents had also been planned on the grounds of other enterprises. The Chairman points out that he has already warned the workers several times against resorting to such methods and has frequently explained that the workshops are primarily employed in supplying the army. Being directly and personally responsible for all disturbances in the workplace and for the resulting losses, the Chairman cannot tolerate such offenses. Consequently, the decision to shut down the workshops was made for the purpose of ruling out any further incidents. The payment owed the workers will be forwarded to them by mail on Friday, Saturday, and Sunday, and must be signed for in person by the employees. In the event of a given worker's absence from his domicile, the mailman will not pay out any funds. In his concern for assuring the livelihood of the workers, the Chairman has spared no efforts in organizing his workshops, whose existence at the present moment makes it possible for thousands upon thousands of people to work in peace. Furthermore, the Chairman promises that he will make every effort to supply the populace with food as regularly and plentifully as possible. It should, however, be taken into account that a series of reasons, including problems caused by the weather, often make it impossible to keep all promises. Irresponsible elements exploit this factor. The individuals creating the discord were arrested and, to avoid a repetition of such incidents, there will be further arrests until peace has been completely restored.

ORDER SERVICE ON THE ALERT

In connection with yesterday's incidents in the carpentry workshops and the closing of all work places, the Order Service has been placed on emergency alert today. No offenses were noted in the course of the day.

SATURDAY, JANUARY 25, 1941

A SONG RECITAL

There was a song recital by the gifted tenor Nikodem Sztajman today at Soup Kitchen No. 2 [for the intelligentsia] at 41 Zgierska Street. Teodor Ryder provided the accompaniment. Arias from the operas of Puccini, Verdi, Tchaikovsky, Leoncavallo and Meyerbeer were sung. The large audience applauded the performer warmly.

SUNDAY, JANUARY 26, 1941

DEATHS AND BIRTHS

Seventy-three people died in the ghetto yesterday and today. No births were registered in the course of these two days.

FACTORIES AND WORKSHOPS STILL IDLE

In accordance with the Chairman's ruling, the workshops managed by the labor agencies continue to be idle. The Order Service remains in a state of alert. Not a single case of disturbance of the peace has been noted.

THE GREAT BREAD THEFT

On Saturday night 91 loaves of bread were stolen from the distribution point storehouse at 4 Jakuba Street. The Bureau of Investigation [of the Order Service] has mounted an active investigation into the case. Several persons suspected of having taken part in the theft have been arrested.

THE DAIRY PRODUCT SITUATION

In accordance with the Chairman's Proclamation No. 201, dairy and bread stores have, since the 24th of this month and after an interruption of many months, been selling butter and oatmeal in exchange for ration-card coupons. In order to make service more efficient, the bread stores are also being utilized to sell these goods and, along with the 17 existing dairy stores, are making it possible to offer these items for sale at 57 distribution points. It is worth noting that until now only children and sick people (with medical coupons) had been able to avail themselves of the butter allocation. At present, the management of the dairy food department is working to renew distribution of dairy products among the entire population. A large increase in the ghetto's supply of butter and margarine has been noted this week. Approximately 2,000 kilograms of each item arrived here in the course of the week. On the other hand, the supply of milk has decreased significantly, at least by one third, and for two days last week there was no milk supplied. There were, however, increased quantities of buttermilk.

MONDAY, JANUARY 27, 1941

THE ORDER SERVICE EMERGENCY ALERT

is still being maintained in connection with the shutdown of the workshops. No disturbances of the peace noted.

PARADOXES OF LIFE

Today, at the provisions [black] market, two almost new tablecloths and a sheet were swapped for a loaf of bread. This unusual transaction is tellingly characteristic of life conditions in the ghetto.

TUESDAY, JANUARY 28, 1941

THE ORDER SERVICE EMERGENCY ALERT

is still continuing in connection with the shutdown of workshops. It is worth noting that the rubber coat factory (at 5 Bałut Market), the fur workshop (at 9 Ceglana Street), and the underwear makers' (at 75 Franciszkańska Street) are not subject to the shutdown and work is proceeding normally there. No disturbances of the peace were noted in the course of the day.

FUEL

The prices of coal and wood in private trade have undergone a decline in connection with the fuel allocation. 1.50 marks are asked for the crudest coal, 0.45 marks for coal dust, and 0.50 marks for a kilogram of wood. The amount of fuel for sale has increased significantly.

WEDNESDAY, JANUARY 29, 1941

A SUICIDE ATTEMPT

In an attempted suicide, 21-year-old Bluma Lichtensztajn leaped from the fourth-story window of the staircase at 60 Franciszkańska Street. The physician summoned from First Aid brought the attempted suicide to Hospital No. 1. Her condition leaves no hope for recovery.

DEATH FROM HUNGER AND COLD

A 15-year-old boy, Kleczewski Hersz (homeless), was found in a state of complete exhaustion from cold and hunger in the basement of the building at 38 Zawisza Street. On the building manager's suggestion, the tenants took charge of carrying the boy to the hospital. The boy, however, died en route without regaining consciousness.

MEAT AND POTATOES FOR THE WORKERS

The proclamation of the Eldest of the Jews posted today on the ghetto's walls institutes an allotment of 580 grams of meat and two kilograms of potatoes as a second ration for janitors, workers employed in public works, the Order Service, and also chimney sweeps. As to workers in factories and workshops, only those who are working at present are entitled to this allocation. The provisions will be issued on the 31st of January.

NEW FUEL RATION FOR THE POPULACE

Made public today, Proclamation No. 204 establishes a second allocation of coal and wood for the inhabitants of the ghetto. This allocation consists of six kilograms of coal dust and two kilograms of wood, sold together at a cost of 0.80 marks. Beginning on the 2d of February, the fuel will be sold for coupon 3 of the food ration card. Payments will be made at the police precincts as was the case during the first allocation.

THE ACTIVITIES OF THE DEPARTMENT OF SOUP KITCHENS

The Department of Soup Kitchens, directed by a commission, supervises the activity of all the public kitchens and eating places, which total some one hundred. The soup kitchens are divided into the following categories: (1) the central kitchens (formerly the Community kitchens), of which there are five; (2) the kitchens run by house committees[24] and recently taken over by the Community; (3) the so-called social kitchens;[25] and (4) eating places or private restaurants. Taken together, the kitchens in operation in the ghetto were serving up to 145,000 midday meals before it became obligatory for an individual to turn over his food coupons to the kitchen where he took his meals. After that the number of meals served dropped to 15,000. Such a significant drop in the patronage of soup kitchens can be explained by the fact that

24. House committees and block committees, tenants' self-government organizations, were created spontaneously on a grass roots level and in elections held by the residents of individual apartment buildings during the first months of 1940, when the ghetto was being established. The house committees were concerned with keeping the properties clean, performing the necessary repairs, organizing the removal of excrement, the cleaning of chimneys, wells, etc., and also with providing care for children, old people, and tenants who were ill. After the ghetto was closed off in May, 1940, the house committees and the block committees were primarily concerned with food distribution, setting up soup kitchens, and certain cultural and educational activities. Initially supported by the Jewish administration of the ghetto, these committees were gradually taken over by the Community's official structure, and later entirely disbanded by the Eldest of the Jews.

25. That is, the soup kitchens that were established and run by members of pre-war Jewish political parties, but principally by the Labor Zionist party (Paole Zion—Workers of Zion) and the Bund. In the early period, the soup kitchens, in addition to serving meals, organized literary and musical evenings and housed gatherings of party members, who operated on a semi-legal basis in the ghetto.

formerly quite a few people took their meals in many different kitchens, which is now out of the question. Moreover, practice has demonstrated that, in general, the populace prefers to receive foodstuffs directly. Given that, the question of the need for the continued existence of any given soup kitchen is being decided by the customers themselves since turning their coupons over to the kitchens makes it possible for them to receive food through the agency of the department.

Under these conditions, a series of kitchens that had clearly been mismanaged have been eliminated, while the kitchens that were organized efficiently and, in particular, those serving good meals, continue to enjoy success. Obviously the deciding factor here is the honesty of the administration and the personnel in various positions, since all the kitchens receive the same foodstuffs and in identical quantities (relative to the number of meals served). There are 18 [privately owned] eating places and restaurants located in the ghetto, 77 soup kitchens formerly run by house committees, five central Community kitchens (30 Młynarska, 26 Zgierska, 10 Ceglana, 10 Jakuba, and 19 Łagiewnicka streets), and three more kitchens under construction. There are, moreover, kitchens run by the shoemakers', carpenters', and rubber coat workshops; the canteens of the police and fire departments, numbering 10, should also be mentioned. The "social" kitchens, of which there are 12, are enjoying great success, particularly the [Labor Zionist party] kitchen at 10 Masarska Street, which serves roughly 2,500 meals a day; two kitchens share second place—the one at 2 Lutomierska Street and that at 59 Brzezińska Street, which are under joint management [with the Bund]—and together serve up to 1,500 meals a day. Of the central Community kitchens, the most popular is the so-called Soup Kitchen for the Intelligentsia (at 10 Ceglana Street) which serves 1,100 meals a day. The kitchens singled out above owe their reputations among their clients to their proper and honest management: "Whatever they get goes into the pot." It is worth mentioning that those kitchens were run to their customers' satisfaction even during the most difficult period of meat and vegetable shortages. The impetus to make use of foodstuffs rather than ready meals is to be explained by the fact that the populace is selling some of its food, contenting itself with only a portion for its own needs;[26] the fuel used to prepare the food is used at the same time to heat a given dwelling. Obviously, had all the soup kitchens been serving the best possible meals, the drop in their use would not have assumed such drastic proportions. When the weather is warmer, it will be time to suspend the allotments, which take the place of meals, and this will be followed by a streamlining of the kitchens' organization as well as by an increase in the number of meals served to two per day. A larger network of kitchens that will be able to serve the entire population of the ghetto efficiently and cheaply is at present being prepared for implementation. The Department of Soup Kitchens' board will discharge the following executive functions: (1) the organization of the kitchens; (2) placing kitchens at suitable points and the liquidation of unnecessary posts; (3) controlling the types of

26. Those ghetto dwellers who did not possess the means to buy the allocations assigned them or who needed their money to buy fuel or other necessities resold a portion of the rations allotted them at prices that were, of course, considerably higher than their nominal value. Moreover, people often resold more essential items, e.g., bread, fat, meat, and sugar, at higher prices in order to then buy, at lower prices and in bulk, low-priced items, such as potatoes, turnips, cabbage, and ersatz coffee. This subject is treated frequently in the course of the *Chronicle*.

meals served; (4) supplying foodstuffs to the kitchens. The Department of Soup Kitchens is a relatively recent creation, existing only since January 12 of this year. The cost of a plate of soup (0.70 of a liter) has been set at 15 pfennigs. The cost of the meals, which consist of two dishes, fluctuates between 25 and 60 pfennigs. The most expensive meals in the restaurants cost 1.20 marks.

THURSDAY, JANUARY 30, 1941

THEY DIED FROM COLD AND HUNGER

Chaim Bielajew has died from exhaustion, cold, and hunger at 26/8 Marysińska Street. Hajman Zukin has died of the same causes in his apartment at 100 Brzezińska Street. The wife of the deceased has succumbed to a life-threatening illness caused by exhaustion.

WORK RESUMES IN THE WORKSHOPS

Today and yesterday the workers in the workshops that were shut down for several days began reporting to work voluntarily and en masse. The majority of workshops are now back in operation. At the same time, the state of emergency alert on which a portion of the Order Service had been placed while the workshops were shut down has been lifted.

NOMINATION OF A PUBLIC PROSECUTOR

Today the Eldest of the Jews named Mr. [Abram] Szwebel as public prosecutor for the local court. The number of public prosecutors in the ghetto has thus risen to four.

TOWARD A SPEEDIER BURYING OF THE DEAD

The Eldest of the Jews has made it mandatory to deliver shrouds and burial planks to the cemetery on the day of the burial. This order was issued in view of the fact that the unpunctual delivery of shrouds and burial planks causes delays in burial.[27]

OPENING OF THE *R* I STORE[28]

Today marked the opening of a new Department of Food Supply distribution point known as *R* I. This store is located at 18 Łagiewnicka Street, and its purpose is to distribute foodstuffs to the sick [and women in confinement] primarily from the funds allocated for social welfare. The Chairman has personally taken charge of this agency. In the near future three more similar distribution stations will be put into operation.

27. In keeping with the old Jewish custom, the dead were buried in shrouds of new linen and in caskets made of unplaned wood, on which only a saw had been used.
28. The letter *R* (*R* I, later *R* II and *R* III) derives from the fact that in the beginning these stores issued food products only upon presentation of a physician's prescription (*recepta* in Polish). Later on their functions changed but the original name was retained.

FRIDAY, JANUARY 31, 1941

REDUCTION OF THE GHETTO'S SIZE

Today, news of the decision by the [German] authorities to remove a quadrant from the ghetto spread with lightning speed. The quadrant in question is formed by Franciszkańska Street (on the odd-numbered side, from 15 to 37), from 29 Brzezińska Street to Oblęgorska Street (also on the odd-numbered side), and Smugowa Street and its continuations, Chłodna and Oblęgorska streets. The supposed cause of the decision is an intention to put a tramline into service on Franciszkańska and Brzezińska streets near the border [of the ghetto]. The barbed wire surrounding the ghetto is to be extended through the middle of Franciszkańska and Brzezińska streets at the above-mentioned sections. Apart from the necessity of resettling the population, the approximately 7,000 people residing in that neighborhood, the loss of that terrain is also especially painful because the largest vegetable and fruit gardens are located there. In exemplary fashion, and at the cost of great effort, those gardens were begun last year on fields that had formerly been used for dumping rubbish and debris. The news about the [planned] reduction of the ghetto had a dispiriting effect on the populace.

FRIDAY, FEBRUARY 28, 1941[29]

DEATHS AND BIRTHS

Forty-five people died in the ghetto today. No births were registered.

"LITZMANNSTADT IN THE FUTURE"

This is the title of an article that has appeared in the *Litzmannstadter Zeitung*.[30] Among other things, this article predicted that the quarter of the city in which the ghetto is presently located will, in the future, be turned into parks and gardens. After the area is leveled, beautiful buildings will be constructed there. The first stage in carrying out these intentions is already occurring—the buildings on Ogrodowa and Nowomiejska streets, which abut the ghetto, are being razed. As to the Jews inhabiting the ghetto, the newspaper article notes that "they will vanish from Litzmannstadt faster than they expect."[31] The news of this article traveled the ghetto grapevine,

29. This is one of three preserved bulletins of the *Chronicle* for February, 1941. The other two are dated February 1 and 8.

30. This was the official daily newspaper published by the German authorities in Łódź. Distributing copies on the grounds of the ghetto was strictly forbidden. Individual copies, however, would make their way in, either smuggled or accidentally left behind by Germans working in or visiting the ghetto.

31. This article, entitled "Litzmannstadt, die Stadt der Zukunft," appeared on January 26, 1941 (no. 57, p. 8). The fragment concerning the Jews and the ghetto reads: "Das gegenwärtige Wohngebiet der Juden, das Getto, wird schneller verschwinden, als die Judenschaft vor dem Beginn des polnischen Feldzuges gedacht haben mag; schon fallen rings um das Getto die baufälligen Häuser in einem breiten Gürtel. Dort, wo sich in Augenblick die hässlichsten Häuser des einstmaligen Lodsch erheben, werden in naher Zeit Grünflächen erstehen, wird ein neuer Mittelpunkt der deutschen Stadt Litzmannstadt geschaffen werden! Mittelpunkt der schöneren, der neuen Stadt wird das Haus der NSDAP mit den Häusern der angegliederten Organisationen werden."

causing moments of great alarm since only negligible quantities of that newspaper make their way into the ghetto and thus the contents of the article were, for the most part, falsely reported. On this occasion it is worth stressing as typical of current conditions that, in general, all information, whatever its source—the newspaper, private correspondence, and even events from life inside the ghetto—is spread in a distorted and exaggerated form.

MARCH 1, 1941[32]

A REVIEW OF THE MOST IMPORTANT EVENTS IN THE GHETTO IN FEBRUARY

The number of people in the ghetto on the first day of February, 1941, totaled 153,995, and the number of rooms fit for human habitation was 49,864, that is, on the average, a room for every three people. In square meters the total area of inhabitable premises comes to 646.30 [?].

As to the weather, the month of February was, fortunately for the residents of the ghetto, relatively mild. The mean temperature was about two degrees below zero; however, in the last third of the month, it rose quite a bit above zero.

The number of deaths in the month of February came to 1,069. Births totaled 52. In comparison with January, when the deaths totaled 1,218, this made for quite a significant reduction. It is worth mentioning in passing that the highest mortality rate (1,366) came in the month of July [1940] and was caused by an epidemic of dysentery. On the basis of information from the Department of Statistics, the primary cause of death in January was heart disease (40 percent) followed by malnutrition (20 percent); around 8 percent of the deaths were due to diseases of the digestive organs, somewhat less than 7.5 percent were caused by tuberculosis and 0.73 percent by infectious diseases.

The increase in criminal offenses has been so great that, in the month of February, 243 persons were arrested for theft, 13 for resisting orders, and 486 for various other offenses. We will supply a specific description of the crimes committed in one of the next bulletins. Because of a ruthless struggle against the criminal element, the figures cited above attest to a decrease since the month of January, when 431 persons were arrested for theft, 29 for resisting orders, and 344 for various other offenses.

The most lurid incident in the area of criminology, one bespeaking a complete return to savagery, was the case disclosed on February 23 by Precinct I of the Order Service. The remains of a child in a state of total decay were uncovered in the building at 42 Franciszkańska Street. The remains had been covered with rags. The doctor summoned to the scene could not determine the date of death precisely, but he did state that it had occurred at least two weeks ago. The child's father, Hersz Aragier, a *batkhn* [wedding entertainer] by profession, did not initially wish to disclose his reason for not burying his only son, a 7-year-old boy, but later confessed that he had done so in order to use his only son's bread and food coupons. The father was

---

32. The *Daily Chronicle Bulletin* for March 1, 1941, is given in its entirety here.

arrested. He is now in prison awaiting the sentence of the court. The mother has been left at liberty in view of her mental illness.

February brought considerable improvement in the food supply. The populace was forced to suffer only at the beginning of the month due to deficiencies in the allocations of kasha and potatoes. On February 7, a new sidetrack was opened up in Marysin for unloading trains carrying food into the ghetto.[33] In the course of the month the provisioning of the ghetto underwent a gradual improvement, particularly in relation to the supply of flour. This situation permitted 15 of the ghetto's own bakeries to be put into operation after a long interruption and, toward the end of the month, three bakeries were nearly ready to begin operations. The populace received bread supplements several times, which caused an increase in the daily ration from 400 grams to 485 grams in one week, and to 457 grams in another. Moreover, all those who were employed received one loaf of bread each. It is worth noting that in the month of February a system for the fair and uniform distribution of bread was introduced.

The official Community prices for necessities underwent no change in February. For the first time in a month the quotations on the private market displayed a downward trend. Only the price of potatoes rose and then declined abruptly toward the end of the month in reaction to the [increased] food rations.

By the second half of January, there was a noticeable improvement in the ghetto's coal supply, which, in the earlier parts of the winter, had constituted a calamity of the first order. At present the coal supply has undergone a conspicuous improvement. Thanks to the efficient organization of the Fuel Department, the populace has been receiving its weekly allotments without having to stand in line and without difficulty. Moreover, it is worth noting that the quality of the coal is significantly higher than it had been previously. Prices dropped significantly in private transactions because the populace was supplied with fuel. Coal, whose price had reached two marks per kilogram this winter, stood at 0.40 marks toward the end of February.

A special sale post known as R I was put into operation in the first few days of February for the purpose of supplying women in confinement and sick people.

In view of the further warming of the weather and the danger of flooding, and in accordance with the relevant order of the Eldest of the Jews, over one thousand unemployed men, directed by administrators and firemen, have been employed in hacking away ice and clearing the sidewalks and roadways of ice.

On the 9th of February the sixth pharmacy of the Eldest of the Jews was opened at 5 Rybna Street.

In the month of February a Divorce Council was formed consisting of two rabbis and a representative of the Department of Vital Statistics.

The number of marriages performed by the rabbis since December has been decreasing—301 in December, 223 in January. Of this number, 101 are marriages concluded since the closing of the ghetto. The remaining number represent the validation of prior marriages.

---

33. Marysin, a section of Łódź, half suburban, half agricultural, with primarily single-story and wooden houses and many gardens. A portion of Marysin fell within the ghetto, forming its boundary on the northeast. The new sidetrack was a branch of the railway which went to Zgierz in the north and to Widzew in the south, thus linking up with the country's main rail lines.

The oldest ghetto dweller, 101-year-old Liba Mokrska of the Old People's Home, died in February. At present, the oldest ghetto dweller is Chaim Tyger, born in 1848, and the oldest woman is Rykla Szarfsztajn, born in 1849.

Most of the cases examined by the court in February involved irregularities in the wholesaling of tobacco. There was also a seven-day trial for welfare abuses.

In February the Department of Vital Statistics issued 466 identity cards; for the entire period [since the creation of the ghetto] 3,673 cards have been issued.

On the 22d of February the Chairman inspected the Central Prison on Czarniecki Street. On the day of the inspection the prison housed 104 prisoners, including 13 women.

On the initiative of NIK [the Supreme Inspection Chamber],[34] a meeting of the directors of the Community's administration was held in order to increase and improve production.

In the month of February there were several literary evenings devoted primarily to Jewish poetry. There were symphonic concerts conducted by Teodor Ryder at the House of Culture and at the Soup Kitchen for the Intelligentsia.

In February the records of the Order Service noted two cases of suicide: on the 18th of February 41-year-old Chaim Dembiński (a resident of 10 Wolborska Street) threw himself from the fourth-floor window of the staircase at 12 Wolborska Street. The emergency physician summoned to the scene administered first aid and then brought Dembiński to Hospital No. 1, where, after a few hours, he died. The investigation by the Order Service determined that the suicide, who had been suffering from mental illness, had already attempted to commit suicide on the 12th of last month and was prevented by members of his household. On the night of February 18, 35-year-old Brana Wajnrech (of 36 Brzezińska Street), the wife of a journeyman baker, committed suicide by strangling herself with a cord. Arrested on a charge of murder, the husband of the suicide was released after questioning.

On the 19th of February, at 8 o'clock in the morning, a fire broke out in the stocking and glove factory in the workshop of the Eldest of the Jews at 3 Kościelny Square. The fire was extinguished as a result of the immediate rescue action taken by the local fire department under the command of Mr. [Henryk] Kaufman. The losses were insignificant.

SATURDAY, MARCH 1, 1941

A DEATH ON THE STREET

Yesterday at seven o'clock P.M. 55-year-old Izrael Wulc (of 15 Brzezińska Street) collapsed in front of the pharmacy on Kościelny Square. In spite of immediate first aid, Wulc died without regaining consciousness.

34. The Supreme Inspection Chamber (*Najwyższa Izba Kontroli*) was convened on November 6, 1940 by the Eldest of the Jews. He also appointed its members, of which there were initially around ten. Later, on July 4, 1941, the NIK staff was disbanded and in its place the Eldest of the Jews appointed only three persons, over whom he presided as Chairman. NIK's task was to oversee the activities of all the bureaus and institutions of the Jewish ghetto administration. The Supreme Inspection Chamber was eliminated in 1943 and its place was taken by the Trade Inspection Section of the Central Workshop Bureau.

WHOEVER HAS HIDDEN ANYTHING IN THE CITY

Proclamation No. 222, posted yesterday, is a reminder of the summons made by the Eldest of the Jews on October 11 of last year for people to surrender, in strict confidence, any articles and objects of value that have been set aside or hidden in the city [outside the ghetto]. As this proclamation states, the Chairman is legally able to retrieve these items. In reminding the populace of this proclamation, the Eldest of the Jews noted that the owners would be paid amounts equal to the values of the retrieved objects after an estimate was made and the appropriate percentage was deducted for the Community. All parties concerned can come forward without fear since they are not subject to any criminal sanctions. Therefore, it is in their own interests to comply as quickly as possible.

PARCELS NOT TO BE SENT TO THE GHETTO

Today a proclamation of the Eldest of the Jews was posted calling on the inhabitants of the ghetto immediately to inform family and friends in writing that they are no longer to mail any parcels of food [to the ghetto] since the Chairman "must confiscate parcels" on orders from the [German] authorities.

CULTURAL LIFE

Today the first symphonic concert conducted by D[awid] Bajgelman[35] took place in the auditorium of the House of Culture at 3 Krawiecka Street. The following works were performed: Bela Keler's overture, Popa's [Popper's] *Suite Orientale* and *Shabes nokhn kugl* [After the Sabbath meal], Bajgelman's *Wiegenlied* and *Chor der Derwische*, the overture from Massenet's *Phèdre*, Ajzenman's Jewish medleys, Siede's [?] intermezzo, Szalit's *Der yosem* [The orphan] and the *Ballet Orientale*. Accompanied by the orchestra, Mrs. [Ala] Diamant sang several soulful Yiddish songs. After the conclusion of the concert, Chairman Rumkowski addressed the audience on current affairs and his own plans.

There was a performance by the violinist Miss Bronisława Rotsztat in the hall at Soup Kitchen No. 2 [for the intelligentsia], and, as usual, it met with great success. Teodor Ryder accompanied. [Nikodem] Sztajman enchanted the audience with his pleasant tenor.

Today, on the premises of the [Labor Zionist] soup kitchen at 16 Berek Joselewicz Street there was an evening dedicated to the work of young Jewish poets.

Today [at another Labor Zionist soup kitchen] at [10] Masarska Street the fifth consecutive *Oyneg shabes* [Joy of Sabbath] evening took place and was dedicated to recitations and songs.

35. Dawid Bajgelman (1887–1944), a composer and conductor, born into a musical family in Ostrowiec, in Kielce province. Like his brothers and sisters, he played many different instruments from early youth, but chiefly the clarinet and violin. In 1912, after his family had moved to Łódź, he became director of the Yitskhok Zandberg Yiddish Theatre Company there. From a young age, Bajgelman had also toured with various Yiddish theaters in Poland and in countries in Europe, South America, and Africa. In the 1920s he was connected with two Yiddish theaters, Azazel and Ararat. He was one of the chief organizers of the ghetto's musical life. In August, 1944, he was deported to Auschwitz.

SUNDAY, MARCH 2, 1941

AN INSPECTION BY THE GERMAN AUTHORITIES

took place today at Precinct I of the Order Service at 27 Franciszkańska Street. The inspectors acquainted themselves with the progress of that institution's work and also visited the jail at the station.

A RESOURCEFUL OLD WOMAN

A certain Mirla Dancygier has addressed a grandiloquent petition to the Chairman requesting that he make it possible for her to live to be . . . one hundred years old. As she states in her petition, she has already lived to be 97 and, as the oldest person in the ghetto, she is counting on the Chairman to summarily order a supplemental food allocation for her "in the name of humanitarianism and out of pity for an old woman." This novel petition acquires special piquancy considering that further investigation revealed that the petitioner had herself chosen to increase her age by 18 years. To live on!

CHILD OF THE GHETTO

The following amusing incident occurred in one of the hospitals of the Eldest of the Jews. A sick 5-year-old boy was brought to the hospital. When he was being undressed before being put to bed, a little sack tied with a string, and containing a good-sized portion of bread, was found under his shirt. The boy absolutely refused to part with his provisions. When it was explained to him that he would receive a complete diet in the hospital, he made it clear that the bread was his property, bought with his own money. "And how did you get the money?" the young patient was asked. "I have my own money because I'm on welfare," replied the resolute little boy.

MONDAY, MARCH 3, 1941

A DAY OF JOY IN THE GHETTO—UNLIMITED LIGHT

The month of March began under the best possible auspices in the ghetto for a whole series of reasons. The first of March brought the populace a pleasant surprise in the form of supplemental food rations, vegetables being especially plentiful. Equally pleasant surprises were the denatured alcohol and the vinegar, neither of which had been available for a very long time. Moreover, the populace received sausage and meat, and the coal allotment came to 20 kilograms this time. In addition, the youngest ghetto dwellers each received one cauliflower. Thus, what the Chairman had said several times in his recent public addresses about an anticipated considerable improvement in the food supply situation has proven true.

The crowning moment among the improvements came on the third of March, a day which will long remain in the memories of all ghetto dwellers. The proclamation that appeared on the city's walls around two o'clock in the afternoon informing the populace that their electric light could be kept on after eight in the evening was itself like a ray of light in the hopeless bleakness of everyday life. This proclamation caused general enthusiasm among the populace, who had thronged the streets on the first real spring day.

Along with all the other cares and afflictions the ghetto dwellers contend with, the prohibition against using electricity after eight in the evening [as of November 14, 1940, by order of the German police] was one of the most painful. There is nothing odd, therefore, in the fact that of the more than two hundred proclamations from the Eldest of the Jews posted so far, none has caused such joy as today's. Large groups formed in front of each [posted] proclamation; the contents of the proclamation were read aloud and the most diverse comments were made, but all with a sense of joy. The reaction produced by this proclamation in all the various strata of the ghetto's populace is uncommonly interesting. It is perhaps the many thousands of working people who will feel this blessing the most. In the past, when a worker returned home after work at eight or even nine o'clock in the evening, he actually had to eat his modest meal in the dark and then go right to bed. In that way, the worker did in fact lead the life of a robot, unable to devote his time off to his own affairs.

This blessing will also be keenly felt by sick people who are not in hospitals. It is a known fact that an incredibly large portion of the ghetto's population falls into the category of the ill.[36] For the sake of their health these people are often compelled to take their medications at night, and they claim that they spend more on candles each week than they do on electric light in three months, and, furthermore, that weak candlelight does not allow them to perform injections, and so on.

Young mothers also received the news about the light with great enthusiasm. Changing their infants in the dark was a genuine ordeal for the mothers. Occasionally, for that reason, a child would lie wet and unchanged until morning, which was a cause of colds.

Even people who are not working commented on the proclamation, adding that it made them even happier than the supplemental bread ration. One woman standing in a small group by a wall, who later proved to be one of the large mass of unemployed white-collar workers, remarked quite aptly that now people would be able to sleep normally and peacefully. Formerly, after a day full of worries and complicated economic maneuvers, it was not possible to read or study during one's free time in the evening because of the lack of light and so, of necessity, people had to sleep. But sleep wouldn't come because adults were not accustomed to going to bed so early; as a result they would lie in bed fully awake and sometimes not get any sleep at all in the course of the night.

Everyone in the ghetto, without exception, is experiencing the benefits of the latest proclamation. We have noted only a few classic examples, but we cannot pass over in silence the reaction this news caused among merchants and storeowners. Since customers frequently demand items which either have to be prepared or made up (for example, cosmetics, baby powder, medicinal powders), the storeowners will now be in a position to fill these orders in the evening after closing their stores, whereas, until now, they could have made bankrupting mismeasurements when using oil lamps or candles for light. What is more important, however, is the fact that this proclamation came just as the days were getting longer.

36. In the original this sentence was crossed out in red pencil.

The slogan "Work and Peace," constantly underscored by the Chairman in his speeches and particularly in his talk on February 1, has again taken on the glow of life. The lifting of the ban on using electricity will allow people to live in more normal conditions and, consequently, create an atmosphere which favors the carrying out of the Chairman's slogan.

TUESDAY, MARCH 4, 1941

TRESPASSING IN THE GHETTO

Today, on the grounds of the ghetto, agents of the Order Service detained a Pole, a resident of Pabianice [near Łódź], named Bronisław Fogt, who had entered the ghetto illegally. He has been put at the disposition of the [German] criminal police [Kripo].[37]

A FUNERAL SERVICE

A funeral service was held at the synagogue at 23 Brzezińska Street[38] for the soul of Izrael Neftalin, of blessed memory. Rabbi [Yosif] Fajner[39] and Mr. Halpern spoke of the deceased and his virtues. The synagogue was entirely filled. C. Rumkowski, Eldest of the Jews, was seated beside the deceased's son, H[enryk] Neftalin, the attorney.

KITCHEN NO. 2 IS ONE OF THE MOST MERITORIOUS POSTS IN THE GHETTO

Anyone who was in Paris between 1920 and 1925 and took a cab from the railroad station driven by a former Russian grand duke, or was given his room key by a liveried porter who had formerly been a chamberlain at the Tsar's court, would certainly recall those moments when crossing the threshold of Kitchen No. 2, the so-called Soup Kitchen for the Intelligentsia at 41 Zgierska Street (10 Ceglana Street).

"There's meat for dinner today," whispers a former bank director to a former gymnasium professor. "There were a lot of potato bits in the barley soup today"—a scrap of conversation from another table, where a few painters were seated together with their former patrons, who were well-known industrialists at one time.

The Soup Kitchen for the Intelligentsia is a likely place to find people who once were something, who at one time held important positions, living life to the fullest, and who have today been torn away from all of that. It is only when we look at the regular customers of Kitchen No. 2 from that point of view that we can appreciate what the kitchen gives them besides food; it is there and only there that they can find

37. The Kripo (Kriminalpolizei) was, together with the Gestapo and Sicherheitsdienst, an integral part of the German security police. See above, pp. xxxix–xl.
38. The synagogues in Łódź, including the two most imposing ones—the Old Synagogue on Wolborska St. and the Reformed Synagogue on Kościuszko Blvd.—were burned down by the Nazis in November, 1939. The synagogue mentioned here was one of the few houses (or simply rooms in some building) of prayer where, after the ghetto was closed in 1940, people could gather for prayer, with the permission of the Jewish administration. Before their elimination in 1942, there were around fifteen such places, not counting, of course, the prayer houses that existed unofficially and were thus not registered.
39. Yosif Fajner [Feiner] (1867–1944), before the war the chief rabbi of Aleksandrów (a small town not far from Łódź), a member of the Rabbinate, and of the Jewish Community in Łódź. He was deported to Auschwitz in August, 1944.

even the illusion of what they had once been accustomed to: a measure of politeness in people's behavior and in the way they are treated—they who today are déclassé and pauperized—a clean and well-set table, dishes that are not nicked, and, finally, pleasant surroundings and good company.

Time is spent in Kitchen No. 2 not only for the consumption of meals but also for the exchange of thoughts; it is a sort of club where these people who once were something meet for the midday meal.

Exactly seven months have passed since the fine idea of a group headed by Helena Rumkowska and Stefania Dawidowicz[40] was put into action, exactly seven months since Kitchen No. 2, the second of its type in the ghetto, began serving afternoon meals.

Initially it served 250 meals per day. At that time the kitchen received no Community allocations and was run independently by the people who had created and instituted it. However, Chairman Rumkowski, on observing its splendid progress, began to aid the kitchen by paying it 10 pfennigs for each meal served.[41] The kitchen was therefore in a position to serve meals at a reduced price to the unemployed and, also, to serve free afternoon meals when so recommended by the Chairman.

With the aim of acquiring ever-increasing funds, the administration of the kitchen has from time to time arranged evenings featuring singers accompanied by instrumentalists, as well as concerts. This was done also to provide some cultural entertainment for the ghetto dwellers and some financial support to the performers. This project was especially appropriate since the kitchen's administration possessed the largest premises suitable for such a purpose at a time when there was still no House of Culture at 3 Krawiecka Street.

Energetic organization and thoroughly dedicated work produced splendid results. After three months in existence, Kitchen No. 2 could boast of serving 1,000 meals a day.

In November of last year, Kitchen No. 2, like the others, was taken over by the Community; however, in view of its founders' special merits, its internal autonomy has been retained. The organization of the kitchen is determined by a committee of over 40 women, volunteer workers in various sections—finance, scheduling, and kitchen. The overall management is in the hands of a 15-person governing board that meets periodically with the presiding officers and devotes itself to the daily business of the kitchen. The presiding officers, who give all their free time to their positions, are Mmes. Rumkowska and Dawidowicz, the chairman of the administration, Mr. Fiszer,

40. The wife of Dr. Józef Rumkowski, the brother of the Eldest of the Jews. The daughter of the well-known Łódź physician, Dr. Fabian Klozenberg, and the wife of Dr. Maksymilian Dawidowicz.

41. In the original *Chronicle*, after corrections were made in indelible pencil, the last two paragraphs read as follows: "Today, exactly seven months have passed since the moment when the splendid idea proposed by the Chairman was picked up by Messrs. Kenigsberg, Gerszowski, and Perelsztajn, who created the organizational committee headed by chairman Fiszer, Helena Rumkowska, and Stefania Dawidowicz. The suggestion went into effect exactly seven months [ago] when Kitchen No. 2—the second of its type in the ghetto—began serving meals. Initially, 350 meals were served per day and, in that period, the kitchen was receiving 1,000 marks from the Chairman and a Community subsidy of 0.15 marks for each meal and was independently operated by its creators and founders. However, when Chairman Rumkowski observed the splendid progress it had made in its first three months, he granted the kitchen additional aid in the form of a 10-pfennig supplement for each meal served."

and the secretary, Mr. F. Kołtoński. The management itself is in the able hands of Mr. Minc.[42]

January 1 was the trial by fire for all the kitchens that had been in existence until that date. In connection with the instituting of ration cards, the greater part of the people who had thus far been boarding at the kitchens chose not to turn in their ration cards to the kitchens and thus, receiving their produce in cooperatives, were forced to cook at home. For that reason business fell by 90 percent in all kitchens. Only Kitchen No. 2 emerged victorious from this trial since it not only did not lose the customers it had before but those customers with the right to choose a kitchen began to compete in large numbers for enrollment on the list of Kitchen No. 2's regular customers. Over 1,000 of the new applications were accepted in spite of the normal, further selection that occurs during registration. In the very near future, upwards of 600 of those who have been registered will be served because new accommodations that will permit the serving of midday meals to the public are being installed at the kitchen. At present, apart from cut-rate meals, the kitchen is serving about 50 free meals a day, which are made up from "leftovers."

The people taking meals at Kitchen No. 2 are divided into four shifts and receive their meals between the hours of one and four P.M., with half an hour allowed for the consumption of the meal. The kitchen's most essential qualities are its tasty food, the ample portions, the cleanliness, order, and punctuality, its fast and polite service, and, most important of all, the special atmosphere of a sort not encountered in any other kitchen: an atmosphere filled with the memories and reminiscences of people who once were something . . .

WEDNESDAY, MARCH 5, 1941

THE FOOD SUPPLY SITUATION

Last week was marked by a great improvement in the ghetto's supply of provisions. Of special significance was the increase in the supply of flour, which makes it possible to raise the number of bakeries to 18. Significant consignments of potatoes, kasha, and other grocery items arrived in the course of the week. On the other hand, absolutely no sugar was supplied. The ghetto received a relatively large shipment of "smokes" [from Croatia] including 1,200,000 Ballerina cigarettes, 300,000 Osta cigarettes, and 750 kilograms of tobacco. Milk is still at about 1,000 liters a day, the supply of horse and ox meat also remains unchanged. There was a significant decrease in the supply of butter this week.

A CONCERT FOR WOMEN WORKERS

Yesterday at the House of Culture, there was a symphony concert conducted by [Dawid] Bajgelman and organized for the women workers of the rubber coat factories. This concert was a repeat of Saturday's première. Chairman Rumkowski delivered a speech concerning his plans for child care.

42. In the original *Chronicle* the last sentence was crossed out.

THURSDAY, MARCH 6, 1941

THE CHAIRMAN

This morning, accompanied by the director of the Central Workshop Bureau, [Aron] Jakubowicz,[43] the Chairman spent some time outside the ghetto dealing with current concerns. Among other things, the Chairman inspected the work being performed by local residents in demolishing the buildings which abut the ghetto.

DEMONSTRATIONS

Around 6:00 P.M. crowds began to form on Młynarska Street in an attempt to organize demonstrations. Handbills were distributed demanding the following: (1) an increase in food rations, (2) a decrease in the prices of products, (3) the abolition of cooperative B,[44] (4) that packages from the provinces be allowed in [to the ghetto], (5) an increase in relief allowances, (6) the institution of free laundries for the poor, (7) establishments for bathing and for disinfection. The crowd sent up hostile shouts against the Community authorities. A series of appeals in Polish and Yiddish were posted condemning the ghetto's own government. Around 700 persons took part in the demonstration. The Order Service succeeded in dispersing the demonstrators in about fifteen minutes. There were some casualties. Several of the civilians were badly roughed up and two members of the Order Service received wounds. Peace had been entirely restored by seven P.M. There have been numerous arrests in connection with the demonstrations.

A NEWSPAPER IN THE GHETTO

The first issue of the Yiddish-language weekly of the Eldest of the Jews, *Geto-tsaytung*,[45] appeared today. The newspaper has four pages, costs 10 pfennigs, and its front page contains the Eldest of the Jews' program of institutions and problems that will be discussed in the columns of the periodical. The newspaper's principal objectives are to shed light on all aspects of life and to inform the public about the Eldest of the Jews' intentions, as well as to indicate what is proper behavior. The newspaper will publish articles on all instances of criminal behavior and corruption.

The article on page 2 is an appeal by the Eldest of the Jews to the youth of the ghetto, and it points out a new path in life for them, namely, professional training in a variety of fields. This is followed by an appeal to people to register themselves. The

43. Aron Jakubowicz (?–1981) was, along with Leon Rozenblat (the head of the Order Service), one of Rumkowski's two deputies. He was the director of the Central Workshop Bureau.

44. Cooperative B (from *Beirat*—advisory council) was a food distribution point for the higher-ranking employees in the Jewish administration, higher police officers, workshop directors and managers. On the basis of lists or special coupons those entitled to use these points collected additional food allocations there in addition to the general ration.

45. *Geto-tsaytung far informatsye farordenungen un bakantmakhungen* (the *Ghetto Newspaper for Information, Rulings and Proclamations*), the official organ of the Eldest of the Jews, was strictly intra-ghetto in nature and published in Yiddish. It was edited by Szmul Rozensztajn, a journalist and a correspondent for the Warsaw newspaper, *Haynt*, before the war. He also managed the printshop in the ghetto.

All together 18 issues appeared, from March 7 to September 21, 1941. A shortage of paper was given as the reason for its discontinuation. A complete set of the *Geto-tsaytung* can be found, among other places, in the archives of the YIVO Institute for Jewish Research, in New York.

article on page 3 is an appeal by the Eldest of the Jews that he not be hindered in the performance of his job. The sections on life in the ghetto contain an article about the Chairman's efforts in providing aid to the ill and also a note on his inspection of Central Prison. On page 4 we find Proclamation No. 228 concerning the food allocation for the 10th through the 20th of this month, as well as a communiqué about a new, large purchase of food, including four million kilograms of potatoes.

The newspaper caused a great sensation in the ghetto. The need for a periodical is best attested to by the first edition's having been snatched up in less than two hours. The public was actually tearing the newspapers out of the newsboys' hands. Only an hour after receiving the papers from the printers, that is, at nine o'clock, the newsboys were requesting additional copies. Throughout the day, the printing house was literally besieged by people competing with each other to be able to sell newspapers. The newspaper's contents, which were literally read from the first word to the last, and assurances by the Eldest of the Jews, which had been printed on its pages, lifted the spirits of the ghetto dwellers and brought them encouragement.

There is yet another positive aspect to the appearance of a newspaper—it will finally suppress the rumors rampant in the ghetto, which have recently reached alarming proportions. The people will at last be accurately informed on matters they should know about. For example, as recently as yesterday completely unfounded rumors concerning a supposedly extraordinary food ration were circulating in the ghetto; even though the newspaper had reported a smaller ration than was being talked about, accurate information about the purchase of the four million kilograms of potatoes, as well as large amounts of other vegetables, because it was authoritative, caused greater satisfaction than the unfounded rumors about increased rations.

SATURDAY, MARCH 8, 1941

TO SUPPLEMENT

the notice of the other day concerning the Chairman's departure for the city, it should be noted that the Chairman held a conference in the central bureau of the [German] Ghetto Administration.[46] The subject of the talks was the further development and intensification of workshops in the ghetto. The talks centered on the ordering and delivery of the materials necessary for further processing, which is a matter of urgency for the factories involved.

THE ELDEST OF THE JEWS FROM PODDĘBICE[47]

Mr. Sosnowski arrived in the ghetto yesterday on private business. Mr. Sosnowski's stay will continue until the 18th of this month. The guest was received by Chairman

---

46. The headquarters of the German Ghetto Administration (Gettoverwaltung) was located at 156 Ceglana St., changed by the Germans to 156 Moltkestrasse.

47. Poddębice, a town located not far from Łódź, to the northwest. The Jewish population of Poddębice, along with those resettled there from the villages in the vicinity, numbered around 2,000 in 1941.

Rumkowski in his office at Bałut Market.[48] A few days earlier, the wife of the Eldest of the Jews of Aleksandrów Kujawski[49] was here in the ghetto. The enormous Stars of David worn by the visitors drew attention everywhere. As it turns out, the Jews residing in Aleksandrów Kujawski are now punished, in many instances, for failing to observe the obligation of wearing their stars by being forced to adorn their clothing with stars twice the usual size.

DEPORTATIONS FROM THE GHETTO

In his speech of February 1, Chairman Rumkowski made it known that he is bringing the most rigorous of methods to bear against individuals who impede him in his work, the criminal element in particular; that is, malefactors and notorious criminals, and thieves of public property are being ousted from the ghetto and sent to do manual labor in Germany. In his speech the Chairman announced that he would be implacable in this matter, and only severe illness could prevent anyone from being deported from the ghetto. This goal is now in the process of being achieved; to wit, on instructions from the Chairman, a special squad of Order Service men, led by [Salomon] Hercberg, the prison commissioner, has in the course of the last three nights carried out mass arrests of thieves, habitual criminals, and disturbers of the present order in the ghetto. All told, over 50 persons were arrested. The prisoners were placed at the Chairman's disposal. A medical examination of 86 prisoners was performed at Central Prison. That number also included others arrested in the last three days. Dr. [Leon] Szykler headed the medical commission. The Chairman was also present during the examinations. The commission found 75 persons fit to be sent to work outside the ghetto.

X-RAY MACHINE COMPLETED

Today, ceremonies were held at Hospital No. 1 at Łagiewnicka Street in connection with the completion of an X-ray machine, which was produced by Messrs. Dawidowicz and Wertheim, engineers who live in the ghetto. This machine will be of enormous service to the Department of Health. The Chairman took part in the ceremonies.

SYMPHONY CONCERT

Today at the House of Culture a symphony concert conducted by [Dawid] Bajgelman played to a full house. The orchestra performed a series of works from the classical repertoire, as well as Jewish music. Mrs. M[inia] Ber sang several songs accompanied by the orchestra. After the program was concluded, the Chairman made a speech appropriate to the occasion.

48. Bałut Market (*Bałucki Rynek* in Polish; *Baluter Ring* in German) was, before the war, the busiest area for market and street trade in the Bałut section of the city. After the creation of the ghetto, the market was eliminated and barracks were built on the vacated area. The offices of a branch of the German Ghetto Administration were established there, as were the offices of Rumkowski and A. Jakubowicz, on explicit orders from the German authorities. The entire center of Bałut Market, surrounded by a fence and guarded by German police, was at the same time a principal transit station, since its northwestern edge was connected with the two "Aryan" roadways, Zgierska and Limanowski streets (see p. 10, n. 16). There, as well as at the station opened later in Marysin, traffic to and from the ghetto was monitored.

49. Aleksandrów Kujawski, a town in the Bydgoszcz province, to the south of Toruń. Before the war, the overall population was over 8,000, of which over 1,000 were Jews.

SUNDAY, MARCH 9, 1941

A SEARCH

Yesterday, officials of the [German] criminal police conducted a search at 14 Brzezińska Street that resulted in the confiscation of pelts and furs worth approximately 30,000 marks.

ARRIVAL OF THE DOCTORS

This week five doctors, specialists hired by the Department of Health here, arrived in the ghetto from [the ghetto of] Warsaw. Dr. [Leon] Szykier, the chairman of the Department of Health, was in Warsaw on this matter a few weeks ago.

MARCH 10–24, 1941

DEATHS AND BIRTHS

Between the 10th and the 24th of March, 529 people died in the ghetto. Twenty-nine births were registered, of which 16 were male, 13 female.

SHOOTINGS

On March 12 at 8:30 P.M., 13-year-old Wolf Finkelstein, a resident of 14 Masarska Street, was shot dead by a sentry. The boy received a fatal wound to his lungs and heart. On the 19th of March, 31-year-old Rafał Krzepicki, a native of Praszka[50] residing at 12 Smugowa Street, was shot dead around midnight at the intersection of Franciszkańska and Smugowa streets. On the 23d of March, at nine o'clock in the evening, 20-year-old Awigdor Lichtenstein of 170 Franciszkańska Street was shot dead near the latrine at the end of the street in the vicinity of the barbed wire. In the incidents cited, the victims were allegedly smugglers.

THEY DIED ON THE STREET

On the 11th of March, Jakub Lew (of 69 Franciszkańska Street) died in front of the building at 33 Wolborska Street. On the 13th of March, the body of Majlech Zelig (of 27 Ciemna Street) was found on the premises of 25 Tokarzewski Street. On the 17th of March, around nine o'clock in the evening, a woman died in the gateway of the building at 3 Kościelna Street. She has not been identified.

INSPECTION OF THE *HACHSHARAH*[51]

On Sunday, the 9th of March, the Chairman conducted an inspection of the agricultural-training center for youth (the so-called hachsharah) which is located in Marysin. The center houses 360 young people of both sexes. The Chairman held talks

---

50. Praszka, a town situated at the extreme southwestern edge of Łódź province, near the pre-war Polish-German border. Out of Praszka's overall population of around 4,500, approximately 1,660 were Jews.

51. *Hachsharah*, the collective garden plots that came into being in Marysin shortly after the ghetto was closed in May, 1940, on the initiative of Zionist youth of every stripe and supported by M. C. Rumkowski. All told, there were more than 20 collective garden plots, including one founded by the Bund's youth and one by the religious youth of *Agudath Israel*.

with the director of the center. During his inspection, the Chairman stated that a very large number of unsuitable persons had made their way into the center, as a result of which the work being done there leaves much to be desired. The Chairman ordered the immediate expulsion of undesirable individuals from the hachsharah and the reorganization of the center, with restoration of healthy conditions as its goal.

OPENING OF A NEW POST OFFICE

On Sunday the 16th of this month there were ceremonies held in connection with the opening of a new post office at No. 4 Kościelny Square. The former station, located at the same address, was too meager to keep pace with its duties. The new station, which has been appointed in a truly comfortable and modern fashion—for the ghetto, that is—is causing a significant improvement in the post office's efficiency and, what is more important, is making it possible to deal with customers without having them wait in line outside, as had previously been the case. The Chairman came for the ceremonies and there was also a large group of invited guests. The director of the post office, [Herbert] Grawe, delivered a speech in which he recapitulated the post office's activities for the year. It should be noted that the opening of the new branch coincided exactly with the first anniversary of this institution of such importance to the inhabitants of the ghetto. The statistical information presented by Mr. Grawe clearly illustrates the range of the post office's activity. From that information we learn that in the period just ended the post office cashed 64,049 money orders, paying out some 1,699,151 marks. In the course of the year the post office delivered 135,062 parcels mailed from the Reich [and territories incorporated into it], and 14,229 from abroad. The telegraph service processed 10,238 wires, and the number of letters and postcards handled reached 1,074,351.

In his highly appreciative speech, the Chairman emphasized the efficient service provided by the post office and its employees. In appreciation of the services rendered by the post office's employees for the benefit of the ghetto's inhabitants, the Chairman granted them a bonus amounting to 50 percent of their monthly salaries and also ordered that the sum of 15,000 marks be allocated for the postal employees' loan fund.

WORK PROHIBITED ON SATURDAY

Instructions issued on orders from the Chairman concerning the organization of work in the carpentry shop anticipate, among other things, a ban against working overtime and on Saturdays. Only the shop managers can override this ban.

WORK FOR WOMEN OUTSIDE THE GHETTO

On March 11, a proclamation from the Eldest of the Jews was posted. It concerned the registration of women from ages 20 to 30 who are applying to leave the ghetto to work. This proclamation was issued on the basis of orders from the German authorities and stipulates that one of the very next transports of workers leaving the ghetto to perform

---

Besides tending the plots and gaining agricultural experience, the hachsharahs engaged in intensive educational activities, the program depending on the nature of a given group. The hachsharahs were eliminated by M. C. Rumkowski not long after the described visit above.

manual labor is to include up to 100 women. Women are being registered at the Bureau of Labor at 11 Lutomierska Street.

SUMMARY COURT

Proclamation No. 233 from the Eldest of the Jews, posted on the 15th of March, informed the ghetto populace that a Summary Court had been created on the 16th of March. This institution will be located at 27 Franciszkańska Street. According to the proclamation, the Summary Court is an entirely independent body whose task is to fight the crime which threatens public welfare. The Summary Court will meet in two groups composed of one judge and two counselors appointed by the Chairman. The trials will not be preceded by an investigation. No prosecutor or defense attorney will take part in the trials. The judges will issue sentences entirely on the basis of their own conclusions.

THE CHAIRMAN'S BIRTHDAY

Chairman M. C. Rumkowski, Eldest of the Jews, turned 64 on the 13th of this month. The Chairman's closest coworkers offered him their congratulations on the evening of his birthday at his private apartment in Hospital No. 1. The Chairman was presented with a whole series of keepsakes made by the employees of the artisans' workshops. The birthday presents displayed a high level of artistic skill and will undoubtedly be of historical importance in the future.

CULTURAL LIFE

On the 11th of this month there was a symphony concert for factory workers in the House of Culture. On the 13th, which was Purim, there was a violin performance by Miss [Bronisława] Rotsztat, as well as a symphony concert conducted by [Dawid] Bajgelman in which the Hazomir[52] chorus participated. On Saturday, March 15, that program was repeated in a performance for invited guests, the Chairman chief among them. This performance had a special ceremonial quality and lasted until ten o'clock in the evening. On March 17 the School Department organized a performance of music and vocals for schoolchildren.[53] On the 18th, 20th, and 22d of March there were symphony concerts for factory workers, and, finally, on the 22d there was a symphony concert dedicated to classical music and conducted by [Teodor] Ryder.

TUESDAY, MARCH 25, 1941

ADDITIONAL BREAD ALLOCATION

The Eldest of the Jews has ordered a one-time additional bread allocation in the amount of half a kilogram, and also 80 grams of margarine and 200 grams of dried rutabaga.

---

52. To some extent this was a continuation of the former Jewish Society of Music and Literature, Hazomir, founded in Łódź in 1899.

53. In the school years 1939–40 and 1940–41, that is, before and after the ghetto was established, there existed a Jewish elementary school system, providing both religious and secular education, and there were also trade and middle-school systems, although all had been severely curtailed and restricted, and functioned irregularly. Overall, the school system included about 7,000–15,000 pupils. Care for the schools and their organization was the responsibility of the Jewish administration, the School Department in particular. That department was headed by Mojżesz Karo, Szmul Lew, and Eliasz Tabaksblat.

ITALIAN OFFICERS

visited the ghetto the other day. They acquainted themselves with the workshops, among other things.

A NEW FACTORY

A few days ago a large factory producing civilian and military caps went into operation at 47 Brzezińska Street. The factory employs a few hundred workers.

CONCERT

Today there was a highly successful symphony concert at the House of Culture which played to a full house.

WEDNESDAY, MARCH 26, 1941

BAKING MATZOTH

In connection with the coming holiday of Passover, a network of bakeries is gradually being put into operation to bake matzoth. Last week, 10 bakeries of this sort were already operational and that number has been doubled this week. Long effort has resulted in the production of relatively good matzoth from rye flour. Two thousand people are employed in baking matzoth, and the daily production of matzoth amounts to 12,000 kilograms. Before beginning operations, the owners and managers of the bakeries took an oath in the prayer house at 23 Brzezińska Street that they would commit no abuses. The matzoth are packed in two-and-a-half-kilogram packages which are supplied with inspection numbers and the address of the bakery. The large soup kitchen at 32 Młynarska Street has been designated as the central storehouse for matzoth. The direction of matzo production is in the hands of Mr. [Mordecai] Lajzerowicz, who, before the baking began, briefed the bakers and called on them to do their job honestly and with a sense of responsibility toward the customer.

A SHOOTING

Tonight, 44-year-old Chana Lewkowicz was shot dead by a sentry at the end of Marysińska Street just beyond the barbed wire. It was alleged that she had been smuggling.

IN THE HOUSE OF CULTURE

there was a musical recital today, performed by Miss [Bronisława] Rotsztat and Mr. Steinman [Nikodem Sztajman].

THURSDAY, MARCH 27, 1941

A WORK SETTLEMENT INSTEAD OF A GHETTO?

There have been rumors that the ghetto will supposedly be changed into a "work settlement for Jews." Moreover, there are rumors circulating that an increase in the bread allocation to 600 grams is supposed to be on the way, and, finally, that the instructors of the Order Service are planning to leave for the Warsaw ghetto. None of these rumors has been confirmed by any authoritative source.

ARRIVAL OF HORSES

Today the ghetto was supplied with eight work horses, and last week it received 32 horses. When possession was being taken of the livestock, Dr. Leichter [Józef Leider], a local veterinarian, examined the horses. The horses purchased are to be used for transporting foodstuff from the Marysin railroad sidetrack. A suitable number of drivers has been hired. The Construction Department is building a stable at 23 Marysińska Street. Apparently, there is now also a project to put a horse-drawn tram into operation that would run from the end of Brzezińska Street to the end of Łagiewnicka Street.

1,050 WORKERS

are employed in demolishing the buildings that abut the ghetto. Eighteen members of the Order Service are in charge of supervising the workers. The work runs from 8 A.M. until 4 P.M.

A CINERARY URN

Today, via Bałut Market, the ghetto received an urn with the ashes of a certain Abram Wajsberg who had been in the concentration camp at Buchenwald. The deceased was 34 years old and his residence here had been at 10 Franciszkańska Street. His widow lives in Tomaszów Mazowiecki [Łódź province]. The urn will be buried in the cemetery here. It is worth noting that this is the second such incident, for, several weeks ago, an urn containing the ashes of Sarna, a lawyer, was brought to the ghetto.

FRIDAY, MARCH 28, 1941

GOODS AND MONEY

that were left behind or hidden in the city [of Łódź] can be reclaimed through the Community and the owners will be paid their cash equivalents. A proclamation from the Eldest of the Jews was posted to that effect today.

RAIDS

A squad of prison guards under the leadership of Mr. [Salomon] Hercberg has continued to conduct raids and make arrests among the criminal element or those engaged in activities inimical to the ghetto authorities.

SATURDAY, MARCH 29, 1941

A SHOOTING

Abraham Dąb, of 8 Podrzeczna Street, was shot in the shoulder at eleven o'clock this morning on Zgierska Street, near the vehicle gate of the Old Market. A First Aid Service droshky took the wounded man to Hospital No. 1. Witnesses to the incident claim that the wounded man had been speaking with the sentry beforehand. It was obviously not possible to establish the substance of that conversation.

SPECULATION IN BREAD

In the course of the day the price of bread has undergone great fluctuation between 4.50 marks and 6 marks. A rumor about the allocation of one loaf of bread to every Community worker influenced the price to fall in the morning hours. Later in the day the rumor proved false and the price of bread was immediately raised. Kasha was being sold for 5 marks. There is an observable increase in the foodstuff offered for sale, which indicates that cash needed to purchase the fixed holiday ration is being sought. This phenomenon goes hand in hand with the appearance of German marks in circulation, which, until recently, had been used specifically for hard currency speculation.

CULTURAL LIFE

There was a concert today at the House of Culture. There were also literary festivities today at the [Labor Zionist party] soup kitchens at 16 Berek Joselewicz Street and 12 Masarska Street.

SUNDAY, MARCH 30, 1941

ABRAHAM DĄB

died after a day in the hospital today as a result of a rifle wound.

A MARRIAGE BY CORRESPONDENCE

One of the clerks employed by the Community concluded her wedding formalities by means of correspondence with her fiancé, who at present lives in Lwów.[54] The current conditions of life create situations that are indeed fantastically paradoxical.

GOSSIP!

Today's topic for newsboy gossip was the "news" that thousands of artisans employed in Community workshops were to be transferred from the ghetto to workshops in other quarters of the city. This rumor, along with a series of others that continue to circulate through the ghetto, is without basis in reality.

TUESDAY, APRIL 1, 1941

REGISTRATION OF CHRISTIANS RESIDING IN THE GHETTO

On orders of the German authorities, a strict registration of Christians residing in the ghetto has again been carried out.[55] On the basis of addresses received from the

---

54. At this time the city of Lwów was occupied by Soviet Russia.

55. The previous official count of non-Jews living in the ghetto had been made on January 5, 1941. At that time there were 61 [or 62?] Christians in the ghetto, including 3 Germans who were citizens of the Reich, 2 ethnic Germans from Łódź (so-called Volksdeutschen) and 57 Poles (9 men and 48 women).

Registration Bureau, the superintendents visited all persons subject to registration and, in that way, data for the questionnaires was obtained. It was thus ascertained that the number of Christians amounts to 110. Of that number thirty-two persons are of Jewish parentage, thirteen of mixed marriages (seven of these people declare themselves Jews); three of the Christians are Germans, citizens of the Reich, and two are local Germans. As to the Germans, four of the cases concern wives who have remained with their Jewish husbands and one case concerns a citizen of the Reich who has settled here without providing any reason for that step. And, finally, there are 60 Polish Catholics who reside in the ghetto. The Christians who reside in the ghetto are, in 45 cases, people who converted, who are of mixed origin and are compelled to settle here;[56] in 10 cases economic considerations inclined them to remain in the ghetto; 37 have various motives, for example, considerations of marriage, attachment to the environment, a reluctance to part with real estate owned here, and so on; in addition, as explained above, there are four German wives and 14 persons who have not made their reasons known for remaining in the ghetto.

FOOD PACKAGES FROM ABROAD

will, according to the notice issued by the Eldest of the Jews today, be purchased by the Community at market prices. The intent here is to protect those concerned against exploitation by shopkeepers on the one hand, and, on the other, to acquire valuable food needed to feed the sick.

WEDNESDAY, APRIL 2, 1941

HOLIDAY FOOD ALLOCATION

In the late evening hours the Chairman held a conference with the directors of the Department of Food Supply and the Fuel Department. The topic under discussion was the determining of a special allocation of food and fuel for the residents of the ghetto in view of the coming holiday.

AT THE SUMMER CAMP IN MARYSIN

In the course of the month of March, 112 children, 65 boys and 47 girls, ages 7 to 14, were sent to the summer camp. Their number consisted for the most part of sick children, cripples, and convalescents.

THE ORPHANAGE

located at 76 Łagiewnicka Street accepted 24 orphans, 9 boys and 15 girls, ages 3 to 7, in the month of March.

---

56. In Poland, as in German-occupied territories in the Soviet Union, the Nazi authorities did not even attempt to create a separate classification for the so-called half-breeds (*Mischlingen*) who had, as they defined it, varying degrees of Jewish blood. In Poland, as opposed to Germany, Austria, and many other occupied countries in Western Europe, each Jew was considered only and exclusively a Jew by the German authorities and was treated accordingly.

FRIDAY, APRIL 4, 1941

A BOOM

Today the private market observed a significant increase in the price of food. For example, the price of potatoes suddenly jumped from 1.20 marks to 2.50 marks, oil from 13 marks to 20 marks, kasha increased to 8 marks from yesterday's 6, and the price of vegetables went from 60 pfennigs to 1 mark. The price increases were influenced by the publication of the food allocations for the holidays, which, in comparison to what had been anticipated, proved extremely meager.

PROCLAMATIONS

Posted today, Proclamation No. 241 establishes the food allocation for the period of the 12th to the 20th of this month and also regulates the serving of meals by the soup kitchens during the holidays. Proclamation No. 242 establishes rules for the sale of bread and matzoth during the holidays and provides the addresses of the relevant distribution points. Proclamation No. 244 provides strict instructions for homes and businesses during blackouts.

MEALS FOR THE RELIGIOUS

By order of the Eldest of the Jews, the three kosher kitchens in the ghetto, namely, those at 26 Zgierska Street, 32 Młynarska Street, and 74 Brzezińska Street, will significantly increase the number of meals they serve during the holidays. The price of those meals, which consist of two dishes, has been set at 30 pfennigs.

SHOT TO DEATH

Sixty-one-year-old Małka Sura Cukier (of 2 Nad Łódką Street) was killed by rifle fire at around ten o'clock in the evening in the vicinity of the barbed wire.

A SUICIDE ATTEMPT

Twenty-nine-year-old Majlech Akerman made an attempt on his own life by opening his veins; he had also taken a large dose of contaminated alcohol beforehand. The attempted suicide was taken to the hospital in critical condition.

A DEATH FROM HUNGER

Kiva Goldberg (homeless) died at Precinct II of the Order Service as a result of hunger.

SATURDAY, APRIL 5, 1941

A DESPERATE LEAP FROM A BRIDGE

In the evening hours, 60-year-old Mojżesz Federman threw himself to the roadway from the bridge above Zgierska Street near the Church of the [Most Blessed] Virgin Mary. The attempted suicide suffered severe injuries to the arms and legs and was placed in Hospital No. 1.

A RAID AT THE MARKET

Today, officials of the Section of Price Control, along with members of the Order Service from the Bałut Market station, conducted a raid on Pilcer Square, where food is traded. In the course of half an hour the dealers engaging in usury had their goods taken from them and the food was then brought to the premises of the Section of Price Control. On instructions of the Chairman, the food seized is to be confiscated and handed over for sale to the distribution points which serve the sick.

SUNDAY, APRIL 6, 1941

SUICIDES

Forty-six-year-old Majer Szajn committed suicide in his apartment at 11 Młynarska Street and 70-year-old Jankiel Henoch Sat attempted suicide in his apartment at 36 Brzezińska Street.

A SHOOTING

Zysla Orensztajn of 7 Kielma [Marysińska] Street was shot in the chest near the barbed wire on Majowa Street.

MONDAY, APRIL 7, 1941

THE STRUCTURE OF THE ORDER SERVICE

was its own creation. As a system, the Order Service is divided into five precincts; a special section services Bałut Market. That section's primary task is to preserve order when food supplies are received in the ghetto, whether they arrive through Bałut Market or from the transshipping station at Marysin. There is also a seven-member team of Order Service men assigned to the German criminal police [Kripo], whose office is located on the grounds of the ghetto. In the so-called Kripo, the Order Service functionaries provide assistance; for example, they bring in people summoned by that office, find addresses, and so on. The police stations operate within the limits of the precincts assigned to them, and their officials provide safety in the streets of the ghetto, as well as within the Community's offices and stores. The Order Service is also in charge of the battle against smuggling. The police precincts are empowered to impose and collect fines when minor offenses take place, and they can also order arrests and detain arrestees up to 48 hours. The Order Service turns over all the more important criminal matters to the Bureau of Investigation, which then pursues these cases in conjunction with the Prosecutor's Office. There also exists a Section of Price Control within the Order Service. This section controls the price of food both in the stores and in the streets and markets. At the same time, this section suppresses any violations committed by the sellers against the regulations on dealing in food issued by the Eldest of the Jews. Furthermore, the Sanitation Section of the Order Service cooperates with the Economy Section in safeguarding health and sanitary conditions in the ghetto. A special section, the Sonderkommando [Special Unit], conducts searches aimed at seizing valuables, furs, hidden merchandise, hard currencies, including German marks, and all items which are subject to [mandatory] sale to the Community (e.g., sewing machines).[57] The valuables seized are sold to the German authorities, and the merchandise also meets the same fate or is put to use in Community workshops. The members of the Order Service receive the following salaries: the chief—300 marks, officers—190 marks, under-officers—150 marks, officer candidates—110–130 marks, senior inspectors—90 marks, inspectors—80 marks, patrolmen—70 marks, department heads—90 marks, clerks—75 marks. The lowest salaries are supplemented with family allowances.

A CONFERENCE WITH THE GERMAN AUTHORITIES

The chief of the Order Service, [Leon] Rozenblat, and adjutant engineer [Julian] Grosbart were summoned to Precinct VI, to which the ghetto is subordinate and which is located outside the ghetto, in a building at the intersection of Limanowski and Zgierska streets. The German authorities held a conference with them to provide them with information on the initiation of sentry duty around the ghetto by a different force, Schupo [Schutzpolizei].[58] From the German side, local police officers and representatives from police headquarters in Radom took part in the conference.[59] The chief of the Order Service was required to present a detailed report on the organization of the Order Service, a map of the ghetto, a breakdown of the ghetto by precincts, an itemized list of the powers of the Eldest of the Jews, the state of the residents' health, addresses of all the Community's offices and institutions, the population density of the individual precincts, and a series of other statistics.

During the conference, the chief of the Order Service provided the requisite answers to a number of questions. In the course of the day, the required statement was worked out, from which it would appear that the number of ghetto dwellers amounts to 154,578, 45 percent of whom are men and 55 percent women. By police districts, the breakdown of the population is as follows: Precinct I—432 buildings with 17,541 rooms, 55,947 inhabitants; Precinct II—684 buildings, 17,435 rooms, 53,458 inhabitants; Precinct III—512 buildings, 8,041 rooms, 27,433 inhabitants; Precinct IV—378 buildings, 5,468 rooms, 16,520 inhabitants; Precinct V (Marysin)—951 buildings, 3,970

---

57. Sonderkommando, later renamed Sonderabteilung, the Special Unit [later the Special Department] of the Order Service, was created by the Eldest of the Jews on July 1, 1940. This department also served as the ghetto's secret police and, though officially subordinate to Rumkowski, in practice it was subordinate to the German authorities, chiefly the Kripo and the Gestapo, from which agencies the Special Department often received direct orders. The role of the Special Department expanded significantly in the second half of 1942, when the Rumkowski administration's so-called autonomy was greatly curtailed; among other functions, this special police unit assumed the supervision of food distribution in the ghetto. It was headed by Dawid Gertler and, after his arrest by the Gestapo on July 12, 1943, by Marek Kligier.

58. One of the many units of the German police.

59. That a representative of the police from Radom, a city not in the territory that had been annexed to the Reich, but in the so-called Generalgouvernement, took part in this conference should not seem odd: a German police unit specializing in all matters of security in the territories of the former Polish state was located in Radom.

rooms, 1,220 inhabitants.[60] Precinct I, located at 27 Franciszkańska Street, employs 117 Order Service men, Precinct II at 56 Limanowski Street employs 131 people, Precinct III at 61 Łagiewnicka Street employs 87 people, Precinct IV at 69 Marysińska Street, 53 people, and Precinct V at Zagajnikowa Street, 60 people. Order Service headquarters, located at 1 Lutomierska Street, along with the Section of Price Control and the Sanitation Section, employs 36 people; the Bureau of Investigation at 22 Gnieźnieńska Street employs 38 people, the section at Bałut Market (27 Łagiewnicka Street) employs 97.

TUESDAY, APRIL 8, 1941

THE FIGHT AGAINST CRIME

On instructions from the Eldest of the Jews, a prison squad is carrying out the systematic arrest of notorious criminals as well as of persons whose conduct poses a threat to order in the ghetto. Those arrested are being transported out of the ghetto in groups as the need for workers in Germany arises. This is how the problem of ridding the ghetto of undesirables is being resolved. At the present moment, a group of 106 arrestees has been prepared for deportation, among whom are people being held in custody and those already serving sentences. According to information from the prison administration, this group is principally composed of professional thieves, fences, pimps, and the like. Those to be deported have been examined by a medical commission, which disqualified 12 persons for reasons of health; the remaining 94, however, were deported. Besides these 94 persons, forcibly expelled from the ghetto to do manual labor, 42 people who had volunteered to work outside the ghetto left here today. The dispatching of the transport of deportees has caused a significant drop in the number of arrestees remaining in prison; at present that number comes to 117 including 12 women and 12 minors. There are nine prisoners in the infirmary.

ALLOCATIONS FOR THE HOLIDAYS

For the Passover holiday, the Chairman has responded favorably to the majority of requests concerning cash relief allowances. The Chairman has assigned a sum of 30,000 marks to pay for holiday allocations or relief supplements.

THURSDAY, APRIL 10, 1941

A SHOOTING

A few minutes after nine P.M. a sentry shot and killed 56-year-old Zelman Hersz Rozental. The victim resided at 18 Zgierska Street and was killed on his way from the

---

60. The conspicuously low number of rooms and inhabitants relative to houses in Precinct V is chiefly a result of the suburban quality of the Marysin district and of its not being fully inhabited. Furthermore, some high-ranking officials of the Jewish administration had summer apartments in Marysin in addition to those in the center of the ghetto.

street to the building next door at 20 Zgierska Street to warm up some coffee on a [public] gas hot plate.

SMUGGLER SEIZED

Yesterday, members of the Order Service apprehended a resident of Pabianice [a town near Łódź], Jakub Gelkopf, as he was slipping through the barbed wire on Niemojewski Street. Contraband food was found on the arrested man. He was handed over to the German criminal police.

THE BAKING OF THE MATZOTH

The baking of matzoth is operating full swing on the eve of Passover. The matzoth are being produced by 27 bakeries, each of which is baking up to 16,000 kilograms per day. Thus far, 180,000 kilograms have been produced. Around 3,000 people are employed in the baking and sale of matzoth. During the holiday each person will receive a package of matzoth weighing 2.5 kilograms at a cost of 1.30 marks per kilo. The matzoth are made of rye flour. The populace will be able to buy bread or matzoth, whichever they prefer. The R II store will be supplied with matzoth baked from wheat flour for the sick.

WORK DURING THE HOLIDAYS

On orders of the German authorities, the Passover holiday is not to be cause for an interruption of work in the factories. On Sunday as well, the second day of the Jewish holiday, which coincides with the first day of the Christian Easter, work in all Community offices will proceed normally.

NO FUEL

Lately, coal deliveries to the ghetto have been reduced to a minimum, and, this week, have been cut off entirely. This was caused by the complete exhaustion of the reserves at the distribution site, which has created an extremely dangerous situation because the public kitchens cannot be supplied with any more coal. The shortage of coal has caused its price to rise to 1.80 marks per kilogram in private commerce. The price of wood has also risen significantly.

THE BUREAU OF PUBLIC GARDENS NOW IN OPERATION

This week a Bureau of Public Gardens was established at Marysin II. Its range of activities includes control over the cultivation of garden plots in the Marysin district. The area under cultivation in Marysin occupies approximately 130 morgens [728,000 square meters]. Those fields have been enclosed by barbed wire. The direction of work in public gardens is in the hands of Engineer Gliksman, as it was last year. An agricultural section has been in operation at the Department of Finance and Economics since the beginning of the planting season. The leasing of plots, the supervision of their cultivation, and the fixing of prices for agricultural products are all under the jurisdiction of the agricultural section.

FRIDAY, APRIL 11, 1941

A TEACHER'S SUICIDE

Today, at daybreak, the body of a man who had hanged himself was discovered at 6 Chłodna Street. The suicide, 46-year-old Mr. Klingbajl, was a teacher by profession. Before hanging himself, he had also ingested an enormous quantity of saccharine tablets.

SEVEN IN THE MORNING

will be the starting time for work in the factories and stores beginning on the 15th of this month.

PROCLAMATION NO. 245

posted on the walls today, prohibits any offer of goods or services made [outside the ghetto] by individuals who bypass the offices of the Eldest of the Jews.

MANUAL LABOR IN GERMANY

Today, 169 men left the ghetto to do manual labor in Germany. The forthcoming transports will, as the need arises, be scheduled as follows: 400 men will leave on the 15th of this month; on the 16th, the first women's transport consisting of 130 women will depart; on the 18th—a mixed transport of 300 men and 100 women; on the 21st—400 men. There will be transports of 400 men each on the 25th, the 28th, and the 30th of April. Thus, all told, it is anticipated that by the end of April 2,700 men and 230 women will be sent out of the ghetto.[61] The office concerned with the registration and dispatch of people to do manual labor, the so-called Arbeitseinsatz, has been empowered by the Eldest of the Jews to register volunteers for work outside the ghetto, to fill the transports, to prepare them for travel, and also to keep accounts of the advance salaries available to the workers' families remaining in the ghetto. Thus far, this office has recorded over 7,000 applications for manual labor. The medical commissions have disqualified up to 40 percent of those desiring to leave, while the German medical review rejected 7 percent of the volunteers who had already qualified. On instructions from the Eldest of the Jews, the families of those who were accepted for work outside the ghetto will regularly receive 12 marks per week as soon as their relatives depart. This advance will be deducted from the worker's weekly wages later on when accounts are settled with the German authorities. The workers' salaries have not yet been precisely fixed; roughly speaking, they will come to 24 marks per week, of which around 6 marks will be deducted for board—that is, after the advance paid the relatives in the ghetto is deducted, 6 marks per week will remain. Thus far, the Eldest of the Jews has not received this advance payment for labor from the Germans, with the exception of 300 marks. Wages will only be paid when work begins. On the basis of information which has arrived here, work on the construction of the Frankfurt am Oder–Poznań highway only commenced at the beginning of March, whereas the first transports had already left the ghetto on the 10th, 13th, and

61. The number of men to be sent out of the ghetto does not add up to 2,700.

16th of December, and the next ones had left on the 9th of January. Others left on the 27th and 29th of March, and, finally, there were those that left on the 8th through 11th of April. All told, there are now 2,418 people outside the ghetto doing manual labor. The families of those workers have received 300,000 marks in all and also, as noted already in the bulletin [of March 27, 1941], a ten-mark bonus during the week of the holidays.

SATURDAY, APRIL 12, 1941

SENTENCES BY THE SUMMARY COURT

Recently, the Summary Court has passed 20 sentences in which the accused were condemned. Punishments were meted out for the following crimes committed by factory workers, primarily tailors, carpenters, superintendents, or workers at distribution points, including managers: the theft of material from workshops, the theft of wood, coal, and foodstuff from stores, the theft of lumber from demolished houses and fences. The longest sentence, six months of close confinement, was received by Mordcha Gdalewicz, who committed a theft from a factory. In addition, there were four three-month sentences of close confinement, five two-month sentences of close confinement, and one instance in which an 80-year-old man was sentenced for willfully demolishing a cottage to sell the wood for profit. There were also seven sentences of one month's close confinement. A 16-year-old coal thief was sent to the Reform School for a period of two months. Finally, there were two sentences of six weeks in prison. A certain Aleksander Chrzanowski received one of the three-month prison sentences for stealing 50 pfennigs from a Community cash box.

SUNDAY, APRIL 13, 1941

WORK

Work proceeded normally in all the Community's departments today, the second day of the holiday.

A BULLET FROM A SENTRY'S RIFLE

wounded Arnold Krysztył, a resident of 6 Jerozolimska Street, in the arm. The incident took place around midday. First Aid brought the wounded man to Hospital No. 1.

MONDAY, APRIL 14, 1941

ORGANIZING AN EXHIBIT

Today at NIK [the Supreme Inspection Chamber] Dr. [Leon] Szykier headed a conference whose subject was the organization of an exhibit in the ghetto that would depict the work done by various factories. The Chairman opened the conference with a few remarks, pointing out that the purpose of the exhibit is to demonstrate the productivity of the ghetto to the German authorities and to stress that the growth of production depends on the receipt of orders and the necessary raw and semifinished materials. The exhibit will be displayed at 32 Łagiewnicka Street, the premises being especially rebuilt for that purpose. The Chairman called upon all those present at the meeting not to neglect their regular responsibilities while organizing the upcoming exhibition. After exhaustive discussion, it was decided that the exhibit will be limited to presenting a cross section of factory output. At the end of the discussion, a three-person organizing committee was elected.

HOLIDAY FURLOUGHS FOR PRISONERS

The Chairman has ordered furloughs for prisoners, both for those serving sentences and those detained on suspicion, during the holidays (the 11th through the 19th of this month). On the basis of that order, 60 prisoners, including eight women, will be home for one week. During the holidays the prison is housing only 27 prisoners (nine of whom are women); of these the majority could not be furloughed because they are at the disposal of Kripo [German criminal police] and several are considered serious criminals.

WEDNESDAY, APRIL 16, 1941

SHOTS FIRED INTO AN APARTMENT

Around eleven o'clock in the evening, Aron Mojsze Tenenbaum was wounded in the arms and the mouth while in his own apartment at 4 Franciszkańska Street. A German sentry in the vicinity of the building had fired at Tenenbaum's window because there was light coming from it.

SHOT TO DEATH ON THE STREET

At 20 minutes to 10 [P.M.?], a sentry shot and killed an 18-year-old boy, Łajba Lewkowicz (of 9 Pałacowa Street), with rifle fire near the building at 9 Zgierska Street.

THURSDAY, APRIL 17, 1941

RETURN OF THOSE SENT OUT TO DO MANUAL LABOR

On the 15th of this month a transport of 400 men was prepared to be sent to Germany. The commission of German doctors found only 347 fit to perform manual labor. Of those, 227 returned to the ghetto today. For the last two days they have been in Konstantynów, in Lutomiersk [two towns near Łódź], and in a former factory building [in Łódź, outside the ghetto] on Kopernik Street. Those two days were spent under very harsh conditions.

A TRANSPORT OF WOMEN

On the 16th of this month a transport of women numbering 146 was prepared by the Bureau of Labor for dispatch to Germany. The local medical commission disqualified six women while the commission of German doctors found only 68 to be fit to be sent out to perform manual labor. Those women left the ghetto, and those who were disqualified returned directly home from Bałut Market.

FRIDAY, APRIL 18, 1941

A POLE IN THE GHETTO

At 1:30 A.M. members of the Order Service apprehended 31-year-old Stanisław Wiśniewski on Niemojewski Street. Wiśniewski, who had slipped in through the barbed wire, was handed over to the disposition of the German criminal police.

"A BLACK LIST"

The Chairman has ordered that a list be compiled of former Community workers discharged from their positions for having committed criminal offenses. This list will be sent by the head of the Bureau of Personnel to the attention of the directors of all departments, offices, and workshops.

THE CLOSING OF *R* I

R I, the food distribution point for the sick on Łagiewnicka Street, will be closed in connection with the opening of *R* II, a similar point, on Lutomierska Street. The *R* II store will be able to serve all the sick people who use food coupons, as well as efficiently serve up to 250 clients per day as it has done so far.

SATURDAY, APRIL 19, 1941

BREAD FOR FIVE DAYS

The Chairman has ordered that five days' worth of bread be sold at a time. This new system will make things considerably easier for the customer and for the distribution system since every customer will receive a full loaf of bread all at once, eliminating all sorts of misunderstandings and abuses produced by the weighing of the bread.

SUNDAY, APRIL 20, 1941

PLAYGROUNDS FOR THE CHILDREN

In the evening, after concluding his daily office work, the Chairman personally inspected a series of building sites searching for a location suitable for a playground, where children could rest and play in the summer. Last year the large area on the grounds of 27 Franciszkańska Street, which is surrounded by the public gardens, fulfilled that role splendidly. This year it is not possible to make use of that space because it is being leased as garden plots to private individuals. As a result of the above-mentioned inspections, the Chairman has ordered that a large, well-maintained area in the very center of the ghetto, on the grounds at 4 Brzezińska Street, be set aside for the purpose in question. That area was formerly a rental and riding space for cyclists. The Chairman ordered that the metallurgical factory be issued special funds to install low, comfortable benches in the area, and also ordered that grass be planted and a soup kitchen installed there. Over 1,000 children will make use of this area.

MONDAY, APRIL 21, 1941

KILLED AT HER OWN REQUEST

At two o'clock in the afternoon, Cwajga Blum, 41, a resident of 21 Limanowski Street, was shot to death next to the barbed wire at the end of Brzezińska Street. The victim was suffering from mental illness and had recently been released from the mental institution on Wesoła Street. According to witnesses, the unfortunate woman had walked up to the barbed wire several times and requested that the sentries shoot her. The Order Service had already pulled her safely away from the barbed wire a couple of times. On the fateful day, the sentry had asked the mentally ill woman to dance in front of the barbed wire. After she had performed a little dance, the sentry shot her dead at nearly point-blank range.

FRIDAY, APRIL 25, 1941

POPULATION OF THE GHETTO

According to information from the Department of Statistics, the population of the ghetto on March 31, 1941, amounted to 150,436: 68,193 men and 82,243 women.

RELEASED FROM PRISON

Between March 26 and April 23, sixteen people have been sent to the ghetto. Thirteen of those who were settled here had been released from various prisons, one had returned from being a prisoner of war, one had been expelled from the city, and there was 1 child, who was sent to the Orphanage. The man who was expelled is a well-known citizen of Łódź, Grzegorz Umański, who had been passing as a Russian possessing a Nansen passport[62] all this time. During formalities connected with registering a change of apartment, his Jewish origin was accidentally discovered, which resulted in his being transported immediately to the ghetto, without any possessions.

---

62. The popular name for the ID cards—passports for refugees and stateless persons—introduced on the initiative of Fridtjof Nansen of Norway, a famous polar explorer and naturalist who was High Commissioner for Refugees in the League of Nations in 1922. He won the Nobel Peace Prize in that same year.

IN THE MONTH OF MARCH

the number of arrests reached 1,011. Four hundred twelve people were arrested for theft, 61 for resisting the authorities, and 538 for various offenses. One thousand twenty-three people died in the ghetto in March (1,069 in February), 55 births were registered (52 in February).

HUNGER

was the cause of death of Abraham Morgensztern, a 21-year-old homeless and unemployed youth who died today in a garret at 30 Wolborska Street.

SUNDAY, APRIL 27, 1941

MARKET STALLS DEMOLISHED

In view of the growing need for, and increasing shortage of, lumber and fuel, all wooden market stalls and booths on squares and markets have been ordered demolished. Beginning today, street peddlers will place their goods directly on the ground or on chairs or tables brought from their homes. Only the stalls belonging to invalids escaped demolition.

DEATH OF THE OLDEST INHABITANT

Today, Dawid Majer, the ghetto's oldest inhabitant, died at the age of 94. The deceased had been living at the Old People's Home.

WEDNESDAY, APRIL 30, 1941

THE ELDEST OF THE JEWS IN OZORKÓW[63]

Today, Mr. Barciński, the Eldest of the Jews in Ozorków, arrived in the ghetto here for a stay of a few days. He conferred with the Chairman.

SATURDAY, MAY 3, 1941

THE GHETTO'S FOOD SUPPLY

Lately the ghetto's requests for food have been matched by the supply. Apart from the current requisitions, considerable shipments of vegetables and potatoes have been arriving here. The ghetto is receiving yellow sugar in addition to the amount requested, which is entirely limited to regular sugar. Coal deliveries remain extremely meager. The ghetto received no coal at all last week while this week it has received scarcely 150,000 kilograms.

---

63. Ozorków, a town to the north of Łódź. In 1941 there were around 4,500 Jews in the ghetto there.

SUICIDE LEAP FROM A BRIDGE

The bridge over Zgierska Street between Lutomierska Street and Kościelny Square is, from time to time, used by suicides to carry out their desperate aim. Today the police blotter noted two suicide attempts from that bridge. At 1:30 P.M. 33-year-old Efraim Regenbaum (of 25 Gnieźnieńska Street) attempted to take his own life by jumping from the upper level of the bridge to the pavement, and two hours later he was followed by 26-year-old Dawid Jakubowicz. They were both taken to the hospital in critical condition.

SUNDAY, MAY 4, 1941

THE POPULATION OF THE GHETTO

on May 1 of this year comes to 148,547.

A SUICIDE

At 10 A.M., 40-year-old Henoch Buterman (of 24 Żydowska Street) leaped from a fourth-story stairwell window to the pavement of the courtyard below at 5 Zgierska Street. He suffered death on the spot.

WEDNESDAY, MAY 7, 1941

A NEW DIRECTOR FOR THE DEPARTMENT OF HEALTH

There has been a crisis for several weeks now in connection with the post of director of the Department of Health, a crisis caused by the resignation of Dr. Leon Szykier. The Chairman accepted that resignation yesterday and has appointed Dr. Wiktor Miller director of the Department of Health.

A SUICIDE

Fifty-one-year-old Laja Arm (of 7 Wawelska Street) has committed suicide by jumping into a deep well.

FRIDAY, MAY 9, 1941

AN INSPECTION OF THE GHETTO

In connection with Gauleiter [of Wartheland, Artur] Greiser's presence in the city, a commission composed of the most important representatives of the municipal administration and the military authorities came to the ghetto today. Among other things, the commission visited a few factories.

SATURDAY, MAY 10, 1941

A TRAVELING GROUP OF GERMAN JOURNALISTS

numbering around fifty persons spent some time in the ghetto today in connection with Gauleiter Greiser's last day in the city. The group arrived in the ghetto by bus and visited the tailor shops at 45 Łagiewnicka Street.

FUEL SITUATION GRAVE

Coal continues to arrive in the ghetto in minimal amounts. The [German] Ghetto Administration has announced that the ghetto will receive no more than 800 tons of coal per month, 500 tons to be used by the soup kitchens and bakeries, 160 tons by factories filling orders for the military, and 140 tons by the hospitals. The [Jewish] local authorities are obliged by the Ghetto Administration to store any amount of coal received in excess of 800 tons per month solely as a reserve, and the German authorities are to be periodically informed as to the status of those reserves. It is worth noting here that the minimal need for the Community's institutions and enterprises requires 1,000 tons a month, and 750 tons a month are needed to make even the most meager of allocations to the public at large, figuring scarcely 5 kilograms per person. These statistics illustrate with perfect clarity the immense disproportion that remains between the monthly coal supply granted the ghetto and the ghetto's most minimal needs.

A BODY ON THE STAIRS

The body of 46-year-old Chaja Jakubowicz, a resident of 17 Zydowska Street, was found today on a stairwell at 31 Nowomiejska Street.

SUNDAY, MAY 11, 1941

REMOVAL OF THE WESTERN QUARTER OF THE GHETTO

The evacuation of the people residing in the western quarter of the ghetto began today. This section, encompassing Generalska, Oficerska, Leśna, and Drewnowska streets (beginning at No. 79 Drewnowska and going up), as well as a few last buildings on Lutomierska Street, will be severed from the ghetto. This quarter has 64 buildings inhabited by 1,330 people. The residents were evacuated to Precinct II of the Order Service.

A BUILDING FOR THE GHETTO ADMINISTRATION

The Construction Department has received an order to begin work on remodeling the building at the intersection of Cegielniana and Piłsudski streets [outside the ghetto], which has been designated for the [German] Ghetto Administration. The department is now sending its engineers, foremen, and workers to the building on a daily basis.

MONDAY, MAY 12, 1941

VICISSITUDES OF THOSE SENT TO PERFORM MANUAL LABOR

A transport of workers sent out of the ghetto last week to perform manual labor, numbering 250, has met with an unpleasant experience. Some of them were sent to Aleksandrów but some were imprisoned [in Łódź] on Kopernik Street. The workers were treated very badly during the several days of their forced confinement and suffered terribly from hunger.[64] They returned to the ghetto today. The majority of them will be sent out to perform manual labor, but a few dozen members of the transport will be returning home. Apparently the transport was held back because a large number of Poles from the city were recruited [instead] for the same purpose.

WEDNESDAY, MAY 14, 1941

A SUICIDE ATTEMPT

At 2:00 P.M. 51-year-old Ides Śmietanka leaped from her third-floor window at 48 Limanowski Street. She broke her leg and also suffered head injuries. She was taken to Hospital No. 1 in critical condition.

ORDERS FOR THE ARMY

The tailor workshops have received large orders from the military. The greater part of the orders is for denim uniforms and pants. The shirtmakers' workshop has received an order for 50,000 military shirts. In addition, orders have been received for several thousand women's dresses and for lingerie.

THE APPLIED ART WORKSHOP

manufactures gloves. A large order to perform alterations on military uniforms is anticipated in the near future. On the other hand, there have been very few orders for men's civilian suits. The rubber raincoat factory is still not operating because of a lack of materials and orders.

MAY 16–20, 1941

DEATHS AND BIRTHS

In this five-day period, 194 persons died in the ghetto. Five births were registered, of which four were boys and one a girl.

---

64. See the account dated Thursday, April 17, 1941.

A SHOOTING

On May 17, at 4:15 P.M., 49-year-old Mordka Moszkowicz was shot dead by a bullet fired by a sentry. The incident took place by the barbed wire at the intersection of Smugowa and Franciszkańska streets.

SUICIDE ATTEMPTS

On May 16, 22-year-old Łaja Ruchla Turko (of 15 Stary [Old] Square) poisoned herself with hydrochloric acid. She died that same day in Hospital No. 1. On the 19th at 7:00 P.M., a married couple, the Gliksmans, attempted to commit suicide together by poisoning themselves with mercuric chloride. They are a young, married couple; the husband, barely 23 years old, is an electrician by trade. His 20-year-old wife, Sara, is a dressmaker. They were taken to Hospital No. 1 in critical condition.

ARRIVALS

Ten people arrived here to take up permanent residence in the ghetto in the period between the 30th of April and the 15th of May. Eight of them were returning from prison. In the same period, with special permission [from the Gestapo], three residents of the ghetto went to [the ghetto of] Warsaw.[65]

MAY 21–26, 1941

DEATHS AND BIRTHS

In this six-day period 200 people died in the ghetto. One girl was born.

THE CHAIRMAN'S RETURN

On May 20, after an eight-day stay in [the ghetto of] Warsaw, the Eldest of the Jews, Chairman Rumkowski, returned to the ghetto. During his time in Warsaw, the Chairman hired 13 doctors[66]—all specialists—who will be arriving in the ghetto in the very near future. The arrival of those 13 doctors will be an enormously important event for the health of the public.

---

65. There was travel between the ghettos of Łódź and Warsaw in the years 1940–42, albeit very little. Leaving aside a few rather official trips made by M. C. Rumkowski and members of his administration, some private persons would, from time to time, travel to the ghetto in Warsaw. The permission of the Gestapo was secured at horrendous cost—gold, diamonds, and foreign currency were often used for payment. The Special Unit arranged these matters in the Łódź ghetto while in the ghetto of Warsaw they were handled by the "Thirteen" (Control Office for Combatting the Black Market and Profiteering), an institution known for its ties with the Gestapo. Trips out of the ghetto are usually described in the *Chronicle* although information on how they were arranged is not provided.

66. In other places in the *Chronicle* (including those dated May 27–31, 1941) only 12 physicians brought from the Warsaw ghetto are mentioned. The number 12 is also given in the *Geto-tsaytung*, No. 11, May 18, 1941. (See also p. 125 and n. 17 below on the death of Dr. Aron Nikelburg.)

SUICIDES

Again on May 20, the bridge at Kościelny Square was the scene of a desperate leap. The incident occurred right before the end of curfew. A 30-year-old tailor, Icek Wajn-blum, made the desperate leap. He was taken to Hospital No. 1.

On the 25th, at 5:30 A.M., a young woman leaped from a third-floor window at 12 Smugowa Street. Her life was saved.

SHOT ON THE STREET IN BROAD DAYLIGHT

In the center of the ghetto, far from any barbed wire, there was a shooting incident on the 22d of May under conditions not previously noted. As is well known, shooting incidents involving residents of the ghetto occur most frequently near border points and primarily after curfew. The shooting is always done by sentries on guard around the Jewish settlement. The scene of Thursday's shooting incident was one of the busiest street corners, the intersection of Franciszkańska and Zawisza streets. At approximately one thirty in the afternoon, near that corner, two men wearing good clothing without Stars of David passed by on the even-numbered side of Fran-ciszkańska Street heading toward Zawisza Street. Right at the corner, one of the men pulled a revolver from his coat pocket and fired two shots indiscriminately. The first shot caused Mordka Brygiel (of 25 Kielma [Marysińska] Street) a slight wound in the arm, while the second bullet took the life of Tauchen Bigeleisen, aged 55, who had been standing on the other side of Franciszkańska Street. The victim lived nearby at 35 Zawisza Street. A nearly indescribable panic broke out on the street while the shots were being fired, but the perpetrator of the incident was not stopped by anyone and set off at a quick pace up Zawisza Street toward Bałut Market. A large squad of Order Service men, lead by [Samuel] Berkowicz, commissioner of Precinct I, arrived on the scene immediately. The victim's body was sprawled in the gutter in front of the corner house. The bullet had pierced his temple, causing instantaneous death. The corpse was floating in an enormous pool of blood. The Order Service blocked off street traffic for an area of some thirty meters from the point where the body lay and allowed no one but representatives of the local authorities into the area they had cordoned off. In the meantime, Brygiel, the wounded man, had been taken by ambulance to the hospital. The German authorities were immediately informed of the incident, and the chief of the ghetto division of the German criminal police soon arrived on the scene accompanied by two investigators and a police dog. They began a detailed investiga-tion on the spot: they questioned witnesses, took measurements, familiarized them-selves with the victim's personal data, and so forth. The chief of the criminal police stated to one member of the Order Service that it was a policeman's duty to identify the person who had done the shooting even if it meant risking his own life. A member of the Order Service stated that, according to a description furnished by one of the eyewitnesses, one of the culprits was dressed in a light-colored overcoat and a light-colored hat and was carrying a cane; the other one, shorter than his companion, was wearing a grey overcoat. Immediately upon the conclusion of the investigation by the representatives of the German authorities, a hearse removed the victim's body, the pavement was washed clean of blood, and normal traffic resumed on the site of the tragic incident, which has shocked the ghetto.

MAY 27–31, 1941

DOCTORS ARRIVE FROM WARSAW

As already noted, during his stay in Warsaw the Chairman engaged the services of 12 doctors (primarily Lodzites) for the ghetto. Herewith is a list of their names: Doctors Michał Eliasberg and Arno Kleszczelski, surgeons; Abram Mazur, throat specialist; Salomon Rubinstein, radiologist; Janina Hartglass and Benedykta Moszkowicz, pediatricians; Józef Goldwasser, Alfred Lewi, Izak Ser, [Izak Mojżesz] Nekrycz, Miss Alicja Czarnożył, and Izrael Geist, internists.

CHAIRMAN OF THE SUMMARY COURT ARRESTED

Recently, an enormous sensation was caused in the ghetto by the arrest, on direct orders from the Chairman, of the chairman of the Summary Court, [Samuel] Bronowski (a former law trainee). Bronowski was arrested on the night of May 12 in his apartment, which was subjected to a thorough search. It appears that 1,000 marks were found in the arrested man's possession, quite a considerable sum in relation to his salary. Bronowski was sentenced to confinement at an Order Service precinct. The detainee has been charged with having accepted bribes from people accused of crimes. As is well known, Bronowski presided at the majority of the Summary Court's sessions and, for that reason, had a deciding influence on the passing of sentences. Issue No. 11–12 of the *Geto-tsaytung*, published on May 30, carried news of the arrest. The Eldest of the Jews will personally decide the fate of the detainee after examining the case in detail.

THE CHAIRMAN

will personally decide the sentences in cases involving any instance of corruption, fraud, and theft committed against the Community. Thus far, such matters had been under the jurisdiction of the Summary Court.

SHABUOTH

Because this holiday falls on the first two days of June, the populace will receive increased food allocations. As to the current state of food supplies, the potato shortage, caused by recent interruptions in rail service, is worthy of note here.

PREMIÈRE OF A REVUE

On Saturday, May 31, the House of Culture put on a revue. The show was composed of skits, genre pieces touching on current events, monologues, and dance performances. Considering the conditions of ghetto life and the lack of professional performers, the revue surpassed all expectations. This show can, without reservation, be ranked with those put on stage by good, pre-war theaters. The revue's success is due to its director, Mr. [Moshe] Puławer,[67] to the author of many of the more successful

---

67. Moshe (Mojżesz) Puławer, born in 1902, in Łódź; before the war, a director in the Łódź Yiddish theater, Ararat. In the ghetto he was one of the organizers of theatrical life, including plays for children. In

pieces, [Szymon] Janowski,[68] and to the truly masterful sets produced by the painter, [Pinchas] Szwarc.[69] The revue was performed entirely in Yiddish. The audience at Saturday's première demanded encores for several numbers with thunderous applause.

After the performance, Chairman Rumkowski delivered a lengthy speech in which he shared his impressions from a recent trip to Warsaw with the audience. There is a striking contrast in the Warsaw ghetto between the tragic poverty of the enormous majority of the people and the prosperity of the small handful who still remain wealthy and have access to every sort of restaurant, pastry shop, and store, where the prices are, of course, dizzyingly high. Aside from that "frippery" and the small number of fortunate people who are dressed in the latest fashion and perfectly well fed, one sees immense crowds of unemployed people whose appearance is simply frightening. Complete disorganization and chaos—such is the image of the Warsaw ghetto.[70] The conclusion of the ghetto leader's speech was dedicated to the new phase of his relentless struggle against the rampant hydra of crime and corruption that is keeping work from being performed in harmony here.

JUNE 1–6, 1941

A THREAT TO SHOOT 100 PEOPLE

The first of June will long remain in the memories of the ghetto's inhabitants. On that day the threat that 100 of its inhabitants would be shot hung over the ghetto. A child's irresponsible act could have had a catastrophic result. At around five o'clock in the afternoon, near 47 Limanowski Street, a window of a tramcar passing [outside the ghetto's borders] was broken with a brick thrown from the sidewalk. The tramcar was brought to an immediate halt. Circumstances were such that when the incident occurred an important representative of the German authorities was in the tram, and, consequently, the initial suspicion was that an assassination attempt had taken place. Within a few minutes the ghetto authorities received peremptory orders to find and hand over the culprit within fifteen minutes; otherwise, 100 people would be shot. Literally without wasting a second, the Eldest of the Jews ordered the mobiliza-

August, 1944, he was deported to Auschwitz and from there was sent to a labor camp in Germany from which he was liberated in May, 1945. In 1963, in Tel-Aviv, he published his memoirs in Yiddish, *Gewen in a geto* (I Was in a Ghetto).

68. Szymon Janowski (1913–44), born in Łódź, a satirical writer in Yiddish, the author of many humoresques and songs published in the thirties. Those published in Łódź included "Feygl in der luftn" (Birds in the Air), 1935; "Tsu zingen un tsu zogn" (For Singing and Saying), 1938. Both before the war and in the ghetto Janowski was connected with the Bund as well as with the Jewish labor youth organization *Tsukunft*. In August, 1944, he was deported to Auschwitz.

69. Pinchas Szwarc (Shaar), a painter, born in Łódź in 1923. In 1944 he was deported to the concentration camp Sachsenhausen-Oranienburg and then to a labor camp, from which he was liberated in May, 1945. He now lives and works in New York City.

70. M. C. Rumkowski's visit to the Warsaw ghetto and how he was viewed there was recorded in many diaries and memoirs. To mention but two: *The Warsaw Diary of Adam Czerniakow*, eds. R. Hilberg, S. Staron, and J. Kermisz (New York: Stein and Day, 1979), pp. 236–38, and *Notes from the Warsaw Ghetto: The Journal of Emmanuel Ringelblum*, ed. and trans. Jakob Sloan (New York: Schocken Books, 1974), p. 180.

tion of an ad hoc investigatory team composed of all representatives of the ghetto's security forces. It would be difficult to describe the tension that seized everyone the moment the emergency investigation began, for the lives of 100 innocent people depended on its outcome. Thanks to what was truly an incredibly lucky accident, they managed to establish the identity of the perpetrator of the act, with its unforeseeably grave consequences, before the fifteen minutes had elapsed. It was learned that a 10-year-old boy, Mojsze Feldman, had thrown the brick at the tramcar. Unfortunately, the boy had been amusing himself by throwing pieces of brick and had absolutely no intention of breaking the tram window. The German police were informed that the culprit had been found. As a result, the fearsome ultimatum was extended for another fifteen minutes. That time was used to question witnesses and the culprit himself. The Chairman personally took part in the investigation. By the use of subtle questions, it was established beyond any doubt, and in little more than ten minutes, that the brick had been thrown by a young boy who had not realized what he was doing. The boy is sick and retarded. A detailed record of the investigation was hurriedly drawn up and the young boy was handed over to the German police before the time period had elapsed. A short while later, after having acquainted themselves in detail with the facts of the matter, the German police released the boy—a happy ending to an incident which could have ended in tragedy.

A SHOOTING

On June 4, at 3:40 P.M., a 46-year-old worker, Kiwa Grynbaum, was wounded by a sentry while he was fertilizing a field at 29 Franciszkańska Street adjacent to Smugowa Street, which is outside the ghetto. Grynbaum was taken in critical condition to Hospital No. 1, where he died the next day.

A SUICIDE ATTEMPT

On June 5, at 3:30 P.M., 36-year-old Gimel Zaks cut his own throat with a knife in his apartment at 22 Dolna Street. He was taken to the hospital by a first aid ambulance.

JUNE 7–9, 1941

HIMMLER IN THE GHETTO

On Saturday, June 7, [Heinrich] Himmler visited the ghetto. At the offices of the [German] Ghetto Administration at Bałut Market, Himmler acquainted himself with the local settlement for Jews and then visited one of the tailoring factories.

ONE-DAY GENERAL HOUSE ARREST

On [Saturday], June 7, on orders from the German authorities, everyone was prohibited from leaving his apartment by the Eldest of the Jews. This ban, according to the relevant proclamation, was ordered as a punishment for the shots fired from the grounds of the ghetto at a sentry booth. The perpetrator of the alleged incident has not been apprehended. No details are known concerning this incident.[71] The ban was in effect from nine P.M. on Friday to eight P.M. on Saturday. The ban even extended to going out into the courtyard. Persons performing community services or going to work on that day were supplied with special passes by the Order Service headquarters. The passes indicated the precise times at which their holders are authorized to be moving about outside. Throughout the day, heavy Order Service patrols were out rigorously enforcing the ban. At Marysin, Order Service men took charge of supplying meals to the resident children. Due to the efficient work of the security forces, the order was executed to the fullest: the ghetto's entire population was forced to spend this hot day of Sabbath in its apartments. Only two incidents were noted; namely, in two cases representatives of the Order Service were struck by individuals not wishing to obey the ban. Those individuals were arrested.

AN ARREST IN THE ADRIA RESTAURANT

The Adria, the most popular restaurant in the ghetto, is located on Bałut Market. Frequented by the best-known representatives of ghetto society, this restaurant became the scene of sensational arrests on Saturday. At a time when the ghetto was under universal house arrest, the Chairman suddenly arrived at the restaurant and made his way to the back room where he found a lively bridge game in progress. Some of the Community's higher officials were taking part in that game, namely: the chief of the Sonderkommando [Special Unit], Commandant [Bronisław] Dancyger, his deputy, [Marek] Kligier, Librach, the director of the bread section, and a certain Mr. Klajnsztajn, who is unemployed. The Chairman was profoundly indignant that on the day when the entire population had been condemned to house arrest, higher officials from his administration were gambling, for it was also determined that high stakes were involved. After a sharp reprimand, he immediately ordered Dancyger and Librach suspended and Klajnsztajn put into prison.

A NEW DIRECTOR FOR THE SONDERKOMMANDO [SPECIAL UNIT]

An acting chief has been named in connection with the suspension of the former Commandant, Dancyger. The acting Commandant is [Julian] Grosbard, an engineer and an adjutant at Order Service headquarters.

KILLED NEAR THE BARBED WIRE

On June 7, at 11:00 P.M., an official from Kripo [German criminal police] informed Precinct IV of the Order Service that the body of a man who was killed around 9:00 P.M. was to be found in a field on Marysińska Street, in the vicinity of the Orphanage. The victim is 17-year-old Elia Hersz (of 11 Zielna Street).

71. The incident and the consequences it entailed are rather enigmatic, especially if one takes into account the fact that Heinrich Himmler, SS Reichsführer, visited the ghetto on the day when people had been prohibited from leaving their houses. The Gestapo first ordered Rumkowski to publicly punish 25 people of his choosing by flogging for the shots supposedly fired. In his reply, a letter dated June 2, 1941, Rumkowski states that this order would be difficult for him to carry out and requests that he be allowed to change the punishment of flogging to 24 hours of house arrest, which, in his opinion, would be both a more painful punishment for the entire population and one that would be possible for him to carry out. (AŻIH) [AJHI] Rum. Records.

JUNE 16—22, 1941

DEATHS AND BIRTHS

Two hundred and six people died in the ghetto during this period. Seven births were registered: three boys and four girls.

MILK FOR THE SICK

Until now only children up to the age of three, infants, and women lying-in have been receiving milk. Now the sale of milk for the sick, suspended since the beginning of the year, has been restored. The proper coupons entitling a person to purchase one fifth of a liter of milk are being distributed to the sick by the office on Bałut Market on the basis of approval from the Department of Health. Milk will be sold to the sick after the children's needs have been satisfied.

TWO WOMEN KILLED

On June 17, at 4:00 A.M., a sentry shot and killed 48-year-old Chajta Nojman, a resident of 23 Urzędnicza Street. The incident took place near the barbed wire at 29 Urzędnicza Street; the victim was mentally ill and had attempted suicide on May 26.

On June 22, around 10:00 P.M., a woman was shot and killed near the barbed wire, outside the ghetto at 11 Zagajnikowa Street.

A FATAL LEAP FROM A WINDOW

Thirty-two-year-old Jakub Nasielski committed suicide on June 19 by jumping from the third-floor window of his father's apartment at 4 Kościelny Square.

JUNE 23—25, 1941

SHOT WHILE ATTEMPTING TO ESCAPE FROM THE GHETTO

At 4:00 P.M. on June 24, 22-year-old Mendel Krygier (of 13 Stary [Old] Market) and 31-year-old Beniamin Siekierka (of 100 Brzezińska Street) were shot while attempting to pass through the barbed wire at the end of Brzezińska Street. The former was shot in the arm, the latter in the shoulder blade. The victims of the incident were taken to the hospital.

A MENTALLY ILL WOMAN SHOT

There has been another shooting incident involving a mentally ill woman near the barbed wire. The victim was 36-year-old Łaja Borensztajn, a homeless person. She was taken to the hospital in critical condition.

A BEARD HUNT

On the morning of June 25, a [German] sentry on guard duty at Bałut Market stopped men with beards and either cut off their beards or sent them with members of the Order Service to the nearest barber shop.

JUNE 26-30, 1941

DEATHS AND BIRTHS

One hundred and sixty-one people died and three boys were born during this period.

SUICIDES

On the 26th, 73-year-old Aron Działkowski hung himself in a lavatory at 18 Ła-giewnicka Street, where he resided. The first aid physician pronounced the victim dead by suicide. On the same day, in a lavatory at 6 Zbożowa Street, 42-year-old Jakub Mordcha Joskowicz attempted to take his own life by swallowing a dose of a powerful poison. He was taken to his apartment in critical condition.

PRICE INCREASES

In connection with the war with the Soviets, in the last ten days of June there has been a sudden increase in the price of packaged goods, which the ghetto had received mostly from the USSR. An upward trend was also reflected in the prices of other food items, sold under the counter. Bread, for example, rose to 12 marks.

A MUSIC SCHOOL

In the very near future the School Department will open a school for music and song.[72] The most distinguished musicians living in the ghetto will be in charge of instruction.

JULY 1–5, 1941

DEATHS AND BIRTHS

One hundred and twenty-two people died in this period. Four births, of which three were boys and one a girl, were registered.

A SHOOTING

On the night of June 30, right after midnight, 23-year-old Jakub Chaim Rzezak was shot near the barbed wire at the outlet on Brzezińska Street. A First Aid Service droshky brought the wounded man to Hospital No. 1 in critical condition. The victim died on July 1, around 2:00 P.M., without having recovered consciousness. Also around midnight on July 3, Anszel Chełmiński, the janitor at 9 Jerozolimska Street (which is located near the scene of the incident) was shot dead by a sentry's rifle fire at the intersection of Franciszkańska and Smugowa streets. The victim was 33 years old. The German criminal police were informed of the incident. They ordered the body buried.

72. The music school was never opened because, as the *Chronicle* will relate, the school system as a whole ceased to exist in the ghetto the next year.

JULY 5–12, 1941

DEATHS AND BIRTHS

In the seven days reported on here, 195 people died in the ghetto (the daily average of 28 constitutes a significant decline in the mortality rate in comparison with previous periods). Twelve births were registered in that week, seven of which were male and five female.

A 14-YEAR-OLD BOY WENDS HIS WAY HERE FROM WARSAW

Recently, a 14-year-old boy, Mendel Temkin, arrived here on foot from [the ghetto of] Warsaw. The brave lad had decided to undertake the dangerous journey, without a cent in his pocket, after the death of his mother. His father had disappeared during one of the roundups. The boy had been on the road for about three weeks, staying with people on the way both in the country and in small towns. The sentry of the German guard, to whom Temkin had reported himself upon arriving at the border of the ghetto, handed him over to the authority of the Eldest of the Jews. The Chairman ordered that the boy be taken care of. The boy likes everything here in the ghetto enormously and says he is happy that he succeeded in getting out of Warsaw where, in his opinion, things are considerably worse.

EVERYONE MUST WORK

The Eldest of the Jews' Bureau of Labor has organized a special office that will be in charge of registering the men and women subject to obligatory labor in public works because they receive welfare. This is the thrust of the Eldest of the Jews' latest order: according to provisional estimates, the order issued will mobilize around 20,000 people for work. Registration is proceeding so briskly that, by the end of the week, 8,000 men and 7,500 women had already registered. Thus far, the office has sent out over 3,000 people, around 300 of them women, to various public works projects being performed in the ghetto. The majority of welfare recipients are being sent to work on the gardens and the agricultural projects, or to dig the reservoirs which were discussed in previous bulletins of the *Chronicle* [June 26–30, 1941].

FROM THE POST OFFICE

The number of food packages arriving from abroad is decreasing from day to day because of the stoppage of packages from the USSR, which had been coming before the outbreak of the war. It is worth noting that the number of packages arriving from the USSR accounted for 50 percent of the entire flow of packages and had reached 4,500 per month. At present the largest number [of packages] is coming from Portugal, which forwards all mail from America.

RACIAL SCIENTISTS[73]

A German commission of racial scientists was in the ghetto on July 8. They visited a factory at 12 Dworska Street (a ladies' dress workshop). Among other things, the

---

73. This refers to officials of the *SS-Rasse und Siedlungsamt* (Race and Resettlement Main Office), one

commission demanded information about the hospital for the mentally ill on Wesoła Street. At present there are about 50 patients in that hospital.

JULY 13–15, 1941

A SUICIDE LEAP FROM THE FOURTH FLOOR

On July 14, at around 6:00 P.M., 23-year-old Iser Gerson Rozenberg (of 43 Zgierska Street) committed suicide by leaping from the fourth floor of the stairwell at 33 Wolborska Street. A doctor from Division II of the First Aid Service pronounced him dead. The German criminal police have been informed of the incident.

A SHOOTING NEXT TO THE BARBED WIRE

On Tuesday, at ten o'clock in the morning, a woman was wounded by rifle fire at the end of Łagiewnicka Street as she attempted to leave the ghetto. Her name has not as yet been determined. She was taken unconscious by a first aid droshky to Hospital No. 1.

A GERMAN COMMISSION

On Monday a German commission visited the primary school at 29 Franciszkańska Street. The commission took an interest in the curriculum and the number of children and teachers, as well as in the subjects being taught.

[SUNDAY,] JULY 20, 1941*[74]

MAIL TO AMERICA

has been suspended since Wednesday the 17th of this month. Apparently, correspondence is not being accepted for Western Europe either.

THE REDUCTION IN THE NUMBER OF PEOPLE SUFFERING FROM CONTAGIOUS DISEASES

in comparison with last year is a truly admirable accomplishment, considering the state of near starvation experienced by the overwhelming majority of the population. The improvement is attributable to the extraordinary and unflagging work that has been done to raise the sanitary level of the ghetto. Only lung diseases increased, a direct result of malnutrition.

---

of the 12 main offices of H. Himmler's SS and Police apparatus, Reichssicherheitshauptamt—RSHA (Reich Security Main Office).

74. Some of the *Chronicle*'s daily entries for the month of July and all entries, without exception, for August, 1941, are not headed *Daily Chronicle Bulletin* but *Rumors*. In the present edition of the *Chronicle* these are marked with an asterisk after the date.

	May 1940	May 1941	June 1940	June 1941
Dysentery	73	40	2,538	45
Abdominal Typhoid Fever	44	4	45	15
Spotted Typhus	84	9	41	11
Meningitis	25	6	10	3
Encephalitis	—	1	—	1
Diphtheria	28	9	15	29
Trachoma	—	—	—	1
Scarlet Fever	15	2	4	7
Measles	7	—	1	—
Puerperal Fever	1	—	—	—
Heine-Medina	—	—	1	—
Chicken Pox	5	—	1	—
TOTALS	292	71	2,656	112
Tuberculosis	144	253	171	253

THE QUESTION OF GARDEN PLOTS

If no vegetables arrive in the ghetto by August 1, all garden plots will be subject to expropriation by the Community. Spring onions have already been requisitioned, and apparently potato plants are being recorded by the Department of Agriculture so that the owners of garden plots do not dig them up prematurely. Only large garden plots are affected by this ruling.

[TUESDAY], July 22, 1941*

SCHOOL BOOKS HAVE BEEN CENSORED

recently by a commission of teachers especially convened for that purpose. All passages and pages relating to Poland have been excised. All accounts of [Józef] Piłsudski, the Legions,[75] and so forth have been removed from the readers, and even exercises in the math books connected with the *PKO*[76] have been deleted. After inspection, the books are stamped *Geprüft* [inspected].

IT WAS RECENTLY DISCOVERED IN THE GHETTO

that the leaves of radishes and young carrots are edible if cooked. Trade in these items has assumed considerable proportions.

THE GOODS SUPPLIED TO THE GHETTO

are, as a rule, of the lowest quality—discards, shopworn, and so forth. The drugstores were recently supplied with powder in packages marked "London." How long had it sat there before finding a buyer? Wheat flour comes here from the most varied

75. Józef Piłsudski (1867–1935), statesman, head of state and marshal of Poland. During the First World War he was the commander of the Polish Legions, a military organization that fought for Poland's independence.

76. The National (Post Office) Savings Bank (Pocztowa Kasa Oszczędności) in Poland in 1919–39.

sources. Small shipments come here from the 10 to 12 mills located a few hundred meters from the ghetto; the sacks are not full, the flour has often suffered serious exposure to heat and is stale and rock hard. In the opinion of experts, this flour is from the cleanups done in the mills in the last weeks before a new harvest, or it is of such defective quality that it found no buyer elsewhere.

THE POST OFFICE

has not been accepting letters addressed to Holland, Belgium, France, and Sweden since Tuesday the 22nd. Letters to America have recently been returned to the senders and stamped: *Zurück. Kein Postverkehr* [Send back. There is no postal service].

THERE IS A CONSTANT INCREASE IN THE NUMBER OF WOMEN

in relation to the number of men. The figures here are influenced by the men's death rate, nearly twice that of the women, and also by the men's leaving the ghetto to perform manual labor. Here we submit data for the last four months:

	April 1	*May 1*	*June 1*	*July 1*
Men	100%	100%	100%	100%
Women	120.5%	122.7%	124.5%	125.2%

N.b. No people were sent out of the ghetto to perform manual labor in June.

[FRIDAY], JULY 25, 1941[*]

THE [GERMAN] AUTHORITIES HAVE DEMANDED

that the personnel of the Department of Health be at their disposal.

JEWS WHO ARE CITIZENS OF COUNTRIES

that recently entered the war continue to reside in the city.[77] Only men of draft age (17–60) have been put in Radogoszcz [prison].[78]

POLES

who had not been furnished with working papers [ID's] were recently expelled from the city in large numbers.

77. This refers to Jews who were citizens of the Soviet Union and also of the former Baltic republics, Lithuania, Latvia, and Estonia. Until war broke out between Germany and Russia on June 22, 1941, those Jews avoided persecution because the Germans, bound by the Ribbentrop-Molotov Pact of August 23, 1939, respected the rights of citizens of the USSR.

78. After occupying the city in September, 1939, the Germans formed a torture prison and later a penal camp (*Straflager*), famous for their refined methods of torturing and tormenting prisoners, in Radogoszcz, a northern suburb of Łódź, first in the former textile factory and brick works belonging to Michał Glaser and later moving to Samuel Abbe's much larger factory (both the former and the latter were Jewish properties). The prison in Radogoszcz functioned until January 18, 1945, almost to the very end of the German occupation of Łódź.

AN INCIDENT

that illustrates the mood of some Poles took place recently. On Monday of this week, a Pole called through the barbed wire to the Jews: "You won't only have nothing to eat but we won't even give you water to drink." It so happened that all the Poles who lived on that street were expelled that same night.

GHETTO HIGH-LIFE SPENDS WEEKEND IN MARYSIN

Any able-bodied person, and especially people with pull, make every effort to be in Marysin on Saturday or otherwise, God forbid, they might not be considered part of the elite.

MONDAY, JULY 28, 1941

REMOVAL OF THE MENTALLY ILL

About two months ago a German medical commission inspected the ghetto's hospital for the mentally ill on Wesoła Street. Yesterday, two German doctors accompanied by Chairman Rumkowski arrived at the hospital where, at present, 60 patients are receiving care. The hospital director presented the German doctors with a list of 12 patients who had been cured. They were examined during this inspection and five (two men and three women) were judged fit to be released from the institution. Today those five persons were sent to their places of residence. However, as to the remaining patients, the hospital received orders to prepare them to be sent from the ghetto in two groups tomorrow. Before their departure, injections were administered to the patients to keep them tranquil. The patients' families were out in front of the hospital the entire day, extremely worried about the unknown fate awaiting their relatives. It is worth noting that patients were evacuated from this same institution in March of last year.[79] At that time there were some 40 patients in the hospital.

[TUESDAY], JULY 29, 1941*

RUMORS THAT THE GHETTO BORDER GUARD IS TO ACCEPT WOMEN

have been gaining increasing currency. Invalids will be included for duty within the city and all men able to bear arms will be enlisted in the ranks. This story is supposedly based on the fact that the tailoring workshops are making women's uniforms. Jokers are exploiting this rumor to pull the legs of the naïve, assuring them that women were already standing guard; more than one person has run to check, only to find himself the butt of a prank.

---

79. All the patients deported, both in March, 1940, and in the action described here, were murdered by the Nazis in forests near Łódź.

IT IS BEING SAID

that a couple of hundred people have been arrested in the city and 40 (or 30) have been shot for attempting to evade military service.[80] The police are conducting numerous searches, apparently looking for persons shirking military service by hiding out in the ghetto. The owner of the building at 6 Pieprzowa Street has been the subject of such talk. It is also possible that they were searching for Zawadzki, a 14-year-old Christian smuggler who had escaped from the hospital. He had been wounded recently when crossing the border of the ghetto and had been in the hospital under guard of the Order Service.

QUITE TYPICAL

of conditions in the ghetto is an event that took place in Precinct III of the Order Service. A woman leaving a distribution point with two long rolls of white bread had them torn away from her by a man who appeared to be starving. He swallowed both rolls so quickly that no one had time to stop him. He was taken to Precinct III station where a discussion began on how to assist the injured party. The simplest solution seemed to be for the malefactor to turn over his ration cards for two days in the upcoming period so that the poor woman would not have to go hungry. There was no question of any loss of money here. But it turned out that his vouchers had already been sold well in advance, and the question of what to do remains.

JULY 29[?]–31, 1941

REMOVAL OF THE MENTALLY ILL

As reported in a previous bulletin, Tuesday, July 29, was the date announced by the German authorities for removing the mentally ill patients who remain under treatment at the institution on Wesoła Street. It is worth adding that the five patients released during Sunday's inspection each received, on the Chairman's orders, a loaf of bread and a quarter-kilogram package of butter upon their release. Sunday's inspection by a German doctor of the 12 patients the hospital had qualified for release was rich in dramatic episodes. The Eldest of the Jews used every argument to gain the doctor's approval for releasing all of the 12 who had been deemed cured by the institution. Specifically, the Chairman spared no efforts in regard to a certain Mr. Ilsberg, whose mental condition was on the good side. Unfortunately, while being examined, this patient became extremely nervous because he was fully aware of the horror of what was happening. His test proved unsatisfactory. Monday night, a night of tragic expectations, left the hospital staff in a state of shock. In spite of their mental confusion, the patients realized what fate was in store for them. They understood, for example, why they had been injected with tranquilizers during the night. Injections of scopolamine were used on orders from the German authorities. The patients resisted in many cases. The above-mentioned Ilsberg arranged his few belongings—

---

80. During the Nazi occupation of Łódź, military service was compulsory only for Germans and so-called Volksdeutschen (ethnic Germans).

various manuscripts—with unusual calm and thoroughness, and then bid a cordial farewell to the doctors and assistants, asking everyone to forgive him for any wrongs he might have committed while under treatment. To rule out the possibility of disturbances, no outside parties and none of the patients' relatives were allowed on the grounds of the hospital from Sunday on. The patients were evacuated in two stages, one at 11:00 A.M. and the second at 2:00 P.M. A covered pickup truck with a squad of five uniformed escorts came for the patients. Thanks to the selfless work done by the hospital staff, the loading of the tragic transport took place with exemplary order.

[FRIDAY], AUGUST 1, 1941*

TANNERS,

the last Jews still working in the city, were sent back to the ghetto yesterday.[81] The reason: an alleged fear of espionage by Jews.

ON THE EVENING OF JULY 31 A RUMOR SPREAD

that the ghetto's medical personnel had received an order at 6:00 P.M. to report to Bałut Market at 9:00 P.M.

RECENTLY, ON GOPLAŃSKA STREET

which is outside the ghetto, the [German] authorities discovered hand and machine guns. Many Poles were arrested, 250 of whom are to be shot.

IN SPITE OF BEING AWARE OF THE SAD FATE

which might be in store for mental patients, the families of people qualified for the hospital for the mentally ill are demanding that they be accepted. Since space is at such a painful premium and conditions are so deplorable in the ghetto, it is a form of deliverance for the families to have their mentally ill relatives in the hospital. Apparently, the first patient since the most recent purge has already been admitted.

TODAY

several police trucks taking Poles in the direction of Radogoszcz passed through the ghetto.

THE PRICES OF VEGETABLES

are becoming incredibly high: the outer leaves of cabbages (which, before the war, were used exclusively for feeding cattle because people would not eat them) today cost 80 pfennigs. A head of cabbage sells for 2 marks.

---

81. After the closing of the ghetto in May, 1940, a small number of Jewish skilled workers, principally rag men—that is, specialists in sorting textile remnants and workers from tailor shops and tanneries—were employed in the city, outside the ghetto. They were quartered in German workshops and were from time to time brought under guard to the ghetto to visit their relatives. In fact, even after September 1, 1941, individual specialists were employed in the city.

THE FUEL SHORTAGE

has caused kitchen stoves in private apartments to go unlit for months. In the morning and evening, [ersatz] coffee (not made to order but ready-made) sells for 5–10 pfennigs a liter and the midday meal is taken at a public kitchen. If by chance someone has something to cook, he goes "to a gas" [gas kitchen] and politely waits his turn in line.

THE SMUGGLER ZAWADZKI

who recently escaped from Hospital No. 1, where he had been under guard by the Order Service, was apprehended in the city and placed under arrest. When interrogated, he stated that he had executed his escape with the aid of a Jew and had paid a policeman 500 marks for his help. The Order Service man who had been on duty in the hospital was summoned to Kripo [German criminal police], and in spite of his passionate assurances that he was innocent, was only released two days later. He is now receiving medical attention. Zawadzki, a fourteen-year-old boy, was the major smuggler both into and out of the ghetto. He supplied saccharine, vaccines, medicines, etc., and earned colossal sums of money. His escape was executed in a highly ingenious manner: Zawadzki stated that he wanted to go to the bathroom, where the stalls were set up so that the user's feet were visible. When, after a rather long time, the patient had not come out and did not respond to knocks, the door was forced open. To their astonishment it was discovered that Zawadzki had left his shoes to deceive the guard while he escaped through a window.

IN SPITE OF THE WAR

communications between residents of the ghetto and their families in non-neutral countries has not been entirely disrupted [and is maintained] primarily by countries which are not participants in the war. Correspondence is relatively easy if one has relatives or acquaintances in those countries. They receive letters saying "say hello to Abram for us and tell him that we're all well," and knowing that Abram is, for example, in Palestine, they send the news and greetings from his family on to him. This was done quite often before but is not now a well-established practice because a significant number of neutral countries (Greece, Yugoslavia) have entered the war. Another route which, moreover, is entirely legal, is the Red Cross in Geneva. The central office of that worthy institution published printed forms on which 25 words of a purely personal nature can be written and sent to families residing in enemy countries and then, after a long wait (from Palestine to the ghetto, one way, takes seven months), replies are received printed on the same form. But most interesting were the letters that arrived directly from those countries, though they were few in number. For example, one postcard written in Yiddish and sent from Kineret (in Palestine) in February, 1941, arrived in the ghetto in May stamped by the English censor and with the *Briefstempel der Oberkommandos der Wehrmacht* [Postal Seal of the High Command of the German Armed Forces]. There was also a label attached to one side of the card which read: "Postsendungen in jiddischer Sprache und in hebräischen Schriftzeichen werden nicht befördert. Auslandsbriefstelle." [Postal materials in the Yiddish language and in Hebrew letters will not be forwarded. Office of Foreign Mail.] Nevertheless it arrived.

700 PACKAGES OF YARN

hidden in a building at 3 Zgierska Street [outside the ghetto] have been reported by the owner. They were brought into the ghetto and appraised during the night. He was induced to this action by the advanced state of building demolition on Nowomiejska Street.

[MONDAY], AUGUST 4, 1941*

ON MONDAY

there was a conference at Bałut Market in which the Chairman and representatives of the ghetto judiciary met with representatives of the German authorities. They discussed expanding the authority of the Court of the Eldest of the Jews to include matters thus far outside it, such as smuggling, crimes connected with foreign currency, the spreading of information injurious to the Reich, and murder both in and outside the ghetto. The court would be authorized to administer every degree of punishment including the death sentence.[82] In cases concerning murder and the spreading of information that could be injurious to the Reich, a motion for a death sentence by the German authorities is to be binding on the court.

AN EXTREMELY CHARACTERISTIC CASE

came before the court not long ago. A dead, flayed horse had been brought to the rubbish area for burial. Because of the lateness of the hour, the burial had to be postponed until the following day and, meanwhile, the carcass was doused with chloride for safekeeping. The next day it was discovered that the flesh had been cut away from the horse's hindquarters. The culprits were apprehended by the police and committed to trial. Their explanation was that they are extremely poor and wanted to store up a supply of meat to allay their hunger. The sentences: four weeks each.

IN VIEW OF THE CESSATION OF MEAT SUPPLIES

and the resulting suspension of sausage production, factory workers will, in the near future, be receiving 300 grams of bread and possibly some margarine as well, instead of the 200 grams of bread and 50 grams of sausage they have thus far been receiving.

THE GHETTO IS FEELING

a shortage of injections of every sort. Certain drugs cannot be purchased for their weight in gold; others, which arrived here in limited quantities, can only be procured through pull and connections. This is the background for an actual event that would

---

82. In practice, the Jewish court in the ghetto did not pass a single death sentence, nor did it even hear a case which could have led to one. Many court officials and lawyers in the ghetto spoke out against the ghetto court's passing sentences of death. Nothing is known about the German authorities' further reaction; it does appear, however, that they did not insist on their demand and let the entire matter rest.

have been unthinkable in other times. One of the best-known nurses bragged to her patient, when giving him an injection, that this time he would not feel anything at all. And, indeed, the treatment went off with extreme ease, but the usual reaction did not occur afterwards. As time passed, the entire treatment began to seem suspicious to the patient; he recalled that the top of the ampule had not been cut off and he could not find the empty ampule. He finally came to the conclusion that the nurse had been tempted to sell the now costly drug to others instead of using it on him, and had injected him with water.

FINAL EXAMINATIONS FOR GYMNASIUM DIPLOMAS[83]

will begin on September 4. The school year ends on September 30 and classes resume on the 15th of October.

NOT A SINGLE LETTER

has arrived here since June 22 from the [Soviet] territories occupied by German troops, contrary to the rumors circulating in the ghetto.

A HEARTENING DEVELOPMENT

is the growth of interest in agricultural work among Jews. Even today new garden plots have been turned over, prepared, and are producing vegetables. Even the smallest scraps of land have been put to use. Bałut never had so much greenery as it does now, nor was it ever so carefully tilled. The profits are also extraordinary given today's prices. For example, the intelligent cultivation of one square meter will yield more than six heads of cabbage; figuring 1.5 marks per head, this can bring in more than 9.0 marks; cauliflowers and onions are considerably more profitable.

"MEN'S COLLARS TAKEN IN AT THE BARBER SHOP AT 13 LUTOMIERSKA STREET"

A timely advertisement since it is now a common occurrence for collars to have become one or two sizes too large. Women with pleasant spherical shapes beyond the help of any Marienbad or Morszyn[84] now have slender, girlish figures. Weight losses of twenty or thirty kilograms, and sometimes even more, are now frequent. Certain ailments (of the stomach or liver, and heartburn, etc.) have entirely disap-

---

83. The Jewish gymnasium continued its pre-war activity to some extent in German-occupied Łódź before the establishment of the ghetto. The gymnasium resumed activity in the ghetto on March 8, 1940, that is, a little less than 2 months before the Jewish quarter (the ghetto) was closed. During the school years 1939–40 and 1940–41, a total of some 700 students of both sexes registered in the gymnasium along with those in the lyceum. The opening of the school on October 15, as announced above, did not occur, for on the next day, October 16, the first transports of Jews deported from the West began arriving in the ghetto. From then on the teachers and the students took part in receiving and finding quarters for the new arrivals, and soon thereafter the school building was put at the disposal of the deportees. Furthermore, during the great deportations from the ghetto in January–May, 1942, the entire school system began to collapse of its own and then was prohibited by the German authorities.

84. Mariánské Lázné and Morszyn were resort towns, the former in Bohemia, Czechoslovakia, the latter in the Stanisławów province in pre-war Poland and now in the Soviet Ukraine.

peared. It is disturbing, however, that for many people these losses have exceeded the permissible limits and are a symptom of muscle atrophy.

[MONDAY], AUGUST 11, 1941*[85]

IN THE COURSE OF THE LAST THREE DAYS

vegetables have been arriving in the ghetto at an average rate of 100,000 kilograms per day. Taken together with the stock in the warehouses this would permit an allocation of three kilograms per person. Yesterday, cabbage cost 80 pfennigs for 1 kilogram at the distribution points, whereas now it can be bought in the free market for 1 mark without standing in line and at a fair weight.

LAST WEEK

a freight car of meat arrived in the ghetto. It had been traveling for three days. The meat was covered with worms. After eating the sausages allocated to their factories, many workers fell ill from food poisoning and ran high fevers (39 degrees and above).

FOR THE PERIOD OF AUGUST 7–10

the Department of Soup Kitchens fixed the following menu: 20 grams of kasha, 20 grams of soup containing pieces of pressed dough, 20 grams of wheat meal, and 50 grams of cabbage per serving.

MINERAL OILS

even for oiling the sewing machines in the tailor workshops are not being sent to the ghetto. People have been trying to use light vegetable oils, that is, oils not containing stearin, as substitutes.

A "MINE" OF OIL IN THE GHETTO

Completely by accident, 10,000–12,000 kilograms of thick diatomite (*Kieselguhr*), which is used to refine oil, has been found in the ghetto. It had been tossed in the junk yard before the war, having been thought entirely useless. Today, 18–20 percent of the white rapeseed [oil], which is highly suited for technical purposes, is being extracted from the oil [found in the diatomite]. The extracts go to the Coal Department. Briquettes of the highest quality, which burn like resinous kindling chips, are being produced from coke dust, sawdust, and wood shavings, and [contain] 10 percent of those extracts; rye flour remnants from the bakeries are used as a binder.

THE MONTH OF SEPTEMBER, 1941[86]

SUICIDES

According to reports from the headquarters of the Order Service, the following incidents of suicide were noted in the ghetto through the 18th of September: On Sep-

---

85. The entry for August 11, 1941, is the last one preserved from that month.
86. Daily entries for the month of September, 1941, were either not made or not preserved.

tember 3, at 7:00 P.M., 35-year-old Efroim Regenbaum (of 25 Gnieźnieńska Street) attempted to take his own life with what is now a commonplace among suicides, namely, a leap from the bridge over Zgierska Street near NMP [Most Blessed Virgin Mary] Church. He was taken to the hospital in critical condition. On the same day, 34-year-old Mojsze Ginzberg (of 4 Koziołkiewicza Street) hung himself in his apartment. The hanged man's body was discovered the next day. On September 13, at 7:00 A.M., 22-year-old Bluma Golda Kronenberg (of 7 Jerozolimska Street) slashed her veins with a razor blade in the bathroom of the building at 8 Koszykowa Street. She was taken to the hospital. On that same day 62-year-old Majer Gelibter died of a heart attack on the street. Gelibter died in front of the building housing the Kripo [German criminal police] office at 6 Kościelna Street where he had been heading in response to a summons.

A POLE SHOT

On the night between the 8th and the 10th [sic] of September, a 32-year-old Pole, Lucjan Mikołajczyk, a resident of the neighborhood closest to the ghetto, was shot near the barbed wire. The wounded man was taken to Hospital No. 1.

THE REMAINS OF THREE MEN BROUGHT TO THE GHETTO

In the first three days of September the German authorities turned over the remains of three men for burial in the ghetto. They were Abram Josek Grossman of 8/6 Dolna Street (his remains came from the city), and Mendel Hannstein and Perec Błaszkowski of 2/3 Mickiewicz Street (their remains came from the Radogoszcz prison). The remains were photographed before burial. There is a supposition, based in particular on the external appearance of one of the corpses, that they died violent deaths.

A REDUCTION IN THE BREAD RATION

Beginning in the last ten days of September the daily bread ration has been reduced from 40 grams to 33 grams. In view of the reduced bread ration each person now receives a loaf for six days, whereas until now a loaf was for five days.

DEPARTMENT OF VITAL STATISTICS INSPECTED

On September 19, the director of the Department of Vital Statistics of the city, the head of the court, and several other German officials came to the Department of Vital Statistics here at 4 Miodowa Street. The ghetto's birth and death records were inspected. The purpose of the inspection was to coordinate procedures in the city and the ghetto.

A DEATH AT THE POLICE STATION

On September 20, a hearse was summoned to the premises of the [German] criminal police to take the body of 55-year-old Artur Berkowicz (of 33 Wolborska Street) to the cemetery. An informer for the criminal police from the very inception of the ghetto, Berkowicz died a sudden death. He had been released from prison in the city a few weeks ago, after having served six months.

POSTAL CHANGES

As of the 15th of September postal communication with France, Belgium, and Holland has been restored. However, in the last ten days of September, special delivery letters of every sort and telegrams to the Protectorate [the Generalgouvernement][87] have been suspended. From now on telegrams may only be sent from the ghetto to the Reich.

SUMMER HOLIDAY

On Saturday, the 6th of September, a show entitled *A Summer Holiday* was staged by the Marysin administration at the House of Culture. The cast of the program, which lasted several hours, was composed exclusively of children who were at Marysin to study or to rest. The program included choral singing, recitations, vignettes of the children's lives in Marysin, dance, farces, and so on. As a whole it was truly impressive. The children displayed genuine talent in all their performances. Guests present by invitation filled every seat and the Community's administration was fully represented. At the end of this pleasant entertainment, the Chairman delivered a short speech in which he indicated that concern for children would remain at the forefront of his activities. There is no sacrifice too great when it is a question of helping the ghetto's youngest inhabitants. After the Chairman's speech, the little children made a ring around him on the stage and danced joyously accompanied by the sound of music and cheers for the ghetto's first citizen. The Chairman gave a present of bread and candy to each of the show's young performers.

TRAMCARS PUT INTO SERVICE

As a result of long-standing efforts by the Eldest of the Jews, the ghetto was provided with a tram system on September 13. Two motor-driven cars (of the old type), as well as several tramcars, were handed over for use in the ghetto. Engineer Dawidowicz has been appointed director of the tram system. The metal workshop announced a few prospective drivers. The [German] authorities have assigned an instructor for one week's time to train the driver candidates. The tramcars will provide transportation between Marysin and Bałut Market. Tramlines will be laid between Brzezińska Street and Marysin (the rails on streets free of traffic will be used for this purpose), and further efforts are also under way to obtain rails from outside the ghetto. The trams caused a veritable sensation in the ghetto when they were used, for the first time, to instruct the drivers.

Two days after the tramcars were turned over to the ghetto, a German commission accompanied by Chairman Rumkowski and Engineer Dawidowicz visited the dress factory at 6 Jakuba Street and considered the possibility of extending the tramline from Franciszkańska Street to the building where the factory is located.

---

87. The *Generalna Gubernia* in Polish; an administrative unit created on the strength of a decree by Hitler on October 12, 1939, initially composed of the Cracow, Warsaw, Lublin, and Radom districts, often popularly referred to as the Protectorate, as was the administrative unit created by the Germans in Bohemia and Moravia on March 16, 1939.

THE JEWISH NEW YEAR 5702

This year the holidays fell on the 22d and 23d of September. The Community's offices were closed on New Year's day. Only the Department of Food Supply and the utility services were in operation. On Sunday and Monday, Chairman Rumkowski could not take part in services due to illness. The leader of the ghetto attended a New Year's service, while convalescing, on Tuesday [September 23] at the House of Culture on Krawiecka Street. The Chairman delivered a speech to those present in which he expressed his joy at being able to pray along with everyone else after an illness that had kept him home on the first day of the holidays. The Eldest of the Jews said that menacing clouds were hanging over the ghetto as the New Year began, and he asked people to pray to God that He spare the Jews of the ghetto from any new affliction. The Chairman assured everyone that he [continued to] stand guard over the fate of the Community and that he trusted that the Community would successfully extricate itself from all its difficulties.

At four o'clock the Chairman received a delegation of officials, who had come to offer him their greetings for the New Year, in his apartment at the Łagiewnicka [Street] hospital. At the beginning of the reception, the apartment swarmed with children who had been sent as delegates from the elementary schools, gymnasiums, orphanages, summer camps, etc. The schoolchildren presented the Chairman with a beautifully made album containing more than 14,000 signatures. Each school had included a decorated card with the name of the school in the album.[88] The Chairman made a short speech to the children thanking them for coming and wishing them a Happy New Year. Then, in the lobby of his apartment, the Chairman heard a report from the section of mailmen and later, in front of the hospital, in ceremonial fashion, he heard similar reports from the Order Service, the Fire Department, and the chimney sweeps. The exchange of New Year's greetings was interrupted shortly after the ceremony began by the summoning of the Chairman to Bałut Market by the German authorities. This happened because, at that same time, final deliberations were under way in connection with the resettling of groups of many thousands of Jews from various locales to the west—some close to the ghetto, others farther away—into the ghetto.

A TROUBLED MOOD

The news about the sudden interruption of the New Year's ceremony at the Chairman's apartment spread like wildfire through the ghetto, creating endless versions of the most varied and, often, panic-producing sort, as well as conjectures as to the new complications that would soon descend on the ghetto. The next few days were marked by a strong sense of anxiety and a mood of general depression. Chief among the flood of rumors circulating under the influence of that mood was that a throng of more than 20,000 Jews, expelled from their small towns, was to be resettled in the ghetto. People even spoke of a possibility significantly worse than that, namely, the forcible evacuation of part of the ghetto's population, the conscription of the entire male population for manual labor, and a division of the ghetto into two parts: one inhabited by workers and artisans from the workshops and the other by the re-

88. The album mentioned has been preserved in its entirety and is presently located in the Archives of the YIVO Institute for Jewish Research in New York (Nachman Zonabend Collection).

mainder of the population. People were also talking about a large section being severed from the ghetto, and about a project to introduce additional identification badges for Jews in the form of two new stars.[89] Obviously, all these Job-like prognoses were devoid of any authoritative basis, and their circulation, which increased the sense of depression, was the result of stupidity and ill will. That fact was often mentioned by Chairman Rumkowski in his speeches and his appeals to ghetto society to struggle against the troublemakers who disturb the peace, the rumor-mongers, the fantasizers, and other such people of ill will. At no other point in the history of the ghetto has gossip run so wild and rampant, so reckless and unchecked. This criminal, anti-social behavior deserves condemnation because it is occurring at a truly important moment that requires complete equilibrium and calm from the ruling circles, whose intense efforts can only produce their best results when they have the social unity of the entire population as their foundation. Chairman Rumkowski's watchword—*calm*—has never been more relevant than in this situation, and the need for calm has now moved to the forefront of the ghetto's problems.

LARGE NUMBER OF NEWCOMERS TO BE SETTLED IN THE GHETTO

Upon the announcement by the German authorities of the supposed forthcoming settlement of large groups of Jews in this ghetto, the enormous machinery of office workers was put into full operation immediately to acquire detailed information as to the possibility of absorbing newcomers, primarily with regard to the housing problem, whose critical state has been a fundamental and widespread sore point from the ghetto's very beginning. The job of determining the density of the population began on Tuesday the 23d and has been going full force, day and night, ever since. Precise figures have been established as to residents, rooms, habitable areas, and types of buildings (stone, wooden, etc.). All results, acquired by truly Sisyphean labor, are communicated at once to the Chairman, for whom they serve as incontestable documents required for his conversations with the [German] officials—who have the final say. As in a series of earlier emergencies, the attorney [Henryk] Neftalin has been called upon to direct this most essential campaign. It is due to his experience and outstanding organizational abilities that the work is proceeding so cohesively and efficiently. Besides officials from the Department of Housing, and workers from the Department of Population Records and the Department of Economics and Finance, other departments also are taking part in this campaign. The result will be that the ghetto will not be caught off guard by any new circumstances connected with the resettlement of the masses of evacuees who are being exiled here, and everything possible will be done so that the new arrivals have a roof over their heads with the least possible trouble.

THE JEWS FROM WŁOCŁAWEK AND ENVIRONS

On September 26 the first transport arrived, as announced, bearing new residents for the ghetto. More than 900 people, almost exclusively women and children, all of whom had been expelled from Włocławek, arrived by rail at the Radogoszcz sidetrack [in Marysin]. The Eldest of the Jews ordered that the newcomers be given the best possible care. They have provisionally been quartered in houses at Marysin and in the

---

89. In the Łódź ghetto, Jews were compelled by an order from the German authorities, issued on December 11, 1939, to wear two yellow Stars of David, one on the right side of the chest, the other on the back.

prison building that had been vacated for the holiday furlough. They have all received food free of charge from the Community. On the day after their arrival, the new residents were sent to the baths. The women say that the orders to abandon Włocławek were distributed on the second day of the New Year's holiday. The ghetto in Włocławek had about 4,000 people. On that day, all those who had received the relevant summons were quartered together (in a building that had formerly been a monastery). Part of the baggage taken by the exiles was, as they have stated, confiscated while they were at the baths in Włocławek. Their remaining property was registered as baggage and will arrive here in a few days. Furthermore, from the women's accounts it appears that the deportations from the Włocławek ghetto included the poorest segments of the population, who had been supporting themselves by working on public works projects. (The men, however, had been separated from their families and taken away to perform manual labor.) The residents of the Włocławek [ghetto] are able to travel outside the ghetto upon presentation of a pass, and their ration cards allow them to receive 25 grams of bread per day (the price of bread is 3 marks on the private market). Other items are at a level not significantly higher than is to be found outside the ghetto. The wages for public works projects are 10 marks per week.

The next transport arrived on the 29th and consisted of over one thousand residents of small towns located in the vicinity of Włocławek,[90] again nearly all women and children. The deportees from the small towns in the Kujawy [region][91] had been wearing different Jewish identity badges: a yellow triangle on the middle of the back and a cut-out Star of David, one quarter meter in size, hung on the chest. The second transport also received full care from the local authorities.

SUICIDE ATTEMPTS

On September 27, at 3:00 P.M., 45-year-old Rywka Rajcher, a worker and resident of 11 Ciemna Street, threw herself from a third-story window at 15 Młynarska Street. She was taken in critical condition to Hospital No. 1, where she died two hours later without having regained consciousness.

On the same day, and also at 3:00 P.M., 58-year-old Majer Federman leaped from the upper level of the bridge at Kościelna Street to the pavement below. He suffered broken arms and legs. He was taken to Hospital No. 1 in critical condition.

OCTOBER 1–15, 1941[92]

WEATHER

From October 1 to 8 the weather remained beautiful and sunny and the sky cloudless.

90. Włocławek, a town situated on the Vistula River, to the northwest of Łódź in Bydgoszcz province. Before the war, around 12,000 Jews lived there, constituting one-third of the population. In December, 1939, during the great resettlement of Jews from the western territories of Poland, chiefly from those incorporated into the Reich, the majority of the Jews were driven out of Włocławek to various towns and cities in the Generalgouvernement.

91. Chiefly from Brześć Kujawski, Chodecz, Kowal, and Lubraniec.

92. The entries for October 1–15, which were preserved in incomplete form, are here given in their entirety. Entries for October 16–31 were either not made at all or have been lost. This explains why the Chronicle has no descriptions of the very moment when some 20,000 Jews from Germany, Austria, Bohemia, and Moravia, as well as Luxembourg, were resettled into the Łódź ghetto. The arrival of the Jews from the West lasted from October 16 to November 4, 1941.

The mornings were cool, with the temperature rising in the course of the day. On October 9 the weather took a sudden turn for the worse; this was the first day of foul autumn weather. The sun came back out on the 10th, but rainy weather marked by frequent showers began on the 11th. The first snow fell on the night of the 12th, accompanied by furious gale winds. Until mid-month, temperatures remained constant, the days were overcast, clearings were rare, and rain frequent.

ARRESTS

During the first half of October, 89 persons were arrested for theft, 14 for resisting the authorities, and 216 for various other offenses. It is worth noting that October 1 was an exceptional day in the ghetto's annals of crime, for there were no arrests that day.

DEATHS AND BIRTHS

In the first half of October, 277 people died in the ghetto. Eighteen births were registered, of which twelve were boys and six girls. One baby was stillborn.

October 9 marked the lowest daily death rate since the inception of the ghetto. Scarcely 11 people died that day. It is worth noting here that the highest daily death rate, 55, occurred in June, 1940, when the dysentery epidemic was at its height.

AN ACCIDENT DURING A DEMOLITION

On October 1, during the demolition of a building that had formerly been a dyeworks, a chimney collapsed at 33 Wolborska Street injuring a 12-year-old boy, Aron Zylberberg, a resident of that building. The accident victim was taken to Hospital No. 1 where, the following day, he gave up the ghost.

SUICIDE ATTEMPTS

On October 1, at 9 o'clock in the morning, Szlama Kluczkowski (of 7 Jerozolimska Street) attempted suicide by swallowing eight Luminal tablets. An emergency physician administered first aid. Kluczkowski is 41 years old and a house painter by trade. On October 6, 25-year-old Izrael Majlech Twardowicz (of 2 Młynarska Street) took a large dose of iodine in the stairway of his building in order to take his own life. He was brought to Hospital No. 1 by the First Aid Service. On October 9, 47-year-old Mojsze Liberman, a weaver by trade, hung himself in his apartment at 66 Zgierska Street. The German criminal police were informed of Liberman's death by suicide. On October 10 at 6:25 P.M., 30-year-old Nuchem Jagoda (of 37 Zawisza Street) leaped from a third-floor window of a building on Franciszkańska Street. The First Aid Service brought him to Hospital No. 1 where he gave up the ghost after two days. On October 11, 21-year-old Szajndla Wyszegrodzka (of [?]7 Żydowska Street) attempted to take her own life. The young woman swallowed Lysol; she was taken unconscious to Hospital No. 1.

A MURDER

A murder was committed on October 9. This is the third murder to be uncovered in the ghetto. The incident took place in the apartment of Szmul Jankiel Litwak, a house painter, at 28 Lotnicza Street. The bloody course of events ran as follows. Litwak's brother-in-law Szlojme Bornsztajn lived close by, specifically at 32 Lotnicza Street. A few days before the incident Bornsztajn had loaned his brother-in-law his jacket, from which he had neglected to remove some ten or fifteen marks. Bornsztajn demanded that his brother-in-law return the money to him, but to no avail. On the fateful day he went to see Litwak, who continued to claim that he had found no money in the jacket and that he had not a cent himself. The injured party (according to his subsequent deposition) requested that Litwak at least give him a few marks to buy some bread. He again met with a refusal from Litwak, who at that moment was playing cards (*stoss* [game of hazard]) for money. When Litwak placed a 5–mark bill on the table, his brother-in-law attacked him with a crowbar. A life-or-death struggle ensued. The exact progress of events has still not been determined because the eyewitnesses, the other gamblers (Bałut riffraff), are clearly not presenting a truthful account of the fight. Apparently Litwak drew his knife in self-defense. He suffered terrible wounds from the crowbar and was taken to the hospital where he died with great suffering. Bornsztajn, the murderer, hid for four days to avoid arrest. He was arrested at 10 o'clock in the evening on the 13th in an apartment at 38 Zawisza Street. He was placed at the disposal of the prosecutor. The murderer is a criminal well known in Bałut by the nickname Szlojma Shnyrl (Shloyme the Rope). He had been living on welfare in the ghetto. According to his own words, he had worked as a peddler before the war, had a long criminal past that predated the war, and had already been sentenced three times by the local authorities for theft and extortion.

THE MONTH OF NOVEMBER, 1941

DEATHS AND BIRTHS

During the month of November, 914 people died in the ghetto and 29 births were registered (13 boys and 16 girls).

PEDESTRIAN RUN OVER

On November 6, 40-year-old Laja Breneskowska (of 48 Brzezińska Street) was run over by a [German] car on Brzezińska Street near No. 48. The accident victim was taken to the hospital where she died.

DEATH IN A LAVATORY

On November 22, at 9:30 A.M., the body of 75-year-old Anszel Gruner, resettled here from Vienna, was found in a lavatory in the building at 34 Żydowska Street. His sudden death had been caused by a heart attack.

RESTAURANTS DOING BRISK BUSINESS

Since the transports arrived from Germany, all the restaurants and pastry shops in the ghetto, half-empty until then, have truly been besieged by newcomers. It should be emphasized, since this is a characteristic phenomenon, that from the moment they arrived, the newcomers began selling their personal property and, with the cash they received, began to buy up literally everything available on the private food market. In the course of time, this caused a shortage in food supply, and prices rose horrendously with indescribable speed. On the other hand, the availability of all sorts of items which had been lacking in the ghetto for quite a while has caused trade to become brisk, and a few of the ghetto's stores have shelves filled with goods that have not been seen in the ghetto for a long time. Because of the newcomers, who are popularly known as *yekes*, stores never really closed their doors in the month of November. They sold their clothing, shoes, linen, cosmetics, traveling accessories, and so forth. For a short while this caused a decline in prices for the most varied items; however, to match the price increase on the food market, the newcomers began to raise the prices of the items they were selling. From the point of view of the ghetto's previous inhabitants, this relatively large increase in private commerce has caused undesired disturbances and difficulties and, what is worse, the newcomers have, in a short span of time, caused a devaluation of the [ghetto] currency. That phenomenon is particularly painful for the mass of working people, the most important segment of ghetto society, who only possess the money they draw from the coffers of the Eldest of the Jews.

264 OF THE NEWLY ARRIVED POPULATION

left in the November transports to perform manual labor in Germany. Of that number 20 were women. Lots had been drawn at their lodgings to determine the candidates.

POSTAL SERVICE TO [THE EASTERN PART OF] POLAND MINOR SUSPENDED

On November 1 the Post Office here received instructions not to accept any correspondence for the eastern [Polish] provinces, which were taken by the USSR [in September 1939]. The restrictions do not, however, apply to mail arriving from the above-mentioned areas. Thus, letters, as well as money orders, continue to arrive in the ghetto from Lwów, Tarnopol, Stanisławów, etc.[93]

BREAD RATION REDUCED

On November 3 the daily bread ration was reduced from 33 grams to 28 grams. This was caused by the increase in the ghetto's population. It should be stressed that the food allocations underwent no change initially because it was not possible to take the newcomers into consideration. Consequently, the ghetto's reserves were stripped bare for the benefit of the new arrivals.

DIFFICULTIES IN RECRUITING WORKERS TO WORK OUTSIDE THE GHETTO

In November the Bureau of Labor received an order from the [German] authorities to make up a transport of 1,000 men to be shipped to Germany to perform manual labor. Preparing this relatively small contingent has presented more serious difficulties than occurred last year, when a few thousand people were being sent from the ghetto each month. The cause of the problem is the terrible state of health among the candidates. The medical commission was barely able to qualify 25 percent of the

93. The provinces of Lwów, Tarnopol, and Stanisławów were incorporated into the Generalgouvernement as the fifth district, in addition to the districts of Cracow, Warsaw, Lublin, and Radom, under the name *Distrikt Galizien*.

candidates for work outside the ghetto and, furthermore, in a final review by German doctors, a portion of them were rejected as well.

THE "GYPSY CAMP"[94]

Beginning on November 5 and continuing for a few days, transports arrived at the Gypsy camp, which has been set up in the blocks of houses on the border of the ghetto at Brzezińska Street and surrounded by Towiańska, Starosikawska, and Głowacka streets. The area earmarked for quartering the "Gypsies" has been separated from the ghetto by two sets of enmeshed barbed wire while the ditches, which had previously been dug in front of the barbed wire and were later to be filled with water, have now been filled in again for technical reasons. The ditches could have posed a threat to the foundations of the buildings located in their immediate vicinity. The transports are arriving at the Gypsy camp via the Radogoszcz station and are under the escort each time of large detachments of storm troopers. The authorities of the Eldest of the Jews have received orders to supply the camp with provisions and medical assistance.

AIR-RAID ALERT

An air-raid alert was ordered for the first time in the history of the ghetto on the night of November 8. The street lights were turned off around midnight after the sirens had sounded three times. As soon as the alert began the local OPL[95] [Air Defense League] immediately ordered lights out in the work places that were open that night. Workshops are not bound by regulation to have their windows blacked out but are obliged to extinguish all lights upon the sounding of the alarm.

SUPPLYING THE GYPSY CAMP WITH FOOD

With regard to the previous note on the Gypsy camp, it is worth adding that during the first six days of its existence the camp was supplied with soup and coffee by the local Department of Soup Kitchens. Thereupon, two kitchens installed by the local

94. The Gypsies resettled into the Łódź ghetto came from Burgenland in eastern Austria, on the Hungarian border, as clearly stated in correspondence between the Reich's Ministry of Internal Affairs and the German authorities in Łódź, who were not particularly pleased that "their" city was to receive Jews from Germany and Gypsies ("20,000 Altreichsjuden und 5,000 burgenländische Zigeuner," letter from Marder, Bürgermeister of Litzmannstadt, to Fuchs, Ministerialdirigent of October 24, 1941).

Before Austria was incorporated into the Reich in 1938, Burgenland was an autonomous, federal province that was inhabited by Croatians, Hungarians, and Gypsies, as well as Austrians. During the war, both in the ghetto and outside it, especially in Resistance circles, it was mistakenly thought that these were not Gypsies but Yugoslav partisans. That is what the Resistance's *Biuletyn Informacyjny*, published in Warsaw on March 2, 1942, wrote of them, for example, as did Jakub Poznański in his memoir of the Łódź ghetto, in an entry dated December 24, 1943. Evidently, the authors of the *Chronicle* were not entirely clear on this matter, which, among other things, explains why, when the Gypsies in the ghetto are referred to, the word *Gypsies* is sometimes, and arbitrarily, placed in quotation marks. The nearly unanimous opinion that these were not Gypsies may have arisen from the fact that some of them knew Serbo-Croatian. It is not out of the question that the Germans included some inconvenient and unruly Croatians residing in Burgenland in the transports.

The English version of the *Chronicle* puts the words *Gypsies* and *Gypsy Camp* in quotation marks wherever they were so used in the original.

95. *Obrona Przeciw Lotnicza*. Here, curiously enough, the chroniclers use the acronym of the prewar Polish anti-aircraft defense.

Building Department were put into operation on the camp grounds. The office of the Eldest of the Jews is passing the cost of supplying the camp with food on to the [German] Ghetto Administration.

A COUNTERFEITER IN COURT

On November 14 the Court of the Eldest of the Jews examined the case of Rauchwerger and his assistants, who are charged with having counterfeited two-mark notes. The Rauchwerger case, whose disclosure was noted in the April [in fact, July 26] bulletin of the *Chronicle*, is the most sensational event in the ghetto's annals of crime. The accused, a prominent professional engraver, had succeeded in counterfeiting 5,500 two-mark notes quite accurately and precisely. The counterfeiting was discovered by chance, someone having noticed two bills with the same number. It became necessary to withdraw all two-mark bills from circulation. The counterfeiter had been etching the plates with acids.

The case against the counterfeiter's assistants, Mr. and Mrs. Cederbaum, has been thrown out in view of the fact that the Cederbaums had left the ghetto before the trial, having been forcibly sent to do manual labor in Germany. The accused admitted his guilt, although, despite the depositions of his codefendants, which were read at the trial, he maintained that he had pursued his underhanded dealings with the knowledge of his "partners." However, it would appear from the above-mentioned documents that the Cederbaums had demonstrated that they were only blind tools used by Rauchwerger to exchange his counterfeit [ghetto] bills, primarily for German marks. The accused had been engaged in counterfeiting from the fall of 1940 until June of 1941, that is, until the time of his arrest. It is worth noting a peculiar factor revealed in the course of the trial, namely, that the accused and his entire family had literally been living in a state of extreme poverty despite his enormous profits. The court sentenced Rauchwerger to a year of imprisonment under severe conditions and a 500-mark fine in lieu of two months of imprisonment. (The accused was deported from the ghetto in the first stage of the deportation campaign in January, 1942.)[96]

ARTISTS AMONG THE NEWCOMERS TAKE PART IN CONCERTS

By the second half of November the House of Culture began to organize concert performances in which the newcomers took part. From the very beginning these concerts have been a great attraction for music lovers. It is worth mentioning that one result of the resettling of new people here is that the ghetto has acquired an array of talented performers—pianists and singers. The piano performances by maestro [Leopold] Birkenfeld of Vienna[97] deserve special mention. Each of Birkenfeld's concerts is truly a feast for the ghetto's music lovers. On orders from the Chairman, the House of Culture had, by mid-November, begun registering all the musicians, actors, singers, and painters who had arrived here in the transports. The number of those registered has now reached some thirty or so persons.

96. The final sentence was obviously added on later.
97. On May 14, 1942, Leopold Birkenfeld was in one of the transports of Jews deported from the Łódź ghetto to the death camp in Chełmno.

SHOOTINGS

According to Order Service reports, the following shooting incidents took place in the month of November:

On the 16th, at 7:30 P.M., Fryderyk Mautner was shot at the barbed wire near the bridge by the [Most Blessed Virgin Mary] church. The victim had arrived in the ghetto on October 22 from Prague and had been living in collective housing at 37 Łagiewnicka Street.[98] A first aid droshky was called for the critically wounded man and he was taken to Hospital No. 1. He died in the hospital at 8:45 P.M.

On the 21st, at 12:15 P.M., Chaja Sura Tragsbetrieger was shot dead at the barbed wire near 27 Zgierska Street. The victim was 52 years old and had lived at 21 Zgierska Street.

On the 25th, at 5:30 P.M., a 43-year-old tailor, Mordcha Józef Wolf (of 21 Wrześnieńska Street) was shot to death at the intersection of Stodolniana and Podrzeczna streets.

On that same day, at 6:30 A.M., 36-year-old Moszek Peres Schlesinger, a tailor and resident of 21 Modra Street, was shot dead in front of 42 Wrześnieńska Street.

On the 27th, 39-year-old Juda Israel Julius (of 16 Starosikawska Street) was shot dead at the intersection of Mianowski and Starosikawska streets. The victim was a native of Poznań.

On the 29th, at 7:00 A.M., a newcomer from Vienna, Lili Wälder, was shot dead near the barbed wire at the intersection of Okopowa and Franciszkańska streets. Born in 1911, she was a resident of 41 Brzezińska Street. The victim had been suffering from nervous depression.

On the 30th, at 9:15 A.M., an unidentified woman was shot dead near the barbed wire on Przemysłowa Street.

A PUBLIC FLOGGING

On November 21 the janitor of a coal yard, who had been caught in the act of stealing coal, was publicly flogged on a square in Marysin.

AN OFFICE FOR RESETTLED PERSONS

On November 24 the Chairman came to a decision to create a special office for the ghetto's new settlers. This office's authority will include all matters relating to the twenty thousand people who have arrived here from Western Europe and the three thousand Jews who arrived here at the end of September from Włocławek and its environs. Henryk Neftalin, the attorney, has been put in charge of running this new office.

HIDDEN FURS AND HIDES DISCOVERED

Searches conducted by the Special Unit in the final days of November have uncovered large reserves of hides, both finished and unfinished, that were being kept concealed.

---

98. The Jews deported from the West were quartered in collectives, often in former school buildings, according to the cities from which they had come. Thus, the housing and transports were given the names of those cities. A transport with the name of a given city and a roman numeral, for example, Berlin I, was sometimes quartered in more than one building. Only a very small number of the new arrivals succeeded in finding individual apartments.

This "warehouse" was located 1.5 meters beneath the floor at 45 Lutomierska Street, at the home of a Mr. Krygier. A large amount of valuable furs, such as astrakhan and broadtail, was discovered at 2 Żydowska Street.

WILL GYPSIES BE WORKING IN THE WORKSHOPS?

On the last day of November there was a rumor circulating in the ghetto that the people who had been placed in the Gypsy camp would be recruited to work in workshops here, specifically, in the tannery and straw shoe workshops. For the sake of accurate chronicling, it is worth noting that the source of that rumor was a plan which, *nota bene*, did not materialize; namely, the authorities had been planning to set up a tannery and a straw shoe workshop on the grounds of the Gypsy camp. There has never been any question of recruiting the inhabitants of the camps to work in the ghetto. The workshops in the Gypsy camp did not materialize, only some preliminary work, like the shredding of old cloth and so on, was done there.

MONDAY, DECEMBER 1, 1941

GHETTO POPULATION 163,623 ON DECEMBER 1

This is the highest the ghetto's population has ever been. In May of last year, at the time the ghetto was closed off, the number of inhabitants came to 160,000, and before the transports arrived from the Kujawy [region], the Reich, Austria, and Bohemia, that is, before September 26 of this year, there had been a constant decline in population which, in percentages, had greater meaning because of the high mortality rate here. The population underwent the following changes in November: On the first, the population stood at 159,505. There were 6,163 new additions in the course of the month—6,084 from the transports, 29 births (one of which was stillborn and one premature), 25 people arrived from the Generalgouvernement and Warthegau, five returned from prison, the bodies of two people were sent back to the ghetto, six returned from work on the railroad, 10 returned from the October 15th and 16th transports that took people out of the ghetto to perform manual labor.[99] The decline in November was as follows: 914 died (including stillbirths and bodies sent back to the ghetto for burial), one woman left the ghetto, 1,130 were sent out to perform manual labor in Germany. All told, the ghetto declined by 2,045 in November. Thus, the increase for November came out to 4,118 people.

INTERMENT OF THE DEAD IN THE GYPSY CAMP

On November 12, the local Department of Burials received orders from the German criminal police to take charge of interring the remains of those persons dying in the Gypsy camp. As of today, the Department of Burials has buried 213 people who had been confined in the above-mentioned camp. In accordance with the orders from the German criminal police, the Department of Burials is obliged to send a hearse to the grounds of the Gypsy camp every day no later than 9:00 A.M. Since there are frequently

99. The numbers do not total 6,163.

many bodies ready for interment, the hearses now arrive at the camp by six o'clock in the morning. On the day when the mortality rate was at its highest, 26 corpses were taken from the camp for burial. In the beginning (transports were rushed to the camp starting November 8 and, according to information in possession here, the population of the camp stood at 5,000) the overwhelming majority of the bodies removed from the camp were those of children. It was only toward the end of last month that there were more adults than children being buried. The bodies of the "Gypsy camp's" residents are buried in a specially isolated portion of the Jewish cemetery which, at the ghetto's inception, had been designated for the interment of the local Gypsies.[100] Thus far, that isolated section has comprised an area of 300 square meters. The Department of Burials does not receive any personal data on the corpses from the camp. The bodies are received without clothing and, most frequently, are in their underclothing. The department is under orders to bury bodies within the course of the day, but quite often, when it is necessary to bury a greater number of bodies, the cemetery carpenters are, for technical reasons, unable to prepare a sufficient number of covered boxes to serve as coffins. In those cases the bodies are buried on planks, as is the normal practice when interring Jews.[101] The Department of Burials reports the number of bodies buried to Kripo [German criminal police] on a daily basis. The hearses do not operate on Saturdays.

As of December 1, three Protestants, part of the ghetto's new population, had been buried, one of whom was a German Christian who, not wishing to be divorced from his Jewish wife, was sent to the ghetto here along with her.

TWO PEOPLE SHOT ON ZGIERSKA [STREET]

Today, at 3:00 P.M., there was a shooting incident on Zgierska Street. A man and a woman were pushing a handcart near number 15 Zgierska Street. Due to the narrowness of the sidewalk at that point, the cart struck a post which supported the barbed wire separating the sidewalk from the street. Directly beside that post is a guard booth where a sentry was on duty at the critical moment. The sentry leaped out of his booth, shot the woman dead with his rifle, without a word of warning, and then trained his weapon on her companion. He attempted to save himself by fleeing into a gateway, but he too was felled by a bullet, receiving a critical stomach wound. Witnesses to the incident, which caused a wild panic on Zgierska Street, have furnished information on other dramatic elements in the situation. In a short while, representatives of the secret police [Gestapo] and the criminal police [Kripo], as well as the chief of the Order Service and the head of the Bureau of Investigation, arrived on the scene. The identity of the woman killed is still not known. The wounded man is Wolf Weder, a 28-year-old bachelor who resides at 86 Zgierska Street. He was taken to Hospital No. 1 in a state near death.

FROZEN TO DEATH AT THE CEMETERY

Yesterday, around 4:00 P.M., 65-year-old Szmul Funkensztajn was found frozen to death. The deceased had been a resident of the Old People's Home, which he had left of his own accord on the 24th of November.

---

100. That is, Gypsies from Łódź and the vicinity who had lived in Poland before the war.
101. Cf. p. 20, n. 27.

AN OLD PEOPLE'S HOME FOR THE NEW POPULATION

Today an extremely important institution for public use came into being. This is an Old People's Home which has been designated for the ghetto's new population. In view of the abnormally large percentage of old people among the ghetto's new population, the establishment of a special shelter resolves one of the most pressing needs created by the increase of the ghetto's population to 20,000. The Chairman has designated a few residential buildings which are—for the ghetto—in exceptionally good condition and are located on Gnieźnieńska Street near Wrześnieńska Street for that purpose. The Construction Department, known for its record speed, is doing the necessary repairs on those buildings, which will house a few thousand old people. Today, the first 46 lodgers took up residence in one of the buildings.

ARRIVALS IN THE GHETTO

Today the following persons were brought to the ghetto: the two Rybicki sisters, 13-year-old Zofia and 17-year-old Zdzisława, who had until now resided outside the ghetto at 114 Brzezińska Street. The girls were brought to the ghetto because their mother is Jewish. The girls were lodged in the orphanage at 76 Franciszkańska Street. The following people were brought under escort from Bełchatów: Chaim Szpiro (b. 1913), a married couple, Icek (b. 1908) and Chaja (b. 1909) Grunbaum; and from Ozorków—Jersz [Hersz] Słotkowski (b. 1887) and Gabriel Majster (b. 1903). The five persons mentioned above were placed in Central Prison here and are at the disposal of the Gestapo.

TUESDAY, DECEMBER 2, 1941

NEW MAGISTRATES SWORN IN

Yesterday, at the Court of the Eldest of the Jews, ceremonies were held on the occasion of the swearing-in of the new magistrates. A few days ago, as the bulletin [of the month of November] has already noted, the court engaged the services of three prosecutors, three judges and one court clerk from among the former lawyers who had arrived in the transports from Germany, [as well as from] Vienna and Prague. It is worth noting parenthetically that at least 500 former lawyers and magistrates have arrived in the ghetto with the transports, and in particular with those from Prague [102] All the new appointees have a command of the Yiddish language in accordance with the court's binding agreement. The full staff of the court was present at the swearing-in, and there were two rabbis present as well, one from the ghetto and the recently appointed rabbi from Germany, who were there to administer the oath. The deed of oath was drawn up in four languages: Hebrew, Yiddish, German, and Polish. The oath ran as follows: "In assuming the post of judge or prosecutor in the Court of the Eldest of the Jews in Litzmannstadt, I, with a pure heart and without ulterior motive, do promise and swear to the Almighty that, with a full sense of my responsibility to the

102. There were also Jews from Germany and Austria, who had emigrated to Czechoslovakia after Hitler took power, in the transports from Prague.

Almighty, to the people, and to the Eldest of the Jews in Litzmannstadt, I will perform the duties I have been charged with in accordance with the dictates of my conscience and the regulations of the law, and in so performing them, and in particular when passing sentence, I will not be swayed by friendship, enmity, or by any extraneous matters, so help me God. Litzmannstadt-Getto. November 3, 1940" [sic]. Then the signatures were affixed to the document.

The new magistrates were escorted to the swearing-in by [Rabbi Yosif] Fajner, a member of the Rabbinical Council. Before the new magistrates were sworn in, Chairman Rumkowski delivered a speech in which he sketched out the duties which issue from the office of prosecutor or judge. The Chairman expressed his satisfaction that his court had acquired new, experienced magistrates who possess excellent backgrounds as lawyers. The Chairman recalled that since the inception of the courts he has adhered to the principle of immunity for judges; however, the regrettable incident which took place a few months ago (a reference to the arrest of ex-judge Bronowski) has, unfortunately, changed his position. The head of the ghetto concluded his speech by expressing his conviction that the new magistrates would discharge their high office with great dignity. The speech was followed by the swearing-in which, besides the new magistrates, also included two other magistrates who had not yet themselves been sworn in. Dr. [Meir Ber] Kitz,[103] a lawyer from Vienna who has been engaged as a judge of the court, delivered a speech in Yiddish. On his own behalf and that of his colleagues, the speaker stated that they had never in their wildest fantasies expected to be able to practice their profession here in the ghetto. Similarly, the lawyers who had come to the ghetto had been surprised by the remarkably autonomous local organization and by the organization of the court itself. He concluded his speech by expressing his admiration for the organizational ability of the Eldest of the Jews and his gratitude for being able to work in his beloved profession, the law. The last speaker was the chairman of the court, [Szaja-Stanisław] Jakobson, a lawyer, who outlined the history of the ghetto's judiciary, its origin, and its development, stressing the fact that the enormous difficulties that had presented themselves to their new judicial system had thus far been surmounted. The ghetto's judiciary enjoys the people's complete acceptance and respect. It has passed its examination in every way.

THE RABBINICAL COUNCIL[104] IS INCREASED

Today the Chairman signed the appointments of four new members of the Rabbinical Council. The appointees were four rabbis—recent arrivals from Germany. To make these appointments to the Rabbinical Council effective, [Henryk] Neftalin, the attorney, as director of the Department of Vital Statistics, held a special conference with the appointees that was attended by officials of the Department of Vital Statistics and

103. Dr. Meir Ber Kitz (1885–1944), a native of Lwów (Galicia), a well-known Viennese attorney, who defended Jews at trial. In the ghetto he was connected with a group that secretly intercepted radio broadcasts.

104. In the years 1940–42 the Rabbinical Council was, to a certain degree, the continuation of an institution that had existed before the war in Łódź, as in all cities in Poland, as part of the Jewish Community: the *Gmina*—or kehillah in Hebrew (see p. 8, n. 12 above). As part of the Jewish administration, the Rabbinical Council in the ghetto was, of course, very limited in power and under-staffed.

the Rabbinical Bureau. In a long speech, Neftalin, who has lately been serving as the Chairman's deputy in matters concerning the new population, outlined the organizational structure of the Rabbinical Council, the duties of its members, and the way in which that body collaborates with the Department of Vital Statistics. The following are the most interesting inferences to be drawn from this exceptionally concise speech: Neftalin said that the Rabbinical Council created in the ghetto has, until now, been composed of fifteen local rabbis. In the field of religious affairs, the council constitutes an entirely autonomous body, whereas in civil affairs it works closely with the Department of Vital Statistics. The Rabbinical Bureau, which is part of the Rabbinical Council, serves as the connecting link between the activities of the council and the Department of Vital Statistics. A year and a half of practice has demonstrated that this collaboration has been proceeding efficiently and harmoniously. There has not, thus far, been a single instance of conflict between these two organizations. The speaker expressed his conviction that, in the future, with an increase in the Rabbinical Council's staff, the collaboration with the Department of Vital Statistics will continue to proceed harmoniously.

The new council members' duty will be to see to the new population's observance of its own customs, customs which may differ from those here. The speaker traced in detail the steps necessary to conclude a marriage in accordance with the ghetto's established principles. The regulations are as follows: (1) Registration of the parties, with their documents, at the Department of Vital Statistics, and in cases where either of the prospective parties is under age, the written consent of the father is required. (2) Notices of intent to marry must be posted twice—on the street and in the synagogue. As for the newly arrived population, printed forms of intent to marry will be provided, when applicable, for posting at collective residences. (3) Upon completion of the above-mentioned formalities, and if no opposition has been voiced, the Department of Vital Statistics will issue the Rabbinical Council authorization to perform the wedding. Since German laws do not permit Jews to contract civil marriages,[105] the wife is not to use the last name of the man she marries in a religious ceremony. Her ID card will, however, be stamped as proof that she is married to the man in question, and the same will be done with the husband's ID.

It is obvious that within the closed ghetto's autonomous social system, a marriage is perfectly legal both in the religious and civil sectors and, thus far, practice indicates that the authorities outside the ghetto also honor marriages concluded here in some areas of everyday concern (for example, a trip out of the ghetto to see one's husband, and, what is more important, in the conferring of the father's last name to a child in cases where the man in question acknowledges his paternity). Clearly this is not applicable to questions arising as a result of marriage, such as property rights and other rights of a specifically civil nature.

The formalities are carried out upon payment of a set fee (6 marks), which can be reduced, or eliminated entirely, in cases of extreme poverty. The Chairman has instituted the excellent custom of presenting each newly married couple with two loaves of bread and one half kilogram of [artificial] honey. The charge for performing a

---

105. According to the Nuremberg laws of September 15, 1935, and their supplementary decrees.

wedding runs from 3 to 15 marks, and the Chairman has lately ruled that these payments be transferred into the Community's coffers since the rabbis, as officials of the Community, receive a monthly salary of 250 marks. Other persons taking part in the marriage ceremony are not permitted to accept any payment. The contracting of marriages by the newly arrived population has been suspended until the enlargement of the Rabbinical Council's staff has been completed. Recently, a collective wedding ceremony was performed for 25 couples from among the new population.

Neftalin concluded his speech by expressing his conviction that the collaboration of the local rabbis with those who are newly arrived here would proceed in an atmosphere of complete accord. After the speech there was a discussion of an informational nature. Among other things, the chairman of the conference promised that the new rabbis would most likely be given private apartments, though they would remain registered in their own collectives. Weddings for the new population will be resumed on the 4th of this month.

WEDNESDAY, DECEMBER 3, 1941

DEATHS AND BIRTHS

Today 42 people died in the ghetto and five births were registered (two boys and three girls).

THE SUICIDE OF A WOMAN FROM PRAGUE

Yesterday, the first aid ambulance was summoned to the Prague IV collective located at 29 Franciszkańska Street. A resident of that collective, 19-year-old Zuzanna Beer, née Freundlich, born in the Sudeten, took poison in order to commit suicide. She was taken to Hospital No. 1 and died a few hours later. She had married shortly before she was resettled. In Prague, shortly before her departure, she had been receiving treatment at an institution for the neurasthenic. Her husband had joined her here voluntarily, leaving Prague in the transport after hers.

REGISTRATION OF RESIDENTS OF COLLECTIVES

All those residing in collectives were registered today. There are at present six residential collectives: the residence of the Prague II transport (at 37 Łagiewnicka Street). Prague III (at 27 Franciszkańska Street), Prague III (at 37–a Łagiewnicka Street), Prague IV (at 48 Marysińska Street), Prague V (at 27 Franciszkańska Street), and the collective for the transport from Cologne (at 14 Otylia Street).[106] The registration was performed by people from Prague who had recently been employed by the Registration Bureau. Beginning at 9 o'clock in the evening, working in pairs, they went around to all the residential collectives. In accordance with the ruling that had been issued, all residents of collectives had to be home on that Tuesday night. Those who worked at night left their ID's at home. On the average, each collective houses 1,000 people. The

---

106. In the original *Chronicle* this entire passage was followed by a handwritten postscript: "error." The addresses of the collectives do indeed contain inaccuracies, as later mentioned in the *Chronicle*.

registration was finished by three o'clock the next morning. It is worth noting that the work was done efficiently in all the Prague collectives whereas difficulties were encountered in the Cologne transport's collective. There the directors had not prepared their materials and the officials performing the registration had to wake all the residents.

THURSDAY, DECEMBER 4, 1941

MAN FROM PRAGUE SHOT TO DEATH

Yesterday, at 7:00 P.M., 21-year-old Piotr Schultz, who had come to the ghetto in the fourth transport from Prague and was a resident of 29 Franciszkańska Street, was shot to death by a sentry near the barbed wire at the intersection of Stefan and Łagiewnicka streets. The victim, a worker, was born in Cieplice [Teplice], in the Sudetenland. Schultz had volunteered for the transport in Prague so as not to be separated from his fiancée, a 16-year-old woman who had been sent to the ghetto here in the second transport. He had given no sign of having any suicidal inclinations. Schultz had applied for work in the saddlery located on the outskirts of the ghetto, in the former Bałut slaughterhouse. On the critical evening he had spent a long time walking about in the vicinity of the slaughterhouse, evidently waiting for someone in connection with his efforts to find employment. Not familiar with the terrain there, he had approached the barbed wire too closely a few times. As usual, Stefan Street was completely deserted when the shooting occurred and thus there were no eyewitnesses to the incident. The German criminal police were informed of the shooting, and after performing an investigation at the scene, they ordered the body taken to the mortuary at Hospital No. 1.

NEW ARRIVALS CAN NOW USE THE MAIL

Beginning today, and with the permission of the [German] authorities, the ghetto's new residents, after more than six weeks since the arrival of the first transport, are able to use the local mail service on an equal footing with the rest of the ghetto population. The general rules for postal correspondence are contained in the following regulations: Only postcards may be used for private correspondence. Their contents can only touch on private matters; descriptions of any sort are not allowed Individuals may only request that pension payments be sent them; drafts may be applied for through the Bank of the Eldest of the Jews. They must be clearly and legibly written. People should be notified not to send packages here, for they are not allowed in. Requests to the [German] authorities for permission to leave are also not allowed. Inquiries to the Red Cross, with pre-paid replies, are only allowed at the window; direct correspondence with the Red Cross is not permitted. The sender's address is Litzmannstadt-Getto. In correspondence going abroad, the sender's address is not to be used (a post office official will fill in the address). Mail cannot be sent across the Atlantic or to Switzerland. The use of intermediaries in correspondence is not permitted. Abbreviations are not to be used in mail going abroad, and it is also impermissible to request packages or money in such correspondence. The margins may not be used for writing. Certificates attesting to residence in the ghetto will be drawn up by the Department of Vital Statistics and, beginning next Sunday, by the Office for Resettled Persons. Money orders are to be negotiated exclusively through the agency of the Bank here.

With the opening of postal service for the new settlers, there were incredible crowds in the post offices throughout the day today, and enormous lines of customers formed in front of the post offices. Approximately 20,000 postcards were sold. Last week, the Post Office received quite a large number of money orders for the "Germans," mostly for small sums in the 10–25 [German] mark range, those reaching 100 were much fewer. Last month, approximately 2,000 kilograms of packages arrived in the ghetto, primarily from Portugal. When the postal service was at its height (before the war with the USSR), 10,000 kilograms of packages arrived here each month.

FRIDAY, DECEMBER 5, 1941

ES GEYT A YEKE MIT A TEKE

So runs the refrain of the ghetto's latest hit song, which is sung to the tune of the popular army song, "The Machine Gun." It makes fun of the adventures of the newly arrived "Germans" [that is, German Jews], popularly known in Yiddish slang here as *yekes*. The song treats their ups and downs with good humor and tells of the *yekes*, forever hungry and searching for food, and the "locals" who make fun of them and quite often take advantage of their naïvete and unfamiliarity with local customs. The song is about women in pants parading through the streets of Bałut. The author and performer of this song is the popular ghetto street "troubadour" [Jankele] Herszko-wicz, formerly a tailor by trade. Last year he composed the extremely popular topical song entitled "Rumkowski, Chaim," and he was able to earn a living for several months by performing that song and once even received a gift of 5 marks from the Chairman himself, who had chanced to hear the song. Another time, the ghetto "troubadour" received a package of matzoth from the Chairman in person when he was performing his song in front of a store which the Chairman happened to be visiting before the holidays. At present the song writer has formed a partnership with a man from Vienna, a certain Karol Rozencwajg, a former traveling salesman. Rozen-cwajg accompanies Herszkowicz on the guitar or zither. And this duo, which, like everything else in the ghetto, is a bit peculiar, being composed of a tailor from Bałut and a traveling salesman from Vienna, is enjoying great success with the populace. This is of course good for their business and the duo sometimes ends up with 6 marks to share after a full day's work, a tidy wage indeed. The partnership has recently launched a new hit song to the tune of a well-known Viennese cab drivers' song (composed, *nota bene*, by a Jew, [Gustaw] Pick). Like its predecessor, this song takes its motifs from the innumerable malapropisms which the *yekes* here commit. The ghetto's song writer has also composed another very popular "hit song" entitled "Lebn zol prezes Khaim" [Long live Chairman Chaim].

SATURDAY, DECEMBER 6, 1941

A WEEK OF CULTURAL DIVERSIONS

The following shows were performed at the House of Culture last week: Revue No. 2, which enjoys ever greater success, was performed on December 1 for the workers of a tailor workshop, on December 2 for the workers in the straw shoe factory, on December 4 for a tailor workshop and, finally, today (for the 39th time). On Wednesday there was a symphonic concert conducted by [Teodor] Ryder. A Viennese, [Leopold] Birkenfeld, lent the concert variety with his absolutely marvelous piano performance. He played the following works with great ability: Schubert's *Unfinished Symphony*, Beethoven's *Moonlight Sonata*, Liszt's *Rhapsody No. 2*, and a few works by Mendelssohn. Birkenfeld's playing literally enchanted the audience. There is no doubt the House of Culture will yet again make it possible for the public to hear such masterful performances.

In accordance with the Chairman's instructions, the House of Culture is registering the musicians and painters who have recently arrived in the ghetto. Thus far, 60 musicians, singers, and actors, as well as 10 painters, have been registered. Of the latter, Gutman of Prague, a well-known portraitist, is worthy of mention. Because of his unique appearance, seemingly direct from Montparnasse, Gutman has already become extremely popular in the ghetto. It is worth mentioning in passing that this painter is a fanatic adherent of Zionism, well-known from his travels on foot to attend Zionist conferences. In 1935, for example, he traveled on foot from Prague to a congress held in Vienna.

SATURDAY, DECEMBER 13, 1941

WEATHER

The tendency of the temperature to increase, abnormal for this time of year yet observable since the end of November, seems today to have reached its culmination. Due to frequent sunny spells the temperature was more than 10 degrees above zero and it felt like a day in early fall. Thus far, the unexpectedly warm weather in December, after November's frosts, has been a real blessing for the people of the ghetto.

THE MORTALITY RATE AMONG THE NEW ARRIVALS

From the 17th of October until today the number of deaths among the newcomers from Germany, Austria, Luxembourg, and Bohemia (all told, 19,883 have arrived in the ghetto in 21 transports) amounts to 270. The overwhelming majority of the deaths are among people of advanced age, 70 and over. The negligible amount of deaths among the young and middle-aged is shown by the fact that, among those under 40, barely ten people have died (and of those, six were instances of violent death, suicides, or shootings) and only one child, aged 6, has died. Among the very oldest people who have died we note the death of a 90-year-old woman from Vienna and also of a man from Frankfurt [am Main] and a woman from Vienna, both 80 years of age. Relatively speaking, it is among the new arrivals from Berlin and Vienna that the death rate is the highest, and among those from Prague that it is the lowest. The illnesses of old age, with heart disease in the forefront, are the most frequent causes of death, while tuberculosis, in first place as a cause of death among the ghetto's settled inhabitants, is close to last among the newcomers.

DEATH OF A WELL-KNOWN BERLIN DOCTOR

Dr. Ernst Sandheimt, who was a health counselor in Berlin and one of that city's grand old men of medicine, died the day before yesterday at the age of 74. He died in Hospital No. 1, where he had been suffering from a duodenal ulcer since his arrival in the ghetto.

A CONCERT

Today there was a symphonic concert at the House of Culture performed by an orchestra conducted by [Teodor] Ryder, which was followed by the second performance by [Leopold] Birkenfeld, the Viennese pianist.

SUNDAY, DECEMBER 14, 1941

A 96-YEAR-OLD WOMAN

who recently arrived in the ghetto has been quartered along with her two daughters, both over 70, at the Old People's Home on Gnieźnieńska Street which, as the bulletin has already noted, was especially designated for the new population [see p. 87]. This woman is, most probably, the ghetto's oldest resident at the present moment.

ROAD TO THE CEMETERY UNDER CONSTRUCTION

The construction of an excellent road to the cemetery has been in progress in Marysin for three weeks now. This road has been set off from Marysin and will run along the cemetery's walls for a distance of 600 meters. The graves located by the walls had necessarily to be respected, and it was not possible to break through the walls, a problem that could only be solved in this fashion. Initially there was even a plan to construct an overpass there, straight as the crow flies and supported by columns. This plan was rejected since, apart from the technical difficulties involved in constructing such a bridge, it would also have been necessary to position the columns in places where graves were located. While the road work was being done, the cemetery walls, which threatened to collapse at many points, were moved. Close to 600 meters of wall stand on cement foundations and approximately 250,000 bricks, retrieved from demolition sites, will be used for this project, enormous in ghetto terms. The road is being built according to the latest in technical design; it will consist of three layers: a foundation of brick, an embankment, and a surface strewn with coal cinders. This road connects with the three-quarter-kilometer road already built that runs along Robert Street. Moreover, Otylia Street, which leads to the factory on Mostowski

Street, is also being paved. The building of exemplary roads under present conditions is a monument to the ghetto's vitality.

TUESDAY, DECEMBER 16, 1941

DEATHS AND BIRTHS

Twenty-seven people died in the ghetto today. Eight births were registered (seven boys and one girl).

The birth of twins, a pair of healthy boys, is worthy of mention here. This is the first instance of live and healthy twins being born here since the ghetto came into existence. Thus far there had been two cases of twins being stillborn. The happy father is Mr. Goldberg, a shoemaker who lives at 4 Gnieźnieńska Street.

AMNESTY

As the bulletin [of December 12, 1941] has already noted, the Eldest of the Jews has declared an amnesty for the Chanukah holiday (the first day of which fell on the 14th of this month). The amnesty is to be applied on an individual rather than a blanket basis. One hundred and nine people have benefited from this amnesty. Specifically, 67 who were under investigation by the prosecutor, 15 prisoners who had been sentenced or were under detention, and 27 who had been convicted in the course of a penal administrative procedure received amnesty.

NEW SETTLERS IN THE GHETTO

Nine-year-old Lech Ryszard Rybicki, who had been left to be raised in the city, has now been brought to the ghetto. As the bulletin noted a few days ago, the two young Rybicki sisters had also been brought to the ghetto in the early part of this month [see p. 87]. The ostensible reason is that their mother is a Jew. The boy was placed in an orphanage.

THE GHETTO'S PAPER SUPPLY

The shortage of paper has recently become one of the most painful sore spots in the ghetto. In spite of the utmost thrift, this shortage has been exerting a negative influence on the work of many of the Community's institutions, at times creating problems which are difficult to surmount. The suspension of the ghetto periodical *Geto-tsaytung* was also dictated by necessity because of the paper shortage. This is a serious loss for the populace, which is now deprived of any up-to-date reading—especially since that periodical did an excellent job of providing information on local affairs and, at the same time, serving as an authoritative expression of the Eldest of the Jews' views and intentions, which are of such lively interest to the populace as a whole. The ghetto has not been receiving paper for six weeks now. Recently a requisition for 10,000 kilograms was approved and has already begun to arrive in installments.

WEDNESDAY, DECEMBER 17, 1941

FESTIVITIES AMONG THE NEWCOMERS FROM PRAGUE

The collective of transport Prague VI, located at 29 Franciszkańska Street, yesterday celebrated the weddings of seven "Czech" couples. The evening, which included a diverting program of music, vocals, and even dancing to the accordion and violin, gave the "exiles" a moment's forgetting. The festivities continued late into the night in an atmosphere of cordial warmth.

PRICES RISING!

This week the prices of basic foodstuffs rose sharply in private transactions. A loaf of bread rose to 12 marks, a kilo of potatoes to 1.30 marks. The prices of margarine and butter reached record highs. Fifty marks was asked for margarine and 75 marks for one kilogram of butter!

FRIDAY, DECEMBER 19, 1941

TYPHUS IN THE GYPSY CAMP

While performing a consultation on the grounds of the Gypsy camp, a ghetto doctor, Dr. Dubski of Prague, himself succumbed to spotted typhus. The doctor, who became a casualty of his own profession, has been placed in the hospital for infectious diseases here. Today, news spread through the ghetto that one of the directors of the local branch of the German criminal police has met a similar fate while discharging his duties as commandant of the camp. Apparently police dogs have also been stricken by this terrible, contagious disease, and have supposedly been shot. Doctor Dubski will be replaced in his work at the Gypsy camp by another doctor selected by the Department of Health by the drawing of lots. The new doctor will take the strictest possible precautions each time he enters the camp and, upon leaving in the evening in a closed vehicle, he will proceed to the hospital on Drewnowska Street to undergo disinfection.

SATURDAY, DECEMBER 20, 1941

TEN THOUSAND PEOPLE TO BE RESETTLED OUT OF THE GHETTO

On the 16th of this month, the German authorities held a conference with the Chairman in the course of which they demanded that 20,000 people vacate the ghetto. Through persuasion and request, the Chairman succeeded in having the number of ghetto residents to be resettled reduced by half. The Eldest of the Jews also won permission to decide for himself, on the basis of his authority over the internal autonomy of the ghetto, who is to leave the ghetto. Apparently, those to be resettled will be sent to the smaller towns in the Protectorate [Generalgouvernement], to centers where food supply is not as difficult a problem as it is in the large cities. Those who are resettled will be replaced by workers and skilled workmen sent to the ghetto from other cities and small towns. After his conversation with the authorities, the Chairman held a conference in strict privacy with a few people who hold the leading positions in the Community's administration and judiciary. That conference resulted in the creation of a commission "of five" [sic] which is composed of the following people: the lawyer [Henryk] Neftalin, director of the Department of Population Records and, recently, of the Office for Resettled Persons; [Leon] Rozenblat, chief of the Order Service; [Szaja-Stanisław] Jakobson, the attorney and chairman of the court; [Salomon] Hercberg, commandant of Central Prison and chief of the Marysin district, [Zygmunt] Blemer, head of the Bureau of Investigation, and Grynberg, director of the Administrative Penal Office. It has been established that the quota demanded by the authorities would be composed of the following groups: about 2,000 of those recently arrived from Włocławek and the surrounding towns of the Kujawy [region] (2,900 people have come to the ghetto from the above-mentioned areas; the people in the oldest age groups will be exempt from resettlement); the so-called undesirable element from the point of view of the ghetto's public interests, including those who are serving sentences and their families; and the families of people sent out to perform manual labor in Germany in the November transports (around 1,000 persons were compelled to leave; cf. the appropriate bulletin [see pp. 81–82]). The drawing up of the list of those to be resettled will be determined collectively, at meetings of the commission. In that way all subjective attitudes toward the candidates will be avoided. The "Germans" [that is, Jews from the West] will not figure in these calculations. A special office has been established in the Precinct I police station that will draw up lists on the basis of conclusions reached by the court, the Bureau of Investigation, and the prison. This office is cooperating closely with the Address Office, which determines the addresses of the candidates for expulsion as well as the addresses of their families. The news of the coming resettlement has created a mood of depression in the ghetto. As usually occurs when a new blow befalls the ghetto, the news has been maliciously and irresponsibly exaggerated and blown out of proportion.

SUNDAY, DECEMBER 21, 1941

CHANUKAH CELEBRATIONS

Many groups have organized festivities for the celebration of Chanukah. Yesterday, the collective of the Prague II transport organized a special Chanukah celebration for children.

A CHURCH EMPTIED OUT

Last week the [German] authorities ordered that the parish church of the Holy Trinity located in the ghetto (at 2 Dworska Street) be emptied of its pews and other church accessories, and these were then taken through Bałut Market to the city. The church building has been designated as a storehouse for fabrics that will be used to manufacture sheepskin coats for the army. It is worth noting that all the other churches located in the ghetto were closed down right at the very beginning—as if to say, they belonged to others and were not an integral part of the ghetto.

SUPERVISOR OF THE FOOD SUPPLY DEPARTMENT SHOT TO DEATH. NIGHT WATCHMAN WOUNDED.

Yesterday at 8:55 P.M., the supervisor of the Department of Vegetables, Lajzer Malin (b. Bielsk, 1890), was shot to death by a sentry. The bullet struck his heart. At the critical moment the victim had been in the courtyard at 28 Zgierska Street, near the vegetable storehouses located at a distance of about 80 meters from the gate. The night watchman who was on duty in front of the storehouse and who was standing beside Lajzer Malin, was wounded by the second shot. The wounded man is Lajzer Heller (of 49 Brzezińska Street). He was wounded in the arm. On orders from the German criminal police, who sent officials to the scene, the victim's body was taken to the mortuary at Hospital No. 3. The victim resided near the scene of the incident, at 42 Zgierska Street. After receiving medical assistance at Hospital No. 1, the wounded watchman was released to convalesce at home.

A SHOOTING BEFORE MORNING

Yesterday at 5:45 A.M., 19-year-old Icek Goldberg (of 56 Brzezińska Street) was shot to death at the intersection of Masarska and Limanowski streets. The victim had been standing in for his sick father, a night watchman at the Precinct II station of the Order Service. On the critical night, the victim had been keeping watch on an apartment at 12 Masarska Street, which had been vacated as a result of the order to relocate. The German criminal police ordered his body brought to the mortuary of Hospital No. 3 at 12 Wesoła Street.

HUSBAND AND WIFE DIE ON THE SAME DAY

Yesterday, a married couple, the Wachtelkoenigs, deportees from Frankfurt am Main, died at nearly the same time in the Old People's Home on Gnieźnieńska Street. The husband was 66, the wife 65.

MONDAY, DECEMBER 22, 1941

A DEATH AT THE POLICE STATION

Thirty-five-year-old Chaim Podomski, a locksmith by trade, died in the German criminal police's building in the ghetto, where he was under arrest. Podomski had resided at 13 Młynarska Street.

FIRST CHILDBIRTHS AMONG THE NEW ARRIVALS

The office of births at the Department of Vital Statistics has thus far registered two instances of childbirth among the new arrivals from Germany. One child was born to a barber from Berlin, the other to a furrier from that same city. Three births have been registered among the newcomers from the Kujawy [region].

DECEMBER 23–25, 1941

SHOOTINGS

On Wednesday, at 6:15 A.M., 31-year-old Wolf Wolfowicz, a tailor employed at the workshop at 53 Łagiewnicka Street, was shot to death by a sentry. The incident took place in front of 28 Limanowski Street. At the critical moment the victim, a resident of 9 Bazarna Street, was on his way to work. On orders from the German criminal police, the victim's body was taken to the mortuary at the hospital on Wesoła Street. A second shooting incident took place on the same day at 8:40 A.M. when 21-year-old Szyja Szylski, a native of Łódź, was shot to death. On the critical day, the victim had arrived here from Brzeziny, where he had been residing. He had been taken under escort from Bałut Market to the building that houses the local branch of the Kripo [German criminal police]. The incident took place at 5 Kościelna Street, in front of the above-mentioned building, when Szylski allegedly attempted to escape from his escort. The victim's body was taken to the mortuary at Hospital No. 1.

Two shooting incidents in a single day have caused a mood of genuine panic in the ghetto, a mood which was heightened by the spread of stories claiming five persons had been killed, a number which, by evening, had increased to seven. The smallest details of these imaginary incidents were passed by word of mouth, and included exact times, the victims' personal data, the places involved (on the bridges), and so forth. The nearly complete cessation of traffic on the streets bordering the barbed wire was a visible sign of how nervous people were.

Given this mood of complete depression and anxiety, it is easy to imagine the great impression made by the Eldest of the Jews' appeal to the people of the ghetto, which was posted late Thursday afternoon. We quote it here in a literal translation [from the Yiddish]: "Sisters and brothers! In connection with the recent incidents, I have chosen this way of informing you that, as a result of my intervention, I have been given assurances that there will be no repetition of such incidents. This obviously does not apply to cases where smuggling or attempts to escape from the ghetto are involved. I appeal to you to remain calm and to report to work punctually as you have been doing so far. Workers and officials can make use of the bridges to go to their places of work and their homes day and night. My slogan, 'Work,' is still in complete effect."

THE CHAIRMAN'S MARRIAGE BANNS

On December 25, the Department of Vital Statistics received marriage banns from the Eldest of the Jews, which were registered in their turn as Number 1,405. The Chairman's plenipotentiary paid the normal charge of 6 marks, 50 pfennigs. Because it is to occur soon, the marriage was exempted from the necessary waiting period. The Chairman's data: Mordecai Chaim Rumkowski, born in February, 1877 in the town of Ilno [Ilino],[107] in Russia; a widower, he resides in the ghetto at 36 Łagiewnicka Street and formerly lived at 105 Kiliński Street in Łódź. His fiancée's data: Regina Wein-

---

107. Ilino, Velikiye Luki province, USSR, near the Western Dvina, once a *shtetl* in the Vitebsk *gubernia*, with a predominantly Jewish population. According to the Russian census of 1897, of the 1,415 inhabitants, 1,105 were Jewish.

berger, born in Łódź in 1907, never married, a lawyer by profession, and a resident of 21 Zgierska Street. The Rabbinate is preparing the marriage contract (*ksube*). The now confirmed news of the Chairman's marriage spread like wildfire "into the city," crowning the rumors that had been circulating for two weeks, and met with a great and positive reaction from the populace. Because the first citizen of the ghetto is to be married, the populace is expecting a supplement to its food rations and, in official circles, rumors concerning bonuses are still making the rounds. This we note for the sake of accuracy in the compilation of this *Chronicle*.

A TRAGIC COINCIDENCE

Recently 72-year-old Beniamin Serejski's death certificate was brought by his family to the office where deaths are registered. Scarcely an hour later, the death of the deceased's 40-year-old son Chaim was reported.

DECEMBER 26–28, 1941

A DEATH ON THE STREET

On Friday, at 8:00 P.M., 31-year-old Cecylia Rubaszki (of 8 Miernicza Street) died of exhaustion in front of 38 Dolna Street. First aid was summoned and the woman pronounced dead.

FORTY THOUSAND PEOPLE IN THE GHETTO

are using the soup kitchens after the recent reorganization of the soup-kitchen system. Before the reorganization, as the bulletin has already noted in a special report [of December 10], 98 percent of the ghetto's entire population was using soup kitchens.

A SERVICE FOR CHRISTIANS[108]

On Christmas Eve, the Chairman granted permission for Christian religious services to be held, designating a modern two-room apartment at 6 Jakuba Street as the place of prayer. Separate services are being held for Catholics and Protestants. The first services were held on Wednesday, the first day of Christmas. The Catholic service, attended by about 40 people, was conducted by [Sister Maria (Regina) Fuhrmann, a Carmelite nun,] a Master of Theology who arrived in the ghetto recently from Germany [in fact, from Vienna]. Apparently there were two Catholic priests among those who came to the service. The service for the Protestants was conducted by a pastor, after which a missionary delivered a sermon in keeping with the holiday. The next services were held on Sunday and services have been announced for New Year's day.

108. Apart from the Christians living in the ghetto, described in the *Chronicle* entry dated April 1, 1941, there were over 250 registered Christians among the newly arrived population from the West.

THE CHAIRMAN'S WEDDING

The wedding of the Eldest of the Jews, M. C. Rumkowski, and Regina Weinberger, Master of Law, took place on Saturday, December 27, in the Chairman's apartment, located in Hospital No. 1. A small group of family and the ghetto leader's closest co-workers took part in the wedding festivities. Rabbi [Yosif] Fajner performed the ceremony. The marriage certificate was written on parchment. The 600 telegrams of congratulations received attest to ghetto society's unusually great interest in the Chairman's wedding. Despite the most varied stories about the grandiose and sumptuous festivities, the wedding was, in fact, extremely modest. The festivities began at 6:00 P.M. and concluded a little after 8:00 P.M.

The next day the Chairman resumed his normal duties, thereby belying the rumors that he intended to take a leave of absence.

FIFTY-SIX THOUSAND WHITE SUITS

The tailor shops are at present filling large rush orders for the army. Fifty-six thousand pairs of pants and shirts with hoods made of thin white cloth, a camouflage for snow-covered terrain, have been ordered.

ONE THOUSAND PAIRS OF CLOGS

were distributed to the neediest, free of charge, by the Department of Clothing on the occasion of the Chairman's wedding.

DECEMBER 29–31, 1941

VICTIMS OF THE TYPHUS WHICH IS SPREADING IN THE "GYPSY CAMP"

On December 29, Dr. Karol Boehm of Prague died in the hospital for infectious diseases as a result of the spotted typhus he had contracted while practicing medicine in the Gypsy camp. The deceased was 50 years old. Three other doctors sick with typhus they contracted in the camp are still in the hospital. They are Dr. Kraus and Dr. Vogel of Prague, and Dr. [Fiszel] Altman, a local physician. The latter is in extremely critical condition. A few days ago, Eugeniusz [sic] Jansen, the German police commissioner who was serving as the camp commandant and who had been assigned to the local branch of the criminal police, died of the same causes. The funeral sashes for the ghetto commissioner's funeral were manufactured in the [ghetto] hatter's factory. In view of the danger of typhus infection, the Department of Health is delegating Jewish doctors to work in the hospital by drawing lots. All doctors up to the age of 45 who are practicing medicine are taking part in this lottery.

CONGRATULATORY TELEGRAMS

on the occasion of the Chairman's wedding were sent by, among others, the Union of Christians in the ghetto located at 6 Jakuba Street (cf. the previous bulletin).

THE ONE HUNDREDTH CONCERT

In 1941 the House of Culture performed its one hundredth in a series of concerts. This jubilee concert took place on the last day of the year and was devoted to a violin recital by Bronisława Rotsztat accompanied by maestro [Teodor] Ryder. The program consisted of works by Bach, Glazunov, and Mozart. Aside from the one hundred concerts, the House of Culture, which was created on March 1, has presented 85 revue performances. The first revue ran 40 performances, the second 45. The second revue is still being performed. In 1941 there were two special shows for children at the House of Culture: one was organized for Purim by the School Department and the other, entitled *A Summer Holiday*, was organized in August by the Marysin administration. Apart from an entire series of speeches delivered by the Chairman on the evenings of concerts and revues, there were three special presentations made by him in the House of Culture's auditorium: on February 1, for the Welfare Department, and on November 1 for representatives of the transports [of Jews from the West]. Around 70,000 spectators have attended these performances at the House of Culture. The cost of a ticket ranges from 30 pfennigs to 1 mark, while shows for factory workers cost from 20 to 30 pfennigs.

RESETTLEMENT

In the last few days of December there were persistent rumors in circulation to the effect that the resettlement was to be suspended. These stories do not correspond to the truth. The special commission's office continues its operations and is compiling lists of candidates for expulsion; the only thing not known is the date for the deportation which is supposed to occur in January, 1942.

WHAT THE GHETTO WAS TALKING ABOUT IN DECEMBER

All local sensations were, in one stroke, reduced to nothing, swept aside, and deprived of all interest, becoming unreal, a sound and fury signifying nothing. . . . All this was caused by a single sentence composed of a mere five words: "The Chairman is getting married . . ."

Probably no wireless telegraph in the world ever functioned as efficiently and swiftly, as intensely and incessantly as the ghetto's "whispering telegraph." The news traveled by word of mouth on the streets, in the lines, in the stores and pastry shops, the market squares, the offices, and the factories; in a matter of seconds it was all over town, from Zagajnikowa to Gnieźnieńska streets, from Żabia to Wolborska.

In seven-league boots, the news ran through the ghetto's gates, barbed wire, and bridges, electrifying everyone without exception, young and old, the healthy and the sick, and even those who had already become insensitive, apathetic, indifferent to everything . . .

After the first sensation had subsided, there was a flood of questions: "To whom?", "Who's the lucky woman he's chosen?", "What does she do?", "Is she pretty?", "When's the wedding?" The questions multiplied and touched on the most intimate matters. And answers to those questions multiplied at the same rate and were, for the most part, contradictory and fantastic . . . An entire pleiad of the "initiated" went about with enigmatic expressions, smiling their "Pythian" smiles in an attempt to heighten the atmosphere of suspense and mystery in which they were glad to steep themselves . . .

Everything that had been a topic of interest before—potatoes, soup kitchens, rations, and briquets—ceased to be of current interest . . .

The next day curiosity had not only not abated but, quite the contrary, had gained strength and momentum. Facts began to crystallize and emerge from the flood of gossip and talk.

Interest grew . . . Just as a voice in a large, vaulted hall reverberates off the ceiling and returns several times in the form of echoes, booming and droning as if trying to smash through the walls and make its way out into wider spaces, so did the news batter up against the barbed wire and the gates, and then, unable to force its way through, return as an echo, magnified many times, and speeding through the ghetto no one knows how many times over.

The city already knew beyond doubt that the Chairman's lucky choice was Miss R. W., that she was a lawyer by profession, that she was young, pretty, and uncommonly wise, that she had already been named legal adviser to the Chairman and been working in the secretariat of the Health Department.

The popularity of the workers in that department increased dramatically. They became the most sought-after people, they were literally chased and inundated with questions . . .

There were those who expressed their doubts, the born skeptics, people distrustful by nature . . . They claimed it was all a fairy tale, a fiction . . . But even those unbelievers had to believe when, on Wednesday evening, the news spread that the lucky woman was sitting in the front row at that Wednesday's concert, that the Chairman had kissed her hand in greeting and, finally, that they had driven off together in a coach which, *nota bene*, had arrived in the ghetto the day before. The unbelievers were dealt the decisive blow on Thursday. The Chairman's carriage stood for an hour in front of the Rabbinate's office on Miodowa Street. And for what purpose? That was no secret. The Chairman was handling the wedding formalities personally . . . And the Chairman was actually inspecting a coat workshop located in that same building!

A new batch of gossip came out. People talked about the fantastic dressing table that had been ordered for the young woman and the apartment they would have, people argued about whether the wedding would be modest or sumptuous, the officials were happy about their prospective raises, and there was talk of an amnesty for the more minor criminals . . .

The ghetto was in a stir. Different people took different views of the step the Chairman was taking, which was, no matter what, a serious one.

In general, everyone approves; but the most interesting thing here is the older generation's opinion. They are in accord in proclaiming that for a man occupying the most prominent position in our society to enter into matrimony is well-advised on all accounts, both in setting an example and as a matter of prestige, as well as for other reasons.

Quite apart from all the individual views and opinions, we must say that the impression made by the news was enormous and brought the interest of 160,000 people to a fevered pitch; and for a long time that news was the sole, the most important, and the most sensational event of the hour.

's of Łódź were ordered to wear Stars of David on their chest and shoulder.

A Jew being frisked and mocked on the street.

vs forcibly harnessed to a horse cart.

The Reform Synagogue on Kościuszko Boulevard, burned down by the Nazis on November 11, 1939.

Jews herded into the ghetto in the winter of 1939–40. Photographer: M. Grossman.

A family on its way to the ghetto.

German policemen at one of the ghetto gates. On the right is a Jewish Order Service man.

One of the three wooden bridges for ghetto foot traffic over an "Aryan" street.
Photographer: M. Grossman.

The camp inside the ghetto, where 5,000 Gypsies from Burgenland, Austria, were incarcerated. Photographer: M. Grossman.

Amtsleiter Hans Biebow, right, the head of the German Ghetto Administration, in his office displaying foreign currency and jewelry seized from Jews. On the bookcase is a confiscated Table of the Ten Commandments.

Biebow at a marketplace in the ghetto.

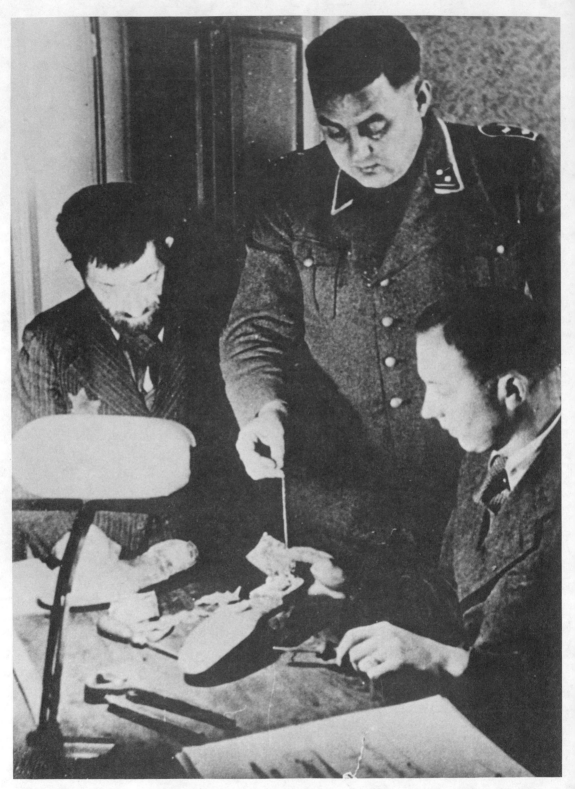

At the German criminal police office. A staged photograph showing valuables removed from a shoe of an arrested Jew.

Brother and sister.

Resting on a doorstep.

Selling homemade "candies."

Selling homemade "candies."

Jankele Herszkowicz of Łódź and Karol Rozenzweig of Vienna, streetsingers, drawing a crowd of spectators.

Ghetto money: one and five-mark vouchers.

The horse-drawn ambulance of the ghetto First Aid Service.

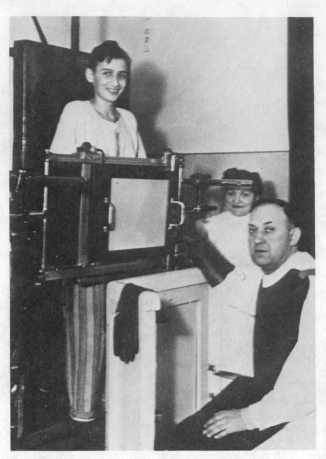

Dr. Daniel Weiskopf, radiologist and gastrologist.

Dr. Wilhelm Caspari, Professor of Medicine at the University of Berlin, who was deported to the ghetto of Łódź.

The Fire Department, the only Jewish institution in the ghetto that was permitted to use a car.

Tram drivers from the city of Łódź supervising the construction of the tramline in the ghetto. Standing in the background and wearing an armband is the Jewish tram-service foreman.

Excrement removal workers. Photographer: M. Grossman.

In front of the office of the Eldest of the Jews.

M. C. Rumkowski at the opening of a new soup kitchen.

...mkowski with children in the ghetto orphanage. Photographer: M. Grossman.

Rumkowski officiating at a wedding ceremony. Photographer: M. Grossman.

Rumkowski at the distribution of gymnasium diplomas. Photographer: M. Grossman.

Rumkowski and Rabbi Yosif Fajner on a visit to a school. Photographer: M. Grossman.

Rumkowski during a visit to the Warsaw ghetto.

PART II: 1942

POPULATION OF THE GHETTO ON JANUARY 1, 1942

On the basis of data from the Registration Bureau, the population of the ghetto on January 1 of this year amounted to 162,681 (66,978 men and 92,703 women).[1] In comparison with the level on December 1, this figure indicates a decrease of 942 ghetto dwellers. In December, 39 births were registered, 35 people arrived here from the Generalgouvernement and Warthegau, 8 from various prisons, and 7 sick people arrived from labor camps in Germany. Thus, all told, there was an increase of 89 souls in December. There was a loss of 1,031 inhabitants (1,029 died and 2 left). Of those who died in December, 195 were part of the ghetto's new population, which had come from Germany and the Protectorate [of Bohemia and Moravia], and 31 were from Włocławek and its environs.

JANUARY 1–5, 1942

FALSE RUMORS CAUSE A PANIC

On Sunday, a rumor concerning the supposed resettlement of the entire population spread through the ghetto like wildfire. Those who spread this story, which, naturally, caused a state of genuine panic in the ghetto, even included details. Specifically, it was claimed that the ghetto would be broken up into districts, similar to what was supposed to have occurred at the beginning of 1940, when the Jews were resettled from the city [into the ghetto, created at that time]. Those who were especially well-informed even announced that the local Address and Registry Office would be supplying the [German] authorities with the relevant data in the next few hours. Fortunately, on that same day, the Chairman delivered a public address in the very introduction to which he gave the lie, in the most vigorous of terms, to those rumors. Such an authoritative denial of the panicky reports caused the populace to regain its calm at once. In spite of the meeting's ending late—late for the ghetto, for it was already after ten o'clock—the ghetto leader's reassuring words managed to reach all of the citizenry that same evening.

WHEN WILL THE RESETTLEMENT OF THE TEN THOUSAND OCCUR?

The deadline, initially anticipated to come in the first few days of the new year, has clearly been extended. No one yet knows for how long. The work of preparing the lists of candidates for expulsion is still in progress. The commission appointed by the Chairman to handle this matter is meeting on a daily basis.

THE MORTALITY RATE IN THE "GYPSY CAMP" BEFORE
THE ELIMINATION OF THE CAMP

On the basis of information from the local Burial Department, which, as the bulletin noted on the first of last month, inters those dying in the "Gypsy Camp" in a separate part of the Jewish cemetery, 400 people from the camp were buried in the month of

---

1. An obvious error; the numbers do not add up to 162,681.

December (213 had been buried between the time they arrived and December 1); that is, their mortality rate was twice that of the 250,000 Jews who had lived in Łódź before the war. The Department of Health has been taking special precautions in connection with the typhus epidemic raging in the camp. Namely, the "Gypsies" who have died recently are not taken to the cemetery in hearses, but in sideless hauling wagons especially constructed for that purpose. The wagons are enclosed by planks and covered from above with tarpaulin. Special chests are also used for transporting the bodies.

It is worth mentioning here that an undertaker, a man by the name of Boms who was employed in transporting bodies from the camp, has now fallen victim to his work. Like some of the doctors, he too became infected with typhus. Fortunately, however, he escaped the tragic end which had befallen the doctors and the Kripo [German criminal police] official. After several weeks of treatment, Boms left the hospital for contagious diseases on January 2, cured.

For the last ten days the "Gypsies" have been taken away in trucks, according to people who live in the immediate vicinity of the camp.[2] The camp, which is practically deserted now, will no doubt be entirely eliminated by the end of this week. Apparently, its elimination was dictated by necessity, since there was a danger that the typhus would spread.

AGAIN, MACABRE LINES

In connection with the significant increase in the mortality rate (compare the relevant sections of last year's final bulletin (p. 107), macabre lines of corpses awaiting burial have accumulated in the mortuary at the cemetery, as was the case at the beginning of last year. The number of the unburied now exceeds one hundred. With a view to eliminating this macabre backlog, the Burial Department has ordered the gravediggers to bury at least 80 corpses on the 6th of this month, keeping only the bodies brought in on that day in the mortuary. On that day, the gravediggers' sole concern will be burying bodies, and they will cease digging fresh graves. At present there are 80 gravediggers employed at the cemetery, a number that will be increased to 200. The workers' poor physical condition, caused by the conditions of life in the ghetto, constitutes the most substantial impediment to intensive work in their sad trade.

MAIL STOPPAGE

On the 5th of this month, the Postal Department of the Eldest of the Jews received orders from the [German] authorities to suspend mail service, regardless of the type of correspondence and the point of origin. Mail service of every sort outside the ghetto has thus been suspended since the 5th of this month. This distressing news spread through the ghetto with lightning speed, causing dejection especially among the ghetto's new population, which, comparatively, was making the most use of the mail service and, most importantly, had been receiving money orders, which were a basic source of support for the majority of them. At present, no one knows what will

2. The Gypsies began to be deported from the Łódź ghetto to the camp in Chełmno (Kulmhof) just before Christmas, 1941, and were all put to death there.

happen to the correspondence and money orders sent to the ghetto. It is worth remembering that since June, 1940, there has been one period of two and one-half months when the ghetto was unable to send correspondence out. During that "curfew" [however] correspondence continued to arrive in the ghetto. There have been various stories concerning the suspension of mail service, and a question of fundamental interest has been whether this was a purely local event or whether there have been nationwide restrictions. There are, in addition, conjectures about the reasons behind this latest restriction.[3]

A DEATH AT THE POLICE STATION

On the 5th of this month there was another incident in which a hearse was summoned to the local branch of the German criminal police. According to the death certificate, at 7.00 P.M., a prisoner, Motek Jabłoński, aged 44 and a former tailor working as a first aid attendant in the ghetto, died in the police station. The cause of death, according to the death certificate, was a cardiac defect. The deceased's brother, the director of one of the distribution points, is also under arrest.

LOVE CONQUERS ALL

The following incident is worthy of note. A certain Edith N., who arrived here in the second Prague transport, had left her fiancé, a Czech (and a Christian), behind in Prague. Longing for his heart's desire, the fiancé did something quite unusual. He set out on a long journey on foot and, after a few weeks, had made his way to the ghetto. He then slipped in successfully through the barbed wire. Once inside the ghetto, he was seized by officials of the Order Service who, in accordance with the ruling on combatting illegal entries into the ghetto, had to turn him over to the German criminal police. His fiancée was summoned to the police station as a witness. The further fate of this courageous daredevil is not known, with the exception of one detail: he has not been admitted into the ghetto.

FUNERAL NOTICE

On January 2, Jakub Szulman, aged 52, well-known in Jewish society as a socially active and indefatigable civic leader in Łódź's Jewish life,[4] departed this world in the prime of his life. Szulman, of blessed memory, enjoyed the same trust and universal respect in the ghetto as he had in pre-war Łódź. Until the last moments of his life he held the important position of chief of Hospital No. 2 on Drewnowska Street. Due to his uncommon abilities and selfless perseverance, the deceased distinguished himself in organizing life in the ghetto, which earned him the fullest appreciation of the

---

3. The reason for the former ban on sending mail out of the ghetto was the epidemic of dysentery that prevailed in the ghetto in the months of June, July, and August, 1940. A new ban on mail to and from the ghetto had, however, been imposed by the German authorities because of preparations for the mass deportation of Jews from the ghetto to the death camp in Chełmno (Kulmhof), which began on January 16, 1942.

4. For understandable reasons the *Chronicle* does not mention that Jakub Szulman was one of the founders and leaders of the Labor Zionist party in Tsarist Russia and in independent Poland, a contributor to the Jewish press, the *Nayer folktsaytung* and the Jewish Telegraph Agency among others, a founding member of many civic, charitable, and scholarly institutions, including the branch of the Vilna YIVO (*Yidisher wisenshaftlikher institut*) in Łódź.

ghetto's leader and of everyone who worked along with him. Among other things, the ghetto owes the creation of the building superintendents' system and successes in the field of hospital management to the initiative of the deceased. Szulman, of blessed memory, was one of those rare people of whom all, without exception, can speak only in superlatives. Ghetto society has lost an extremely useful, righteous, and noble man of great merit. The funeral took place on Sunday, proceeding from the mortuary to the cemetery. Hundreds of people from all walks of life, as well as Chairman Rumkowski, took part in the funeral ceremony. The deceased is survived by his wife and son.[5]

A TRAGEDY IN A RABBI'S FAMILY

Rabbi Müller, his gravely ill wife, and his two daughters arrived in the ghetto in one of the transports from Prague. The rabbi's wife died on January 2. One of the daughters, Herta, aged 36, whose married name was Gernerov, in despair at the loss of her mother, asked the sentry on duty at the border of the ghetto at the end of Brzezińska Street to take her life. She was shot dead at a distance of 10 meters from the barbed wire at a point outside the bounds of the ghetto. She had been shot in the head and the arm. By order of the German criminal police, the body was taken to the mortuary in the Łagiewnicka [Street] hospital. Upon learning of this new blow to him, the rabbi was close to madness.

A DEATH FROM HUNGER

On the 4th of this month, at 5:00 P.M., the body of 31-year-old Rubin Broncher (of 32 Drewnowska Street) was found in a building on Bleigasse (Mianowski) Street. A physician from the First Aid Service determined the cause of death to have been exhaustion and hunger. Informed of the incident, the German criminal police gave permission for the body to be buried.

DEATH OF AN ORDER SERVICE PRISONER

On January 4, at 5:00 P.M., 43-year-old Anszel Szmulewicz, who had been at the procurator's disposal, for theft, since September 19, died while a prisoner at Precinct II of the Order Service. He was due to be released soon.

AN ATTEMPT TO ESCAPE FROM THE GHETTO

Eighteen-year-old Mojżesz Pinczewski (of 86 Brzezińska Street) was apprehended by the German police [while attempting to escape from the ghetto] and remanded to the prison here. This was Pinczewski's second attempt to escape from the ghetto.

UNREGISTERED PERSONS CANNOT BE GIVEN ACCOMMODATIONS

Proclamation No. 347 by the Eldest of the Jews has been issued in reference to this matter. Persons who, in defiance of this order, admit anyone into their dwellings or grant anyone who is registered elsewhere accommodations for the night are subject to a punishment of forcible resettlement out of the ghetto. The publication of this

5. Pola Szulman (1900–44), Jakub's widow, was deported to Auschwitz. Jakub's son, Aron Elias Szulman, survived the war, having gone to England in 1938 to study medicine. At present, he is a professor at the Medical School of the University of Pittsburgh.

order has caused great anxiety, principally among the newcomers to the ghetto, a great many of whom are registered at their collectives and are being sheltered in private apartments, without permission, by the local populace. This order most affects old and sick people, for whom conditions in the collectives are simply unbearable. Those people prefer to allocate the last of their money to pay for accommodations in private apartments. However, this ruling does not intentionally refer to that type of case; rather, it is dictated by the necessity of carrying out the campaign, now under way, of preparing 10,000 people for evacuation. And the lists of candidates for deportation are obviously being drawn up from addresses furnished by the Registration Bureau.

THE CHAIRMAN'S SPEECH ON THE THRESHOLD OF THE NEW CALENDAR YEAR (JANUARY 3, 1942)[6] [Special Report]

Work for Everyone is the Program for 1942
As noted in *Daily Chronicle Bulletin* No. 2 for January 3 [in fact, January 1–5] the Chairman delivered a long speech concerning his programs in the auditorium of the House of Culture to especially invited representatives of the Community's administration, the workshops, and the transports of the newly arrived segment of the population. The meeting was opened with a few remarks from the Chairman's deputy, [Leon] Rozenblat, chief of the Order Service.

The Eldest of the Jews began his speech by stressing that the New Year, in spite of its not corresponding to the traditional Jewish year, did, however, mark the beginning of a new calendar year in the ghetto. And that factor provided a reason for devoting some time to a review of the events of the past year, 1941.

"I don't know what interests my esteemed audience more, the past, the future, or just plain gossip. We all know that in the course of what has been almost two years in the ghetto we have lived through a great many bad periods. When I cast my mind back I am first filled with pride by the record speed at which the ghetto was turned into a place of work. Indeed, from nothing we have created enormous establishments for productive labor, we have put the most varied enterprises and factories into operation. Today we employ an army of close to 50,000 people. Such a number of workers has to be treated seriously by everyone, including, first and foremost, those who make policy. Everyone here should realize that the policy makers I have just mentioned categorically demand that the ghetto be dedicated to work. Our life in the ghetto would be much more peaceful if the Jews were not, as is their custom, too clever by half. From the beginning I have been striving to achieve one basic goal. That goal is to be able to demonstrate to the [German] authorities that the ghetto is composed exclusively of working people, that every able-bodied ghetto dweller has his own line of work. Unfortunately, a large portion of ghetto society has not wished to understand this, my basic intention. At times, people have even ridiculed my intentions, taking neither my age nor my position into account. In that respect my efforts have been a

6. An error; the speech was not delivered on Saturday, January 3, but on Sunday, January 4. Like all the rest of Rumkowski's public pronouncements, this one was also delivered in Yiddish. The Polish version of the *Chronicle* presents them in a Polish translation and the German version in German.

complete fiasco. The difficult task of correcting the evils caused by that lack of under-standing on the part of the public now awaits me.

"The question of food supply is undoubtedly one of the most difficult problems, the most urgent of problems, not only in the ghetto but everywhere in the country. I would like to say a few words about the fuel supply situation. Last year we struggled with very great difficulties in that area. You will recall that when we were facing the winter I was far from optimistic in regard to the question of fuel. I made no assurances then, though I was optimistic in regard to food. Fortunately, I succeeded in supplying the ghetto with fuel. And as to the question of food supply, things could be worse. Nevertheless, prices have risen wildly. Closing stores and increasing penalties have not helped in the struggle against this orgy of inflation. Profiteering is mushrooming. I do not mind in the least if someone takes the food out of his own mouth to sell it. But I cannot and will not tolerate the hyenas who serve as middlemen, just as I will continue to show no tolerance for the unparalleled exploitation practiced by those hyenas on members of the new population who are selling off their possessions. As I have stressed many times before, the newcomers are leading a life that is simply unforgivably frivolous. They still suffer from the mistaken belief that the present situation is already coming to an end and, under the influence of that delusion, are living from hand to mouth, selling off everything that they had brought here with them. Unfortunately, the present situation will go on and on. . . . Given that, reason would suggest the necessity of spending one's money as cautiously as possible.

"It will be a bad day when the newcomers need to start receiving relief. It is out of the question for me to institute special relief programs for them. Indeed, they are now receiving relief of every sort in their collectives, while those who have individual dwellings are availing themselves of the same food rations as the rest of the ghetto. Nevertheless, profiteering is flourishing. Before the transports arrived in the ghetto, I had succeeded in eradicating parasitic trade in food. I would also remind the new-comers that I will ruthlessly apply strict repressive measures against those who attempt to avoid selling their furs, and so on, to the bank.[7]

"Last year my monthly balance exceeded three million marks and, of that sum, more than one third was absorbed by social welfare. Financially, I am in much better shape than many of Łódź's important pre-war manufacturers. It is certain that I will always have sufficient resources to cover my obligations and to improve my financial situation. The balanced budget is supported by two pillars—work and requisitions. In any case, if I have any need for credit, I will receive it without difficulty because I have the best currency in the world at my disposal. That currency is work. My current concern is to be able to provide work for everyone. At the same time, I will not be discouraged in my efforts to stabilize life in the ghetto. There will be a new registra-tion, which will again employ thousands willing to work. Everyone in the ghetto must have work as his passport. If new work battalions are to be prepared, I will report to the authorities that my reserves are mobilized and waiting to be employed. In the very near future there will be far-reaching changes in my administration, both at the top

7. The confiscation or compulsory sale of various items, such as furs, cameras, bicycles, and musical instruments, was a frequent occurrence in the years that the ghetto existed. The same occurred when the compulsory reporting of valuables within or outside the ghetto was involved.

and below. And now I will turn to the plague known as gossip. Once again a gang of scoundrels are launching stories with the intention of disturbing society's peace. Perhaps the authors of those panic-producing stories are even lurking about here, in this audience. I would like to murder them," (said the speaker emphatically, losing his temper).

"I don't like to waste words. The stories circulating today are one hundred percent false." (On the day of the speech there was a persistent rumor concerning the alleged deportation of the entire population.) "I have recently agreed to accept twenty thousand Jews from the smaller centers, setting as a condition that the territory of the ghetto must be enlarged. At the present time, only those who are, in my opinion, deserving of such a fate will be resettled elsewhere. The authorities are full of admiration for the work which has been performed in the ghetto and it is due to that work that they have confidence in me. Their approval of my motion to reduce the number of deportees from 20,000 to 10,000 is a sign of that confidence. I have complete confidence in the Resettlement Commission. Obviously it too is capable of making mistakes from time to time.

"It is regrettable that the officials holding the most important posts engage in the unforgivable act of spreading gossip. I will give special attention to this and, with the aid of special confidential agents, I will be taking an interest in whether people are working or gossiping in the offices. I will be merciless to the guilty. Indeed, in the course of our two years in the ghetto you have seen for yourself what value such gossip has had. In the very near future a newspaper will be appearing again and, among other things, it will contain changes in the regulations concerning financial and economic matters, which were instituted on the first of January: changes in rents (see the relevant bulletin [of January 6, 1942]), the centralization of the ghetto's entire bookkeeping system with only auxiliary bookkeeping departments remaining in the individual workshops, and so forth.

"Bear in mind that at the center of all my projects is the aspiration that honest people may sleep in peace.

"Nothing bad will happen to people of good will." (Thunderous applause.)

"It is a characteristic sign that one workshop inflicts damage on another as if viewing it as a competitor. Odd things occur—if one workshop has a machine that another needs, the former is not willing to consign it to the latter. The creation of mutual impediments is even worse than theft because it strikes directly at the work process. The troubles connected with the attempt to put a dry cleaner's into operation, an establishment providing employment for a few thousand people, were truly grotesque. It could not be put into operation . . . for lack of a motor.

"I appeal to the directors to eradicate these injurious practices and to remember that they are not working for the benefit of one establishment or another but for the overall good of the ghetto. The narrow, petty point of view must be entirely overcome; we are a single, united community here in the ghetto. Here it is one for all and all for one.

"Comrades, friends, I predicted that hard times, perhaps very hard periods, would be coming, but I am certain that we will struggle through them if we eradicate the evil in ourselves; you would be very grieved if you knew what I have been through lately. And the gossips knew nothing about that, I assure you. Remember the recent mandatory repressive ruling against Jews and Poles. Had the strike attempts that took place here recently come to the attention of the [German] authorities, the snow would have been red with blood.[8] Using tough methods of my own, I put a stop to those attempts in a factory where, comparatively speaking, the workers earn the best wages. Remember, comrades and friends, that day and night my mind is concerned with improving the situation in the ghetto, and I am near the breaking point from constant exertion. I am certain that if the ghetto does its work well and in earnest the authorities will not apply any repressive measures. I want to be even more firmly grounded in that certainty, and an increase in, and improvement of, production is the road that leads there. The achievement of results in this area depends on you, with the Trade Commission in the lead. Let us, without making much ado about it, take pains in the service of the public good and not for me, its servant. Stop dealing in food, stop all the conniving. Remember that when a new contingent of deportees is demanded, I will include all the parasites on the list. Exert yourselves in your work and help each other at work. I will be instituting working papers for everyone. And it is no mere fantasy that another ten thousand people will find employment in the very near future. I give you my word of honor that there is no evil waiting concealed in the wings of the new registration. It is an ordinary precaution against any eventuality, and in case the wind changes direction. . . .

"I swear to you that at the present moment I am not on the threshold of any new danger. A great deal has already been saved through foresight. . . . The shooting incident which took place recently was just a regrettable misunderstanding [see pp. 98–99]. The guarantee obtained from the authorities prohibiting the shooting of innocent people is still in force. In that particular case a passerby, a newcomer from Germany, had not yet learned the set-up of the streets, and his actions gave the impression that he was a smuggler. They respect us because we constitute a center of productivity. I remember my reply when repressive measures were applied to the Community workers who had buried objects that were subject to compulsory sale in the bank. Persons of that sort will be ousted from work on the spot. I will bring the same methods to bear on a shoemaker or a physician; they will lose the right to work here.

"The loss the ghetto suffers through those people who, motivated by extreme selfishness, evade selling the articles subject to requisition by my bank, is attested to by the fact that units of the Kripo [German criminal police] have confiscated approximately 1,500 fur coats whose monetary equivalent could have been used for the public coffers, and whose owners would have received appropriate compensation from me. But now those assets have been irretrievably lost. And another characteristic abuse has been uncovered: a certain ghetto resident who possessed a significant hidden fortune has availed himself of welfare and special supplements for some time. Necessity compels us to come up with the goods that have been hidden, and it makes no difference, after all, whether these buried objects are discovered today, tomorrow, or in a week. It is far more sensible, therefore, to present them for sale voluntarily and

---

8. The strikes had taken place in the ghetto in October, November, and December, 1941. At that time, the principal strikers were from the boiler workshop at 17 Krótka St. and the metal workshop at 56 Łagiewnicka St. Those strikes were suppressed by the Jewish police, who arrested some of the workers, especially those they considered to be its organizers.

on time. The common interest of the ghetto demands this. At the present time our workshops have sufficient orders. Isolated shortcomings could not be under more serious scrutiny. I am planning to put new factories into operation. I will again be able to employ a large number of those thus far without work, which will, at the same time, relieve the budget of some social welfare expenses. I repeat, once again, that the ghetto's honest citizens can sleep in complete peace and need not fear anything.

"The obligatory school vacations extended past the quarter fill me with the greatest concern for the fate of the children. However, I hope that after the conclusion of the resettlement campaign I will succeed in putting the schools and kindergartens back into operation. Fathers and mothers, believe me, my heart bleeds when I see your children roaming the streets, and, thus far, I have not been able to open the school's doors for them. All the same, it did once make me so happy to see the ghetto's youngest citizens hurrying to school with their little briefcases . . .

"An old people's home for 1,500 people is not a fantasy. It is a reality close to realization.

"Representatives of the new population, I appeal to you again to finally adapt to the conditions of life in the ghetto. Aren't you ashamed that I have had to use policemen to force you to work? That I had to resort to confining you to your work crews? I wanted to give you the best apartments in the ghetto. The officials of the Housing Department can best testify to that.

"Representatives of the factory workers, work conscientiously and guard yourselves against harmful agitation. Remember that I cannot always intervene directly and that the fatal effects of provocation will not be long in coming.

"A plan on the threshold of the new year! The plan is work, work, and more work! I will strive with an iron will so that work will be found for everyone in the ghetto—it doesn't matter if it is work in a cooperative or a factory, whether the job be that of a janitor or tramcar driver. In carrying out the general program, I will be able to demonstrate, on the basis of irrefutable statistics, that the Jews in the ghetto constitute a productive element, and that they are, perforce, needed. Help me search out the harmful individuals. This will facilitate my carrying out my task, and will make it possible for you to lead a more tranquil life. I will dedicate a great deal of attention to finding employment for all our young people. I assure the workers that I have done everything to wrest at least the minimum needed for their survival. I am doing everything possible. I should not be required to do what lies beyond the bounds of the possible. Brothers and sisters, I maintain the position that without your help I cannot achieve anything. But with your help I am certain that I will succeed in carrying out my mission: to create conditions that allow us to live through the current period in good health, and to preserve the lives and the health of the people of the ghetto society and its young generation."

With those words the leader of the ghetto concluded his New Year's address. The speech, summarized above, produced a great impression on the audience and, for a long time after the meeting, was commented upon with the greatest interest by the populace of the ghetto.

A DEATH FROM HUNGER

Thirty-six-year-old Chaim Kirsztajn (of 4 Żydowska Street) died at 11 o'clock, in the gateway of the building at 8 Żydowska Street. The doctor summoned from First Aid determined the cause of death to be exhaustion.

A CONCERT

Today there was a concert conducted by Teodor Ryder, with an expanded symphony orchestra. Works by Massenet, Beethoven, Humperdinck, and Puccini were performed. In addition, the well-known Prague [in fact, Viennese] pianist [Leopold] Birkenfeld enchanted the public for a third time with his performance of Chopin's masterpieces: Variations in B Major, Nocturne in D-flat Major and the Scherzo in C-sharp Minor.

BOOTS MUST BE TURNED IN

Today, Proclamation No. 350 was posted and, by order of the [German] authorities, directed that ski and mountain boots in sizes 40 and up should be presented for sale at the Bank of the Eldest of the Jews. All boots of this type should be presented to the bank no later than the 15th of this month. In the event that boots are discovered after the above-mentioned deadline, they will be subject to confiscation, and their owners will incur the appropriate penalties.

THURSDAY AND FRIDAY, JANUARY 8 and 9, 1942

A HORRENDOUS RISE IN PRICE OF NECESSITIES ON THE MARKET

For the last few days the prices of food in the ghetto's private market have been increasing from one day to the next, and even from one hour to the next. Both the level of the prices and their rate of increase are without precedent in the history of the ghetto. Obviously one should not exaggerate the significance of the high price of food for the life of the community as a whole. As opposed to normal conditions in the pre-war period, there is no direct correlation between prices and people's lives for the simple reason that, in normal times, the private food market is the sole source of food, whereas in the ghetto's circumstances it is rather an entirely secondary factor. Indeed, the great majority of the ghetto's residents, even in periods when prices are at a low level, is too poor to be able to shop in the private market and must necessarily be satisfied with obtaining food solely on the basis of ration cards for bread, food, and vegetables. It is not, however, possible to negate the significance of transactions on the private market, since that market plays the extremely important role of regulating commodities in relation to the needs of the broad sphere of ghetto society. That role of regulator is extremely important considering the negligible role of the local market as a supplier. When reflecting on the subject of the food situation, it must be realized that the private market and the phenomena connected with it have great significance only for a negligible portion [of society]—the most prosperous element in the ghetto.

On the other hand, while stressing the role of the private market as a regulator of commodities, which is of considerable significance from a general point of view, it should be realized that this market makes it possible for the public at large to engage in transactions that are advantageous from the point of view of bettering one's own economic situation. Although these are cash transactions, they have all the characteristics of barter. One sort of food obtained on rations is sold to buy another sort. The difference in price makes it possible to obtain a larger quantity of a cheaper item, that is to gain quantity at the expense of quality. This is the attitude of the majority of the population who are not well-off. What can roughly be called the middle class, that is, the entire class of office workers receiving "middle" incomes and better, participates in transactions on the private market as a contracting party (in actual practice, as an intermediate contracting party) for the above-mentioned segment of society, the largest and the poorest. For example, members of the ghetto's middle class will frequently sell off completely, or in part, the vegetables they have obtained from the general allocation or from supplements received at their offices in order to acquire bread, sugar, margarine, or other such things. Conversely, a member of the largest class of the population is glad to buy vegetables with the money obtained from the sale of fat, meat, sausage, and even bread. This example clearly illustrates that the private market is a regulator of commodities in transactions that revolve around an exchange of quantity for quality, or quality for quantity. Obviously, there is yet a third class in ghetto society—a relatively small number of people who are especially well-off (representatives of the Community's highest administration, including the world of doctors); naturally that class takes part in transactions on the food market only as buyers. However, because the so-called upper ten thousand are a negligible number in relation to the society as a whole, that class has not played a very important role in making transactions and fixing prices. The type of situation in which food is bought and sold has been in existence since the inception of the ghetto. It is also a fact that the leader of the ghetto has many times issued orders to suppress the food trade in stores and on the streets. The Chairman, as he has often stressed in his public statements, is concerned with eliminating the merchant middleman from the food trade and with neutralizing the element that exploits both the buyer and the seller. Besides, special penalties, including the confiscation of property and the closing of stores as a means of destroying the temptation to engage in speculation, have been applied many times against the professional middlemen and merchants in the food market. At the same time, however, the Chairman himself has emphasized in his speeches that he neither will nor can forbid people to sell food they have acquired legally. Because of such a practical approach to the matter, the food market has existed without interruption, although it has recently assumed a more primitive character and the Community authorities are closing their eyes to its existence. Until recently, the Department of Food Supply, which, of course, depends on food supplies received from outside the ghetto, has exerted the deciding influence on the food market situation. Every food allocation increases the items for sale on the food market and thereby reduces prices. The prices are determined by the law of supply and demand: thus, for example, a greater availability of vegetables when fat was in shorter supply caused their respective prices to stabilize, reflecting the relationship between supply and demand, fats and vegetables. The trend in prices for the most important foodstuff, i.e., bread, goes along with the populace's supply of potatoes and also reflects the general cross section of prices. In that regard, the price of bread can always be considered an authoritative indicator of the situation in the food market.

It is only in the last few weeks that circumstances have completely changed the role and the character of the private food market. Since December, when the postal limitations on the deportees from Germany were lifted, there has been a constant avalanche of money orders. In December, over three quarters of a million [German] marks flowed into the ghetto. A whole new factor has come into existence, one which eludes the control of the Community's autonomous authorities who, thus far, had been fully able to dominate the economic situation within the limits of their means, and who are, as noted above, dependent only on the delivery of food. Recently, as the bulletin's special report notes, the provisioning of the ghetto had been displaying a tendency towards complete stabilization. In the area of basic items, the ghetto is quite regularly receiving food in quantities which correspond to the stated need. Accordingly, for many months now the distribution of food allocations to the populace has been displaying considerable uniformity and stabilization. But, at the same time, there are rampant price increases on the food market that are unprecedented in the ghetto. The new population, funded with money from outside the ghetto, is, in addition to selling its own possessions, buying up whatever is available on the food market, regardless of price. There is nothing surprising in this since the greater part of the new population is living in collectives and not receiving allocations directly. Thus, a completely new element has entered the picture and is at present playing the fundamental, almost monopolistic role of customer in the food market, a fact that has destroyed the role the food market has thus far been playing, that of regulator of commodities. Last week that new element had turned the market into a hotbed of speculation, where even the possibility of fixing precise prices was disappearing. Until recently, and throughout the ghetto's existence, those prices had displayed an admirable uniformity (both in time and in relation to the ghetto's various far-flung districts). And now chaos has set in. Clearly, although the food market—either in its present chaotic state or in its former, more stabilized state—does not play much of a role as a food supplier to the broadest elements of society (a role which still falls exclusively to the Community's administration), it does possess great significance in the life of the society (devaluation of the currency). Although the devaluation has no practical effect on the society's standard of living, it nevertheless has a depressing influence on that portion of society which receives its sole funds from the Community's coffers. Psychologically speaking, this is perfectly comprehensible: even though many people do not buy bread in the market, satisfying themselves with their rations, they are, nevertheless, subject to depression and to concern about the future in the face of the alarming disproportion between the price of a loaf of bread and a monthly salary. No one can rest easy when he finds that his monthly earnings are equal to the cost of a few loaves of bread. If only for morale and the need to maintain the currency's value at an appropriate level fixed by appraising people's labor and by official prices, it would be advisable to put a stop to the phenomena in the trade of foodstuffs which have started to become increasingly flagrant.

The following quotations, made today, illustrate the furious increase in the cost of living:

bread	19–21 marks for a 2 kg loaf
potatoes	3.5–4 marks for 1 kg
rye flour	16 marks for 1 kg
wheat flour	20 marks for 1 kg
kasha	30 marks for 1 kg
oil	35 marks [for 1 liter]
sugar	10 marks [for 1 kg]
margarine	50 marks [for 1 kg]
butter	120 marks [for 1 kg]
honey marmelade	8–10 marks [for 1 kg]
beets	2 marks [for 1 kg]
turnips	1.80 marks [for 1 kg]
horse meat	above 10 marks [for 1 kg]
saccharine	0.10 marks [for] 6 tablets

There is yet another confirmation of the idea contained in the above-quoted reflection on the influence of a new factor on the market situation. Since the newcomers for the most part live in collectives, they have no influence on the increased demand for fuel in the market. Here the market still plays the deciding role of regulator. Since fuel is presently being issued, the price of briquettes, regardless of the situation on the food market, is holding at 0.60–0.70 marks with a weak tendency [?], and the price of coal at 1 mark.

The price of at least one type of food is showing a downward trend: blended [ersatz] coffee, whose price has fallen beneath the Community's price to 2.20 marks. The newcomers, for the most part, do not purchase this item. Apparently their collectives prepare sufficient coffee for them.

JANUARY 10–13, 1942

DEATHS AND BIRTHS

In the course of four days, 216 people died in the ghetto. From the beginning of the year to January 14, the death rate has reached an average of 46 per day. There were births registered only on the 13th of January—three, to be precise (two boys and one girl). In January, with its marked increase in the mortality rate, the principal causes of death were exhaustion, tuberculosis, and heart disease.

A PHOTOGRAPHERS' COLLECTIVE

The Eldest of the Jews has granted a license for photographers who are union members to form a cooperative.[9] Eleven photographers have joined as co-partners;

9. Although cameras and photographic equipment were confiscated from the Jews almost at the very beginning of the German occupation in 1939, there were isolated photo shops in the ghetto. They were, however, gradually taken over by the Jewish administration. The cooperative met a similar fate. And so, officially, photography was to be the exclusive domain of the Jewish administration and the Photography Section it had created at the end of 1941. Yet the people in that section, aside from the work they did to order for various departments and workshops, photographed all aspects of life in the ghetto, often

photographers employed in the Community's institutions are not allowed to join. The cooperative has two photography shops: one at 11 Brzezińska Street and one at 34 Lutomierska Street. Supposedly, the cooperative will be taken over by the Community at some point in the future.

THE SITUATION ON THE CIGARETTE MARKET

The second half of last week was simply catastrophic for smokers. The tobacco available practically disappeared when the price of one 50 gram pack of *Ultra* brand cigarettes was raised to 20 marks. This drastic situation caused the street peddlers, who had until recently been thronging the sidewalks and gateways, to nearly disappear from view. It was possible, though difficult, to obtain miniature cigarettes for 20 pfennigs apiece, whereas the price for factory-made cigarettes, without mouthpieces, was 50 pfennigs. What was mostly being sold at a price of 10–12 pfennigs was a diminutive "cigarette" made from leaf of unknown origin. On Friday, such a crowd of smokers gathered in front of the store of the Eldest of the Jews on Brzezińska Street that the director had to call the police. The store is still not selling anything while it creates a stock of cigarettes made of tobacco blended from French cigarettes and from packs of *Ultras*. On January 10, a memo was sent by the Eldest of the Jews to all departments and work places, recommending that, in order to make cigarette distribution equitable, a list be drawn up of all smokers who are working and that their addresses be supplied to the Central Secretariat on Bałut Market.[10]

EVEN THE NEWSPAPER HAS GONE UP IN PRICE

Recently, a negligible number of copies of [the *Litzmannstädter Zeitung*,] the newspaper published in the city, has been reaching the ghetto by illegal means. At the same time the price of a copy increased from what it had been, 2.50–3 marks, to 5 marks, and the Sunday edition went from 8 marks to 10.

THE RESETTLEMENT ACTION

On Friday, the special commission for resettlement, which has its office in Precinct I, began sending out the first two thousand warrants. Those who have been sentenced and their families, the people who arrived here in October from Włocławek and its environs, the families of those forcibly sent from the ghetto to perform manual labor, prostitutes, and other "undesirable elements" have received summonses. The summonses are in German and Yiddish. They are marked with the date on which the

---

using hidden cameras. Mendel Grossman (1913–45), a painter and artistic photographer, was, in particular, occupied with that work. His photographs of the ghetto, some of which have been preserved, are now among the most valuable records of that time, both from a documentary and an artistic point of view. See Mendel Grossman, *With a Camera in the Ghetto*, ed. Zvi Szner and Alexander Sened (New York: Schocken Books, 1977).

10. The Central Secretariat was one of three secretariats of the Jewish administration of the ghetto, and the most important. Correspondence with the German authorities passed through its offices, as did the Eldest of the Jews' correspondence with all internal departments and workshops in the ghetto. The Central Secretariat was headed by Dora Fuchs, a Jew from Germany who had come to Łódź in October, 1938, when around 15,000 Jews were deported from Germany to Poland. After being liberated from the concentration camp to which she had been deported when the Łódź ghetto was being liquidated, Miss Fuchs emigrated to the United States.

recipient must present himself at the assembly point that has been established at 7 Szklana Street, in the vicinity of Central Prison. The first summonses enjoin their recipients to report on the 13th of this month and on the following days. It is anticipated that the first transport will leave the ghetto on Friday, the 16th of this month. The transports will be comprised of 700 people per day. Those being resettled are allowed to bring along 12.5 kilograms of baggage each. All money possessed by deportees will be exchanged for German marks at the assembly point. The summonses contain a clause that anticipates that people will be forcibly conducted to the assembly point in the event that they do not report there by the appointed time. In such cases a deportee will lose the right to take his baggage along with him.

Proclamation No. 353, of January 9 of this year, informs the families being resettled that they can offer their furniture and household effects of every sort for sale at the Eldest of the Jews' carpenters' shops. After an appraisal by experts, the furniture and household effects will be purchased there. At the same time, the proclamation permits furniture to be left for safekeeping in the carpenters' shops instead of being sold. Where sets of furniture are involved, the parties concerned may request that the experts performing the appraisals be sent to their apartments, in which cases the carpenters' shop will itself remove the furniture it purchases. The sale of furniture must occur in the interval between the receiving of the summons and the date for reporting to the assembly point.

Because of the resettlement action, the Rabbinate has been authorized to grant divorces in a simplified fashion, that is, by bypassing the Divorce Collegium in cases where the parties are subject to resettlement. There has been an influx of such cases to the Rabbinate. Most cases stem from a desire for a divorce when a married couple has been previously separated and when one of the parties is being compelled to leave the ghetto.

The fact that the resettlement action has been launched in a period when frosts are increasing has caused severe depression in the ghetto after a short-lived state of calm caused by a false rumor that the action would be suspended.

NEWCOMERS FROM ZGIERZ

On Monday morning, 85 Jews from Zgierz were transported to the ghetto.[11] For the most part they are tradesmen and their families, primarily tailors and shoemakers. They traveled the nine kilometers between Zgierz and the ghetto on horse-drawn wagons. They brought all their movable goods with them, including their furniture, bedding, and so forth, and even a relatively large amount of coal, potatoes, onions, and products of every sort. The fuel and the food were confiscated at Bałut Market for the common needs of the Community. Some of the people from Zgierz had brought up to 10 bushels of coal with them. After undergoing disinfection at the baths, the entire group from Zgierz was brought to the school building at 25 Młynarska Street.

A RUSSIAN IS SETTLED IN THE GHETTO

At two o'clock on Tuesday afternoon, January 13, officials of the secret police [Gestapo] brought a quite unusual newcomer to the central office of the Eldest of the

11. Before the war, the Jewish community of Zgierz numbered about 5,000 out of the town's total population of some 27,000. Toward the end of 1939, the greater part of them were resettled in Central Poland, to the Generalgouvernement.

Jews on Bałut Market. This was Mr. N., a Russian, of the Orthodox Church, the son of the director of industrial enterprises, who is well known in Łódź, and a descendant of a Cossack family. Mr. N's wife is Jewish. And that is the reason he is being settled in the ghetto. He is supposedly charged with having converted to Judaism, but that is simply not the case. Until now he had been living in the city with his wife without any problems. He has been settled in the ghetto along with his wife, whose parents live in the ghetto, and their 10-year-old son. The arrival of the Russian, who has many friends and acquaintances here, has caused something of a sensation. It is worth noting that Mr. and Mrs. N. arrived here without any possessions.

A WEEK [OF FESTIVITIES] FOR THE GRADUATES OF CHAIRMAN RUMKOWSKI'S LYCEUM[12]

Everyone in the ghetto knows that children and young people are the apple of Chairman Rumkowski's eye. His pre-war activities left him with an excellent reputation as a most sensitive patron and protector of children; that reputation is directly linked to his current activity in the ghetto. The manifold child-care institutions that have been developed in the ghetto with a genuine sense of reverence and such talent clearly correspond to the ghetto leader's wishes; they are and they will remain monuments to his ardent love for children and young people. As for the Chairman's relation to young people, there is no doubt that he has established and maintained both an elementary and a secondary school system that will stand out like golden threads in the history of the ghetto. According to information in our possession today, in other centers where, in many respects, conditions are much better [than here], the young people have been doomed to delinquency almost since the beginning of the war, when the doors to the schools were locked.[13] The Eldest of the Jews' love for young people and his concern for their future were symbolized by the special festivities for the ghetto's lyceum graduates—the Week of Festivities for Youth. Those festivities will long be remembered in the dismal history of the ghetto. There is no doubt that they instilled considerable courage in the hearts of those for whom the festivities were organized under such difficult conditions. And there is also no doubt that those 85 graduates will for many years recall the debt they have incurred to ghetto society and its leader. Surely that handful of young people will, from the moment they receive their diplomas, strive to divest themselves of their debt through their work.

On January 4, the House of Culture was filled with a most unusual audience—the 85 graduates of the Eldest of the Jews' Lyceum, their parents, representatives of the teaching staff, and members of the school's administration. The Chairman was seated at the ceremonial table on the stage, which had been decorated modestly but effectively. Also seated at that table were the Chairman's deputies, Messrs. [Leon] Rozenblat and [Aron] Jakubowicz, the heads of the School Department, and the

12. See above, p. 36, n. 53.
13. The schools of the Łódź ghetto were actually a rare phenomenon in the Polish territories that had been incorporated into the Reich. Yet, both secular and religious schools did exist, although limited, until their elimination in mid-1942, in many of the Generalgouvernement's ghettos, including those in Warsaw, Cracow, Lublin, Rzeszów, and Nowy Sącz.

principals of the secondary schools. There was a series of speeches by the principals, representatives of the School Department, parents, and graduates. In their speeches, the graduates expressed their gratitude to the Chairman for enabling them to receive their diplomas. The final speech was delivered by the Chairman. His was an ardent appeal to the young people just crossing the threshold of maturity.

JANUARY 14–31, 1942

FOR RESISTANCE

On January 19 of this year the walls of the ghetto were, by order of the [German] authorities, plastered with notices concerning the "legal"[14] shooting of Dr. Ulrich Schulz, who had come to the ghetto in the second transport from Prague. From the time of his arrival in the ghetto, the victim had been in Central Prison on Czarniecki Street. En route from Prague to the ghetto, he had flown into a rage and slandered the [German] police officials who were on the train as escorts. The execution took place in Central Prison, in the presence of Commandant [Salomon] Hercberg. Schulz was shot by German policemen. Dr. Schulz was born in Prague in 1897 and was a lawyer by profession.

A SHOOTING

On January 15, at 8:00 P.M., 38-year-old Lajzer Kaffeblum (of 72 Zgierska Street), a shoemaker by trade, was shot in front of 60 Zgierska Street. The sentry's bullet wounded him in the left cheek. The wounded man made his way home under his own power and from there was taken to Hospital No. 1 by an ambulance.

A SUICIDE

On January 21, at 6:45 P.M., Jakub Majersdorf (born in 1909, a resident of 25 Rybna Street) threw himself from a fourth-floor staircase window at 17 Zgierska Street. He suffered death on the spot. The German criminal police has been informed of the incident.

A DEATH IN THE STREET

On January 21, after 8:00 P.M., Chaim Jakubowicz (b. 1909, a resident of 5 Brzezińska Street) was found unconscious at the intersection of Franciszkańska and Brzezińska Streets. An ambulance was summoned and brought him to the first aid station at 41 Łagiewnicka Street. Jakubowicz died three hours later without having regained consciousness. A heart attack was the cause of death.

THEY LEFT FOR WARSAW

On January 19, 27 residents of the ghetto left for Warsaw with special permission.

---

14. In the original the word "legal" was crossed out in red pencil.

INTERMENT PROBLEMS

Because of the record increase in the mortality rate, over 200 unburied bodies had accumulated by the end of January in the cemetery mortuary. The Burial Department has ordered that immediate steps be taken to bury the corpses as quickly as possible. Special conferences have been held on this matter with the Rabbinate.

A RETURN TO JUDAISM

In the period covered, Mr. E., a 50-year-old doctor of medicine from Vienna, presented himself to the Rabbinate in connection with his desire to return to Judaism. The applicant had converted to Christianity in 1913. After carrying out the religious formalities, Dr. E. undertook to conclude a marriage.

THE BEGINNING OF THE RESETTLEMENT ACTION

The resettlement of the first 10,000 people began in the second half of January. As the BKC [*Biuletyn Kroniki Codziennej—Daily Chronicle Bulletin*] has already noted, it was decided that the undesirable elements would be used to fill the deportee quota, beginning with people under judicial or administrative sentence. The first transports would also include prisoners who are in Central Prison and those who are at the disposal of the German authorities. The formation of the transports has been determined according to the following procedure, which, incidentally, will also be maintained without change for the next stages of the resettlement. The deportees received deportation orders by mail, and all persons named (as is well known, for that entire period, those qualified for deportation were resettled along with all members of their families, and, in many cases, even with those persons who lived with them and were not members of the family) were summoned to report on a given day—more or less three days after the serving of the summons—to the assembly point at 7 Szklana Street. There, from 9 o'clock in the morning until 9 in the evening the formalities of registration proceed uninterrupted, performed by teachers and by officials from other departments summarily mobilized for the job. One thousand summonses are sent out each day. The assembly point has been in operation since the 13th of January. On the first day, scarcely half of those who had been summoned reported. From the start of the campaign the deportees have been brought in forcibly. This has occurred most frequently at night. It is worth noting that a clause in the resettlement order provides that anyone who fails to present himself voluntarily will lose the right to take 12.5 kilograms of baggage and 10 marks with him. In the first days of the campaign a dozen or so people reported voluntarily; these were for the most part homeless people. After their personal data was recorded at the meeting point, the deportees' bread and food ration cards were taken from them. At the same time, certificates concerning the health of the seriously ill family members or cripples who had remained at home were accepted. The Department of Health has mobilized a special team of doctors [for this purpose]. Day and night, the doctors, accompanied by orderlies, have been visiting the apartments where sick people have been left behind. Cripples and the bedridden have been placed in hospitals or in the Old People's Home. They have been saved from the certain death that threatened them as a result of their families' leaving. Because the hospitals are overcrowded at this time, the Department of Health has nearly been forced to suspend admitting sick people into the hospital, giving absolute priority to the above-mentioned category.

After registration, the deportees are confined in three places: the building adjacent to Central Prison at 6 Czarniecki Street, in Marysin, and in the school at 25 Młynarska Street. In the prison office, the deportees' local mark vouchers [*Markquittungen*] are exchanged for German bills. While confined at the above-mentioned quarters for a period of two to three days, the deportees were provided with food by the Community. They received a normal bread ration, soup with meat, and coffee. In addition, the Clothing Department has received orders to supply the deportees with the necessary clothing and with clogs. The free distribution of clothing, which included some twelve thousand pairs of warm underwear, earmuffs, gloves, stockings, socks, and clogs, took place in Marysin right before the transport left. The deportees were given half a loaf of bread and a sausage for the road. Every day, a train carrying deportees has left in the early morning hours. The trains are made up of approximately 20 passenger cars (55 people per car).[15]

A VICTIM OF HIS PROFESSION

On January 26, there was another case of the death of a doctor who had been sent to the Gypsy camp to combat the typhus raging there. The latest victim of his own profession was Dr. Aron Nikelburg. He had drawn his turn by lot during the final phase of the camp's existence on Brzezińska Street. The deceased was scarcely 32 years old. He received a degree from the German gymnasium in Łódź,[16] and then did his studies in Berlin. He worked in the Anna-Maria Hospital before the war as a pediatrician. He had been in the ghetto only a short time, having come here last summer as part of a group of doctors hired by the Chairman for the Department of Health.[17]

REPRESENTATIVES OF THE JEWISH COMMUNITY OF KALISZ HERE IN THE GHETTO

In the second half of January, the Chairman of the Jewish Council of Kalisz, Mr. Gustaw Hahn, spent some time in the ghetto together with his deputy. The representatives of the Kalisz Jewish Council provided information about the fate of the Jews of Kalisz. The following account has been pieced together from what they said.

Before the war, the Jewish population of Kalisz stood at 23,000. The mass evacuation of Jews from Kalisz began as early as September, 1939. In the final quarter of last year there were still 700 Jews left in Kalisz. They were all living in communal quarters that were formerly part of a hospital. During this period there were two evacuations, which included all persons unfit for work, as well as children up to the age of 14. Thus far, no one knows anything about either the fate or the current whereabouts of the

15. All were deported to the camp in Chełmno (Kulmhof), where they were put to death.

16. In pre-war Poland, every national group—Poles, Jews, and Germans—had its own schools, which existed alongside the public schools. There were a few German gymnasiums, the first of which, the Männliche Gymnasium, was founded in 1887. Some Jews attended German schools before and after the First World War.

17. Dr. Aron Nikelburg was probably the thirteenth physician brought by M. C. Rumkowski from Warsaw to the Łódź ghetto. (See above, p. 55, n. 66.)

evacuees.[18] At the present moment there are only 160 Jews in Kalisz. A camp with around 1,500 Jews has been set up near Kalisz, 23 kilometers away, in the small town of Koźminek. Those remaining in Kalisz inhabit a block formed by three buildings, without being walled off from the rest of the city. However, with the exception of the three-man Jewish Council, the inhabitants of that block do not travel out into the city. The municipality of Kalisz is in charge of supplying them with food. Model workshops, which receive civilian and military orders, have been set up in that block. The food supply leaves nothing to be desired. The food rations are as follows: 2.25 kilograms of bread per week; unlimited potatoes at the market price of 8 pfennigs per kilogram; bread, which costs 27 pfennigs per kilogram with a ration card, can also be bought easily without a card at the price of 50 pfennigs; 250 grams of sugar per week; 100 grams of fat; 100 grams of marmalade; 200 grams of cottage cheese; and 250 grams of meat. The workers receive a 50-gram pack of tobacco and soap for each two week period. The coal allocation comes to 90 kilograms per person per month. There is a communal kitchen located in the block. Each family has one room at its disposal. In addition, the Jewish Council supplies the residents with bedding and work clothes. The wood needed by the residents is supplied by the municipality from demolished buildings in the city. Two doctors and one medic provide health care. They have a pharmacy and an infirmary at their disposal. There is a canteen in the block stocked with haberdashery goods, stationery supplies, and so forth, which also sells beer and other beverages. All the residents receive food free of charge. The Jewish Council settles accounts concerning wages and food with the municipality. In addition, people who are working receive 3 marks a week.

Mr. Hahn and the deputy who accompanied him, Majer Landau, were glad to share their impressions of their nearly 10-day stay in the ghetto. It is worth mentioning that, during their visit, the Chairman put an Order Service official at their disposal who showed them around the ghetto and its institutions. And so the guests from Kalisz had the opportunity to acquaint themselves with conditions in the ghetto, with the organizational structure of the Eldest of the Jews, and also with the work of the most important enterprises here. In their own words, they were simply amazed by what they had seen. They were particularly taken with the exemplary organization, the order they observed, and the hospital system. When sharing their impressions, the representatives of the Kalisz Jews lay special emphasis on their admiration for the leader of the ghetto. So much for the "splendor of life here." The shortcomings, on the other hand, principally the problem of hunger, had a depressing effect on our guests. It is also worth noting that quite false information had been spread in Kalisz concerning conditions in the ghetto here, and the representatives of the Jewish Council decided to reveal it as such immediately upon their return to Kalisz. To be precise, it has been said in Kalisz, completely without any basis, that all Jews not originally from Łódź are treated negligently in the ghetto here. According to those stories, the ghetto authorities have established a rule of allowing only Łódź Jews to work, thus condemning Jews from out of town, including those from Kalisz, to death by starvation.

18. From September to December, the Jewish population of Kalisz was resettled to the Generalgouvernement in Central Poland. In December, 1941, however, Jews unfit for work and the children were deported to the death camp in Chełmno (Kulmhof).

Our guests stated that they had seen with their own eyes that those rumors were false because the Chairman applied a policy of complete equality towards all the ghetto's inhabitants.

THE RESETTLEMENT ACTION IN JANUARY

Resettlement occurred in January from the 16th to the 29th, and included 14 transports. All told, 10,003 persons left the ghetto—4,853 men and 5,750 women.[19]

POPULATION COUNT AS OF FEBRUARY 1, 1942

On February 1 of this year the ghetto numbered 151,001 inhabitants: 64,717 men and 86,284 women.

Population Changes in the Month of January

	Total	Men	Women
Population on January 1, 1942	162,681	69,978	92,703
Births in January	34	18	16
Stillbirths in January	3	2	1
Arrivals from Warthegau and the General-gouvernement in January	15	11	4
Arrivals from Zgierz in January	83	40	43
Returned from prison in January	7	7	
Returned from manual labor in January	14	14	
Total	156	92	64
Deaths in January	1,787	1,083	704
Left for Warthegau and the Generalgouvernement in January	46	17	29
Resettled in January	10,003	4,253	5,750
Total	11,836	5,353	6,483

In the course of the month of January the population of the ghetto declined by 11,680 (5,261 men and 6,419 women).

THE MONTH OF FEBRUARY, 1942

DEATHS AND BIRTHS

During the 28 days of February, 1,875 people died. The average daily mortality rate exceeded 67. This is the highest number of deaths for one month in the history of the ghetto. In the month of February, 1,124 men and 751 women died.

Forty-five children were born in the ghetto in February—21 boys and 24 girls.

---

19. An error; there were 5,353 men (cf. the table below).

THE RESETTLEMENT ACTION

The resettlement action, begun last month and renewed in the last ten days of February, is one of the most important events recorded in the *Chronicle* in February. In that period, the authorities demanded 10,000 people for resettlement from the ghetto. The deportation took place from the 22d to the 28th of February. Ten thousand people were deported from the ghetto in seven transports. A special commission was in charge of evaluating candidates for deportation. The list of deportees included prisoners serving sentences who were still in the ghetto. In February, people on relief also began to be deported. The second stage of the resettlement (the resettlement campaign began in January) involved even greater severities. Thus, among other things, a person's right to take the sum of 10 [German] marks with him was rescinded. As background to this restriction, there was a rumor in the ghetto to the effect that in February people were being deported to the Generalgouvernement where, as is known, German marks are not the currency in circulation.[20] Many widely varied stories appeared in the ghetto concerning the fate of the deportees. It was said, for example, that the deportees were set free in Koluszki; those who spread this unverified information claimed that this news had come from many deportees in Warsaw. Another rumor had it that the deportees were in Koło county and also in the vicinity of Brześć Kujawski.[21] We mention these stories only for the sake of accuracy in chronicling events, for in reality the ghetto has not received any precise information on which to base an idea as to the fate or even the whereabouts of the deportees. This mystery is depriving all the ghetto dwellers of sleep. The resettlement in February was significantly more severe than the one in January; most of the guards ordered the deportees to throw away their knapsacks and often even the bundles they were carrying by hand, including the food supplies they had taken with them for their journey into the unknown.

SUICIDES

The records of the Order Service indicate the following incidents of suicide in the month of February, 1942:

On January 31, 46-year-old Icek Pinkus Kopel, a spinner by trade, hung himself in his apartment at 7 Berek Joselewicz Street. A doctor from emergency aid pronounced him dead.

On February 2, at 3:00 P.M., Rubin Starozum, a 56-year-old worker and resident of 36 Drewnowska Street, hung himself from the doorway in the attic at 34 Lutomierska Street. He died on the spot.

On the same day, at 9 o'clock in the morning, a 57-year-old former merchant, Wilhelm Blum, resettled here from Frankfurt am Main, attempted to take his own life

---

20. Initially, the pre-war Polish złoty was the currency of the Generalgouvernement, which was later replaced by the złotys issued by the Bank of Issue in Poland (*Bank Emisyjny w Polsce*), founded in Cracow by the Germans.

21. While the information about the town of Koluszki, one of the main railroad junctions in Poland, was false, the story that the Jews resettled from the Łódź ghetto had been sent to Koło county was true, for Chełmno (Kulmhof) was located in that county.

by taking Veronal. He was placed in the infirmary of his collective at 70 Zgierska Street. He died after several hours. The cause of his depression: destitution.

On February 20, a 58-year-old man resettled here from Breslau,[22] Siegberg Erich Friedrich (of 39 Wolborska Street), a tram driver by profession, attempted suicide by taking an overdose of Luminal tablets. He was taken to Hospital No. 1, where he died after suffering two days.

On February 27, Gabriel Józef Frydman, aged 59, an insurance agent and a native of Warsaw, committed suicide by jumping from a fourth floor window at 33 Młynarska Street. He was taken to the hospital beyond hope of survival.

SHOOTINGS

On February 3, at 3:30 A.M., a 34-year-old woman resettled here from Prague, Edyta Czerkowska (a resident of the collective at 29 Franciszkańska Street), was shot and killed. The incident took place at the intersection of Smugowa and Franciszkańska streets near the barbed wire.

On February 18, at 5 o'clock in the afternoon, two officials of the German criminal police presented themselves at Precinct I of the Order Service to report that the body of a man was lying near the barbed wire at 38 Smugowa Street. Officials of the Order Service went to the scene where they found that the death had resulted from a gunshot wound in the mouth. Identification found on the victim provided information as to his name and profession. He was Fiszel Wolf Kuperman, born in Łódź in 1920 and a tailor by trade; he had recently been living in Tomaszów, where he was engaged in commerce. According to explanations furnished by agents of the [German] criminal police, Kuperman had attempted to enter the ghetto illegally. By order of the German police the victim's body was carried to the mortuary at Precinct I [it was actually Hospital No. 1] at 8:00 P.M.

On February 24, at 6:00 P.M., Ludwig Rabl, born in 1881 in Bohemia, was mortally wounded in the head by a sentry's bullet in the vicinity of the barbed wire at the intersection of Franciszkańska and Smugowa streets. The wounded man lived in a collective at 13 Franciszkańska Street, that is, in a building in the immediate vicinity of the incident. Physicians from First Aid found the body as it was already growing cold. By order of the German sentry, the body was taken to the mortuary at Precinct I [should be Hospital No. 1].

AN EXECUTION

Saturday, February 21, will long remain in the memories of the ghetto's inhabitants because the first public execution took place on that day. The large square at Bazarna and Lutomierska streets was chosen as the site of the execution. People did not know until the last moment that an execution was going to take place on the square. However, there was a rumor circulating the previous evening that a public meeting would be called for Saturday morning on Bazar [Square]. The cause of this rumor was the order the Office of Resettled Persons received from the [German] authorities on Friday: namely, the office was ordered to have the residents of all collectives and

22. There were no resettlements directly from Breslau to the Łódź ghetto. S. E. Friedrich probably arrived there in one of the transports of Jews from the West.

transports of West European Jews appear on Bazar [Square] at 10 o'clock in the morning. In the early morning hours, groups of German Jews could be seen marching there in ranks. They were led by the directors of their collectives, escorted by Order Service men, and were headed toward the square on Bazarna Street. At precisely 10 o'clock, three large groups of Jews lined up around the square. Numerous Order Service patrols maintained order. Only people who were ill (and possessed medical certificates) were exempted from having to report to the square. A gallows had been erected in the very center of the square. A few minutes after 10:00 a droshky containing a shackled convict, escorted by officials from Central Prison headed by Commandant [Salomon] Hercberg, pulled up in front of the building on Rybna Street in which the Office of Resettled Persons is located. The condemned man was brought to the office. Right up to the last minute, he had no idea of the fate awaiting him because he had arrived in a droshky that had bypassed the square where the gallows had been erected. While the convict remained in the office, the final preparations were made near the gallows, under the eye of the [German] authorities who had arrived by car. At precisely 10:30 the condemned man was taken from the building at 8 Rybna Street to the place of execution located nearby. The condemned man remained completely calm to the end. A few officials from Central Prison accompanied him on his final walk. He did not break down, even when, coming out of Rybna Street, he caught sight of the crowds (about 8,000 German Jews had been brought there as spectators) arranged in rows of two around Bazar Square. It was at that moment that the condemned man realized that he was being taken to his execution. Only when he threw off his coat and jacket did he quietly and humbly request that he be granted his life. The hangman, the only person taking part in the execution who did not wear [yellow] patches, slipped the noose around the condemned man's neck. There are several stories as to his identity. Some claim that he was a Pole brought in from the city. Another rumor has it that he was a Jew. The representatives of the [German] authorities issued instructions at a distance of about two meters from the gallows. At the moment when the body was hanging from the rope, many of the men assembled at the place of execution began to recite the prayer for the soul of the dead (*kaddish*). Having taken photographs after the execution, the representatives of the authorities returned at once to their automobiles and left the ghetto. The crowd too began to disperse almost at once. The hanged man's body remained on the gallows for a few hours. Around 4 o'clock, a covered [horse-drawn] hospital ambulance drove up and took the corpse away. At the same time, the gallows were removed—as was the condemned man's clothing, which had been lying just nearby the entire time. It is worth noting that, during the execution, a considerable number of the forced spectators suffered nervous shocks. The condemned man's wife and daughter were also forced to be present at the execution.[23] The execution has shocked the ghetto. The hanged man was Maks Hertz, resettled here from Cologne, born September 27, 1888, in the city of Gangelt. He had received a secondary education and was a printer by profession. He arrived in the ghetto with his wife and nine-year-old daughter on October 23 of last year in the first transport. A few weeks before his execution Hertz

---

23. In the original, the words *forced to be* were crossed out.

had slipped out of the ghetto and apparently had spent several days in the city, where he managed to acquire letters of recommendation to be used in Cologne. He was arrested at the railroad station while he was buying a ticket to Cologne. At that moment the patch which adorns the clothing of the ghetto's inhabitants fell out of his wallet. The cashier noticed this, which was to have further consequences. After his arrest he was placed in Central Prison in the ghetto, where he spent about three weeks before he was executed.

TO SUPPLEMENT THE NOTE

on page 3 [p. 129] concerning the shooting of Fiszel Wolf Kuperman, we can add the following details. Kuperman, a young man of 21, had recently been residing in Tomaszów and had been roaming the country in the two years since his flight from Łódź. His father, whom he was intending to visit, lives in the ghetto. It was during his attempt [to visit] that he was shot and killed.

THEY WERE DELUDED

One day during the resettlement action a rumor spread through the ghetto that the resettlement was to be suspended and that the head of the ghetto would deliver a public speech on that subject after a long silence. Unfortunately, the rumor proved false; resettlement proceeded according to the plan announced in advance, which—as we note on page 1 [p. 128]—stipulated that 10,000 people were to be deported from the ghetto during the month of February. The much anticipated speech by the Chairman concerning the desired changes did not, of course, take place either. Parenthetically it is worth mentioning that among the deportees were a good number of socially harmful individuals, including notorious [German] informers, for example, the well-known Mr. G.

THE PREPARATIONS FOR THE RESETTLEMENT ACTION

which was conducted in February—as we note on page 1 [p. 128]—began on February 12, and [the resettlement] commenced on the 22d. Sewerage workers,[24] numbering 300, 300 [other] people who had committed various offenses, people on welfare and extra workers were in the forefront of those entered on the deportation rolls. The original list of candidates for deportation included 3,000 names. Until the moment when the order to commence deportation was received, the ghetto had continually deluded itself by believing, as noted above, that the resettlement would not occur. Those rumors were true only to the extent that the date for the resettlement was delayed for some eight days: it began on the 22d instead of the 14th.

TYPHUS

The danger of a typhus epidemic, brought here from the Gypsy camp, hung over the ghetto during the first days of February. There were 28 cases of spotted typhus in this

---

24. Excrement removal, a difficult and dangerous job that for some was a means of obtaining additional food allotment, was also used to punish people who had been arrested for a variety of offenses in the ghetto; most often, however, for the theft of food, embezzlement, or for resisting the authority of the Jewish administration and for organizing strikes in the workshops (see also pp. 229–30).

period. This was an exceptionally severe period for the health service, for, at that time, the majority of doctors had succumbed to illness as a result of exhaustion.

ABRAM FUKS

born in Opoczno in 1903, owner of a stationery store at the intersection of Młynarska and Zawisza streets, died suddenly in the office of the [German] criminal police on February 27 of this year.

PROFESSOR FELIKS HALPERN

a pianist esteemed in Łódź, a piano teacher, and for many years a music critic in the Łódź press, died on February 3 of this year at the venerable age of 76. Halpern was a very popular figure among the intelligentsia of Łódź. Among other things, he was known in society as the creator of peerless puns and stories.

COPPER COINS TAKEN OUT OF CIRCULATION

By order of the authorities, the Eldest of the Jews has informed the population of the ghetto that copper coins, such as 1 and 2 *Reichs* and *Rentenpfennige*,[25] will be taken out of circulation beginning on the first of March. All copper coins, including [Polish] *groszy* and [Czech] *koronas*, should be exchanged at the bank or at Order Service precincts.

POPULATION COUNT AS OF MARCH 1, 1942

On March 1, 1942, there were 142,079 Jews residing in the ghetto: of that number 60,829 were men and 81,250 were women.

Population Changes in the Month of February

	Men	Women	Total
Level on February 1, 1942	64,717	86,284	151,001
Born in February	21	24	45
Stillbirths	—	—	—
Miscarriages	1	—	1
Remains from outside the ghetto	1	—	1
New arrivals from the Generalgouvernement and Warthegau	14	4	18
Arrived from prison	8	—	8
Correction in the number of new arrivals from Zgierz	—	1	1
Total new arrivals in February	45	30	75
Deaths in February	1,128	745	1,873
Left for the Generalgouvernement and Warthegau	46	52	98
Correction of the previous list of those sent to do manual labor	1	—	1
Resettled in February	2,758	4,267	7,025

25. *Rentenpfennigs*, like *Rentenmarks*, were introduced in Germany in November, 1923, to combat inflation. Though later withdrawn, they remained in regular circulation as a form of small change.

Population Changes in the Month of February (cont.)

	Men	Women	Total
Combined loss for February	3,933	5,064	8,997
Actual loss for February	3,888	5,034	8,992

THE NUMBER OF WEST EUROPEAN JEWS

On the last day of March of this year there were 17,628 Jews deported from Germany, former Austria, former Czechoslovakia, and Luxembourg residing in the ghetto. That figure breaks down into 6,768 men and 10,860 women. In the fall of last year, around 20,000 Jews came to the ghetto from the West; a few hundred of them have left to perform manual labor, a dozen or so have gone to the Generalgouvernement, and thus, of those remaining, around 3,000 have died here in the course of 5 months.

THE MONTH OF MARCH, 1942

DEATHS AND BIRTHS

In March, 1942, 2,244 people died in the ghetto (in January of this year 1,877 died, and in February, 1,875). The figures in parentheses make it evident that there was a shocking increase in the mortality rate in March. The causes are hunger, the protracted winter, and the resettlement campaign. 1,411 men and 833 women died in March.

There were 54 births registered in March: 25 boys and 29 girls. One child was stillborn and there were two cases of premature birth.

SUICIDES

The universal mood of depression and panic that reigned in March as a result of the resettlement action provided fertile soil for acts of desperation. The following chronicle of the suicides committed in March illustrates the state of affairs.

On March 1, a married couple, Wiktor and Daisy Heller, resettled here from Prague, committed suicide together by taking an overdose of Luminal. Wiktor Heller was born in Bohemia in 1882 and his wife, in London in 1886. In the ghetto they lived in the collective at 10 Jakuba Street, which was where they also committed suicide. The husband died before the doctor arrived, and the wife, a few hours later in Hospital No. 1. They left a letter from which it appears that Heller was driven to his desperate act by illness and anguish, while his wife wished to share her husband's fate.

Gabriel Frydman, the insurance agent who jumped from a fourth-story window on February 27 in an attempt on his own life, died in the hospital on March 1.

On March 4, Sara Tenenbaum (of 26 Gnieźnieńska Street), born in 1886 in Brody, took her own life by leaping to the road from the bridge over Zgierska Street, near the church.

On March 2, Elza Bender (born in Prague in 1889) jumped from a fourth-story window in the building at 10 Jakuba Street, where the collective of Jews from Prague is located. She was taken to the hospital, but there was no hope for her survival. She died in agony after twenty-four hours.

On March 9, at 8:00 P.M., Rola Pacanowska, a widow, born in Warsaw in 1877, committed suicide by taking an overdose of sleeping pills. She died in the hospital after a few hours without having recovered consciousness.

On March 11, at 2 o'clock A.M., Johann "Israel"[26] Schultz (born in Frankfurt in 1885), who had been resettled here from Frankfurt am Main, committed suicide in his lodgings at 70 Zgierska Street by taking Veronal. He was taken to Hospital No. 1. The motive for his desperate act has not been established.

On March 12, Dwojra Rubinsztajn, aged 48, born in Piotrków, hung herself in her apartment at 61 Brzezińska Street. The doctor, sent by ambulance, pronounced her dead.

On March 15, a 63-year-old woman, Julia Altschul, who had been resettled here from Prague, jumped from a fourth-story attic window of the Old People's Home to the pavement below. She had been exhibiting signs of a nervous breakdown, caused by the most recent ordeals. By order of the German criminal police, the body was placed in the mortuary at Hospital No. 1.

On March 19, Luzer Gartner, a street cleaner (of 32 Dworska Street), born in 1892, jumped from a third-story window at 29 Dworska Street. He was taken by a first-aid droshky to the hospital in critical condition.

On March 18, 20-year-old Bela Wilk threw herself from a third-story window. Due to a fever caused by typhus, the young suicide was not [fully] conscious when committing the act. The incident took place at night, when all the building's residents were asleep. The body was taken to the mortuary at the hospital.

Luzer Gartner, whose suicide attempt we mentioned earlier, died after a few hours in the hospital.

On March 22, Jankiel Wolrauch (born in Łódź in 1910), by trade a cashier, recently unemployed, leaped from a third-story window at 12 Łagiewnicka Street. He was taken to the hospital in critical condition.

On March 23, Julia Falk (of 23 Urzędnicza Street), who was born in 1898 and resettled here from Berlin, poisoned herself with sleeping pills. She was taken to the hospital.

On March 24, a widow, Jozefina Beck (b. Vienna, 1885) and her son Egon (b. Vienna, 1924) committed suicide together. The mother and son together drank a strong dose of poison on the staircase of the building at 13 Limanowski Street. They lived together at 6 Miodowa Street. The son had been working in the fire department. The mother died on the spot, the son was taken to Hospital No. 1, where he died after a few hours. The above incident is unparalleled in its horror.

On March 25, Ruchla Pasamonik (b. Tuszyn, 1904), a resident of 13 Żydowska Street, committed suicide by jumping from the fourth story of the building where she resided. She was taken to the hospital with no hope of survival.

Edward Silberstein (b. Vienna, 1910), resettled here from Vienna and a resident of 7 Lotnicza Street, committed suicide by cutting the arteries in his left arm. He was taken to the hospital.

26. According to the Nuremberg Laws (Second Decree Implementing the Law of Concerning the Change of Family Names of August 17, 1938), Jews in Germany were forced to adopt additional names: *Israel* for males, *Sara* for females. This law was extended to Austria and the Protectorate of Bohemia and Moravia, but not to occupied Polish territory.

On March 27, Tauba Nachma Piotrkowska (b. Łódź, 1870), a midwife, poisoned herself in her apartment at 14 Limanowski Street. The first aid physician pronounced her dead.

ILLEGAL BORDER CROSSINGS INTO THE GHETTO

An incident of this type was recorded in March. The details are as follows: On March 8, at 10:00 P.M., officials of Precinct II of the Order Service found a man critically wounded by two rifle shots on Dolna Street. An ambulance took the victim to Hospital No. 1, where he died in the morning. From the documents found on the victim it appears that he was a Pole who resided in the city. His name was Marian Osiecki (b. Bełchatów, 1909) and he was a barber by profession. He was shot while crossing the border of the ghetto.

A SHOOTING

On March 12, at 5:30 P.M., two officials of the German criminal police appeared at Precinct IV of the Order Service to report that the body of a woman who had been shot and killed was to be found on Ogrodowa Street, on the far side of the barbed wire. By order of the German police, Order Service men brought the woman back into the ghetto. No personal data has been established for the victim. There were no documents in her possession. The body has been placed in a hospital mortuary at the disposal of the German authorities.

A FOOTNOTE TO THE RESETTLEMENT

There were strong frosts just after the middle of March that caused a large number of fatalities among the deportees. A great number of deportees froze while still waiting for the train at the Radogoszcz station. During the resettlement campaign, the corpses of five deportees, evidently frozen at the beginning of the journey, were sent back to the ghetto.

POSTCARDS

As is well known, postal service to and from the ghetto has been suspended since the beginning of the year. On March 9, the Post Office received permission from the [German] authorities for local residents to send out printed postcards containing brief statements concerning the sender's health. 1,000 such postcards are allowed to be sent out per day.

RUMORS

Toward the end of the first ten-day period in March a rumor spread through the ghetto that the Community authorities intend to withdraw currency from circulation in order to curtail speculation on the food market. Time has proven this rumor to be without foundation.

Several times during the resettlement action there were rumors that it would be interrupted. These rumors, however, proved untrue since the action continued uninterrupted through the month. In that respect, March 21 will be a day to remember. On that day, which was a Saturday, after the transport had left, the authorities informed the Eldest of the Jews that further transports were suspended. The deportees quartered in Marysin to await their turn were released at once and returned home. The joy, however, was short-lived. Early Monday morning a new contingent of 11,000 people was demanded for deportation. That incident had a depressing effect not only on the populace but on the higher officials here as well. After this incident, the Eldest of the Jews often stressed in his statements that because of the change in decision by the authorities, which had occurred in the course of a few hours, he was not able to provide authoritative assurances as to how long the resettlement action would continue.

ON MARCH 25, 120 PEOPLE LEFT FOR WARSAW [GHETTO]

In the context of the resettlement action, their departure made an impression like that of rats abandoning a sinking ship. Everyone in the ghetto envied those leaving for Warsaw of their own free will.

ON MARCH 24, 687 PEOPLE (9,267 MEN AND 15,420 WOMEN) WERE RESETTLED FROM THE GHETTO

The resettlement action continued uninterrupted throughout the month, Sundays excepted. Thus, each of the transports, on the average, comprised 900 people per day. For the most part the deportees were welfare recipients, including, in large measure, people who had recently been working and had even been working for quite a long time, but who had formerly been on welfare. All persons listed on the rolls of the court or in the Bureau of Investigation and also in the office of administrative punishment were resettled. In general, the nature of the offense was not taken into consideration, since the demand by the [German] authorities for increasing numbers of deportees imposed the obligation of continuously supplying more and more thousands of people on the authorities of the Eldest of the Jews. March will long be remembered in the annals of the ghetto as the month of resettlement. From morning on, for twenty hours nonstop, processions of deportees headed on foot for Marysin . . .

ARREST AND RESETTLEMENT OF THE PRISON COMMANDANT

The Hercberg affair has made for one of the greatest sensations in the annals of the ghetto thus far. The "Hercbergiada" will no doubt stand out in bold relief in the history of our ghetto.

Who was Hercberg? A tall, obese man of some forty-odd years, bursting with health, splendidly dressed, he was one of the most popular figures among the leading representatives of the ghetto's administration. His prison commandant's cap, adorned with thick gold braid, like the beautiful gold-embroidered armband he wore, set him apart from those around him. He was a child of the Bałut neighborhood. In this neighborhood, he had worked as a projectionist in a third-rate theater before the war. It is said that he was initially taken on for the post of Order Service commissioner on the basis of documents he presented that showed him to have been an officer in the Polish army. The authenticity of those documents is doubtful, to say the least. In June, 1940, he was arrested by the German authorities on a charge of concealing a radio. He was kept in the Radogoszcz camp for several months. After his release in the fall of 1940 he was appointed to the post of commandant of the prison here, which was, at that time, in the process of being established. After some time Hercberg's authority increased significantly. He became chief of the Order Service precinct in

Marysin and, at the same time, head of the administration of Marysin II. In that manner Hercberg became the lord and master of Marysin as if he were the governor of that most beautiful section of the ghetto. He was granted great powers; he had the right, for example, to hire personnel and policemen on his own. Besides directing the prison and exercising the highest authority in Marysin, Hercberg took a lively and active part in various campaigns on the grounds of the ghetto itself. He was charged with special assignments in connection with the rounding-up of the ghetto's undesirable elements. And he had often personally organized and directed night raids on apartments, as well as raids that were carried out on the streets in broad daylight. He played a significant role in the execution of the resettlement action, and so on, and so forth.

Thus, there is nothing surprising in the ghetto residents' outright dismay on learning of Hercberg's arrest. It turned out that Hercberg had been ignobly abusing the trust that the authorities had placed in him. The memorable incident took place on the night of March 12. The arrest was made by representatives of the German criminal police, causing no small sensation in the ghetto. On the next day, Friday, March 13, Hercberg was released; after a few hours he was again brought to the [German criminal] police's branch office on Kościelna Street. The ghetto was almost immediately aware that searches had been conducted in Hercberg's apartments, of which he possessed as many as three (at 9 Drukarska Street, on Czarniecki Street across from Central Prison, and in Marysin), and had yielded fantastic results. As people in the ghetto put it, a regular subsection of the Department of Food Supply was discovered in his apartments. People said—and this seems to be entirely well-founded—that he had cached away the following supplies: 70 kilograms of salt bacon, sacks of flour, several dozen kilograms of sugar, candy, and marmalade (he had been in charge of a candy factory in Marysin), an array of liquors of the highest quality, a box of oranges, innumerable canned goods, a few hundred boxes of shoe polish, 40 pickled tongues, a very large stock of toilet soap, and so forth. Whole sets of clothing and linens—for example, three magnificent fur coats and nine pairs of high boots—were found in his apartment; and, moreover, people in the ghetto maintained that more than 20 kilograms of gold, in the form of various objects were found there, as well as a large amount of valuable jewelry, including some genuine stones. Apparently, the most valuable items were found concealed in loaves of bread. It is not hard to guess the source of this lurid booty . . . The raids and night searches evidently provided him with far-reaching opportunities to commit crimes that harmed not only the parties involved but, first and foremost, the populace of the ghetto, for whose use the confiscated goods should have been employed. In addition, according to rumors which, in this case, seem not to be without foundation, over half a million marks in the form of German banknotes were found at Hercberg's. Where did these astounding sums come from?[27] Therein lies Hercberg's most heinous crime. Out of concern for the fate

27. An enormous fortune, by ghetto standards, was indeed found in the apartment or apartments of Salomon Hercberg, the head of Central Prison. Clearly, the chroniclers had only a rough idea of what he had actually amassed, and that may have been based, as they themselves say, on the stories that were circulating in the ghetto. Hence, the sometimes quite exaggerated reports, such as, "more than 20 kilograms of gold in the form of various objects were found there," or "over half a million marks in the form of German banknotes" were found there. However, a complete invoice of the items confiscated from Hercberg was made by the German criminal police (Kripo); comprising 162 categories, it was typed in two

of the deportees, the Chairman had endeavored to furnish them with cash for their journey. We should recall that, at the beginning of the resettlement campaign, each deportee was allowed to take 10 [German] marks with him. The discretionary fund for that noble purpose, which had literally exhausted the ghetto's treasury of its reserves of German banknotes, had been entrusted to Hercberg. The members of Hercberg's family, which consisted of his wife, his three sons, and his mother-in-law, were arrested along with him. After several days under arrest at the local branch of the [German] criminal police, Hercberg, his wife, and his children were unexpectedly taken to the Radogoszcz train station. That was on Tuesday, March 17, of this year. A few minutes before the train departed with the deportees, a private car containing Hercberg, his wife, and sons, as well as police escorts, drove nearly right up to the train car assigned to the police escort. The eyewitnesses say that Hercberg's appearance left much to be desired. His head was no longer graced by his splendid cap, which had now been replaced by an ordinary cycling cap. The next day the former commandant's mother-in-law was deported under similar conditions. Since his deportation, there has, of course, been no information about his subsequent fate; indeed, no precise information has been established about the fate of any of the people who were deported from the ghetto. The "Hercbergiada" was, however, long discussed in the ghetto, and rumor had it that, shortly after his departure, he took his own life.

Fear began to reign over the ghetto's inhabitants the instant the news of his arrest spread through the ghetto. People were afraid that the entire population might have to atone for his guilt. When, a few days after his deportation, the authorities ordered the resettlement suspended and then revoked the decision a few hours later, people remarked that this was the result of the Hercberg affair. It is difficult to determine whether that rumor accords with the facts. Jakub Tintpulwer had been appointed by Hercberg as his deputy. He was arrested along with Hercberg and incontestably charged with knowing about all of his chief's sinister machinations. According to his death certificate, Tintpulwer died of a heart attack on March 18 of this year, in the offices of the [German criminal] police. Seven prison officials were arrested in connection with the Hercberg affair; they were released after being held under arrest for a few weeks. One of them, the prison victualler, Kamiński by name, died in the hospital shortly after his release.

HOW THE DEPORTEES SOLD THEIR PERSONAL PROPERTY

On the basis of the relevant proclamation, the deportees were able to sell their household property and furniture at a special purchasing point in the carpenters' shop, and also in stores set up ad hoc at 35 Franciszkańska Street and at the Main Purchasing Agency (at 4 Kościelny Square). In March there were swarms of deportees in front of those institutions' stores, where they had brought their goods and chattels

---

columns, on four sheets of paper. The inventory mentions no half-million German marks, but 2,955 Reichsmark, nor 20 kilograms of gold, but 15 various items made of gold, like rings, watches, signets, and earrings (*Aufstellung der sichergestellten Gegenstande zum Vorgang Hercberg*, Litzmannstadt, March 3, 1942). The original document is in the Archive of the Jewish Historical Institute in Warsaw, and there is a copy in the YIVO Archives in New York.

on the day before their forced departure. Independent of the above, there was also lively trade in the streets and gateways. At every turn these unfortunates could be seen selling their household articles, a sight which has been deeply engraved in the memories of the ghetto dwellers. Naturally, everything was sold dirt cheap, often just to be rid of those things that, although useless now, had belonged to the same family for several generations, just to get a little money to buy food for the road. The possibility that he might succeed in bringing that food with him was the hope of every deportee on the day before his departure.

The deportees could deposit their cash at special points the Chairman had established in Marysin, near where they were to assemble. At those points the deportees could name the persons to whom they wished to remit their remaining money.

THE RESETTLEMENT CONTINUES

Twice, the Eldest of the Jews has ordered the publication of proclamations stating that, by order of the [German] authorities, the resettlement will continue. The first proclamation of this sort, dated March 22, points out that it is mandatory that all deportees appear punctually at the assembly points; anyone failing to do so will lose the right to take his baggage with him. The second proclamation, on March 25, points out that the rumors about the suspension of the resettlement are false. This proclamation also includes a clause on punctual appearance at the assembly points.

POPULATION COUNT AS OF APRIL 1, 1942

On April 1, 1942, the ghetto's inhabitants numbered 115,102.

Of this number, 50,094 were men and 65,008 were women. 17,628 Jews from Germany, the Protectorate [of Bohemia and Moravia], and Luxembourg were resettled into the ghetto in October and November. That number includes 6,768 men and 10,860 women. It is worth recalling that in the same months last year, 19,953 people (8,263 men and 11,610 women [?]) came to the ghetto from Western European cities. In the course of nearly five and a half months there were 2,061 deaths among the new population (1,251 men and 810 women); 264 people left to do manual labor (244 men and 20 women). According to these figures, close to 10.5 percent of the new population has died. During the first quarter of this year, 5,204 people died in the ghetto.

Population Changes in March

	Total	Men	Women
Level on March 1, 1942	142,079	60,829	81,250
Births	54	25	29
Stillbirths and miscarriages	3	2	1
Remains brought in from outside the ghetto	1	—	1
Arrivals from Warthegau and the General-gouvernement	18	13	5
Released from prison	4	—	4
Total arrivals in March	80	44	36
Deaths*	2,244	1,411	833

*This is the highest number of deaths in a month since the establishment of the ghetto.

Population Changes in March (cont.)

	Total	Men	Women
Left for Warthegau and the Generalgouvernement	118	51	67
Resettled	24,687	9,267	15,420
Total decline in March	27,049	10,729	16,320
Population decline in March	26,969	10,685	16,284

LITZMANNSTADT-GETTO, APRIL 1, 1942[28]

Resettlement continues: 1,000 people are sent from the ghetto each day. If there is a certain number lacking one day, it must be made up on the next. Conditions are becoming more severe every day; recently, the deportees have been leaving the ghetto without baggage and without money. They receive small sums from the buyers at the Main Purchasing Agency for their household odds and ends, bedding, clothing, etc., and out of these small sums they pay enormous prices for bread and other food items. Two kilograms of bread were selling for 150 marks and even higher, whereas a kilogram of wood fell to 20 pfennigs. Figuring that a large wardrobe or dressing table weighs around 50–60 kilograms, how much furniture does a person have to sell to buy one loaf of bread for the road? The Main Purchasing Agency pays next to nothing for wringers, dishes, linen, and so forth; for example, they pay 2–5 marks for the oldest type of wringer, and a few marks for a pile of linen! Appraised by eye! Such tears, such wailing, such wrack and ruin! The last possessions of ruined people going for a pittance.

In recent days there have been instances of deportees throwing their ghetto money off the train at the last minute, having no further use for it outside the ghetto. The Main Treasury used to change any amount into German marks, then it would only change 10 marks' worth, and recently, it would not change any amount whatsoever. Initially, the exchange rate was 1.50 ghetto marks for 1 German mark; later it went up to 2–3 marks and has now reached 4 *Rumkis* for 1 German mark. A kilogram of sugar costs 100 marks, a kilogram of flour (rye flour—for that's all there is!) costs 140 marks. The prices have been driven up by those leaving the ghetto, who are trying to save themselves by purchasing food "at any price."

Had the Community been able to exchange the Rumkis of those leaving the ghetto for German marks, the problem would have been solved. People would have collected money instead of food, there would not have been such a demand for food, prices would have had to fall, and life would have remained more or less in order.

A second terrible plague in the ghetto is the shortage of small change. Since 5- and 10-pfennig coins are in circulation throughout the Reich, people exchange them and buy them up for their departure. On the other hand, the cooperatives are not selling the allocated food unless the consumer pays the exact amount; yet nobody has any small change. The cooperatives are also insistent in refusing to accept round figures; they do not want to be keeping notes and settling accounts with their clientele. They

---

28. This is the third in a series of essays on current events which began to appear in the *Chronicle*, along with the daily bulletins, on March 3, 1942.

are displaying no empathy for the populace and are creating a situation that is simply tragic. Small change appears out of nowhere and is paid into the cooperatives; thus, a large amount of small change flows into the cooperatives, yet they do not give anyone any change. So, where is that change ending up?

In the [ghetto] city, people are now saying that news has arrived from a few of the deportees, and it would appear that they are working in conditions that are bearable. This has been of some reassurance, and the menace of deportation has ceased to be as terrible as it was before. There are even known incidents in which individuals who had succeeded in having themselves removed from the lists have voluntarily applied for deportation in the belief that fairly soon everyone will have to leave the ghetto and that, the sooner they do it, the better it will be for them. They have come to this conclusion on the basis of the treatment received by deportees in the initial and the most recent periods. Formerly the deportees could take everything with them (at least from the ghetto), while, at present, they can take practically nothing.

While formerly the processions of emaciated old people and children with cadaverous faces made a macabre impression on passersby, now the eye has already grown accustomed to seeing spring-carriages pass loaded with people who are more dead than alive. Wrapped in rags, barely visible, they lie motionless on the wagons. Their blank gazes fixed on the sky, their faces bloodless and pale, hold a silent but terrible reproach to those who have remained behind and are bustling anxiously about the ghetto.

April 3 of this year had been designated as the day when the resettlement was to stop, but again, new numbers for further resettlement are being mentioned, and there is even talk about the ghetto's being liquidated entirely.

The ghetto is under the sway of uncertainty, which is disrupting ghetto life to a significant degree, because everyone figures that he may be deported and is acting accordingly.

The Chairman has made no speeches lately, and the populace has not heard any authoritative statement on the question of deportation. This situation has caused all manner of supposition, for, until now, the Chairman has never missed an occasion to deliver a speech.

Something is in the air and, for the time being, no one can tell what it is.

RESETTLEMENT ACTION INTERRUPTED

Rarely do the inhabitants of the ghetto have occasion to experience moments of joy. And for that reason April 2 will be vividly inscribed in their memories; because on that day the resettlement action was suspended. It should be stated that, two weeks before then, a suspension or elimination of the resettlement had been announced. However, in view of the fact that an interruption of the resettlement had taken place on [March 22] which had also been announced ten days before and then, scarcely a few hours after the entire ghetto had been seized with joy, the ruling was rescinded and on that same day the Resettlement Commission again returned to its normal work, on April 2 everyone feared that a similar incident could occur. That factor attenuated the mood. People were simply afraid to allow themselves to be carried away with joy, only to experience an even more grievous disenchantment. On that memorable day, from morning on, there were signs that the resettlement had been suspended. The skepticism which took hold of the populace, now schooled by sad experience, impeded the spreading of the news. It is interesting that while the people of the ghetto usually place their faith uncritically in any trumped-up rumor, this time utter disbelief held sway in spite of information originating from qualified individuals, such as members of the committee, policemen, and so forth. The ghetto was seized with joy only when, by order of the Chairman, at around ten o'clock in the morning, the police began to inform the populace that the resettlement had ceased and expressly quoted the Chairman himself to that effect. By the bridge, in the lines, in front of stores, in the offices, wherever people congregated, the police, acting on instructions from their supreme commander, spread the joyous news. People were happy as children and gave public expression to their excitement. "We've lived to see happy holidays," (Thursday, April 2, was the second day of Passover, which came early this year) said people throughout the ghetto, "God willing, everything's taking a turn for the better!" More or less on that same day, the distribution of the first potatoes from the mounds was begun. These two incidents combined to produce the very optimistic conclusion that the greatest worry after resettlement, the problem of food supply, would be alleviated. By afternoon, everyone was aware that the Resettlement Commission had been liquidated. Many of the officials who had been summarily delegated to that commission returned to their old departments that very day. For the sake of accuracy, it should be noted that the commission, its size reduced, will continue to work for a short time after April 2, finishing up various matters, terminating its work, and so forth. It is worth noting that news about the commission's final tasks even became the basis for rumors of a supposed resumption of the resettlement. Throughout the day, one could see entire pilgrimages of people carrying bundles on their way home. If, during the many-week-long course of the resettlement action, the sight of people with knapsacks caused a feeling of depression, this time, those affected, and others as well, were overjoyed that they had managed to avoid deportation at the last minute. It is worth adding here that, in the final days of the resettlement, the number of people in hiding to avoid deportation had increased significantly, and their number had reached something like 3,000. Of course, those who were in hiding were unable to receive provisions at the distribution points. From what has been said above, it appears that the ghetto at large had a deadly fear of resettlement (there were exceptions—people who, desperate over the food situation here, had applied voluntarily). It was a noble gesture on the part of the Eldest of the Jews to order that no measures be taken against the deportees who had failed to report, and that no obstacles be put in the way of their receiving food and bread allocations retroactively for the entire period. There were incidents of people who had been in hiding for a few weeks. Such persons received their food all at once, which, in ghetto terms, amounted to receiving a fortune.

The orders issued a few days later by the Chairman to the board of the Main Purchasing Agency should also be noted. As is generally known, the deportees sold off all their belongings to people they knew or on the streets, and, to a very significant degree, at the Main Purchasing Agency. During the deportations, the number of purchases made by that institution increased by 150 percent. The most intense activity was noted in the second half of March. The deportees brought primarily dishes, utensils, and other such household items to the agency. Linen and clothing were second. There were also many articles that had not been offered in more than a year, such as white cloth, hides, and so on, that were put up for sale.

In this regard, the Chairman issued instructions that in the event that any would-be deportee requested the return of any items he had sold, his request should be complied with as liberally as possible. On this basis former owners are in all cases receiving their property back. And even if they do not have money, the Main Purchasing Agency is waiving the money it had paid out.

In concluding this account of the suspension of the resettlement action, it should be added that transport No. 39 left on April 1 and transport No. 40, the last transport, left on April 2. Together those transports included 2,349 deportees. According to the original plans, the last transport before the suspension of deportation was to have left on April 3. That transport did not materialize but an additional 300 or so people were included in the final [fortieth] transport.

All told, the number of deportees (since January of this year) amounts to 44,056 people.[29]

FOUR DOCTORS LEAVE THE GHETTO

On the final day of last month four doctors left the ghetto: [Icie] Lebowicz, Przytycki [Dawid] Margolis, and [Michał] Urbach. They have been hired by the [German] authorities and are to depart for Pabianice, Łask, Bełchatów, and Zelów.[30] They left along with their families, taking all their possessions, including their medical instruments, with them.

A footnote to the doctors' departure: a story circulated through the ghetto that this incident was related to the spread of a typhus epidemic among the population that had been resettled from the ghetto to the above-mentioned towns. As is well known, there is still no authoritative information as to the whereabouts of the deportees. The most persistent story is that they have been assigned to a camp in Koło county.[31]

PASSOVER SERVICE

On April 3, during services for the Passover holiday, the Eldest of the Jews went to the synagogue at [23] Brzezińska Street, where he delivered a short speech for the occasion.

A CONCERT

On Saturday, April 4, the leading representatives of local society gathered to attend a concert. Everyone was awaiting the Chairman's arrival and the speech he would deliver on the present state of affairs since the interruption of the resettlement campaign. Those expectations were, however, disappointed. This did not impede "copies" of the speech that did not take place from being circulated the next day.

29. They were all deported from the ghetto during the resettlement action, which ran from January 16 to April 1, 1942, and killed in the death camp in Chełmno (Kulmhof).

30. The combined Jewish populations of these four towns in the Łódź province numbered around 20,000.

31. For the second time the *Chronicle* mentions Koło county by name as the place where the Jews deported from the ghetto were staying, that is, the area where the Chełmno (Kulmhof) death camp was located.

According to one version, the leader of the ghetto was supposed to have said in his speech that a new resettlement was on its way.

APRIL 10–14, 1942

DEATHS AND BIRTHS

In the four days reported on here, 220 people died in the ghetto. Eight births were registered in those four days.

THE NUMBER OF THE ELDEST OF THE JEWS' CLERKS

According to the Personnel Bureau's data, the number of people employed in the Eldest of the Jews' departments, workshops and institutions on March 1 came to 11,293. During March, 929 people were hired, 184 were taken off the rolls of the employed, and 46 died, which brings the number of workers on April 1 to 11,992.

SUICIDES

On April 10, Herszke Goldsztern, a worker, born in Łódź in 1901, hung himself in his apartment at 16 Wróbla Street. He was pronounced dead by the first aid physician. On April 11, Adolf Epsztein, born in the Sudetenland in 1880 and resettled here from Prague, hung himself in his apartment at 35 Zawisza Street. The attempt proved fatal. On April 11, Fajga Pachciarek (b. 1881, in Łódź) jumped from a third-story window at 63 Lutomierska Street. She died in the hospital. On April 10, Julius Borhard (b. 1867, in Neustadt), a resident of the Old People's Home (at 26 Gnieźnieńska Street) cut the veins in his arms and, also, leaped from a window.

NEWS FROM LUBLIN

News of the resettlement of 70,000 Jews from the Lublin ghetto has reached this ghetto.[32] Apparently, the resettlement took place in the space of two hours. Only 5,000 Jews remain in Lublin. This news has caused Jobean prognoses to begin circulating. The report has been stretched to mean that there will be a new resettlement action here that is to include 70,000 people. According to other versions, the Jews of Lublin were to be driven to the [Łódź] ghetto. Each day brings new rumors that new groups are expected to come into this ghetto. "Those in the know" have spread stories that 15,000 Jews, principally from Holland and Belgium, will be arriving here. It is worth noting that, in several speeches recently delivered in various factories, the Chairman

---

32. The news of the deportation of Jews from Lublin was noted in the *Chronicle* four weeks after the event and, as was usual if the information came from without, the report was very inaccurate. In fact, the deportations from the Lublin ghetto began on the night of March 17 and lasted, with some interruptions, until the 14th of April, 1942, when about 30,000 Jews were deported to the death camp at Bełżec and killed. After the deportations, some 4,000 specially selected Jews remained in the Lublin ghetto. After being supplied with special work cards, on April 17–20, 1942, they were resettled to a new ghetto in Majdan Tatarski, 3.5 kilometers from Lublin. The liquidation of the Lublin ghetto was an integral part of the large action to exterminate Jews that the German authorities had undertaken at that time in the territory of the Generalgouvernement (the so-called Aktion Reinhard directed by SS Brigadeführer Odilo Globocnik, chief of the SS and the police (*SS und Polizeiführer*) in Lublin.

has mentioned these auguries concerning the resettlement of new groups in this ghetto. It would appear, from the ghetto leader's authoritative statements, that this matter has not yet taken any definite form.

TO SOW UNREST

On Sunday April 12, distressing reports about a supposed further resettlement were circulating through the ghetto. To confirm their accuracy, those spreading the reports cited the fact that the Chairman, under new orders, has canceled his speech at Saturday's concert. It is worth noting that the Chairman was not scheduled to attend the concert.

A SHOOTING

On April 11, at 4:30 A.M., Irma Teresa "Sara" Lewental[33] (b. 1882, in Ausbach), resettled here from Frankfurt [am Main], was shot dead while attempting to escape from the ghetto, at the intersection of Majowa and Drewnowska streets, on the other side of the barbed wire. The victim had been staying in the Old People's Home on Gnieźnieńska Street. She was shot in the head. Her body was taken to the mortuary at Hospital No. 2.

THE FIRST NEWS ABOUT THE DEPORTEES

On April 12, a high officer of the secret police [Gestapo], who is serving as the commander of the camp where the people deported from this ghetto are now located, was briefly at Bałut Market. This is the first definite source of information concerning the deportees; for the record, it is worth adding that the story of their whereabouts that circulated with the most persistence has, this time, been confirmed. It has now been irrefutably established that the camp is located in the region bordering directly on the town of Koło, now called Warthbrücken. The camp houses about 100,000 Jews, indicating that besides the 44,000 resettled from this ghetto, Jews from other cities have been concentrated in that camp. This gigantic camp was formerly a living site for Germans from Volhynia. Apparently 30,000 people had been living there. They left the barracks in perfectly decent order, and even left their furniture for the Jews to use. The food supply at the camp is, apparently, exemplary. Those fit to work are employed on the camp grounds repairing roads and performing agricultural tasks. Workshops are to be set up in the very near future.[34]

LITZMANNSTADT-GETTO, APRIL 11, 1942

A rainy, overcast day, the temperature 6–8 degrees above zero.

A story spread through the ghetto that the 70,000 Jews resettled out of the Lublin ghetto in the space of two hours were supposed to arrive in this ghetto. That seems a bit improbable, for the Lublin ghetto was projected to be the central ghetto for all

---

33. See p. 134, n. 26 above.

34. All this information, with the exception of the location of the camp (near Koło, Warthbrücken in German), is fictitious. Moreover, this was one of the many false reports about the deportees that were spread in the ghetto by officials of the Gestapo, Kripo, and the German Ghetto Administration.

Poland,[35] whereas the ghetto here—to judge by the resettlements that have occurred thus far—would seem to be slated for liquidation after a certain amount of time.

Such new resettlements here would obviously be a catastrophe for the local population, not only because of the disorganization it would cause in the workshops, which are the ghetto's material mainstay, but by creating too great a population density. 43,500 Jews have, thus far, been resettled from this ghetto, thereby causing hygienic conditions to improve somewhat, but thousands of newly settled Jews from the West are still waiting for their collective-camps to be liquidated so that they can move into private apartments, which, however, they have not yet been able to obtain. The spotted typhus epidemic is spreading, new doorkeepers are constantly being hired to enforce the quarantine, there are houses which have already been quarantined for a third time, and a new resettlement of people here could simply have fatal consequences.

People are also talking about the [German] authorities' demand that the part of the ghetto bounded by Smugowa, Franciszkańska, Brzezińska and Widok streets be turned over to them. But that demand has been dropped because several workshops, like the hosiery workshop, the saddlery, and so forth, had been transferred to that area. The Mariavites' building at 29 Franciszkańska Street has also been occupied by a workshop.[36]

On the other hand, there is a story in circulation that, on the 20th of this month, resettlement of people into Germany and the Protectorate (of Bohemia [and Moravia])—even including people newly resettled here—will supposedly begin again.

Taken together, all this has created an atmosphere of uncertainty and confusion in the ghetto once again, for no one can be sure of the morrow.

The Chairman had announced that he would deliver a speech yesterday on Krawiecka Street; quite a few people from the neighborhood had gathered there, but the news from Lublin caused him to cancel his plans.

The ghetto is once again under the sway of anxiety.

WEDNESDAY, APRIL 15, 1942

A SUICIDE ATTEMPT AT THE OLD PEOPLE'S HOME

Yesterday evening, there was another suicide attempt at the Old People's Home on Gnieźnieńska Street, which had been established for the ghetto's new population. Fifty-five-year-old Alfred Freund, from Vienna, attempted to take his own life by

---

35. That is, the so-called Lublin Reservation, which the German authorities had intended to create in the period between Fall, 1939, and Spring, 1940, in the Lublin province on territory bounded by the Vistula, San, and Wieprz rivers and, at that time, right on the border of the USSR. The Germans spoke and wrote publicly about their plans for the reservation, and by October, 1939, had already begun sending transports of Jews to that area from Germany, Austria, Bohemia, and Moravia, as well as from Polish territories that had been incorporated into the Reich. In the spring of 1940, the German authorities gave up the plan.

36. This was one of the most imposing apartment buildings in the ghetto and, before the war, had belonged, along with the adjacent church, to the Mariavites (admirers of the life of the Virgin Mary), a sect that originated in a Catholic organization that was founded in 1893 and was independent of Rome.

cutting open the veins in his right arm. He received assistance on the spot from the First Aid Service and was not removed from the Old People's Home.

SHE RETURNED TO COLOGNE

On April 11, by order of the [German] authorities, Emma Stock (b. 1894), a cook by profession, left the ghetto en route to Cologne. In the ghetto, she had lived with her husband and 7-year-old daughter at 34/36 Zawisza Street. This is the first case of someone's returning to a former place of residence.

THURSDAY, APRIL 16, 1942

COLLECTIVES ELIMINATED

The collectives inhabited by the newly arrived population continue to be eliminated. The quarters at 13/15 Franciszkańska Street, where the resettled persons from the second transport had been residing, were vacated today. The collective of the Prague V transport, located on Jakuba Street, is the next to be vacated. The Transportation Department is making flat, horse-drawn wagons available free of charge to residents of collectives to transport their baggage to private apartments. Yesterday, a large soup kitchen was put into operation at 32 Młynarska Street to provide the residents from Prague with meals.

FROM THE POST OFFICE

Because of the continued suspension of postal service, the local Post Office, in addition to handling local mail, forwards 1,000 to 1,100 pre-printed postal cards, which carry information about the state of the sender's health and/or request that money be sent. The return address on the pre-printed postal cards is *Eldest of the Jews*. Money orders, totaling a half million [German] marks per month, arrive in the ghetto continuously. Since March 20, Maurycy Goldblum has been in charge of running the Post Office.

AN INSPECTION

At around 2:00 p.m., high-ranking representatives of the [German] authorities visited the ghetto, their inspection having been announced a few days in advance. In the course of two hours, the inspectors visited the following enterprises of the Eldest of the Jews: the textile workshop (on Drewnowska Street), a hide and leather workshop, a carpenters' shop, and a boot-top workshop. Eyewitnesses state that the inspectors left with a most favorable impression after visiting the local enterprises.

CAUSES OF DEATH

Among today's 66 deaths (37 men and 29 women), 5 persons died of dysentery, 11 of tuberculosis, 2 of lung disease, 2 of nervous ailments, 8 of old age, 1 from loss of blood, 16 of heart attacks, 11 of exhaustion, 7 of heart problems related to exhaustion, 1 of cancer, and 2 of other causes.

FRIDAY, APRIL 17, 1942

SETTLED IN THE GHETTO

Yesterday, 15-year-old Apolonia Piątecka was brought to the ghetto under escort. She has been placed in the ghetto because she is suspected of being Jewish by origin. At an early age Piątecka, as the child of unknown parents, became a ward of the municipal orphanage. The sound of her last name has had an influence on her current situation.[37] For 12 years she was raised by foster parents, the Grabowskis, who lived at 39 Brzezińska Street before the war and who have lately been living at 280 Piotrkowska Street. Until yesterday their foster child had been working as a milliner in an establishment in the city. Before being placed in the ghetto, she was examined by a special committee. She was brought to the ghetto without any of her things. For the time being, she has been quartered in the orphanage on Franciszkańska Street. This new ghetto dweller will no doubt be employed in the hat factory.

APRIL 18–20, 1942

WEATHER

On Saturday and Sunday, the 18th and 19th, the weather continued to grow significantly warmer, and both days were sunny. On Monday, the 20th, the weather grew a bit cooler and the sky was slightly overcast.

On the first Saturday of spring, in the full sense of the word, the ghetto's mood seemed to adapt itself to the weather. On that day, all the people in the ghetto were in a cheerful mood. Hope and optimism overtook the populace with the first breath of spring. On that day most conversations were dedicated to working on one's garden plot and, since a significant portion of the populace had the day off from work, they intently set to work tilling their garden plots. Despite local custom, no Job's news was to be heard on Saturday. The populace apparently remained ignorant of the new blow it would receive from the street posters the next day, for the task of forming a medical commission, which was to cause universal dejection and depression, was not delegated to the ghetto authorities until Saturday afternoon. By late Saturday, a plan for carrying out that harsh order had already been worked out. A certain practical conclusion can be drawn from this, namely, that the "street's" rumors are, clearly, far from the real state of affairs—both the good and the bad. And the Chairman has emphatically called attention to this more than once in his speeches.

AN INCREASE IN THE JOB NETWORK

Recently, there has been a large influx of new orders to the Central Workshop Bureau. Consequently, new enterprises are now being put into operation and those already existing are being enlarged. It is worth particular note that the resumption of operations, after a few weeks' interruption, in the manufacture of straw shoes in the

---

37. There seem to be no grounds for this assumption. Variations on Piątek (Friday)—Piątecki (a), Piątkowski (a)—are rather common names in Poland.

workshop at 7 Widok Street, the founding of a second furriers' section exclusively for army commissions at 6 Smugowa Street, of a knitted goods workshop at 41 Brzezińska Street and a shoemakers' workshop producing plaited shoes at 1 Bałut Market.

A MEDICAL INSPECTION

A German health commission visited the ghetto on the 17th of this month.

TWENTY-ONE MARRIAGES

were contracted on the 17th of this month because of the curtailment of such ceremonies for religious reasons until May 5.[38]

MILK HAS ARRIVED

After a 10-day suspension, milk began arriving in the ghetto on April 18. For the time being, milk is only being issued to children, and because of an insufficient supply, its sale to the sick has been suspended until the end of the month.

THOSE NOT WORKING TO FACE MEDICAL EXAMINATION

On the morning of April 19, Proclamation No. 374, dated the 18th of this month, announcing that all of the population above the age of 10 that is not working is subject to medical examination, was posted on the ghetto's walls. This proclamation has had a staggeringly depressing effect on the population of the ghetto, which is already steeled by two years of experience and is accustomed to blows of various sorts. There is nothing surprising in the fact that Sunday's proclamation made such a strong impression if one considers that all inhabitants of the ghetto, nearly without exception (apart from the new population), have already faced the danger of families being separated. So, the public treated the medical examinations in this fashion right from the very start. The proclamation contains the following provisions: According to the order by the [German] authorities, people of either sex and over the age of 10 who are not working are obliged to appear before the medical commission. When reporting, they are required to have their ID's or bread ration cards with them. People should present themselves for the examination in a state of cleanliness. The bedridden will be brought to the examination by members of the Department of Health. To expedite matters to that end, people are to report to their precinct police stations. The following categories are exempt from appearing before the commission: (1) those who are employed; (2) those who possess certificates of work allocation issued by the Bureau of Labor or by the Personnel Bureau; (3) persons who came here from the old Reich, Luxembourg, Vienna, or Prague. People are to report for the examination at 7:30. The examining commission is situated on the grounds of the large soup kitchen at 32 Młynarska Street. In the proclamation, the following plan, based on the street of residence, provides for the commission to work from Monday through Thursday, the 23d of this month: the plan includes people living on streets to the right of the bridges, that is, in a direction running from the center of the city toward the ghetto with the exception of the Marysin district.

38. This was the *Sefirah* period between the two Jewish holidays, Passover and *Shabuoth*, with the exception of *Lag ba'Omer*, i.e., May 5 in the year 1942.

Within the dry framework of a chronicle it is extremely difficult to render an account of the situation created in the ghetto by the proclamation in question here. To be brief, one can only say that everyone is ruled by the specter of calamity that hangs in the air. People are walking around in a state of utter helplessness, seeking salvation, help, and advice from everyone they meet, friend and stranger alike. It could be observed that the merchants, that is that small portion of the population not employed by the Community, were, for the most part, closing their stores. A frenzied confusion reigned in the offices as well. It comes as no surprise that, on that day, no one, no matter how great his sense of duty, was in any state to discharge his duties normally; and besides, daily cares and everything which had seemed so important the day before, had now passed into oblivion. A sole concern absorbed every mind: the fate that awaits those who have to report for the examination. With lightning speed, the grapevine spread the news, not mentioned in the official proclamation, that the commission will be composed entirely of German doctors. Naturally, these stories exaggerated the significance of that ruling. After initial deliberations and consultations, large crowds began to head toward the Bureau of Labor and the Welfare Department, which are located at 11 Lutomierska Street. The crowd of thousands in front of those offices was clearly in a state of extreme anxiety. People seemed to be deranged. Everyone wanted to get inside the building to obtain a so-called work passport, the document which the Chairman in his every speech, whether delivered this month or more than a year ago, had called the guarantee of peace. On April 19, he convinced the ghetto that those were truly prophetic words. Unfortunately, a painful disappointment was in store for everyone there. The Bureau of Labor has suspended the taking of applications. Nevertheless, the crowds did not leave the courtyard at 11 Lutomierska Street. There was some relief when the office posted an announcement there and on walls throughout the ghetto stating that applications would be taken for work on public projects, but only from persons who are not subject to a mandatory appearance before the commission, in accordance with the street plan contained in Proclamation No. 374. The loophole of a work passport was thus created for people living on the left side of the ghetto's streets. Immediately after this announcement was made, a line of a thousand people had formed in front of the Department of Public Works, which is also located at 11 Lutomierska Street. Anxiety increases as the situation develops.

APRIL 21–24, 1942

THE MEDICAL COMMISSIONS

performed their functions in accordance with the plan for six days, from Monday, the 20th of April, to Saturday, the 25th. On Friday, the 24th, the [German] authorities informed the Eldest of the Jews that the examinations would be broken off until Friday, May 1. The commissions were composed of a few German doctors and representatives of the secret police [Gestapo]. Administrative functions were performed by officials of the Eldest of the Jews and of the Jewish police, who were primarily engaged in maintaining order. In addition, attendants sent by the Department of

Health served as assistants. The women were examined on the top floor of the soup kitchen at 32 Młynarska Street and the men, in the hall below. During the six days, the examinations proceeded in complete peace, without incidents of any sort. After the examination, each person registered received a plate of soup free of charge. The examinations were performed very cursorily; persons over 60 were not obliged to remove their clothing, and only those in fairly good condition underwent a heart examination.

The commissions were in session from about 9 o'clock until 2 P.M. In spite of the relatively small number of people involved, on practically no day were all those reporting examined. The doctors stamped a letter on the chest of everyone who had been examined. There were 16 different letters, 8 for the men and 8 for the women. Apparently, one of the letters (allegedly "L" for the women) signified an inability to perform work of any sort. On the third day of the commissions' operation, the authorities made it known that too few people were reporting. On the same day, a few hundred residents of the Old People's Home were brought in for examination. Throughout the campaign, large groups of children under the age of 14 were brought to be examined. It is worth noting here that children over the age of 13 can be accepted as apprentices in Community enterprises. The appropriate commission of the School Department, which is assigning children to work in the factories on the basis of questionnaires, has therefore been working day and night, and with double intensity, for the entire week. On the 23d, Order Service men forcibly brought in over 500 persons to be examined as a result of the roundup they conducted to search out everyone who was in hiding. The next day the number of those forcibly brought in amounted to around 300 and, finally, on the last day, Saturday, around 250 persons were brought in. Roughly 65 percent of those examined were women, which more or less coincides with the proportion, by sex, of those employed in the ghetto. On the 20th, 1,375 people were examined, 1,567 were examined on the 21st, 1,847 on the 22d, 2,090 on the 23d, 1,719 on the 24th, 1,358 on the 25th, and, all told, the number examined was 9,956. The ghetto is of the general opinion that the [German] authorities had demanded that 20,000 people report for examination. After the break was ordered, the minds of ghetto dwellers were absorbed by a single riddle—what basis will the commission be operating on when it continues its work and how many people will be examined?

TO WARSAW

On April 23, 1942, 147 people left the ghetto for Warsaw [ghetto]. In the morning, the streets which intersect Łagiewnicka Street in the section bordering on Bałut Market were closed to foot traffic. Over 200 persons had received the appropriate papers authorizing them to travel to Warsaw, a record-high number in comparison to all other group departures. This fact has caused a great throng to come to Bałut Market, where those who are leaving are inspected in small outbuildings and are obliged to bathe. Three large trucks have been assigned to transport the people and their baggage. However, there was not enough room for everyone and a considerable portion had to give up on the much-desired journey. All of this did not pass without incident. By order of the German authorities, around 20 people were named the next day to report for a medical examination. The order was carried out.

In an atmosphere of general anxiety because of the examining commission operating in the ghetto, the events connected with the trip to Warsaw were a subject of lively discussion for the entire population. A rumor is circulating that any further such trips will be suspended because of the disorder that prevailed during the departure.

THE "CZECHS"

are saying that the nearest place where the transports from Prague have been resettled is Izbica, on the Wieprz [River].[39] Apparently, authentic information has come in by an indirect route, from the "Czechs" in that location to their friends who have been settled in this ghetto.

MONDAY AND TUESDAY, APRIL 27 AND 28, 1942

DEATHS AND BIRTHS

In these two days, 157 people died in the ghetto. Three births were registered (one boy and two girls).

TO SUPPLEMENT

the information about Friday's departure to Warsaw, it is worth adding that 104 people had been on the list of those authorized to leave. Forty-six persons were removed from the list but, in fact, 127 people left.

RESETTLED IN THE GHETTO

The following persons were recently brought to the ghetto: on the 23d, 11-year-old Zenon Lewczuk was brought in from the city. The boy was placed in the Orphanage. On April 25, Hedwig "Sara" Meyer (b. Essen, 1893) was brought to the ghetto. She was placed in the quarters for resettlees at 15 Rybna Street. This is the first case of a person from the Old Reich being resettled individually in the ghetto. On April 25, 44-year-old Zela Lachman (born in Poddębice) was brought to the ghetto from the bureau of investigation in Magdeburg. She has taken up residence at 42 Lutomierska Street. Finally, on April 22, 12-year-old Aleksander Neuman of Częstochowa arrived in the ghetto. He is now living with his parents at 15 Zgierska Street.

RUMORS

On Monday, there was a rumor that people who are not working and thus possess no stamp on their bread cards will be treated as second-class citizens and will, for example, receive 80 grams of bread.

---

39. A small, predominantly Jewish town in Lublin province and the seat of the rabbinical dynasty founded by Rabbi Mordecai J. Leiner. According to the census of 1921, 2,862 of Izbica's total population of 3,085 were Jews. During the German occupation, Izbica was turned into a ghetto where, in addition to the local Jews, those from other Polish territories annexed by the Reich and those from Bohemia and Moravia were concentrated. Toward the end of 1942, the ghetto in Izbica was liquidated and its inhabitants deported to death camps in Bełżec and Sobibór and exterminated.

WEDNESDAY AND THURSDAY, APRIL 29 AND 30, 1942

MEDICAL EXAMINATION

In the evening hours of the 28th, the populace learned from public proclamations by the Eldest of the Jews that those subject to medical examination will also be registered at 32 Młynarska Street on the 29th, between the hours of 9 and 3. The registration was completed in these two days.[40] On Tuesday, the commission performing the registration recorded the personal data of 1,080 people, and on the second day, that is, on Wednesday, another 700 people passed in front of the commission's table. The registration commission is composed of the chief of the Order Service and the directors of the Department of Social Welfare and the Bureau of Labor. The commission questioned those reporting for registration about their family situations; its primary interest was in the number of family members working and the qualifications for work of those reporting. The commission made notes on these matters. One may conclude from this registration system that, if possible, people without work who are burdened with large working families may be exempted from having to appear before the commission. This will become clearer as events develop. The great majority of those reporting for registration are women, and primarily elderly women. Some unusual and noteworthy incidents took place while the commission was in operation: for instance, a few people who had previously undergone a medical examination and been stamped, reported for registration, needlessly bringing utensils with them. Apparently, during the medical examinations, as well, there had been cases of people reporting to the commission several times in order to receive an additional free meal. Such persons were sadly disappointed at the registration, for no soup was given out there.

The Main Commission has continued to work on dealing with the list of complaints submitted by individual departments.

UNEMPLOYED WESTERN EUROPEAN JEWS ARE LEAVING THE GHETTO

The ghetto had still not recovered its equilibrium from the medical examinations when, on Wednesday, surprising news, of great importance, shocked everyone. On Wednesday, at around 1 o'clock, word spread through the ghetto that the unemployed "Germans" were being resettled. This news has caused renewed excitement. A few hours later, the yellow poster of Proclamation No. 380 confirmed that this unexpected and sensational news was accurate. The substance of the proclamation is as follows: By order of the authorities, the Chairman is making it known that on Monday, May 4, the resettlement of Jews from the Old Reich, Luxembourg, Vienna,

40. From other information in the *Chronicle* it appears that, according to the proclamation by the Eldest of the Jews on April 25, 1942, all persons with work assignments issued by the Bureau of Labor who were still not working, were to appear on April 26 before special commissions that were to determine precisely how many people in the ghetto were actually working and how many others were fit for work. Those who were working were to be inspected in their workshops and individual departments by specially created commissions. The work of those commissions was not concluded, however, on April 26. Hence, the new proclamation by the Eldest of the Jews, which was an extension of the registration deadline for those not working—who would have to report for a medical examination if the German commission resumed its work.

and Prague will begin. Those who have been decorated with iron crosses or received decorations for wounds and those who are working will not be resettled. The first two categories should present their documents at the Office for Resettled Persons. Those being resettled will be able to take 12.5 kilograms of luggage and can sell their belongings at the Main Purchasing Agency and at the bank. A bureau for matters connected with the resettlement will be opened at the Office for Resettled Persons at 8 Rybna Street. This bureau will provide all information and will also accept petitions and complaints.

It is worth stressing that the news concerning the resettlement of the non-working segment of the new population was truly a bolt from the blue, as opposed to the other blows the ghetto dwellers have met with, blows which were foretold by the facts a short or long time in advance. Nevertheless, despite what might have logically been expected, the news did not, on the whole, have a shattering effect on those to be resettled. Compared to the fear that usually dominates the ghetto's old population when they are faced with resettlement, the news produced a relatively minor impression on the new population. This is the result of a series of factors whose explanation does not fall within the limits of the *Chronicle*.

Immediately after the proclamation appeared, crowds of those whom it affected began to besiege the Office for Resettled Persons. The office was not, however, able to offer any definite explanations on Wednesday. Conferences of the leading representatives of the local authorities, with the Eldest of the Jews himself taking part, went on late into the night. General plans were made during those conferences, and the work of organizing the resettlement operation, which got underway first thing Wednesday morning, proceeded in accordance with those plans. Apparently, the resettlement is to include a minimum of 10,000 people. There is a possibility of employing a few thousand people from the new population, which numbers over 17,000. About 3,000 of that total figure are employed at present. It is clear that employment will depend on the number of positions that become available and will proceed on the principle thus far applied of favoring persons the majority of whose family members are working. For that reason, the Office for Resettled Persons has compiled informational material and has also drawn up a list of families in which no one at all is working. The list of those to be resettled will be drawn primarily from the latter category. On Thursday, the directors of individual departments and workshops presented the Office for Resettled Persons with lists of the family members they employ. On Thursday afternoon it was being said in circles close to the Office for Resettled Persons that newcomers from Bohemia, with the sole exception of the members of the Prague V transport, which is still a collective, would not be considered for the first stages of the resettlement action. On the other hand, members of the Cologne II collective quartered in Marysin will, it seems, be in "the first line of fire." And, finally, a third version has it that transports of 250 people are to leave each day.

On Thursday, contrary to what might have logically been expected, no increased sale of belongings was noted either at the Main Purchasing Agency or on the street. The populace anticipates that the resettlement action will drive the already high price of food on the private market to astronomical heights.

THE PRISONS FILL

On Wednesday night the Order Service was on emergency alert. For on that night, a roundup was executed throughout the ghetto in order to imprison people hiding to escape medical examination. Those arrested were sent to various precinct stations where they were checked for a second time. Ultimately, 800 people were sent from the precincts to Central Prison. Everyone in the ghetto is interested in knowing whether the grapevine is right that medical examinations will be resumed on May 1 and what sort of contingent will be sent to them.

The number of "regular" prisoners is 14, of which 5 remain at the disposal of the German authorities. The prison staff at present consists of 38.

A WAIF

Krystyna N., born January 2, 1939, was brought to the ghetto recently (on suspicion of being of Jewish origin). The waif was placed in the Orphanage.

FROM TUREK

A postcard from a village near Turek has arrived in the ghetto by indirect means. It was sent by a family resettled in January and reports that they are in good health.[41]

MEDICAL EXAMINATIONS TOMORROW

On Thursday evening, Proclamation No. 381 of the Eldest of the Jews was posted informing the public that the medical examination commission will be in session on Friday, May 1. All persons obliged to report for an examination should appear at 7:30. In accord with previous proclamations, newcomers from the Old Reich, Vienna, Prague, and Luxembourg are not subject to the examination.

SEWING MACHINES

have arrived in the ghetto in great quantities via Bałut Market over the last few days. On the basis of evidence in the form of notes and printed matter found in the drawers of these machines, one may conclude that they were sent here from small towns in Koło and Kutno counties.[42]

LUGGAGE

On Wednesday, a few people employed at Bałut Market observed a large truck that had stopped to refuel en route from Zgierz to the city. The truck was fully loaded with luggage of various sorts, but chiefly with knapsacks belonging to the people recently resettled from the ghetto. The truck was allegedly on its way from Kutno to Pa-

---

41. This is another example of the misinformation campaign waged in the ghetto by officials of the German authorities on the subject of deported Jews.

42. These machines had originally belonged to the Jews in the towns, small and large, of Koło and Kutno counties, for, between December, 1941, and the end of April, 1942, Jews from the following towns in those two counties were deported to the death camp in Chełmno (Kulmhof): Koło, Bugaj, Dąbie, Izbica Kujawska, Kłodowa, Sompolno, Kutno, Krośnice, and Żychlin.

bianice.[43] It is difficult to determine whether or not this information is accurate. Thus, the bulletin notes it with obvious qualification.

A NEW PROCLAMATION CONCERNING RESETTLEMENT

Proclamation No. 380, printed on yellow paper, was posted in the late evening. This proclamation was posted over a proclamation bearing the same number, in the same format, and on the same yellow paper, that had been posted 24 hours before. These circumstances indicate that the newer proclamation invalidates the text of the previous one. The contents of the new "edition" of Proclamation No. 380 are identical to those of the original proclamation No. 380 (see the current *Daily Chronicle Bulletin No. 22* entitled, "Unemployed Western European Jews are Leaving the Ghetto") with the difference that it does not specify the categories of the new population exempt from resettlement. However, all other provisions concerning the resettlement action remain in effect. Thus, among others, the section about the Office for Resettled Persons receiving petitions and complaints has been retained. The fact that this section has been retained would make it appear that the entire new population will not be subject to resettlement. Decisions about filling the transports remain under the authority of the office on Rybna Street. There is no doubt that the principle that has been observed lately of justly favoring (exempting from deportation) people who are working and their families will be strictly applied this time. The posting of a proclamation with altered terms caused great consternation among those affected, and the doubts that naturally arose caused numerous rumors.

PROCLAMATION NO. 380

of April 29, 1942, has caused a panic among those newly settled here, and the most diverse comments are to be heard on this account. The prevailing sense is that the local population has been tucked away in workshops and offices to be saved from resettlement, while the Western Jews have been pushed to the fore. Enormous bitterness prevails in certain circles of those recently settled here, whereas others have taken a sober view of the matter and have begun at once to seek means of remaining in the ghetto. In spite of the fact that many newcomers had not been permitted to take any documents with them, a great many of them brought evidence of their valor in World War I and, indeed, one must wonder at the number of Jews who were decorated. On the other hand, a great many people intend to decline the privilege of remaining here and have decided not to disclose their decorations. More than five months of hunger and cold, on bare floors, does not in the least dispose them to fight for life in the ghetto. They say that wherever they may find themselves, things will not be any worse for them, and so they are ready and willing to leave their current residence. There are many among them who were not only formerly very well-to-do, but, moreover, held prominent positions in society. The majority of them have been

---

43. Those trucks bearing the belongings of the victims of the death camp in Chełmno (Kulmhof), as well as of those from the Jewish settlements who were liquidated, were sent to Dąbrowa, a village not far from and to the north of Łódź, next to the town of Pabianice. Enormous sorting houses were built in Dąbrowa, where Jews performed forced labor, sorting the items that had been seized and sending the best of them to Germany. There will be additional information about Dąbrowa in the course of the *Chronicle*.

doing manual labor in the ghetto, a great many of them working at garbage and excrement disposal, and there is tremendous bitterness on that account! The situation in certain transports is simply tragic. If, for example, we take the Berlin III transport, of the approximately 1,100 newcomers to the ghetto (that was the number when their collective was formed) only 980 remain. Of those, about 180 have died in the course of a few months and about 150 of the elderly were transferred to the Old People's Home. Furthermore, some 100 persons have found employment of one sort or another and, of the amount remaining, more than half are suffering from swollen legs. They cannot move and are unfit for travel. There are around 50 people among them who have received decorations; yet, they have all unanimously decided not to attempt to remain here and to leave together in the same transport. They have had enough of this paradise!

In connection with the state of panic, the price of food on the free market has risen with dizzying speed. Today, a loaf of bread costs 180 marks, 1 kilogram of rye flour—150 marks, 1 kilogram of margarine—450 marks, and so forth.

The new settlers have frantically been selling off their possessions, taking foodstuffs from the local population in exchange. A good suit goes for half a loaf of bread, a pair of shoes, for 2 kilograms of potatoes, half a kilogram of flour or some other such item. A tragedy! On the one hand, they have to get rid of those things because they cannot take them with them, but, on the other hand, they might have been able to exchange them elsewhere for enough food for the long weeks ahead! The ghetto is full of activity and tension, and no one is talking about anything else . . . New dark clouds hang over us!

POPULATION COUNT AS OF MAY 1, 1942

On May 1, 1942, the ghetto was inhabited by 110,860 people (48,068 men and 62,738 women [?], of which 16,959 were new settlers.

Population Changes in April

Level as of April 1, 1942   115,102 (17,628 new settlers)

	Men	Women	Total
Births in April	31	34	65
Stillbirths	—	3	3
Arrived from the Generalgouvernement and Warthegau	6	2	8
Arrived from the Old Reich	—	2	2
Total arrivals in April, 1942	33	45	78
Deaths in April, 1942	1,116	772	1,888
Left for Generalgouvernement and Warthegau	61	71	132
Left for the Old Reich	—	1	1
Resettled	873	1,476	2,349
Total losses in April	2,050	2,320	4,370
Actual loss	2,017	2,275	4,292

After the corrections of the Resettlement Commission are included (9 men and 5 women fewer), the level as of May 1 comes out to 110,860, as above.

CHANGES IN THE POPULATION OF NEWCOMERS [FROM THE WEST] IN APRIL

The number as of April 1, 1942, was 17,628 (6,768 men, 10,860 women). In April, 669 died, 2 arrived, and 1 left. After the single-digit correction is included,[44] the number of new settlers on May 1, 1942, comes to 16,959, as above.

LITZMANNSTADT-GETTO, MAY 1, 1942

The ghetto remains in a state of anxiety. It appears that we are now faced with some fundamental changes in a situation that seemed to have already been settled. On the one hand, the medical commission at 32 Młynarska Street is examining the long-time residents of the ghetto, a small portion of whom are even reporting voluntarily, but the majority of whom had been arrested by the Order Service over the last two nights. All told, some 1,200 people passed before the medical commission today.

The commission has apparently concluded its work with today's examinations, and now the resettlement of 8,000 local and 12,000 foreign Jews is to ensue. At the moment, there is no movement among our own Jews, for each one is counting on it not being him but someone else who will be deported; and besides, there are all sorts of stories going around, and people have been placed into such a variety of groups by the commission that no one has a sure sense of anything—whether they are sending people who are fit to work out of the ghetto or, just the reverse, the sick and the weak! Since there is talk that both the weak and the fit are being considered [for resettlement], the mood is not so fearful, and those who still have some life in them are, thus far, managing somehow or other. In any case, there has been no need to use too much "pull" here; a little has sufficed to obtain a work allocation. Among the "foreign Jews" (as we call them), as we have already seen, an entirely different sort of mood prevails. Some are in despair because they feel endangered by a new journey into the unknown, while others are pleased to be leaving the ghetto. Those who had already somehow made themselves at home in the ghetto regret leaving the most; others believe resettlement will improve their lives. They are, however, filled with concern when wondering if they have the strength to make the journey. The majority are walking shadows who find it hard to make the "distant" journey to Marysin. And what will happen if they have to go further than that on foot? [At the moment] this concern overshadows all others. They are selling off their best possessions for a little margarine, bread, and potatoes, taking only small bundles with them so that they can travel light.

And besides . . . the regulation states that they are only allowed to take 12.5 kilograms with them, and they have grown accustomed to conforming to regulations strictly.

Hyenas and predators have been making the rounds of the camps and the collectives since early morning. There have been many speculators who have made a good

---

44. It is not known which single-digit correction is meant here.

profit off the misfortunes of their brothers from the West. Ruthless and cruel, they have flocked around their victims like vultures on a battlefield.

Our own Jews, men and women, have been seen in the ghetto wearing peccary-skin gloves and raincoats—blue ones, red ones, green ones, and so on—and burdened with newly-acquired clothing, suitcases, briefcases . . . A change of clothes, or a change of roles as well? And for how long? No one thinks of that!

MAY 1–3, 1942

A SUICIDE

On May 1, a newcomer from Vienna, 66-year-old Ryszard Izrael (of 5 Jakuba Street), committed suicide. The reason: despair over the loss of his wife, who had died the previous night.

RESETTLEMENT

has marked the first days of May for the Jews from the West. The deportation of the new settlers, which begins on Monday, has become the fundamental question of the moment for the ghetto. The Office for Resettled Persons on Rybna Street has been working without respite on organizing the action. Thousands and thousands of petitions are pouring into that office from the parties who are affected and who wish to avoid deportation from the ghetto. The first few thousand deportation cards, known in ghetto slang as "wedding certificates," have been sent to families in which no one at all is working. There is a persistent rumor in the ghetto that the first two transports of deportees will be sent to occupied France and the remainder, to Bessarabia. People who are employed are not receiving deportation cards. Moreover, priority in the forming of a *supra-quota* not subject to deportation will be given to those who are directly related to people who are employed, with particular consideration given to those employed in workshops producing goods for the army and those who have been decorated. At the same time, commerce in possessions of the deportees is now occurring in the ghetto. It should be recalled that they arrived in the ghetto having been permitted to bring 50 kilograms of baggage with them. Now, when leaving the ghetto, they can take 12.5 kilograms. Naturally, in the course of six months they had already sold a considerable portion of their possessions, and on the eve of resettlement they began to sell everything they could not take along with them. The ghetto has simply been possessed by furious commerce. In front of the gateways to the collectives, on the squares, in the streets, and inside the gateways, all people are doing is selling, trading, and examining goods. For the most part, it is clothing, linen, and shoes that are being sold. For the somewhat better things, including clothing and boots, the deportees are demanding their equivalent in food. In this chaos, it is difficult to determine any standards of value, whether measured in marks or in food. The deportees receive marks and use them to buy up everything available in the way of food from the population which is remaining here. The same chaos in the food market makes it impossible to determine price levels. For the sake of context, it is worth remembering that people are saying that a pair of boots has been sold for a loaf of bread, that a loaf of bread has brought from 300 to 350 marks, that new, luxurious clothes have been swapped for a kilogram of margarine, a kilogram of margarine has sold for 60 marks, a workshop soup ticket for 20 marks, and a 50-gram piece of sausage, for 10 marks. So that there be trade and exchange! The Community's official purchasing institutions, like the main agency at 4 Kościelny Square and the bank, are handling hundreds of sellers. It would seem that the crowds in front of these institutions ought to be larger; however, such expectations were undone by the shift to barter. The cause of this is to be sought in the rather low prices paid by those institutions, and the fact that the sellers cannot buy much of anything with the money they receive. Agencies of the Order Service have received orders not to allow undesirable traffic jams on the street and to disperse groups trading on the spot. There has been a series of arrests; of course, it is the buyers who are brought to justice for frequently preying on the misfortunes of their neighbors.

MONDAY, MAY 4, 1942

DEATHS AND BIRTHS

A disproportionately large number of deaths among the new population, in relation to the general mortality rate, has been observed in recent days, as indicated by yesterday's entry [*Deaths and Births for May 1–3, 1942*]. The new population amounts to no more than 15 percent of the whole, whereas it has been accounting for 50 percent of the number of deaths in the last few days. There is no doubt that the resettlement action affecting the newcomers is having a significant influence on the increase in the mortality rate.

Sixty-one people died today, 27 of them newcomers. On the other hand, there were no births.

LAST DAY OF MEDICAL EXAMINATIONS

On May 1 the German medical commission examined those people who failed to appear before the commission during the past week. On the last day about 1,200 people came to be examined, thus a total of over 11,000 people in the ghetto have had their bodies stamped.

FIRST DAY OF THE RESETTLEMENT

On Monday, at around 8:00 A.M., the first transport of the Western European Jews, who are being resettled after being settled in the ghetto half a year ago, pulled out of the Radogoszcz sidetrack station. At the moment, one important detail has been established in connection with the departure of the first transport: all those departing (the transport consisted of one thousand people) had their baggage, knapsacks, and even their hand-held parcels taken away from them. This news has cast a chill over the ghetto.

A SUICIDE

This morning, in the collective house at 70 Zgierska Street, 60-year-old Julia Baum from Frankfurt am Main hanged herself. The reason: fear of deportation.

TUESDAY, MAY 5, 1942

THE SECOND DAY OF RESETTLEMENT

The second transport of Western European Jews being resettled from the ghetto left today. Their baggage was taken away from them, as it was from those who left yesterday. It is worth noting that doctors and health personnel were included in the transports. The selection of candidates among doctors for deportation was performed by the directors of the Department of Health. All told, 15 doctors are being resettled. There have been cases of local people volunteering for the transports. Naturally, their applications are rejected because the deportation is comprised solely of members of the new population. Trade in the possessions of the deportees continues, but on a much smaller scale. In exchange for their more valuable possessions, the deportees are accepting only food, and even soup tickets (whose price fluctuates from 12 to 15 marks), or German marks figured at a rate of 1 RM [Reichsmark] to 8 [ghetto] marks. The rate for small bills is two points higher than that for hundred mark notes.[45]

WEDNESDAY, MAY 6, 1942

THE THIRD DAY OF THE RESETTLEMENT ACTION

Today's transport, the third of Western European Jews, and composed, as usual, of one thousand persons, was also completely dispossessed of its baggage. People are telling stories of the tragic incidents the deportees experienced just before entering the trains. The guards ordered them to step back five paces from the train, and then to throw all their baggage to the ground, not only their knapsacks and suitcases but their hand-held parcels, bags, etc., as well. They were only allowed to keep their bread. The property discarded by the deportees was turned over to the Order Service which, on instructions from the local authorities, transported it all on flat, sideless, horse-drawn wagons to the Office for Resettled Persons on Rybna Street, where the ownerless items were secured in storehouses that had been cleaned out especially for that purpose. The sight of the wagons pulling up in front of the office, loaded mostly with small packages, nearly all of which contained the most essential items—bedding and blankets—caused a feeling of hopelessness among passersby.

The work of organizing the action has been going on nonstop, day and night, in the Office for Resettled Persons. The office's principal responsibility is sending out depar-

---

45. In another copy of the original *Chronicle* the last sentence was corrected, and rightly so, to read: "The exchange rate for smaller bank notes is two points lower."

ture warrants and then examining petitions and complaints concerning exemptions from deportation. The office has been cooperating with the Resettlement Commission, which has been operating for several days and is located at the registration point on Szklana Street. Final decisions concerning petitions are made by a special commission consisting of the directors of the Office of Resettled Persons, the chairman of the court, the director of the Department of Population Records, and the director of the Department of Penal Administration.[46] In accordance with the principles established, deportation cards are not being sent to: (1) those decorated with the iron cross, classes I and II, and those decorated for their wounds (this immunity also includes veterans of the former Austrian army), and also a few of their family members; (2) those who are employed, with particular consideration for skilled workers with permanent positions, in that order. The fate of day workers has not yet been determined precisely. The rule for those who are employed includes one member of the immediate family (wife, parent, child). The directors of the transports [collective houses], as workers without permanent positions, do not in principle benefit from this immunity; many of them have already received deportation warrants and some have applied voluntarily in the hope of bettering their lot.

The resettlement is proceeding according to the following plan: each day, beginning on the third of this month, the following transports are being filled: Berlin II, Vienna II, Düsseldorf, Berlin IV, Hamburg, Vienna IV, Prague I, Prague III, Cologne II, Berlin III, Prague V, Berlin IV, Vienna II, Vienna V, Prague II, Prague IV, Vienna I, Frankfurt, Cologne I, and the final transport, Luxembourg. In accordance with the request of the Association of Christians, they will be resettled as a group, which involves some 300 people. The plan is for this group to be included in Saturday's transport. When speaking of categories not subject to resettlement, it is worth noting that the group of translators registered at the office, and their families as well, have been ordered exempt from resettlement by the secret police [Gestapo]. In the month of March, the secret police demanded that a list be drawn up of translators from and to Hebrew, English, French, Serbian, modern Greek, Spanish, and Latin. After a very large number of applications, the list was closed at 20 candidates for future work; after the list was approved by the ghetto's highest authorities, it was submitted to the German authorities. At present that list consists of 17 persons, three having died in the meantime. The orders from the German authorities make no provision for any possible enlargement of this list.

A LIST

of all those people residing in the ghetto who perform the religious rite of circumcision, and who are currently practicing it, and who practiced it before the war has been demanded by the [German] criminal police.[47]

---

46. In another copy of the original *Chronicle*, the last sentence reads: "Final decisions in cases of resettlement are rendered by a commission composed of the directors of the Resettlement Commission, the chairman of the court, [Szaja-Stanisław] Jakobson, and persons appointed by the Chairman [the Eldest of the Jews]."

47. Circumcisers (*moylim*) were frequently compelled to perform circumcisions while being filmed or photographed by the Germans for purposes of anti-Jewish propaganda. (See the entry entitled "Filming" on June 8–10, 1942).

FORTY-TWO WEDDINGS

were performed yesterday in a new hall designated especially for that purpose at 4 Kościelny Square, where the Department of Vital Statistics and the Rabbinate are located. It should be explained that, in the current 49-day period between Passover and the Feast of Weeks [Shabuoth], marriages can only be performed on two days— the 5th and the 17th of this month. Twenty of the 42 marriages were concluded between couples who had been deported to the ghetto from the West. The fear of being separated because of the resettlement campaign is behind these large numbers. In assuming the bonds of matrimony, the couples made written declarations stating that they did not wish to be separated, whether they are resettled or remain in the ghetto. One of the unions concluded yesterday was a "mixed" marriage: he had come here from Germany (he is now a policeman in the ghetto), she was a local girl. One subject of immediate interest to the newlyweds is whether or not they will be granted a special food allocation in keeping with the tradition that has been observed thus far.

LITZMANNSTADT-GETTO, MAY 6, 1942

Today the third transport of Jews who had been settled here from Germany left the ghetto. The conditions of departure have not changed. Those departing are not permitted to take any packages and, thus, their hand-held baggage has remained at Marysin station.

During the last resettlement, the local Jews were also at times forbidden to take their packages with them and people's knapsacks were cut off their backs, but, somehow or other, our Jews found a way to cope with that. In response to the order, they would lay down their larger packages and keep the smaller ones, and then, later on, they would put the smaller ones down and pick the larger ones back up. And, if someone were quick-witted enough, he would take advantage of the guard's inattention and save the rest of his baggage as well. This was not a universal phenomenon, but it was, nevertheless, quite commonplace.

It was a somewhat different story with the well-disciplined German Jews. For them an order issued by a uniformed authority is sacred, and at the first command they all set their baggage down without a thought of trying to retrieve any of it. As consolation they were told that they would receive their baggage on the next train.

The news of the conditions prevailing at departure is, to a significant degree, causing possessions to continue to be sold. Once again, clothing, linen, shoes, and other odds and ends have been placed on the market and, once again, barter is flourishing in all the gateways on Bazar [Square], Wolborska Street, and in the "transports." Whatever people fail to sell in the "city," they either have to throw away on Szklana Street or in Marysin, or, in the extreme, at the train station. Schooled by the experience of recent days, some people have struck on the old idea of putting on a few suits, a few changes of underwear, and, quite frequently, two overcoats. They tie the first coat with a belt from which they hang an extra pair of shoes and other small items.

And so their faces, cadaverously white or waxy yellow, swollen, and despairing, sway disjointedly on top of disproportionately wide bodies that bend and droop under their own weight. They are possessed by a single thought: to save the little that remains of what they own, even at the expense of the last of their strength. Some people have been overcome by utter helplessness, whereas some still believe in something.

Fewer and fewer people loaded down with sacks are to be seen, and the later transports are practically without luggage when they come to Marysin. Abandoned umbrellas and canes are strewn over the grounds of the prison.

The last and final privilege—to take a "bag and a stick"—has also been retracted from them.

THURSDAY, MAY 7, 1942

PEOPLE ARE SAYING

that, in the immediate future, up to 30,000 skilled workers and laborers will arrive in the ghetto (without their families). These Jews are supposed to be coming here from the small towns in the vicinity.

THE FOURTH DAY OF RESETTLEMENT

A transport of former residents of Hamburg and Düsseldorf left the ghetto today. Possessions, down to the smallest parcels, continue to be taken away. They are only left their bread and, at times, bits of some other food as well.

The transports are conveyed in the following manner. In the afternoon hours, the deportees make their way to Central Prison or to the small buildings surrounded by barbed wire on Szklana Street. There they remain for the night, and the next day at noon they are assembled into groups and escorted under guard to the camp in Marysin, where they are lodged in the school building on Jonscher Street and in five small buildings on Okopowa Street. They receive food at these assembly points—a ration of bread, [ersatz] coffee, and soup. Each person is supplied with a loaf of bread for the journey, free of charge. At four o'clock in the morning, special detachments of the Order Service, already expert at performing such onerous tasks, transport the deportees by tram to the Radogoszcz sidetrack station. Half an hour before the train departs—which occurs at 7 o'clock on the dot—secret police [Gestapo] officials, accompanied by regular [German] police, arrive by automobile. By then the deportees have been lined up by the Order Service, in groups of ten in front of the compartment doors, at a distance of two meters from the train. Then they take their places under the eye of the police. It is then that they are ordered to throw away the things they had brought with them. The largest pieces of luggage have already been taken away by the Order Service at the assembly points; those items, and those taken away at the station, are later sent to the office on Rybna Street. Porters carry the sick and the very elderly onto the trains. There are medical stations in operation at the assembly points, and a medical team is on duty at the train station as well. The story circulating through the ghetto concerning the beating of deportees is worth correcting. Such incidents, with minor exceptions, are not taking place. The train is made up of third-class carriages, as in the previous resettlements. Each person leaving the ghetto is given a seat. The train returns the same day, at 8 o'clock P.M.

[THURSDAY, MAY 7, 1942]

A FOOTNOTE TO THE RESETTLEMENT OF THE HAMBURG TRANSPORT

Barely Half a Year . . .
Barely half a year has passed since they arrived in the ghetto. At that time they arrived here in long lines, festively-attired people whose appearance contrasted so sharply with our native squalor. We were struck by their elegant sports clothes, their exquisite footwear, their furs, the many variously colored capes the women wore. They often gave the impression of being people on some sort of vacation or, rather, engaged in winter sports, for the majority of them wore ski clothes. You couldn't tell there was a war on from the way those people looked; and the fact that, during the bitter cold spells, they strolled about in front of the gates to their "transports," and about the "city" as well, demonstrated most eloquently that their layers of fat afforded them excellent protection from the cold.

Their attitude toward the extremely unsanitary conditions in which they were quartered was one of unusual disgust, though perhaps that was not without justification; they shouted, they were indignant, and beyond the reach of any argument. At that time they were not concerned that the ghetto's entire meager transportation system had been paralyzed as a result of their arrival, which also caused the entire winter allocation of vegetables to freeze at Marysin. They could not see that quartering 20,000 newcomers in the ghetto's meager terrain could only be done at the cost of reducing the area inhabited by the old population. It is true that this problem was not solved at once as it should have been and became a great sore spot, but, in all fairness, one must admit that to solve that problem would have required a certain amount of time, even under the best of conditions. However, they were very impatient and swore a blue streak!

Somewhere along the line they had been led astray . . . They had not been informed of where they were going and what would happen to them. They had heard that they were traveling to some industrial center where each of them would find suitable employment, which was why they were disappointed when they found themselves in a situation that was entirely different from what they had expected. Some of them even asked if they mightn't reside in a hotel of some sort. There were, indeed, some arrogant and ill-mannered people among them, but, at bottom, losing their bearings had made them feel small and helpless. Upon their departure, they had been allowed to take along only 50 kilograms of baggage (things were not the same everywhere!) but they rarely observed the rule, and that is why the Department of Transportation was busy for six weeks transporting their luggage.

Nearly all of them brought extra food with them, but those who, for whatever reason, were unable to do so, found considerable amounts of bread, margarine, and other products offered for sale by the old population. New customers, a wealthy market which absorbed everything on sale each day. Prices shot up from one hour to the next, and in a short time the price of a loaf of bread had risen to 25 marks, whereas in previous conditions a price of 10 marks would have seemed sky high.

The newcomers could see the poverty of the local population; they knew that, due to their own financial advantage, they could tear the last bite of bread from the mouths of their brothers from the East, but that did not faze them. Large numbers of people in front of butchers' stalls sold them their rations for next to nothing, initially for some thirty-odd pfennigs. They looked with disgust at the soups served them, and it was rare for any of the newcomers—at least in the beginning—to be seen eating a meal in any of the Community's soup kitchens. They would give away their soup to our local paupers in exchange for various favors and services.

Part of the Hamburg transport was quartered in the building where the Bajka Cinema was formerly located, at 33 Franciszkańska Street. This took place on Thursday evening, the 20th of November, and on Friday morning the Chairman arrived to greet his guests. They were spread out on the floor, sleeping on their bundles, the old people and the women sitting in chairs lining the walls.

They rose to his greeting and the Chairman delivered a short speech, perhaps the shortest speech in the history of the ghetto. It contained but a few sentences, but it was so warm and sincere that not only the women but many dignified men wiped tears of emotion from their eyes. It was a genuine brotherly greeting, as well as an assurance that he would share his humble roof and his bread with them.

That evening, the newcomers from Hamburg arranged a Friday service. Dressed in their best clothes, with many candles lit, they said their first prayer to God with uncanny calm and in a mood of exaltation. Those who had left Judaism a long time before, even those whose fathers had broken any connection with their forefathers, stood there that day, festively attired, in a sort of grave and exalted mood, seeking consolation and salvation in prayer. When their prayers were concluded, they went out into the lobby, the same words on all their lips: "Now we see that we are all equal, all sons of the same people, all brothers." This was either mere flattery or, perhaps, a genuine compliment to the old population—or perhaps a premonition of the not-too-distant future.

Events outpaced time, people changed visibly, at first outwardly, then physically, and finally, if they had not vanished altogether, they moved through the ghetto like ghosts . . .

The rutabagas and beets they [the newcomers] had at first disdained, they now bought at high prices, and the soups they had scorned became the height of their dreams. Once it had been others, but then it was they who prowled the "city" with a cup or a canteen on a chain to *shnorn* [beg] a little soup.

Conditions changed enormously in that short span of time, and a soup kitchen meal became a luxury; the price of such soup had reached 15 marks, and no one was in any hurry to sell his soup, even though it bore no resemblance to the soup available six months before. They sold off the last of their possessions to secure themselves food of any sort, which they now saw as their last salvation from doom.

And indeed, it was only half a year, only six months, that had proven to be an eternity for them! Some of the metamorphoses could not be imagined, even in a dream . . . Ghosts, skeletons with swollen faces and extremities, ragged and impoverished, they now left for a further journey on which they were not even allowed to take a knapsack.

They had been stripped of all their European finery, and only the Eternal Jew was left . . .

The premonitions they had had that first Friday in the ghetto had proven all too true . . .   [Józef] Kl[ementynowski]

FRIDAY, MAY 8, 1942

THEY PREFERRED DEATH TO A SECOND EXILE

In the last two days the records of the Order Service note five suicide attempts by people resettled here from the West who were faced with deportation from the ghetto. On May 5, at 4:00 P.M., Aber Hugo, single, hung himself in his apartment at 8 Pieprzowa Street. The First Aid Service recorded the death of the 66-year-old man, who had been resettled here from Bohemia. On the same day at 3:00 P.M., 66-year-old Teresa Adler took an overdose of Luminal in her apartment at 8 Gnieźnieńska Street. She was taken to Hospital No. 1 in critical condition. A married couple, the Landsbergers, took Veronal together in their apartment at 18 Ciesielska Street during the night of the 7th. The husband, Artur (aged 63), died before the doctor arrived; his wife, Kathe (also 63 years old), was taken unconscious to Hospital No. 1 and died twenty-four hours later. On the 7th of this month, at 4:00 A.M., Malwina Frisch (of 13 Krzyżowa Street) poisoned herself by taking Gardenal. She was taken to Hospital No. 1. A footnote to these suicides is the view, shared by local society, that these incidents constitute yet another proof that, compared to Polish Jews, the Jews of Western Europe display considerably less resistance and strength of spirit. Remarks about the local Jews, to the effect that they are more steeled to the vicissitudes of fate, both physically and mentally, than they are, are frequently heard from newcomers: it should be remembered that the martyrdom of local society dates from the outbreak of the war, while the sufferings of the newcomers, at least in the material sense, began only half a year ago, when they were herded into this ghetto after having been expelled from their native lands.

THE DEPARTMENT OF SOUP KITCHENS

has made the meals in all of the ghetto's soup kitchens conform to a pattern. Porridge will be cooked on odd-numbered days while canned beet or sauerkraut soup will be prepared on the even-numbered days. The soups' composition will be as follows:

Porridge		*Vegetable Soup*	
Potatoes	250 g	Potatoes	150 g
Flour	10 g	Canned beets (or 100 g of beets and 100 g of sauerkraut)	150 g
Rolled oats	30 g	Flour	4 g
Margarine	2.5 g	Margarine	2.5 g

RESETTLEMENT

A group of 260 Western European Jews professing Christian religions was included in Saturday's transport. As the bulletin has noted [p. 162], this occurred because the ghetto authorities complied with the wishes of the parties involved. Beginning on Saturday, the baggage situation improved somewhat. People were allowed to take smaller knapsacks and haversacks of food along with them. In cases where deportees were carrying relatively large pieces of luggage, they were ordered to throw them all away. On Sunday people in the ghetto were saying that, apart from taking knapsacks away, the Order Service, watched over by a [German] secret police official and acting on his orders, conducted body searches, pulling the last of the deportees' possessions from their pockets. This rumor has no foundation in fact.

Because the commission at the Office for Resettled Persons complied with many of the appeals, the number of additional departure warrants (known in the ghetto as wedding certificates) sent out has increased significantly in the last few days; thus, for example, a very large number of people, even those who are working, have received such warrants. On Sunday, 156 warrants arrived at the Düsseldorf collective at 15 Rybna Street, the greater part of which had already been evacuated. It is worth noting that even the doctors are all receiving warrants one after the other, and they were only exempted from deportation after an investigation of their appeals, which were based on the fact that they were practicing their profession in the health service. On the other hand, all unemployed doctors are subject to forcible deportation; there are 15 such doctors. The commission that deals with complaints is working day and night. Punctually at eight in the morning, crowds of petitioners fill the courtyard of the building where the office is located, for it is at that time that an official of the office reads out the names of those who have been given exemptions and those subject to deportation or to some postponement. The crowd listens in an atmosphere of the most extreme anxiety; the impression is of people waiting for either a reprieve or a death sentence. Tears of joy or of terrible despair—everyone reacts one way or the other upon hearing his name called. It is no exaggeration to say that the morning hours in the courtyard at 8 Rybna Street are, by their nature, profoundly tragic.

THE OLD PEOPLE'S HOME FOR NEW SETTLERS (ON GNIEŹNIEŃSKA STREET)

has received a summons for 300 pensioners to leave the ghetto, and the shelter on Krzyżowa Street has received orders for around 30. It is worth stressing that over 750 people reside on Gnieźnieńska Street and, thus, 40 percent are subject to deportation.

A SERVICE

During the Saturday prayers in the Düsseldorf transport's collective, Rabbi Dr. Klein delivered a sermon dedicated to the fate of [our] deported brothers.

A MUCH SOUGHT-AFTER ITEM

Potato peels have become a much sought-after item. The soup kitchen directors are approached in a wide variety of ways and all strings are being pulled, just to somehow or other obtain a little of this food, which is the only nourishment apart from bread for some people. Up until Saturday, the directors could dispose of potato peels as they saw fit, and, most frequently, they divided them among their staffs. As of Saturday, that prerogative has been taken away from them.

HUNGER IN THE GHETTO

Hunger is the most tragic fact of the moment. The potatoes for May, distributed in the first half of April, were eaten a long time ago. In only a small number of families is there anything left to eat, and those who have enough for the rest of the month can be counted on the fingers of a hand. To evaluate the situation objectively one should not forget that, after relatively generous rations in the first half of April, there was a suspension of all vegetable deliveries, and the population was left with only 280 grams of bread and 250 grams of potatoes (and besides, the latter were, to a considerable degree, in a state of rapid decay and had to be consumed quickly). On the other hand, premature consumption was, in many cases, caused by the recklessness of people who are constantly underfed and who were counting on further allocations in the immediate future. Whatever the reason, the great majority of the ghetto is starving.

AN ACT WORTHY OF RECOGNITION

A few doctors have recently foregone the special food allocation due them by virtue of the profession they practice; those allocations are now being sold by the R stores, formerly distribution points for the sick. Their refusal to avail themselves of special privileges was motivated by the general state of hunger.

A RAID AT THE ADRIA

On Monday, at around eleven o'clock, a few officials of the German criminal police, with revolvers drawn, entered the Adria restaurant on Bałut Market. At that moment the restaurant was incredibly packed, its small rooms containing at least one hundred people. Trade—in goods, food, barter, and money—was going on in the restaurant as if nothing unusual were happening. The restaurant was mostly filled with German Jews who had taken a special liking to the Adria from the moment they arrived here and made it a general place to meet. One can easily imagine the effect caused by the surprise visit. On the basis of a list in their possession, the representatives of the police were especially interested in a few particular individuals. All the customers were subjected to a body search, and not only were their possessions, brought there primarily for sale, confiscated, but so were personal items, such as watches, pens, and cigarette cases, as well as their money (including ghetto marks). There were no serious beatings. The worst of it was the fear and the material losses suffered. Only four customers were taken away by the police. The criminal police's spring carriage, well-known to ghetto dwellers, was loaded with the confiscated property.

DOLLS

Typical ghetto dolls are fashioned from clay and modeled after puppets. This is done by order of the [German] authorities. When a set is completed, the models are turned over to the authorities.[48]

48. The Research Department (*Wissenschaftliche Abteilung*) was engaged in the production of dolls to be used by the Nazis in anti-Jewish propaganda. The *Chronicle* will later provide a very detailed account of this department, along with information about its disbanding in June, 1943. (See also, pp. 209–10, n. 70.)

PEOPLE ARE SAYING . . .

that a new resettlement from this ghetto will take place. The latest versions would have it that at one point the authorities assigned a quota of 90,000 to be resettled. About 45,000 people had left the ghetto before the 2d of April and the second group of 45,000 has been demanded recently. After taking great pains, the Chairman succeeded in bargaining that figure down to 25,000. To be included in the above number are the 11–12,000 resettled here over the last year, the rest coming from the local population, principally from those who were stamped during the last examinations performed by the medical commission.

TUESDAY, MAY 12, 1942

THE RESETTLEMENT ACTION

still continues. The 9th transport left today. 900–1,000 people fill each transport, which means that close to nine thousand Western European Jews have left the ghetto.

As the bulletin has already noted, rumors persist in the ghetto about further resettlement, a possibility which has been denied in private conversation by representatives of official circles. Today those rumors seem to have taken on a definite form. A mood of genuine panic set in among the ghetto's permanent population when it was ascertained that, since yesterday evening, deportation cards had begun to be sent out to the local population as well. And that means an across-the-board resettlement. However, after a few hours, the populace learned through the grapevine that in this particular case only a very small category is affected, that is, persons especially undesirable to society—notorious criminals, "prisoners serving sentences," and so forth. Apparently, this number is not to exceed 100, and will be subject to deportation with the final transports. There is no question at the moment of any further resettlement of "Poles." When the action now underway will end is the question of the day. In the afternoon, a story spread through the ghetto that the resettlement will be concluded on Wednesday and not on Friday, as anticipated. This is being neither confirmed nor denied on Rybna Street. Meanwhile, work continues nonstop at the office on Rybna Street, and it should be stressed that, in spite of the incredible difficulties that have accumulated, the commission is scrupulously and punctually dealing with thousands of complaints in strict accordance with the principles established. Moreover, all the office's divisions are functioning normally and handling the usual problems of the new population.

The train that takes all the deportees away each day heads for Widzew.[49] There is a change of locomotives in Widzew and the train is shunted onto a side track.

On the 10th, a train car of Jews from Sieradz[50] pulled up on the Marysin sidetrack.

49. Widrew, a suburban industrial settlement in Łódź whose railroad station had been enlarged.
50. Before the war, around 5,000 Jews lived in Sieradz, a town situated to the southwest of Łódź. During the Nazi occupation, the Germans established a labor camp for Jews in Sieradz and a ghetto, which existed from 1940 to 1942; they also took over and expanded the nineteenth-century prison there. In August, 1942, around 1,400 Jews from Sieradz were deported to the death camp in Chełmno (Kulmhof).

That car, which contained about 40 people, was attached to the transport. They made signs through the window from which one could conclude that they had been deprived of food for three days. They had no packages. They were probably Łodzites who had recently been housed in the Sieradz prison. One day the following incident occurred: before the train departed [German] secret police officials noticed that one of the porters was intending to pick up something from an abandoned package. They immediately ordered him included in the transport. After a few minutes, the unlucky man attempted to save himself by fleeing from the train. His flight was observed and he was placed in the car occupied by the train's guards (the only second-class car).

WHERE ARE THE JEWS?

This is the question sent here by the Jewish Council of the town of Inowrocław. From its card it is evident that the council has its seat in a monastery in the small town of Mogilna. They inquired as to whether the Jews who were resettled from Piotrków Kujawski and Świątnica in October of last year might not be in the ghetto here.[51]

A FRENZY OF SUICIDES

During the course of the resettlement action the records of the Order Service note daily instances of suicide among the new population. Thus: Hedwig Kupidlarska, from the town of Horandovice in Hungary, a resident of 7 Widok Street, poisoned herself on the 8th of this month. She was taken to Hospital No. 1 in critical condition. On the 9th of this month, a married couple, the Fischers, 75-year-old Ignaz "Israel" and 60-year-old Karolina "Sara," took Veronal together to poison themselves. They were taken unconscious to the hospital. The husband died after 24 hours; the wife is now in her death agony. On the 11th of this month, at 6 o'clock in the morning, Irma Wesela, born in 1885, a seamstress by trade and resettled here from Bohemia, hung herself in her apartment at 67 Franciszkańska Street. On that same day, Teresa Adler, who, as the bulletin has reported, attempted suicide by taking an overdose of Veronal on May 6 of this year, died in the hospital. Malwina Frisch, a native of Vienna who poisoned herself with Gardenal on the 7th of this month, also died on the 11th. On the 11th of this month, Rosa Kaldor (of 25 Wolborska Street), a 63-year-old woman resettled here from Hungary,[52] threw herself from a fifth-floor window, dying on the spot. Finally, on May 12, at 10:30 A.M., a local resident, Maria Jakubowicz, born in Łódź in 1892, cut the arteries in her right arm. She was taken to the hospital by an ambulance. She had resided at 23 Młynarska Street.

A SIGN OF THE TIMES

People are gathering in front of the entrances to the soup kitchens in search of potato peels. They accost the help for them; they will not leave the managers in peace. Thus,

51. Jews from Piotrków Kujawski and Świątnica, small towns in the vicinity of Inowrocław, were not resettled to the Łódź ghetto. As for the Jewish population of Inowrocław itself, it was, by the end of 1939, deported to various cities and towns in the vicinity, including Mogilno. There it was quartered in the cellars of a Benedictine monastery, which the Germans had turned into a police jail and where people marked for deportation were held.

52. Jews were not deported directly from Hungary to the Łódź ghetto. The women mentioned probably arrived in Łódź in a transport from the West.

the latter were pleased by the ruling of the Department of Soup Kitchens on the 11th of this month, forbidding the distribution of potato peels to anyone whatsoever. Potato peels may be obtained solely on the basis of medical certificates stating that they are necessary to the restoration of a given individual's health, and when approved by the director of the Department of Soup Kitchens, Mr. Kaufman, who, at the same time, sends them to one of the soup kitchens. So many formalities for potato peels!

B[ernard] O[strowski]

WEDNESDAY AND THURSDAY, MAY 13 AND 14, 1942

RESETTLEMENT

On Wednesday morning, a story spread through the ghetto that the [German] authorities had withdrawn their decision of the previous day, to speed up the resettlement action and conclude it by Thursday, and that they had demanded that transports be sent to the train station on Friday and Saturday as well. This would make it appear that around two thousand more people are to be included in the deportation—that is, all told, this resettlement [of May, 1942] will comprise some 12,000 people. Consequently, the office on Rybna Street began to send out masses of deportation warrants on Wednesday to people selected from the list of those hitherto exempt from the quota. (In view of the fact that, during the entire course of the resettlement action, the ghetto authorities have not been kept accurately informed as to how many people they are to assign for resettlement, there have been incidents where deportation cards have been sent out to people whose petitions had already been approved.) Then, on Wednesday night, the Order Service was put in a state of instant readiness, just as when the medical examinations were taking place. During the night, Order Service men forcibly removed some 500 people from their dwellings who had not reported to the assembly points by the deadline. Most of these people were taken from collectives, where people are most easily caught. It should be noted that, thus far, when people resettled here from the West were being deported, the Order Service had not forcibly removed anyone from a private apartment, confining themselves to people in collectives. It is worth adding that, during the resettlement of Western European Jews, there had been no need to forcibly remove those who had received summonses because they obeyed orders as a matter of principle. In the last few days, in the building on Rybna Street that houses the collectives of refugees from Düsseldorf, there have been cases of infectious diseases, which have caused a quarantine to be ordered: fortune in misfortune. Their isolation is saving many Düsseldorf Jews from deportation.

The train that bears the deportees away each day is made up of seven passenger cars. In each car, the first and last compartments are assigned to the escorts. The number of Polish Jews [whose presence in the ghetto is] considered undesirable (see bulletin No. 30 [Tuesday, May 12, 1942]) who have been included in the final transports amounts to some 400 persons. This number includes both the undesirables and their entire families.

FRIDAY, MAY 15, 1942

SIGNS OF A RETURN TO STABILITY

By yesterday there were observable signs indicating that the economic situation in the ghetto, which had been thrown into complete chaos over the last few weeks, was being brought under control. The sudden drop in the prices of necessities is the first harbinger of a return to normalcy. Bread fell, yesterday, from close to 600 marks to 450 and lower, margarine went from over 1,000 to below 400. Other items followed suit. Saccharine displayed a somewhat weaker tendency to fall, its price dropping only to 50 pfennigs per tablet. The cigarettes placed on the market by the Community have, for the time being, satisfied demand entirely, as is eloquently demonstrated by the fact that those wishing to speculate in resale were forced to content themselves with barely 25 pfennigs per cigarette. The best German cigarettes have appeared for sale at 1.75 marks a pack. The German mark, whose exchange rate has acted as a barometer of tension during the deportation action, fell to below 7 [ghetto marks] on the eve of the action's conclusion, with no buyers whatsoever. These signs have made the population of the ghetto a bit optimistic after having recently been in a state of complete depression and exhaustion. With increasing frequency, one hears the opinion that the Community authorities' forceful measures will achieve their goal and bring the situation back under control. Just so long as there is no new calamity to shatter the equilibrium, which has been patched up once again—this is the devout wish of the ghetto's inhabitants.

PEOPLE ARE SAYING . . .

Yesterday evening people were saying that today's transport of deportees would be suspended. Their prediction was not, however, borne out, since a transport left today as well. It may be the last.

SATURDAY, MAY 16, 1942

POTATO PEELS

The demand for potato peels, obtainable with medical certification, has recently been so great that the director of the Department of Health was forced to forbid doctors to issue any more such certificates. However, it is not always possible to refuse to give people cards. By Friday, the Department of Soup Kitchens had given out 350 authorizations for potato peels at various public kitchens. Control of the potato peels in workshop kitchens, which are exclusively for the workers employed in those enterprises, has been left to the directors.

HOLDERS OF THE IRON CROSS

were summoned yesterday to report to Bałut Market today at 8 A.M. Around 100 of these summonses went out, both to those who had been decorated with iron crosses and to those with medals for wounds suffered while serving in the German or Austrian army during World War I. The Office for Resettled Persons was the assembly point. Those reporting were conducted by the [Jewish] police from the office to Bałut Market. A few hundred old men marching down the streets of the ghetto by fours, military style, drew everyone's attention. Representatives of the secret police [Gestapo] examined their documents at Bałut Market, and quite courteously, too. Everyone was able to properly establish his identity with the decorations in his possession. Clearly the point here was to learn if anyone was illegally avoiding resettlement by virtue of this privilege. The chief of the secret police has spoken to the Chairman about assuring work to those with decorations. The next group of 100 has been summoned for tomorrow. The Office for Resettled Persons had barely caught its breath after the last resettlement, when new work was imposed on it; for the same office has been burdened with summoning the medal holders, performing the preliminary examination of their documents, and compiling lists. The work continued through the night until 7 o'clock in the morning. The total number of those registered and possessing documents comes to 289, which constitutes a very high percentage if one considers that this figure does not include the series of transports whose members, for a variety of reasons, did not manage to bring their documents with them [especially those from] (Berlin). In the days ahead, we will return to this discussion of the percentage of people with decorations relative to the total number of those who had been resettled here.

SUNDAY, MAY 17, 1942

AFTER THE RESETTLEMENT ACTION

As noted in the previous bulletin, the final transport of Western European Jews left from the Radogoszcz station on Friday, the 15th of this month. According to the authorities' original order, 1,500 people were to be deported in the final two days; in the end they agreed to accept 1,300. Of these, 706 left on Thursday and 600 on Friday. At 7:30, right after the train's departure, the representatives of the secret police [Gestapo] at the train station informed the chief of the Order Service that the resettlement was finished and that, on Saturday morning at 4 o'clock, a transport consisting of two thousand people would arrive from the small towns in the vicinity. During the process of resettlement, 250 local residents were forcibly added to the next-to-last transport of deportees. Included in that transport were people who were to have been resettled during the previous deportation action, which they had avoided by hiding. Among the 250 are individuals burdened with sins of one magnitude or another. On the final day, the German guards treated the deportees in relatively mild fashion, allowing them to take their possessions with them.

Informed during the night that only 600 more people were needed for the final transport, the Order Service released 80 people at 4 o'clock in the morning—people, no longer needed, who had reached the final stage before resettlement, that is, they had been in Marysin. The selection of the fortunate proceeded on the basis of a list received from the Resettlement Commission and cleared by the Office for Resettled Persons. It is worth noting here that, each night during the deportation action, and in the final moments before people were sent to the train station, complaints were still being examined at the assembly points, Central Prison and Marysin, by authorized individuals from the commission and the office. It is difficult to describe the joy of the 80 candidates for deportation who were released at the last moment. Their joy is analogous to that of people sentenced to death who are pardoned right before the execution. The Order Service attended to the chosen 80 until daybreak, distributing bread and [ersatz] coffee among them. Apparently, throughout the entire action, the deportees were supplied with food—a bread ration, coffee, and soup containing meat—at the Community's expense. During the final days at the assembly points, there were places where cigarettes could be bought only by deportees, in unlimited amounts, and at a reduced price of 50 pfennigs apiece.

One night, there was a suicide attempt on the grounds of the prison. The person making the attempt cut the veins in his arms; however, this did not help him avoid deportation. After bandages were applied and the bleeding stemmed, he was sent to the train station. There was another instance of a failed suicide attempt. On the whole it must be said that in these tragic moments before another journey into the un-known, the exiles from the West preserved their equanimity to a greater degree than have their brothers here in similar situations. Lamentation, screaming, and wailing at the final assembly points were characteristic features of the previous deportations, whereas during this deportation the Western European Jews made an outward display of considerably greater self-control. On the other hand, they lost that self-control at the train station and, by causing confusion, drew down repressive mea-sures from the guards. There was one case in which the German authorities ordered the arrest of a [Jewish] policeman who had attempted to hand an abandoned package to a compatriot from Prague. By order of the authorities he was punished with three days of arrest.

Some figures: the resettlements took place between the 4th and the 15th of May, inclusively. Twelve transports containing 10,915 people left here. The office sent out around 15,000 deportation warrants and 4,500 complaints were approved. In the meantime, 94 candidates for resettlement died. Twenty-five people were sent from the hospital for resettlement. There were about 300 volunteers from among the local population.

POTATO PEELS

The quest for potato peels is an eloquent symbol of the hunger prevailing in the ghetto. The starving populace is competing for this delicacy with admirable tenacity. On the basis of medical certificates, the Department of Soup Kitchens distributes allotments of three kilograms of potato peels [per person?] a day. Such large lines form in front of every kitchen when the peels are distributed that there is no way of providing everyone with a full portion. The peels are given out free of charge. The desirability of this item which, in normal times, is completely useless for consump-tion, is attested to by the recent price orgy—people willingly paid 15 marks for 1 kilogram of potato peels. People make soup from the potato peels or make them into flat cakes. *Signum temporis.*

MEDICINE

A certain amount of medicine arrived in the ghetto on Saturday. This delivery will alleviate, albeit for a short time, the shortage of the most essential medicines. Vitamin and liver injections, as sources of nutrition and strength, are the most sought-after in the ghetto. The lack of these preparations and the furious demand for them has caused the price of one ampule of the most sought-after injections, such as Campollon forte, for example, to reach 15 marks in unlicensed trade. The vogue for vitamin injections has, to a great degree, captured the minds of ghetto dwellers. Of late people have been discoursing on Campollon, yeast, and strychnine as much as on the now classic subject of soup. Opinions are divided among the ghetto's doctors. While some consider injections highly advisable, others maintain that they are only a whim of fashion. The head pharmaceutical office has divided the medicines received among the hospitals and health agencies.

THE DEATH OF A FAMOUS SCIENTIST

On May 5, Professor Jakob Edmund Speyer died in the ghetto, at the age of 63, as a result of exhaustion and weakening of the heart. Professor Speyer, a doctor in chemistry, is ranked among the greatest inventors in the field of medical chemistry. His name became famous at one time in connection with the discovery of Eukodal, a preparation that constitutes an improvement over morphine. In addition, he rendered science and humanity great service with his research into sensible nourishment by the use of vitamins. He collaborated for many years with the well-known German chemical company, Merck. The deceased was originally from Frankfurt am Main.

THE VIENNESE JOURNALIST RICHARD BEER,

an official working under the Eldest of the Jews, contracted a marriage today with Zofia Wajnsztajn, a painter well known in Łódź society, who is a clerk in the Department of Housing. Numerous guests, representing the elite of local society, attended the wedding ceremony performed by Rabbi [Yosif] Fajner.

WEATHER

May weather in all its splendor. 30 degrees at noon. A light breeze. Not a cloud in the sky.

DEATHS AND BIRTHS

Fifty-seven people, 22 of whom had been resettled here, died today. That latter figure is striking if one considers that, at the present moment, the approximate proportion of Western European Jews in relation to the remainder of the population is no more than 7 percent, whereas today's mortality rate represents a rate of 40 percent in relation to the overall number of deaths. No births were registered.

A SHOOTING

Last night at 3 o'clock, 30-year-old Josek Bernard Zajtman (of 11 Urzędnicza Street) was shot to death a few feet from the building where he lived, which is located right by the barbed wire.

THE RELOCATING

of residents of collectives to apartments continued yesterday. Residences were found for 100 people from Berlin III and 100 from Düsseldorf, along with the 360 relocated in the first two days, out of an overall number of 1,500.

Yesterday, the Chairman issued an order that they be allocated vacant apartments and that they be relocated in apartments which had been partially vacated by foreigners who have been resettled. That has caused a temporary suspension in work, since those affected have to be listed. Nevertheless, as soon as a dozen or so apartments became available, the people who were relocating left for their collectives at once, with porters and wagons, to move.

LITZMANNSTADT-GETTO, MAY 18, 1942

The final transport of new settlers has scarcely left the ghetto, and already there are new dark clouds on the horizon. Yesterday at daybreak, a transport of Jews deported from Pabianice arrived here, and a second such transport arrived today. All told, some 3,800–4,000 people have arrived thus far.

It was primarily women and men in the prime of life who came to this ghetto, for children up to the age of 10 and the sick had been separated out and sent off in another direction.[53] As the new arrivals tell it, they knew nothing about plans for a deportation, for the majority of them had been employed in their own professions for nearly two years and had been acquitting themselves to the complete satisfaction of their employers. It was true that, in the recent past, fewer orders had been coming in from the military authorities; nonetheless, they had been doing work for the German (civilian) populace, receiving their commissions from two Aryan firms in Pabianice: Kelle and Günther and Schwarz. Those firms divided the orders among the Jews they employed and were, in theory, in competition with each other. Both firms, but especially Kelle, had been slow in making payments, but the Jews had not been overly upset by this, for they had been able to get by one way or another as long as they could maintain contact with the outside world. Their ghetto had not been closed, so they had had contact with the Aryans when they left the ghetto to go to work and were also in touch with them when they came to the ghetto to consign one job or another.

The Jewish Community's allocations had included only basic items like flour, sugar, margarine, bread, etc., but rations had been issued erratically. The newcomers are of various opinions about those allocations. What one basically hears is that the Community possessed rather large supplies but was capricious in distributing them. Much of that food was sold on the private market, at much higher prices, and thus there is talk of considerable corruption. The Germans would often ask the Jews coming to work if they were receiving their food rations, getting enough to eat, and so on. That, however, could prove to be a source of trouble. If a worker replied that he had been wronged, that wrong could be partially rectified, but, on the other hand, the Community would settle accounts with him in another way, and this would result in his being deported from Pabianice. In that context of various internal intrigues, many Jews had had to leave Pabianice even earlier, going to perform manual labor in parts unknown. Formerly, the Chairman of the Pabianice Community had been a certain Mr. Rubinstein, and the newcomers had greatly deplored his arrest, for they had lived

---

53. That is, to Chełmno (Kulmhof).

in considerably more peace during his administration. He had apparently fallen victim to some low intrigue.

The newcomers are agreed on one point: that the members of the Council of Elders had been living well, right up to the last minute. Apparently, the Community administration's budget had been based on a 10 percent tax taken out of employees' wages and, therefore, the administration was interested in employing as many Jews as possible. However, it took little interest in their fate.

As we have already seen, for those Jews food was not a pressing issue, for they obtained more than enough food through their contacts with the civilian population. However, it was a fact that in recent times the prices on the free market had been, relatively speaking, quite high in Pabianice as well: a loaf of bread cost around 8 marks, one kilogram of potatoes—80 pfennigs to 1 [German] mark; flour, poultry, and meat were at roughly comparable prices. The prices of foodstuffs on the free market were very low in comparison with prices in our ghetto; on the other hand, clothing, shoes, and other items were extremely expensive, and it was enough to sell a little something from your closet to live well for a few weeks.

On the whole, conditions in Pabianice were like those here before the ghetto was closed. People there could buy a great variety of food, even geese, ducks, bacon, chicken fat, eggs, etc., and many of the newcomers had considerable food stocks in their apartments—but these comforts were not unaccompanied by incidents. Time and again they were forcibly dragged out to work, and their apartments were sometimes searched on one pretext or another and everything they owned taken. However, for the most part, they were tradesmen who made their livings by working with their hands, so their spirits were soon restored and they compensated for their losses the next chance they had by doing private work. Those who gave them private commissions paid them, for the most part, with food for their tailoring, shoemaking, and other such work. As a rule, the Jews of Pabianice did not bemoan their fate, for none of them went hungry and they say that no one died of hunger there. They engaged in unselfish mutual aid and lived like one big family. That was possible because they were not suffering from hunger, although they lived in constant fear, which united them.

On Saturday, the 16th of this month, they were ordered to assemble in front of the buildings where they lived at 4 o'clock P.M., and from there they were taken in groups to the Krusche and Ender company's athletic field. They thought a census was going to be taken. They had not been ordered to bring anything with them, and so—although it was a Saturday—some of them considered it unsuitable to wear their best Sabbath clothes. They went out in their everyday work clothes, thereby wishing to demonstrate the extent of their loyalty. They were placed in the center of the field, in a very small area, and segregated according to the letters that they had received during their recent medical examinations. Thus, people with the letter "A" (*Arbeitsfähig*) and those who possessed working papers were ordered to pass to one side, while the unfit, the aged, the sick, the children, and those marked with the letter "B" were placed on the other side. Shocking scenes were played out there, for children were not allowed to go to persons in group "A," infants were torn from mothers, children ran crying and screaming around the field looking for their parents, while their parents, unable to regard these scenes with composure, beseeched the guards to allow them to take their children with them. In response, they were shoved back, their children were torn from their arms and thrown to the grass like balls, and even thrown over the fence. They remained on that field until evening; it was a day of heavy rains and they were all drenched to the marrow, not to mention the fact that they hadn't even had a drink of water since they had left their houses. In the evening, they were informed that they were leaving for Litzmannstadt-Getto, while those unfit to work and marked with the letter "B," as well as the children, had been loaded onto peasant wagons and taken away in a different direction, to parts that remain unknown. At first 50 strong men were mobilized from group "A" to load those unfit to work onto the wagons, and another 50 were added later on. In a state of terrible tension, those left behind in group "A" waited for their comrades to return to learn something from them about the fate of those who had been carted away, but those hopes were to no avail for, of those one hundred men, none returned before their departure. The worst conclusions were drawn . . .

By order of the [Jewish] authorities, the hospital had been accepting patients on a much more liberal basis and, thus, on the eve of the deportation it housed some 150 patients. One of the men from Pabianice told of the patients' fate, of which he had heard from someone close to the authorities. Their end was brief and extreme. Disturbed by what he had heard, he implored his employer to make it possible for him to leave for the Łódź ghetto, even though he was not under threat of deportation. His employer, who was an official, furnished him with the requisite certificate and, in this way, enabled him to join the next transport, which arrived in Litzmannstadt on Monday, May 18, at four o'clock in the morning. Before departing, the man in question had intended to drop by his apartment to take something with him, but he learned that the majority of the apartments had already been searched, so he preferred to join the transport just as he was. He ascribed the deportation to the competition and animosity between the two German firms mentioned above. Mr. Kelle is, he says, a Landrat [head of a county in Prussia]; the firm of Günther and Schwarz, on the other hand, is an enterprise with branches in Germany. A while back a conflict had arisen between the two firms, the result of which was that some 150 workers employed by the Landrat were resettled. The Landrat avenged himself by causing higher officials to resettle all the Jews, thereby including those who had been employed for a long time by the firm of Günther and Schwarz.

On the other hand, a rumor is afoot that this resettlement, and particularly the employment of Jewish children, had been demanded because of [German] public opinion and the [Nazi] party in Pabianice, which had been outraged by the idleness of the Jewish children at a time when German children over the age of 16 had to fight at the front, and those over 10 had to work in the fields.

The new arrivals have been assigned to 7 Widok Street, 22 Masarska Street, and 25 Limanowski Street in the ghetto; additional locations are being prepared. The newcomers seemed well-fed, but it is terrible to see these desperate, lamenting women and men, wringing their hands, from which those nearest and dearest to them had been rudely torn. Rather good food was prepared for them, but many of them did not even touch it and did not reply to the questions addressed to them.

On the second day of the deportation, a few children and a few people not in category "A" made their way into the ghetto. It turns out that the Jews of Pabianice quickly got their bearings and used small gifts—watches, wallets, cigarette cases, etc.—to save the lives of a sizable handful of their brothers.

A transport from Brzeziny is expected tomorrow, to be followed by one from the other small towns in the surrounding area. A new wave of resettlement, a new wave of suffering!

FIVE THOUSAND WESTERN JEWS

remain in the ghetto after the conclusion of the resettlement action. And thus, roughly speaking, the movement of Western Jews in this ghetto can be reduced to three figures: about 20,000 arrived here, nearly 4,000 have died (20 percent!), and close to 11,000 have been resettled out of the ghetto.

ARRIVALS FROM PABIANICE AND BRZEZINY

After the people were deported from Pabianice, Brzeziny's turn came. The first rail transport from Brzeziny arrived today, at the Radogoszcz station at 9 o'clock in the morning. The 64 tallest men among them were selected and sent at once by tram to Bałut Market, from which they had, by 9:30 A.M., already left the ghetto by tram.

Apparently, they have been sent to perform manual labor in Dąbrówka [Dąbrowa], near Pabianice. One hundred people from Pabianice who had arrived here a few days ago also left to perform manual labor that morning. At noon, and in the afternoon, other transports of people resettled from Brzeziny arrived here. They traveled on the main road, some on foot, some in wagons. Their baggage has been brought to the ghetto and is under the supervision of the local authorities. In Brzeziny, each person was allowed to take 12.5 kilograms of baggage. Children under the age of 10 were—to the despair of their parents—taken from them and sent off to parts unknown. The tragedy of a local pharmacist, who left this ghetto a few months ago for a position as a pharmacist in Brzeziny, has become well known here. He returned here yesterday in a state of utter hopelessness, because his only son, a 5-year-old, was taken from him. [Michał] Urbach, a doctor of medicine who had left for Pabianice two months ago, in accordance with the authorities' demand for a physician, has returned to this ghetto. He had left here with all his instruments, and even with some expensive therapeutic machines, and has returned with nothing. Toward evening, the good news spread that 200 children had arrived from Brzeziny. This brought a ray of hope to the hearts of mothers and fathers, but it turned out that all these children were over the age of 10.

In the course of two days, 2,370 plus 920 people, that is, 3,290 people, all told, have arrived here from Pabianice. Today, 1,420 arrived from Brzeziny making for an overall total of about 6,000. Only 300 people remain in Brzeziny. There were also 300 people from Stryków among those arriving here from Brzeziny.

FALSE RUMORS

Today there was a story afoot that beginning tomorrow, May 20, 6 kilograms of potatoes per capita would be distributed for June. The Vegetable Distribution Center denies this. Besides, this would not be possible, if only because there are not sufficient reserves for such an allocation. Another rumor, one which has the whole ghetto talking, concerns a resumption of resettlement that is to begin on Friday. The names of the people able to confirm this information are mentioned, and the rumor specifies that children and people stamped by the medical commission will be the first to go. Those close to Bałut Market categorically deny this report.

WEDNESDAY AND THURSDAY, MAY 20 AND 21, 1942

A SPECIAL ALLOCATION

For several days now there have been hints in the ghetto that, to mark the Feast of Weeks [Shabuoth] (which begins on the 22d), the Chairman would distribute the much-desired gift of a special food allocation to the populace. Those wishes have been answered. Although the allocation is modest, including only 200 grams of white sugar, 70 grams of margarine, 50 grams of [ersatz] coffee, 50 grams of candy and 150 grams of meat, it nevertheless caused intense satisfaction. It was also said that 0.5 kilograms of bread would be issued against supplement cards numbered 1 and 2; unfortunately, that rumor remained an unfulfilled wish.

Recently, Community employees received from 4 to 10 kilograms of firewood at a cost of 25 pfennigs per kilogram, and also 200 grams of vegetable salad for 50 pfennigs. Not much, but something. . .

LARGE ORDERS

are constantly being placed here in the ghetto. I have learned from reliable sources that the dry cleaners have received consecutive consignments of 300 train cars of dirty underclothes for cleaning and, thus, are assured of work for a very long time (many months). The woodwork factory, apart from its current orders, is to produce a million pairs of clogs. 800 people work there in three shifts. The metal workshop is supposed to have work enough for two years. The straw-shoe workshop has been manufacturing straw boots for the army since Tuesday. Its location at the outskirts of the ghetto presents a serious problem to its workers, who are recruited from among the women and the elderly. The long walk exhausts the workers, who are not exactly radiant with excess strength and health these days. Further orders are expected for other workshops

B[ernard] O[strowski]

THE MOOD OF THE GHETTO

has changed completely since Sunday. Reports of resettlements from the provinces have had a depressing effect on the entire populace. Nothing could be more shocking than to visit the site at 22 Masarska Street, where over a thousand (1,082) women from Pabianice have been quartered. In every room, in every corner, one sees mothers, sisters, grandmothers, shaken by sobs, quietly lamenting for their little children. All children up to age 10 have been sent off to parts unknown. Some have lost three, four, even six children. Their quiet despair is profoundly penetrating, so different from the loud laments we are accustomed to hearing at deaths and funerals, but all the more real and sincere for that. It is no surprise that anyone with small children or old parents awaits the days to come with trepidation. The greatest optimists have lost hope. Until now, people had thought that work would maintain the ghetto and the majority of its people without any breakup of families. Now it is clear that even this was an illusion. There were plenty of orders [for new work] in Pabianice and Brzeziny, but that did not protect the Jews against wholesale deportation. Fear for our ghetto's fate is keeping everyone up at night. Our last hope is our Chairman; people believe that he will succeed, if not totally, then at least in part, in averting the calamities that now loom ahead.

B[ernard] O[strowski]

RESETTLEMENT

Talk of further resettlement becomes increasingly definite. It is said that it will begin on Friday, and other stories say not until Sunday. The Chairman is supposed to have said that he will make an effort to keep the suffering of local people to a minimum. The first to be resettled are the most recent arrivals, that is, those from Pabianice and Brzeziny, followed by the "Germans" [i.e., Jews from the West]. Insofar as necessary to fill the quota, people from Łódź will go in the following order: those who hid from the last resettlement and then those who were stamped at the medical commission's examinations. As for the residents of the Old People's Home and children under 10 in the Orphanage,[54] the Chairman is making assurances that he will spare no efforts to keep them here. This information is supposed to originate from the most authoritative sources.

B[ernard] O[strowski]

HUNGER IN THE GHETTO

The recent incidents (the resettlements into and out of the ghetto) have eclipsed all else to such a degree that hunger, ever more widespread and grievous now, is forgotten or not talked about. An official occupying a very important post says (as background, I add that this occurred at three o'clock in the afternoon), "I've already eaten my bread for today and tomorrow, and I'm horribly hungry." In one family, the sole daily meal from Monday to Thursday is the soup they are given at work. They have nothing to cook at home since their potatoes for May were consumed a long time ago, in April, and they attack their bread with such greed and voracity that by Sunday there is none left.

B[ernard] O[strowski]

LITZMANNSTADT-GETTO, MAY 20, 1942

Around 5,700 people from Brzeziny, near Łódź, have been resettled of which around 4,000 have been sent to Łódź and the rest to parts unknown. The resettlement from Brzeziny is somewhat different in appearance [from that of Pabianice]. The ghetto there was surrounded by a fence, and the houses whose windows looked out onto streets not included within the ghetto's boundaries were entered from their courtyards, through openings in walls, fences, etc. The ghetto was guarded, and attempt-

---

54. In the original, the word *Orphanage* was crossed out.

ing to leave it, especially recently, was punished severely. Recently, ten Jews were sentenced to death for smuggling food into the ghetto, and the sentence was executed in front of the populace which had been assembled on a square. After that incident, the Jewish Police punished Jews caught smuggling with enormous severity. Nightmarish stories are told about Perlmutter, the police chief there, and the punishments he meted out were often bizarre. It was a generally accepted custom that the Jewish Police would confiscate the goods seized, and the smugglers would have to pay a ransom for their release, the price depending on the person seized. Unfortunately, our compatriots did not acquit themselves honorably in that town either.

The civilian population, the Aryans, and particularly the Poles, were very favorably inclined toward the Jews and, in large measure, the Jews from Brzeziny owe them their lives. They tell of one baker who baked a special quota of bread for the Jews, which he would have little children bring into the ghetto. The little children would bring one batch of bread into the ghetto, and then, before anyone knew it, they'd be back with another. Aryan friends would pass the Jews bacon, meat, and other products through the ghetto fence, more often than not without being paid for it. The Jews from Brzeziny see no analogies with the pre-war situation; anti-Semitism seemed to have vanished completely there. As to their regular food, it was markedly different from ours here in the ghetto. Their daily bread ration came to 280 grams and, in addition, they received around 250 grams of sugar, 200 grams of flour, and 150 grams of margarine, etc., per week. When they left their ghetto, their Community storehouses were still full of food. All told, around 6,000 Jews were living in the Brzeziny ghetto most recently, and to feed such a handful presented no great problems. Everyone worked for the same company, Günther and Schwarz, and the director of the company saw to it that the workers were suitably fed. Whenever there were rumors of resettlement, he would assure his employees that things would not reach that pass.

No orders had been arriving lately, and disturbing rumors of resettlement had begun to spread. At the time, the director was not in Brzeziny. Suddenly, the Jews of Brzeziny were informed that they were to be prepared to travel on Monday, the 18th of this month. They were told that they could bring 11 kilograms of baggage with them and that the resettlement would proceed by apartment blocks. Their packed bags were to be set out in front of their buildings, and people were to assemble in groups of five to make it easier for the authorities to count them. On Monday, the 18th of this month, the groups assembled in front of their buildings; clearly, some bags contained more than 11 kilograms, and this caused a violent reaction on the spot—such bags were thrown back into gateways or apartments, which were then at once shut and sealed. Those who were strong and healthy, regardless of sex, were assigned to one side, while the weak, the sick, the elderly, and little children under 10 were assigned to the other. If parents belonged to group "A", that is, were healthy and fit to work, their small children were taken from them, even babies at the breast, and placed in group "B." And so, those who realized what was happening at once joined their children in group "B," even though they were fit to work, and left with group "B" for parts unknown. Apparently there were 1,700 people in that group. The women, the older people, and the children in group "A" were brought to Gałkówek [south of Brzeziny], in peasant wagons, while the younger people proceeded on foot. After a few hours' wait at the station in Gałkówek, they were lined up, ordered to set their baggage down, and then loaded on trains. There were some physical injuries. The baggage was loaded onto the same train and sent to Litzmannstadt. Upon receiving their baggage in Litzmannstadt, that is, the ghetto, the Jews from Brzeziny were pained to find that their food supplies were gone, though their other things had arrived. The newcomers complain that their bags were ripped open and the traces of theft were obvious. The majority accuse our police who had been in charge of receiving their baggage.

The newcomers from Brzeziny look considerably worse than those from Pabianice: they are poorly dressed and emaciated. This is to be explained by the fact that even before the war the tailors of Brzeziny belonged to the most exploited segment of the proletariat and rarely earned enough to support themselves, to say nothing of wartime, when they earned starvation wages and it was no easy matter to obtain food. According to the newcomers, they had already gone through the hell of resettlement before this, and many of them, wandering from ghetto to ghetto, had only arrived in Brzeziny during the last months. It cost them great effort to get themselves started there, that is, they got hold of some odds and ends, pillows, pots, etc., expending the better part of their paltry earnings on such things, while others had lost all their possessions to fire during the [German-Polish] military campaign [of September, 1939] and were left with nothing but ashes. In this respect, the Jews of Pabianice had fared better, which is why they look so different. There is one other feature characteristic of the Jews from Brzeziny, namely, a complete lack of any solidarity among them, whereas such solidarity is the most attractive feature of the Jews from Pabianice, and all one hears about is the services they rendered each other.

Quartered in buildings on Szklana Street, the new settlers still do not know what fate awaits them. Their guess is that they will soon be resettled to work, and for that reason they do not seem too desperate. They cannot imagine how they could live in the ghetto here on such small earnings and with food prices so high—on the open market, of course. For them, food rations were usually a matter of secondary importance, and there was no worker who would not buy at least one additional loaf of bread a week at a price of 5–8 [German] marks, a few kilograms of potatoes for 1 mark, and so forth. A worker's daily wage fluctuated between 3 and 4 marks for piece work; the masters made 7–8 marks a day and, in addition, had all sorts of opportunities for "economizing" on thread and merchandise. They were able to buy extra food privately with their additional income.

The despair of parents and other family members who had been parted from their brothers and sisters is beyond description, and their sole consolation is that they have been assured that their children will be arriving shortly. They also find consolation in the promise that, when the children arrive in the ghetto, they will be housed in dormitories and shelters, and they are constantly asking if they can believe that promise.

They do not believe that there will be a quick end to their suffering, and they see a future veiled by dark clouds . . .

FRIDAY AND SATURDAY, MAY 22 AND 23, 1942

THE WAREHOUSE IN DABROWA

The Jews from Pabianice who were recently settled in the ghetto say that in the village of Dąbrowa, located about 3 kilometers from Pabianice, in the direction of Łódź, warehouses for old clothes have recently been set up on the grounds of a factory idle since the war began. Thus far, five gigantic warehouses have been set up there. They contain clothing, linen, bedding, shoes, pots and pans, and so on. Each day, trucks deliver mountains of packages, knapsacks, and parcels of every sort to Dąbrowa. Everything is broken down into groups and put in its proper place in the warehouses. Each day, thirty or so Jews from the Pabianice ghetto are sent to sort the goods. Among other things, they have noticed that, among the waste papers, there were some of our *Rumkis*, which had fallen out of billfolds. The obvious conclusion is that some of the clothing belongs to people deported from this ghetto. Apparently, some of the residents of Brzeziny, who had been sent out to perform manual labor directly upon their arrival in the ghetto [of Łódź], had been sent to work in Dąbrowa.

YESTERDAY (THE 22ND OF THIS MONTH) AFTERNOON

an order arrived from Pabianice to send back three watchmakers and jewelers who were specified by name. They left for their destination by truck on Saturday. This is the second time people have been sent out of the ghetto (the first was on Tuesday, and included one hundred people who apparently went to Dąbrowa); in addition, two other groups, of 250 and 50, will be leaving soon.

B[ernard] O[strowski]

ON FRIDAY NIGHT

six hundred and forty people arrived here from Ozorków [north of Łódź] by tram. This is the second transport from that small town. The first, which arrived 24 hours earlier and consisted of 747 people, was quartered at 15 Rybna Street because cases of typhus had been found among them.

The sites for the newcomers from Brzeziny, located on Otylia Street and at 7 Widok Street, have also been quarantined for the same reason.

B[ernard] O[strowski]

SUNDAY AND MONDAY, MAY 24 AND 25, 1942

TRAMLINE INTRODUCED

Now under discussion is a project to introduce a tramline in the ghetto that would run first to Marysin, where many workshops are located. The [German] authorities have nothing against the project in principle. A small matter such as tickets is not even a problem since the city's municipal trams have enormous quantities of tickets printed in Polish that they are willing to give the ghetto free of charge. There are no technical obstacles. Figuring that 25 pfennigs per ride is 5,000 marks per day if 10,000 people ride in both directions, this will provide considerable reinforcement to the

Community's coffers. And it will be a great convenience for ghetto society. The Chairman's decision is expected in a few days. For the time being, from Thursday of this week on, anyone not belonging to the Department of Transportation is prohibited from using the trams.

LITZMANNSTADT-GETTO, MAY 24, 1942

FROM THE LIFE OF THE PABIANICE GHETTO

Despite notions common here, not all Jews fared well in Pabianice; it was rather the reverse. Those who fared well can be counted on the fingers of a hand and, for the most part, they were members of the community council (*Beirat*), the higher officials, the people who had succeeded in saving money, valuables, or other things from some time back, and tradesmen. The general population suffered poverty and want in varying degrees, which, in some cases, led to starvation. The so-called illegals were in the worst situation. Those were people who, at one time, had been deported to the Protectorate [the Generalgouvernement] and had managed to return to Pabianice. Since they could not be registered, they possessed no ration cards and received no food allocations. And clearly, they possessed no means of buying food on the open market. They lived on their fellow Jews' mercy. Their number is estimated at around 300. Furthermore, there were many people who were unemployed; they subsisted by selling their bread, butter, and sugar, buying potatoes, beets and other vegetables with the money. The Jews from Pabianice joke about this category of ghetto citizen, saying that resettlement in Łódź has raised his standard of living. Here they eat bread, which is, moreover, free of charge, whereas in Pabianice they could not afford to eat that costly item. It should not be thought that those who were employed in the workshops were much better off. The pay rates were very low. An apprentice earned 2–3 [German] marks per week. A *Gruppenführer* [foreman] earned up to 12 marks. And that was absolutely not enough to subsist on. Three months' delay in payment was more the rule than the exception. So then, why did so many people apply for work in the workshops or at home? The reason was simple: it was believed that a work card constituted a safe conduct, enabling its possessor to remain where he was; moreover, it could also be used to camouflage the work or commerce done on one's own. The municipal government (*Stadtverwaltung*) allocated work to tradesmen working in their apartments. An Aryan with work to be done would apply to a municipal office, pay the stipulated charge, and commission a Jewish tradesman to fill his order. The payment was divided as follows: the municipality collected 50 percent, of the remainder the Jewish Community took 20 percent, and the person filling the order received only what was left. This affected all categories of workers without exception, regardless of whether they were employed in workshops, outside the ghetto, or in their own private workplaces. In essence, Jews were not allowed to receive orders or payments directly. Thus, there is nothing odd about tradesmen barely being able to make ends meet. Quite frequently, those commissioning the work were aware of this, particularly when the work in question required careful execution. They would not pay any extra money but they would provide the worker with half a loaf of bread, or butter, meat, sausage, or something else, at times risking their own safety. For example, one person would bring wheat bread, but he was afraid of being caught bringing Jews white bread since Germans had been threatened with serious punishment for doing so; so he would cut the bread into slices and wrap two slices in a piece of paper as if it were a sandwich for himself. I heard of many other such cases. The tradesmen who received orders directly from peasants and were paid in kind also fared well.

It is worth adding that for more than a year the Jews in Pabianice were limited to using only the Yiddish or German languages. For conversing outdoors in Polish they could be clubbed on the head; they paid a fine of 20 pfennigs for saying one word of Polish in the workshops. When children were going out their mothers would remind them that God forbid that they should speak Polish, and so the Jews from Pabianice were surprised on their arrival here that our police spoke Polish volubly and publicly, and that it was the language used most often in the ghetto's offices.[55]

[Bernard] O[strowski]

WEDNESDAY, MAY 27, 1942

NEWS FROM THE CAMP NEAR POZNAŃ

Today copies of a postcard were posted in front of the Bureau of Labor. The bureau received the card from a resident of the ghetto who had been sent to a labor camp near Poznań on May 15 of this year. The postcard was stamped: Posen [Poznań], May 23, 1942. Today, many of the people reporting to the bureau on Lutomierska Street read the copy of the postcard with great interest. Here are its contents (translated from the German): "To the Eldest of the Jews of the Litzmannstadt-Getto, Baluter-Ring [Bałut Market]. Gutenbrunn [Kobyle Pole], May 19. To the Eldest of the Jews, C. Rumkowski: Please forward this card to my sister, Bronka Dąb, 28 Zgierska Street for which I thank you.—Nachman Dąb. My dear sister Bronka, I am writing you a few words just after arriving in the camp. I am well and satisfied that I have gone to do manual labor. I am working very hard at laying concrete and I eat three times a day. I get two good soups and bread. Other than that, there's nothing new. Next time, I will write you more but now I am tired from my trip. I kiss you and send my regards. Your brother." This is followed by greetings for relatives and friends. On the other side of the card he jotted down a few words to his girlfriend, stressing that he was not hungry. The camp's address: Gemeinschaftslager D.A.F. [Deutsche Arbeitsfront], Gutenbrunn bei Posen.[56]

AN ATROCIOUS FRAUD

After a preliminary investigation, agents of Precinct III of the Order Service have eliminated an unlicensed manufacturer of "salad" produced from scraps retrieved

55. As distinct from the Generalgouvernement, on Polish territories incorporated into the Reich, the Polish language was barely tolerated by the occupier, and then only out of necessity. On the other hand, in the hermetically sealed Łódź ghetto, it was a matter of complete indifference to the German authorities which language people spoke—Yiddish or Polish. Moreover, a large portion of the correspondence in the Jewish administration's own internal departments was conducted in Polish.

56. This was a branch of the large labor camp in Poznań-Stadion.

from the garbage. The investigation showed that this item, whose deceptive appearance made it seem similar to the popular Community salads, but which, in terms of contents, consisted of rotting matter in the final stage of decay, was being sold in mass quantities, primarily to the new settlers who, as is well known, make great efforts to obtain food in unlawful transactions. Up to 9 marks a portion was paid for this poison, in the literal sense of the word. When the police entered the apartment at 5 Ceglana Street where the above-mentioned operation was located, they found the air to be incredibly foul from the large clumps of raw material ready for production and from the salads already made. Two families numbering about a dozen people were arrested.

POTATO PEELS

Despite the Department of Health's having forbidden doctors to send certificates allowing the purchase of potato peels to the Department of Soup Kitchens, the kitchens are still giving out peels to those with the proper documents. Demand continues to be absolutely furious.

COD-LIVER OIL

Today the pharmacies received cod-liver oil in 100 gram bottles to be sold solely on the basis of special certificates issued by pediatricians. This item, so important to a child's health, was sold out in something like half an hour.

6,310 WESTERN EUROPEAN JEWS

still remain in the ghetto after the last resettlement campaign. In connection with deportation, the statistics, in round numbers, on that segment of the population are as follows: There were 17,225 Western European Jews in the ghetto before the resettlement. 10,915 were deported. As stated above, 6,310 have remained here. Here is the breakdown by city: five transports from Prague—2,470, the five Vienna transports—1,100, the four Berlin transports—745, the two from Cologne—730, one from Hamburg—340, one from Düsseldorf—400, from Frankfurt am Main—325, and from Luxembourg—200.

THURSDAY AND FRIDAY, MAY 28 AND 29, 1942

ELIMINATION OF THE PUBLIC KITCHENS

On Thursday, the Chairman ordered the elimination of the public kitchens as of June 1, meaning all those preparing soup for laborers and office workers, as well as those designated for private customers. Only five of the larger kitchens for consumers will remain. Among others, the so-called Soup Kitchen for the Intelligentsia, the kosher kitchen, and the Department of Health's kitchen (serving both office workers and registered consumers) will be retained. Two other kitchens will also be retained (depending on the number of customers remaining on June 1). Until now, there had been 50 kitchens in operation, serving over 40,000 laborers and office workers and as many as 7,000 registered consumers. That latter figure had increased because of the serving of soup to the ghetto's newly arrived residents (they receive meals on credit, as the newcomers from the West had before). The kitchens employed around 1,700 workers, who have now been discharged. They will undoubtedly be given other employment. The elimination of the kitchens, and with them the so-called factory soups, which under today's conditions were a form of recompense for the working population, has become the most important event of the day. Everyone is absorbed by the question of what alternative will replace the soup.

In this regard, the Chairman followed his usual custom and immediately delivered a speech, on Thursday afternoon, in the courtyard of the saddlers' workshop on Jakuba Street, on the progress of events. The details of the issue have still not been resolved, but, in all probability, all employees will receive an additional 150 grams of bread in place of the soup and workers [in factories] will, in addition, receive 40 grams of sausage. It is still not known whether those not employed in workshops will also receive sausage. That will be determined tomorrow. Since Thursday, the residents of the ghetto have been racking their brains solely on this most pressing question: which is better, a plate of soup or a piece of bread and sausage. The prevailing opinion is that bread with sausage is better but that soup is better than bread alone. This reform has supposedly been introduced only as an experiment, for a period of one month.

A CONCERT

On Wednesday, there was a concert performed by the symphony orchestra conducted by T[eodor] Ryder at the House of Culture. Beethoven's works (excerpts from *Egmont*) were on the program. Miss [Bronisława] Rotsztat, the favorite of ghetto audiences, enchanted the public with her beautiful violin performance.

THE SEWING MACHINES

from small towns in the surrounding area have been placed at the disposal of the Central Workshop Bureau. A consignment of army denims, which had previously been given to the now-dissolved ghetto in Brzeziny for tailoring, has now arrived here.

DR. LEON GLAZER, M.D.

has left the ghetto for Pabianice to serve as a physician to the Jewish population remaining there, which still numbers over 150.

SETTLED IN THE GHETTO

The German police have brought 13-year-old Jakub Kessler to the ghetto from Stryków.[57] He has been lodged at 63 Łagiewnicka Street. A foundling, Halina Bogdańska (aged 2) has been placed in the orphanage at 82 Franciszkańska Street. And, finally, a one-month-old infant from the city, Estera Laskowska, has been placed in Hospital No. 1.

---

57. Before the war, around 2,000 Jews lived in Stryków, a small town northeast of Łódź. The majority of them were resettled to the Generalgouvernement in the autumn of 1939. The Jews remaining in Stryków, some 300, were placed in a ghetto that was liquidated in May, 1942; its inhabitants were then resettled to Brzeziny.

MEAT

Recently a very substantial amount of high-quality meat, including some veal, has been coming into the ghetto. Since Thursday, the populace has been able to receive 100 grams of meat per capita against the proper ration ticket.

SATURDAY AND SUNDAY, MAY 30 AND 31, 1942

INSPECTION OF THE GHETTO

On Saturday, the mayor [of the city of Litzmannstadt, Werner Ventzki,][58] inspected the ghetto accompanied by a number of people both in uniform and in civilian clothes. The representatives of the authorities inspected a series of workshops and took photographs.

LARGE SHIPMENTS OF BAGGAGE

have been sent to the ghetto since May 25. The people of the ghetto are tremendously puzzled by the arrival of these shipments, which contain clothes of all sorts and other things and which are transported here each day by trucks, including five-ton vehicles. The Department of Used Articles has been ordered to store all this material. The department has assigned some enormous warehouses for that purpose, namely those at 75 Brzezińska Street, 20 Marynarska Street, 93 Franciszkańska Street, and 32 Dolna Street. What is it that these large trucks are carrying? It would be difficult to enumerate the contents. One reason is the tonnage involved, which, in every case, exceeds 100,000 kilograms and is perhaps even higher. Among their contents, the things most frequently encountered are improvised sacks made from rugs, blankets, sheets, and so on. This type of bundle indicates that they were not packed by their owners but by other hands. These bundles for the most part contain clothing, linen, and bedding. This latter has passed through disinfection. Among other frequently encountered items are shirts and slips rolled together, three or four at a time, and also two pairs of pants rolled up with a few pairs of unmentionables. Nearly all the jackets and coats bear traces of having been ripped along their seams . . . There are a lot of goods, for example, curtains, which are brand new. There are also a great many *taleysim* [prayer shawls]. There are no knapsacks or suitcases to be seen. Documents—letters, papers, ID cards, and so on that had been issued in Western European cities—often fall out of the bundles, but there are also a great many from Włocławek, and often there are papers that were drawn up in this ghetto as well.

A very significant percentage of the items are brand new. For the time being, these things have been placed in storage; they will be distributed to the deportees from the

---

58. Werner Ventzki (1906–) was the *Oberbürgermeister* in Litzmannstadt from May 6, 1941, to August 15, 1943. He had studied law at universities in Heidelberg, Königsberg, and Greifswald. He joined the NSDAP in 1931, in Stettin, where he fulfilled various functions in the city and county administration. Formally speaking, the Łódź ghetto was directly subordinate to him, as was Hans Biebow, chief of the German Ghetto Administration. After the war Ventzki settled in Bonn, where he was an official in the Bonn ministry for displaced persons (*Bundesvertriebenenministerium*).

surrounding areas, to the residents of the Old People's Home and orphanage, and perhaps even to the Clothing Department.

MAY, 1942

was marked in the ghetto by a difficult food supply situation, the resettlement of the Western European Jews, and the settling here of Jews from neighboring towns— Pabianice, Brzeziny, and Stryków.

On one hand, 10,915 people were resettled, on the other, 7,046 were settled here. Not all of the settlers remained in the ghetto, however, for some of them were immediately sent from the ghetto to perform manual labor, while others were included in various groups later deported to build the highway near Poznań and to work in Dąbrówka [Dąbrowa] (near Pabianice), sorting baggage of the most diverse sorts.

At the beginning of May a medical commission arrived in the ghetto. The commission evaluated the health of the long-time ghetto residents, marking their bodies with Latin letters, an act whose significance remains unknown. The number qualified by the commission (for resettlement and for work as well) came to around 11,000, with no distinction as to sex (and with an age limit of 10!).

Recruitment for jobs of every sort increased enormously because of the medical examinations; several new positions, along with those already existing, absorbed some 10,000 people in this period. The Chairman's slogan that everyone in the ghetto must work, for only work can assure the populace peace, had begun to be proven true. Whole families registered for work—from 10-year-old children to grey-haired old people; they were all beating on the doors of the Bureau of Labor to get assigned somewhere, anywhere. Due to a shortage of suitable positions, many people applied to do ditch-digging and agricultural labor, just to be registered and to benefit from having their work cards stamped. Some workshops were not able to provide space for the newly accepted workers and, of necessity, a whole battalion of reserve workers was created. It is worth remembering that only one workshop, the straw-shoe workshop, anticipates being able to employ around 10,000 workers. It has proved necessary to reduce working hours for certain categories of workers. The first to be affected were the teenage workers, whose work day was reduced to four hours. At the same time, the Chairman has ruled that supplemental food be issued them in special kitchens, under the supervision of a so-called workshop guardian. This was also done to ensure that the young people did, in fact, consume their food on the spot and not take it with them to barter with later. Nearly all strata of the ghetto's population have been caught up in bartering.

As to prices, on the so-called free or, rather, unlicensed food market, the ghetto experienced outlandish price hikes in this period—the price of a loaf of bread rose to 600 marks, one kilogram of margarine to 1,000 marks, one kilogram of potatoes to 90 marks, one cigarette, without mouthpiece, to 4 marks, and so on. Simultaneous with these perturbations, which shook the entire ghetto, causing both chaos and gloom, there were also displacements in various other areas of ghetto life. Practically all the public kitchens were closed with the exception of four, and there had been 50; the vegetable distribution points were eliminated, to some degree because of the shortage of vegetables, which have nearly ceased coming in from the city, and because of the need to carry out a certain reorganization. For the time being the personnel from those points have been placed at the disposal of the Personnel Bureau. Rations have become more meager because of the vegetable shortage and, in consequence, the mortality rate has increased. The number of deaths per day has not, in fact, risen in absolute numbers; however, if one takes into account the warmer weather, which has helped stave off a typhus epidemic, then the rate has not only not fallen in percentage, but has held at the prevailing level, which should be taken as a deplorable sign from every point of view. In connection with the threat of resettlement, many people suffered nervous breakdowns, and hence the significantly higher number of suicides. There were also large numbers of marriages concluded between people threatened by resettlement and those who were not—another means of saving oneself from resettlement.

Characteristic of this severe period of hunger was the enormous demand for potato peels. To obtain them, a doctor's certificate, verified by the Department of Soup Kitchens, was required. Finally, even that limitation could not restrain demand and, to save the doctors from constant onslaughts by the populace, the Department of Health was forced to rescind their right to issue the certificates.

The total lack of small change was also a great plague and a factor in the price increases. Small [German] change had been taken by the deportees, to be used as hard currency outside the ghetto. The currency in circulation, which had formerly amounted to only 1.2–1.5 million marks, rose to 5.5 million marks in May, because, on the one hand, no rations had been announced for a long time and, on the other, the deportees had been paid around 1.5 million marks for the possessions that they had sold. That money made its way to the populace of the ghetto in exchange for food and did not return to the Community's coffers; so there is nothing surprising in the fact that those coffers were soon emptied. For the first time in quite a long while the payment of salaries was delayed, and the last ten day period in May was pushed ahead to June.

In order to counteract this abnormal situation, the ghetto authorities undertook a series of different measures. The shortage of small change was brought under partial control with coupons issued by the Post Office, the Meat Department, and several cooperatives. To prevent the larger families from amassing too much bread, and to avoid creating temptations to barter, the system for distributing bread was changed (to three times a week, instead of two).

To counter inflation, the Community authorities raised the prices of all foods by 50 to 100 percent, and, in the case of cigarettes, over 1,000 percent (from 8 pfennigs to 1 mark). They put a few hundred thousand cigarettes on the market and, in this way, brought the greater part of the money in circulation into the Community's coffers.

At the same time, the rates for electricity and gas were raised but, for the convenience of working people, two shifts were introduced in the gas kitchens (seven hours each) and business hours in the cooperatives [Community food stores] were extended. Permanent barber shops were created in the Community workshops, and those who were persistently unclean were compelled to go to the baths to be deloused.

Housekeeping suffered tremendously because of the increase in employment, and there was a shortage of people to do cleaning and laundry, and to carry large packages, etc. There is now a project to found a domestic help bureau that would, at a cost fixed by the Community's administration, help bring order to apartments that are not being cared for.

For some time, rumors continued to spread concerning further resettlement, and this caused people to hold on to their jobs with all their might, viewing them as their only salvation from resettlement.

A certain easing of tension set in at the end of the month.

On the 23d of this month, after a long break, the Chairman delivered a speech at the prayer house at 23 Brzezińska Street, bringing considerable reassurance to people's troubled minds and, a week later, he used a microphone to address a crowd of several thousand in the fire department's courtyard, which helped to further calm the populace.

A great deal of clothing and footwear has been brought to the Department of Clothing at 30 Franciszkańska Street, and the populace rushed there to buy up articles that were relatively cheap in ghetto terms. Money has again begun to return to the Community's coffers, because food rations, even rather plentiful ones, have also been announced. Money had started to become more valuable, while prices had been falling due to a lack of buyers.

The growing season is in progress, work in the fields proceeds at a furious pace, the first early vegetables have appeared, and the first relaxation in the food supply situation has occurred and was soon reflected in the state of the ghetto's health.

Newcomers from the small towns, whom fate had saved from deportation, were rapidly relocated in the private apartments that had been occupied by the Western European Jews who were resettled. The Tram Department laid new branch lines to several squares and public transportation has now begun.

The stormy waves have been subsiding gradually, a certain calm looms on the ghetto's horizon, and all of life has begun to return—on the surface, at least—to what had been the norm before the resettlements.

POPULATION COUNT AS OF JUNE 1, 1942

On June 1, 1942, 104,469 people were residing in the ghetto, of which 45,294 were men and 59,175 were women; there were 7,046 new settlers from three small towns in the surrounding area.

The exact number of Western European Jews still remaining in the ghetto will be determined in one of the next bulletins.

Population Changes in the Month of May, 1942

	Men	Women	Total
Level on May 1	48,068	62,738	110,806
Births	31	27	58
Stillbirths	3	2	5
Miscarriages	1	7	8
Arrived from the Generalgouvernement and Warthegau	1	3	4
Arrived from prison	1	—	1
Arrived from Pabianice, Brzeziny, Ozorków	2,677	4,369	7,046
Total Increase	2,714	4,408	7,122

Population Changes in the Month of May, 1942 (cont.)

	Men	Women	Total
Decrease			
Deaths in May	1,068	711	1,779
(Deaths in April—1,188)			
Left for the Generalgouvernement and Warthegau	5	3	8
To manual labor in Poznań	758	—	758
Resettled	3,657	7,257	10,914

(The number of resettled indicates a decrease in Western European Jews; it also includes about 500 who volunteered or were forcibly resettled from the ghetto's permanent local population.)

Total decrease in May	5,488	7,971	13,459
Actual decrease	2,774	3,563	6,337

The number of 104,500 [104,469] inhabitants is the lowest level of population since the ghetto came into existence.

MONDAY, JUNE 1, 1942

ORDERS FROM THE ARMY

Last week, the Central Workshop Bureau received very large orders from the [German] Ghetto Administration, particularly tailoring work to be done for the army. Until now, the majority of the tailor workshops have been filling civilian orders. Because of these new orders the production work in all tailoring establishments is now for the army.

SEWING MACHINES

by the hundreds have recently been supplied to the ghetto from small towns in the surrounding area, and probably coming from the liquidated ghettos. The sewing machines have been placed on the grounds of the former Bałut slaughterhouse, which is now occupied by a saddlery. A certain percentage of the machines has already been distributed to various tailor shops.

FOUR FIVE-TON TRUCKS

brought enormous quantities of civilian footwear here on May 29. By order of the [German] Ghetto Administration, the footwear has been stored at 63 Łagiewnicka Street, property which is occupied by a saddlery. The shipments arrived here from the direction of Brzeziny. The taps, or the entire heels, on each pair of shoes— women's, men's, and children's—had been torn off. While unloading one truck, the guards from the city rounded up passersby on Bałut Market to help with the work.

LITZMANNSTADT-GETTO, JUNE 1, 1942

Chairman M. C. Rumkowski delivered a public address to the people of the ghetto yesterday after not having done so for quite a long time. A crowd of some 5,000 people gathered in the fire department's courtyard at 13 Lutomierska Street. Loudspeakers and a podium had been set up.

The Chairman arrived at 6:15 P.M., accompanied by his wife, and director Józef Rumkowski.

The crowd was calm and orderly, the weather was lovely—sunny and warm.

The Chairman had not delivered a speech for quite a while so the announcement of the speech understandably caused curiosity on the part of the entire populace. The Chairman's public addresses have nearly always been marked by a certain optimism, at least for the immediate future, and for some time now, everyone has been hungry for a bit of encouragement.

In his speech, which lasted about an hour and a half, the Chairman summarized the events of recent months, briefly discussed the resettlement of about 55,000 people, and emphasized that considerable blame is to be borne here by the populace itself for having been reluctant to work. The populace had been summoned to work last year by the Chairman, when he spoke in the same place and warned them of the potential consequences of idleness.

The idea of working papers as authorization for remaining in the ghetto had, indeed, been propounded by the Chairman many times, and if it formerly lay within his powers to decide on the resettlement of one group or another, the progress of events has caused that power to slip from his hands, so to speak. In a situation such as this, it is to his credit that he succeeded in keeping another thirty thousand or so people in the ghetto who may in fact have been registered, but who had not, thus far, been employed. All told, the population of the ghetto at the present moment amounts to around 100,000 people, of which 70,000 are employed. The problem of resettlement has still not been resolved, even with such a high number of people working, and the Chairman intends to find employment for another 10,000 people in the very near future. He spoke of the creation of new workshops, of easy work for children and old people, for he would then be able to place those who have registered but have not been assigned, or have not been assigned to suitable positions.

The problem of work ran like a red thread through the Chairman's entire speech, creating the impression that although the question of resettlement has been averted for the time being, it could crop up again if the labor reserves are not entirely exhausted in the ghetto's workshops.

Besides this main theme, the Chairman touched on a whole series of local problems, which we quote *in extenso* in the shorthand record of his speech.[59]

TUESDAY, JUNE 2, 1942

REORGANIZATION OF FOOD SUPPLEMENTS FOR WORKING PEOPLE

Beginning today, 55,000 workers and Community employees will be receiving supplemental meals in the form of a 150-gram slice of bread and a 40-gram slice of sausage in

59. The short record of M. C. Rumkowski's speech was not preserved in the *Chronicle*. There is, however, a copy of it in the Jewish Historical Institute in Warsaw.

exchange for special coupons. These meals are being issued at 32 distribution points set up yesterday by the Department of Soup Kitchens at locations which, until now, had been assigned to the soup kitchens. In addition, around 6,000 workers and laborers in Marysin are availing themselves of these rations. The staff of the distribution points is exclusively composed of workers appointed by the Department of Soup Kitchens.

Before the kitchens were eliminated, the Department of Soup Kitchens still employed 300 permanent workers, who will now be placed at the disposal of the Personnel Bureau, as well as 1,000 day workers, who will be sent to the Labor Bureau upon dismissal. Four kitchens remain to serve registered consumers, whose number has fallen in the present ten-day period to its lowest level (3,000). Those kitchens are the so-called Kitchen for the Intelligentsia, the former doctors' kitchen at 1 Łagiewnicka Street, the so-called kitchen for the orthodox at 74 Brzezińska Street, and the Department of Economics' Kitchen at 11 Lutomierska Street. The Kitchen for the Intelligentsia and the Health Department's kitchen have the most customers—1,000 each.

The experiment of baking rolls from 150 grams of flour to avoid abuses has not succeeded since the chunks came out too hard and could not be made in uniform weights. Today, 5,000 pieces of the experimentally baked bread were given out in the workshops. The customers have themselves introduced controls with worker-delegates, who spot check the weight of the meals at the distribution points. Yesterday was a "fast" day because of technical considerations; a few thousand workers did, however, receive 60 grams of sausage (8 marks' worth) for 50 pfennigs. The price of the bread and the sausage is 40 pfennigs. Canteens have been set up for children apprenticing in the workshops. This has been done at the largest kitchens—at 10 Masarska, 32 Młynarska, 26 Zgierska, 6 Flisacka, and 76 Franciszkańska streets, and there are still six kitchens in Marysin. The children are taken to the canteens in groups by their guardians, and there they consume their bread, sausage, and sweetened [ersatz] coffee. The rumor that the children are to receive soup and bread with margarine is not true.

On the first day, the working population expressed its satisfaction and accepted the innovation as beneficial, for there was general agreement that bread, sausage, and coffee provided more nutrition than a bowl of soup. It is the sincere wish of everyone that, under the new system, meals will not be stolen.

THE TANNERS

until now working and residing in the city and numbering three, were recently brought to live permanently in the ghetto. Their names: Henoch Rzepnik, Motek Mrozek, and Szmul Winkeluszer. There are still a few Jewish tanners left in the city.

SHOOTINGS

At midnight on Sunday, the first of this month, a woman whose personal data has not been established was shot to death in the immediate vicinity of the barbed wire on Drukarska Street. The body was taken to the mortuary at Hospital No. 1.

On Monday at 4:30 A.M., 19-year-old Mojsze Roter was shot and killed on the roadway, having first passed through the barbed wire. The incident took place in the vicinity of the building at 56 Zgierska Street. The victim, who had resided at 9 Bałut Market, was mentally retarded.

GOSSIP AND STORIES

have not been circulating in the ghetto the last few days. Could this be the result of a certain stabilization in conditions and peace of mind? The only thing people are talking about is an extremely generous supplemental "sugar" ration that is supposed to be allocated in the very near future.[60]

WEDNESDAY, JUNE 3, 1942

THE COURTYARD OF THE CHURCH OF THE NP [MOST BLESSED VIRGIN] MARY

Today, the most varied packages of clothing, underwear, and so on were brought by truck to the courtyard of the Church of the Most Blessed Virgin Mary. In the main, those packages were wrapped up in tablecloths, sheets, and other linen. They are being sorted there, possibly for storage.

TO WARSAW

This afternoon, 160 ghetto dwellers left for [the ghetto of] Warsaw, with special permission.[61] They left in two trucks, which had arrived the previous evening from Warsaw. As is generally known, until now departures for Warsaw have originated at Bałut Market. Today, however, for the first time, a departure originated at the ghetto gate in Marysin. Apparently, the [German] authorities issued this order to avoid the confusion that usually accompanies departures from Bałut Market. The Chairman made a special point of coming to Marysin before the departure. It proceeded without disturbances, with the possible exception of the fact that some of the suitcases remained on the wagons due to a lack of room [in the trucks].

A DELIGHTFUL SURPRISE FOR SMOKERS

Yesterday evening, after a break lasting a few hours, the kiosks run by veterans, where Community employees sell Drawa cigarettes (without mouthpieces), in a surprise move, lowered the price from 1 mark to 25 pfennigs per cigarette (four to a customer). Long lines of smokers immediately formed in front of the kiosks. Street peddlers were in a state of genuine consternation, and they began a price war on cigarettes of every type. Joy reigned among the thousands and thousands of smokers, however, which is completely natural if one considers that, in a life as difficult as the ghetto's, every improvement plays a great role. That's how it started. Today brought smokers an even more delightful surprise; the kiosks were now selling 12 cigarettes for three marks and, at the same time, notices were posted in front of all the dairy distribution points announcing a cigarette and tobacco allocation. From these notices it would appear

60. The "sugar" or "sweet" ration, as it was popularly known in the ghetto, was a food ration that, along with other items, also included sugar.
61. See above, p. 55, n. 65.

that, starting at twelve noon today, those possessing special cards may obtain the following for next week at the dairy distribution points: with Coupon No. 1—20 Drawa cigarettes for 3 marks, with Coupon No. 10—a 20-gram package of tobacco for 2 marks and 100 Solali cigarette papers for 50 pfennigs.

The greatest optimists did not expect such a generous allocation of "smokes." And it was not long ago that smokers in the ghetto found themselves in tragic straits, in pursuit of cigarettes whose price had reached 5 marks. In the lines that thronged the kiosks from seven o'clock in the morning on, there were words of great respect for the Community's leaders, the Chairman chief among them, for finding such a happy solution to the cigarette problem in the market. It is worth noting parenthetically that, after 7:30, lines were no longer forming in front of the kiosks and everyone could obtain cigarettes at 25 pfennigs apiece, which, although high compared to the old price of 8 pfennigs, was nevertheless sensationally low compared to previous prices.

THURSDAY, JUNE 4, 1942

TO WARSAW

For the sake of accuracy, 187 people, not 160 as bulletin No. 46 mistakenly reported, left for Warsaw [ghetto] yesterday.

NEW SETTLERS

Thirty-year-old Erika Grahs, with her 2-year-old daughter, Ruta, was settled in the ghetto by police agents from Poznań.

POTATO PEELS

In connection with the elimination of the soup kitchens, the distribution of potato peels has automatically come to an end. The steady customers for that food substitute peculiar to wartime are lamenting the loss. Those emaciated stomachs will no doubt make up that loss, with plenty to spare, on the early locally grown vegetables that are appearing on the market in ever larger amounts. In addition, it is anticipated that yeast, which is irregularly on sale at one store on Kościelna Street, will, due to the frantic throng of buyers, be distributed in the future by the Department of Food Supply through appropriate distribution points, naturally, upon presentation of a medical certificate.

Yeast remains enormously sought-after by the ghetto's emaciated populace because of its vitamin B content. It is worth noting that, in recent days, the utter lack of vitamins, liver, or glucose injections has been sorely felt here.

THE NUMBER OF PERMANENT EMPLOYEES [OFFICIALS AND CLERKS]

amounted to 12,063 on June 1 in the records of the Personnel Bureau. The level on May 1 came to 11,989. In May, 325 were hired, 171 removed, and 80 died.

THE PHARMACEUTICAL DIVISION

In view of the shortage of glucose for medical purposes, attempts have been made to produce this preparation on our own; for the sake of economy, it is being produced from potato peels. At present, the production of this substance has passed from the experimental stage to manufacture; a daily production of around half a kilogram is anticipated, which ought to satisfy the needs of the ghetto.

The production from other preparations of ferrous oxide saccharine, calcium chloride and other substances is in the planning stage.

LITZMANNSTADT-GETTO, JUNE 4, 1942

Because of the arrival of a commission of German authorities, the ghetto has taken on a nearly festive appearance. From early morning on the janitors have been at work cleaning the sidewalks, whitewashing the gutters, and sweeping the streets.

Around ten o'clock 10 private cars arrived bearing, among others, Gauleiter [Artur] Greiser and minister Schwarz.[62] The head of the Central Workshop Bureau, A. Jakubowicz, accompanied by the Chairman as leader of the ghetto, escorted the guests about.

The commission first visited the workshops on the right, that is the Bałut Market side (of the ghetto) and, later on, went to the other side to visit the Textile Department, which is located in the buildings of the [former] Kaszub company.

Traffic in the city was very limited, no children were to be seen in the streets, and neither were the weak and infirm old people who make for an indispensable part, to be encountered everywhere, of daily life in the ghetto. In a word, the ghetto seemed to be a labor camp where idle people are not seen on the streets during the day.

The populace knows and understands that this is not an ordinary inspection but concerns something larger, more important—the question of its very existence. The result of today's inspection is still unknown, but a positive impression could be read on the visitors' faces.

But what precisely is it that the citizen of the ghetto desires; what does he want and what does he expect from that commission? He wants only to be left in peace, not to be torn from his family, to be allowed to endure in these severe conditions, and to have his work acknowledged. If he is acknowledged, he will be granted the right to remain in the ghetto and, consequently, will be allotted a modest food ration.

As indicated by the Chairman's last speech, of the 100,000 Jews residing in the ghetto, around 70,000 have already found employment and—if one discounts children and old people—the human resources here have already been used up. However, the fear of the possible resettlement of the unemployed, which would mean the break-up of families, runs deep in the ghetto dwellers' minds, weighs on them, and prevents them from working normally. Were it not for that worry, it could all somehow be endured, for, on the whole, our people are greatly inclined to optimism and to believe in the power of the spirit in spite of physical exhaustion.

Thus, the news of the inspection's results is awaited with enormous suspense.

The experiment in baking 150-gram rolls has not been entirely successful, for it is difficult to make accurate measurements when such a small weight is involved. Some of the rolls are over the weight whereas others are under, and the Department of

62. The Nazi party treasurer, *Reichsleiter* Franz Xaver Schwarz from Berlin.

Bakeries will probably desist from any further baking of such rolls, even though they had turned out extremely well. Things look somewhat worse as far as the sausage, which is not of the highest quality, is concerned. The meat has not been cured, it won't keep, and must be consumed immediately. In general, however, everyone is more content with the present allocation, especially since, in recent times, the soup had been extremely thin.

The demand for potato peels, which had been having ill effects on people in a weakened condition, has disappeared along with soup. There were fairly frequent cases of poisoning and volvulus, which required serious surgery; for the eating of potato peels had recently assumed near universal proportions, and they were being prepared in a great variety of dishes.

Bread and sausage! The populace has already grown accustomed to the idea, just as it had once grown used to soup. Now things are a little easier and more convenient, because it will no longer be necessary for people to bring along a container for the soup. But those vessels cannot be put aside entirely, for in the ghetto constant change is the rule. Will there always be meat or sausage? Will there be a flour shortage with the coming of summer or, on the other hand, more vegetables?

Then there will be a return to soup, and the pots and spoons with which the populace has now parted company will be needed again . . .

FRIDAY, JUNE 5, 1942

YESTERDAY'S INSPECTION BY THE AUTHORITIES

As bulletin No. 47 reported, high-ranking representatives of the authorities from Berlin, Poznań, and Łódź, accompanied by a large number of escorts, spent time in the ghetto yesterday. Among those inspecting the ghetto were minister [Franz Xaver] Schwarz (*Reichsschatzmeister*), and [Artur] Greiser (Reichsstatthalter), as well as the mayor of the city [Werner Ventzki, Oberbürgermeister]. For the most part, the representatives of the authorities were in uniform and arrived in a line of 10 automobiles. While they were inspecting the workshops, a bus filled with uniformed men also drove up to the ghetto. The automobiles began arriving at Bałut Market around noon. The inspection party headed immediately for the workshops. A[ron] Jakubowicz, the Eldest of the Jews' deputy and director of the Central Workshop Bureau, drove in the first car and led the way. Chairman Rumkowski, accompanied by his deputy [Leon] Rozenblat, the chief of the Order Service, followed the cars in his own [horse-drawn] vehicle.

The following enterprises were visited: the saddlery that occupies the grounds of the [former] Bałut slaughterhouse on Łagiewnicka Street, the carpentry shop at 12 Drukarska Street, and the newly created tailoring division in the large building at 29 Franciszkańska Street. While inspecting those workshops, the representatives of the authorities displayed great interest in the progress of the work, the equipment, and the goods produced. Workers who witnessed the inspection state that the establishments shown the authorities made a great and favorable impression on them. Photographs were taken everywhere.

After nearly an hour, the automobiles returned to Bałut Market, where a few pictures were also taken. Before leaving the ghetto, the representatives of the authorities expressed their satisfaction in what they had seen to the Eldest of the Jews.

YESTERDAY IN THE GHETTO PEOPLE WERE SAYING

that, after the inspection by the authorities, the Chairman remained in a good mood. The distribution of a supplemental "sweet" ration in the evening was viewed as a token of the ghetto leader's excellent humor. We note this rumor, of course, as part of our duty as chroniclers; but it is typical as well, for, as we have already stressed several times, it indicates that the people of the ghetto have grown accustomed to treating the leader's mood as an authoritative barometer in any situation. Thus, there is nothing surprising in the above-noted rumor's having given a lift to the entire populace's mood.

SATURDAY AND SUNDAY, JUNE 6 AND 7, 1942

RESETTLED TO PERFORM MANUAL LABOR

In spite of the calmer mood prevailing in the ghetto lately, a few days ago the malicious tongues of troublemakers began to spread dire predictions about new plans for a resettlement action. Fortunately, those rumors are the product of fantasy. All that is true is that on Friday the authorities demanded that two transports be prepared to be sent out to perform manual labor in Poznań. A week ago, the authorities had announced that they would be ordering over 500 men to be sent out to perform manual labor. The two transports will consist of 560 people (men), with 280 in each. The first leaves the ghetto tomorrow, that is, Monday, June 8 (from Bałut Market), and the next one on Monday, June 15. The Bureau of Labor has recently had a 300-person reserve of volunteers at its disposal. That number fell to 130 candidates for departure since the workshops did not want to release the remaining volunteers because they were indispensable skilled workers. It should be borne in mind that, before the completion of tomorrow's transport, 30 of the above-mentioned 130 will be reclaimed by the [ghetto] workshops, leaving 100. The remainder will be made up by new settlers from the surrounding area who are not working and, also, a small number of those arrested for various offenses or those who have committed transgressions in the past. Men from 18 to 60 years of age are eligible for the transports. They are not to be subjected to medical examination by local doctors this time. (They will face a medical examination by German commissions in the city.)

[TUESDAY,] JUNE 9, 1942

A HUNGER FOR THE PRINTED WORD

is now making itself felt more strongly in the ghetto. To ascertain how hungry people are for books it is enough to take a look at the kilometer-long line at Sonenberg's lending library (even there!). Borrowers are treated as if they were in a cooperative [ghetto grocery] store. Each reader walks up to the table, requests a couple of titles, finds out if a given book is available (it usually is not), receives a couple of books to choose from, and has to make up his mind in a hurry. There is no time for long deliberation, as there once had been. It is worth noting as a feature of the times that the library staff, headed by the owner, is working in the workshops for reasons that are well-known and understandable. The additional hours they put in at the reading room are burdensome but very lucrative. A monthly subscription at present costs 2 marks and, in addition, there is an enrollment fee of 3 marks or a book as a non-refundable deposit.

B[ernard] O[strowski]

JUNE 8–10, 1942

DESCRIPTION OF THE RESETTLEMENT OF THOSE TO PERFORM MANUAL LABOR

As the *Daily Chronicle Bulletin* announced, 280 healthy men were to leave for Poznań to perform manual labor on Monday. However, scarcely 150 left. This occurred because of the following circumstances: the Order Service had supplied the German authorities with the full contingent demanded, 280 men. When filling the transport the representatives of the authorities ordered that all those who possessed working papers issued by the Eldest of the Jews remain in the ghetto. As is known, apart from the Jews from small towns in the surrounding area, these had been volunteers to perform manual labor, but this time the [German] authorities, nevertheless, took the unequivocal position that people who were employed should remain in the ghetto. This incident ought to be regarded as extremely important and significant. For it confirms in practice the accuracy of the Chairman's position that working papers are the passport to safety and an indispensable document guaranteeing the right to remain in the ghetto.

Of the 159 men taken, nine returned the same day, having been rejected by the medical commission. Because Monday's transport was under quota, the Bureau of Labor has prepared a second group of 124 people for Tuesday. That group also was composed of Jews from the small towns in the surrounding area and of volunteers from the local population. The necessity of filling this unforeseen quota forced the ghetto's [Jewish] authorities to apply "summary recruitment" measures (dragging people out of their beds at night). A group of 50 people also left on Tuesday to work in the peat bogs in the vicinity of Zgierz.

PEOPLE ARE REJOICING IN THE GHETTO

This is not fiction, but the unvarnished truth. On Wednesday at noon, circulars were posted in front of the distribution points and in the display cases of the Chairman's Secretariat[63] announcing a special food allocation for working people. It has been

---

63. The Chairman's Secretariat was the second of the above-mentioned three secretariats connected to the Jewish ghetto administration and was rather technical and auxiliary in nature. Initially it was housed at 4 Kościelny Square and later at 1 Dworska Street. The secretariat was headed by S. Cygielman. (See p. 120, n. 10).

more months than anyone can remember since a special allocation has had such a positive effect on the populace. People were so pleased to receive the special supplement that literally all other topics and cares receded into the background. The universal joy was not even diminished by the fact that the allocation had not for the most part been a surprise, had not taken the populace unaware, but had been announced via the grapevine, by "those in the know," a few days before the last allocation for the second ten-day period of this month (see the bulletin for June 6 [and 7]). And so, this time a commonly believed prediction came true. The supplemental ration includes the following items: 2 kilograms of potatoes, 50 grams of margarine, 100 grams of white sugar, 100 grams of rye flakes, 100 grams of [ersatz] coffee, and 100 grams of marmalade. The ration costs 2 marks and all those working on the 7th of this month are entitled to it. From tomorrow on, the ration will begin to be issued on the basis of a certificate from a person's place of work.

THE INFLUX OF ORDERS

to the workshops has been constantly increasing, particularly in the area of orders for the army. The increase in orders has been observable since the time when the ghettos in the neighboring small towns were eliminated.

FILMING

In the last few days considerable filming has been done in the ghetto [by the Germans], as it was last year as well. They filmed outside in the streets and inside in workshops, institutions, and hospitals. Among other things, a circumcision ceremony was filmed in Hospital No. 1.[64]

[JANKELE] HERSZKOWICZ, THE GHETTO TROUBADOUR

has recently composed two songs of current interest. One of them is dedicated to Hercberg's memorable misdeeds [see pp. 136–38], a sad entry in the annals of the ghetto, whereas the second song concerns the latest reorganization of the soup kitchens. Herszkowicz, deprived of his former partner [Karol Rozencwajg], the Viennese traveling salesman who accompanied his singing on the zither, has recently not had the time to perform for crowds in the streets because at present he is working as a messenger. He can only gladden chance listeners with his song on various enterprises during work breaks.

THURSDAY, JUNE 11, 1942

A POLISH WOMAN

who, until now, had been living in the ghetto at 63/65 Drewnowska Street has been removed from the ghetto by order of Precinct VI of the German police and taken to a penal institution in Rawicz.[65]

---

64. See above, p. 162, n. 47.

65. An old but still operative prison established in 1819 by the Prussian authorities (at the time of Poland's partition) in buildings that had formerly belonged to a monastery in Rawicz, Poznań province. They were taken over by the German authorities in September, 1939, to be used as a *Zuchthaus* (penitentiary) for men and a *Frauengefängnis* (prison for women).

THE PAPER SHORTAGE

The price of waste paper is reaching unprecedented heights in the ghetto. It is not surprising that in such conditions every scrap of paper is valuable. As a sign of the times we can quote the notice in the waiting room of one of the ghetto's most popular doctors: "Patients are requested to bring their own paper for prescriptions and certificates" (authentic).

THE DISTRIBUTION OF YEAST

which has recently been generally acknowledged as one of the most important medical agents in this period of vitamin deficiency in the ghetto, has been subjected to new changes. For three days now, yeast has been issued solely at the milk distribution points, on the basis of medical certificates stamped by the Department of Dairy Products.

SATURDAY, JUNE 13, 1942

WEATHER

After an entire week of beautiful weather, Saturday was marked by rain. The "farmers" were happy on that account, but many of the people who had a day off from work and were intending to spend their Saturday in Marysin (in the lap of Nature) were sadly disappointed. The weather cleared up by late afternoon and became sunny again.

A LECTURE ON THE GROWING OF VEGETABLES

was delivered at the Department of Economics by director engineer [Józef] Zylberbogen. This was the fourth lecture this year for people who cultivate garden plots. As usual, Zylberbogen's talk inspired great interest. His lecture was devoted to the following agricultural problems: (1) scarifying the soil, (2) weed removal, (3) hoeing plants. In the discussion, in which the audience participated, the lecturer explained how to water properly. At this same meeting, another agronomist, resettled here from Germany, delivered a lecture on edible weeds. Agricultural lectures at the Department of Economics are published in the form of mimeographed notes and contain professional instructions on the growing of vegetables. Thus far, four sets have been published. They are sold at a price of 10 pfennigs per copy.

SUNDAY, JUNE 14, 1942

BEARDED MEN IN TROUBLE

Today, in accordance with the announcement made by the Chairman in his most recent public address, a campaign was initiated against men with beards, who, despite all warnings and past experience, have not wished to voluntarily divest themselves of their "adornments."[66] A veritable hunt for "bearded men" occurred, and those who were caught were immediately sent to the nearest barber shop.

ON WEDNESDAY

a German commission composed of representatives of the Gettoverwaltung [Ghetto Administration] and the authorities, including, among others, [Hans] Biebow and [Günter] Fuchs,[67] inspected the hospital on Wesoła Street. As a result, the commission proposed that the building be released for use as a workshop. To his objection that he had to have a hospital for the sick, the Chairman received a reply to the effect that there were plenty of small buildings in Marysin, and, as for the sick, there was no possibility of saving their lives as things stood now. The Chairman is making every effort to avert the elimination of the hospital; the danger of that happening is, however, quite real.

B[ernard] O[strowski]

A CAMPAIGN TO SAVE CULTURAL VALUES

has been initiated by [Henryk] Neftalin, the attorney, on consultation with the Department of Economics. There has been a ruling that superintendents and janitors are to inform the Department of Population Records of all books found left behind by deportees in unlocked apartments. In such cases the department will send its own people to the addresses cited to retrieve the books. Thus far, the overwhelming majority of the books found have been of a religious nature, whereas there have been barely a few volumes of other types.

B[ernard] O[strowski]

MONDAY, JUNE 15, 1942

ARRESTS

Two people were arrested for theft today and 10 for various other offenses. The latter arrests were made when agents of Precinct I discovered a secret workshop producing pancakes from rotten vegetables and potatoes retrieved from the garbage. Two families residing at 13 Lwowska Street were engaged in producing this delicacy, most probably for profit. They were arrested by order of the public prosecutor. In the course of the investigation the prisoners denied that they had engaged in the sale of pancakes.

TO POZNAŃ FOR MANUAL LABOR

A transport of 280 young men left Bałut Market by tram this morning at 8:30 A.M. The transport was in part composed of 172 residents of Bełchatów and Zelów who had

---

66. The *Daily Chronicle Bulletin* for June 1, 1942, gives the following fragment from a summary of Rumkowski's speech: "Children must absolutely cease wandering the streets. Parents must help root out this problem. . . . It is equally necessary to do away with capotes and beards, a reform that will be enacted over the [next] 8 days."

67. See above, pp. xl–xli.

arrived in the ghetto a day or so ago.[68] The remaining 100, for the most part day workers employed on public works projects, were forcibly assigned to the transport. Aside from people employed by the Department of Public Works, day workers in Marysin were also incorporated into the transport, as were workers from the coal yard. It is known that 211 people have come here from Bełchatów and Zelów. Those who were not included in the transport (39 in number) are craftsmen of various sorts and the elderly or the sick. Such people are also found among those resettled out of Bełchatów and Zelów. Most of those resettled from those towns had been working on public works projects for a few weeks. Upon leaving their ghettos, those in this category were treated so tolerantly that they were allowed to take their household effects and even food with them. Aside from the workers, people who had been dragged right out of bed were sent to the ghetto, and among them, as noted above, were many elderly people and even some who were half crippled. The newcomers say that in regard to food supply, the situation in Bełchatów and Zelów left nothing to be desired. For example, a loaf of bread not bought on a ration card cost 80 pfennigs while a bushel of potatoes was 10 marks. There was no problem with poultry, including geese. The newcomers have been quartered in Central Prison. They learned at once of the grave food supply situation prevailing in this ghetto, which caused them to set out very readily on the next stage of their journey today.

TROUBLEMAKERS

were spreading stories today about a forthcoming resettlement action.

THURSDAY, JUNE 18, 1942

CLEANSHAVEN AND BEARDLESS

Men should report to work in the workshops and enterprises cleanshaven and beardless. The circular to that effect from the Central Workshop Bureau has been posted in the doorkeepers' quarters in all work places. The circular stipulates that failure to conform to this decree will result in immediate job loss.

IN FRONT OF THE POST OFFICE

A notice was posted in front of the post office to the effect that the pre-printed postal cards that are allowed for use in the ghetto can be sent only to Jews. At the same time, the notice calls attention to the fact that when addressing pre-printed postal cards to Jews residing in the Old Reich, it is absolutely mandatory to add the names "Israel" or "Sara." This is the personal responsibility of the sender.

PEOPLE ARE SAYING

that, with the start of the vacation period, the so-called category of hard workers who have recently been receiving special allocations in the R stores will be given a four-

---

68. Practically all 8,000 Jews from Bełchatów and Zelów, towns in Łódź province to the south of the city of Łódź, were deported to the death camp in Chełmno (Kulmhof). Only a selected group of people was resettled to the Łódź ghetto.

week vacation; the vacationer's rest will consist of being sent for a period of four weeks. . . to work in the bakeries. There his work will last only four hours, but it will include what everyone in the ghetto dreams of: the chance to consume as much bread as his heart desires right on the spot. This is, as everyone knows, the privilege of those who work in the bakeries. That privilege has recently caused many workers, including white-collar workers, to make intense efforts to switch to physical labor in the bakeries. A symptom typical of the times.

The rumor noted above, for the sake of accurate reporting, is obviously the product of a too-fertile imagination.

The convalescent home that operated in Marysin last year is sparking interest among clerical workers. No one knows for certain yet whether that convalescent home will open its hospitable doors again this year to office employees exhausted from work.

FRIDAY, JUNE 19, 1942

THE PURCHASING AGENCY AT THE CARPENTERS' SHOP

The peculiar conditions of ghetto life have made it necessary to create agencies and institutions that were never known in normal times. It is possible to have lived in the ghetto from the beginning and still not be entirely aware of what type, and, frequently, of what extremely curious agencies it contains. The so-called buy-up stand at the carpenters' workshop, in existence since January of this year, falls into that category. This agency was put into operation by the Community's authorities at the same time the resettlement action began. We recall that proclamations concerning resettlement informed the deportees that they could sell their household effects and even their furniture at the carpenters' workshop before their departure from the ghetto, or that they had the right to leave their belongings on deposit there. The buy-up campaign lasted until the resettlement of the local population was completed, that is, until the end of April of this year. The resettlement of the newcomers from the West was not affected by the operations of the agency in question for the simple reason that the newcomers possessed neither furniture nor household effects; they sold only clothing, linen, or objects of value, which were purchased, as is known, by the Main Purchasing Agency and the bank. During the several-month-long campaign to buy up household effects and furniture, superhuman labor was performed in the warehouses of carpenters' shops and, in the beginning, in the courtyards. There, at the Main Purchasing Agency, all the deportees' despair and resignation unfolded, as in a color film. The unwearying workers in that agency say that they were not so much oppressed by the work, which exceeded their strength, as by the sight of immense human misery, the daily contact with the deportees forced to sell their possessions, which, in so many cases, had been in their families for decades. Typically, the entire family being resettled would be present at the sale of its household effects. Before the decision to sell was made, the families would come (to the agency) day after day for information, explanations, and so forth.

Naturally, this increased the incredible chaos that prevailed at the purchase agency. There was a shortage of space, a shortage of personnel and painful frosts, which made life miserable for those waiting outside in the open air. Only after the buy-up campaign was concluded was it possible to move on to sort the items purchased and to place them in the storehouse that had been set up in the meantime. The most diverse items had been purchased from some 3,000 people. The value of the items purchased reaches nearly 150,000 marks. The appraisals were made by experts in various fields, and it is worth noting that used furniture was bought for its wood content, at 20 pfennigs per kilogram. Of the 3,000 sellers, hardly any left their goods for deposit, a fact that is both highly eloquent and symbolic.

The goods purchased have, in large part, been sent to public service institutions, such as the agencies of the Department of Health, the Orphanage, and so on. Recently, the new settlers from the surrounding area have been availing themselves of these household effects and furniture.

SATURDAY, JUNE 20, 1942

THE MEAT SHORTAGE

has made it necessary today to issue meals consisting solely of bread and [ersatz] coffee to those working in the various departments. Those employed in workshops received bread and butter. Naturally, this incident has caused great anxiety among working people, although blue-collar workers were rather satisfied with the replacement of sausage (whose quality had been a cause of widespread complaints recently) by a slab of butter.

The reduction of the ghetto's meat supply has been making life miserable for over two weeks now. Fortunately, a shipment of various types of meat, including veal, beef, and mutton, arrived the other day. This meat is of very low quality because it is not from animals slaughtered in the city but comes from outlying areas. The necessity of subjecting this meat to chemical disinfection caused a one-day delay in sausage production. However, tomorrow, all workers will receive fresh and relatively good sausage due to the competence of the management of the Meat Clearinghouse. The ghetto has recently been receiving supplies of horse meat in minimal amounts. The limited meat supply makes it impossible for it to be sold against ration cards, as shown by the recent allotment, which has still not been bought up by the greater part of the populace.

THE CARPENTERS' WORKSHOP

has received an order (from the German authorities) to construct a gallows for 10 people. The structure was built and was picked up today.[69]

69. The German authorities' demand for gallows was connected with an extensive preventive police action, whose slogan was deterrence (Abschreckungsmassnahmen). During the liquidation of the ghetto and the deportation of the Jewish population to Chełmno (Kulmhof), on instructions from the Reich Security Main Office (RSHA) and from Himmler himself, randomly selected Jews were hung in order to sow fear and discourage others from resisting deportation by hiding or fleeing. The German criminal police (Kripo) in Łódź, in a report to the police and security service in Poznań on June 9, wrote: "Thus far, 95 Jews have been hung publicly here. The measures taken have caused the Jew to understand the severe order here, and from now on he will obey all orders completely and peacefully." In another report, on August 15, the Kripo reported: "All told, and in accordance with the RSHA's instructions, there have been 13 public executions in July, of which 9 were in Warta (Sieradz county), 2 in Łask county, and 2 in the Litzmannstadt ghetto, of those escaping forced labor (Biuletyn Żydowskiego Instytutu Historycznego, 54 [1965], pp. 39–40).

SUNDAY, JUNE 21, 1942

THE GREETING OF GERMAN OFFICIALS

The circular of June 19 from the Eldest of the Jews, addressed to departments, enterprises, and workshops, reads as follows: "Concerning mandatory greetings. By order of the authorities, I am informing you that residents of the ghetto are obliged to greet all German officials, whether they are in civilian clothing or in uniform. When workshops or offices are inspected or during visits from members of the Ghetto Administration, everyone must rise upon hearing the command 'Attention!' The suspension of work during an inspection will continue until the moment when the command 'Back to work' is heard. Workshop directors should appoint persons to deliver these two commands during an inspection or visit. So that these greetings may proceed smoothly, I recommend that trial runs be made after receipt of this circular."

MONDAY, JUNE 22, 1942

A SHOOTING

At around midnight on June 19, 24-year-old Rafal Kutner was shot to death on the other side of the barbed wire. The incident took place in the area between Marysińska and Krawiecka streets. By order of the [German] authorities, the body was placed in the mortuary at Hospital No. 1.

A MUSEUM

A newly created department, of which literally no one in the ghetto is aware, was recently established on the former premises of the Department of Vegetables on Łagiewnicka Street, at the corner of Bałut Market. This is the Research Department, operating by order of the [German] authorities.[70]

The director of this department, unique in the ghetto, is a rabbi—Prof. [Emanuel] Hirszberg. Until recently, Professor Hirszberg and his daughter had been working, by order of the authorities in the city, as experts in the field of Judaism. This department is at present occupied in preparing exhibits for a prospective museum, which is to be set up in the city. Meanwhile, the department is attempting to have a similar museum created in the ghetto and, toward that end, is planning to produce all exhibits in duplicate. The museum's task will be to portray the life of the Jews of Eastern Europe. The department has a further, long-range plan to create a museum of the ghetto. The

70. The Research Department was really the only ghetto institution that functioned outside the administration of the Eldest of the Jews because it was established directly, bypassing M. C. Rumkowski, by the Łódź branch of the Institute of the National Socialist German Workers Party for Research into the Jewish Question (*Institut der NSDAP zur Erforschung der Judenfrage*), in Frankfurt am Main. The Łódź branch, directed by Adolf Wendel, a professor of biblical studies from the University of Breslau, was located at 33 Sienkiewicz St. The specialty of the Łódź branch was, as they put it, research into the East European Jewish Question (*Erforschung der Ostjudenfrage*) and the agency set up in the ghetto was supposed to prepare specimens for anti-Jewish exhibitions and for "scientific" study. See also "Dolls", p. 169 and n. 48.

primary emphasis is to be given to production of an artistic nature, so often encountered in certain branches of the ghetto's workshops. The department now has a workshop in operation where painters, sculptors, and their assistants are creating remarkably artistic dolls that represent the most diverse figures in the Jewish world. The execution of these dolls demonstrates a very high artistic level and precision, not only in the rendering of the heads and hands (which are made of porcelain) but in the garments as well. The first in the series, which depicts a Jewish wedding, will be finished in a matter of days. The department is not only seeking exhibits and souvenirs of every sort, but is also actively looking for artists—painters, sculptors, graphic artists. Thus far, the department has a staff of 17. The humorous, satirical element dominates in their motifs.

A ROBBERY AT THE FLOUR STOREHOUSE

Today at noon, the premises at 2 Łagiewnicka Street, which were the scene of a daring night robbery, were examined by the Bureau of Investigation, accompanied by one of the crime's perpetrators. Agents of the Bureau of Investigation led by commander [Zygmunt] Blemer, representatives of the Public Prosecutor's Office, the director of the Department of Food Supply, and a judicial expert, Dr. Kwiat, took part in the investigation at the scene of the crime. The culprit, 17-year-old [Icek] Adler, gives the impression of being a bright young man. One need not be much of a psychologist to observe that he is the type of wiseguy commonly found on the sidewalks of big cities. It turns out that he returned here after escaping from doing manual labor near Poznań, not three weeks ago as we reported yesterday, but only last Wednesday. When asked why he fled manual labor, he explained that the bad treatment and poor food he was receiving there had compelled him to flee. According to him, the workers are forced to perform extremely intense labor and are fed only 250 grams of bread and one serving of soup. His deposition states that he was caught on the road and placed under arrest in Pleszew [Poznań province]. He succeeded in escaping from Pleszew after two days, taking two loaves of bread from the jail's storehouse with him. He committed the robbery here in despair over the impossibility of obtaining a food ration card. He claims that he solicited the most important representatives of the Community's authorities about his cards, but to no avail. Order Service headquarters has informed the German authorities of the robbery. The dozen or so kilograms of flour missing from the sack (which had been recovered) were found today. The investigation at the scene of the crime drew crowds of onlookers in front of the building on Łagiewnicka Street. No other arrests have been made in connection with this case thus far. Adler was then taken in shackles to the hospital, where a confrontation with the victim [Lajb Bornsztajn, the night watchman injured during the break-in] occurred in the presence of a medical expert. Today, the wounded man Bornsztajn's condition took a slight turn for the worse.

TUESDAY, JUNE 23, 1942

GOSSIP AND REALITY

The rumor of a supposed forthcoming resettlement of children up to the age of 10 still persists. Once again we stress that authoritative circles are not confirming this rumor.

Certain persons, representing the ghetto's higher official spheres, are even categorically denying the rumor. Today there was a rumor that the Bureau of Labor has stopped accepting applicants, who are competing for work. This rumor is basically inaccurate, for the bureau is functioning normally, but is only allocating work to people who are specifically requested by particular workshops. In recent days the bureau has not been sending people out to work en masse only because the enterprises that made the larger requisitions to the bureau have temporarily suspended taking new workers on for technical reasons. It is a matter of premises being under reconstruction for future workshops, as is the case, for example, in various departments of the rag-sorting workshop and in the newly created departments of the home footwear workshop. Nevertheless, even now the bureau is sending out about 200 people a day to work.

Since yesterday there has been another disturbing rumor in circulation, [this time] about the registration of people who were stamped not long ago, during the examinations by the German medical commissions. There is a grain of truth in this latter rumor: the Department of Social Welfare—as is frequently the case—is conducting a check on people receiving welfare in order to bring to light any instances where welfare recipients have jobs. This, obviously, has nothing in common with the registration of people who had been examined by the medical commissions.

For a week, a story has been spreading that the Bureau of Labor has received a list of thirty or so workers from the ghetto who have died in the camp near Poznań (some are supposed to have died violent deaths). This rumor too is false. The Bureau of Labor denies having received any correspondence whatsoever on that subject, although notification of deaths in the camp is a normal occurrence since it is on the basis of such notification that the appropriate entries are made in the workers' files and that their families are informed. With the many thousands of workers sent out of the ghetto, cases of death, followed by official reports, are an entirely normal occurrence.

WEDNESDAY, JUNE 24, 1942

ADLER,

the 17-year-old perpetrator of the nighttime break-in at the flour storehouse, was today sent from the jail at the Bureau of Investigation to Central Prison.

THE RUMORS

about a resumption of resettlement that began to circulate through the ghetto on Saturday afternoon, causing widespread anxiety, were probably caused by the Chairman's demand that he be presented with a list of the number of children over the age of 10 who had been stamped by the medical commission and who have been given jobs. His concern was that, if need be, he would have at his disposal statistical material to present to the authorities. A second rumor sprang up at once in connection with the Chairman's having supposedly ordered that children between the ages of 8 and 10 who had been stamped be employed. Both of these rumors are entirely without foundation. Mr. Goldberg of the Central Accounting Office was arrested for disseminating false information concerning resettlement.

THURSDAY, JUNE 25, 1942

THE FOOD MARKET

is displaying complete inertia. The cause of the stagnation in the unlicensed food trade is the daily decrease of the food offered for sale. It is easy to imagine that with the increase in employment, there are increasingly fewer people who are selling off their food supplies because of a lack of means. The fury for buying goods that seized the ghetto a few weeks ago is also a thing of the past. It is possible that summer is reducing people's search for clothing. These circumstances make it senseless to sell off one's food. Pieprzowa Street, the center of the food exchange, has been completely deserted of late. This is clearly not unrelated to the campaign against unlicensed trade conducted by the Price Control section of the Order Service. Such being the state of affairs, it would be pointless to mention prices, for prices, even in the most insignificant transactions, have lost the ability to provide any general indications. Apparently, under current conditions a loaf of bread still sells for 100 marks. Clearly, such a relatively high price for bread and the similarly high prices for other necessities are only a reflection of the shortage of food being offered for sale, as mentioned above. The few semi-legal food stores still hanging on have been cleaned out, and their owners, the last food profiteers in the ghetto, are wringing their hands in despair and making strenuous efforts to find more reliable occupations.

SIXTY-SIX THOUSAND

is the number of meals served to working people over the last few days. This number includes the 6,000 served to working people in the Marysin district. This figure irrefutably demonstrates that we are not far from the moment (promised by the ghetto's leader in his memorable speech of March 2 of this year) when the entire population of the ghetto will become one army of workers.

FIFTY-SEVEN WORKERS

arrived in the ghetto by car yesterday from labor camps. Among them were not only local residents but Jews from small towns in the vicinity as well. For the most part, the new arrivals were sick people. They have been placed in Central Prison for the time being.

A WAIF

Danuta Adamczewska, aged 15, has been remanded to the ghetto. The reason: she is suspected of being Jewish by origin. The new ghetto resident was placed in the quarantine room of the Orphanage in Marysin.

FRIDAY, JUNE 26, 1942

FUR PURCHASES

The fur purchase drive came to an end yesterday. It had run for 10 days (from the 14th to the 24th of this month). As is generally known, absolutely all furs, including those exempted six months ago, were to be brought to the bank for sale. No exceptions were made to this rule. The first days of the buy-up were relatively sluggish, with scarcely a few dozen clients appearing at the bank each day, but the turnout increased dramatically during the final days. Thus, during the final day, for example, the bank purchased furs from 325 people, paying out 25,000 marks. It is worth noting that on the basis of a rough estimate, the number of furs sold significantly exceeds the number of furs that had been exempted. This circumstance was determined to a considerable degree by the furs put up for sale by the German Jews, who, as is well known, have only lately arrived in the ghetto. Evidently, they had not complied at the proper time with the order, issued especially for them, to surrender their furs. It is worth mentioning that, early in the campaign, Chairman Rumkowski and members of his family, as well as the head of the Department of Health, Dr. [Wiktor] Miller, had presented their fur coats to the bank. Today, over 50 people reported to the bank with furs to sell. The bank accepted the furs, making the appropriate entries on the release forms, but it made no payment for the furs. Persons who did not present their furs to the bank will be subject to a search by agents of the Special Unit [of the Order Service].

THE OLD CEMETERY IS ENDANGERED

On Thursday, the 25th of this month, a session of the Rabbinate was suddenly called, and Mr. [Boruch] Praszkier, by order of the Chairman, read a letter sent by the Gettoverwaltung [Ghetto Administration]. Because of the need to increase the area occupied by the woodwork factory, due to the very large orders it has received, the Gettoverwaltung is ordering that the old cemetery that abuts the grounds of the workshop be used as a lumberyard. The gravestones are to be used for paving passageways. Since it is impossible to avert these orders, the Rabbinate has requested that efforts be made simply to save whatever can be saved. In any case, the Rabbinate has ordered that work on a precise map of the arrangement of the graves begin at once, so that, if need be, at some point the pattern can be reconstructed.

The hospital for the mentally ill also is to fall victim to the reconstruction of the workshop. It is possible that the same fate is also in store for the tuberculosis hospital. Both hospitals [and the old cemetery] are located on Wesoła Street.

B[ernard] O[strowski]

SUNDAY, JUNE 28, 1942

A SHOOTING

Yesterday at 9:15 P.M. Ewa Landau (of 1 Bazarna Street) was shot to death near the barbed wire at 21 Podrzeczna Street. A story is circulating in the ghetto that she had asked the sentry to shoot her and had attempted to make her way through the barbed wire right before his eyes.

A SUICIDE

Yesterday, Sara Fajga Lewin jumped from a fourth-floor window at 12 Rybna Street. She died on the spot.

MANDATORY GREETING

Proclamation (No. 387) concerning the obligation to greet all German officials, both in uniform and in civilian clothing, has again been posted. This proclamation directs the populace's attention to the fact that the obligation is not being observed scrupulously. Clerks driving past in automobiles should also be greeted. Order Service men and firemen are obliged to express their respects by coming to attention. The civilian population is obliged to remove any head covering. Women and persons not wearing hats are to perform the greeting by inclining their heads forward. Those failing to observe this obligation are under threat of severe punishment.

[LITZMANNSTADT-GETTO,] JUNE 28, 1942

The last food ration, issued on June 26, 1942, for the period of July 1–10, 1942, includes a greatly reduced allotment of sugar and flour. The supplemental ration for working people was also skimpier this time, containing only 1 kilogram of potatoes. We are in the period before the new harvest, and the reduced allocations are, to some extent, reasonable. In fact, reduced rations ought to have been expected in June, but everything was pushed a couple weeks ahead because of the belated spring this year.

It seems a bit odd to be making use of the stockpiled potatoes at this time of year: in fact not very many have come in and not many are coming in now, but, be that as it may, the ghetto's surplus, which amounts to about 400,000 kilograms, will suffice for another ten-day period if nothing more arrives. It also seems strange that the sugar ration has been reduced at a time when the reserves of sugar, given the size of the allocations thus far, should suffice for a few months. The ghetto recently received 180,000 kilograms of yellow sugar, which is short in this ration, and therefore the price of sugar rose at once on the unlicensed market to 120 marks per kilogram. Due to the shortage of other nutriments, sugar has become the most sought-after item in the ghetto; after consuming sugar, people experience a marked improvement in their state of health, and doctors have been tending to advise people to consume as much sugar as possible. They are no longer prescribing liver extract, for they know it cannot be obtained, and consequently they are advising people to consume as many green vegetables as possible in addition to sugar. But here too the populace has met with disappointment. The cool June this year has caused enormous delays and even postponements in vegetable deliveries, and the prices on the open market have been extremely high. Yesterday, a kilogram of spinach was selling for 13 marks, 1 kilogram of lettuce for 10 marks, and a bunch of radishes (10 pieces) for 1.50 marks, and even at those high prices there were enormous lines in front of the private sales points. A weed like pigweed was selling for 4 marks per kilogram and radish leaves, for 2 marks a kilogram.

After the optimistic outlook at the beginning of June, when it seemed that everything was returning to a normal state, hunger again prevails in the ghetto and this time is even more grievous than before. The number of deaths, which rarely exceeded 50 at the beginning of the month, and often fluctuated around 40, shot up at once to between 70 and 80, and it is primarily those who were exhausted by the winter that are dying off now. The hospital used to be an inviting place for those whose own homes did not bode well as places in which to endure an illness, but now the food in the hospital discourages anyone who can otherwise avoid it. Surgery cases constitute the sole exception. The tuberculosis hospital on Wesoła Street has been receiving reduced food allocations, most glaringly evident in the case of bread, whose daily allotment amounts to only 200 grams per patient.

Last year, the first bridge on Zgierska Street was still a measure of the intense communication among the ghetto's divided parts, most eloquently demonstrated by the long lines of pedestrians on both sides of the bridge. Today, traffic on the bridge is minimal, and what there is of it is slow and sluggish. People often give up one thing or another to spare themselves crossing the bridge, so debilitated have they now become. It should be recalled that this bridge is only 5.40 meters high, that is, barely two and a half stories tall.

There is more and more work in the workshops, more and more hands are being mobilized for labor, but productivity is constantly falling, the individual worker's productivity is decreasing in spite of the fact that production is being held at a high level in the majority of cases. At present, more than 65,000 people in the ghetto have made use of the supplemental bread and sausage allocation, but that does not compensate for their loss of strength over the winter months, nor even for the energy used up at work. Laborers and blue-collar workers are completely exhausted and disinclined to work, but they are in a no-exit situation. If, after seven days of illness, a worker reports back to work, he must present a medical certificate stating that he has recovered his health; if he continues to be ill, he is then subject to being stricken from the rolls of the employed and put on welfare, the consequences of which are clear to him. As a laborer or blue-collar worker, he receives an additional 150 grams of bread and 40 grams of sausage a day, but without it? He would be under the same threat as the remaining 30 percent of the population, which is composed of the elderly, the sick, and children; first, hunger and then, if something should happen, possibly deportation as well.

The ghetto has not only become a labor camp, where there is no place for people who are not working, but also some sort of Nietzschean experimental laboratory from which only the "very strong" emerge in one piece . . .

MONDAY, JUNE 29, 1942

DEATHS AND BIRTHS

Today 74 people of which 40 were men and 34 women died in the ghetto. It should be mentioned that, lately, men have been accounting for the majority of the deaths. The principal cause of death is tuberculosis, the second—diseases of the alimentary canal, and third—heart failure.

Five births (two boys and three girls) were registered today.

ADLER'S ESCAPE

The official [German] ghetto authorities have been informed that [Icek] Adler—perpetrator of a daring nighttime break-in at the flour storehouse—had escaped from a labor camp near Poznań. Consequently, it has been established that Adler had entered the ghetto illegally. He remains in Central Prison. Because his escape from the camp has now officially been disclosed, his fate has assumed tragic dimensions.

DEATH OF AN EDITOR

The dean of Viennese journalists, the editor Stephan Deutsch, died on Wednesday, the 24th of this month, in the ghetto. The deceased had an illustrious record as a publicist, writing for newspapers and magazines with a nationalist-Jewish orientation.

THE WELL-KNOWN FORMER ŁÓDŹ MERCHANT, KAPITULNIK

died on Friday in the offices of the [German] criminal police on Kościelna Street. The death certificate states that the deceased suffered a heart attack. He and his son had been under arrest for two weeks.

POPULATION COUNT AS OF JULY 1, 1942

On July 1, 1942, there were 102,546 people residing in the ghetto. 58,495 women were living in the ghetto, and 44,051 men. Of that number 90,113 were local Jews, 5,672 were German Jews [and Jews from Vienna, Bohemia and Luxembourg]. 6,761 had been resettled here from Pabianice, Brzeziny, Ozorków, Bełchatów, and Zelów.

By sex, the ghetto was inhabited by 39,355 men and 50,758 women of local origin; of the "German" Jews, 2,434 were men and 3,238 were women, and of the Jews from the small towns in the surrounding area, 2,262 were men and 4,499 were women.

Population Changes in the Month of June This Year

	Men	Women	Total
Level on June 1, 1942	45,294	59,176	104,470
Births	63	36	99
Stillbirths	3	—	3
Miscarriages	4	1	5
Arrivals from the Generalgouvernement and Warthegau	3	3	6
Returned from manual labor	33	—	33
From Bełchatów and Zelów	211	—	211
Arrivals from 17 towns in Warthegau (see Note 1 below)	37	—	37
Addendum to the number from Brzeziny	130	138	268
Additions to the population count from Pabianice and Brzeziny (see Note 2)	1	2	3
Increase in residents in June	485	180	665
Deaths	960	754	1,714
Left for Warsaw [ghetto] and Warthegau	95	106	201
To prison (see Note 3)	—	1	1
To manual labor in Poznań	622	—	622
Addendum [?]	1	—	1

Population Changes in the Month of June This Year (cont.)

	Men	Women	Total
Decrease in June	1,678	861	2,539
In June the population decreased by	1,243 [?]	681	1,924 [?][71]

The number of ghetto residents—102,500—is the lowest since the ghetto came into existence.

Note 1: In the final days of June, as the corresponding *Daily Chronicle Bulletin* notes, 57 men were transported to the ghetto from a labor camp near Berlin. They were placed in Central Prison at the disposal of the German police. Twenty of the 57 men are residents of the ghetto here who had at one time been sent out to perform manual labor; the remaining 37 are residents of 17 small towns, for the most part from the former provinces of Łódź and Warsaw.

Note 2: On May 21, a transport of residents from Brzeziny arrived here and then left the ghetto almost immediately upon arrival. Evidently, 268 Jews from Brzeziny had been in hiding, since, in the meantime, they have reported their presence in the ghetto. The list of people from Brzeziny presently residing in the ghetto has been increased by the supplementary figure above.

Note 3: A Polish woman, Zofia Ziomek, who had been living in the ghetto since the beginning of the war, was remanded to the penitentiary in Rawicz by order of the German police.

THURSDAY, JULY 2, 1942

A SUICIDE

Last night, 39-year-old Gitla-Hinda Zylbersztajn hung herself in her apartment at 11 Zbożowa Street.

THE GHETTO'S DISEASES

On the basis of a short report from the head of the health service, Dr. [Wiktor] Miller, we are able to give a general description of the health situation in the ghetto. In Dr. Miller's opinion, the danger of spotted typhus has recently been entirely averted. A typhus epidemic had been hanging over the ghetto while the so-called Gypsy camp was in existence, that is, in the months of November, December, and January. Decimating the inhabitants of the camp, the typhus had begun to make its way into the ghetto. Fortunately, at that time, the danger of an epidemic was successfully staved off. Recently, typhus was brought into the ghetto by people resettled here from Brzeziny. Fortunately, this time the epidemic was nipped in the bud by immediately isolating the Jews from Brzeziny in Marysin. Since that quarantine ended, the number of cases occurring in the ghetto has become quite rare. Dysentery, which made life so miserable this time of year two years ago and, to a lesser degree, a year ago, is at present not a problem. Obviously, the shortage of fruits and vegetables has had an influence on the situation. The ghetto is plagued by starvation edema. No doctor and no medicine is able to combat this disease, since only better nourishment could provide an effective cure. Starvation edema has, in recent times, constituted one of the most frequent causes of death. On a par with starvation edema, tuberculosis (of

71. The numbers do not add up to 1,243 and 1,924.

the lungs and of the entire organism) is increasing the number of deaths. The health service is nearly helpless in its struggle against this terrible disease. The number of patients in the hospital amounts to about 1,600. If one adds to this figure the number of patients in the sanatoriums and the Old People's Homes, then it will exceed two thousand by a considerable amount. For a poor ghetto, the number [of beds here] is extremely impressive. And yet, unfortunately, sick people have to wait a long time for a hospital bed.

OUR [FOOD] SUPPLIES

1. Yesterday a shipment of 800 kilograms of meat in a state of advanced decay arrived in the ghetto. Some pieces were green, yellow, or white. Upon receipt of the meat, Community officials, after consultation with the Meat Clearinghouse, called the shipment into question, stating that they were unable to use this meat, which had been earmarked to be made into sausage for working people, because of the disastrous effect it could have on their health. The Gettoverwaltung delegated two officials to the Meat Clearinghouse to check the meat, but the spoilage was so obvious that they acknowledged that it was unfit and ordered processing suspended and the meat kept under refrigeration until an official veterinary surgeon arrives from the city.

2. Not long ago, we noted the arrival of 10,000 kilograms of butter. The butter was completely rancid and black in color. Experts state that it had been lying around for at least six months. After washing the butter several times, the Milk Department succeeded in removing the bitterness from it and in rendering the butter relatively pure and digestible by the stomachs of ghetto dwellers, which are used to everything.

3. Recently, one of the bakers of Litzmannstadt, using his own horses and wagons, sent a sizeable quantity of flour, which had begun to spoil in his own storehouse, to Bałut Market. This he did not do philanthropically but, it would seem, out of fear of the punishment that would have awaited him for allowing the flour to spoil. It was unusable in the city, but more than good enough for the ghetto.

B[ernard] O[strowski]

THE DRIVE TO EMPLOY CHILDREN OVER THE AGE OF 10

is making vigorous progress, particularly in relation to the children who had been "stamped." Practically all of the latter have found work. The negligible number of the still unemployed will be given jobs in the next few days. A curious thing has come to light at the present moment. Around one hundred children have used fictitious names, that is, names which were never to be found in the ghetto or were the names of people resettled or deceased. Rumors are circulating among the populace that the Chairman is also attempting to find employment for younger children as well—those from 8 years old and up. This is categorically denied by authoritative circles.

B[ernard] O[strowski]

MONDAY, JULY 6, 1942

DEATHS AND BIRTHS

Eighty-six people died in the ghetto today. (The death rate continues its alarming increase.) One child was stillborn.

A SUICIDE

At ten o'clock in the morning, 20-year-old Sara Ser (of 38 Młynarska Street), a clerk in the Coupon Department and a resident of the ground floor of that building, threw herself from the fourth floor of a stairwell at 1/3 Dworska Street. The incident had a staggering effect on the suicide victim's large circle of friends at work. She fell to the courtyard pavement, suffering a fractured skull and a broken arm. She was taken to Hospital No. 1 past any hope of recovery. Tragedies in her family inclined the young woman to suicide. Her mother died a few months ago, her father had recently suffered a nervous breakdown, and her sister is ill with tuberculosis. It was evidently more than her nerves could bear. She had been working in the Coupon Department for nine months.

PROCLAMATION No. 388

posted yesterday is notice that the Eldest of the Jews should be informed about any places in the city [outside the ghetto] where merchandise or objects of value are being kept or hidden. This proclamation is a reminder of those already issued several times in regard to this same matter. This time the Eldest of the Jews called attention to the fact that houses are being demolished in certain districts of the city. Persons who, in confidence, reveal places where merchandise is hidden will, upon the discovery of the objects in question, receive their cash equivalent based on an appraisal, with a certain percentage deducted for the Community. No one should fear punitive sanctions, and those parties affected are therefore advised to report at once.

THE RUMOR

about soup replacing the meals thus far served to working people is patently false since the Department of Soup Kitchens knows nothing about any such innovation.

TUESDAY, JULY 7, 1942

WEATHER

A second scorching day. Not a single cloud in the sky. The temperature reached 37 degrees. The dry spell continues with no rain in sight.

DOCTOR OF MEDICINE IZYDOR BETTE

died today at the venerable age of 74. Right up until the very end of his life, the deceased was seeing patients at the clinic at 17 Zgierska Street in his capacity as a specialist in internal medicine.

A HEART ATTACK

caused the death of 58-year-old Szaja Zylberszac a day ago, in the office of the [German] criminal police. The deceased was well-known in the Bałut section under the nickname "Szaja Magnat" [Magnate], and was linked to the famous pre-war cases involving "Max the Blind". Until his arrest, Szaja Magnat was living in the building at

14 Młynarska Street that had been his property before the war. Recently he had been serving as the building's janitor.

On July 1, 39-year-old Szymon Kaszub, a master weaver by profession, died in similar circumstances.

A STORM

As noted in our weather report today, there was no sign of rain to be seen and not the slightest cloud in the sky. And so the heavy rain that began falling suddenly at around five o'clock in the afternoon came as a complete and pleasant surprise. The heavy rain fell in sheer torrents while the sun continued to shine. There were also a few claps of thunder. A sun shower is an extremely rare meteorological event. Most important, the parched soil was thoroughly watered and after a day of scorching heat people could breathe freely again.

WEDNESDAY, JULY 8, 1942

UNDER A TRAM'S WHEELS

Yesterday, at two o'clock in the afternoon, through her own carelessness, a young woman fell under the wheels of a trailer attached to a tram. The weight of the trailer crushed her head. The tram driver bears no responsibility for this accident. Only today was the body identified. The woman run over was Rojzla Sochaczewska (of 12 Piwna Street) who was born in Kalisz in 1903. Sochaczewska was a seamstress by profession. She had recently been working on garden plots in Marysin. Immediately after the incident, photographs were taken of the victim lying beneath the trailer. The [German] authorities permitted the woman to be buried without an autopsy.

THURSDAY, JULY 9, 1942

DOCTORS ARRIVE FROM KALISZ AND THE SURROUNDING AREA

Yesterday, at ten o'clock in the morning, a train arrived at the Radogoszcz station carrying deportees from Kalisz[72] and the settlement of Koźminek.[73] Around 500 Jews—men, women, and a small number of children—were deported from those two areas to the ghetto here. Informed of the arrival of new residents, the Community authorities sent representatives to the train station along with a good-sized squad of Order Service men and porters. The children, the sick, and the elderly were taken by

72. Before the war, Kalisz, a town in Poznań province, included over 20,000 Jews, that is, about 35 percent of its total population. Nearly all of them were resettled to various locations in the Generalgouvernement immediately after the occupation of Poland in the fall of 1939.

73. The ghetto in Koźminek, a small town in Kalisz county, existed from January, 1940, to July, 1942. Both the local Jews and resettlees from the surrounding towns and villages, including Kalisz, Stawiszyn, and Ostrów Kaliski, were concentrated there. All told, more than 2,500 people passed through that ghetto, of which around 1,000 were deported to the death camp in Chełmno (Kulmhof) between January and March, 1942.

tram from the train station to their temporary housing on the grounds of Central Prison. The others traveled to the prison by [horse-drawn] wagon. In terms of physical appearance, the newcomers looked rather good. Their outward appearance indicates that until now they had been fed normally. The fate of the Jews from Kalisz is as follows: In the last half of January, the Chairman of the Kalisz Jewish Council, Mr. [Gustaw] Hahn, along with his deputy, Mr. [Majer] Landau, had spent two weeks here. Their purpose in coming to this ghetto at that time had been to establish contact with the Eldest of the Jews concerning the possible resettlement of the Kalisz Jews to this ghetto. At that time there had been hints in Kalisz that the city would be completely "cleansed" of Jews. In that period, there were 160 Jews in Kalisz, practically all of whom were working in the various workshops operating on the grounds of the block of buildings where those same Jews lived. The *Daily Chronicle Bulletin* from the second half of January of this year contains exhaustive information about the situation of the Kalisz Jews. Little had changed there since that time. In the meantime, the number of residents in Kalisz had been reduced by 27. All the rest, that is 140 people, were included in the transport which arrived in Marysin yesterday. 1,500 Jews deported from Kalisz and the surrounding area had been concentrated in the settlement of Koźminek (23 kilometers from Kalisz) in January (see the *Daily Chronicle Bulletin* from the second half of January of this year). Over the last six months Jews had been deported from Koźminek several times. During some of the deportations men were sent out to perform manual labor, mostly to Inowrocław;[74] in other cases children and people unfit for work were deported. The last group was included in the transport which arrived here. The newcomers maintain that recently all the cities and small towns in Wartheland had been "cleansed" of Jews. Apparently, a whole series of deportees from various small towns are to be sent to this ghetto. This applies in particular to Sieradz and Zduńska Wola.[75] A great many shoemakers, tailors, electricians, cutters, locksmiths, sandal-makers, and so on have arrived here from Kalisz and the surrounding area; they will undoubtedly find work in their own trades in the next few days. The Jews of Kalisz had lived the last few months in constant fear of deportation. In concert with a certain German manufacturer they had created a sizable workshop for mending army uniforms, expecting that this establishment would protect them from deportation. The order to vacate Kalisz, a result of instructions from Poznań, came without a moment's notice. It happened on Monday, the 6th of this month. Secret police [Gestapo] agents came to all the work places informing the Jews that they had to prepare to leave the ghetto there within the next hour. Everyone went back to their apartments and, under the eyes of the police, began to pack their belongings in feverish haste. The Jewish Council hired wagons and even an

74. There were a few forced labor camps in Inowrocław, including one for prisoners of war that held some British prisoners, and one for Gypsies and Jews. The Jews worked on the railroad tracks, broke stone for the highway, and built municipal swimming pools; they also worked in the camp's artisan workshops. (See also p. 171, n. 51)

75. Zduńska Wola, a town in Łódź province, included over 9,000 Jews before the war, that is, about 38 percent of its overall population. Jews from a few of the surrounding towns and villages, including Sieradz and Maciszewice, were concentrated in the ghetto established there in the spring of 1940. The ghetto in Zduńska Wola was liquidated in August, 1942, and its inhabitants were either murdered on the spot or deported to the death camp in Chełmno (Kulmhof). Only specially selected individuals were resettled to the Łódź ghetto.

automobile to transport people's things. For the most part, the police allowed the deportees to take everything with them. After about two hours had elapsed, all the Jews of Kalisz had been concentrated on the square in front of the train station. At the same time, a few hundred deportees from Koźminek were brought to the square. After an entire night spent on the square, the departure began at 7:30 in the morning. It is worth noting that during the night 100 people, both men and women, were sent from the assembly point to Inowrocław to perform manual labor. Only people without work skills were selected for that transport, from which fact it seems beyond dispute that it was principally skilled workers who were sent to the ghetto here. We mentioned above that there was a small percentage of children among the new arrivals. According to information from the deportees, these children had been kept in hiding during the last few months to avoid their resettlement. Thus, these children were not officially registered. Four passenger cars had been provided for the deportees. Obviously, nearly 500 people along with their baggage could not be seated in four cars. And so, when leaving, they encountered a now familiar disappointment. Before entering the cars, they had to part with the last of their belongings. Only smaller hand packages could be taken. The representatives of the [German] authorities promised that the baggage left behind would arrive after the deportees. The Jews from Kalisz say that they were touched by the cordial care they have received since first arriving here in the ghetto. They say that they will readily suffer the privations that are the lot of the local inhabitants since they are certain that here they will find the peace and safety that were hard to come by in Kalisz because of the constant threat of resettlement. It is worth emphasizing that, as soon as the Jews from Kalisz were quartered in Central Prison, they were paid a personal visit by the Chairman. The leader of the ghetto took an unusually lively interest in the distress of his newest citizens; he questioned them about all the details of their lives up to that point. The Chairman promised the deportees from Kalisz that he would do everything in his power to ease their situation. First, of course, he promised that they would all be given work. He then promised them that in the event that their baggage did not arrive here, they would be provided with clothes, bedding, and so forth.

The bulletin from the second half of January of this year contains information about the food supply situation in Kalisz, which took a certain turn for the worse this year. Recently, the standard per capita food allocation for the Jewish population ran as follows: bread—1.90 kilograms per week, potatoes—2.5 kilograms per week, unlimited fuel, 100 grams of fat, 220 grams of sugar, 100 grams of marmalade, 200 grams of meat per week, and so forth. Apart from his rations, each person received 1 kilogram of sausage per week. It was a simple matter to buy bread for 8 [German] marks, a bushel of potatoes for 15 marks, and 15 eggs for 5 marks from Poles on the open market. The canteen in the Jewish block always had an excellent supply of fruit (garden strawberries, gooseberries), groceries of various sorts, haberdashery goods, and beverages such as beer and lemonade.

SATURDAY, JULY 11, 1942

BARRACKS AT THE TRAIN STATION

On instructions from the German authorities, the Construction Department has begun erecting large barracks at the Radogoszcz side-track station. To that end, finished materials are brought in and the work there consists solely of laying foundations and assembling the parts. The barracks occupy some 900 square meters. These barracks will be a storehouse for the materials and the semi-finished materials that are brought to the ghetto. There may be yet another purpose in constructing these barracks. It is likely that, if need be, these barracks will be utilized as a point where deportees or new settlers can be concentrated. The authorities have issued an ultimatum that the barracks be completed this month. The barracks for storing vegetables that are planned for construction—as the *Daily Chronicle Bulletin* has already reported—in the vicinity of the Marysin gate [to the ghetto] on Zagajnikowa Street are not, for the time being, under construction due to a lack of sufficient quantities of wood. When it has stored a suitable amount of wood from demolished buildings, the Building Department will begin constructing the barracks for storing vegetables.

UNDER THE WHEELS OF A TRAM

There has been another fatal incident involving a tram. On Friday at 12:30, near 49 Łagiewnicka Street, a trailer came uncoupled from the lead car. As a result, a 4½-year-old boy, Akiba Buki (of 9 Ceglana Street), a tailor's son, found himself under the wheels of the trailer. By order of the public prosecutor, the worker responsible for placing safety bars on the temporary track was held under arrest. An investigation is under way.

PEOPLE ARE SAYING . . .

A rumor is afoot in the ghetto to the effect that in the next few days new residents will supposedly arrive in the ghetto—specifically, 10,000 deportees from Prague.

SUNDAY, JULY 12, 1942

A LEAP FROM THE FOURTH FLOOR

was the means used by 42-year-old Chaja-Ruchla Zydier (of 21 Pieprzowa Street) to commit suicide today. No motive has been established for her desperate act. She died on the spot.

A RETURN TO SOUP

Yesterday, the Department of Soup Kitchens received an order from the Eldest of the Jews to put kitchens into operation, beginning on the 14th of this month, to prepare soup for working people. 10,000 servings of soup will be prepared on the very first day. Over the next few days, the entire working population, that is, some 70,000 people, will receive soup. The supplementary meal of bread, sausage, and [ersatz] coffee is thereby abolished. The kitchens will be put into operation at what are, at the present time, the B. W. K. [*Brot, Wurst, Kaffee*] distribution points. The sizable shipments of vegetables the ghetto has received makes it easier to carry out this so-called reorganization. Today bread and butter were distributed in the Community workshops; [those employed in] departments once again had to be satisfied with unbuttered bread. The Meat Clearinghouse has been able to produce enough sausage for tomorrow for everyone who is working. There will be no sausage the day after tomorrow since not one gram of meat has arrived in the ghetto. This is a rare occurrence.

MONDAY, JULY 13, 1942

FROM KOŹMINEK, NEAR KALISZ

The other day, 39 more Jews were brought to the ghetto from Koźminek, near Kalisz. Yesterday four persons arrived from there. The deportees from Koźminek, like their predecessors, have been temporarily quartered on the grounds of Central Prison. The Jews from Kalisz, as we have already reported, are now being given apartments, the most essential furnishings, and, in many cases, are receiving clothes and undergarments free of charge. The Office for Resettled Persons on Rybna Street, which, as is generally known, is in charge of dealing with the ghetto's new populations, is procuring clothing for the newcomers, both from the Clothing Department and from the storehouse where the shipments of clothes that recently arrived in the ghetto are stored.

THEY GAVE HER FOOD AND DRINK

The [Jewish] policemen employed at the precinct at Bałut Market tell of the following incident. Yesterday, around one o'clock at night, a German sentry at Bałut Market observed a 5-year-old girl wandering in the vicinity of the barbed wire fence. In response to his questions, the little girl explained that at nine o'clock she had gone to see her mother, who was working in a Community workshop, and had gotten lost on the way back home. To the policemen's horror, the German sentry took the girl to Precinct VI [outside the ghetto]. She was released after a few hours and committed to the care of the Order Service. The girl told them that, during the night she spent in the German precinct, she had been very well cared for and had been fed until she was full.

WEDNESDAY, JULY 15, 1942

A SHOOTING

Yesterday, at nine o'clock in the evening, 44-year-old Ignacy Smolenski was shot to death outside the ghetto, near the barbed wire. A sentry's bullet inflicted a mortal wound on Smolenski's heart. He was shot while attempting to make his way into the ghetto. The victim's history is as follows: A teacher by profession, he was a native of Łódź. He had emigrated to Lwów at the beginning of the war. He had left his wife behind; also a schoolteacher, she lives in the ghetto. He had not corresponded with his wife for the entire time of their separation. From the papers found on him it appears that he had taken up residence in Vienna several months ago and had recently been living in Warsaw, outside the ghetto. The documents he possessed did not indicate that he was of Jewish origin. It would appear from his attempt to enter the ghetto that the victim intended to return to his wife.

THURSDAY, JULY 16, 1942

FUNERAL NOTICE

One of Łódź's oldest doctors, Dr. [Wolf] Kocen, a specialist in internal medicine, died today. A respected man of achievement, he had devoted himself to his profession almost until the very end of his life.

Szmul Boniowka, the cantor in the great synagogue, died yesterday. From the moment he arrived in the ghetto, the deceased performed services during the high holidays at the [former cinema] Bajka and at 26 Zgierska Street. Cantor [Szmul] Boniowka was gifted with a splendid tenor voice.

SATURDAY, JULY 18, 1942

A SUICIDE

On the 18th of this month, Filip Vohssen (b. 1889, in Holland), who had resettled here from Germany and had resided at 9 Jerozolimska Street, poisoned himself with an overdose of Veronal.

BARRACKS INSTEAD OF A HOSPITAL

After weeks without too many incidents of significance, menacing clouds once again hang over the ghetto. There is a more than justified fear that an order eliminating one hospital, and perhaps even more, will be issued in the immediate future. The hospital buildings will have to be turned into Community workshops. Hospital No. 3, at the intersection of Bazarna and Wesoła streets, is the most likely choice for evacuation.

This would be an incalculable loss for the ghetto. Hospital No. 3 is second in importance to the hospital for internal illnesses on Łagiewnicka Street. Hospital No. 3, whose existence is now threatened, was designated for the treatment of people with tuberculosis. That fact alone is sufficient indication of its importance for the health of the ghetto's populace. Today, tuberculosis, the greatest enemy of the Jews residing in the ghetto, is the cause of at least three quarters of the deaths, which are literally decimating the ghetto's population at a rate faster than that at the front or during an epidemic.

Hospital No. 3 has 400 beds that are permanently assigned to tuberculosis patients and, in addition, a psychiatric ward where about 50 mentally ill people are receiving treatment. It would be difficult to describe the great expenditure of money and labor that went into the creation of that hospital. Immediately upon the resettling of the Jews in the ghetto, the authorities ordered that a hospital for contagious diseases be created in the building on Wesoła Street, which had housed an ORT [Organization for Rehabilitation through Training] factory before the war. The remodeling of the factory into a hospital with exemplary modern facilities in record time was the Eldest of the Jews' first monumental achievement. A hospital suitable for contagious diseases was created only later, on Drewnowska Street. And still later, the Department of Health's central institutions were established, along with Hospital No. 1, in the former City Hospital and Ambulatorium building on Łagiewnicka Street. In 1941, the director,

Józef Rumkowski, undertook the remodeling of the third and fourth floors of Hospital No. 3. Thanks to this recent Sisyphean labor, wards containing about 10 beds each were created. And today this hospital is threatened with liquidation by being transformed into a division of the wooden shoe workshop, which is located in its immediate vicinity. The hospital will be replaced by barracks, of the modern field-hospital type. One such barrack has already been sold to the Community by the [German] authorities (at a cost of many hundreds of thousands of marks). It will occupy an area of 60 by 15 meters. In all probability it will be installed on the square at the intersection of Franciszkańska and Tokarzewski streets. The authorities had suggested constructing that barrack in the cemetery. Fortunately, the Eldest of the Jews succeeded in getting that order annulled. At the present, sick people frequently wait for several weeks for each hospital bed since the 1,550 hospital beds are already occupied. The probable liquidation of a hospital is disastrous for the ghetto.

SUNDAY, JULY 19, 1942

A REVUE

On Saturday, the 18th of this month, the House of Culture presented Revue No. 3 for the twentieth time. Some 10,000 spectators have already attended the House of Culture's presentations of revues. This week, only the revue will be performed; the traditional Wednesday concert will not take place. The House of Culture's orchestra recently suffered an irreparable loss in the death of its first violinist, Kantor, of blessed memory, the former concertmaster of the Łódź philharmonic orchestra.

TUESDAY, JULY 21, 1942

GERMAN COMMISSIONS

have been visiting the ghetto in very large numbers in the last few days. Among others, representatives of the trade council from Poznań visited the Community workshops. Representatives of the military visited the tailor workshops, which are producing 10,000 pairs of pants and tunics from light-colored, flannel-lined cloth (for camouflage in snowy terrain), as well as the Community tailor workshops where jumpsuits for paratroopers are being manufactured. Another commission also spent some time here on behalf of the OPL [Air Defense League]. After completing its inspection, that commission was entirely satisfied.

13,000 CHILDREN

had, by the 20th of this month, been employed by the School Department in various Community workshops as apprentices. The intensity of the work done by the Reclassification Commission [of the School Department] is attested to by its succeeding in finding employment for 1,800 young people between the ages of 10 and 17 in the first 20 days of July. That is a record for the ghetto.

PROVIDING THE NEWCOMERS FROM THE PROVINCES WITH CLOTHING

As is well known, the deportees from the provinces, Pabianice in particular, arrived here with only the clothes on their backs. Now, on instructions from the Chairman, they are being given about 75,000 pieces of underwear, on the basis of need, which are issued by the director of the Office for Resettled Persons. This underclothing comes from the shipments of underwear, clothing, and shoes sent here by the authorities.

B[ernard] O[strowski]

SINCE THE END OF MAY THE GHETTO

has been receiving colossal amounts of clothing. Thus, as of the 16th of this month, the following had been shipped here:

clothing and rags	798,625 kg
feathers, eiderdown, and pillows	221,035 kg
furs and hides	8,130 kg
used shoes	69,350 kg
used stockings and socks	50 kg
used neckties	12 kg

B[ernard] O[strowski]

ORDERS FROM THE GETTOVERWALTUNG

The Gettoverwaltung [Ghetto Administration] has ordered 250 sets of bedding and linen made for it out of the articles recently sent to the ghetto. This order was filled with the greatest of care and using the best materials in the best condition. In the meantime, a second order arrived from those same authorities for ready-made clothing, underwear, and shoes for workers. It would appear that this consignment is intended for the Jewish workers who have been sent out of the ghetto to perform manual labor. This order is intended for three groups: (1) men, (2) women, (3) children up to age 14, and includes 1,260 [items] for the first group (without shoes), 1,265 for the second (including 200 pairs of shoes), and 205 for the third group (including 6 pairs of shoes).

B[ernard] O[strowski]

WEDNESDAY, JULY 22, 1942

A MURDER

Yesterday, at five o'clock in the afternoon, 55-year-old Chawa Rosenblit was found murdered in her apartment at 9 Ceglana Street. A physician found four fatal head wounds on the victim that had most likely been inflicted by a one-kilogram weight. The incident was immediately reported to officials of the German criminal police, who assumed control of the entire investigation, excluding the ghetto security forces from the case for the time being.

AN EXECUTION

Today, around eleven o'clock, the second public execution in the ghetto took place on the square on Bazarna Street. Two men were hung on the gallows: 16-year-old Grynbaum from Pabianice and 45-year-old Markowski. They were executed for escaping from a labor camp near Poznań.

THURSDAY, JULY 23, 1942

COURSES FOR YOUNG PEOPLE IN TAILORING

Since the beginning of this month, supplemental trade courses for young people in tailoring have been underway in the tailors' workshop building at 29 Franciszkańska Street. Putting such an institution into operation has provided a rational solution to the problem of completing the education of children and young people in tailoring, which is a basic trade in the ghetto. At present, the tailoring workshops employ around 2,000 children as apprentices. All the tailoring divisions, as well as the related manufacturers (the hosiery factory, the saddlery workshop, and so forth), are sending their most gifted children to attend the courses. The ghetto's specific conditions, which, in all areas, require people to adapt to severe conditions, also make it imperative that the courses be given at lightning, "American" speed. Nowadays, it is impossible to plan out lessons for years in advance as in normal times—the children have to be taught their trade in record time. For that reason as well the course has been scheduled for only two months and each course will be attended by 300 children. The course's classes run from 8 to 4 o'clock; there are 12 groups. Two hours of classes each day are assigned to lessons in sewing by machine and two hours to sewing by hand. In addition, the children are taught cutting and how to make technical drawings. Two hours per week are devoted to the study of materials, and they also learn about their machines. They also receive a one-hour lesson each week in the accounting and mathematics necessary to their profession. One hour a week is also dedicated to lessons in occupational hygiene. In developing the curriculum, the director of the Reclassification Commission did not, in spite of everything, abandon the more general subjects, so there is a lecture in Yiddish each day. On Saturday there are courses from eight to twelve o'clock. The staff is composed of instructors and teachers. For the convenience of the students there is a dining area on the premises where they consume the meals normally provided to working people in the ghetto. The establishment of these educational courses must be acknowledged as an event of far-reaching importance for the future of the children who reside in the ghetto.

B[ernard] O[strowski]

READING ROOMS FOR CHILDREN AND YOUNG PEOPLE

Through the efforts of [Henryk] Neftalin, the attorney and director of the department of population records, a few book collections, which are without owner and under no one's care, have been taken over by the Archives. Some two hundred books have been selected from among them. A pair of mobile libraries has been created for various institutions that are concerned with the welfare of children and young people. The first library, consisting of 150 volumes, was today sent to the residents of the Reform School. A further collection has been prepared for residents of the youth hostel. It is to be expected that this enterprise will be of great value for those affected; in any case, it will make their time pass more pleasantly.

B[ernard] O[strowski]

FRIDAY, JULY 24, 1942

LETTERS FROM THE LABOR CAMPS

Recently, the Information Bureau has been receiving a great many postcards from ghetto residents who had been sent out to various labor camps. Most of the correspondence has been coming from Jews originally from small towns around Łódź who have remained in the labor camps and whose families are at present here in the ghetto. The Information Bureau's announcements, which are posted at the busiest intersections, are a sure sign that correspondence [has arrived]. These announcements contain long lists of the names of people to whom correspondence has been sent. In cases where the Bureau of Information possesses the addresses, it forwards the correspondence directly. The Information Bureau also segregates correspondence arriving from the families of local residents in the Protectorate [General-gouvernement]. As a rule this latter type of correspondence is limited to a stock phrase about the sender's health, as in the pre-printed postal cards that are sent from the ghetto. However, the cards from the labor camps are more extensive. They are not, for the most part, of any general interest since nearly all of them are confined to purely family matters. However, one card, from a labor camp near Inowrocław, was spotted the other day in which the sender, apart from personal matters, includes the following sentence translated literally from German: "I am receiving such plentiful food here that I would be happy if you, my dear ones, were receiving even anywhere near as much."

SUNDAY, JULY 26, 1942

EXCREMENT REMOVAL

One of the Economics Department's greatest problems is the shortage of a sufficient staff of cesspool cleaners and, first and foremost, of horses, a problem from which the department, despite the best of intentions, finds it difficult to extricate itself. The shortage of horses has thinned the ranks of those engaged in excrement removal. The most painstaking attention should be given to this problem, for here the dry statistics are both eloquent and horrifying. To replace a draft horse is beyond human power, which has caused, and continues to cause, a mortality rate that is record high, even under ghetto conditions. Last year there were 250 cesspool cleaners, while now there are less than 120, or 130 at most. And none of them has quit his job. Some of them have died, and some, bedridden, have been placed in hospitals. Thus, for example, last week alone six cesspool cleaners died of complete exhaustion while 12 were sent to the hospital. Last year there were 30 wagons available, now there are 20 at most. Due to intense work by the Department of Economics, the entire set of wagons has been put into exemplary order. As we have already noted, the department recently set up a smithy and an assembly area for wagons. At present, a fourth wagon has already received rubber wheels. The situation can only be resolved by allotting a larger number of horses or by a considerable increase in manpower to perform the work connected with excrement removal.

RUMORS AGAIN

On Saturday a story was circulating in the ghetto that relatives of new arrivals from the provinces (children and elderly people in category "B"), who had been deported directly from those provinces, are alive and well in various camps in the vicinity of Poznań. Exact addresses and some people's serial numbers were even mentioned. As for the children, it was claimed that they had been placed in Poznań itself, in the so-called *Judenkinderlager* [Camp for Jewish Children] at 5 Rudolfstrasse.[76] Considering the wild rumors about the supposed fate of the above-mentioned deportees, these stories caused understandable interest in the ghetto and had a great calming effect as far as the deportees from our own ghetto were concerned. Unfortunately, the post office knows nothing about any such letters. Neither is there any knowledge of whether this news arrived here by some other route. In any case, it may be supposed that these rumors, like so many others, are without any foundation whatsoever.

MONDAY, JULY 27, 1942

A VENERABLE OLD WOMAN'S SUICIDE

Seventy-two-year-old Ema Toruńczyk, a resident of 74 Zgierska Street, took her own life today. The venerable old woman jumped from the fourth floor of the building in which she lived. She had been suffering from a nervous breakdown.

FROM WARSAW

Alarming news has reached the ghetto from Warsaw, causing a general feeling of depression. According to the report, mass deportations were carried out in Warsaw last week. Apparently, 10,000 people per day were removed from the Warsaw ghetto. The deportation proceeded block by block. Tragic incidents apparently occurred during those deportations. The chairman of the Warsaw Jewish Council, Adam Czerniakow, committed suicide as a result of this situation. According to information received today, the deportation action lasted three or four days.[77]

---

76. Those stories were, like the ones circulated earlier about the people deported from the Łódź ghetto, entirely fictitious. There was also no street in Poznań named Rudolfstrasse.

77. In the period from July 22 to October, 1942, over 300,000 Jews were deported from the Warsaw ghetto to the death camp at Treblinka, in the Bug River valley in Warsaw province.

Adam Czerniakow, the Chairman of the Warsaw ghetto Judenrat, committed suicide on July 24, 1942.

TUESDAY, JULY 28, 1942

NEWCOMERS

This morning 112 men from Turek were brought by truck to Bałut Market. They were placed in Central Prison at the disposal of the [German] authorities. The newcomers had no baggage in their possession.

WEDNESDAY, JULY 29, 1942

IN THE BAKERIES

The office personnel and all unskilled workers in the bakeries are to be replaced. Those who have been working there until now, or a certain number of them, will be replaced by white- and blue-collar workers who are physically exhausted. The point here is that work in the bakeries comes with the privilege of consuming as much bread as a worker wishes, obviously, while he is on the job, that is. Thus, sending people who are especially exhausted to work in the bakeries constitutes a real blessing for them. The Chairman, who initiated this important project, has charged a special commission with putting it into practice. Details of the project's implementation will follow in a day or two after [the commission] fully coordinates the rules with the Chairman.

THE SORTING HOUSE

The other day a sorting house and a storehouse for the shoes that have recently arrived in the ghetto in enormous quantities, along with shipments of clothes and underwear, was put into operation in a building at 9 Brzczińska Street. As we reported before, multi-ton trucks brought these shoes to the premises on Łagiewnicka Street where the saddlery is located. Now the shoes have been transported in lots to the new sorting house. Mr. [Izak] Zonabend, the technical director of the felt-shoe workshop and a leading expert on shoemaking, has been named director of the sorting house.

SZYMON MA[R]KOWSKI

who was hung in public last Tuesday, was 51 years old. He arrived in the ghetto in a transport of deportees from Pabianice. After one day here, in quarters at 7 Widok Street, he was sent out of the ghetto with the Pabianice group to perform manual labor. He escaped en route near Kutno. The other man who was hung, 16-year-old Josek Grynbaum, had escaped along with Makowski. Both men were caught and remanded to Radogoszcz, where their death sentences were passed. The condemned men were brought to the ghetto on the day of their execution. Makowski's wife and two of his children, who had been classified in category "B" (unfit for work), were taken away to parts unknown on the day before he was brought to the ghetto. Makowski's 16-year-old daughter lives here in the ghetto and works in the straw-shoe workshop. His two other young children are on the outskirts of the ghetto [in Marysin]. The daughter learned of her father's fate at the Bureau of Labor. Among other documents, exit papers for Palestine were found in Grynbaum's clothing. The bodies of the hanged men were buried in the cemetery here and their personal data was entered in the Burial Department's registry. There is no information as to where the body of Hertz, who had been hanged earlier (on February 21), has been buried, and his personal data does not appear in the local records.

THURSDAY, JULY 30, 1942

BREAD FOR EIGHT DAYS

The news hit the populace like a bolt from the blue. After the ample vegetable supplies of recent weeks, after entirely unexpected allocations of young potatoes (1 kilogram per person), optimism had begun to prevail among the populace. It was believed that the difficult pre-harvest period had already passed. Unfortunately, that joy was premature. Due to the meager stock of flour, on which we reported [yesterday], it has been necessary to reduce the daily bread ration. One loaf for eight days, not seven. To make matters worse, the vegetable supplies have also undergone changes. If this situation is not corrected with all possible haste it could prove fatal. The death rate, at present around 70 per day, could increase very sharply. Productivity is declining in the workshops. After the working person's allotment had been changed from 150 grams of bread with possibly either sausage or butter to vegetable soup, a marked drop in productivity was observed at once. Ordinarily bread would be distributed today for the new period. As usual, a great many people had eaten the last of what they had yesterday figuring that they would be able to go on living and eating "on credit," so the change in bread distribution has been a disaster for them. There will be many people, a great many, whose only meal will be their soup at work—if they are working. The rations for the last ten-day period were also consumed some time ago. The immediate future will tell what effect this change will have on the populace. For quite a number of ghetto dwellers the bread ration was only enough for five to six days, and they fasted the remainder of the period. Now things will be even worse.

FRIDAY, JULY 31, 1942

DEATHS AND BIRTHS

Today 95 deaths were registered. That figure, so high in relation to the number of deaths that have been occurring in recent days, is eloquent testimony to the populace's making every last possible use of the ration cards belonging to the deceased. It should be realized that today bread was issued for an eight-day period, and that until yesterday one could obtain a ten-day allotment of food. This is a sad but nonetheless telling sign of life in the ghetto.

One boy was born.

A SUICIDE

Today at nine o'clock in the morning, 19-year-old Bluma Rozenfeld (of 78 Zgierska Street) leaped from the fifth floor of the building at 8 Łagiewnicka Street. The young woman was taken to Hospital No. 1 by ambulance, past any hope of recovery.

THE HORRIFYING MORTALITY RATE

In seven months this year more than 13,000 people have died in the ghetto, whereas in the entire past year, 1941, 11,500 people died and, in 1940, 8,200, both before the ghetto was established and after. The mortality rate in recent months has simply been horrifying.

DEPORTEES FROM TUREK COUNTY

A few days ago we reported the arrival of 112 men in the ghetto from Turek county and some from Kalisz county. These are residents of Turek, Uniejów, the villages of Dobra, Koźminek, and Kalisz. After staying in Central Prison a few days, they have been given work in various local enterprises and, in a few days, will be quartered in private apartments. There are many tradesmen among them—tailors, shoemakers, locksmiths, and, *inter alia*, one doctor, Dr. Michał Haber from Turek. They had all lived in a village [of Kowale Pańskie] that was in direct proximity to Turek. In September of last year about 3,000 Jews from Turek and its environs were quartered in that village. They fared quite well in that settlement and were able to live rather freely. They would be sent out in groups to perform manual labor in the neighboring villages for the day. Their settlement was not enclosed in barbed wire and only the requisite signs at its outskirts revealed that it was inhabited by Jews. They had self-government, a canteen, an Order Service, a Council of Elders, and so on. Provisions were supplied by the municipality of Turek. Aside from their work in the village, the residents of the settlement engaged in trade, and, relatively speaking, wanted for nothing. As background, it is worth adding that, until the moment they left, the price of bread not purchased with ration cards was 2.50 [German] marks; the most expensive item was first-quality creamery butter, which cost 25 marks there. Everyone could afford to eat as many eggs or as much meat, not to mention the necessities, as he wished. During the settlement's existence of nearly a year, people were sent out several times to perform manual labor, chiefly to Inowrocław and Poznań, so that the number of residents in the settlement amounted to less than 2,000. The fittest-looking men, primarily the young men, were selected to leave and come to this ghetto. They worked as usual on the day of their departure, and that evening they were summoned to what was supposed to have been a meeting. For that reason none of them had brought any of his things and only a few of them arrived here with some small supplies of food. One of the new arrivals is a man who had been shot in the leg, a result of incidents accompanying their [impending] departure.

INTERMENT PROBLEMS

Recently, there have been instances in which bodies have remained unburied at the cemetery for three to four days. The macabre lines in the mortuary often consist of up to 110 corpses. The Burial Department barely has four horses at its disposal—one of which, moreover, is in poor health. After the recent inspection, the Burial Department was allocated horses that are not fit for work, while those that had been trained to pull hearses have been taken to perform other jobs.

The staff of the cemetery service, consisting of 140 people, is inadequate (under the circumstances) since it is, for the most part, made up of people in poor health, while those with more strength were recently sent to Poznań to perform manual labor.

ELIMINATION OF THE LAST VESTIGES OF TEACHING

The day before yesterday, the Chairman ordered the suspension (until further notice) of all the lectures, talks, and readings still being given at the reading room for young people in Marysin. Thus was all continuing education in the ghetto eliminated. This order was initiated from without.

B[ernard] O[strowski]

NEW RUMORS

I can offer an unconfirmed report from other sources that the populace is supposed to have bread for 10 days; the surplus thus gained is to serve as a supplement for the workers, in the quantities [150 grams] I have previously indicated.

During an inspection of the vegetable lot on Lutomierska Street, [Maks] Szczęśliwy is supposed to have said that, in view of the large surplus of potatoes and cabbage, the allocation in the first ten-day period of September will be increased to 5 kilograms.

B[ernard] O[strowski]

POPULATION COUNT AS OF AUGUST, 1942

On August 1, 1942, there were 101,259 people living in the ghetto; of that number, 43,220 were men and 58,039, women.

Population Changes in the Month of July

	Men	Women	Total
Level on July 1	44,051	58,495	102,546
Births	32	32	64
Stillbirths	1	—	1
Miscarriages	—	1	1
Arrivals from the Generalgouvernement and Warthegau	8	8	16
Arrivals from prison	3	—	3
Remains brought here (see Note 1)	1	—	1
Returned from manual labor	26	—	26
Arrived from Kalisz, Koźminek, and the settlement near Turek (Heidemühle [Kowale Pańskie])	333	302	635
Total increase in July	404	343	747
Deaths (see Note 2)	1,227	798	2,025
Left for Generalgouvernement	1	2	3
Left for manual labor	7	—	7
Total decrease in July	1,235	800	2,035
Actual decrease	831	456	1,287

Note 1: [Ignacy] Smoleński, the teacher who was shot to death while attempting to enter the ghetto (cf. the corresponding bulletin) and was buried in the cemetery here, is not included in the population statistics.

Note 2: In recent months the death rate has been disproportionately higher among men than among women. This was especially true in July.

THE NUMBER OF PEOPLE EMPLOYED BY THE ELDEST OF THE JEWS

According to data from the Personnel Department, the number of permanent employees [in Community offices throughout the ghetto] on August 1 of this year amounted to 12,880. There were 7,061 on August 1, 1941. In July of this year, 601 employees were hired. Their number on July 1 came to 12,620, that is, during the month of July it rose to 13,221, but 185 were taken off the rolls and 156 died; that is, the decrease came to 341, producing the figure of 12,880 cited above.

On January 1 of this year there were 9,776 permanent employees. The overall number of people working in the ghetto comes to nearly 80,000.

SUNDAY, AUGUST 2, 1942

A SUICIDE ATTEMPT

Lota Hirszberg, aged 56, a deportee from Berlin and a resident of 13 Urzędnicza Street, poisoned herself by taking an overdose of sleeping powders. Taken to the hospital, she died after a few hours without regaining consciousness.

PASSENGER SERVICE ON THE TRAM SYSTEM

which had been progressing so well right from the start and which was a real blessing, especially for the men and women workers employed in Marysin, has been, by order of the [German] authorities, eliminated.

FOOD QUOTAS FOR THE GHETTO IN AUGUST OF THIS YEAR

As we have already noted the quota for all types of flour (rye, potato starch, and whole wheat grain) has been set at 155,000 kilograms per week instead of the previous 202,000 kilograms. This represents a decline in quantity. Previously, the decline had been one of quality. Last year the ghetto received pure rye flour for baking its bread; later on, a 6 percent addition of potato starch became mandatory and was gradually increased to 15 percent; then the ghetto was ordered to use the so-called wheat grain flour, which has very little nutritional value. More recently, these additives have been accounting for as much as one-third of the weight of the bread. The above-mentioned quota is the entire amount of flour the ghetto will receive and, therefore, it must suffice for the baking of bread, home use, and use by the soup kitchens. The reason for the reduction is that this is the period before the new harvest and reserves have been exhausted. It is hoped that when grain is obtained from the new harvests this situation will improve.

B[ernard] O[strowski]

MONDAY, AUGUST 3, 1942

THE TELEPHONE WORKSHOP

Two days ago the ghetto was visited by a German commission that inspected the telephone workshop at 12 Smugowa Street, which was recently created by order of the [German] authorities, and the telephone exchange, which is called the Department of Low Voltage Equipment. The commission ordered that the workshop be put into operation at once, promising to send it the proper machinery. A number of tools have already been delivered. Consequently, the Bureau of Labor has, in recent days, been hiring workers for the new workshop.

FROM PRISON

During the last month the [German] authorities have brought quite a large number of Jews to Central Prison. They arrived here from various small towns in the surrounding area, such as Stryków, Łęczyca, Pabianice, and Lutomiersk; most of them had been in the prison in Łęczyca or the Bureau of Investigation in the city. They are all men, the youngest of them, fifteen years old. They remain in prison at the disposal of the secret police [Gestapo]. During the month, 16 other men were brought to the prison in the same capacity. In addition, three men were handed over by the Bureau of Investigation and were released on their own recognizance. Four children were handed over by the German police. They have been placed in a dormitory for people who work in the ghetto (at 19 Żydowska Street). They are: the Boczko sisters, 19-year-old Urszula, 15-year-old Gerda, and 14-year-old Dora; they were brought here from Kalisz. Born in Breslau, the sisters had recently been living in Bremen. In addition, 14-year-old Blima Kuper, from the small town of Dobra, was also handed over to the dormitory from the summer camp near Turek (see bulletin no. 102 [of July 31]).

RESULTS OF THE INCREASE IN THE DEATH RATE

The horrifying and unprecedented mortality rate in the ghetto has forced the Burial Department to issue rulings to prevent a recurrence of a recent problem, namely, often a body will remain at home for several days before a hearse arrives. There are known cases of a body remaining at home from a Thursday to a Monday, and that during a July heat wave. These delays are a result of problems with transportation. To resolve this situation the ruling provides that funeral processions and services may also be held on Saturday afternoons [at the close of Sabbath], a phenomenon very rare in the history of the Jews.

Beginning today, due to the shortage of hearses, ordinary flat wagons will be used to transport the dead.

B[ernard] O[strowski]

TUESDAY, AUGUST 4, 1942

THE DEPARTMENT OF LOW VOLTAGE EQUIPMENT

that recently went into operation, as we have already noted, has received a very substantial order from AEG [*Allgemeine Elektrizitätsgesellschaft*], a company in Berlin. Because of the order, the department has set up a pearling mill for mica, which is to be produced in large quantities, as contracted. Eighty people have already found employment in this project. That number will be increased to 500. This is an ideal occupation for older people since it does not require much physical effort.

OUTPATIENT CLINIC ELIMINATED

Since the ghetto's inception the Community outpatient clinic has been located at the pre-war specialists' ambulatorium at 17 Zgierska Street. Quite recently that outpatient clinic was eliminated because a new workshop needed to be installed in the area occupied by the clinic. The doctors who had been receiving patients there will continue their treatments afternoons at the outpatient clinics at 40 Brzezińska and 36 Łagiewnicka streets.

SEVENTY-SEVEN JEWS FROM A SETTLEMENT NEAR TUREK

arrived in the ghetto last Friday evening. Like their predecessors, this second group has been quartered in Central Prison.

WEDNESDAY, AUGUST 5, 1942

A SUICIDE

was attempted today by a deportee from Prague, Kurt Lichtenstein (born 1888 in Wartenburg, Bohemia), a former bank director. He cut the veins of his right wrist in his apartment at 2 Gnieźnieńska Street. He was taken to Hospital No. 1 in critical condition.

THURSDAY, AUGUST 6, 1942

A FLAT WAGON HEARSE

For a few days now, a new kind of "hearse" has been circulating about the ghetto. These are very large platform wagons harnessed to a single horse. The platform is covered with a box, made of unplaned boards, which opens from the center out. This unique type of "hearse" can pick up as many as 30 corpses in one run. Sad but true.

FRIDAY, AUGUST 7, 1942

ORDER SERVICE MEN ON ASSIGNMENT

For several days a group of 50 policemen has been leaving [the ghetto] each morning by order of the [German] authorities and returning late at night. They leave from Bałut Market by truck. In Pabianice, their job is to supervise and monitor the final details connected with the disposal of portable goods belonging to the Jews who had been driven from that town. It is still not known where the Pabianice Jews' belongings, or the clothing, bedding, and furniture they left behind, will be sent.

SATURDAY, AUGUST 8, 1942

A SUICIDE ATTEMPT

Today Ruchla Lichtenstein threw herself from the third-story window of her apartment at 8 Łagiewnicka Street. She had just turned 18 this spring. She was taken by droshky to Hospital No. 1, her condition hopeless.

MONDAY, AUGUST 10, 1942

EXTENSION OF TRAM SERVICE

Yesterday work was completed on laying the "loop" (the so-called S-ka) [an S-shaped track that allows trains to pass each other on a single rail line] at the intersection of Brzezińska and Łagiewnicka streets. A second sidetrack will be laid at the corner of Brzezińska and Marysińska streets when the required elbow-joint arrives from Germany. As we have already reported, the laying of sidetracks makes tram traffic possible on both tracks on Brzezińska Street, with no need to stop traffic when the tram goes to Bałut Market and back. It is worth stressing that the technical services of the Department of Transportation proved to be the most efficient in laying the sidetrack. This work was handled in less than three days, to the complete satisfaction of the technicians from the head office in the city. A good deal of credit in this goes to tram-service foreman Binem Kopelman, who, from the first, directed the laying of new tram tracks in the ghetto. This was no small job if one considers that the length of the rails in both directions, running along Marysińska Street to Radogoszcz station, amounts to 7 kilometers. In addition, an entire series of branch-lines were installed in record time, and under incredibly difficult conditions since it was winter, a time when tracks are never laid; [the branches run] to the station, the Bałut slaughterhouse, the tailors' clearing house, the vegetable and coal [storage] yards, and to the tailors' section on Jakuba Street. All this work was performed in the course of barely nine months. Another ghetto work record.

TUESDAY, AUGUST 11, 1942

SUICIDE ATTEMPTS

Fifty-year-old Izrael Sztern attempted to take his own life by hanging himself in his apartment at 51 Młynarska Street. He was saved at the last minute and taken to the hospital in critical condition.

Fifty-three-year-old Klara Weinberg (of 36 Dolna Street), a deportee from Vienna, slit her left wrist in an attempted suicide. She was taken to Hospital No. 1, her condition hopeless, and died there the next day.

JEWS FROM PABIANICE ARRIVE

Yesterday, 186 residents of Pabianice were brought to the ghetto. They are the last of the Jews from that town. There are very few women among them and scarcely five or six children. As is usually the case, the physically weak, the elderly, and the children—those in category "B"—have been resettled elsewhere. For the time being, the Jews from Pabianice have been quartered in Central Prison.

REMEDIES FOR EDEMA

As we have noted earlier, Mr. H[enryk] Wosk had presented the Department of Health with a series of preparations that, in his opinion, could cure people suffering from starvation edema, of whom there are, unfortunately, a considerable number in the ghetto. Thanks to the intervention of persons interested in this matter, so vital for the public at large, the director of the Department of Health, Dr. [Wiktor] Miller, decided to submit a few patients to a cure based on these preparations, which was monitored by doctors at Hospital No. 1. The results have been extremely encouraging. Nevertheless, Dr. Miller has acknowledged that the preparations are too costly since they must be made from food, which is in short supply in the ghetto. For that reason, he has taken a restrained attitude toward this plan of action. The day before yesterday this affair entered a new phase. Accompanied by the director of the Department of Health, Mr. [Henryk] Neftalin, the attorney, reported on this matter to the Chairman of the Eldest of the Jews. The Chairman decided that they should proceed at once to test the preparation's effectiveness on a larger number of people—even if only fifty—and, if it proves effective, to begin producing it immediately on a large scale. This experiment is to begin in the next few days and will be tried initially on only ten people.

LIQUIDATION OF THE PROVINCIAL GHETTOS

Aside from the news coming from Warsaw about the renewal of mass expulsions of Jews from the ghetto, transports of people resettled from small towns have been arriving here since yesterday, when about 180 people from Pabianice came. They were the last of the Jewish inhabitants of that town—mostly tailors who had been detained there until they finished their orders still outstanding. It should be noted that the sorting warehouse in Dąbrówka [Dabrowa], near Pabianice, in which about 250 Jews are working, is still in operation. People from Bełchatów arrived today: almost exclusively men, very few women, and all young people or people in the prime of life; they had almost no packages with them. At two o'clock, two other trucks filled with evacuees arrived here. It has been announced that 5,000 more resettled persons will be sent here tomorrow. We still do not know from where they are coming.

THE CENTRAL WORKSHOP BUREAU

can complain neither of a lack of orders nor a lack of work. Orders arrive constantly and, in many cases, as soon as one order is filled, another arrives. It sometimes happens that some workshop will have no work for a short period of time, but, in general, the ghetto has a great many orders, sometimes even more than it can fill. As usual, orders from the army are in the fore, whether procured directly through the commissary or through private companies. Recently, the entire ghetto has been talking about the winter uniform for the army, the so-called *Tarn-Anzüge* [camouflage dress]. The winter outfit consists of three parts: a shirt, pants, and hooded cap with drawstrings. One of its features is that it is reversible: the white side is for combat in snowy terrain and the grey side, for normal terrain. In all, the orders amounted to 140,000 pieces, and new orders may well be still on their way. Not long ago an order for 100,000 khaki uniforms for the *Überfall* [attack units] was filled. Aside from orders for the army, civilian orders continue to flow in but, unfortunately, they cannot always be filled since army orders have priority. Last week a curious incident occurred. Due to a shortage of buttons, it was impossible to send out an order of 200,000 otherwise completed pairs of pants. However, to demonstrate to the authorities that the workshops had done their part, the pants were sent to a storehouse on Bałut Market.

In the meantime, a small number of buttons arrived; they were entirely unsuitable, but since nothing better was to be had and this was a rush order, they began sewing them on at once. An improvised tailor shop was set up on Bałut Market, where up to 150 people worked for 24 hours straight. On the whole, it must be said that the Central Workshop Bureau has many problems because of a shortage of all the essential raw materials and prepared products. If one type of material is received, another is lacking. If, by some stroke of luck, they are both on hand, then there's a shortage of buttons or thread or tape. A great deal of time is wasted on constant correspondence, constant requisitioning, and constant monitoring of undelivered materials.

The hat department is turning out 15,000 padded winter caps for the armored [troops]. The metal workers have plenty of work. Enormous presses for stamping out army helmets are now being assembled. The carpenters' workshop is producing children's beds in quantities of 10,000 per month.

THURSDAY, AUGUST 13, 1942

FOUR HORSES

There were four wagon drivers in the group of 186 Jews who arrived in the ghetto on Monday from Pabianice. They drove here with their own horses and wagons. The horses and wagons have now become Community property and the owners of the horses have been employed as drivers. The ghetto possesses 101 horses at present. After the control of horses was assumed by the German authorities, the number of horse-drawn droshkys in service in the ghetto was reduced to 30.

MONDAY, AUGUST 17, 1942

SUICIDES

On Friday, Maks Kraus, a doctor of medicine resettled here from Prague, leaped from a fourth-story window at 14 Podrzeczna Street. He was killed on the spot. This is the first instance of a doctor committing suicide in the ghetto. Kraus was 63.

Anna Garfinkel, born in Łódź in 1902, swallowed a large amount of match heads in an attempted suicide. Taken from her apartment at 26 Dworska Street to Hospital No. 1, she died after suffering a few hours.

On Sunday, 57-year-old Szlama Rubin hung himself in his apartment at 38 Franciszkańska Street. Before the war, Rubin was well-known in Łódź as a man of commerce. The presumed cause of his suicide was depression at the loss of his wife, who had died a few days before.

On Sunday, 61-year-old Luiza Bloch, resettled here from Prague and a boarder at the Old People's Home at 56 Gnieźnieńska Street, poisoned herself with Veronal. Attempts to save her proved fruitless.

On that same day, 21-year-old Mosze Goldsztajn jumped from a second-story window at 13 Limanowski Street. He was taken to Hospital No. 1 in hopeless condition.

Herta Fiszer, resettled here from Prague, committed suicide by leaping into a well. She died on the spot. The incident took place at 9 Rymarska Street, where she had been living.

REMOVAL OF FIGURES AND CROSSES

By order of the [German] authorities, a group of workers arrived here from outside the ghetto on Saturday and removed the figure of Christ from its pedestal in front of the Church of the [Most Blessed] Virgin Mary on Zgierska Street. They also cut down four large wooden crosses in that church's courtyard. At the same time, other groups were dismantling a figure at 17 Zgierska Street. Because access was difficult, the process took several hours.

B[ernard] O[strowski]

RUMORS

There is a story circulating that, during the recent events in Warsaw [ghetto], the well-known Łódź rabbi, Dr. [Symcha] Treistman, took his own life. In addition, another Jew from Łódź, Laskowski, an engineer who had recently left here for Warsaw, is also supposed to have committed suicide.

TUESDAY, AUGUST 18, 1942

SHOOTINGS

Idel Zysman (of 10 Rybna Street) was shot to death yesterday at 8:00 P.M. The incident took place at the intersection of Podrzeczna and Stodolniana streets, just outside the barbed wire fence. Since the Zysman family are known smugglers, it can be assumed that the victim was killed while engaging in that practice.

A few days ago a 68-year-old unemployed woman, Fajga Kersz, of 7 Młynarska Street, was shot to death in Marysin at the intersection of Bracka and Przemysłowa streets at a point also outside the barbed wire fence. The incident took place at eleven o'clock in the morning.

WEDNESDAY, AUGUST 19, 1942

SUICIDES

Yesterday at 6 o'clock P.M., Gitla Basia Lipszyc threw herself from a third-story window at 4 Widok Street, where she resided. Death occurred on the spot.

Today, at one o'clock in the afternoon, Kuna Leska, born in 1915, jumped from a fifth-floor window at 22 Łagiewnicka Street. She was taken to Hospital No. 1, her condition hopeless.

AN EXTRACT FROM THE DEATH RECORDS

1.	Tusk, Machla Golda	aged 17	died July 10, 1942 (daughter)
2.	Tusk, Chaim Kasriel	aged 22	died July 26, 1942 (son)
3.	Tusk, Cywia	aged 45	died August 11, 1942 (mother)
4.	Tusk, Majer	aged 47	died July 28, 1942 (father)

Still Alive:

Tusk, Abram	aged 21
Tusk, Rywka	aged 15

RESETTLEMENT

Not a day passed last week without the authorities sending a number of Jews from small towns to this ghetto. Usually they arrive here straight from work, having had no opportunity to bring any clothing or linen with them. The painful responsibility of supplying them with everything they need has fallen to our ghetto. An organization has already been created which is so efficient that the newcomers are being absorbed without problems, even imperceptibly, and are being provided with the most essential items—apartments, furniture, bedding, etc., etc. After a few days they become regular ghetto residents. Upon their arrival, the newcomers are in the care of Order Service headquarters, which directs them to assembly points, and of the registration office of the Department of Vital Statistics, which compiles lists of the newcomers and, at the same time, provides them with cards for meals and coffee.

As soon as a newcomer receives an apartment and bread and ration cards, he can report to the Office for Resettled Persons, which issues him a voucher for clothing, underwear, and bedding. Then he takes that voucher to the distribution point at 2 Bazarna Street, where, at the discretion of that department's director, he receives bedding, blankets, covers or quilts. Upon presentation of another voucher at the Clothing and Underclothing Storehouse at 7 Widok Street, he receives the clothing and underclothing he requires.

Recently, any newcomer, regardless of any sum he had been paid [on arriving in the ghetto?] receives an advance of 10 marks for his current expenses.

FRIDAY, AUGUST 21, 1942

THE FIGHT AGAINST CRIME

Today the Chairman ordered the publication of the following circular, which is quite telling: "I have recently discovered that thefts are still on the increase in workshops, distribution points, bakeries, and kitchens. Since in today's harsh circumstances those acts strike at the vital interests of the populace as a whole and can result in dire consequences, I have decided that my court will mete out punishments of increased severity for such crimes. Toward that end, I have ordered a special disciplinary section established at Central Prison. Prisoners in this section will be deprived of the right to leave their cells and of conversation with, or visits from, relatives. Those who break the law will lose the right to work, which in turn will cause their food allocations to be decreased. I have also discovered that in many instances crimes are going unpunished because workshop directors or the criminal's fellow workers are concealing evidence. Justice is also being thwarted, by means of intervention, by agencies of the Order Service. Therefore, I will again make it known that any intervention whatsoever is forbidden and anyone who intervenes in a criminal matter will be held as responsible as the criminal himself. Superiors who knowingly conceal from the prosecutor a criminal act committed by a subordinate will be punished with equal severity. At the same time, I am forbidding anyone to conduct investigations in his own area. In such cases sole jurisdiction belongs to the prosecutor's office or the Bureau of Investigation and, when speed is of the essence, to the appropriate sections of the Order Service. The settling of such matters by a dismissal from work does not constitute sufficient punishment."

MONDAY, AUGUST 24, 1942

WEATHER

The hottest day of the year. The temperature reached 42 degrees.

DANGER OF TYPHOID

The increasing number of cases of typhoid fever has made it necessary to post proclamations containing universally known means for maintaining cleanliness and safety in order to safeguard against the threat of typhoid.

LITZMANNSTADT-GETTO, AUGUST 25, 1942

For nearly two weeks we have been experiencing a great drought, with temperatures reaching as high as 40 degrees. This beautiful August heat wave has had a disastrous effect on agriculture in the ghetto. First to be negatively affected was the cabbage, which has literally been devoured by an enormous mass of caterpillars throughout nearly the entire ghetto. Where, yesterday, beautiful heads of both regular and so-called Italian cabbages were green and growing, today, there are only the skeletons of leaves and stalks.

The owners are clearing away the remains of the vegetation with uncommon speed; what were once beautiful garden plots, a real credit to intense, unflagging labor, are now desolate, abandoned.

The Agricultural Department had, in fact, at one point recommended a remedial chemical known as *Spruzit*, but it proved of little use due to the heat wave, when thousands of caterpillars settled so thickly on the leaves as to make them seem a different color. Those familiar with such matters could not recall any such insect invasion having happened for a long time. Worst of all, it happened so suddenly and so rapidly that it was impossible to combat the crisis directly. The infestation developed faster than people were able to clear their vegetables away, for it is difficult to pick everything at once and bring it to an apartment before it wilts.

In spite of the fact that lately very few vegetables, in fact next to none, have been coming into the ghetto, and that until now [cabbage] leaves were a much sought-after item, there had of late been such a great supply that it proved difficult to find buyers, and a large portion of the leaves simply have rotted. They rotted and perished, and the work of so many hands, so much energy, and the last ounce of people's strength were lost along with them! This can only be understood by those who fell victim to the plague, little people without resources, who worked alone or with their families, giving every free minute they had to that tedious, back-breaking work.

And now those little people are helpless, in distress . . .

They had thought that by Sisyphean labor they would be able to set a little something aside for the hard winter months to come, they believed in some better tomorrow, assured them by the labor done in the hours free from the demands of the ghetto, and now, suddenly, disillusionment and despair!

But a Jew is a fatalist. He believes that if something happened, it was meant to be.

And, besides, he consoles himself with the knowledge that he has already suffered greater losses and ordeals and somehow survived them too. He must only think of how to protect his remaining vegetables from this plague, since the caterpillars are already moving on to the beets (for lack of anything else to feed on), so those too will soon be under serious attack.

Perhaps a salt, or even a soda solution will be found so that we can somehow go on living and survive this grievous affliction while we wait for a better tomorrow. Such is our mentality!

LITZMANNSTADT-GETTO, AUGUST 28, 1942

As a rule, until now, the rations for the next ten-day period have been announced before the end of the current period and all the ghetto populace's conjectures are focused on the amount and the quality of that next allocation. Will there be a lot of potatoes in the ration, how many groceries, will there be any meat? and so forth . . . The ghetto's equilibrium and peace of mind have been violated, something is wrong, for here we are on the day before the new ration and, for some reason, no one is talking about it. Perhaps that's a slight exaggeration; people are talking about it, but not as they used to. Here and there one hears questions about what's come in and whether there's more this time, but the makeup of the new rations is not emerging as one of the leading current concerns. Something has happened that has overshadowed that concern and shoved it into the background: the new deportees being settled here, an action abounding in nightmarish stories.

Jews have arrived here from Pabianice, Bełchatów, Ozorków, Zelów, Wieluń, Stryków, Sieradz, Łask, and, recently, from Zduńska Wola, and the process continues.

At the same time, bedding from those small towns has no longer been arriving by truck but by tram dump cars, and this new phenomenon has come to dominate everyone's thoughts. The newcomers tell all sorts of stories about their recent experiences, but the same note of pain and despair runs through all their accounts. Not everyone has arrived here—families have been separated and it is difficult even to determine why some were sent to this ghetto while others had to take another, more dolorous journey. It is difficult to discover any guidelines in all of this, which is precisely what grieves everyone most. Once again a cloud of uncertainty has seized the ghetto; people are shaken by the tales the newcomers tell and by the great unknown, which is worse than the worst reality. In such circumstances, can one ascribe great importance to the composition of the new rations? It is known that there are striking deficiencies in the provisions, that the food to be distributed is arriving in the ghetto at the last minute, and that it is rare for the average ghetto dweller to have any food left for the last day in a ten-day period. Today, the composition of the new ration is an important—no, a most essential matter; for 95 percent of the population it is a vital question, a matter of survival, and yet in this ten-day period that question has receded from the foreground and rations are discussed only in whispers. The survival of one's fellow Jews from the small towns and their pain and suffering are, after all, more important.

Pale shadows trudge through the ghetto, with edemic swellings on their legs and faces, people deformed and disfigured, whose only dream is to endure, survive—to live to see a better tomorrow without new disturbances, even if the price is a small and inadequate ration.

SUNDAY, AUGUST 30, 1942

WEATHER

No change in the weather. The sky is cloudless and the temperature reached 45 degrees in the afternoon.

DEATHS AND BIRTHS

On Saturday and Sunday, 105 people died in the ghetto. Three boys and two girls were born.

A SUICIDE

A 61-year-old former resident of Berlin, Hilda Schultz, of 18 Ciesielska Street, has attempted to take her own life by ingesting Veronal. She was taken to Hospital No. 1.

LITZMANNSTADT-GETTO, AUGUST 30, 1942

Strange are the ways of life in the ghetto, abounding in surprises of every sort. Nothing is logically predictable, and people often wrack their brains over one or another turn of events that had seemed completely clear but underwent a change at the last minute. Thus, the decentralization of our ghetto by means of mass resettlement remains, to this day, unexplained, and the fact that Jews are being resettled here from small towns in the vicinity as well defies reason. This constant movement of populations creates enormous uncertainty, undermines normal life, and has a very negative effect not only on people's frame of mind (which, at the present time, is not even taken into account!), but has a dramatic impact on production in the workshops. At present, about 75 percent of the ghetto's population is working, working and barely keeping body and soul together, but it does all this for an illusory peace, which is, however, regularly disturbed either by resettlement or by constant rumors of resettlement.

The problem of the ghetto's food supply is not the least of the many surprises.

When everything indicates some stabilizing in the food supply, when there is every basis for a favorable resolution to that problem, all hopes are suddenly dashed and the populace is faced with a reduction in what are already "hunger" rations. And, vice versa, when the populace has already gotten used to thinking that it is now receiving the maximum that could be expected, a ration that is not only quantitatively greater but of a higher quality than its predecessor is announced. The ghetto's populace receives this news not only with joy but with a kind of enthusiasm, as a promise of improvement, salvation . . .

Thus, the ration announced yesterday, in which the amount of groceries was increased by 50 percent (!) came as a genuine surprise. Not only was there no reduction as people had been saying there would be, but there was an increase, and by 50 percent at that! At the same time, 4 kilograms of potatoes per capita have been announced for the next ten-day period, whereas, thus far, the official allocation had amounted to only 2.5 kilograms. Moreover, an allocation of fresh vegetables has been promised—if they arrive—and that too may include potatoes.

What is the determining factor here? What influences this situation? Why do omens of improvement so often end with things becoming worse and vice versa?

These are questions that disturb the entire population and for which no answers can be found, answers that may not even be found before the war is over!

It could be whim, and it could be necessity!

MONDAY, AUGUST 31, 1942

DEATHS AND BIRTHS

The death records indicate that there were 97 deaths today, a fact which is connected with bread having been distributed yesterday. The births of two boys were registered.

A SUICIDE

Sara Felicja Weinberger, born in Łódź in 1912, leaped from the third floor of her residence at 73 Franciszkańska Street and died on the spot.

A SHOOTING

Liba Charłupska, a seamstress, of 21 Rybna Street, born in 1911 in Sieradz, was shot to death at 10:30 A.M. The incident took place outside the ghetto, in the vicinity of

Hospital No. 3, at 75 Drewnowska Street. By order of the [German] authorities the victim's body was placed in the hospital's mortuary.

[TUESDAY, SEPTEMBER 1, 1942][78]

Population Changes in the Month of August, 1942

	Men	Women	Total
Level as of August 1, 1942	43,220	58,039	101,259
Increases in the month of August			
Births	25	17	42
Stillbirths	2	—	2
Miscarriages	1	—	1
Arrivals from the Generalgouvernement	17	16	33
and from Warthegau prison	—	1	1
Remains from outside the ghetto (from the Zduńska Wola transport)	22	5	27
Returned from [camp at the] *Reichautobahn* [in construction from Poznań to Frankfurt]	77	—	77
Resettled from labor camp (see Note 1)	88	—	88
Resettled from various towns in Warthegau (see Note 2)	3,188	3,056	6,244
Total increase in August	3,420	3,095	6,515
Decreases in August, 1942			
Deaths (see Note 3)	1,012	726	1,738
Left for Reichautobahn [construction]	75	—	75
Total decrease	1,087	726	1,813
Actual increase	2,333	2,369	4,702
Level as of September 1, 1942	45,553	60,408	105,961

Note 1: Laborers [who had been sent out of] this ghetto and Jews from other towns arrived here from the Eberswald camp, not far from Berlin.

Note 2: From the following towns: Turek, Pabianice, Bełchatów, Zelów, Wieluń, Ozorków, Sieradz, Warta, Zduńska Wola, and Łask. In July, 1942, there were 635 Jews resettled here from Kalisz, Turek, and Koźminek; in the month of June—over 200 Jews from Bełchatów and Żelów; and in May—some 7,000 from Pabianice, Brzeziny, and Ozorków; the total number resettled here from the smaller towns by September 1—14,350.

Note 3: The mortality rate has decreased since July; in July, 2,025 people died, whereas 1,738 people died in August; this comes to a daily average of 56 in August compared to 65 in July. The reduction in the mortality rate is probably due to the improved food situation.

78. Beginning on September 1, 1942, all the daily bulletins, with only one exception, are in German. The German portion of the *Chronicle* for the final quarter of 1942 does, however, include a few essays on current events written in Polish. And thus, for purposes of clarity, each text that was translated from Polish will be marked by a dagger.

TUESDAY, SEPTEMBER 1, 1942†

PATIENTS EVACUATED

Yesterday evening the [German] authorities demanded that a delegation of 50 policemen be sent to Bałut Market at 5 o'clock this morning. The Order Service headquarters thought it was a matter of sending policemen to small towns in the vicinity to supervise the vacating of apartments of Jews who were being deported. It is known that for several weeks officials of the local Order Service have been ordered to perform such duties, but that they have always returned to the ghetto in the evening. However, it turned out that they were to perform a function of a completely different nature. At precisely five A.M. trucks pulled up to Bałut Market accompanied by numerous policemen, both in uniform and in plain clothes, and hospital orderlies. The police were ordered to close off the street at the points where the vehicles were to park. The vehicles were first sent to the hospital on Wesoła Street, where the patients were evacuated. Other hospitals (there are four in the ghetto) were evacuated during the day, in addition to the children's hospital on Łagiewnicka Street, the sanatorium in Marysin, and Central Prison. During the night of September 1, the night staff of orderlies and nurses was present at the evacuations, whereas the day staff, doctors included, was not allowed into the hospitals. The hospitals were cordoned off by the Order Service, which had received orders to allow no one near the places being evacuated. There were many cases of patients, especially those not seriously ill, making escapes under dramatic circumstances. In connection with the escapes, the authorities demanded that all escapees be brought in for deportation. To execute that order, there were searches for escapees that very night. Since it was impossible to catch them all, people who had obtained the so-called hospital qualification [that is, admission] were also brought in. The evacuation of the patients has shocked the ghetto and brought on a mood of panic. The darkest predictions are on everyone's lips.

LITZMANNSTADT-GETTO, SEPTEMBER 1, 1942†

Today, on the third anniversary of the war, the ghetto awoke to a sort of eerie nightmare.

Before curfew, a truck with two trailers, escorted by representatives of the authorities (in a private car), pulled up in front of the hospital on Wesoła Street and all patients were ordered loaded onto the truck and trailers. These vehicles then went from Wesoła Street down Lutomierska Street to the corner of Pawia Street, and turned by the hospital on Drewnowska Street, and the patients were then taken outside the ghetto. This action was repeated on Łagiewnicka and Mickiewicz streets. All the patients were evacuated from the first hospital, in the second, it is said that some of the patients saved themselves by fleeing, while in the other two hospitals some patients apparently jumped over the hospital fence.

Upon entering a hospital, the authorities apparently demanded a list of the patients and then, after the evacuees were loaded and counted, insisted, under threat of the most severe sanctions, that the escapees be turned over to them.

The tragic plight of the patients, and their families, is beyond description.

Each of them was leaving someone behind—a brother, a sister, a father, a mother, a cousin, an aunt. Such despair was not even seen during the resettlement actions at their most intense, nor was so much weeping and lamentation heard [as from] those little groups of tearful women, children, and helpless men who had been separated from their loved ones in such nightmarish fashion.

And how much effort and maneuvering had been required to get them into the hospital in the first place! Pull was needed to obtain a bed, even one in a corridor, a passageway. How happy was the family that was able to place a loved one in the care of a hospital! Then, all of a sudden . . .

No one knows the reason behind this event except, perhaps, that new workshops are to be installed in the hospitals. But weren't there barracks being built for patients on Krawiecka and Tokarzewski streets that were to be completed soon? Then why the haste? Why so suddenly?

People are terribly agitated, a macabre mood prevails, and it is still difficult to arrive at any definite sense of the situation. The Jewish authorities were shocked by this new ruling and are completely unable to express any opinion on the subject. No intervention is possible, for the vehicles have already left and are far from the ghetto now. The Chairman was in the hospital on Drewnowska Street since early morning (no one has heard any report on the outcome of his intervention) and Mr. [Dawid] Gertler [the head of the Special Department] has been busy at the hospital on Łagiewnicka Street, surrounded by petitioners of every sort.

But meanwhile, life goes on. Wagons of potatoes are arriving, overshadowing other concerns. Anyone who has not been directly affected thinks of tomorrow, believing that fate may protect him from new trials. People's minds have been blunted—the stomach rules over everything!

Sad, painful, but, unfortunately, true!

[Józef Zelkowicz]

LITZMANNSTADT-GETTO, SEPTEMBER 2, 1942†

All of yesterday, day and night, the populace was affected by nightmarish experiences.

The authorities have ordered the Eldest of the Jews to hand over all those who fled the hospitals and, in the end, the number of persons who were to be rounded up for deportation today was set at 200. Consequently, the Order Service has been issued strict orders to round up the hospital escapees who are in hiding or to arrest members of their families if they fail to determine where the escapees are hiding. On the alert, the Order Service rounded up more than 200 and the extras were released today.

There were, however, instances in which the escapees were not found, and [in one case] a wife was taken instead of her husband, but, as it turned out, the husband had already been evacuated the day before. In accordance with the authorities' ruling, people who had applied for admittance to the hospital were also taken. The hospital prepared a list of their names, on which basis the Order Service brought in candidates for deportation from their apartments.

Terrified that his aged mother would be evacuated, a son died of a heart attack and, two hours later, the mother, as a person who had qualified for admission to the hospital, was taken away by the Jewish police. One woman fled the hospital the day after having been sutured following childbirth (the child had been stillborn!), crossed over the bridge and, today, died. The exact number of victims cannot be determined yet: there were those who were direct victims of the evacuation and others who were affected indirectly, as well as accidental victims. Nurses who tried to help patients escape were fired on but, fortunately, none were hit.

In the case of children's diseases, the patients had intentionally been kept in the hospital a little longer to avoid spreading the infections, and those children, who were essentially cured and healthy, have fallen victim to this terrible ruling. All those who had used special "pull" to stay on at the hospital were also among the victims. This is the reason that so many patients were able to escape by their own strength and drag themselves to their apartments.

Today, at around 10 A.M., that same truck with two trailers loosely covered with boards reappeared, and the evacuation of the above-mentioned 200 escapees began.

Again there was despair, weeping, and lamentation on the streets. These were people who had been saved from the lion's jaws once, and who, now, voluntarily or under constraint, reported for a journey into the unknown.

The events of the last two days have eclipsed all other problems, even ones as important as food supply. Potatoes continue to arrive in the ghetto, and in increased amounts, but this seems of no interest to anyone. Everyone has a loved one who has been affected since, besides the hospitals, there were evacuations at the sanatoriums and at Central Prison, where some people were serving a sentence of 48 hours for failing to observe the regulations concerning blackouts.

Depression and sadness reign in the workshops, in many of which no work is being done—all people are doing is sharing impressions and making the most diverse conjectures.

A sad page in the history of our ghetto.

[Józef Zelkowicz]

LITZMANNSTADT-GETTO, SEPTEMBER 14, 1942†

The period of September 5–12, 1942, will leave indelible memories among that portion of the ghetto's population on whom fate smiles and who survive the war.

One week, eight days that seem an eternity!

Even now it is difficult to grasp what has occurred. An elemental force has passed through the ghetto and swept away some 15,000 people (no one knows the exact number yet) and life appears to have resumed its former course.

In his speech of September 4, 1942 (at 4:00 P.M.), the Chairman announced that, by order of the authorities, about 25,000 Jews under the age of 10 and over 65 must be resettled out of the ghetto. Those were the instructions received by the Resettlement Commission which is composed of the following: commandant [of the Order Service, Leon] Rozenblat, [Szaja-Stanisław] Jakobson, [Henryk] Neftalin, the attorneys, commissioner [Zygmunt] Blemer, Grynberg, a legal trainee, and a clerical staff. The commission was located on the third floor at 4 Kościelny Square (on the premises of the Main Trade Commission), while the preparatory work was done on the second floor, on the premises of the Department of Statistics, and consisted of copying out the names and exact ages of families on separate cards, going through the 19 volumes of the population records, building by building, apartment by apartment. The work was initially done in two 12-hour shifts; later, the 38-person crews (two people for each volume) were changed every eight hours. The preparatory material, arranged by streets, then went up to the third floor from which it was sent to individual Order Service precincts for execution.

In accordance with the Chairman's proclamation on the 4th of this month, pedestrian traffic after 5 P.M. has been suspended until further notice since the 5th of this month, and it was then that the Jewish police's action to round up all persons subject to resettlement began. The arrest of persons to be resettled proceeded on the basis of lists supplied by the Resettlement Commission, which in turn received information from the above-mentioned[?] commission on population records. Upon receiving the cards, the Jewish police collected people in different parts of town and delivered the children, the elderly, and the ill—on foot or by wagon—to the assembly points. It was said that had this action encountered any difficulties or resistance, the German authorities would have stepped in. The action, however, had scarcely begun when on Monday, the 7th of this month, there was talk that the German authorities, who were not relying on lists but were guided solely by visual impressions, had taken the initiative.

In point of fact, the operation proceeded as follows block after block was surrounded by the Jewish police and then each building surrounded by a host of police and Jewish firemen and entered by a representative of the authorities (the Gestapo). A shot was fired as the signal to assemble, and then all the residents of a given building were assembled in the courtyard, arranged in two rows, and subjected to inspection by representatives of the authorities. In the meantime, the Jewish police were searching the apartments and bringing out anyone who had been hiding or people who were ill. In the smaller buildings, this operation often took only a few minutes. The deportees and those who were to remain were separated into two groups. Those selected for resettlement were sent by wagon to the assembly points. The hospital on Drewnowska Street was the assembly point for the left side of the ghetto while the hospital on Łagiewnicka Street served the right hand side. Since this operation took place at an extremely rapid pace and wagons were constantly leaving from and arriving at the hospital, the clerical workers sent to the assembly points to make lists of the deportees were unable to list all the people brought there and only a portion were included in their lists, while others were taken from the ghetto by vehicle and their personal data was not, and may never be, established.

In light of these incidents, the work of the Resettlement Commission and the work done in conjunction with the commission on population records have proven entirely superfluous, even though that work continued without interruption throughout the entire resettlement action. The entire population has been listed on some 60,000 cards, which remain in the commission's hands and may possibly serve as a point of reference when the next census is taken.[79]

79. In another copy of the *Chronicle* the last sentence reads: "Information has been taken down from more than 60,000 [ration] cards and is being kept for reasons unknown."

To carry the weak and the sick to the wagons, the so-called white guard, i.e., the porters from the Department of Food Supply, headed by Jankiel Rozenberg (*Chmol*) were mobilized; the porters' families were exempted from resettlement.

When the wagons were being loaded, there were incidents in which people, either because of a misunderstanding or intentionally, attempted to join the group that was remaining here; retribution was very swift in such cases (such people were shot without warning), and took place right before the eyes of the assembled tenants of a building. That, however, did not prevent people from escaping from the wagons or while en route, or from being rescued from the hospital by means both legal and illegal. For the most part, it was people employed in workshops who were rescued legally. In such cases the appeals went from a representative of a workshop to Aron Jakubowicz, who during the operation played a very active role in exempting the so-called workshoppers, finding positive solutions in many cases.

To encourage the Jewish police and the firemen to conduct the operation conscientiously, promises that their closest relations would be spared had been made. Thus, their children were placed in a hospital and isolated from the rest of the population, and an isolation ward was set up in Marysin for those relations who were elderly or under special protection. There were some 1,500 of these lucky ones who, in spite of their age and infirmity, were spared resettlement. Of course, these were not people who were making any contribution to society, not even people able to perform any especially valuable work in the ghetto but were, we repeat, people with connections.

But if being loaded onto a wagon did not block off every avenue of escape, being loaded onto a 5-ton truck whose trailers have high plank siding meant that every hope was crushed. These vehicles would leave the ghetto at once and return in less than an hour. From this one may conclude that the deportees were let off somewhere not too far from the ghetto.[80]

Dramatic scenes were played out in the hospitals. Escape attempts came to a bloody end. Anyone who attempted to save himself by fleeing and was spotted by the authorities had to pay for that attempt with his life. Because the operation proceeded so rapidly, the authorities gave no thought to the motives or causes for any particular act. At 38 Zgierska Street, an elderly woman from Sieradz did not understand if she had been ordered to go to the left or the right and, instead of going to a wagon, she walked over to a group of "remainers." This the authorities interpreted as an escape attempt. The woman was shot to death on the spot. At 3 Zgierska Street, Rozenblum, a 13-year-old boy, attempted to hide in a dustbin; he was seen and shot dead. There were many such victims but even more numerous were cases of people who were wounded when a crowd was fired on.

On Wednesday, the 9th of this month, the operation seemed to have concluded on the left side of the ghetto and people had even been permitted to come out in

---

80. The 5-ton trucks took deportees to a railroad station outside of Łódź, where the victims were loaded onto railroad cars and sent via Kutno to Koło, and from there taken directly by vehicle to the death camp in Chełmno (Kulmhof), a distance of 14 kilometers. Sometimes the victims were also transported by narrow-gauge railway from Koło to the village of Powiercie, from which they were all either taken by vehicle or herded on foot to Chełmno.

groups to be given bread. People rushed to the co-ops, but not all the distribution points had bread in their stock rooms and orders were rushed to the bakeries. On the whole, things ran rather smoothly here. But it was another matter with the collection of the 8-kilogram potato ration, the lion's share of which the ghetto had not managed to obtain before the *szpera* [Gehsperre: curfew]. People were simply starving. They had no bread, no potatoes, there had been no deliveries, and it is understandable that when potatoes and cottage cheese began to be distributed in the dairy stores—on the Bazar [Square], and on Wesoła and Rybna streets—enormous lines formed. Suddenly, a few representatives of the authorities drove up from the direction of Limanowski Street. Seeing crowds of people on the street when the szpera had not yet in fact been rescinded, they opened fire; the crowd quickly scattered to the adjacent buildings and hid in apartments. Among these people were some who had already been "commissioned" and exempted from deportation. The authorities, however, summoned everyone outside from the buildings on Rybna Street. And here, again, people were lined up in twos on the street, separated into groups, and some earmarked for deportation. Those attempting to flee were shot. Apparently, 17 people were wounded. At another point, on Wesoła Street, people were driven from the line-up to the old Jewish cemetery, while those on Bazarna Street were brought to a building at 10 Bazarna Street where, through an opening in the fence, they were also told to go on to the cemetery. Suddenly, five representatives of the authorities came running up from the direction of Krótka Street and seized three [women] escapees. The crowd assembled at the cemetery was called on to hand over any escapees under threat that they would all be shot if they refused to obey. Since that was purely a random gathering of people, there was no question of determining who the guilty parties were.

Those people were kept at the cemetery for about two hours. Many were selected for deportation, and five were shot dead. Those who were present at the scenes played out at the cemetery have had much to say on the subject.

After the conclusion of the regular operation, a so-called random verification took place. It was not carried out in the courtyards of buildings this time, rather, all residents (on the smaller streets) were called out to the street and, again, many people who had formerly been exempted were taken away to the wagons. There were many victims among those who, in disregard of the curfew, found themselves by chance in a neighborhood that was being checked.[81] On the whole, however, the repeated inspections did not produce much of a yield, and there were buildings from which not a single person was seized.

The criteria for specific inspections varied greatly, as is demonstrated by what occurred at 38 Zgierska Street. This building, which has many outbuildings, is inhabited by more than 200 families. One of the outbuildings on the right-hand side also has an exit and windows that face No. 40. The inspection of 38 Zgierska Street was already completed, while the one in the neighboring building was still in progress; the inhabitants of the first outbuilding who had been exempted from resettlement

81. In another copy of the *Chronicle* this sentence reads: "Since the szpera [curfew] had been partially rescinded on the left side of the ghetto and people were moving about freely there, many ghetto dwellers ended up, by chance, in an entirely different section and were there subjected to examination."

returned to their apartments and, out of curiosity, looked out their windows at the operation in progress in the building next to theirs. This was noticed by the inspecting officers, who then ordered everyone out into the courtyard. During this new inspection 40 of the 50 people present were selected for deportation. It was only due to intervention by A[ron] Jakubowicz that many of those people, workshop employees for the most part, were released. A few, however, did fall victim to chance.

Intervention was possible on the spot, and, in many cases, actions taken by our police proved effective. A person could be rescued before the loading took place or after; everything depended on the individual [German] police officer. There are known cases of direct personal intervention. A 40-year-old woman employed by the Community, when selected for deportation, asked the inspecting police officer, in good German, why she, a woman in her prime, was being deported. The officer thought for a moment, glanced over at her, and ordered that she be allowed to remain in the ghetto. There were cases of quite haggard people being allowed to remain because representatives of our police stated that they were good, useful ghetto workers, and in other cases it sufficed for a Jewish policeman to claim a deportee as a relative. Clearly, all this was a matter of chance, the exception, not the rule. In many cases, however, outward appearance was the deciding factor in obtaining an exemption. It was observable that people who looked better, and particularly those wearing clean clothes, were not taken. There were cases of people over 70 being allowed to remain, while middle-aged and even young people were taken if their appearance betrayed weak health.

As we have already seen, names were not listed when people were seized in the buildings, and they were often taken so quickly to the trucks at the assembly points and driven away that the officials assigned to draw up the lists were barely able to record a small percentage of those being resettled. Since no other lists had been drawn up—at least no such lists have been sent to the ghetto—it is impossible to speak with any accuracy about individuals or about the number of people who have been resettled out of the ghetto. The figure 14,432 has been mentioned, but it does not seem likely that such an exact number could be determined. It may be possible to determine the total resettled after another census is taken, but none are under consideration at the moment. Besides, it is doubtful whether the authorities would agree to an interruption of work, without which a census campaign is unthinkable.

No one knows what will happen next. Things have to be put into some sort of order because many families have been using, and continue to use, ration cards belonging to resettled family members, while in other instances, deportees have inadvertently taken an entire family's food ration cards with them. People are talking about horrific incidents in this regard; in one case, a wife who was resettled along with her three children took all their cards with her and her husband starved to death after five days of nothing whatsoever to eat. The people seized by the authorities from the potato lines on Bazar [Square] and from in front of the dairy co-ops had their [vegetable] coupons and food cards in their possession, so here again families were left without rations. The Ration Card Department has had enormous work to do in connection with these cases, but only after a new census is taken will it be possible finally to determine who is entitled to rations.

This could not be of less concern to the populace itself, for it is still under the effect of the shock it has experienced and, moreover, is accustomed to associating every new development with yet another calamity. So it was wise to let things stand as they were until people regained a certain calm.

Incidentally, the populace's strange reaction to the recent events is noteworthy. There is not the slightest doubt that this was a profound and terrible shock, and yet one must wonder at the indifference shown by those—apart from the ones who were not directly affected and who returned to normal life at once—from whom loved ones had been taken. It would seem that the events of recent days would have immersed the entire population of the ghetto in mourning for a long time to come, and yet, right after the incidents, and even during the resettlement action, the populace was obsessed with everyday concerns—getting bread, rations, and so forth—and often went from immediate personal tragedy right back into daily life. Is this some sort of numbing of the nerves, an indifference, or a symptom of an illness that manifests itself in atrophied emotional reactions? After losing those nearest to them, people talk constantly about rations, potatoes, soup, etc.! It is beyond comprehension! Why this lack of warmth toward those they loved? Naturally, here and there, there are some mothers weeping in a corner for a child or children shipped from the ghetto, but, as a whole, the mood of the ghetto does not reflect last week's terrible ordeal.

Sad but true!

[Józef Zelkowicz]

SEPTEMBER 1–19, 1942[82]

WEATHER

During the first twenty days of September the weather was lovely and sunny, with only a few brief showers. Cool autumn mornings, the nights mostly very cold; only in the last ten days have the nights become warmer, the average daily temperature rising to 25 degrees. This spell of fine weather has caused the crops to ripen—tomatoes, potatoes, and other vegetables—and there are already many empty, harvested fields to be seen.

DEATHS AND BIRTHS

On September 1—56 deaths, no births.
On September 2—46 deaths, no births.
On September 3—62 deaths, 2 births (1 boy, 1 girl).
On September 4—35 deaths, no births.

On [September] 5 and 6, Order Service headquarters did not submit a report since, because of the curfew, it did not receive the relevant data from the Department [of Vital] Statistics.

On [September] 6, Order Service headquarters submitted its report to the authorities based on the figures supplied by the Burial Department.

82. The *Daily Chronicle Bulletin* for September 1–19, 1942, is given in its entirety here.

On September 5 and 6—93 deaths, no births.
On September 7—47 deaths, no births.
On September 8—53 deaths, no births.
On September 9—68 deaths, no births.
On September 10—72 deaths, no births.
On September 11—51 deaths, no births.
On September 12 and 13—68 deaths, no births.
On September 14—29 deaths, 1 boy born.
On September 15 and 16—29 deaths, no births.
On September 17—26 deaths, 2 boys, 3 girls born.
September 18—16 deaths, no births.

ARRESTS

September 1—robberies, 1.
September 2—robberies, 2, miscellaneous, 1.
September 3—robberies, 4.

During the period of the curfew, from September 5 to 7, there were no arrests. The Order Service was entirely occupied with the evacuation.

September 13—robberies, 2.
September 15—robberies, 2, miscellaneous, 7.
September 16—robberies, 9, miscellaneous, 9.
September 17—robberies, 13, miscellaneous, 12.
September 18—robberies, 6, miscellaneous, 11.
September 19—robberies, 2, miscellaneous, 3.

SUICIDES

On August 31, around eleven P.M., Hendla Biterman, born in Tomaszów in 1893, a resident of 25 Ceglana Street, attempted suicide by hanging herself. The First Aid Service brought her to Hospital No. 1.

On September 4, in the Old People's Home at 25 Gnieźnieńska Street, Stefanie Kapper, of Prague, born in 1880, committed suicide by taking poison. Depression was the probable motivation.

On September 5, there was a joint suicide [attempt] by a mother and daughter. Mariem Kraus of Prague, born in 1903, and her daughter Kwieta, born in 1937, tried to commit suicide together by taking phenobarbital. After first aid was administered, they were able to remain in their apartment at 5 Rybna Street.

That same day, at 3:30 P.M., Maksymilian Zereski, born in 1905, his wife Maria, born in 1907, and their son Jean Albert, born in 1937, attempted to commit suicide together by taking phenobarbital in their apartment at 21 Wawelska Street. Emergency Service II provided first aid. The probable cause of their desperate act was fear of evacuation. Zereski comes from a well-known family of Łódź industrialists.

On September 8, Fanni Halpern, born in 1871, a resident of 7 Bazarna Street, committed suicide by taking a sleep-inducing drug. The physician who arrived on the scene could only pronounce her dead.

On September 14, Szmul Jacob Szmol, born in Zduńska Wola in 1924, hanged himself in his apartment at 6 Masarska Street. [On its arrival] the Emergency Service determined that he was already dead.

On September 15, around twelve noon, a drowned woman was sighted in the pond near the intersection of Dworska and Towiańska streets. When the dead woman was pulled ashore, working papers made out to Bluma Selzer of 2 Wincenty Street were found on her person.

We have been informed that during the evacuation several people tried to escape from the trucks by jumping into the pond. It is possible that the above-mentioned woman died in this manner.

A WORK ACCIDENT

On September 3, at eleven-thirty A.M., while repairing the gas line in the building at 15 Limanowski Street, the following mechanics suffered poisoning from the inhalation of lighting gas: Faiwel Szejndling, a resident of 4 Limanowski Street, originally from Chemnitz, and Szlama Szladowski, a resident of 14 Wrześnieńska Street. After receiving first aid, the victims were taken to their homes.

FIRES

In the period covered by this report, the following fires were noted:

In the textile factory at 77 Drewnowska Street, a wooden machine caught fire. The blaze was extinguished by the Jewish Fire Department. The suspected cause of the fire was a tin button or nail among the rags, which somehow ignited.

On September 15, around twelve noon, a fire broke out in the apartment house at 12 Jakuba Street. The Jewish Fire Department was called, the German Fire Department also rushed to the scene, and both set to work at once. The fourth floor of the building was completely destroyed by the flames. By four P.M., the firefighters had made sufficient progress for the German Fire Department to leave the scene.

The Jewish Fire Department continued to fight the blaze until four-thirty P.M. This has been the largest fire in the history of the ghetto. The neighboring buildings were in great danger, especially the one containing large sub-sections of the tailors' workshops. Fortunately, they were all saved. During the fire-fighting action the following people appeared at the scene of the blaze: representatives of the authorities, [Hans] Biebow, head of the Ghetto Administration, officials of the [German] criminal police, and representatives of the Community, with Chairman Rumkowski at their head.

On September 16, at ten-thirty P.M., the Jewish Fire Department was again called to Jakuba Street, where a ceiling between the third and fourth floors had caught on fire. After fighting the blaze for some three and a half hours, the Fire Department was able to leave the scene. The fire had been caused by material still smouldering from the previous day's fire.

NO REPORTS ON CONTAGIOUS DISEASES

On the first and fifteenth of every month, Order Service headquarters delivers a report on contagious diseases in the ghetto to the German authorities. On September 14, Order Service headquarters reported to the German authorities that, since all hospital [patients] had been evacuated from the ghetto on September 1 and hospitals and outpatient clinics had not been in operation between September 1 and 14, no reports on contagious diseases were available.

MONDAY, SEPTEMBER 21, 1942

DEATHS AND BIRTHS

Today, seven deaths were registered. This is the lowest number since the ghetto was established. Without a detailed study of the causes for this figure, one must assume that it is due to the evacuation of the sick and the old. Furthermore, we must bear in mind that yesterday [evening and today] was the Day of Atonement, the highest Jewish holiday and a day of fasting, so that many religious people would not have reported a death. As for births, two boys were registered.

NORMAL WORK ON THE DAY OF ATONEMENT

All Community [vegetable and coal] storage lots, distribution points, workshops and offices were open during today's holiday. Great appreciation and gratitude were felt for the especially good and substantial midday meal—a potato and pea dish cooked with bones—that was served to mark the holiday. This midday meal was the sole evidence of the holiday, which is normally celebrated so solemnly. Only a few private stores were closed.

ARRIVAL OF LARGE MACHINES

Today, large crates were observed arriving in the ghetto by rail; they contained the component parts of the gigantic machines that are to be used at the carpentry shop, and the boot-top and metal workshops. A new era is thus commencing in the ghetto: the passage from handicrafts to machine work.

LARGE-SCALE ORDERS FOR THE GHETTO

Recently, the ghetto received large orders from the military administration. In particular, fur coats and other clothing made with fur were ordered.

TUESDAY, SEPTEMBER 22, 1942

A REDUCTION OF THE GHETTO

No sooner had the wounds of the horrible last ten days ceased bleeding than dreadful news again swept through the ghetto. The local authorities have been ordered to evacuate a large part of the ghetto within a few weeks, and they are now responsible for relocating the tenants of the buildings. The ghetto was supposed to have been reduced in size in February, 1941. However, after great effort, the Chairman succeeded in obtaining a delay because, at that time, [the ghetto] had a population of 150,000. But now, with Litzmannstadt undergoing great changes and modernization, the removal of a part of the ghetto by the [German] authorities can no longer be delayed. The section in question is a large square area in police Precinct I and is comprised of the following streets: Franciszkańska, from the corner of Smugowa (No.

13) to the corner of Brzezińska (No. 33), that is, all the odd-numbered buildings; and then Brzezińska, from the corner of Franciszkańska toward the cemetery; and likewise, the odd-numbered side as far as Oblęgorska, the last street before the fence, opposite the [former] so-called Gypsy camp. The removal [of this part of] Brzezińska Street causes the ghetto the loss of an artery second in importance only to Zgierska Street. Just recently a two-track tramline to Marysin was laid on Brzezińska Street. To relocate [the people living in] this part of the [ghetto] city is at present a far more difficult undertaking than it would have been in February, even though the number of inhabitants there that month was 8,000 as opposed to the 5,000 today. The problem is that there are 14 large workshops located in that district. The large buildings there, particularly suitable for workshops, had been put to use toward that end. Metal workshop II, among others, had been installed at 12 Smugowa Street, in a former factory building; the Low Voltage Equipment Department [was installed] in another building; not far from there, at 21 Franciszkańska Street, we have one of the ghetto's most important workshops, the fur workshop, also in a large building; Precinct I of the Order Service is housed at 27/29 Franciszkańska Street, a six-story building that formerly belonged to the Mariavites and in which a large section of the tailors' workshop had only recently been installed;[83] another building on the section of Brzezińska Street that is to be cut off contains one of the largest and most important divisions of the shoemakers' workshop; the Department of Dairy Products is located on Źródłowa Street, right by the barbed wire fence. We cannot overlook the fact that the district to be removed contains the largest amount of cultivated land [in the ghetto], an area of some 30,000 square meters. It had cost great effort to change what had once been a huge garbage dump into fertile soil. All this demonstrates what a great loss [the removal of] this district will be for the ghetto.

The loss of this district will have an especially severe effect on the [ghetto's] housing problem. It is not simply a matter of finding new apartments for the five thousand people living there; far more difficult is the problem of providing housing for the thousands of tenants who will have to leave their apartments because new buildings are required for the workshops that will be moving—not to mention the fact that new transports of evacuees from the surrounding area are arriving in the ghetto almost every day.

The relocation action—that is, the necessary preliminary work—is already well under way. The Chairman himself is busy from early morning until late evening; along with the head of the Department of Housing and the heads of individual workshops, he has been looking for buildings suitable for rehousing the workshops. Wolfowicz, the head of the Department of Housing, will assist them in executing this difficult operation with the least possible damage.

At the same time, preparations are being made to cut off a section of the ghetto in Marysin, in the vicinity of Otylia Street.

83. See p. 146, n. 36.

WEDNESDAY, SEPTEMBER 23, 1942

FROM THE LABOR CAMP

Today, 151 Jews (from Łódź and other towns) arrived here from the [Neustadt-]Ebers-walde labor camp, located not far from Berlin. They have all been lodged in Central Prison. The German authorities have ordered this transport to leave the ghetto again in the next few days. Several Order Service men have been assigned to Central Prison to make the necessary preparations.

PEOPLE ARE SAYING . . .

A rumor spread through the ghetto today that fifty children who have returned here are saying that all the children who have been resettled are now in the garden of Helenów [Helenówek].[84] This report is pure fantasy.

A SUICIDE ATTEMPT

Rojzla Rotlewi, of 2 Nad Łódką Street, has attempted suicide by taking poison. The Emergency Service brought her to the hospital on Mickiewicz Street. She is 35 years old.

THURSDAY, SEPTEMBER 24, 1942

A TRANSPORT FROM THE PRISON

As we noted in yesterday's report, 151 persons have been brought to this ghetto from a labor camp near Berlin with the condition that these people not remain here but be transported elsewhere. That fact has given rise to a variety of panicky rumors, which have been spreading since early this morning. Nightmarish stories are being told: among others, that a motorized raiding squad consisting of three vehicles had entered the ghetto to clear out the entire prison, that, en route to Bałut Market, the squad had picked up passersby and people at their windows had been dragged out of their buildings; that several children had been added to the transport; and that, especially on Tokarzewski Street, many people had been rounded up and taken away. [Allegedly,] more than 200 people left the ghetto in that transport.[85]

Actually, the raiding squad arrived at eight A.M., as mentioned above, and demanded the 151 workers who had been brought to Central Prison from the labor camp. The squad also took 23 prisoners who had been remanded to the custody of the prosecutor's office or the Bureau of Investigation. All told, 174 people were transported out of the total of 207 in prison that day. It is therefore obvious that the entire prison was not evacuated. The 23 persons from Central Prison included the three men from Pabianice whose death sentences had been commuted on September 7,

---

84. The pre-war Jewish Community (kehillah) Orphanage of which Rumkowski had been the director was located in Helenówek, a suburb in the northern part of Łódź.

85. This entire paragraph beginning with "As we noted" to "in that transport" had been crossed out in red pencil in the original.

when eighteen men from Pabianice were hanged; these three men had been re-manded to the custody of the [German] authorities in Łódź.[86]

During the course of yesterday, some 17 persons were sent to Central Prison, including 9 women who have either been sentenced by the local court or turned over to the Jewish authorities. Thus, the number of those detained at Central Prison now stands at 50.

FRIDAY, SEPTEMBER 25, 1942

DEATHS AND BIRTHS

Today 28 people died. Five children were born: four boys and one girl.

PEOPLE ARE SAYING . . .

People are still saying that some 10 children have returned to this ghetto; even the addresses of the children and their parents are mentioned. Yet, it has been deter-mined beyond doubt that none of these claims has any basis in fact. Absolutely nothing is known about the fate of any people resettled from this ghetto.

LITZMANNSTADT-GETTO, SEPTEMBER 25, 1942†

After the last resettlement there is [almost] no one in the ghetto over the age of 65 or under the age of 10. The hospitals have been liquidated—but does that mean there are also no sick people left? Unfortunately, many people are sick, with abdominal typhus predominating among infectious diseases. In some buildings there are several apartments where people are suffering from typhus, but the crowded conditions preclude quarantine. The auxiliary medical service has also been abolished; neither family members nor an apartment can be isolated, which advances and spreads the epidemic.

The very considerable number of vegetables on hand and the relatively warm weather provides the conditions for typhus to run rampant, but it is filth that is the dominating factor in this situation! One lives in filth, one sleeps in filth, and one eats without observing the basic rules of hygiene. Vegetables are not being washed as they should be, for there is no hot water to boil them and there is no time to do that and then prepare the food. After a whole day at work, people don't care about washing vegetables thoroughly, don't wait for them to be cooked properly and, out of hunger, consume half-cooked food, and that, in the majority of cases, is the cause of the illness.

If domestic hygiene does not undergo a radical change or improvement, a wave of spotted typhus cases can be expected with the onset of winter.

There has been considerable discussion in the ghetto about setting up a public laundry, but that idea has died. The laundering of underclothes is at least as impor-

---

86. In the original *"Lodzer"* (in Łódź) had been crossed out in indelible pencil.

tant as the problem of food supply, and considering the bad, cramped conditions in apartments, to postpone dealing with it endangers the entire population.

If to that situation we add the recent, total lack of a number of medicines, such as tannalbin, opium, and other astringents, we will find it easy to comprehend the danger facing us. Many mild cases have already ended in death because of such trivial reasons.

The total number of deaths has decreased, but it is still very high relative to the population, while the typhus epidemic, which is not talked about but is a reality, will no doubt gather in a plentiful harvest.

The [German] authorities have taken a negative attitude toward people suffering from tuberculosis and other incurable diseases, considering them unproductive individuals; but the most valuable workers can temporarily fall ill with an infectious disease, and there ought at least to be an isolation ward for such workers. The problem is becoming more and more urgent every day and may turn into a genuine epidemic if it is not nipped in the bud and no thought is given to effective countermeasures.

If the authorities could be shown the necessity of putting a public laundry into operation and a proper case were made for it, there is no doubt that they would accept the project without reservation, because the authorities value cleanliness in general and because they depend on our people to fill military and civilian orders for them. After all, it is not difficult for an epidemic to spread and for germs to travel beyond the ghetto.

The sooner such a laundry is in operation, the more people will be saved from extermination. Time is short and this problem cannot be postponed!

SUNDAY, SEPTEMBER 27, 1942

A SHORTAGE OF MONEY

Recently, and especially in the past few days, the populace has been suffering from a severe shortage of money, which makes life in the ghetto much more difficult. During these past few days there have been several rations [issued] that cost almost twenty marks per person. This is a large sum for the populace and therefore some people cannot even purchase rations. For this reason, during the first few days after the distribution of the rations, the lines at the vegetable [storage] yard, as well as at the cooperatives, have been very short—almost nonexistent. As a result, there has been very brisk trade in merchandise—linen, clothing, etc.—at very low prices, simply so that people can obtain money for rations. Such trade is to be seen on every street. Naturally, a few people are exploiting this situation. In any event, some departments have been lending their employees ten to fifteen marks to help remedy the situation a bit.

IMPROVEMENT IN FOOD SUPPLY

Immediately upon the lifting of the szpera [curfew], the Chairman promised an improvement in food supply and, indeed, improvement is to be observed everywhere.

Lately, much larger quantities of vegetables, potatoes, and meat have been arriving. As a result, the Meat Clearinghouse has been issuing 150 grams of sausage and 100 grams of good quality meat every week. In the past few days, tripe (1000 kilograms [daily]) has been distributed without ration cards. Vegetable salad has not only been sold for coupons but for regular vegetable cards as well. The soup too has been much improved. Not only does it contain 500 grams of potatoes, but rye flakes have been added instead of flour. On the whole, hunger is, fortunately, no longer an immediate concern.

LITZMANNSTADT-GETTO, SEPTEMBER 27, 1942†

In his recent speech, on the 19th of this month, the Chairman alluded to the ghetto's loss of its former autonomy, but he did not go into detail and he offered no commentary. This would seem to be an issue of little importance, but it affects a number of other issues.

The Chairman made that allusion in reference to the recent resettlement action. Previous resettlements had taken place on the basis of instructions from the Chairman, whereas this one occurred outside of his jurisdiction and abounded in unforeseen developments that could not be remedied. This was a hard and painful blow to the Chairman, for he felt helpless before a variety of events which had formerly borne the imprint of his will.

But, apart from the resettlement action, the loss of the so-called autonomy is expressed in a series of other events and phenomena.

As a religious person, the Chairman respected various traditions and displayed a certain reverence for the clergy, which explains their relatively privileged position. Therefore, he had to have had a profound reaction to the recent campaign against the rabbis and the official ban on the reciting of prayers during holidays. Until recently, representatives of the [German] authorities would even attend the recitation of prayers, and the Chairman took it as a kind of victory that, in the second and third years of the war, he had been able to win such concessions from the authorities.[87] All that has changed radically now, as is emphasized by the order that people must work on holidays. What is important here is not religious sentiment but the sort of freedom of action allowed by that now-lost autonomy. The Chairman's assurance, which was always manifest in his numerous speeches, in spite of all the warnings and threats he made, had a calming effect on the populace. People believed in his power and authority and that, if they had to go to him, his intervention would produce positive results. On the basis of the plenipotentiary power granted him, the Chairman was the sole master of the ghetto and was in charge of everything that happened here, with the exception of cases under the jurisdiction of the [German] criminal police. The authorities were strangely accommodating of him in that respect.

Today, things have changed in that respect as well, and every large workshop is now, to some degree, in direct contact with the authorities or the customer. In some

---

87. The Gettoverwaltung would sometimes take visiting members of German commissions to watch and photograph the prayers.

workshops, the so-called desk officers of the [German] Ghetto Administration have been inspecting the work since early morning, others are visited by surprise inspection commissions, which are regularly reviewing production; they speed up delivery and even intervene in organizational matters. In the workshop at 10 Jakuba Street, a commission checked up on the staff in individual posts and sections and decided that there should be some reduction in the number of employees, whereas, until quite recently, the Ghetto Administration had never interfered directly in the affairs of the workshops, leaving all the ghetto's internal affairs to the sole jurisdiction of the Chairman.

Thus, little by little, the ghetto is losing its internal freedom, which may not have been sufficiently appreciated before. Perhaps nothing will change in the lives of given individuals, and for some this may even be a change for the better; significant changes have, nevertheless, occurred in the entire moral framework that will have indirect significance for the entire population and will increasingly make themselves felt.

WEDNESDAY, SEPTEMBER 30, 1942

WEATHER

One of the most beautiful days of the wonderful autumn weather we have been having. Not a single cloud in the sky the entire day. In the afternoon it was as hot as a summer's day, [the temperature reaching] about 35 degrees. The night too was like a summer's night.

A TWELVE-HOUR WORK DAY IN THE DEPARTMENTS

Today the Chairman issued a circular whose contents were as follows:

"Circular to all internal departments and distribution points in the ghetto. For *all* internal departments and distribution points in the ghetto, I decree that as of Friday, October 2, 1942, daily working hours [will be] from 7:30 A.M. to 8 P.M., with one hour off for lunch. On Saturdays, working hours will be from 7:30 A.M. until 2 P.M. Applications will be accepted from 8 A.M. until 7 P.M., while the remaining time, that is, from 7:30 to 8 A.M. and from 7 P.M. to 8 P.M., will be reserved for internal work. Employees are to take turns for the one-hour lunch period to avoid interrupting work in the internal departments and distribution points. On this occasion, I would like to point out that applications are to be processed swiftly to prevent long waits. From time to time I will check the situation personally, and I will *dismiss without notice* all employees who fail to observe these instructions."

This circular has come as quite a surprise, causing great panic[88] and consternation among office workers. All of them, of course, maintain that, if this directive is strictly observed, they will have absolutely no time for themselves, for example, to pick up their rations or to prepare meals. It is hoped that this circular will be revised, so that work will be done in two shifts, since no one can endure a twelve-hour work day for

88. In the original, "panic and" had been crossed out in indelible pencil.

very long. Office employees are very interested in knowing why the Chairman has issued such a directive.

A REDUCTION IN SENTRIES

In the evening there was a report circulating that, beginning on October 1, the police force around the ghetto will be reduced; sentry duty at the barbed wire will be taken over [in part][89] by the Jewish police. It has already been observed that sentry booths have been removed in various places; the booth at 38 Zgierska Street is one example. This change, which is of great importance for the populace of the ghetto, will be clarified by tomorrow.

LITZMANNSTADT-GETTO, SEPTEMBER 30, 1942†

Despite seemingly efficient organization, laxity among blue- and white-collar workers is having a ripple effect. Apart from the mental factors influencing this state of laxity, health is not insignificant, for it has an increasingly negative effect on an individual's ability to work. Organization and productivity at pre-war standards are out of the question, for people now have a different mental attitude and their ability to work is constantly changing *in minus*. Without exaggeration, one may assume that the current potential of a given worker has fallen by 50 percent in comparison to a year ago, a warranted inference given that actual production is unchanged while staffs are significantly larger. Although this is difficult to determine in individual workshops due to the diversity in [types of] production between last year and this year, it is striking in the work performed in the offices, whose range has shown little increase, while the number of clerical workers has more than doubled. From pre-war experience we know that expanding production to two or even three shifts requires only an insignificant increase in the number of white-collar workers, while the third shift will present no problems to a businessman, aside from raw materials. A third shift leads to capitalization and is the most lucrative shift for the businessman. Actually, the ghetto is moving in a somewhat different direction since, due to a lack of private initiative, there are no precise calculations made for production and commerce. Given workshop directors do, in fact, make efforts to show a profit in their enterprises and to demonstrate it statistically, but (so we have heard) at bottom, when accounts are settled later on with the customer, those calculations are always upset. There is a whole series of items which are known in advance to be deficit-producing, while others are known to be so not only to the workshop but to the Central Workshop Bureau. But that does not matter, the ghetto does not and should not count on being profitable. The only point here is the exchange of labor for a sufficient amount of food, and if there are budgetary problems, they can be covered by raising the prices charged by the Community for food.

The excessive number of workers in particular workshops and the reduction in the scope of their work become comprehensible, however, once profitability is no longer an issue. In specific workshops, such as the *Altmaterialien* [*-betrieb*—plant for sort-

89. In the original, "in part" had been added in indelible pencil.

ing used textiles] for example, work has been reduced to a minimum and yet, in a great number of cases even that minimum is not being done. Not because people are so exhausted that they are unable to perform the work, but simply because they do not want to. Their wages are of little concern to them and, besides, they are day workers and receive soup no matter what—and it is the soup that is the magnet drawing them to work, to the workshop. Thus, this time of affliction has not taught people to work; on the contrary, it has disaffected them from work, demoralized them, dispossessed them of their fundamental sense of obligation to their employer. An employee does not want to give his employer anything at all in return, no matter how easy the work, covering himself with one excuse or another, most frequently, poor health. The employer is faced with an onerous alternative: dismiss the worker, which means condemning him to death by starvation, and it is not everyone who can bring himself to [do] that. And so he tolerates the existing state of affairs and contributes to further disintegration and laxity. It is now commonplace for a worker to refuse to do what he is told if it means going up to another floor or climbing the stairs on a [ghetto] bridge, and the subordination that every organization requires is fast disappearing from daily life. Refusals are heard from blue-collar workers, white-collar workers, and, finally, even from messengers, whose very [Polish] name [goniec—runner] implies that ability. People refuse when a thing cannot be done and also when they do not feel like doing it. The latter always predominates.

What can be done about this? Police measures will not help because every step in that direction means death by starvation, and no one wishes to condemn anyone to that. An end to the war would be the best solution, but as long as the war continues we must make the public aware of the fatal consequences of such laxity.

A certain social discipline must exist, especially in times as hard as these!

Population Changes in the Month of September, 1942

	Men	Women	Total
Level as of September 1, 1942	45,553	60,408	105,961
Increases in September			
Births	19	13	32
Stillbirths	—	1	1
Arrivals from Generalgouvernement and Warthegau	13	6	19
From prison	1	1	2
Returnees from outside the ghetto	130	—	130
Returnees from labor in various towns in Warthegau	103	—	103
Additional people resettled here in August	51	80	131
Total increase	317	101	418
Decreases in September			
Deaths	608	466	1,074
Deportees	174	—	174
Total decrease	782	466	1,248
Actual decrease	465	365	830
Resettled in September (9/1, 9/2, and 9/7–9/12)			15,685
Level as of October 1, 1942			89,446

Regarding resettlement in September, see *Chronicle*, September 1 and 2: evacuation of the hospitals, sanatoriums, and Central Prison; September 7–12: evacuation of the children, the sick, and the elderly [Litzmannstadt-Getto, September 14, 1942].

FRIDAY, OCTOBER 2, 1942

DISEASES: DISBANDING OF THE DEPARTMENT OF HEALTH'S STAFF

The typhus epidemic continues. Because of the elimination of the Department of Health and the hospitals, it is impossible to form an accurate picture of the number of cases of typhus and of other diseases in the ghetto. The physicians who make house calls have determined that there have been numerous cases of typhoid fever, gastric illnesses, and jaundice during the past few days. Also, the [work] attendance records show a high number of people out sick, even though nowadays no one fails to report to work willingly, since such [absence] can be very dangerous.[90] The lack of hospitals and other health-care institutions is, of course, catastrophic for the ghetto populace. Perhaps this problem can be solved in the future, when the barracks on Czarniecki Street are completed. Fortunately, most of the recent cases of typhus appear to be mild. On October 1 of this year the Department of Health and Hygiene dismissed nearly all its employees. Nurses are sent on house calls only for cases of typhus. Unfortunately, it is not possible to make any of the remaining auxiliary staff available to anyone suffering from any other disease, thus, the sick in the ghetto are left to their own devices. The Department of Health's employees, of whom there are a great many, are, of course, being given new jobs by the Bureau of Labor, but solely on a day-to-day basis. Very few of them have permanent positions yet.

SUNDAY, OCTOBER 4, 1942

DEATHS

The Mortality Office reported today that 56 people have died in the ghetto. This number includes the 18 men who were hanged on September 7 of this year, that is, on the second [third] day of the last evacuation.[91] Although these men were buried that same day in the cemetery here, their personal data was not registered until today. In the Mortality Office, their place of death is listed as Bazarna Street [where the execution took place]. Since all these men had arrived here from outside the ghetto, their place of residence is listed as "outside the ghetto." The medical death certificate does not indicate the cause of death. Of these 18 people, two were inhabitants of this ghetto, one came from Zelów, one from Pabianice, nine from Pajęczno, one from

90. In the original *Chronicle*, the conclusion of this sentence, "such [absence] can be very dangerous," was crossed out in red pencil.

91. In a report to the police and security service in Poznań on October 1, 1942, the German criminal police (Kripo) in Łódź wrote that in the month reported on, August, 35 Jews had been executed by hanging after being caught attempting to escape deportation, for sabotage, or for illegally leaving the ghetto or their place of work. *Biuletyn Zydowskiego Instytutu Historycznego*, 54 (1965), p. 40. Cf. above, p. 208, n. 69.

Wieluń, and four from Lutomiersk. The oldest of these men was born in 1871 and the youngest, in 1924.

No births.

EVACUATION

We have learned that the number of ghetto inhabitants who are to be evacuated from the section being detached from Precinct I comes to about 3,750. The Department of Housing is doing such excellent work that nearly all these people have already found apartments. Those who are not satisfied with their newly allocated apartments will have the opportunity to apply for another apartment at the Department of Housing around the twelfth of this month, that is, after completion of this action. Some of the workshops have already been relocated, and in such a way that there has been almost no interference with their work; for those remaining, the Construction Department is completing the work with [American] speed,[92] so all workshops will shortly be relocated.

SENTRIES

As already mentioned, the number of German sentries around the ghetto was reduced as of October 1. Until October 1 of this year, there were some 300 policemen on duty at those posts, all shifts included. Now, less than half remain. Today, a guard is posted at roughly every 400 meters. As of October 1, the Jewish Order Service men have been out on patrol.

PEOPLE ARE SAYING . . .

The Special Unit has recently been given greater powers so that it has become a separate department, entirely independent of the Order Service.

TSHOLENT

Today, instead of soup, tsholent was served in all the soup kitchens, which was, of course, to the great satisfaction of all the workers. Let us hope that this [treat] will be repeated once a week.

CHILDREN WITHOUT GUARDIANS

The commission responsible for finding homes for children left untended because of the evacuation has been hard at work and has already found homes for about 200. Some 500 families have expressed interest in taking in children.

TUESDAY, OCTOBER 6, 1942

AN ILLEGAL CROSSING OF THE GHETTO BORDER

The day before yesterday, two women succeeded in entering the ghetto in broad daylight through the fence on Głowacki Street. The two women were from this ghetto

---

92. In the original, "American" had been crossed out in red pencil and replaced by "with quick."

and for a year had been in a labor camp not far from Poznań. Recently, due to illness, these women, together with other sick women, were being transported in a sealed car to another camp. At a railroad station, they managed to open the car and get out. They had not had any water for two days and were terribly thirsty. In the meantime, however, the train pulled away and the women came to this ghetto, where they have relatives. They arrived here after three weeks on foot. Immediately upon their arrival, they learned that they no longer had homes here because their families had been evacuated. So they went to the Order Service and told their story. The Order Service was forced to report this matter to the authorities, and the women were therefore handed over to the Kripo.

A SUICIDE

Sala Regenberg, a resident of 38 Drewnowska Street, born in 1908, attempted suicide today. She jumped from the fifth floor at 48 Limanowski Street. She suffered serious injuries and was taken to the hospital by the Emergency Service.

NUMBER OF GHETTO INHABITANTS

Yesterday, the number of ghetto inhabitants was 89,325. On October 1 of this year, the number of ghetto inhabitants was 89,415.

THURSDAY, OCTOBER 8, 1942

TOTAL POPULATION

89,271. Eleven people arrived here from [the ghetto of] Warsaw.[93] They had received special permission to enter this ghetto, a fact which is connected with the events in Warsaw, about which the most diverse rumors are circulating in [our] ghetto, forming the main topic of conversation. It is claimed that of the 600,000 Jews in Warsaw, only about 30,000 are left. Unfortunately, there is no reliable information available.[94]

SATURDAY, OCTOBER 10, 1942

A WARNING

A great sensation has been caused by a proclamation signed by the [German] Ghetto Administration (Biebow). It reads:

"A warning that concerns every inhabitant of the ghetto:

"Recently, there has been an increase in robberies that (1) constitutes a serious offense against the wartime economy, (2) causes irreparable damage to [German]

---

93. See p. 55, n. 65.
94. Even today there is a lack of precise statistical information. However, by relying on various authoritative sources—German, Polish, and Jewish—one may state that, after the deportation of over 300,000 Jews in the summer of 1942, some 40,000 people remained in the Warsaw ghetto.

private business, (3) interferes with the orderly distribution of food to the population, especially the workers.

"Effective immediately, severe action will be taken against any person misappropriating anyone else's property; it makes no difference whether the articles in question are [spools of] thread, cloth scraps, fur remnants, or other such trifles. To offer another example: [it is a crime for] any person to steal from shipments within the ghetto, particularly from horse-drawn vehicles carrying vegetables or other foodstuffs. It is, furthermore, [criminal] for any person to attempt to appropriate food illegally—items in food storehouses, at vegetable distribution points, bread shops, etc. As of today, the Special Department [Unit] of the ghetto has been ordered to make doubly sure that such extremely reprehensible offenses no longer occur. From now on, every instance of theft will be punished with the harshest possible penalty."

This announcement has made a great impression on the populace, for it is the second proclamation not signed by the Chairman. As is well known, the first such proclamation concerned the ending of the September evacuation. It has therefore been inferred that, from now on, the Ghetto Administration will be in charge of all internal matters in the ghetto. We have learned that workshop signs will no longer say "The Eldest of the Jews," but "Ghetto Administration," department (factory), such and such. We have also learned that, in certain factories, workers are being issued new identity cards, made out by the Labor Office of the Ghetto Administration. People have noticed increased supervision in the workshops by commissions and representatives of the Ghetto Administration.[95]

SUNDAY, OCTOBER 11, 1942

SPECIAL UNIT INCREASED

Since, as stated in the latest proclamation by the Ghetto Administration, the Special Unit is assuming general supervision of the ghetto, this branch of the police is now recruiting new members. The Chairman summoned the young men who had obtained their gymnasium degrees in the ghetto to the Personnel Department and hired those who were physically fit on the spot. The inspectors in the Special Unit are already occupying all the posts in question—that is, those at the vegetable yard, distribution points, etc. At the same time, the supervisors and inspectors from the Supreme Inspection Chamber are still officiating, and it would appear that these two agencies are competing with one another.

TUESDAY, OCTOBER 13, 1942

A DELIVERY OF POTATOES

On the night of October 12, shipments of potatoes arrived here unexpectedly, and in amounts unprecedented for the ghetto. 118 loads arrived and thus, overnight, the

---

95. In the original, this entire paragraph, from "This announcement" to "of the Ghetto Administration" had been crossed out in red pencil and marked with a question mark.

ghetto was faced with difficult problems. These precious goods had to be stored immediately. Obviously, the Department of Food Supply was unable to cope with all this, with the staff it had at the Wares Acceptance Post in Radogoszcz. The Chairman therefore ordered a sort of general mobilization of all available manpower. On the first day, Order Service men, rank and file as well as officers, had to report there for duty. Then, all departments had to contribute a specific contingent of manpower for this job—to wit, about fifty percent of their employees. The office workers thus delegated had to report to Marysin by 6:30 A.M. There, a commission from the Bureau of Labor was in charge and exempted all those not physically fit for this sort of labor. Office workers by the hundreds were registered at the wares acceptance point and had to report for this work every day. Women were assigned to the wheelbarrows or to the sorting of potatoes, which were stored in mounds, or to the camp barracks that were recently built on Zagajnikowa Street. The Construction Department is still working on the construction of these barracks. The men were assigned to the Radogoszcz railroad station, where they unloaded the potatoes in two shifts. While on this assignment, the office workers received a daily wage of only three marks and two [bowls of] soup. The Chairman charged Commander [Zygmunt] Reingold with the overall authority for storing the potatoes, while Izrael Silberstrom, the present director of the coal yard, was placed in charge of manpower.

WEDNESDAY, OCTOBER 14, 1942

A FIRE SET BY A SICK MAN

Froim Borenstein, a sick man who was receiving no care, set fire to his bedding, in his apartment at 17 Dolna Street, with the intention of committing suicide. The Fire Department was called and managed to put out the fire in time.

CONTAGIOUS DISEASES

According to a report from the hospital for epidemic diseases recently established in Marysin, there were 50 patients there on October 1. Today, that is, two weeks later, there are 122. During these two weeks the following cases were diagnosed: typhoid fever—56, typhus—4, dysentery—1, and pulmonary tuberculosis—1.

SATURDAY, OCTOBER 17, 1942

SIGNS IN THE GHETTO

In accordance with a Ghetto Administration directive signed by [Hans] Biebow and addressed to all workshops, factories, and departments, now all signs and signboards of any kind in the ghetto may only be in German. "If possible, Hebrew [Yiddish] inscription is to be cut off, or else covered up or painted over so that none of it remains visible." This directive has wiped out the Jewish administration's most important characteristic—the Yiddish language. Since the last evacuation, there has been a noticeable increase in intervention by the [German] Ghetto Administration in the ghetto's internal affairs. This has been shown by the proclamations and by increased supervision of all workshops by the Ghetto Administration.

In this connection, a circular penned by secretary [S.] Cygielman has been issued to all workshops, factories, and departments informing them that, by order of the Chairman, the Department (workshop) of Sign Painting, which had previously operated at the Used Materials Purchasing Agency, will be independent as of October 1 of this year. This department is headed by Mr. Sz[mul] Rozenstein and is located at 10 Brzezińska Street (the printing shop).

SUNDAY, OCTOBER 18, 1942

FOOD ALLOCATION

Today, the ration for the ten-day period from October 20–31 was published. It represents a slight improvement over the previous ration, and the populace is satisfied. This ration costs 4 marks, 20 pfennigs for those who cook at home and contains: 300 grams of rye flour (an increase of 50 grams), 200 grams of rye flakes (an increase of 50 grams), but no peas, 360 grams of sugar (an increase of 40 grams), 50 grams of oil, and 60 grams of melted butter, the latter included again after a long absence, 300 grams of [ersatz] coffee mixture, 50 grams of artificial honey, 50 grams of marmalade and 250 grams of salt, 10 grams of paprika, 20 grams of baking soda, and a half-package of soap powder. For those registered at the kitchens, the ration costs 2 marks, 50 pfennigs. It contains 140 grams of sugar, 300 grams of coffee, 100 grams of salt, 50 grams of artificial honey, 50 grams of marmalade, 60 grams of butter, 15 grams of baking soda, and a half-package of soap powder. Beginning on October 20, there will be 100 grams of meat and 100 grams of sausage per person.

TUESDAY, OCTOBER 20, 1942

THE CLOTHING CAMPAIGN

Yesterday, it was announced that the shoes and clothes made available by the Ghetto Administration to the Eldest of the Jews are to be distributed only to workers in workshops.[96] Meanwhile, a directive from the Chairman to the effect that other employees should also be so supplied was issued today. From the Chairman's directive it appears that the word *workers* is to be understood to mean *employees*, that is, everyone with a job. For the moment, however, only ten percent of each [workshop's] staff is to receive this allocation. Aside from the shoes already issued, some nine thousand pairs are to be allocated during the next few days. Applications for shoes

---

96. The clothing, underclothing, bedding, boots, etc., that came from the ghettos liquidated in the villages and towns of Wartheland, as well as from the death camp in Chełmno (Kulmhof), and which were considered by the German authorities to be of little or no value, were sent to the Łódź ghetto. The German Ghetto Administration (Gettoverwaltung) debited them to the account of the Eldest of the Jews, as was done with all other supplies, e.g., food, brought to the ghetto from without. (Cf. p. 6, n. 10 above.)

are to be made to the director of a department or workshop. Shoes may be issued only to applicants who do not possess a single pair of wearable shoes. The agency for used shoes has some 250,000 pairs, some of which[97] can serve as material for repairs. The shoes literally come from all over the world and are in all conceivable styles, the oldest to the most modern are represented among them. The sorting agency's principal task is to find matching pairs in this gigantic mass of shoes. The work of sorting the shoes is being performed by several hundred women. First, the shoes are divided into men's and women's shoes. Next, brown shoes are matched with brown, black with black, shoes with shoes, boots with boots, and only then is the correct left shoe paired with the correct right. There is also a section for overshoes. Various leather pocketbooks and briefcases supply the material necessary for repairs and even for new shoes. The required lasts are likewise made on the spot to help cope with this enormous repair operation. Thanks to excellent planning and organization, the work is proceeding apace. It would be difficult to find another such factory anywhere in the world. It is run by the well-known Łódź shoe expert, Pruszycki. At present, some 700 pairs of serviceable shoes are produced each day; seeing them, no one could imagine the woeful state in which they came to the ghetto. The prices have been set as follows: men's shoes: shoes—30 marks, boots—35 marks; women's shoes: shoes—20 marks, boots—25 marks. The pair one receives is, however, entirely a matter of chance.

BARRACKS CONSTRUCTION

Several weeks before the hospitals were closed down, the Department of Health was notified by the [German] authorities that several hospital barracks were to be constructed and would initially contain 600 beds. Construction has been in progress on Krawiecka Street for over two months now. The work is being done by a German firm, which employs not only ghetto workers but its own team of Polish workers as well. This latter group is escorted into the ghetto every morning and out of the ghetto every evening by the German police. The roof on the first of these barracks was completed yesterday. However, we have learned that these barracks will not be used for their original purpose; they are to be allocated to the fur workshop which is being relocated from 21 Franciszkańska Street [cf. pp. 225–26].

WEDNESDAY, OCTOBER 21, 1942

IMPRISONMENT

Three women who attempted to leave their places of work in Poznań have been lodged in Central Prison where they are the prisoners of the German authorities.

A SUICIDE

Icek Dobrzyński, of 38 Zgierska Street, resettled here from Zduńska Wola, forty-six years old, jumped from the fifth floor at 40 Zgierska Street and died instantly. The Order Service listed a nervous breakdown as the cause.

---

97. In another edition of the *Chronicle*, the words, "some of which," were changed to, "the majority of them."

NO NEGROES IN THE GHETTO

Precinct VI of the German Police has inquired of the Chairman whether there are any Negroes or mulattoes in the ghetto. The Chairman was able to report that there are no Negroes in the ghetto.

AN HONEST FINDER

A female worker in a ghetto sorting office found a gold necklace weighing 26 grams in an old piece of clothing. She turned the item over to the management. This is not the first case of valuables being found in clothes that were shipped here for use within the ghetto.[98]

THURSDAY, OCTOBER 22, 1942

A LEAP FROM A BRIDGE

After a relatively long time, the bridge on Kościelny Square has once again become the scene of a suicide. Forty-five-year-old Fraidla Ruchla Dobrzyńska, of 38 Zgierska Street, a native of Łódź, jumped from the upper platform of the bridge to the roadway of Zgierska Street at 5:45 A.M. She suffered very serious injuries. The Emergency Service physician had the woman brought to Hospital No. 4 on Mickiewicz [Street]. As reported yesterday, her husband, 46-year-old Icek Dobrzyński, of Zduńska Wola, was killed when he leaped from a fifth story. Fraidla Ruchla first tried to join her husband in death by attempting suicide near the barbed wire fence. She did not succeed, however, because the sentry was not willing to shoot her. So, she leaped from the bridge. The cause of both suicides goes back several weeks. The couple's two children were taken away during the evacuation in September.

FRIDAY, OCTOBER 23, 1942

PRICES RISE

For quite a while now, prices on the open market have been soaring. Bread now costs 100 marks, potatoes, 8, sugar is unavailable even at 100 marks, and butter is hard to find even at 400 marks; the best way to obtain food is through barter. Vegetables—legally priced at 2 marks for the current ration—now cost 6 marks. The price of briquettes has suddenly risen to 3.50, wood is over 2 marks, matches are up to 1 mark, saccharine—8 tablets for 1 mark. Soup kitchen tickets have risen to 3.50. This increase in prices is due to strict supervision by the Special Unit. Since no illegal bread is reaching the market, the other prices are rising accordingly.

98. Cf. note 96, above.

SATURDAY, OCTOBER 24, 1942

DEATHS

One [death reported]. For the first time in the history of the ghetto, only one case of death has been reported (due to the fact that today is a Saturday). In reality, of course, there were several deaths; but they were not reported because of the Sabbath. Yet, taking even that into account, the mortality rate must have been very low today.

No births.

MARRIAGES

There have been no marriages in the ghetto since the September evacuation. But now, prospective parties are being notified that, as of next week, the Chairman will personally perform marriages.

PEOPLE ARE SAYING . . .

As of November 1 there will be further restrictions on the use of electricity in the ghetto. Supposedly, the use of electricity in private apartments is to be prohibited after 9 in the evening. Authoritative circles in the ghetto claim to know nothing about any such restrictions.

The next ten-day [ration] period is supposed to include white flour and hard [unrefined] sugar—the latter in addition to the normal ration of refined sugar.

There are supposed to be further potato allocations for the months of April, May, and June in the next few days. A potato allocation has apparently been issued outside the ghetto as well.

The next few days will show how much truth there is to these rumors.

DIFFICULTIES IN RECEIVING POTATOES

The prices for home deliveries of potatoes are rising phenomenally. They have already reached 10 marks for a 40-kilo ration. This is all the more burdensome since, given the shortage of potatoes in the [ghetto] city's warehouses, buyers have to pick up their potatoes in Marysin. On the other hand, the potatoes there are in better condition.

SUNDAY, OCTOBER 25, 1942

DEATHS

Forty-one (compare Saturday). Births: one boy. Since nearly all recent deaths have the same cause, we offer, by way of illustrating the mortality rate, a survey of the causes of today's deaths. Typhus: one man, one woman; pulmonary tuberculosis: four men, four women; tuberculosis of other organs: one man; diseases of the nervous system: two women; marasmus: one woman; diseases of the digestive system: three men, two women; heart diseases: six men, six women; malnutrition: one woman; hydrophobia: one man; suicide: one man; debilitation: one man.

A SUICIDE

Israel Meier Bonom (original name: Horowitz), of 2 Lotnicza Street, born in 1883, hanged himself in his apartment. Motive unknown.

A DEATH

Yesterday, Irene Weiss, a former Łódź journalist, died at the age of 33. She had no relatives in the ghetto. In the end, stricken with typhus, she took poison.

FOOD PRICES

Unlicensed trade continues unabated. Bread costs 90 [marks], potatoes—8, oil—2.50, butter—3.50 to 4.00, sugar—100, saccharine—8 tablets [for 1 mark].

MONDAY, OCTOBER 26, 1942

SUICIDES

Alfred Fink, of 67 Marynarska Street, took poison and was brought to the hospital. His condition is hopeless. Chaja Rifka Blada, born in 1878, of 21 Zgierska Street, jumped to the street from a fifth floor and died instantly. Motive unknown. Lajb Ehrlich, of 30 Wolborska Street, 38 years old, jumped to the street from the second floor and died instantly. Motive unknown.

HEADS OF DEPARTMENTS AND WORKSHOPS [ASSIST IN] POTATO [STORAGE]

The call for volunteers to help store the potatoes has been entirely successful. Some 100 leading officials and ghetto employees assembled at the [former] movie theater in Marysin. These included the highest functionaries, for example, [Salomon] Ser, head of the Main Treasury; [Chaim] Lipnowski, head of the Main Purchasing Agency; Dr. [Józef] Klementynowski, head of the Archives; Minc, head of the Office for Resettled Persons; [Mojżesz] Karo, head of the School Department;[99] [Szaja-Stanisław] Jakobson, an attorney, and a presiding judge of the court; and many others along with their staff members. Work groups were formed of department staffers who were assigned wagons. The volunteers had to haul potatoes and vegetables from the railroad cars to the storage yards and sheds. The leading officials of the Jewish administration now had occasion to see for themselves what an enormous amount of work the Wares Acceptance Post has to do. One has to witness such work personally in order to appreciate the technical problems involved in feeding the population. On the Radogoszcz freight station's many tracks there are entire trains composed of railroad cars from a great variety of countries. One sees former PKP [*Polskie Koleje Państwowe*—Polish State Railroad], German, Austrian, Belgian and French freight cars; they all deliver potatoes and vegetables, mainly kohlrabi, radishes, red beets and rutabagas. Although the volunteers were not recruited from among the young, they performed their work energetically to pull their wagons to and from the unloading

---

99. In the original *Chronicle*, the words, "head of the Archives," were crossed out in red pencil, and "School Department" had been replaced by "The Revaluation Commission," also in red pencil.

points as frequently as possible. After 12 [midnight] they were served soup, which was either the best in the ghetto or else tasted unusually good because of the strenuous work they had done out in the night air. Relatively well organized, the work is hampered only by a lack of unloading equipment. The shift ended at 6 A.M. and each worker received his 400 grams of bread.

The scope and importance of the work done in Marysin are demonstrated by the fact that 600 workers were employed there each day. During the next few days, all departments will take turns sending their office workers to this important project directed by the heads of the Bureau of Labor, [Bernard] Fuchs and [Kiwa] Sienicki. Reingold of the Department of Food Supply is the specialist in charge; [Izrael] Silberstrom of the Coal Department and Kleinman, head of the Transportation Department, are the technical directors.

TUESDAY, OCTOBER 27, 1942

A SUICIDE

Dr. Walter Kraus, born in 1914, a lawyer from Reichenberg, Sudetenland, has committed suicide by taking phenobarbital. In his homeland, he was well known as the representative of the Danish ministry of information. He leaves a wife who, like the deceased, has been ill for a long time.

A DEATH

The senior Łódź physician, Dr. Chorec-Brotman, a specialist in venereal diseases, died today at the age of 68.

LITZMANNSTADT-GETTO, OCTOBER 28, 1942†

Our life is composed of a whole series of rather inconspicuous things which we frequently fail to notice but which have many times represented a turning point in our situation and have even shattered the long-standing traditions, so assiduously maintained and cultivated by our ancestors. Hundreds of years of normal life had not been able to breach those traditions and even the slight evolutionary changes were not noticed. Here, in the ghetto, sudden and radical changes have occurred, changes which would have normally been beyond the range of any imagination.

We will not reflect here on the whole series of changes which have occurred in Jewish life in the ghetto, but will discuss only the latest sensation, caused by the marriages performed by Chairman M. C. Rumkowski.

After the resettlement action in September of this year, the Rabbinate was abolished in the ghetto, which in turn meant the end of religious marriage ceremonies. This made for a somewhat touchy situation, for, on the one hand, it was impossible to oppose the ruling by the [German] authorities, while, on the other, life demanded its own rights too. Then, after consulting with people competent in such matters, the Chairman decided to take the role of chaplain upon himself and make it possible for couples to conclude marriages that were legal in the Mosaic sense.

Yesterday, the first seven couples were married according to the new rite in the auditorium of the former Rabbinate at 4 Kościelny Square, in a second annex on the third floor. After 6 P.M., in the beautifully lit hall, the Chairman seated himself at a table covered with a green cloth. A small table with a typewriter had been placed beside the larger table. The young couples were called out in turn from the other room, and led in by their witnesses, who arranged them in a semicircle at the table. The presence of outside parties was ruled out in advance and entrance was allowed only to invited guests upon presentation of a proper invitation.

The Chairman addressed a few brief remarks to the assembly, explaining the new situation to them, including the ban on religious marriage ceremonies. He told them that the new marriage ceremony had been adapted to the needs of the moment and the present situation, but, at the same time, did not in the least transgress the requirements of Jewish ritual. Everything had been set up with the agreement of persons competent in these matters and was absolutely obligatory for those entering into matrimony. The most important parts of the wedding ceremony are the vows and the blessing, and it is precisely those that have been maintained while the rest are remnants of an old tradition, which has had to yield to the necessities of the moment.

A new ksube [marriage contract] has been composed; it is considerably shorter and also contains no references to gold, diamonds, and other valuables, which new-lyweds here, *de facto*, do not possess. And thus it is more realistic and truer than the previous version which, of necessity, was a fiction. The Chairman concluded his remarks by cordially wishing the newlyweds happiness and success in their new life. Then each couple was called in turn to the table, where they signed the ksubes prepared for them and the Chairman asked each of them individually if they were marrying of their own free and unconstrained will. Here we see not only the external changes, the abolition of the wedding canopy and other such ceremonies, but an innovation which far exceeds the limits of Jewish ritual, for, in the custom as it had stood until now, the person performing the marriage never asked this of the bride and groom.

The newlyweds answered the question put to them affirmatively and signed the ksube.

While the signing of the ksubes was taking place, Miss [Tusia] Ejbuszyc, the director of the Coupon Department, who had come to the ceremony with the Chairman, was writing out the marriage coupons at a feverish pace and attaching them to the ksubes. This was a surprise that brought radiant smiles to the faces of the newlyweds, for it was a known fact that marriage coupons had been abolished. When I asked the Chairman about this, he explained that it was difficult for him to abandon that new "tradition" which he himself had introduced and even though he had felt obliged to reduce the coupons slightly (one loaf of bread instead of two) he still did not want to deprive the newlyweds of the pleasure of a good dinner.

Then it was time for the wedding ceremony. The Chairman asked the couples if they possessed their own rings; in two cases, the couples wished to use fountain pens with gold nibs instead of rings. After consultation with [Rabbi Moshe Dovid] Dąb and Bauman, the Chairman agreed that the pens could be used instead of rings.

Raising a glass of wine in his right hand, the Chairman blessed the newlyweds and then poured the wine from the glass, which had been blessed, into the seven nearly full glasses on the table. After the couples had exchanged vows, the Chairman told each groom to drink the wine and to share his glass with his bride. Upon completion of this ritual, the Chairman handed the grooms the ksube, which they in turn handed to their wives, along with the coupons.

Another *signum temporis*—not one glass but seven were used! The Chairman explained to me that this was due to health conditions among the ghetto's populace. In these times, he said, it is difficult to maintain the tradition of using a single glass; with rampant disease and epidemics in mind, he had ordered a separate glass for each couple.

These religious rituals were followed by the Chairman's reading of the seven blessings, which he pronounced volubly but with a note of sadness in his voice. That sadness was very much a reflection of the mood of those present at the ceremony, whose faces were marked by uncertainty and dejection; their expressions gave no indication that they were on the threshold of an important change in their lives. Then the newlyweds stood before an official from the Department of Vital Statistics, B. Rajngold, and entered their signatures in his ledger.

As is usually the case in other circumstances, this time too the newlyweds did not wish to waste the opportunity offered by close proximity to the Chairman to entreat him for a gift or a favor, be it an apartment or an improvement in their material situation and, in one case, a bride even requested a pair of shoes. The Chairman heard out the petitioners with exceptional patience, his kindly feelings toward them quite evident. He commended special requests to Miss [Tusia] Ejbuszyc, whom he instructed to make note of them so that they could be dealt with later on.

After the ceremony was concluded, the Chairman bade everyone farewell and advised them to hurry to the *RI* cooperative to cash in the coupons they had received and to celebrate with a proper dinner that evening.

And so that seemingly modest wedding ceremony attended by a small number of guests has written a curious page in the history of Jewish society here!

FRIDAY, OCTOBER 30, 1942

THE LABOR OFFICE

For the first time, a circular issued to all factories, workshops, and departments bears the signature: "The Ghetto Labor Office." This circular demands a list of workers who:

(1) have been dismissed at their own request;

(2) have been dismissed on the basis of a doctor's certificate, when there are grounds to suspect that the medical certificate is not fully justified in regard to the bearer's ability to work; or who

(3) have remained absent from work for more than one week without an excuse or with an insufficient excuse.

ORPHANS

Homes have been found for about 520 of the children left parentless after the resettlement. There have been offers of 500 more. The commission is now providing these children with clothing.

SATURDAY, OCTOBER 31, 1942

A NEW HOSPITAL

Yesterday, a new hospital for contagious diseases was opened at 71 Dworska Street. Prior to its evacuation in September, this was the location of an Old People's Home. It is anticipated that the hospital will have a total of 300 beds. 180 patients have already been admitted. This institution will have a very significant effect on sanitary conditions in the ghetto because the hospital facilities in Marysin are quite primitive— small, unconnected wooden houses with no sewerage system. However, since the typhus epidemic is still raging, these facilities will be maintained for the time being. Whether or not the new hospital on Dworska Street will suffice depends on the epidemic's being brought under control.

At the moment there are 130 patients in the hospital on Mickiewicz [Street]. It is characteristic of the situation that very few people now seek admittance to the hospital, whereas earlier, hundreds of patients eligible for hospitalization had to wait for beds. The reasons [for the lack of applicants] are that, on the one hand, the shock of the hospital evacuations is still in the air and, on the other, the hospital is only accepting cases that can be cured swiftly, mainly surgical cases. Neither patients with tuberculosis, the most widespread disease in the ghetto, nor those with hunger edema are being admitted.

NEW SIGNS FOR WORKSHOPS

The new signs for the workshops have already been put up. They indicate the kind of workshop and the factory number, and are signed: Gettoverwaltung [Ghetto Administration].

FROM THE PAPER WORKSHOP

This workshop recently received a large order for decorative lampshades. 5,500 are to be produced. The prototypes are excellent and their quality compares favorably with those produced in peacetime. A large collection of the latest in toys has recently been produced. Several million such toys are to be manufactured. These products are so imaginative that no one can tell that they are made largely of paper and refuse.

Population Changes in the Month of October, 1942

	Men	Women	Total
[Level as of] August 30, 1942	45,088	60,043	105,131
Resettled on September 1–2 and 7–12	6,016	9,669	15,685
Level as of October 1, 1942	39,072	50,374	89,446
Increases			
Births	7	14	21
Miscarriages	1	—	1
Arrivals from the Generalgouvernement and Warthegau	13	9	22
From manual labor outside the ghetto	40	3	43
Total increase	61 [60]	26	87 [86]

Population Changes in the Month of October, 1942 (cont.)

	Men	Women	Total
Decreases			
Left for manual labor outside the ghetto	22	—	22
Deaths	474	332	806
Actual decrease [?]	414	305 [306]	719 [720]
Level as of November 1, 1942	38,658	50,069	88,727

SUNDAY, NOVEMBER 1, 1942

PRISONERS EVACUATED

A motorized squad appeared at Central Prison early this morning and took the prisoners being held for the German authorities. These 19 prisoners included such infamous representatives of the Jewish underworld as Jankiel "Chmol" [Rozenberg], a notorious thief. He was the leader of the gang that tunneled into the food warehouse some time ago and then stole sugar by the sackload. He had previously run a large-scale smuggling operation. "Chmol" has faced hanging once before. These prisoners also included the gangster "Didika."

TOTAL POPULATION

Correction from August 16. Instead of the 72 people indicated as resettled here from Bełchatów, there were only 57. Corrections from the month of August: from Zduńska Wola—6, from Wieluń—1, and from Łask—1. In light of these corrections, the total population today is 88,703.

A SUICIDE

Salomon Małkes, the head of the Information Department and one of the ghetto's most senior officials, committed suicide by jumping from a fourth floor [window]. At the hospital, he succumbed to his serious injuries. Małkes had recently been in a state of severe depression that dated from the deportation of his mother. The suicide of this official has had a profound effect on the ghetto.

MONDAY, NOVEMBER 2, 1942

SUPREME INSPECTION CHAMBER ELIMINATED

As already reported, confusions as to areas of responsibility resulted when the Special Unit began performing inspections while the *NIK (HKK)* [Supreme Inspection Chamber][100] was still formally in existence. The situation has now changed, however. The *HKK* no longer exists. The Chairman has issued a circular announcing that the Main Trade Commission has been integrated into the Central Workshop Bureau and now bears the title, Central Workshop Bureau and Trade Inspection Section. This

100. NIK—Najwyższa Izba Kontroli; HHK—Höchste Kontroll-Kammer. Cf. p. 24, n. 34.

section now consists of: Bernard Koppel, an engineer, Łuzer Neumann, Mieczysław Rozenblat, and Józef Rumkowski. Thus, the entire presidium of the Supreme Inspection Chamber has been incorporated into the Central Workshop Bureau as the Trade Inspection Section.

DEMOLITION OF WOODEN HOUSES ON BRZEZIŃSKA AND FRANCISZKAŃSKA STREETS

By order of the Ghetto Administration, the one-story houses on the sections of those streets that have been separated from the ghetto are to be torn down. The demolition work on those wooden houses has already begun. Today, workmen began demolishing the building at the corner of Franciszkańska and Brzezińska streets. A building of this size yields some 70,000 kilograms of wood, which is to be allocated for heating purposes by the demolition department of the coal storage yard. The razing of this corner building and two further properties on Brzezińska Street will leave a vacant area here. The work should be completed in one week.

TYPHOID

As we have learned from Dr. Wiktor Miller, head of the Department of Health, the causes of the typhoid epidemic are to be sought in the following abuses: fecal matter contaminating the well water; insufficient means of transportation for removing excrement; and the devastating effect that the shortage of adequate housing is also having; the low level of sanitary conditions; the filth in apartments; the impossibility of combatting typhoid because no compulsory hospitalization exists. No precise statistics are available since many people do not summon physicians. [The number of people with typhoid] is now estimated to stand at one thousand. The form of typhoid now most prevalent is relatively mild, however, and the mortality rate is low. It is expected that the onset of cold weather will put an end to the infestation of flies, and it is also feared that convalescents will then be highly susceptible to pulmonary diseases. At present, tuberculosis and hunger edema are the main causes of death.

TUESDAY, NOVEMBER 3, 1942

AN EXHIBITION IN THE GHETTO

An exhibition of ghetto products was already in the planning stage one year ago. The idea was to mount a large-scale exhibition in a special building to be constructed in the vacant area between Łagiewnicka and Ceglana streets. All the design work was completed by the Construction Department but was never executed. Now, the Ghetto Administration has once again resumed this project and given the Eldest strict orders to proceed immediately with the exhibition. The two modern five-story buildings at 37 and 37a Łagiewnicka Street, the former site of the children's hospital, are being made available for this purpose. It will probably take several months to adapt these [two] structures as well as equip them with essentials, such as furniture, glass cases, etc., and, finally, to choose and prepare the objects for the exhibition.

INTRODUCTION OF DAYLIGHT SAVINGS TIME

Until now there have actually been two kinds of time in the ghetto. Generally, clocks were set fifteen minutes ahead of the time outside the ghetto. Individual departments, however, went precisely by city time. With the introduction of daylight savings time, public clocks, like the one at the [ghetto's] Main Post Office, have been adjusted so that we are now on correct Central European time. Oddly enough, however, the ghetto population has ignored this change and continues to go by the old time. It is expected that the large three-faced clock soon to be installed opposite the entrance gate to Bałut Market will normalize time throughout the ghetto.

A NEW REST HOME

Yesterday, for the first time, the Vacation Commission sent workers to the new rest home on Gnieźnieńska Street (formerly the Old People's Home) for a normal week of vacation. Since the new rest home can accommodate 150 (as opposed to 26 in the old), the vacation schedule can be rotated at a faster rate. Thus, we now have four rest homes: three in Marysin and the new one on Gnieźnieńska Street. The Chairman inspected this new home today. So far this season, some 1,000 people—blue-and-white-collar workers—have spent their vacations there.

WEDNESDAY, NOVEMBER 4, 1942

DAYLIGHT SAVINGS TIME

From now on the only valid time is that indicated by the electric clock in the lobby of the Main Post Office. This clock is to be regulated by a signal transmitted twice a day from Bałut Market.

PEOPLE ARE SAYING . . .

A persistent rumor has it that ghetto inhabitants will be allowed on the streets solely on the basis of workshop and office work schedules, that is, only during a change of shifts. These rumors are probably due to the conditions that prevailed in Warsaw [ghetto] immediately following the deportations there.[101] According to information arriving here, a total curfew is in effect there such that people cannot even contact their closest relatives. Postcards have been arriving in this ghetto with the terse message: "We are working."

---

101. After the great deportations of July–October, 1942, the area of the Warsaw ghetto underwent a considerable decrease and barely comprised a few blocks. Those blocks formed the so-called residual ghetto (*Restgetto*) which was more reminiscent of a labor camp than of the former Jewish quarter. The residual ghetto's population of some 40,000 was roughly divided into two groups: those who were employed and were, along with their families, registered, and the so-called "wild" or unregistered residents, that is, those who had by some miracle avoided deportation. The former were chiefly employed in German workshops and were quartered there as well, and separated from the members of their families who were either employed in other shops or lived in the so-called residential sector of the residual ghetto, thus making any contact extremely difficult.

FROM THE POST OFFICE

The average monthly total of money orders arriving here is approximately 250,000 [German] marks. The greatest number comes from the Protectorate of Bohemia and Moravia. As for foreign countries, money is being transferred here from Holland and Hungary, about 10,000 marks per month. Remittances from Warthegau and the Generalgouvernement have decreased considerably because of the resettlements. Scarcely 15,000 marks per month are arriving here [from those areas]. The flow of funds from the Generalgouvernement has always been smaller since no money orders could be issued [there] for more than ten marks. However, there was no restriction on money sent from the towns in Warthegau. This is why the above-mentioned decrease [in money orders] from Warthegau is a heavy blow. Money order stubs bearing messages are removed by the Gestapo[102] for they are viewed as violations of the mail embargo.

Printed matter: Previously, the ghetto was allowed to mail out 30,000 pre-printed postal cards. Now the limit has been reduced to about 20,000. This number now suffices, unfortunately, because the overall volume of mail has automatically declined as a result of the resettlements.

After two weeks of a total mail embargo, postcards are again arriving from Warsaw [ghetto].[103] It has been noted that these cards no longer bear the postmark of the Jewish Postal Service but only the postmark C2 (Warsaw, Center). Most of the mail from the small towns in the Generalgouvernement and Warthegau is in German, or Yiddish in Latin letters, or in Polish. The majority of the correspondence makes reference to *khasenes* [weddings].[104] From this mail, one can infer that nearly all Jewish centers have been liquidated apart from a small number of industrial towns, for example, a small town in the Cracow area where Jews are working in a munitions plant. It appears that the Kielce district is the only area that has so far been spared drastic resettlement actions.[105]

Large amounts of mail have also been coming in from local ghetto residents who are now in labor camps outside the ghetto. Principally, their letters contain requests for warm clothing. This is the only kind of package sent outside the ghetto. These clothing packages, amounting to 25 every week, are expedited by the post office on

102. In the original *Chronicle* the word, "Gestapo," had been crossed out in indelible pencil.

103. During the great deportations to Treblinka in July–October, 1942, the Jewish postal service in the Warsaw ghetto practically ceased functioning, although the institution as such had not been entirely eliminated. Its staff decimated and its activity extremely curtailed, the post office in the ghetto continued to function until the ghetto was liquidated in April, 1943. As late as February, 1943—according to a report by the Warsaw Judendar—4,162 letters came in to the ghetto. AZIH (AJHI)—E. Ringelblum's Underground Archives, II, no. 280).

104. *Khasenes*, literally *weddings*, but here the word is used with a code meaning: unfortunate events.

105. In 1942, after deportations from villages, towns, and cities throughout occupied Poland to the death camps in Chełmno (Kulmhof), Treblinka, Sobibór, Majdanek, Bełzec, and Birkenau-Auschwitz, the Reich Security Main Office (RSHA) allowed the so-called secondary ghettos and also the Jewish labor camps working for the German war economy to remain for a certain time in the five districts of the Generalgouvernement. In the Cracow region (*Distrikt Krakau*), these included the ghettos (*Arbeitsgettos*) in Cracow, Bochnia, Tarnów, Rzeszów, and Przemyśl, as well as the forced labor camp (*Zwangsarbeitslager SS*) in Płaszów and its various branches. In the Kielce region (the wartime *Distrikt Radom*), these were the ghettos in Sandomierz, Szydłowiec, Radom, Ujazd, and others, as well as the labor camps, including one of the largest, in Skarżysko.

the basis of certificates from the Bureau of Labor. The mailing of food is not permitted. No packages whatsoever come into the ghetto.

Telegrams are a rarity. At Rosh Hashanah, a wire arrived from South America.

Local mail: Since the various departments communicate with one another by mail, the volume of local mail has increased greatly. The post office processes up to 4,000 items daily, including a rather large number of food coupons. A mailman often has to deliver as many as 550 items per day.

Since the most recent cutbacks, the postal service employs 130 people.

THURSDAY, NOVEMBER 5, 1942[106]

WEATHER

Further cooling. High temperature of the day—11 degrees, the low—5 degrees.

DEATHS

Twenty. Births: one girl.

COMMITTED TO PRISON

Eleven men from the camp at Radogoszcz have been transferred to Central Prison. The person reported as remanded here from Litzmannstadt on the 3d of this month is a 6-year-old boy of unknown background; he is suspected of being of Jewish descent.

TOTAL POPULATION

88,636.

MEAT AND SAUSAGE

Beginning tomorrow, November 6, 150 grams of meat and 100 grams of sausage will again be distributed.

CIGARETTES ARRIVE

Yesterday and today, new shipments of tobacco and cigarettes arrived in the ghetto. Altogether, we have received 5,000,000 cigarettes in brands known here (Bregava, Rama, Drava) and some 2,400 kilograms of tobacco (Croatian state monopoly). This shipment will meet the needs of the ghetto for roughly one year. Demand will decline somewhat because new cards for smokers will be issued next month and, thus, the cards of people resettled or deceased will be taken out of circulation. It is possible that the weekly ration will be increased.

WHAT HAS CAUSED SO MUCH GASTRIC DISEASE?

A bacteriological examination of the most essential foods has revealed the following: The potatoes used in the soup kitchens for thickening the soup were being grated one

106. The *Daily Chronicle Bulletin* for Thursday, November 5, 1942, is given in its entirety here.

day in advance. They were turning black overnight and were therefore injurious to health.

VALUABLES FOUND IN OLD CLOTHES

The workers who sort the old clothes delivered to the ghetto frequently turn up valuables such as jewels, gold objects, and foreign currency. All such items are duly handed over to the [German] authorities.

POST OFFICE: PHILATELY DEPARTMENT

The Philately Department is located in the post office branch at 1 Rybna Street. During the next few days, this department is to be incorporated into the Main Post Office. The reason for this change is that [Jakub] Dawidowicz, an engineer and expert in philately, had previously served in the branch office and is now head of the main office. The Philately Department has just received its Christmas order and is now preparing collections and packets of stamps. As we reported earlier, these stamps come from collections that have been purchased in the ghetto. The new order's estimated value is approximately 7,000 marks. Rare stamps have been very hard to come by lately.

THE ORGANIZATION OF THE DEPARTMENT OF HEALTH

Forty medical districts have been established, one for each 2,000–2,500 inhabitants. The district physicians make house calls and are also on duty for certain hours in the outpatient clinics. These physicians also refer patients to specialists. Two clinics have been established for this purpose: one at 40 Brzezińska Street and one at 40 Lutomierska Street. In keeping with the motto: "To the front lines—the workshops," physicians have been assigned to all factories. Each plant having more than 1,000 workers will get one doctor who will be on duty there for seven hours. He will refer bedridden patients to the appropriate district physicians.

The Department of Health also maintains two emergency stations, one at 41 Łagiewnicka Street, where the department's head office has been located since the resettlement actions—and the other at 13 Lutomierska Street. The ghetto now has 161 physicians; 31 of them have been dismissed as Community physicians and placed at the disposal of the Personnel Department. This group is not practicing at the moment, but there is some prospect that these doctors will again be employed. The [facilities of the] X-ray Department, which were confiscated by the German authorities after the hospital's patients were evacuated, are now to be returned. Two of the six X-ray machines, as well as some of the other equipment, will be returned. Since the liquidation of the hospitals, the ghetto has been deprived of this medical equipment. The medical supply situation grows worse from one day to the next. The shortage of injections and chemicals is becoming greater all the time.

SATURDAY, NOVEMBER 7, 1942

WOMEN POLICE

A week ago, the Chairman decided to establish a women's police unit. Summonses were sent solely to gymnasium graduates who had received their diplomas here in the ghetto. Today, the medical examinations took place. Some sixty girls were examined. The duties of this unit will consist of looking after children and taking care of minors whose parents work in the factories. Dr. [Karl] Bondy, until now the head of all the transport collectives of Jews resettled here from the Reich [and the Protectorate of Bohemia and Moravia], will assume the administrative leadership [of the women's police unit] on behalf of the Order Service.

A CONCERT AND A SPEECH BY THE CHAIRMAN

Today, after an interval of over two months, a concert once again took place in the House of Culture. Conducted by [Dawid] Bajgelman, the program consisted of his latest compositions, nearly all of them concerto fantasies and variations on popular Jewish themes. The soloist was [Miss Bronisława] Rotsztat. Since its concertmaster has died, the orchestra was incomplete, and a few of its members, for example, Professor [E.] Wachtel (viola), have been resettled. Now, the musicians can play only in their spare time, since the House of Culture no longer exists as an independent department and all musicians are employed in workshops or departments. After the concert, the Chairman delivered a speech covering three main points. He spoke about the newly established women's police [unit] as a means of dealing with the problem of [orphaned] children, about the medical service, the obligation to report contagious diseases, and, finally, about the food situation. In regard to the latter, he stressed that no further allocations of potatoes are to be expected apart from the rations already distributed. He cautioned the populace to be as thrifty as possible with its supplies. He flatly denied the rumors that are now spreading panic. After the long period [during which the House of Culture was closed], the Chairman's speech in the crowded auditorium caused a sensation. Nearly all the Community's leaders were present. As the Chairman announced, regular concerts will again be performed from now on.

MONDAY, NOVEMBER 9, 1942

NO WINDOW PANES

We have already written about the great shortage of window panes in the ghetto. The authorities promised to deliver one railroad car full of glass for window panes. However, the [German] Ghetto Administration has now notified the Construction Department that this delivery cannot be counted on and, in a lengthy letter, explained that all this glass has been requisitioned for the needs of the Eastern Front. This development places the Construction Department in a serious predicament in a period when numerous transfers and reinstallations of workshops are occurring. Many of the apartments allocated to the people from the evacuated [portion of] Precinct I are without window panes, and the tenants are freezing.

MEAT FROM DANZIG

Frozen meat (veal) of very high quality has arrived in the ghetto from Danzig, and some of it is already being distributed at allocation centers. We have already noted that canned meat is being distributed again. However, only manual laborers are receiving canned meat. 35,000 kilograms of canned meat were still in the ghetto. The Ghetto Administration gave permission to distribute this supply, realizing that it could no longer keep without spoiling. The Veterinarian Department examined the cans of meat two weeks ago and divided them into three categories: meat no longer edible, meat suitable only for cooking, and meat that can be eaten without being cooked.

TUESDAY, NOVEMBER 10, 1942

RESETTLED HERE

The man from Waldhorst (in the Old Reich) mentioned the day before yesterday, is a plumber, Chaim Bygeleizen, born in Łask in 1907. The man registered yesterday as resettled here from Litzmannstadt is named Mrozek; until now, he had remained in the city working as a tanner.

A CAMP NEAR THE CEMETERY

The terrain along the cemetery wall, part of the area removed [from the ghetto] and now enclosed by a high plank fence, is, according to confidential information, to be used as a camp for Polish teenagers.

BREAD

The hope that bread would be distributed for six days this week has come to naught. As of this moment, there have been no changes.

WEDNESDAY, NOVEMBER 11, 1942

RESETTLED IN THE GHETTO

Tauba Sochaczewska and her 5-year-old daughter, Estera, have arrived in this ghetto from Warsaw. They are residing here at 9 Drewnowska Street. Twelve-year-old Teresa Salaszki, whose parents are unknown, has been resettled here from Litzmannstadt on the suspicion that she is Jewish. She has been placed in the home for working adolescents in Marysin.

SATURDAY, NOVEMBER 14, 1942

AN OBITUARY

Dr. Dawid Helman, a laryngologist well-known and respected in Łódź, died today at the age of sixty-eight. As one of the first members of the Chairman's staff and as his representative in the city, he had a leading part in organizing the Department of Health in the ghetto.

Also, today, Aleksander Nower, head of the Tobacco Department, died of angina pectoris.

LABOR CAMP

Lejzer Prichacki, of 14 Brzezińska [Street] has been deported to the labor camp at Waldhorst (the present name for Kolumna, a former resort near Łask). Thus, Waldhorst is not located in the Old Reich, as was noted in one of the previous bulletins of this *Chronicle*. Workshops have been set up in Waldhorst, mainly for tailoring, and Jews from nearby Pabianice have been working there. Jews (craftsmen) from [our] ghetto are sent to that camp from time to time.

MILK AND COTTAGE CHEESE

No milk has been delivered to the ghetto for two days now. The distribution centers have so little cottage cheese that employee coupons are presently not being honored, and cottage cheese is being distributed only to sick people possessing the appropriate coupon. In private commerce, a portion (200 grams) of cottage cheese already costs five marks.

A RISE IN PRICES

Noted in private commerce: bread—100 marks; potatoes—11 marks; sugar—110 marks; other items essentially unchanged.

THE CALENDAR FOR 1943

The ghetto calendar for 1943 is now in preparation. Wall, table, and pocket calendars are being printed in editions smaller than last year's; the editorial director is Mr. S[zmul] Rozenstein, head of the ghetto printing office. This year, the calendars will again contain interesting notes about the development of the ghetto, forming a concise history of the ghetto through the end of 1942.

A CONCERT

The second symphony concert since the resumption of activity by the House of Culture has taken place and was directed by [Dawid] Bajgelman. Jewish compositions by the conductor were performed. Afterwards, the Chairman spoke about the ghetto's current problems, chiefly the placing of homeless children and the food situation. He again emphasized that no more potatoes would be distributed.

SUNDAY, NOVEMBER 15, 1942

A THROUGH-TRAM

Today, tramcars from outside the ghetto began running along Franciszkańska and Brzezińska streets to the edge of the city. This makes for an entirely new picture: trams from the city, filled with Germans and Poles, running along ghetto streets not enclosed by barbed wire. There is only one regulation: Jews are not allowed to walk on the odd-numbered side of Franciszkańska Street from Smugowa [Street], the ghetto border, to Brzezińska Street (odd numbers) and from that corner to the end of the [ghetto] city. Policemen are making sure that this regulation is observed. The Jewish tramcars run on the left side. It is assumed that this section, which has been severed from the ghetto, will not be fenced off for technical reasons, since it is impossible to place a fence between the two sets of electric tracks. For the moment, the vacated apartments in the section separated from the ghetto remain unoccupied. Work is continuing in the workshops located in this section of Precinct I.

FOSTER CARE OF CHILDREN

The special commission has placed 624 parentless children with various families. This project is still in progress.

THE TAILORS' TRADE SCHOOL

The Tailors' Trade School at 29 Franciszkańska Street, which had 60 children enrolled in its courses, is now to be expanded to accommodate several hundred children. For this reason, [Dawid] Warszawski conferred with the heads of workshops, who are being asked to lend a hand in expanding this extremely important institution.

THE HOUSE OF CULTURE

After yesterday's concert in the House of Culture, the Chairman has definitely resolved that regular performances again be given there, as before the last resettlement. This week, there will be three evening revue performances beginning on Tuesday (Revue No. 3), and a concert on Saturday. Preparations are already underway for the performance of Revue No. 4.

MONDAY, NOVEMBER 16, 1942

THE THROUGH-TRAM

In regard to the information that tramcars from Litzmannstadt are to pass through the ghetto (Franciszkańska–Brzezińska streets), it should be added that all these trams are closed and do not stop anywhere in the ghetto, not even at street corners. On the second day, an attached car jumped the rails, and it took quite a long while to deal with the accident. First, a special unit of the German police had to come to the scene in order to let the passengers out of the car and guard them, keeping them from any contact with the Jewish population, while the tramcar was being put back on the track.

In several of the workshops remaining in the area now separated from the ghetto, a German commission has checked to make sure that no private individuals, except for those employed there, are to be found in any of those buildings.

The portion of Smugowa [Street] now separated from the ghetto is still fenced in.

PEOPLE ARE SAYING . . .

That the next food ration will include an allocation of wheat flour. Also, rumors that bread will be distributed for six days still persist.[107]

---

107. In one of the copies of the *Chronicle* this sentence was crossed out in indelible pencil.

Supposedly, news from the people resettled from [this ghetto] has arrived here from [the region of] Polesie, including, as well, news from recent deportees from Warsaw [ghetto]. At present, there is no way to determine whether these rumors are based on fact.

TUESDAY, NOVEMBER 17, 1942

THE THROUGH-TRAM

Previous information could well be supplemented by a description of the way the tram enters the ghetto. A gate has been made in the fence at the corner of 13 Franciszkańska Street and Smugowa [Street] where the ghetto ends. A [German] sentry is posted at this gateway. Whenever a tram arrives, it halts, the cars are sealed, the gate is opened and the closed tramcars pass through the ghetto. Order Service men patrol the Jewish side. For that reason, in order to get the derailed car running again, they had first to obtain permission from the German police to unseal the tram. It took a while to obtain this permission because [the German] police are located on Bałut Market in Precinct VI. A great many people use this line (No. 9) which goes to the cemetery; the trams carrying Poles are so crowded by 7 P.M. that a tram train often consists of three cars. The difference between the German trams, which are of the latest construction, and the mostly open Jewish trams is so striking that they seem from different eras.

AN INCREASE IN [THE PRICE] OF CLOTHING

In the few [private] shops remaining in the ghetto, there has been a markedly sharp increase in prices for clothing. Thus, a pair of winter gloves now costs 15 marks, while just a short time ago they cost only 5 marks. This rise is due to the fact that now all available material is brought to the Central Storehouse at 10 Jakuba [Street] and the buying outlets have been eliminated. The items are no longer accessible to the populace since they are processed and used exclusively for export.

THE WOMEN'S POLICE

The women's police [unit], established on November 1, 1942, and known as the FOD [*Frauenordnungsdienst*—Women's Order Service] is headed by Dr. Karl Bondy. So far, 56 women have been accepted. This unit has no direct contact with Order Service sections.

WEDNESDAY, NOVEMBER 18, 1942

FALSE RUMORS

For the entire day there has been a pleasant rumor circulating that 5 kilograms of potatoes and 5 kilograms of vegetables are to be added to the usual ration. This rumor specifies that the potatoes and vegetables are of inferior quality and will be distributed in Marysin. Even after the printed proclamation concerning the food allocation, people have been saying that others have seen potatoes and vegetables being allocated. This sort of false rumor, especially in a new ration period, leads us to conclude that these are not chance tales but a deliberate attempt to mislead the population, especially in regard to potatoes. The Chairman has repeatedly denied [the rumor of] any new distribution before April. Apparently, in order to increase profits later on, people are trying to drive prices down in private commerce, which, unfortunately, has not yet been eliminated entirely.

MONDAY, NOVEMBER 23, 1942

CENTRAL PRISON

By order of the [German] authorities, some 50 people were brought from the prison to Bałut Market, and were then taken out of the ghetto. One of these people was the former Order Service man, Torończyk, who was being punished for taking an amount in excess of his ration when picking up his vegetable ration at the market. Because of these events, various rumors about new resettlements are already circulating. Some 30 people remain in the prison.

THE WOMEN'S POLICE

Today, for the first time, one could see members of the Women's Order Service in the streets. The young girls wore special green uniforms—short trousers, short waistless jackets, and round caps, all made from the same material with yellow stripes. They bear the insignia of the Order Service on one arm and carry nightsticks.

SECURITY FORCES IN THE GHETTO

The figures concerning Order Service men in the ghetto run as follows: 528 in the five precincts and the Bureau of Investigation; 35 in the Isolation Service; 298 hall and house fire prevention [units]; Fire Department—176; chimney sweeps—39; Central Prison—35; total—1,111 men.

THE USE OF ELECTRICAL APPLIANCES

is prohibited. Because of the constant recent power failures caused by the use of hot plates, etc., searches have been increased sharply, and any appliances found are confiscated. The Kripo [German criminal police] are also carrying out such searches and confiscating any hot plates, irons, or other [electrical appliances] that they find.

Severe penalties are provided for using electric light during the day. As a result, a rumor is circulating in the ghetto that this has been made a capital offense. Needless to say, this is an exaggeration.

PEOPLE ARE SAYING . . .

A rumor is afoot in the ghetto that the Ghetto Administration has granted permission for the establishment of a movie theater. A similar rumor circulated two years ago but the wish did not come true then and will not come true this time either.

THURSDAY, NOVEMBER 26, 1942

A SPECIAL ITEM

On November 25, at 7:20 P.M., two Kripo officials ordered the Order Service man on duty at the corner of Środkowa and Głowacki streets to retrieve the body of an unidentified woman shot just outside the ghetto. There are no details as to her identity. The body was taken to the mortuary at Hospital No. 1.

THE STANDARD CLOCK ON BAŁUT MARKET

whose installation has already been reported here, will be in operation as of Thursday. This clock will make things easier for the ghetto's population since, until now, every office and workshop has gone by a different time. The directors were not happy with this situation because of the resulting lack of punctuality [among workers]. It is to be hoped that this standard clock will bring about a single time system [in the ghetto].

WORKSHOP SOUP

has again been prepared with vegetables during the past few days. Because of the large deliveries of cabbage that must be used up, the Department of Soup Kitchens has ordered a reduction in the soup's potato and starch content.[108] They are to be replaced with cabbage. And thus, since Thursday, the afternoon soup has been prepared with cabbage. The soup is tastier now but its nutritional value is lower. The "black market in soup" reacted to this with an immediate drop in price. A [bowl of] soup now costs 3.50 marks as opposed to [the earlier price of] 4.0 to 4.50.

THE CARES OF DAILY LIFE

At present, the food problem is eased by the larger vegetable allocations; however, we now must deal with the problem of heating. Aside from the fact that the amount and the frequency of cooking has been increased by the larger allocations, the heating of dwellings is now of prime importance; as a result, fuel is in great demand and very expensive, with briquettes and wood costing 3 marks. A further crucial fact is that the distribution of [sawdust] coupons in the woodwork factories has stopped, and inspections there have been increased.

FRIDAY, NOVEMBER 27, 1942

PEOPLE ARE SAYING . . .

The local population is still extremely nervous. People are talking about further resettlements. Supposedly, the staff of the straw-shoe workshop is to be transferred to Poznań. The reason given is that it is much easier for the authorities to implement a one-time transfer of workers than to keep shipping the straw materials from Poznań

---

108. In the original the words, "and starch content," were crossed out.

to the ghetto. As we have learned from the best-informed of sources, no resettlements of any sort [are scheduled] at this time, and this rumor has met with a complete denial.

Supposedly, 6 kilograms of potatoes and 4 kilograms of vegetables are to be added to the next ration.

Regarding the now rather normal number of deaths, it should be noted that, among the deceased, there were persons who were not suffering from shortages of any kind. It has been demonstrated that the mortality rate drops as soon as the food market comes to life and rations are increased. Characteristic examples are the deaths of Mrs. Kleiman, the wife of the head of the Department of Transportation, and Miss Kaufman, the daughter of the head of the Fire Department, that is, people who were certainly well-to-do.

DISEASES

The characteristic ghetto disease during the past few weeks has been typhoid, occurring with a high fever of 40 degrees for up to four weeks. If no complications ensued, the typhoid as such has usually been curable, but, in cases with very dangerous complications, the disease has been fatal. Most recent deaths were caused by this disease.

TUESDAY, DECEMBER 1, 1942

Population Changes in the Month of November, 1942

	Men	Women	Total
Resettled September 1–2, and September 7–12, 1942	6,016	9,669	15,685
Level as of September 1, 1942	44,674	59,738	104,412
Level as of November 1, 1942	38,658	50,069	88,727
Births	3	8	11
Arrivals from the Generalgouvernement and Warthegau	13	7	20
Remains discovered (Note: the remains of Estera Fraja Schulsinger, born in Wieruszów in 1923)	—	1	1
Resettled here in August	2	—	2
Increases	74	18	92
Deaths	397	292	689
Left for the Generalgouvernement and Warthegau	—	1	1
From manual labor outside the ghetto	75	—	75
Resettled	8	11	19
People erroneously registered as resettled here in August	—	9	9
Total decrease	470	313	783
Actual decrease	396	295	691
Level as of December 1, 1942	38,262	49,774	88,036

TUESDAY, DECEMBER 1, 1942

WE HAVE LEARNED

from sources in good standing with the [German] Ghetto Administration that no resettlements are anticipated before the New Year, that work cards are to be issued to all workers between the ages of ten and sixty-five, and that a motion picture theater is to be set up to provide working people with entertainment and diversion from daily life. People are also saying that there will be a further potato allocation in every ration, so that 10 kilograms of potatoes per capita will be distributed to the population every month. Of all this news, which we heard several days ago, the last item was confirmed by the potato allocation in the last two rations. It is to be hoped that the other rumors are also based on something like fact.

WEDNESDAY, DECEMBER 2, 1942

MILK AND COUPONS

Contrary to the optimistic expectation that milk would be coming into the ghetto again, as of last Sunday no milk had yet been delivered. The ghetto is still without milk. The expiration date of the various coupons given to [blue-collar] workers, instructors, policemen, firemen, and a few office employees has been extended indefinitely.

FOOD PRICES

On the free market, bread costs 130 marks, onions, 150, and leeks are simply unavailable. Sugar costs 120, but, at present, this item is not being offered for sale. The fact that it is unavailable may be linked to the rumor that in the future only brown sugar will be allocated.

FUEL

Because of the great shortage of fuel, [the price of] wood has already risen to 4 marks per kilogram.

IMPRESSMENT

As we reported earlier [on November 30], single men, a list of whom has been drawn up in the Department of Ration Cards based on the vegetable books, are being impressed for night duty at the vegetable storage lots in Marysin. It is assumed that these men will be housed in barracks there, performing their normal jobs during the day and then taking turns at night duty. At the moment, there is a great shortage of manpower in the ghetto. The [German] Ghetto Administration has demanded 388 men for demolition work outside the ghetto, but this demand could not be met, which made for some terrible scenes. It was therefore decreed that a number of office workers should be discharged in order to create the necessary manpower. For example, 30 men were released from the post office, 51 from the Resettlement Office. Further impressment is under way.

THURSDAY, DECEMBER 3, 1942

TRAFFIC JAMS

have occurred inside and outside the ghetto because of the heavy snowfall. In particular, the ghetto's bridges were so jammed because of the difficulty in crossing them that only one person at a time could be allowed over; as a result, many workshop and office workers have been arriving at their jobs an hour late.

In the city, the tram line has been taken out of service because of the accumulation of snow. Thus, for the first time, Germans and Poles were forced to travel on Zgierska and Limanowski streets on foot, which resulted in a rare sight—Aryans walking on the roadway while Jews walked on the sidewalk.

PEOPLE ARE SAYING . . .

Various rumors are again circulating. Supposedly, the entire Jewish population is to be impressed for the construction of the highway between Litzmannstadt and Warsaw, resulting in a complete evacuation of the ghetto. It is also said that, due to interventions of various sorts, this danger has, however, been averted until January 1.

THE GHETTO AS A LABOR CAMP

The ghetto was gladdened to learn that, by decision of the highest authorities in Berlin, it is being declared a labor camp. It is hoped that this [new status] will make various things easier [for the populace] and cause an improvement in the food supply.

SATURDAY, DECEMBER 5, 1942

A REDUCTION IN THE ORDER SERVICE

The Order Service was again reduced in size several days ago. Fifty-two Order Service men were dismissed, including people who were sick or weak, or who had committed some minor offense. Sixteen new Order Service men were taken on so that the total number of Order Service men on December 1 (not counting the Special Unit) came to 562.

A CONCERT

Today, as on every Saturday, a concert took place in the House of Culture and, as usual, the ghetto's elite attended. [Dawid] Bajgelman conducted the performance of light Jewish music and there was also a violin solo by [Miss Bronisława] Rotsztat.

SUNDAY, DECEMBER 6, 1942

A SUICIDE ATTEMPT

Today, Gabriela Jacobskind, born in Nieszawa in 1872, a resident of 4 Kościelny Square, attempted suicide by taking poison. She was brought to the hospital in critical condition.

ELIMINATION OF THE OFFICE FOR RESETTLED PERSONS

The Office for Resettled Persons, now located on Rybna Street, will be eliminated on January 1, 1943. This office is no longer needed since no new population transfers to the ghetto are planned. This office was of great importance when 20,000 West European Jews were brought to this ghetto in October and November, 1941, and also when thousands of Jews were resettled here from various small towns in Warthegau. Organized by [Henryk] Neftalin, the attorney, in November, 1941, this office will have existed for over a year by the time it is eliminated. There is no question that this institution will have a place of major significance in the history of the ghetto.

MONDAY, DECEMBER 7, 1942

CARING FOR ORPHANS

The Special Commission to provide care for orphans, which was created on September 22, has already placed 720 children with families. Its card index still contains some 100 offers from families and more are added every day. We can see that the Chairman's appeal to the hearts of ghetto dwellers has met with complete success. The remainder of the 300 children registered will soon be placed with families by the commission, and a portion of those adolescents still in hostels for teenage workers will also eventually find homes. The five hostels for adolescents now house about 300 children. [The commission] plans to leave only the older children of 16 and 17 there, and gradually to place the others with families. The exceptions are those children who, because of ill health or because of their classification as problem children, cannot be placed with families.

Also, for the first time, an attempt has been made to place the older children—the 16- and 17-year-olds—in small groups of four and five in apartments of their own, where they would be supplied with furniture and all the necessary household articles. The hostels or the commission will continue to supervise these small groups.

The commission also supplies clothing, linen, shoes, or money to children who earn too little themselves or whose foster families do not earn enough to buy rations.

WEDDINGS

Weddings took place this Sunday as they do every Sunday; the Chairman married fourteen couples. From now on, along with the food coupon each couple receives, newlyweds will be given a coupon worth 30 marks toward the purchase of linen and clothing. The buying power of this coupon is further increased by the 25 percent price discount that has been granted to newlyweds.

TUESDAY, DECEMBER 8, 1942

NEW COINS

Today, new 10-pfennig pieces went into circulation in the ghetto. The Main Treasury minted the coins several months ago, but production was halted after a short while.

At the time it was said that continued minting of these coins had been prohibited by the authorities, because these 10-pfennig pieces were very similar to the German Reich coin of the same value. Recently, there has been a great shortage of small change [in the ghetto] because the 10-pfennig vouchers issued by the Post Office were not sufficient for 88,000 people. The newly minted 10-pfennig pieces are smaller in size than the Reich coin. On the first day, 100,000 coins were put into circulation, and more are being produced by the metal factory every day. One side bears the inscription: *Quittung über 10 Pfennig* [10 pfennig voucher]; on the other side, the words: Der Älteste der Juden in Litzmannstadt [The Eldest of the Jews in Litzmannstadt] form a circle in whose center is a Star of David and the year, 1942. The coins were manufactured from electrum, a light metal.

OFFICE WORKERS IN THE GHETTO

According to the files of the Personnel Department, as of December 1, there were 13,396 office workers employed [in the ghetto]. During the month of November, 637 office workers were dismissed and 86 died, thus reducing the total number by 723. Seven hundred two new office workers have been hired, so that the overall number was reduced by 21 during the month of November.

FROM THE POSTAL DEPARTMENT

During the past few days, postal cards have arrived here from [the ghetto of] Warsaw and from various cities in the Generalgouvernement. The mail from Warsaw is postmarked *Warsaw C2*, presumably at a post office outside the ghetto, and thus, this correspondence may be assumed to have arrived here purely by chance.[109] Many senders use the German firms for which they work as their return addresses. No mail comes from any city in Warthegau, for all Jews have been vacated from that area. On the other hand, a small amount of mail does arrive from cities in Galicia, such as Tarnopol or Lwów. In the postcards from labor camps, the senders request clothing parcels.

Only pre-printed matter can be sent from this ghetto, and no more than approximately 400 items a day. About 70 packages are sent from the ghetto every week to relatives in labor camps. Lately, very few money orders have been arriving in the ghetto; totaling no more than 150,000 to 200,000 German marks, they are chiefly from Bohemia. The individual amounts run between 20 and 50 marks, with occasional larger sums up to 300 marks.

On December 1, the postal service staff was again reduced; of 130 employees, 100 remain. On November 25, Abramowicz, of the Bureau of Investigation, assumed charge of the post office; as we have already reported [on November 20], Abramowicz was installed as commissioner by the Chairman after embezzlements were discovered, and he is now the director. The former director of the post office, [Jakub] Dawidowicz, an engineer, has returned to his former position as head of the post office's Philately Department on Rybna Street. Schweizer, the postman who was

109. See p. 284, n. 103.

involved in the embezzlements, was removed from Central Prison during the last resettlement.

THURSDAY, DECEMBER 10, 1942

RESETTLED HERE

In the past few days, six people from Zelów and a woman from Holland have been resettled in this ghetto. The woman was remanded to Central Prison, where she has been lodged as a prisoner of the German authorities.

A POLISH SMUGGLER ARRESTED IN THE GHETTO

The Order Service has been notified that there was a Pole in the apartment of Kiwa Herzberg, of 12 Nad Łódką Street, apt. 27. The Pole had entered the ghetto illegally through the barbed wire fence at around 10 in the evening, shortly before the report was made. He was carrying a large sack. The Pole, who was immediately arrested, is Jan Jaworski, who resides in Litzmannstadt, at 25 Ogrodowa Street, (that is, in close proximity to the ghetto). The following were in his possession: 4.75 kilograms of lard, 1.5 kilograms of butter, and 4 loaves of bread. The smuggler was turned over to the state criminal police [Kripo].

EXTRA FLOUR RATION

Quite unexpectedly, and unpreceded by rumor, it was announced today that every inhabitant of the ghetto will receive one half kilogram of flour in exchange for ration card coupon 81. This is a Chanukah present.[110]

Children will receive 200 grams of candy from the Eldest of the Jews, as they have on holidays in previous years.

The extra flour ration has caused immediate price drops of about 30 percent on the open market; bread has dropped from 120 to 85 marks, flour from 80 to 55 marks, potatoes from 12 to 10 marks. Butter remains constant at 450, oil, 250, sugar, 100, matches, 1.50, briquettes, 3, and wood, 2.50.

FRIDAY, DECEMBER 11, 1942

FROM HOLLAND

A person from Holland has been resettled here in the ghetto, as we have already reported [yesterday].[111] This man is a 40-year-old Dutch Jew [by the name of] Behr. He was transferred to Central Prison here from a prison in the Poznań district. He had been arrested in Holland a year and a half ago and has been in various prisons since that time.

110. In the original *Chronicle*, this last sentence was crossed out in indelible pencil and marked with a question mark.
111. In yesterday's entry, presumably the same individual was identified as a woman from Holland.

A SPECIAL DISTRIBUTION POINT FOR THE ORDER SERVICE AND FIRE DEPARTMENT

The members of the Order Service and the Fire Department are to have two special distribution points, one on Wolborska Street and the other on Lutomierska Street. These two services will receive all their rations there, including the food that they previously received in food store *R*. This is a very welcome reform since there have always been altercations in the cooperatives and other stores whenever the Order Service men and firemen wished to pick up their rations without waiting in line.

THE NEW 10-PFENNIG PIECES

One hundred thousand marks' worth of the new coins have been minted, that is, 1 million coins. Since this will eliminate the shortage of small change, all 10-pfennig vouchers are to be withdrawn and will no longer be valid.

Most of the [ghetto] marks [Markquittungen] are now in the Community's coffers. Because of the frequent food rations, the population cannot hold on to the money.

MONDAY, DECEMBER 14, 1942

THE ARYAN WIDOW

of Judge Neumark, a member of the local court who died several weeks ago, has left the ghetto. The widow, an ethnic German, had succeeded in contacting her family; her brother is a pilot. Before her departure, she said that she was going to Berlin.

Before the war, Neumark was secretary of the Łódź Association of Rag Dealers.[112]

PEOPLE ARE SAYING . . .

The entire ghetto is saying that a delegation of the Swiss Red Cross will be coming here.

35,000 WOODEN CLOGS (*TREPKIS* [TREPY])

for the local population have been produced in the ghetto within less than two weeks. There had been a great shortage of shoes. Not even the 10 percent quota could be met, since not enough leather soles were available. Because of this shortage, the Chairman succeeded in obtaining permission from the authorities to manufacture 35,000 pairs of trepkis for the ghetto. The Used Materials [and] Sorting Point supplied the necessary material; the tops were to be made chiefly out of knapsacks. This large number is expected to satisfy entirely the demand for shoes.

AN UMBRELLA FACTORY

The Main Purchasing Agency, at 4 Kościelny Square, recently established an umbrella factory. During its first few weeks in operation, this factory produced over 1,000

---

112. In the original *Chronicle*, a question mark was placed in the margin beside the last sentence.

umbrellas, entirely modern in design. These umbrellas have been earmarked for sale outside the ghetto.

That same agency has also established a workshop for manufacturing clothes at 4 Kościelny Square; it chiefly produces women's clothes from materials supplied by the Main Purchasing Agency. These articles too have been designated for "export" out of the ghetto.

AN ORDER FOR 50,000 PAIRS OF INSOLES MADE FROM RAGS

was received by the Used Materials and Sorting Point, which has opened a special workshop for this project on Źródłowa Street.

The general cutback in the Used Materials and Sorting Point has affected 600 blue- and white-collar workers, so that now there are only 2,000 left.

A new way has been found to put rags and iron to good use; they are used in manufacturing covers for glass flasks, which were previously wrapped in wicker.

WORKSHOP SOUP

During the past few days, midday meals in the workshops have taken a considerable turn for the worse, since their potato content was reduced from 400 grams to 100. As a result, the price of soup on the open market has dropped to 2.50 marks.

TUESDAY, DECEMBER 15, 1942

ERIKA NEUMARK

an ethnic German and the widow of the local Judge Neumark, has, as we noted yesterday, left the ghetto; her address has been officially changed from 48 Wrześ-nieńska Street to Litzmannstadt.

FORTY-TWO MEN FROM THE NEUSTADT [EBERSWALDE] LABOR CAMP

arrived in this ghetto yesterday. They were lodged in Central Prison as prisoners of the Gestapo. Thirty-two of them are residents of this ghetto and 10 are from such small towns as Warta, Krośniewice, Zduńska Wola, and Lututów. All of them are skilled workers.

A POSTCARD TO RELATIVES

has arrived here from a local Jewish woman in the women's labor camp near Munich. Postcards have also arrived from people's relatives in Sulejów near Piotrków [Trybunalski].

FORTY PEOPLE ARE REGISTERED IN SOUP KITCHENS

in the entire ghetto; most of them take their meals in the Soup Kitchen for the Intelligentsia.

Since no special rations for these individuals were mentioned in the past few ten-day periods, it was believed that they received the same rations as those who eat at home. However, they have to pick up their reduced rations at two special distribution points.

WEDNESDAY, DECEMBER 16, 1942

BROUGHT TO THIS GHETTO

A local Jew who left the ghetto illegally one year ago has been lodged in Central Prison as a prisoner of the Gestapo.

A SUICIDE

Szymon Najdat, of 32 Wolborska Street, born in Żychlin in 1907, threw himself from the fourth story of 13 Żurawia Street. The Emergency Service physician determined that he was dead.

A BARBER

Szmerling, a local barber, has been hired for the Camp for Polish Teenagers in Marysin, where he is now working full time at his profession of barber, and receiving full board. He was apparently recommended for this position by a German barber in the city.

PEOPLE ARE SAYING . . .

The ghetto populace hopes that special rations will be distributed for the coming Christmas holidays; thus, people are talking about one egg per person, fat, sugar, bread for six days, and the like.

THURSDAY, DECEMBER 17, 1942

HOW RUMORS GET STARTED

Among the many rumors concerning special rations by the year's end, one is especially persistent: namely, that every inhabitant is to receive one egg. Eggs have become entirely unknown in the ghetto. How did this rumor get started? In the past few days, the Department of Food Supply received 1,000 eggs, which are being used to bake *farfel* [a type of noodle] for sick people.

SUNDAY, DECEMBER 20, 1942

BROUGHT TO THIS GHETTO

Józef Herszkowicz, born in Zelów in 1913, Mariem Najman, born in Gombin, and Dwojra Schenwald, born in Gombin in 1890, have been brought to Central Prison, where they have been lodged as prisoners of the Gestapo.

A SUICIDE

Eliasz Rozenblum, born in Warta in 1909, a resident of 4 Bazarna [Street], jumped from the fifth story of the building at 3 Bazarna [Street]. He died instantly. The suicide victim was an office worker in the tailors' workshop, where he had embezzled meal tickets. When this was discovered, he took his own life for fear of the consequences.

A MILK SUBSTITUTE IN POWDERED FORM

A milk substitute in powdered form has been distributed free of charge to some 100 persons in exchange for special coupons. Real milk is still not coming into the ghetto.

AT THE CAMP FOR POLISH TEENAGERS IN MARYSIN

which was opened ten days ago, various specialists from the ghetto have been hired to teach in the camp's trade school.[113]

RUMKOWSKI'S SPEECH

delivered after the concert in the House of Culture on Saturday evening, was extraordinarily[114] optimistic in tone. He again denied the various rumors about a possible resettlement action. He also spoke about sanitary conditions in the ghetto, explaining that it was every inhabitant's duty to keep himself and his home clean. By order of the Chairman himself, dwellings are to be inspected. Dirt is particularly dangerous in winter, since it can easily cause typhus. Large laundries will be established, so that the populace can have its clothes cleaned; likewise, bathing [will be] compulsory. If necessary, compulsory haircutting (including for women) will be decreed.

The Chairman also spoke about employing 9-year-old children in the workshops. Every workshop will set up a special area for younger children where they can receive professional supervision and be fed while their parents are working. The parents are to bring their children there each morning and then take them home after work.

In conclusion, the Chairman dealt with the special potato rations; he pointed out that, despite these and possible further rations, people should economize on their consumption in order not to be faced with hunger.

PEOPLE ARE SAYING . . .

A rumor has spread throughout the ghetto that, by order of the German authorities, no work will be done here during the Christmas holidays and that even the soup kitchens will prepare no soup; bread and sausage are to be distributed instead.

The Central Workshop Bureau knows nothing about any of this; nor has the Department of Soup Kitchens been notified yet of any such measures.

---

113. The Camp for Polish Teenagers (officially *Polen Jugendverwahrlager*) was located in Marysin at 72 Przemysłowa St., an area that had been separated from the ghetto. The camp was designated for Polish youths from territories incorporated into the Reich who had been arrested for various offenses or even for those committed by their parents against the German authorities. The average number of boys and girls up to the age of 16 in that camp came to two to three thousand. The camp existed from December, 1942, to January, 1945, that is, until the city was liberated from the Germans.

114. In the original *Chronicle* the word, "extraordinarily," was crossed out in red pencil.

MONDAY, DECEMBER 21, 1942

CHILDREN WILL BE WORKING

Conferences were held in various workshops concerning the creation of jobs for nine-year-olds. A special workshop may perhaps be created for these children. In the Used Materials and Sorting Point, the possibility of having the children wind warps for carpets was discussed.

FOR SHAME!

As we reported some time ago, the youth care commission has, for the first time, attempted to place 17-year-olds outside the hostel in their own apartment on Gnież-nieńska Street. As reported to Order Service headquarters yesterday, these children have been robbed of all their belongings and all their food.[115]

CONSEQUENCES

As we have reported [on December 18], Dr. S. from Düsseldorf[116] used his deceased parents' ration cards for himself for some time. As a punitive measure, *B* rations for physicians have been canceled.

PEOPLE ARE SAYING . . .

The rumors about the two days off [at Christmas] are no longer prevalent. On the other hand, there is increasing talk about a general curfew to be ordered on Sunday so that all homes and courtyards may be cleaned.

AGRICULTURAL WORK

The agricultural section of the Department of Economics is already making preparations for next season's farm work. The following measures have been decreed: In Marysin, the tilling of garden plots will no longer be solely a community concern; plots will now be distributed to the populace. All fruit trees are to be put in good order. All relevant literature [guidebooks] should be prepared. Plants are already being ordered from outside the ghetto, etc.

TUESDAY, DECEMBER 22, 1942

DEATHS

Eleven; births, none.

The following diseases were responsible for the 11 deaths (7 men and 4 women): pulmonary tuberculosis—3 men, 2 women; other lung diseases—2 men, 1 woman; digestive diseases—1 woman; cardiac disease—1 man; tuberculosis of other organs—1 man. Tuberculosis remains the leading cause of death.

---

115. In the original *Chronicle*, a question mark in red pencil had been placed in the margin beside this information.

116. The bulletin for December 18, 1942, mentions that Dr. S. was originally from Prague.

WORKSHOP SOUP

In regard to the preparation of the midday meal, the Department of Soup Kitchens has decided that, henceforth, on odd-numbered days soup will be made with 300 grams of cabbage, 200 grams of potatoes, and 20 grams of starches, while on the even-numbered days, it will be made with 400 grams of potatoes, no cabbage and 20 grams of starches. This regulation has influenced the soup market; prices rise as high as 4 marks for soup on the "good days," but hold at around 2.50 on "cabbage days".

The number of soup kitchens in the ghetto remains unchanged at 45. Five of them are in Marysin. The soup kitchens employ about 2,000 people.

MEDICINAL HERBS

The four different species of herbs (for cardiac, gastric, and other ailments), which were planted last summer by the Department of Economics, have now been distributed to the pharmacies. The pharmacists believe these medicinal herbs to be of very good quality. This particular planting will be highly beneficial to the ghetto in view of the great shortage of drugs.

WEDNESDAY, DECEMBER 23, 1942

A FIRE AT THE WOODWORK FACTORY

All of today the ghetto has felt the effect of the enormous fire at the woodwork factory on Wesoła Street. The fire had caused a virtual panic in the morning hours, since the discovery of its cause, which had not yet been determined, could easily have had dire consequences. During the afternoon, people regained some calm upon learning that the director, a few office workers, and other people arrested by the criminal police [Kripo] had been released; they had been ordered to report the next day so that the investigation could continue. The same [orders were given to] the two firemen who had been on night duty during the night of the blaze.

The four-story building, which used to be a hospital, had been transformed into a highly modern small-furniture factory after the last evacuation and had been equipped with modern machines. The entire factory was destroyed by the fire. It was very difficult to halt the flames because the building was old and made largely of wood (the staircases, for example). The plumbing, wiring, and a freight elevator that was still under construction, had been installed at great expense, in part when this building was adapted for use as a hospital and in part when it was converted into a carpentry workshop. This building is considered to be the second most valuable structure in the ghetto (the first is the former hospital on Łagiewnicka Street). The machines installed there a few weeks ago had not yet been put into operation since the 80 or so motors needed had not been delivered. A large number of motors had been installed just one day before the fire.

The blaze was first noticed around 5 A.M. Presumably, it had begun much earlier inside the building but, because of the blackout procedures, which prevented anyone from seeing in, the fire was not discovered until 5 A.M. by the air-raid warden and the guard. Normally, the building is locked up after inspection at the end of the work day and then guarded only from the outside.

The Jewish Fire Department, which arrived at the scene of the fire one minute after the alarm, immediately notified the Municipal Fire Department which then arrived with 15 [fire] trucks. The chief of the Municipal Fire Department directed the fire-fighting operation, in which members of the Jewish Fire Department performed with utter disregard for their own personal safety. It is interesting to note that the source of water was a hydrant located over half a kilometer away, in the [former] Poznański Factory,[117] outside the ghetto. The firemen immediately realized that it was impossible to save the building because the raw and the processed wooden materials were rapidly feeding the flames—not to mention the fact that the building itself, as already reported, was old and largely made of wood. Furthermore, the factory contained benzine, alcohol, and paint, which caused explosions continuously into the next day, thus placing the firemen in great jeopardy.

It was the most sensational blaze anyone had witnessed for some time. During the early morning hours, the fiery glow could be seen for miles around, like the golden rays of the sun.

A fire watch by air-raid wardens was ordered at many buildings in the surrounding blocks to prevent any further spreading of the flames.

The firemen's primary effort was to remove the finished furniture from the warehouse in a second building and from the courtyard, and to save the raw material, which was of inestimable value. A secondary consideration was to prevent the fire from spreading to the greatly imperiled building at 7 Bazarna [Street], which also contains a warehouse for the carpentry workshop. Both goals were attained. Nor was any human life endangered throughout the entire fire-fighting operation.

However, the four-story building burned down to its foundation. The damage was enormous, since not only the new machines but all the other equipment, wooden material, and completed products (lately, as many as 3,000 cribs and some baby carriages were being manufactured each week) were destroyed by the flames. The scope of the fire can be inferred from the fact that the Municipal German Fire Department fought the flames from 5 A.M. until nearly 5 P.M., at which time they left the scene. The Jewish Fire Department, under the personal direction of its chief, [Henryk] Kaufmann, remained at the scene throughout the night and next morning, during which time several explosions occurred.[118]

In the early morning, leading representatives of the [city] authorities, the mayor, state police [Gestapo], et al., appeared at the scene. The Chairman, accompanied by his principal aides, arrived at the beginning of the fire and returned several times in the course of the day.

Thanks to the Order Service, under the leadership of Commandant [Leon] Rozenblat, complete peace and order were maintained at the scene of the blaze; normal traffic flow in the immediate vicinity of the fire continued without incident.

The investigation into the cause of the fire is, of course, being conducted by the

117. One of the largest textile plants in Łódź, established in 1873 by I. K. Poznański.
118. In the original *Chronicle*, a question mark in red pencil was placed in the margin beside this sentence.

German authorities. Although their investigation is not yet complete, they have enough information to know that no one can be held responsible for the fire since it was caused by a short circuit. This finding has afforded the ghetto's population great relief.

It has been decided that work in the woodwork factory will be resumed tomorrow, since the other building, at 6 Bazarna [Street], was entirely spared by the flames, as were several other departments. The factory has large orders to fill. It employs some 1,500 workers, none of whom is to be dismissed. Initially, only the elderly and children will be exempt from working, but they are to continue receiving their midday meals until production is fully under way again.

THURSDAY, DECEMBER 24, 1942

TWO PHYSICIANS DIE

Dr. Hugo Clement and Dr. Altschul [a university lecturer], both of whom practiced in the ghetto after their resettlement here, have died. The two physicians were from Prague.

AN ANNIVERSARY CELEBRATION IN THE WORKSHOPS

Aside from the departments we have already mentioned as taking part in the anniversary celebration this Saturday at the House of Culture, we must also add the Sewing Machine Repair Department. This department is of major significance to the tailors' workshops. Dawid Warszawski, director of the Tailors' Central Office, the initiator of Saturday's celebration, tells us that the goal of this celebration is to demonstrate publicly, and for the first time, the work done by the tailors' workshops. Some of these workshops are, after all, among the oldest in the ghetto. The first tailors' workshop was founded on May 1, 1940, and began with less than 100 workers. It was at that time that all tailors in the ghetto began to be registered. Today, the tailors' workshops in the ghetto employ 2,500 [8,500][119] craftsmen and have 12 sections (the military, civilian, and mixed work sections), the Tailors' Central Office, and 7 warehouses. The most interesting aspect of the work done by these sections was the introduction of the assembly-line system which was employed for the first time in the ghetto in tailoring.

The ghetto in Pabianice, then still in existence, sent representatives here; later they were to introduce this same system in their own tailoring workshops. As a result of pamphlets that were subsequently printed, factories in the Reich also introduced the assembly-line system, which makes it considerably easier to employ people who are not skilled in tailoring.

The anniversary celebration's program will consist of two parts. In the first, official part, speeches will be delivered by the directors of the departments involved in this celebration; in the second part, an album will be presented to the Chairman, who will

119. The number 2,500 was corrected to 8,500 in the original *Chronicle*.

then speak; the intermission following his speech will be used for viewing the exhibition of graphics; later on, there will be interludes of singing.

FRIDAY, DECEMBER 25, 1942

BROUGHT TO THIS GHETTO

Four men from the Radogoszcz camp were transferred to Central Prison here, where they have been lodged as prisoners of the Gestapo.

CLOTHES TO BE MENDED FOR THE POPULACE

Some time ago, we reported that the tailors' workshops had been prohibited by the Ghetto Administration from doing private work for the local populace. But now an exception has been made: a special section of the tailors' workshop has received permission to do mending for ghetto inhabitants who are on special assignments. This work is to be performed without using material or accessories belonging to the workshop, but only such material and equipment as is provided by the customer.

MONDAY, DECEMBER 28, 1942[120]

WEATHER

Cold again. Temperatures ranging from 6 degrees below zero to 1 degree above zero. Dry.

DEATHS

Nineteen. Births: one girl.

TOTAL POPULATION

87,651.

A SUICIDE

Today, at 4 P.M., a woman jumped from the third floor of the building at 21 Drewnowska Street and died instantly. Her identity has not as yet been determined.

FOOD ALLOCATION

This afternoon, the food ration for the first ten-day period of 1943 was made public. All rumors about special rations before the end of the year have been definitively quashed by this announcement. The new ration is somewhat smaller than the previous ones, mainly because the population has not been allocated any more potatoes. The ration costs 4.60 and contains: 400 grams of rye floor (100 grams less than last time), 200 grams of rye flakes (100 grams more), 320 grams of sugar, 100 grams of oil,

---

120. The *Daily Chronicle Bulletin* for Monday, December 28, 1942, is given in its entirety here.

300 grams of coffee, 200 grams of artificial honey (last time: 250 grams of marmalade), 250 grams of salt, 10 grams of citric acid, 10 grams of paprika, 10 grams of baking powder, half a bar of soap, and one tenth of a liter of salad dressing. In addition, 5 kilograms of turnips per person are to be distributed for 2 marks. Laundry soda is to be sold on the open market.

The announcement does not indicate when meat and sausage are to be distributed.

A ghetto bridge at rush hour.

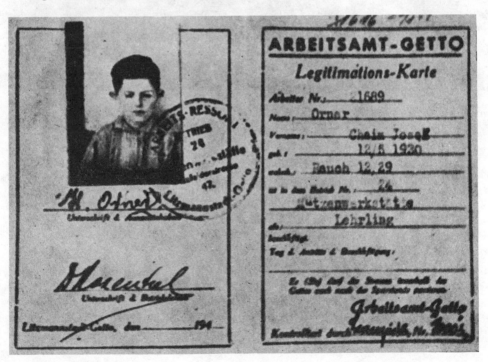

Working card of a young boy.

A warp maker. Photographer: M. Grossman.

the carpet workshop Y. Zylberstajn, the old
eaver, teaches Perec Zylberberg the craft. Perec
urvived the war and now lives in Montreal.
hotographer: Henryk Ross.

In the carpet workshop.
Photographer: M. Grossman.

In the metal workshop.
Photographer: M. Grossman.

Low voltage equipment workshop. Standing at
the right is Michał Samelson.

In the lingerie workshop.

her stitchers.

dren working. Photographer: M. Grossman.

A break for midday soup. Photographer: M. Grossman.

PART III: 1943

PART III. 1945

EPILOGUE TO A CELEBRATION

The festivities surrounding the exhibition that opened on December 12, 1942 [at the House of Culture on Krawiecka Street], and in which five workshops took part, were held on January 7, 1943, in the Soup Kitchen for the Intelligentsia. The reception, to which five of the ghetto's highest officials were invited, was quite sumptuous and in very good taste. A variety of delicacies, including wine, was served; a truly copious dinner caused the people of the ghetto the greatest surprise. The party did not break up until 2 A.M. The populace has made a wide variety of comments on this odd affair.

RESETTLEMENTS

During the last few days people have again been rounded up to be sent out of the ghetto to perform manual labor. The prime targets are unattached individuals, pre-selected on the basis of their vegetable cards,[1] as well as persons guilty of any sort of infraction. Most of the people brought to Central Prison thus far have been men, though there were a few women among them. A special commission will review each case. If a particular individual possesses special abilities or skills essential to the ghetto, he will be released. The number of people involved in this action and their destination are not yet known.

This renewed resettlement has created great panic among the populace, particularly in the absence of any guidelines and details.

MONDAY, JANUARY 11, 1943

RESETTLEMENT

As we have learned, this is not a case of resettlement in the true sense of the word. Rather, the [German] Ghetto Administration has instructed the Eldest to furnish it with 150 strong, healthy men. The Chairman succeeded in having that number reduced to 80, but then additional people were demanded and were dragged from their beds at night and placed at the commission's disposal. For the most part, those selected were persons who were unattached or who, for one reason or another, had come into conflict with the authorities. Persons essential to the ghetto were exempted from resettlement, but mistakes have, of course, been made. Since the quota demanded has not yet been filled—the ghetto does not have that many strong, healthy people—it is to be assumed that the roundup will continue tonight as well.

TUESDAY, JANUARY 19, 1943[2]

WEATHER

A frost set in suddenly during the night, bringing the morning temperature down to minus 17 degrees. In the course of the day the thermometer rose to minus 8 degrees, where it remained until nightfall.

1. Unlike the bread and food cards, which were issued to each person individually, the vegetable cards were allocated to the family, marked for the number of people in a given family.
2. The *Daily Chronicle Bulletin* for Tuesday, January 19, 1943, is given in its entirety here.

DEATHS

Thirteen.

BIRTHS

None.

POPULATION

87,164.

WHITE-COLLAR WORK ORIGINATING OUTSIDE THE GHETTO

For the first time in the history of the ghetto Jews have been assigned to white-collar jobs originating outside the ghetto. This contrasts with the established practice of assigning ghetto dwellers exclusively to physical labor. The explanation is to be sought in the following:

As is the case in the rest of Germany, the fuel allocation for the Warthegau is to be based on a survey conducted by questionnaire between April 1, 1942, and March 31, 1943. The questionnaire seeks to determine the number of members in each household, the number of rooms to be heated, past fuel consumption, and also whether the dwelling in question has a gas or electric cooking range.

Because the gathering and analysis of the figures on fuel consumption requires extensive personnel and because of the labor shortage in the Warthegau, the job was given to the ghetto. The organizing of this bureau, which will employ a substantial number of clerical workers for a limited time, has been charged to [Henryk] Neftalin, the attorney, who has already begun to select the required personnel. This "white-collar workshop" will be located at 8 Rybna Street.

WEDNESDAY, JANUARY 20, 1943

A GHETTO CURE

The Eldest of the Jews has arranged recuperative opportunities for people in great need of rest who have the right connections by obtaining employment for them in a bakery for a period of eight weeks. Since these workers will receive a half kilogram of bread per 12-hour workday plus a special allocation of an additional 2 kilograms per week, this type of cure is much in demand and has met with great approval, especially since bread sells for 60–70 marks per kilogram on the private market.

On Friday, the chief of the Special Department, [Dawid] Gertler,[3] had a discussion with the Chairman, as a result of which 60 individuals, mostly from the Department of Gas-Kitchens, have been given positions in the bakeries.

3. Although Dawid Gertler (1911–1977) was one of the most influential men in the ghetto and was considered by the populace to be Rumkowski's rival for the office of the Eldest of the Jews, he is mentioned here for the first time. From now on he will appear frequently in these pages. In July 1943 Gertler was arrested by the Germans and deported to Auschwitz. The circumstances of his arrest are not fully known; the most often cited reason is that he was smuggling food into the ghetto, having bribed the Gestapo and Kripo. Cf. also p. 43, n. 57.

SUNDAY, JANUARY 24, 1943

OTHER NEWS

Last summer a number of transports to [the ghetto of] Warsaw were organized.[4] Those transports were principally composed of ghetto dwellers whose transfer to Warsaw had been requested by friends or relatives who possessed some wealth—for this journey costs from 1,000 to 6,000 [German] marks. The main reason for such journeys was the fact that living conditions in Warsaw were superior to those here.

But, because of the changes that have occurred in the Warsaw ghetto's overall situation, the trend has now been reversed. There is talk that the same group that had taken the transports from here to Warsaw is now to bring them back from Warsaw. The first people are supposed to be returned here within the next few days.

THURSDAY, JANUARY 28, 1943

ONE DAY OFF

per week has been arranged for the populace. Workers and clerks in the workshops are to work 10 hours per day, and Sunday is to be entirely free. According to the pertinent circular, January 31, 1943, is to be the first such Sunday off.

UNPLEASANT INCIDENTS

have been occurring in the ghetto lately. Random passersby are being stopped [by Germans], asked for their opinions [on various matters], and, according to their answers, beaten up. These incidents have occurred in markedly deserted areas.

FRIDAY, JANUARY 29, 1943[5]

SIDEWALKS TO BE CLEARED

Because a Kripo [German criminal police] officer fell on a slippery sidewalk (without suffering any injury, however), janitors from the adjacent buildings were summoned to the Kripo [office] and beaten. Then they, and all janitors along the main streets, were ordered to clear the sidewalks and remove all traces of ice.

TO WORK IN THE CITY

Eight tramcar workers from the ghetto have been sent to the city to fill vacancies created by the labor shortage. More detailed information concerning their working conditions is not yet available.

4. See p. 55, no. 65 and p. 197.
5. In the original *Chronicle*, both of the entries dated Friday, January 29, 1943, were crossed out.

SATURDAY, JANUARY 30, 1943

INJECTIONS AND MEDICATIONS

are now being dispensed by a special section of the Sonderkommando [Special Unit]. To receive them one has to line up early in the morning with a doctor's prescription; then, after another long wait in line, the following day the prescribed medication is dispensed. This procedure has been instituted to eliminate private trade in medicines at exorbitant prices.

Unfortunately, the amount of medicine made available, however, has proved insufficient and, thus, by the following day injections that previously sold for 15 marks on the private market are being sold for 35 marks.

SUNDAY, JANUARY 31, 1943

TYPICAL OF THE TIMES

is the fate of young people who are not yet old enough to be employed in workshops. They spend much of their time indoors, not getting out into the open air; their games, even their songs, are, accordingly, sad and serious. Their songs are less like children's songs than they are like plaints and lamentations over rations, resettlement, and the hard life in the ghetto, of which even the youngest among them are already aware. One has a sister who has been resettled, or a brother, or even a father or mother, and so these children all know the meaning of life in the ghetto. It is not unusual to hear them say: "If we are still alive, then . . ." Words such as those have a particularly tragic ring when spoken by a child.

On the other hand, this precocity, unfortunately, has hampered the progress of their education. Since there is no formal instruction and the schools are closed, we find children aged nine or ten, and even older, who lack even the most elementary skills in reading or writing, who cannot read books and thereby acquire knowledge. On the whole, the education of the young bears the imprint of the war.

FOR MANUAL LABOR OUTSIDE THE GHETTO

The [German] authorities have again demanded a sizable number of able-bodied men, and the Bureau of Labor has worked through the night compiling a list of eligible men, that is, men not employed here as skilled workers. In view of the debilitated state of the populace, it will, however, be necessary to summon more people [than are actually needed]. The first contingent of 70 men is supposed to start work soon.

MONDAY, FEBRUARY 1, 1943

A FREE SUNDAY

January 31, 1943 was officially the first day off given to all white- and blue-collar workshop employees. In part, this is to allow them to pick up their rations and clean their living quarters and, if there is any time left, to get some rest. The distribution points, which were open from 7 A.M. to 9 P.M., were, consequently, very busy.

ABSENTEEISM

most frequent at the highly strenuous demolition jobs, but occasionally occurring at the workshops as well, has meant the loss of ration cards and a report of absence to the Bureau of Labor for workers absent not due to illness but of their own volition. If a "striker" has wished to return to work, he has had to report to the Bureau of Labor. Some have been sent to Central Prison and from there assigned to perform manual labor outside the ghetto. The police have also been sent to search out those who failed to report to work. Loss of their ration cards is the only form of pressure that will compel them to return to work.

TUESDAY, FEBRUARY 2, 1943

A SHORTAGE OF FATS

Recently, the shortage of [animal] fats in the ghetto has become particularly notice-able because even the most privileged people (doctors, pharmacists, high-level employees) have not received their allocation. This is proof that the ghetto has no fat reserves whatsoever; 700 kilograms would be needed to cover the rations past due. At first, fat [smalec] was issued instead of butter, but the last allocation included no fats whatsoever.

THE DEMAND FOR WORKERS

to perform manual labor outside the ghetto is great. This has caused widespread alarm among the populace; additional forced resettlements are feared.

SATURDAY, FEBRUARY 6, 1943

OTHER NEWS

According to a well-informed source, all ghetto enterprises not engaged in work for the German military or for plants in the military sector are to be closed due to the general situation. This would be a painful blow to a significant number of ghetto dwellers, who would be left without work and would consequently have to fear possible resettlement or, at best, work assignments outside the ghetto.

There is talk that new (tailors') workshops will be opened, but in the immediate future it will be impossible to find positions for all those not engaged in work connected with the war economy.

PEOPLE ARE SAYING

that the death penalty for people who read newspapers is being considered. It has not been possible to learn whether this is in fact true, but it is known that people with connections who have had access to daily papers [published by the Germans outside the ghetto] are no longer to be found reading them.

TODAY'S PRIMARY SOURCE OF FOOD

is rutabaga. This highly sought-after item has stimulated not only the populace's appetite but also its resourcefulness; people prepare all sorts of palatable dishes from this often very tasty sweet root, which is sometimes yellow, sometimes white. Rutabagas are used in cakes in place of apples and, with the addition of some lemon juice and sugar, do indeed simulate the taste of apples. Rutabagas are used in soups, prepared as a vegetable "à la asparagus," or, according to personal preference, instead of carrots. They are, however, primarily eaten raw because of their nut-like flavor; white rutabagas, in particular, taste like coconut. On the other hand, rutabaga has been jocularly termed "ersatz cheese" because of its typically yellow or white, honeycomb appearance.

SUNDAY, FEBRUARY 7, 1943

A SUNDAY OFF WITHOUT THE MIDDAY MEAL

Today, the second Sunday off in the ghetto, differed from the first in that no midday meal was distributed either in the workshops that were closed or in those that were open, with the exception of the Fire Department, the carpenters' and the straw-shoe workshops. There is talk that, instead of these midday meals, potatoes and flour products will be distributed to the populace in the next food allocation.

The Sunday off has yet another drawback. Instead of the previous seven 8-hour days, the work week now consists of six 10-hour days, making a total of 60 hours. People are so exhausted after these long hours that they are almost incapable of performing the most pressing domestic chores, picking up their rations, etc. All this is therefore left until the free Sunday, which hardly suffices for dealing with everything that has piled up during the week: housework, laundry, rations, and so forth.

PEOPLE ARE SAYING

that even this day of rest with no rest will not last for long, and that 10 hours of work will be required on Sundays as well.

THOSE WHO RETURNED

from Kreuzsee near Reppen [Rzepin][6] and who are, as we have already noted, in very poor condition, are to receive additional daily allocations of soup and better nourishment to help them get back on their feet. Fifteen of them required hospitalization because they needed special care and better food if they were to survive. The doctor has prescribed one meal a day containing meat for them.

6. The labor camp to which Jews were regularly sent from the Łódź ghetto to perform manual labor in the construction of the Frankfurt-Poznań highway (*Reichsautobahn*) was located in Reppen (Rzepin), in Brandenburg.

MONDAY, FEBRUARY 8, 1943

PEOPLE ARE SAYING

that working and living conditions in the ghetto will become even worse because the workday will be increased from 10 to 12 hours, and Sundays, now free, will once again become workdays. As compensation, the working population is to receive soup twice a day.

Considering the populace's already extremely poor state of health and the discrepancy between the amount of work demanded and the food allotted, the effects of these rumored changes are easily imaginable.

THE PROBLEM OF MATCHES

remains acute. Matches were again not included in the last allocation. Their price on the free market has risen to 3 marks per box, and they are still very scarce. This has also affected the price of lighters and flints. Lighters are being sold at prices reaching 30 marks, depending on quality, and flints cost between 1 and 1.50 marks per flint.

This shortage is not without its comic aspects, particularly in one-person and small households, since matches are allocated according to the number of people per household. When the last match in a household has been used, people may be seen going from neighbor to neighbor, at all hours of the day, from early morning until late at night, kindling in hand, in search of fire.

THE PROBLEM OF LAUNDRY

in the ghetto is being solved by the periodic issuing of coupons to those who work; those coupons entitle them to hand in 20 to 25 items of laundry to one of three laundries, which are located on Drewnowska Street (the former Kaszub factory), 68 Zgierska Street, and on Mickiewicz Street. Unfortunately, the laundering is not done very carefully, nor is the clothing treated with particular care. On the whole it comes back dirtier than it was before laundering, bearing traces of the dust and dirt usually found on laundry that has fallen down when it was hanging to dry, and so on. There is nothing surprising in that if one considers the means at the laundries' disposal.

THURSDAY, FEBRUARY 11, 1943

A SUICIDE

One of the two people resettled here from Białystok has hanged himself in his apartment. The man, [Chaim] Jankelewicz by name, committed this desperate act because his wife was killed while attempting to leap out of a train while it was passing through Litzmannstadt. His daughter, who broke her leg in the attempt, is in the hospital. All three were to be resettled in this ghetto.[7]

7. Around 20,000 Jews were deported from the ghetto in Białystok to the death camps in Treblinka and Auschwitz between the 5th and 12th of February, 1943. Most likely, the Jankelewicz family was on a train heading from Białystok via Łódź to Auschwitz. In the personal papers of Dr. Oskar Rosenfeld, one of the authors of the *Chronicle*, there is the following entry dated February 18, 1943: "*Ad* Białystok: around 2,000 people were loaded onto a train car and taken away; a father, mother, and daughter jumped off the train. The mother was shot dead, the father and [the] daughter (with a broken arm) are in the hospital. The father [committed] suicide. The Chairman [Eldest of the Jews] has taken over the care of the girl."

VIGANTOL

The popular remedy for rickets and softening of the bones is only being given to infants, following orders issued by the Special Department, since there is at present no milk for them in the ghetto. However, this vital drug is also available to those with connections.

THE BLACK MARKET IN DRUGS

not available in pharmacies or through the Special Department is, unfortunately, flourishing in the ghetto, and prices are astronomical. For example, the going rate for 10 grams of Vigantol is 30–35 marks. The ordinary ghetto dweller living on his earnings cannot afford this, short of selling his midday meal and a part of his food ration. The source of the black-market drugs is not known: they may be smuggled in, or may come from people fortunate enough to have obtained them with a doctor's prescription.

MONDAY, FEBRUARY 15, 1943

PEOPLE ARE SAYING

that the new chief of the Gestapo [SS-Sturmbannführer, Dr. Otto Bradfisch][8] has ordered an inspection of the [ghetto's] living quarters and that those whose dwellings do not meet certain standards of hygiene are to be put on a list for future resettlement.

A directive is also said to be under consideration banning women from using makeup and nail polish, and also from wearing hats. Kerchiefs are to be the only head covering permitted.

ARREST OF A SMUGGLER

An Order Service man in the Special Department has arrested a Polish [Aryan] smuggler who had planned to bring a large quantity of [animal] fats and drugs into the ghetto. Despite his pleas and promises, the man was not released. He was instead handed over to the [German] authorities. One hundred eighty people have already been arrested in the ghetto in connection with this affair. Fats and drugs are vitally important to the ghetto, particularly for the treatment of the sick.

FRIDAY, FEBRUARY 26, 1943

PRO DOMO

Because Dr. Józef Klementynowski is about to leave the Archives to assume his new position in the Credit Bank,[9] [Henryk] Neftalin, the attorney, has reorganized the

---

8. Otto Bradfisch assumed the position of chief of the Gestapo in January, 1942. See above, p. XL.

9. Toward the end of 1942 all the debts incurred by workers and clerks in the workshops and departments because of loans made to them by the Jewish administration in the ghetto were nullified. Afterwards, the Credit Bank, created in January by the Eldest of the Jews, was to handle low-interest loans. To that end, the newly created bank was given a grant of 250,000 marks by the Jewish administration. (Cf. the bulletin of Wednesday, September 15, 1943.)

Archives as follows: Ghetto History—Engineer Bernard Ostrowski; Administration of the Archives (Document Collection)—Józef Zelkowicz; the Chronicle and Current Affairs—Dr. Oskar Singer. They assumed their new duties on the 24th of this month.

SMALL LAND-PARCEL LEASES

We have learned from the Department of Economics that a final decision regarding the leasing of parcels for the coming growing season has already been reached. Old lessees have priority for the parcels they tilled last year. Furthermore, in view of the scarcity of usable land, leases will be limited to 50 square meters per capita. If this regulation helps combat the ghetto's "landed aristocracy," it will be highly welcome to those who had been wronged by the old system. In the last growing season, large parcels were leased out to a relatively small group of people who only rarely worked the land with their own hands. Thus, some private individuals received unprecedentedly large profits from their parcels without, at the same time, being affected by the obligation binding on commercial farmers to turn over their agricultural products [to the Community]. This time the Chairman has instituted a just rule. Now parcels will be allocated so that any duplication is avoided. All members of any group taking part [in this activity] will have a notation placed on their vegetable card. It should be assumed that the so-called declarations required for this purpose will be distributed rapidly.

SATURDAY, FEBRUARY 27, 1943

WORK IN THE GHETTO

The conjectures that [Hans] Biebow will bring the ghetto factories sizable orders have been confirmed. We have already presented a survey [in the bulletin of February 25] of the productivity of the most important workshops for the month of December. The following is a list of the January orders for the 26 most important workshops:

Tailors'	145,923 items	Blankets	10 kg of feather
Textiles	40,778 "		comforters
Furs	1,784 "	Underwear and	
Caps	5,485 "	dresses	70,579 items
Boot tops	54,024 pairs	Gloves and	
Metal	92,421 items	stockings	1,438 dozen
(Department I)		Shoemakers (Depart-	
Rugs	645 "	ments I and II)	213,960 pairs
Rubber coats	9,647 "	Metal	6 crates of
Carpentry	44,849 "	(Department II)	small items
Cloth shredding	7,500 "	Corsets and	
Paper goods	350,000 "	brassieres	97,492 items
Brushes and bristles	78,000 "	Special wares	395,000 "
Low-voltage		Woodwork	120,155 "
equipment	2,739 "	Upholstery	244 "
		Leather and saddle-	
		making	4,000 "
		Woodshavings	50,000 "

If to this we add the orders still being processed as of January 31, we get a fairly complete picture of the probable total production in the first month of the year 1943:

Tailors'	173,458 items
Furs	11,226 "
Caps	15,847 "
Leather and saddlemaking	147,560 "
Shoemakers	1,354,172 pairs (771,308 [pairs of] straw shoes)
Shoe factory	400 "

WEDNESDAY, MARCH 3, 1943

OFFICIAL COMMISSIONS IN THE GHETTO

Two commissions arrived in the ghetto today. One was shown the demolition sites (the area bounded by Franciszkańska and Brzezińska streets) by the chief of the Ghetto Administration, [Hans] Biebow. The mayor of Litzmannstadt, Werner Ventzki, was also present. The second commission consisted of military experts from the so-called Armaments Commission of Posen [Poznań]. This group was shown around the most important ghetto plants by the assistant chief of the Ghetto Administration, [F. W.] Ribbe. Its objective was to determine whether, and which, plants in the ghetto could increase their production for the German Armed Forces, or which ones could be switched at once to such work. The tailors' workshops, metal departments, and nail factories were inspected. The Jews were represented by [Aron] Jakubowicz.

DISBANDING OF THE FOD [FRAUEN ORDNUNGSDIENST—WOMEN'S ORDER SERVICE]

The disbanding of the Women's Order Service was announced yesterday evening and carried out this morning. Sentries and patrols of the women's police still posted by the Jewish police at various stations yesterday were recalled early this morning. The women were allowed to keep only their coats and shoes; all other parts of their uniforms had to be turned in. The short life of this institution is a heavy blow to those involved, since it means the loss of the Order Service coupon privileges that they had recently obtained.

In its early days the Women's Order Service did commendable work in combating street commerce, especially insofar as minors were concerned. Such minors have now disappeared from the scene. More recently, the FOD was performing routine auxiliary police duties.

SUNDAY, MARCH 7, 1943

OTHER NEWS

The Department of Population Records has been instructed by Bałut Market to obtain supplies for taking 80,000 photographs. These pictures are intended for the new worker-identification cards that are soon to be issued on behalf of the [German] Ghetto Administration.

The Chairman performed 13 weddings in the House of Culture today. Zwilling, a member of the Order Service, was also on the Department of Vital Statistics' marriage roster, but he failed to appear. The department had received no advance warning of this.

SATURDAY, MARCH 13, 1943

NEWS OF THE DAY

The Chairman Speaks

At 7 P.M. this evening, in a crowded hall at the House of Culture, the Chairman addressed department and workshop delegates. The meeting was opened by the chief of the Order Service, Leon Rozenblat, after which the Chairman took the floor.

After a few opening remarks about the constantly changing situation in the ghetto, the Chairman came to his actual subject. "At one time," he said, "we had autonomy. But, step by step, that autonomy was curtailed, so that today only a paltry few remnants of it remain. As you know, my brothers and sisters, orders from the authorities are not subject to discussion. There is a war on and there is total mobilization in the Reich; new factories must be created, for which additional workers must be found. From where are those workers to come? The problem can be solved only by reorganization, and it is better that we face this inevitable fact soberly and undertake the necessary steps ourselves in order to prevent chaos. What is the real issue here? Is it a tragedy if today we [reassign] young people, most of whom have been sitting in offices for the last three years, that is, for as long as the ghetto has been in existence, while people aged fifty and over have been utterly exhausted by hard physical labor? It is not a tragedy to move people around and allow older people a bit of rest. We are in a labor camp, yet it is possible for us to regulate things in our own sphere. Don't make this difficult for me. Try to put yourselves in my place and you will see that it is better to tell me what your occupation was before the war, so that I will not be assigning skilled workers to the wrong jobs. In these difficult times, when productivity on our part is essential, it is a sin against society for experienced, skilled workers to hide in offices instead of putting their skills into service for the good of all. We too must begin a total mobilization. Of course, this cannot be done overnight. We must first form some idea of the workers available to us. They are, so to speak, our reserves. As soon as the factories open, this entire human resource will be put to work. Office staffs will become smaller, or older people will replace the young. I am aware that in many cases the change will be a very difficult one, particularly with respect to actual living conditions. But we have coped with more difficult situations, and we will also surmount this problem—which can only be solved by changes in the budget. With a monthly budget of 5.5 million marks, we will definitely find a solution. Trust me! But also bear in mind that the mobilization of people up to the age of 40 does not mean the end of this process. We do not know how things will develop or whether older age groups will also have to be mobilized in the near future. And, above all, do not think that this move is limited to the departments alone. We will have to restaff the offices in the factories as well. Yes, if need be, I will even take a director's secretary away from him, regardless of the tears he sheds over the loss of his trusted right hand. And so-called "diplomatic" illnesses will also be of no help during this campaign. We will have to be firm, for everything is at stake here. For the time being, we have a three-month plan. What happens after that remains to be seen. Don't pull strings in an attempt to avoid these changes. Don't provide us with false information, for here, as everywhere, honesty is the best policy."

Having said this, the Chairman then touched on the food supply problem, the stringent blackout regulations, and the all-too-lively street life. He further announced that commissions from the city will be checking up on the use of electricity here and that hot plates are not to be used. He closed his address, which had made a strong impression, with a few words about the nursery.

SUNDAY, MARCH 14, 1943

FROM THE COURTROOM

A new factor has been introduced into criminal trials. In addition to the prosecutor, we now frequently find a representative of the Special Department present at criminal trials, principally in those cases which were sent to court by this department. At first, the Special Department's representatives intervened in the trials, but an end was soon put to that. The representative is now confined to the role of observer. It is not known how great an influence the Special Department exerts in the appellate actions taken by the prosecution in cases of acquittals or overly lenient sentences. We note this fact merely to indicate the existence of a certain double standard in this area as well.

MONDAY, MARCH 15, 1943

MUCH ADO OVER A HEN

Stern, a commercial gardener on Urzędnicza Street, was the owner of a hen, a thing of enormous value in the ghetto, where there is no fowl to be found. Stern received no less than 25 marks for each egg his faithful hen laid for him. Today, his feathered treasure was stolen from him. Following the tracks of his beloved hen, Stern arrived at his neighbor Szatan's door, where he spotted some familiar feathers. Stern was able to establish that Szatan's daughter had abducted the hen and taken it to her sister's house on Bałut Market. There, the faithful creature was found dead, having suffocated in transit.

This sensational case of theft will have to be settled in court.

FRIDAY, MARCH 19, 1943

FOOD SUPPLY AND DISEASE IN THE GHETTO ACCORDING TO MEDICAL OBSERVATIONS

We have been interviewing a number of doctors in an attempt to determine the major causes of the various illnesses occurring in the ghetto. Dr. Hugo Natannsen commented on this subject as follows:

If we examine the problem of food not merely from the nutritional (caloric) point of view, but also from the standpoint of health (vitamins), a number of significant factors emerge:

1. The appearance of diseases formerly less prevalent or rarely observed leads to the conclusion that their cause is connected with nutrition. In the past year, we have seen an increase in scurvy, pellagra, hunger edema, and abscesses and furuncles. Scurvy is caused by a vitamin C deficiency, pellagra, by a vitamin B deficiency, hunger edema, by a vitamin B and albumen deficiency, and furuncles, by a vitamin A and C deficiency.

Food *per se* is not of much help here. In the summer, however, fresh vegetables, dairy products, etc., have helped reduce the incidence of these diseases.

2. For the moment, scurvy and hunger edema have declined, but, on the other hand, there is an observably acute increase of bronchitis and pleurisy, and not always in connection with tuberculosis.

Since vitamin C is an antiseptic agent, products containing this vitamin, such as sauerkraut, beets, and so forth, may be considered medicines.

3. A new and frequent phenomenon is the so-called softening, that is, decalcification of the bones. It has been discovered that the cause of this problem is a vitamin D deficiency. Our food products contain only a very minute amount of vitamin D (in butter).

Sunlight and sunbathing, and ultraviolet rays as well, are sources of vitamin B. Vigantol and cod-liver oil are sources of vitamins. But since the mass of ghetto dwellers do not have ready access to ultraviolet radiation or Vigantol and cod-liver oil, the above-mentioned diseases cannot be fought successfully with the means at our disposal.

4. Diseases caused by a vitamin B and C deficiency could be alleviated by the addition of sauerkraut (a source of vitamins B and C) to the ten-day food ration. But people would have to be informed that cooking destroys vitamins and that the sauerkraut should be eaten raw.

Red beets, red cabbage, and turnips are also sources of high-grade vitamin C. However, at this time of year (March) those vegetables are no longer rich in vitamins, and therefore the addition of foods containing vitamins [to the rations] is essential.

SATURDAY, MARCH 20, 1943

NEWS OF THE DAY

By order of the chief of the Ghetto Administration, [Hans] Biebow, the sacred shrine at the intersection of Brzezińska and Młynarska streets is to be demolished. This is the second such demolition. About a year ago, the statue of [the Most Blessed Virgin] Mary in front of the main gate of the large church on Kościelny Square was removed.

The visit of Reichsleiter Dr. [Robert] Ley:[10] Bałut Market and the workshops expect a visit. Ten clerks of the Department of Statistics are very busy compiling tables.

Return from Poznań: the 850 workers who have returned from Poznań were to be assigned immediately to workshops or demolition sites. They were, however, ordered held in isolation in Central Prison, and are neither allowed to leave the area nor to have visitors.

FROM THE POLICE BLOTTER OF MARCH 7–14, 1943

Three Smart Turkeys

On March 7, a man came rushing into Precinct III and breathlessly reported: "Three birds have entered the ghetto through the barbed wire." This caused some surprise at the precinct. What? In broad daylight and despite the guards? The birds will have to be arrested and brought to the precinct. How old are these birds, these impudent escapees? About two years old, and so fat they are barely able to waddle around.

The police were dumbfounded. This was no joke! The three birds that passed through the barbed wire at Okopowa Street (Marysin) were now playthings for Jewish children. One of the children said that huge ravens with scarlet beaks, birds with red crops, had flown into the ghetto! There was nothing surprising about that [description]—the child had never seen a turkey before and had no idea what they looked, or tasted, like.

Electrified by the news, the precinct staff jumped up and, accompanied by a volunteer search party, set out [in search of the birds]. Their hunting instincts had been aroused, and the prospect of a juicy piece of turkey, if their efforts were successful, also [motivated them].

The patrol went down Tokarzewski Street (Goldschmiedegasse) into the courtyard, where the three turkeys had supposedly taken refuge. The entire precinct was seized by tension and excitement. What would the hunt yield?

Absolutely nothing. There wasn't a trace to be found of those desirable feathered creatures. The clever turkeys had forsaken their freedom in the ghetto and had returned to captivity in Litzmannstadt.

SUNDAY, MARCH 21, 1943

NEWS OF THE DAY

The Birthday of the Eldest of the Jews

Today was the Chairman's birthday, his 66th, and as a result the post office and the Secretariat (Miss [Rebeka] Wolk)[11] were very busy. A large number of telegrams and

---

10. Robert Ley (1890–1945), *Reichsorganisationsleiter* of the *NSDAP* and founder and chief of the German Labor Front (*Leiter der Deutschen Arbeitsfront*). He committed suicide in prison in Nuremberg, where he was to be tried for war crimes before the International Military Tribunal.

11. The third and last of the Eldest of the Jews' secretariats, this one was chiefly concerned with relief. In addition, its offices handled correspondence from ghetto dwellers, as well as their petitions for work, additional food rations, coal, clothing, etc. Miss Rebeka Wolk was the head of the secretariat, which was located at 1 Dworska St., as was the secretariat headed by S. Cygielman.

letters of congratulation were handled.

Iron Collection
Order Service headquarters has received an order from the Ghetto Administration, signed by its chief, [Hans] Biebow, to the effect that all iron fences and cemetery fences in the ghetto are to be removed and brought to the collection centers that were set up, in accordance with the Reich ordinance of March 17, 1943. The Order Service immediately contacted the Bureau of Labor to supply the necessary number of workers. The largest object in question would seem to be the fence along the street facing the church on Kościelny Square. Whether this fence will also have to come down is not yet known.

Further Limits on Living Space?
The [German] authorities have ordered a survey to determine which houses belong to Poles or Germans in the following areas: Franciszkańska, Brzezińska, Żydowska, and Jakuba streets, and the Stary [Old] Market. These blocks are to be razed to create a zone safe from fire. This would mean yet another catastrophic shrinkage of living space in the ghetto, which is already at a premium.

MARRIAGES

Today, the Chairman performed 15 marriages in the House of Culture.

MONDAY, MARCH 22, 1943

NEWS OF THE DAY

Even though nothing of particular significance has happened in the ghetto and everything is proceeding in its usual fashion, the populace's morale is very low. There is a general feeling of anxiety and tension because of the forthcoming visit of Dr. [Robert] Ley and because of the uncertain fate of the workers who returned here or were resettled here from Poznań. They are still interned. It is feared that they will be resettled.

GALLOWS HUMOR

Even the ghetto has its wags who can sum up an entire situation with a single well-aimed joke. Their sense of humor is typically Jewish—sarcastic and critical. Food, of course, is the paramount theme.

Lately, the abominable food situation has begun to be reflected in people's outward appearance. The sight of people swaying as they walk down the street has given rise to macabre humor. With tears of laughter in his eyes, a ghetto Jew will remark in jest: "Before the war we ate ducks and walked like horses, now we eat horses—and waddle like ducks." Of course, this witticism is not altogether accurate, since people "waddle" only because they are allotted barely 200 grams of horsemeat per ten-day ration period. If there were more horsemeat the joke itself wouldn't have a leg to stand on.

Another joke makes for an even more incisive comment on the situation. One Jew meets another and asks: "Why do you think I've lost my drive?" The other answers: "In the ghetto, if you don't have pull, you don't have drive."

TUESDAY, MARCH 23, 1943

PEOPLE ARE SAYING . . .

It is being bruited about the ghetto that Reichsorganisationsleiter Dr. Robert Ley has already arrived in Litzmannstadt, that the inspection schedule has already been drawn up, and that the ghetto is not included in it. This rumor has naturally given rise to the usual nonsensical speculations.

It is whispered that about 1,000 persons are soon to be resettled. That would mean that the approximately 855 people from Poznań now in Central Prison would be supplemented by about 150 people from the ghetto.

WEDNESDAY, MARCH 24, 1943

NEWS OF THE DAY

Spirits in the ghetto remain low. In the course of three hard years of ghetto life, people have developed a nose for impending disaster. It is known for a fact that, in addition to the people from Poznań, ghetto dwellers are also scheduled for resettlement. The uncertainty about their numbers and categories weighs like lead on the souls of the people as they move anxiously about the streets.

The general nervousness mounted in the evening hours, as word circulated that the Special Department had been placed on alert.

Some of the people from Poznań had been released and allowed to stay in private residences; a search for them has now been launched. People here have become skilled in hiding, and the police, who have been issued strict orders, have no choice but to imprison relatives as hostages. One can sense that the next 24 hours will tax the nerves of the ghetto.

THURSDAY, MARCH 25, 1943

NEWS OF THE DAY

Today was marked by the roundup conducted by the Special Department. It began in the early morning hours and lasted until 12:15. Special Department patrols roamed the streets; passersby were stopped and asked to show their working papers. Since there had been no [prior] announcement of this action, many people out for brief errands did not, of course, have their working papers with them. Women out shopping, or hurrying to get some soup for a sick husband or some medicine for a child, were stopped by the young men of the Special Department. They were rounding up people like dogcatchers after strays. The four precincts and the guard house at Bałut

Market were filled. Many of these people even had their working papers with them and others had theirs rushed to them by relatives or friends. But all to no avail. The precinct stations are only functioning as storehouses for the "goods" delivered there by the Special Department. The Special Department brings in a certain number of heads and the Order Service issues a receipt. Terrified, these prisoners attempt to convince the Order Service to release them by shouting, crying, whining, and begging. But the Order Service has no say in the matter. The situation is in the hands of the Special Department.

A field commission was to inspect this human merchandise. Naturally, part of this merchandise is in miserable condition: worn, bedraggled, gaunt. However, scattered among them are some good-looking, still well-dressed women to whom the boys of the Special Department had, for some reason, taken a dislike. All these people are guilty of one thing: being in poor physical condition. The commission, composed of Messrs. [Zygmunt] Blemmer, [Szaja-Stanisław] Jakobson (court), and Commissioner [Józef] Kohl began its tour of inspection in Precinct I. About 80 percent of those detained were released. Precinct III was the last to be inspected, at around 7 P.M. The people detained there had to endure their ordeal until the evening; most of them had been under arrest since 8 that morning. The psychological state of these people defies description. All of them had someone ill or infirm at home awaiting the return of a mother, father, son, wife, or sister. Not only were the people under arrest kept in the dark about the fate of those awaiting their return, but most of them had to wait all day without any food. The commission does its job efficiently. Those men have a practiced eye for the difference between usable material and "scrap." Those who looked halfway fit for work were sent home, to be met with tears of joy by their waiting families. Others, however, waited in vain for their relatives to return. The telephones in the precinct stations were ringing nonstop. People with connections could count on being released. Before the commission arrived, only a select few were released—by order of [Dawid] Gertler or [Marek] Kligier [the chief and deputy chief of the Special Unit of the Order Service].

The Background

It is known that 855 people arrived here from Poznań. Fifteen of them died from exhaustion in the first few days; four were released. A considerable number, provisionally released from the police jail, went into hiding. In addition to those who died and those who were released, about 120 of the original group are missing from the police jail. A few skilled workers have also been released. Since about 1,000 people are scheduled for resettlement, the balance had to be obtained by roundup. The situation in Central Prison today is something like this: from Poznań (including hostages), 683; in the hands of the Gestapo, 15; in detention by the courts, 49. The roundup netted about 120 persons. It is hoped that this number will be sufficient.

FROM THE POLICE BLOTTER OF MARCH 15–21, 1943

Central Prison

A sad morning, the 17th of March. Five Order Service guards were on duty in Central Prison, which has been housing the 850 workers from Poznań who are soon to be dispatched once again, [this time] from the ghetto. The prison is being inundated by people in search of relatives and friends they haven't seen or heard from in years. One person is looking for his father, another for his brother, a wife for her husband. Scenes of reunion alternate with scenes of suffering when someone making inquiries learns of the death of a close relative or friend. The crowds were no smaller on the 18th and 19th. The police attempt to assist those seeking information, but the task exceeds their powers. In addition to its normal function, Central Prison had, for a few days, become the scene of countless tragedies.

FRIDAY, MARCH 26, 1943

NEWS OF THE DAY

The action connected with the scheduled resettlement has, unfortunately, not yet come to an end. More people have been taken from their homes in nighttime police raids, most of them unemployed persons in the older age groups or persons with fictitious jobs. The prolongation of the campaign has greatly dejected the populace.

SATURDAY, MARCH 27, 1943

MATZOTH FOR PASSOVER

Contrary to our previous report [of March 27] we have now been informed by the Department of Bakeries that matzoth are to be distributed. However, the total will be about 10,000 kilograms, which means that only a small segment of the populace will be supplied.

THE RESETTLEMENTS

The incidents of March 26, that is, the street roundups executed by the Special Department, continue to color the mood of the ghetto. Although the streets have again resumed their everyday appearance—and the picking up of rations makes for some liveliness around the distribution points—the ghetto populace is still inwardly agitated.

Nothing has changed in the situation on Czarniecki Street. The 850 people from Poznań, as well as those from Litzmannstadt who were added to their number, remain under lock and key, victims of cold, dirt, and vermin. Because of the shortage of beds, hundreds of men and women are forced to spend the night leaning against doors and walls or in a crouched position

As yet, no orders have come from the German authorities, and nothing definite can be learned about what lies in store for the internees. In the ghetto itself conjecture is rife. Optimistic speculation alternates with profound pessimism. The fact that the street arrests included individuals of various ages and professional skills has given rise to the greatest anxiety. That makes it more difficult to determine the criteria for the March 26 action and fuels rumors of further "resettlement." There is already increasing talk that, within the next few days, a Jewish commission will visit the departments and remove human material unfit for work and prepare it for transport.

The fate of the approximately 1,000 internees at Central Prison will probably be decided on Monday, March 29, and thus provide some indication about any further actions.

SUNDAY, MARCH 28, 1943

NEWS OF THE DAY

The ghetto's anxiety continues to rise. As of today, no decision has been reached concerning the transport [to be] composed of the internees now in Central Prison. Further actions regarding the completion of this transport are expected, but, since the people assigned to this affair are pledged to secrecy, no detailed information is available. The populace is, of course, tormented by all sorts of fears and conjectures.

MONDAY, MARCH 29, 1943

NEWS OF THE DAY

The situation in the ghetto remains unclear, and morale is even lower than before—If that is possible. In the evening it became known that a meeting of the precinct chiefs had been held at police headquarters. Absolutely nothing has been learned about the purpose of that meeting. People have concluded that night raids will resume, but no one knows who their target will be. Consequently, all sorts of rumors are, of course, circulating in the ghetto; figures ranging from 6[000] to 15,000 are being bandied about without any basis whatsoever. The most realistic assumption is that this action will encompass some category of the critically ill. Tension was further exacerbated by the news that both the Order Service and the Special Department will be on full alert. There is no chance that the night will pass calmly.

TUESDAY, MARCH 30, 1943

NEWS OF THE DAY

As was expected, the night did not pass calmly. A rumor had already circulated through the ghetto that there were plans to fill out the transport with the critically ill, particularly with patients suffering from tuberculosis. As a result, a great many sick people fled—primarily from the two hospitals—and went into hiding. In point of fact, however, the hospitals were not affected, and only a few hopelessly sick people at the hospital infirmary on Dworska Street were taken. All told, the Order Service brought about 90 sick people from private apartments to Central Prison. The list of these people was checked at Bałut Market and only those with active tuberculosis were designated for resettlement. A number of people were also brought into the precincts and, in the afternoon, were taken to Central Prison in horse-drawn carts. One such group sang "Hatikvah" en route.[12]

In the early afternoon a 20-car train was assembled at the Radogoszcz sidetrack. The train was loaded in the late afternoon. The action was carried out by the Order Service with the assistance of the Special Department.

The scenes that were played out in front of Central Prison and the precincts almost defy description. Although most of the people involved were hopelessly sick, the despair of their families knew no limit. (The police blotter [of March 22–25][13] gives more detail.)

A small number of skilled workers from the Poznań contingent, primarily shoemakers, were spared resettlement. Thus far, 23 men have been assigned to the shoe factories.

MONDAY, APRIL 5, 1943

POPULATION

85,804.

NEWS OF THE DAY

The day passed routinely and without incident in the ghetto.

The Chairman is not feeling well, and yet he performed 17 weddings at the House of Culture yesterday.

WEDNESDAY, APRIL 7, 1943

NEWS OF THE DAY

Mr. Julian St[anisław] Cukier-Cerski died today, at the age of 43. The deceased was one of the first members of our staff and directed the *Chronicle* from its inception until January, 1943, when he was stricken by tuberculosis. He came from a well-known Łódź family; his father, Ludwik Cukier, who still lives in the ghetto, was president of a synagogue.

The staff of the Archives mourns the loss of a colleague, friend, and co-worker.

PEOPLE ARE SAYING . . .

The popular imagination is already envisioning the changes in the [anticipated] new ration. There is talk that this time there will not be any grain or sago or such products but, instead, only flour, at 800 grams per person.

---

12. "The Hope," the anthem of the Zionist movement and later the national anthem of the State of Israel.
13. In the *Chronicle*, the text, under the heading *Police Blotter*, was incorporated into the bulletin for April 2, 1943.

At the same time it is hoped and rumored that there will be a potato allocation, or that sizable quantities of potatoes will arrive here in the ghetto.

THURSDAY, APRIL 8, 1943

NEWS OF THE DAY

Today did not pass very calmly. To begin with, the large commission of SS officers that arrived in the ghetto created the sensation one might expect. Twenty-six high-ranking SS officers, presumably from the Berlin Sicherheitsdienst [Security Service], arrived by car at Bałut Market and inspected the most important workshops. As they drove into the ghetto they were stopped by a Schupo [Schutzpolizei] man because they did not possess a written entry permit. Not until such a pass arrived from the city were they able to enter the ghetto.

According to reports from various workshop directors, the commission was very satisfied, even astonished [by what it saw].

SATURDAY, APRIL 10, 1943

RELIGIOUS LIFE IN THE GHETTO

The first blow to religious life in Łódź had already been dealt in September, 1939, when all houses of worship, synagogues, and shuls were ordered to close. Communal religious services came to a halt; even prayer in private dwellings and the smallest *minyonim* was prohibited. Prior to that, the Jews had been dealt a severe blow by the order that shops had to remain open on the high holidays. Ritual slaughter was prohibited; religious people did not, however, eat meat that was *treyf* [non-kosher]. This was still possible, in view of the overall food situation at that time. After the ghetto was closed the situation changed rapidly. The great majority of Jews lived on welfare; the influx of agricultural products, meat, etc., diminished day by day. Endangered by starvation, even religious Jews, including the most Orthodox, began to eat the soup distributed at Community soup kitchens. The needs of religious Jews were met, as much as possible, with the opening of kosher kitchens.

In the closed ghetto, in accordance with Proclamation No. 108, of August 12, 1940, public religious worship was allowed after prior permission had been obtained from or granted by the Chairman. After the resettlements in the spring of 1942, this form of religious life also came automatically to an end.

The pious were persuaded to shave their beards by suggestion from within the Community. Later, these religious Jews also modified their customary dress. *Kashruth* [dietary laws] at Passover had disappeared in practice by 1941. It was impossible to supply the entire population with matzoth in 1942 due to insufficient quantities, and now, in 1943, a scant 15,000 kilograms of matzoth is all that will be available. The Sabbath is no longer a day of rest; Sunday is now the day off. At best, pious Jews can give expression to their religious beliefs in the privacy of their homes. The slender candles that street peddlers offer for sale to passersby for Friday evenings are a pitiful symbol of this [religious] life. Another such symbol is the Chairman's prohibition of the sale of cigarettes in his shops on Saturdays.

MONDAY, APRIL 12, 1943

NEWS OF THE DAY

The Chairman has more or less recovered and has resumed his normal duties at Bałut Market. The day passed calmly in the ghetto.

FOOD SUPPLY

The situation remains very tense. As regards staples, apart from flour, only one carload of potato meal has arrived in the ghetto. The rye meal expected for the announced ration has not been received. There are few vegetables and even fewer potatoes.

Obviously, greater supplies of potatoes had been expected, but since the [German] authorities seem to think that the ghetto has been supplied with mounds of potatoes through the end of April, they evidently do not view the matter as urgent. The Chairman is making every effort to come to grips with the situation. To begin with, he has abolished the coupon system. Neither sick persons nor any others will be issued coupons; he took this step in concurrence with Dawid Gertler. For the first time in its existence, the Department of Food Supply has received written instructions from the Chairman to cease *all* distribution of food to the so-called small market. Thus, for a while at least, even the privileged will not be receiving any supplementary food, despite the limited under-the-counter practices that have existed until now. Of course this measure will not greatly alter the overall food situation; its significance is, rather, a moral one.

TUESDAY, APRIL 13, 1943

NEWS OF THE DAY

By order of the chief [of the Ghetto Administration, Hans] Biebow, the Research Department on Łagiewnicka Street will be disbanded.[14] This ruling was probably connected to the request of its director, [Emanuel] Hirschberg [Hirszberg] for wire, which he needed to make figurines for the various display-case groups. As we know, this department was primarily engaged in producing figurines depicting scenes from Jewish life and other visual representations of themes from folklore and other Jewish motifs. This department had been formed on instructions from the Ghetto Administration and had nothing to do with the institutions of the Eldest. The closing of this department is not in itself regrettable. It only means that the various draftsmen and model-makers employed there will lose their jobs in the near future. But we assume,

14. Cf. p. 209, n. 70.

or rather, hope, that these craftsmen will find employment elsewhere and their skills be put to use.

WEDNESDAY, APRIL 14, 1943

FOOD SUPPLY

For the Passover holidays it will be possible to exchange bread for flour or to receive matzoth for bread. This means that 1.25 kilograms of matzoth will be distributed against Coupon No. 44 at a price of 2.50 marks, or ¾ kilogram wheat and ¾ kilogram rye flour, that is, a total of 1.5 kilograms flour at 1.70 marks in place of the 2-kilogram loaf of bread. To that end, one must declare one's preference—flour or matzoth—at the proper bread and grocery distribution point.

FRIDAY, APRIL 16, 1943

NEWS OF THE DAY

The ghetto is calm. A supplementary ration announced today (see below) has raised spirits somewhat. Nevertheless, the general picture is bleak. Things are worse than in the spring of 1942. People can barely drag themselves down the street. Everyone complains about great weakness in the legs. This may in part be due to the spring weather, but the principal reason is the lack of potatoes, which has ill effects on people's bones. In contrast to last year, hunger edema is more rarely to be seen but, conversely, one sees a striking number of emaciated faces and typically tubercular faces but not the full, characteristically hectic ones seen in normal times. These are people to whom death has merely granted a respite. It is feared that if the food situation fails to show some fundamental improvement in the near future, there will be a rapid increase in the mortality rate.

FOOD SUPPLY

A supplementary food ration was announced today. Even though the hopes pinned on this ration were not fulfilled, the event was greeted with joy. The ration includes the following items:

200 grams brown sugar, 200 grams marmalade, 150 grams sago, 50 grams fruit tea, 500 grams canned red beets, 3 kilograms vegetables and 1 cake of soap—against Coupon No. 56 of the food ration card. In addition, beginning tomorrow, Saturday, April 17, the dairy shops will issue 50 grams margarine, 50 grams skimmed milk powder, and one piece of cheese against Coupon No. 62 of the food ration card. These two supplementary rations cost a total of 4.50 marks. The vegetables must be picked up by April 18. After that date the vegetable coupons become invalid. Naturally, a new myth is growing up around that deadline, namely, that it will supposedly be followed by further rations.

PUBLIC HEALTH

The Department of Health has furnished us with the following figures on contagious diseases in the ghetto:

	January	February	March
Typhus	6	—	7
Typhoid fever	163	51	49
Paratyphoid	1	—	—
Diphtheria	1	1	2
Tuberculosis	185	215	256
Dysentery	1	1	—
Scarlet fever	1	1	—
Meningitis	1	—	—
Encephalitis	1	—	—
Whooping cough	1	—	—

It must be pointed out that these figures do not present an accurate picture of the actual situation, for they include only the cases that the doctors must report. The figure for tuberculosis is, of course, completely erroneous. Doctors estimate the number of active cases at about 10,000, and an equally large number are in immediate danger [of contracting tuberculosis]. In this connection it is of interest to consider the data related to the public health department's efforts to carry out its difficult task after the drastic cut it suffered in personnel in September [1942]. We have already reported on the number of public health doctors. The following is a listing of the remaining personnel: Director's office, 2 doctors and 1 administrative chief; head nurses, 3; nurses, 197; patient-care staff, 185; office workers, 114; manual laborers, 47; technical personnel, 36; medics, 22; druggists, 3; sanitation controllers, 45; sanitation inspectors, 9; students, 10; pharmacists, 69; chemists, 2; bacteriologists, 11; dentists, 36; X-ray technicians and physical therapists, 4; porters, 10; kitchen personnel, 26; laundry workers, 17; seamstresses, 2; dental technicians, 16. (In addition, there are the previously mentioned 151 doctors including 36 workshop doctors.) Until the liquidation of the hospitals in September, 1942, the Department of Health employed approximately 2,000 people.

SUNDAY, APRIL 18, 1943

THE JUDICIARY

Lately, the courts have, to a certain degree, been relegated to the background. Thefts, the province of the investigatory section of the Special Department, are handled in administrative criminal procedures. For example, three days ago the theft of a sack of sago was discovered while [a shipment of] goods was being received at the Radogoszcz sidetrack. All but a few kilos were recovered. The Special Department promptly sentenced the guilty parties to work at excrement removal. The defendants do, however, have the legal right of appeal to the Eldest. The Eldest has probably not overruled a single sentence passed by the Special Department. *Fiat iustitia, pereat getto.*[15]

15. A paraphrase of *fiat iustitia, et pereat mundus*, the law must be done even if the world perish, words attributed to St. Augustine or to the Emperor of the Holy Roman Empire, Ferdinand I (1556–64).

WEDNESDAY, APRIL 21, 1943

NEWS OF THE DAY

Nothing of significance. The day passed without incident.

The situation of the ghetto populace in regard to shoes is truly desperate. The ghetto dwellers who have been behind barbed wire since May, 1940, have, of course, used up the last of their reserves since that time, if they had brought any at all with them to the ghetto. The small number of good shoes brought in by later arrivals [which replenished the local supply] has also been used up by now. Except for a small elite that has everything and can obtain everything, ghetto dwellers are literally "dragging their shoes behind them," even though there are hundreds of thousands of shoes here in the ghetto—Jewish shoes—some in good shape, some in poor shape and more or less useless, these are shoes from the Jewish communities that were evacuated in the Warthegau. What is lacking is skilled, qualified shoemakers to put this stock into circulation.

FRIDAY, APRIL 23, 1943

GHETTO IDYLLS

On the road from the city [ghetto] to Marysin, among puddles and sand pits, graze three goats and six sheep. These rare creatures are feeding on the first blades of meadow grass. Above them, butterflies and one stork. . . . A vision of spring and peace amid the gray melancholy of ghetto life.

MONDAY, MAY 3, 1943

FOOD SUPPLY

The Potato Problem: Excitement in the Ghetto
Will potatoes be distributed tomorrow afternoon at 4 o'clock?

A large crowd began to gather in the early morning hours near Łagiewnicka Street, gazing longingly as potato carts rolled by. Children ran after the carts, pleading with the drivers: "Give us a potato."

Suddenly the Chairman appeared at the vegetable market at the intersection of Łagiewnicka and Pieprzowa streets with Dawid Gertler immediately behind him. Both men inspected the potato storehouse and then got into a droshky, where they engaged in a lively conversation. People tried to decipher the expressions on the faces of these two men of authority. The mood is somber.

On the evening of May 3 we learn that the kitchens need about 37,000 kilograms of potatoes daily, that is, a total of 110,000 kilograms for three days. However, so that the starving masses do not suffer from an interruption in potato supplies, the kitchens will not use any potatoes for three days, namely, on May 5, 6, and 7, 1943, which also means that they will not be serving any soup whatsoever. On these three days, all those entitled to soup will receive 150 kilograms of bread in place of the soup. The 110,000 kilograms of potatoes saved by the kitchens will be distributed to the ghetto population, which otherwise would have had to wait. On Sunday, May 8, soup will again be distributed.

TUESDAY, MAY 4, 1943

NEWS OF THE DAY

A day without incident, but the mood has improved substantially with the hope of greater potato shipments. Hundreds of people waited on Pieprzowa Street, in front of the gate to the vegetable yards, since early morning. In spite of the fact that the Order Service was beefed up, the usual commotion prevailed.

FRIDAY, MAY 7, 1943

PEOPLE ARE SAYING

that the amount of potatoes coming into the ghetto will be large enough to allow potato rations for the next few weeks. An authoritative source is supposed to have said that due to the available and expected quantities of potatoes, the price of black-market soup will fall to 0.50 marks and the people of the ghetto will have to move their furniture out into the courtyards to make room for such vast quantities of potatoes. This grand-sounding declaration has brought hope to the hearts of 80,000 hungry people; [and]

that, henceforth, the Chairman will hold his receptions directly in the workshops and departments; and

that, in compensation for the soup lost in the last three weeks, 3 kilograms of potatoes per capita will be distributed.

SATURDAY, MAY 8, 1943

NEWS OF THE DAY

The ghetto is in a vastly better mood. The continuing potato deliveries are still the main topic of the day. Groups of adults and children will pounce on any potato that falls off a potato cart. The guards try to protect every last potato against these street attacks.

FRIDAY, MAY 14, 1943

OTHER NEWS

As we know, there is no normal trade in the ghetto. The shops of the Eldest merely handle the distribution of foodstuffs. There are, however, shops in the ghetto that offer a variety of goods. Their windows display a real jumble [of things]—books, marmalade, old combs, cosmetic powders. Rations are the source of almost all the foods on sale there. People who are forced to divest themselves of part of their rations sell them to stores of precisely this type. The difference between the legal and the private market price is so great that, for example, someone selling a single sausage ration can, with the money obtained, buy two or more rations [in the Community stores]. But what is most interesting is the trade in merchandise that transpires both in the shops and through middlemen, professional traders, or agents who work on commission. For example, the briefcase of such a trader might contain a toothbrush that had formerly been the property of someone resettled in this ghetto. That toothbrush can cost from 25 to 30 marks. A pair of ladies' fine-mesh stockings costs 50 marks, and genuine silk stockings sell for 80 to 100 marks.

A decent suit (made to measure), also the former property of a recent arrival, can, if new, cost 400 marks. At the time of resettlement, a suit of this sort would have cost about 50 marks.

Used shoes with good soles cost from 200 to 250 marks; new shoes run as high as 500 marks. Thus, an elegant suit can be traded for 3 kilograms of bread.

Razor blades, in great demand, now bring 1 mark each. Shaving soap has disappeared from the market altogether. Instead, people use the soap powder that is brought into the ghetto surreptitiously. Cosmetics for women are practically unobtainable. A man's tie in decent condition sells for up to 25 marks. Despite all their problems, the more worldly sorts attempt to maintain appearances. It is surprising that one can still see many well-dressed people who are evidently able to pay those high prices, but they may also be new arrivals or persons who have not yet sold everything they own.

People with connections are still able to acquire clothing legally. No one receives a pair of shoes without permission from the chief of the [central bureau of] workshops. The same holds true for suits. Obviously, only the select few with close ties to that office enjoy this privilege.

THURSDAY, MAY 20, 1943

NEWS OF THE DAY

A Gestapo commission went to the cemetery in Marysin this afternoon to open a grave in which objects of value had been buried.

Three smugglers attempted to enter the ghetto but were frightened away. No arrests were made.

A woman succeeded in entering the ghetto at the intersection of Żurawia and Kościelna streets. Although a large police squad was dispatched, it failed to apprehend her.

FRIDAY, MAY 21, 1943

NEWS FROM THE WORKSHOPS

For some time now the mortality rate in the tailors' workshops has been rising perceptibly, particularly among those working at machines, where it has reached unprecedented levels. This phenomenon has naturally come to the workshop directors' attention; they have begun to reflect on this evil and to analyze its causes.

On May 24[?], 1943, the heads of the tailors' workshops met to discuss the problem of the rising mortality rate among tailors. They determined that, aside from the poor hygienic conditions in the workrooms and other poor working conditions, inadequate nutrition was responsible for the tailors' poor health. Their 10-hour workday and the energy they expend in their work requires different, and more substantial, nourishment than has thus far been granted to this category of workers. It is an established scientific fact that operating machines (including typewriters) consumes far more calories than any other similar type of physical or mental activity.

The meeting of the directors was held to find a remedy for this situation, since the rising mortality rate among workshop tailors could have disastrous results for the ghetto if it caused the production of the tailoring workshops to fall below the norm. The ghetto's food supply depends entirely on productivity here. If the orders from the German authorities are not filled, on time and in the desired quantity, the ghetto faces enormous danger. For all these reasons it is essential to assure suitable conditions for the tailors' workshops. Better nutrition and higher wages for tailors are two items of business that must be dealt with by those responsible for production. Again and again, the facts demonstrate that the group of especially privileged avail themselves of all possible consumer goods, thereby diminishing [the amount] received by the great mass of workers, which in turn undermines the elite's own existence.

THURSDAY, JUNE 3, 1943

A PUZZLING RAID

After a long interval, the calm prevailing in the ghetto has once again been disrupted by a rumor whose basis is not yet entirely clear. Today, in the early morning hours, word spread that something had happened in the vicinity of Talweg (Dolna) Street. Passersby had observed people standing in formation near Łagiewnicka Street, behind the hospital, waiting for orders from the German authorities. As usual, the ghetto has interpreted this event in a great variety of ways and linked it to a possible resettlement action, which has made for widespread anxiety.

According to reports from reliable sources, that is, eyewitnesses, at around 5 A.M., Schupos in "field gray" uniforms knocked on the doors of apartments in the Dolna–Łagiewnicka Street block, as far up as the passage on Dolna Street, and ordered the occupants out into the courtyards to await further instructions. Thus, it was in this neighborhood that people were to be seen standing in groups for an hour, which attracted the attention of passersby hurrying to their workshops at around 6:30 A.M. The Schupos ordered the people in those groups to show their work permits and bread-ration cards as proof of identity. But the main intent of the action was the police search for people in hiding in the apartments that had been left open. The people in the courtyards obviously had no idea of the meaning and purpose of this action, and they too viewed it as a harbinger of resettlement. It is not difficult to imagine their anxiety. The story that prevailed in the end, however, was that the

Schupos were searching for persons from Litzmannstadt who had sneaked into the ghetto to engage in smuggling or for other reasons, and were to be found in that particular neighborhood.

In view of the fact that, when searching the apartments, the Schupos also opened wardrobes and dresser drawers, this raid seemed to extend beyond a search for persons. Because the action was conducted politely, with no arrests or confiscations, the ghetto soon regained its calm.

FRIDAY, JUNE 4, 1943

NEWS OF THE DAY

The Chairman was not feeling well again today and did not appear at Bałut Market.

The Dolna Street Raid

In connection with the raid discussed yesterday, the Special Unit [Department] has, by order of Dawid Gertler, closed the extant private shops and confiscated their merchandise. This measure is, in effect, a concession to the German authorities. It would seem that the main purpose of the house search of June 3 was, in fact, a search for smugglers and smuggled merchandise. The closing of the private shops, some of which allegedly traded in smuggled goods, is intended to put a stop to all smuggling.

The Surrender of Bicycles[16]

By proclamation of the Chairman, on June 1 all bicycles in the possession of private individuals are being called in. These bicycles must be presented for sale to the Main Purchasing Agency by June 15. After that date, any bicycles found in private apartments will be confiscated without compensation. All bicycles in workshops and departments are also to be presented for sale by that date.

SATURDAY, JUNE 5, 1943

A COMMISSION INSPECTS THE WOODWORK FACTORY

Amtsleiter [Hans] Biebow accompanied a military commission on an inspection tour of the woodwork factory at 9 Pucka Street. On this occasion particular attention was paid to the recently instituted production of a new material. As we have reported, master locksmith [Henryk] Wosk has invented a sort of bakelite material suitable for producing utensils, lamp bases, etc. The principal ingredients in this material are sawdust and kaolin clay. The commission spoke with the inventor. There is a plan to produce this material in large quantities. Amtsleiter Biebow, who had just returned from a trip on official business, has probably brought back large orders for this material.

16. According to the German police authorities' order of 1939, Jews were not allowed to have bicycles. Cf. p. 10, n. 17.

SUNDAY, JUNE 6, 1943

THE JUNE 3 RAID

In connection with the raid of June 3, the following additional information has been brought to our attention: when blocking off the buildings, Schupos with rifles in hand were posted 20 meters apart, effectively preventing anyone from leaving the area. In the meantime, Gestapo men entered apartments to check whether anyone was still inside. It was a cloudy but warm spring morning; the first workers were hurrying to their workshops. Since the action was carried out so quickly and unexpectedly, as in the never-to-be-forgotten days of last September, many people assumed that a resettlement action was under way. As a precaution, people put on several shirts and suits, as they had done before. IDs were checked swiftly and efficiently. Passersby were also required to present identification. By 7:30 A.M. the action was over. The residents of the area had gotten off with a scare.

FOOD SUPPLY

The *Daily Chronicle* [*Bulletin*] has already noted [several times] that, in contrast to the same period last year, rather large shipments of potatoes have begun to arrive in the ghetto since the beginning of May and have accordingly been distributed to the population. This has produced welcome effects. Stomachs are full, hunger pangs have subsided, and, after a long period of starvation, people have begun to recover gradually and to gain some weight. A better psychological state of mind has come with physical recovery. There are sparks of hope in people's eyes since they have started believing that hunger will not return for the duration of the ghetto and that at least the greater part of the ghetto population would survive this last and most difficult stage. Conversations with people have confirmed this observation. Individuals suffering from pronounced hunger edema, with swollen legs and faces, have shown considerable improvement. Others have found that they are now able to cross bridges and climb stairs without the old feeling of exhaustion. As already mentioned, the mortality rate has declined rapidly. Thus, there exists the hope that the increased potato supply will mitigate the terrors of tuberculosis, that most insidious of ghetto diseases.

MONDAY, JUNE 7, 1943

RESETTLED TO THIS GHETTO

As reported earlier, on Saturday, June 5, sixteen Jewish workers from a labor camp in Jędrzejów (Warthegau) were brought to this ghetto. For the time being, those people are at the disposal of the Gestapo. One of the sixteen, scarcely 20 years of age, has already died, and a second is also hopelessly ill. The rest are in terrible physical and mental condition. These people were in a labor camp that had been a ghetto of a sort. They had been employed in building a railroad track, physically taxing labor which had to be performed nonstop, regardless of the weather. Working 10 hours a day, they were given 250 grams of bread, two servings of soup, coffee, and, from time to time, a small helping of meat. Here in the ghetto these workers, who survived their ordeal, will receive better nourishment to make them fit to resume work and again be at the disposal of the German authorities. It is not, however, out of the question that, once their health has been restored, they may remain in this ghetto and be integrated into the labor force here.

FROM THE POLICE BLOTTER

A suicide: Precinct IV, Order Service. On May 26 the hospital at 74 Dworska Street released a mentally ill woman [Chana Schwager née Goldstein, born 12/2/1896 in Serock, Warsaw province]. On May 28 her body was retrieved from the pond on Dworska Street. This was a suicide (see our report of May 29).

SUMMER IN MARYSIN

The first ripe fruits in Marysin, gooseberries, have already roused the greed of one passerby, who tore off a few branches bearing berries. The search for the culprit continues.

A LOVELY DAY

June 6 was a lovely, warm Sunday. As if nature were for everyone and we not in a ghetto, thousands streamed out of the [ghetto] city to the green grass of Marysin. The police had to remind the hikers that between 9 and 10 P.M. it would be necessary for them to return to their airless "metropolitan" apartments.

TUESDAY, JUNE 8, 1943

NEWS OF THE DAY

The Chairman is well again and, once more, can be seen riding through the streets in his droshky.

FOOD SUPPLY

Small shipments of potatoes have begun arriving again; there is a good supply of lettuce and large amounts of dill. The prices of fresh vegetables on the private market have declined considerably. Spinach costs 2 marks, at the most.

SOCIAL WELFARE

By order of the Chairman, children in hostels will, as of June 9, be given two servings of soup [per day] at a cost of 0.50–1.0 mark.

NEWS FROM THE WORKSHOPS

Juvenile workers: By an ordinance of the FUKR [*Fach und Kontrollreferat*—Trade Inspection Section],[17] all juveniles between the ages of 13 and 17 who have been working as so-called messengers have been removed from those positions and as-

---

17. Cf. p. 24, n. 34.

signed to the metal workshop. Exceptions are to be made only in cases of general debility or for other health reasons confirmed by a doctor's certificate. Only juveniles up to the age of 13 can be employed as messengers. In general, however, only people unfit for production should be employed in that capacity. Naturally, this also includes messengers with permanent positions. The FUKR will not authorize any further granting of permanent positions to juveniles.

AGRICULTURE

Thus far, only spinach, radishes, and small amounts of lettuce have been harvested in the ghetto's vegetable gardens. The spinach harvest was ample. As already mentioned, sizable quantities have remained unsold. After the recent rains, the [vegetation] situation improved considerably. But it will still be a fairly long time before the ghetto will be able to consume its own vegetables. During this season of the year the ghetto is particularly short of onions. The agricultural section of the Department of Economics has been distributing onion seed. It was easily available on the private market, but at fantastic prices—between 15 and 75 marks per 10 grams. The tomato seedlings have not done well.

Unfortunately, the Department of Statistics will no doubt fail again this year to photograph these small vegetable gardens in the heart of the [ghetto] city. And that is a pity. The ghetto has many unique features, but the fencing around the small garden plots in the [ghetto] city is unforgettable. Anything that can protect a scrap of ground from being trampled or pilfered is put into service. Ordinary posts with plain or barbed wire are not, of course, to be found. What does exist in large quantities is scraps from the metal workshop, such as metal strips stamped into all possible shapes which, if joined together, make something like a garden fence. One also sees old iron bedsteads fastened together with some stretched-out mattress springs or other scrap metal. Wood cannot, of course, be used for things like fences, and so people rummage through demolished houses searching for rusted iron bedsteads to make into ingenious "iron fences" that, naturally, cannot withstand the gentlest kick. They only constitute a sort of moral barrier.

A CITY WITHOUT FLOWERS

The ghetto, with its approximately 85,000 inhabitants, is probably the only city in the world without any, or almost any, flowers. While flowers are still to be seen in gardens or in windows on the other side of the barbed wire, the ghetto itself is at a disadvantage here as well. In the center of the [ghetto] city and in the nearby vegetable gardens every square inch of ground is, of course, used to grow vegetables. But if flower lovers even wished to grow some, they would not be able to; there are no seeds, bulbs, or seedlings. Only outside the city, in Marysin, can one still see some gardens, a touch of color—mostly perennials like lilies and peonies. The few lilac bushes that bloomed in the courtyards and in Marysin in May were quickly stripped of their blossoms, to the detriment of the city's appearance and the [Marysin] landscape. Window boxes are very rare; at most, one sees an occasional sorry-looking asparagus plant. Yet many windows do have some sparse greenery: sweet peas, good old sweet peas climb up threads, clinging to them with their fragile bodies. In some windows people have simply planted red beets. They will not bloom but one day their leaves will end up in a soup. Red beets as decorative house plants—that's the ghetto.

OTHER ITEMS

Today, on the eve of Shabuoth, there is no sense of holiday atmosphere. A Jewish city without Jewish holidays.

TODAY'S DRESS REHEARSAL FOR THE ORDER SERVICE REVUE

The dress rehearsal for tomorrow's Order Service revue was held today in the House of Culture. The auditorium was filled to overflowing and the police had to restrain the press of curious onlookers.

FRIDAY, JUNE 11, 1943

A MINOR INCIDENT: A FLAP OVER BEARDS

A group of Jews obtained food illegally by using the ration cards of people who had been resettled. For months the group—seven men—remained in hiding while members of their families supplied them with their daily needs. During that time, they grew long beards and, thus, again became Hasidic Jews. There is no Hasid without a beard.

On June 7 the fraud came to light and the entire group was arrested—the young, the old, the middle-aged. After their arrest their beards had to be shaved off. The [German] authorities have long prohibited the wearing of beards, supposedly for reasons of hygiene. But what is a pious, traditional Jew without a beard?

SATURDAY, JUNE 12, 1943

NEWS OF THE DAY

Today three Jews were executed in Central Prison: Abram Tandowski, born 1912 in Zduńska Wola, Hersz Fejgelis, born 1920 in Tomaszów Mazowiecki [and] Mordecai Standarowicz, born 1914 in Faustynów. The first man was from the ghetto. He had escaped recently and had briefly been in hiding with peasants in the vicinity. He was captured and brought to Central Prison. Fejgelis and Standarowicz were workers who allegedly had escaped from their labor camps and also hidden with Polish peasants in the vicinity. No details concerning the executions are known. All that could be learned thus far is that all Order Service section heads were obliged to attend the execution.

FRIDAY, JUNE 18, 1943

JEWISH SKILLED WORKERS SENT TO THE REICH

Today, five Jews were dragged from their beds to be resettled in Germany. This was not an administrative, punitive measure but, rather, the resettlement of five workers, three printers and two engravers, needed in plants in Leipzig. One of the two engravers was taken from Central Prison, where he had been forcibly lodged for having illegally employed his skills as an engraver.

Their Jewish stars [of David] were removed from the five skilled workers at Bałut Market, and they were assured that as "economically valuable Jews" they would be better provided for in the Reich than in the ghetto. They were also allowed to take along 50 [German] marks each and personal necessities (clothing, linen, shoes).[18]

TUESDAY, JUNE 22, 1943

A DEATH

On June 21, 1943, the well-known Jewish scholar and writer Abram Szoel Kamieniecki died in Hospital No. 1. The burial took place today, the 22nd, at 1:30 P.M. The Chairman attended the funeral, after having personally gone to the cemetery in the early morning hours to select a suitable burial site. The burial took place in absolute silence. It was attended only by a few people who at one time had been part of the Zionist circle of Łódź and who wished to honor the memory of an outstanding Hebraist.

The original plan to have the eulogy delivered by Mosze Karo was canceled after consultation with the Chairman.

Since April, 1942, Dr. Kamieniecki had been a coworker of ours here in the Archives. The harsh blows dealt him by fate took their toll on his creative energy. Within the space of a few weeks he lost his wife and his sister-in-law and was then compelled to live a life of utter solitude. He was a quiet, modest person who had been entirely devoted to the life of the mind. Recently, however, his creative work had begun to suffer. With his death the Archives lose a fine, kind colleague. We honor his memory.

(We will present a biographical sketch of Dr. Kamieniecki in tomorrow's bulletin of the *Chronicle.*)

WEDNESDAY, JUNE 23, 1943

DR. ABRAM S. KAMIENIECKI

Our co-worker in the Archives, Dr. A. S. Kamieniecki, has died at the age of 69. Born in Słonim in 1874, he attended a kheder, where he received his early Jewish and Hebrew education. This enabled him to do the necessary studying on his own for the matura

---

18. In the ghettos, as in the concentration camps, officials of the Foreign Political Department in the Nazi Security Service of the Reich Security Main Office (*Amt VI* of the *RHSA*) recruited from among the prisoners highly skilled printers and engravers who were employed in counterfeiting dollars, British pounds, foreign passports, and other such documents. Bernhard Krüger directed this section, known by the cryptonym "Operation Bernhard" (*Unternehmen Bernhard*). Its top-secret production unit (*Geheime Reichssache*) was located in Block No. 19 in the Sachsenhausen-Oranienburg concentration camp. Engravers and printers from the Łódź ghetto were among those who worked there. One of them—Seweryn Tiefenbach—is mentioned by name in the book by Anthony Pirie, *Operation Bernhard* (New York: William Morrow and Co., 1962), p. 115.

[the qualifying examination for university admission], as a so-called "outside student." Having passed the matura, he began his university studies. He attended the universities of Heidelberg, Berlin, and Berne, studying Semitic philology and philosophy, at the same time embarking on independent research in these fields. His doctoral dissertation, submitted at the University of Berne, was on the *Peschitta zu Koheleth*. Its publication in *Zeitschrift für [die] Alttestamentarische Wissenschaft* (Berlin, 1904),[19] brought the young scholar to the attention of the academic community. In 1908 Kamieniecki published a critical essay entitled "Deux lettres de l'époque du dernier exilarque." Kamieniecki contributed an essay on Bible exegesis to the *Zeitschrift für Alttestamentarische Wissenschaft* (1909) entitled "Das Koheleth-Rätsel".[20] Furthermore, he contributed to critical studies of the Bible, including an introduction to the Psalms of Solomon (תהלות שלמה) [Tehilot Shlomo] and (עלית משה) [Aliyat Moshe—Ascending of Moses] in Hebrew (*Hashiloach*, 1904).

These works established his reputation as a Hebraist, Bible scholar, and philological literary critic. Naturally, he was invited to collaborate on the great *Jewish Encyclopedia [Evreiskaia Entsiklopediia]* published in Petersburg; he edited the sections on the Bible and on Hebrew and Chaldaic grammar. This Russian-language encyclopedia was created under the auspices of the renowned Jewish scholars Dr. A. Harkavy and Dr. [J.] L. Katzenelson.

The Chairman, M. C. Rumkowski, held Dr. Kamieniecki in high esteem and enlisted his services in developing the ghetto's educational system. For as long as the ghetto had elementary schools and its Hebrew Gymnasium, Dr. Kamieniecki acted as the supervisor of schools within the School Department. After the breakdown of the entire school system, the late scholar was without employment for a while until the Chairman summoned him to the Archives.

In the Archives Dr. Kamieniecki devoted himself to problems of Jewish tradition, as well as to Yiddish and Hebrew culture in the ghetto. The modest, reserved manner of this renowned scholar in relation to his colleagues earned him widespread admiration.

A year ago Dr. Kamieniecki lost his wife. Broken by that loss and consumed by illness, he lost his will to live, which hastened his end. The Chairman looked after him, saw that he received supplemental food rations and was admitted to the convalescent home, but, sick and embittered, the scholar was beyond help. He died in the hospital on June 21, 1943.

Dr. A. S. Kamieniecki was buried in the Marysin cemetery on June 22. His colleagues and friends accompanied him on his last journey. The Chairman arranged for a suitable burial site.

THURSDAY, JUNE 24, 1943

A SUICIDE

On June 24, Fritzi [Friederike] Mukden, born December 28, 1901, in Prague, a resident of 19 Lutomierska Street, committed suicide by jumping from the fourth floor of the building at 7 Bazarna Street. The Emergency Service physician pronounced her dead.

19. Full title: "Die P'šita zu Koheleth textkritisch und in ihrem Verhältnis zu dem massoretischen Text, der Septuaginta und den anderen alten griechischen Versionen untersucht" (1904).
20. Entitled: "Das Koheleth-Rätsel" (1909) and "Der Rätselname Koheleth" (1914).

REGARDING THE MUKDEN SUICIDE

Mrs. Friederike Mukden, who committed suicide today, had been resettled here from Prague. Her husband, Alois Mukden, an engineer, born October 15, 1894, had died on November 12, 1942. Her 14-year-old daughter Emilie René had been ill for some time and died today of tuberculosis, that most insidious of ghetto diseases. After the death of her husband, [she] had lost much of her will to live, and the death of her child was a crushing blow. So the unhappy woman chose death that same day. Yet another family wiped out!

RESEARCH DEPARTMENT DISBANDED

On May 2, 1943, the Eldest of the Jews received a letter from the [German] Ghetto Administration in regard to the Research Department. That letter stated that the request for wire used in the figurines this department produces would not be granted because wire was a rationed item available only to enterprises engaged in war-related work. The Research Department is, therefore, to suspend work until the appropriate commission reaches a decision on the matter. That decision was made a few days ago, without the promised inspection by a special commission from the Ghetto Administration, or by its chief, Amtsleiter Biebow. The Chairman appeared in person at the Research Department and ordered its director, Emanuel Hirschberg [Hirszberg], to cease all work and make the completed figurines, pictures, and showcases available to the Ghetto Administration. Thus, after 13 months of work, the Research Department must be disbanded as of June 24. At present, all the folkloric material produced by this department still remains in the ghetto. As of today, nothing is known about its possible removal to Litzmannstadt.

At one point, in a special report [pp. 209–10], we wrote about the origin, development, and cultural significance of the Research Department, noting that the figurines and groups depicting the traditional life of Eastern [European] Jews were intended for an exhibit which was to serve as a sort of museum of East European Jewry in Litzmannstadt. We stressed that this department had been formed not at the suggestion of the Chairman but by order of the Ghetto Administration and that the ghetto made a point of remaining aloof from this department, not approving of the direction in which it was moving.

THE DISBANDING OF THE RESEARCH DEPARTMENT

On Thursday, June 24, we reported that the Chairman had disbanded the Research Department on Bałut Market headed by Emanuel Hirschberg [Hirszberg]. We now learn that the Chairman has ordered all members of this department to be available for assignment to workshops. Of the [department's] 35 employees, 28 have already been assigned to various workshops with some relation to arts and crafts (rugs, paper, and wood notions). The remaining seven, headed by Rabbi Hirschberg, will remain in place until the operation is liquidated.

FOOD SUPPLY

The situation is extremely critical. Naked hunger once more reigns in the ghetto. The sparse vegetable shipments are inadequate for the preparation of a meal. The last potato ration of 15 kilograms, announced on May 20, was to last until July 18, and even the small supplements of classes I and II were by far too small. On the one hand, it was feared that the potatoes would rot and, on the other, it was impossible to come anywhere near stretching the allotment to the date scheduled because of the hunger situation. Today, there is hardly a household in the ghetto that still possesses even one kilogram of this ration. Only the privileged holders of supplementary rations, such as B[eirat], B[eirat] I–III,[21] and CP[Ciężko Pracujący—Hard Working], had a little more, but they too, naturally, have no reserves either. It is no wonder that long lines form at the distribution points, where some miserable scraps of lettuce are being distributed; no wonder that people once again make their way to the larger and smaller vegetable gardeners to buy or barter a couple of beet leaves; no wonder that the price of soup is also rising rapidly. Workshop soup is listed at 8 marks today. The price is certain to rise higher. At the moment there is no hope of any significant vegetable shipments. Although vehicles carrying cabbage, even cauliflower, have been seen on the ghetto's thoroughfares—such as Zgierska and Limanowski streets— these seasonal vegetables are merely an advance guard and will not be arriving in the ghetto for quite some time. Meanwhile, the health of the ghetto's people will, unfortunately, deteriorate, and the mortality rate will of course rise again.

MONDAY, JUNE 28, 1943

OTHER NEWS

Lately, more and more messages have been arriving here from people who left this ghetto in the course of various resettlements. These are postcards with brief messages that indicate that the senders are not faring too badly. At any rate, it is a reassuring sign that these people are alive and able to work.[22]

TUESDAY, JUNE 29, 1943

FOOD SUPPLY

The situation is growing steadily more acute. The last remnants of the ration have now been used up. People are living, inasmuch as they can, on their daily soup. But that soup has also declined markedly in quality. The soup kitchens are now producing the first cabbage soup from the small quantity of cabbage that has just arrived in the ghetto. Small rations of fresh vegetables are being distributed in the cooperatives. Four hundred grams of carrots, a bit of lettuce, and, in some shops, even some fresh pea pods. But only about 140 grams out of 400 grams of carrots gross weight are usable. Considering that absolutely no potatoes are to be had, it is obviously impossi-

21. See p. 31, n. 44.
22. In Chełmno (Kulmhof), as in the other death camps, the SS men and staff members frequently forced their victims to write postcards to their families. "We're doing well," "We're working in the Reich"—thus read some postcards. (See Serwański, Obóz zagłady w Chełmni nad Nerem, p. 41.)

ble to prepare an adequate meal from those 140 grams of carrots. Naturally, most people consume their bread rations more quickly, so that at the end of the bread ration [week] there is literally nothing left to eat. The ghetto's vegetable gardens continue to yield only small quantities of young red beets but, since their price has been set at 2.50 marks, the market is empty. These leaves are available only in illicit trade, at exorbitant prices (8–10 marks per kg).

DR. BERNARD HEILIG HAS DIED

This afternoon, one of our colleagues in the Archives, Dr. Bernard Heilig, died at the age of 41. Dr. Heilig had been working in the Archives since January, 1942. He was stricken by tuberculosis in March of this year. Tomorrow's daily report will present a biography of the deceased.

WEDNESDAY, JUNE 30, 1943

ON THE DEATH OF DR. BERNARD HEILIG

With [the death of] Dr. Bernard Heilig, our department has lost its third member this year, following the deaths of [Julian-Stanisław] Cukier-Cerski and Dr. A. S. Kamieniecki. The loss is all the greater because Dr. Heilig was one of the few economic experts engaged in studying the economic history of the Jews while, at the same time, performing statistical work. While working in our department, the deceased had studied the fate of the Western European Jews thus far settled here and had compiled some extremely informative statistical tables. Since our work system here is arranged so that each individual's area is intrinsically connected to that of his colleagues, the death of Dr. Heilig has left a gap that will be hard to fill.

Dr. Heilig had already made a name for himself in his early years as an authority in the field of the economic history of the Jews of Western Europe; he wrote a number of valuable and informative studies of the subject.

His pamphlet, *Zur Entstehung der Prossnitzer Konfektionsindustrie*, is an important contribution to Jewish industrial history. This study expertly explains the origins of this specifically Jewish industry and, at the same time, refutes the myth that Jews were unproductive in industry. This study was translated into Czech, Dutch, and English. Dr. Heilig dealt with a related topic in *Die Vorläufer der mährischen Konfektionsindustrie in ihrem Kampf mit den Zünften* and *Die Prossnitzer Juden als Begründer der österreichischen Baumwollindustrie*. His studies *Urkundliches zur Wirtschaftsgeschichte der Juden* and *Ziele und Wege einer Wirtschaftsgeschichte der Juden in der Tschechoslowakischen Republik* are extremely informative. His monograph, *Faith Ehrenstamm, ein jüdischer Repräsentant des Frühkapitalismus in Österreich* portrays the most important Jewish figure in commerce in eighteenth-century Austria, a man he discovered in the course of his research, and whom he likened to such men as Jew Süss [Joseph Süsskind Oppenheimer], Rothschild, Wertheimer, *et al.*

These outstanding, original contributions attracted the attention of Jacob Lestschinsky, a well-known journalist specializing in economic affairs, who treated them in detail and approvingly in the journal YIVO *Bleter* (Yidisher visenshaftlikher institut,

Vilna). Lestschinsky wrote that "in Dr. Heilig, West-European Jewry has now found a spokesman for its economic history."[23]

Dr. Heilig's writings grew out of his extensive practical experience as the manager of a ready-to-wear clothing factory, as director of the largest Central European exporter of hides, and finally as an independent exporter to South and Central America. In recent years, the deceased had contributed articles in his field of expertise to numerous Prague journals, contributions which solidified his reputation as a writer on economic affairs.

The same conscientiousness and expertise that Dr. Heilig brought to his writings marked his contribution to our department. His personal graciousness, his sober demeanor, and his spirit of cooperation also earned him the friendship of many people outside his immediate circle.

Dr. Heilig fell seriously ill in March, 1943. His health had already been impaired by the generally catastrophic situation. His malnutrition resulted in tuberculosis, despite heroic efforts by his wife, Vera Heilig, who sacrificed everything still left to be sacrificed. But, as is always the case here in the ghetto, fate could not be averted. We buried our colleague Dr. Bernard Heilig today, Wednesday, June 30. We honor his memory.

THURSDAY, JULY 1, 1943[24]

WEATHER

Temperature range: 18–30 degrees; sunshine.

DEATHS

Nineteen.

BIRTHS

None.

ARRESTS

Miscellaneous, two; theft, one.

FIRE ALARM

On June 30, at 7:30 P.M., the Fire Department was called to the building at 4 Ciesielska Street, where it was able to quickly extinguish a floor fire.

---

23. Jacob Lestchinsky, among others, published extremely favorable reviews of the following works by Bernard Heilig: *Ziele und Wege einer Wirtschaftsgeschichte der Juden in der Tschechoslowakischen Republik* (1932), *Die Vorläufer der Mährischen Konfektionsindustrie in ihrem Kampf mit den Zünften* (1931), *Urkundliches zur Wirtschaftsgeschichte der Juden in Prossnitz* (1929), and *Eine mährische Stadt und ihr Ghetto* (1932) (YIVO *Bleter* V (1933), pp. 152–57; VII (1934), pp. 117–21).

24. The *Daily Chronicle Bulletin* for Thursday, July 1, 1943, is given in its entirety here.

TOTAL POPULATION

84,495.

NEWS OF THE DAY

The Chairman remains ill; it seems to be a stubborn cold, which was exacerbated by his going outdoors prematurely.

NEW ARRIVALS

Today, another group of workers (some 50 persons) arrived in the ghetto; these are ailing workers from the labor camp in Jędrzejów. The men were driven in two trucks to Central Prison; from there some of them had to be transferred immediately to the hospital on Dworska Street. Everything had been prepared for receiving them. Though not much was seen of the returnees as they were being transported through the [ghetto] city, their particularly poor condition was, nevertheless, apparent. It is to be hoped that careful nursing and better nourishment will put them back on their feet. The Chairman has made the necessary arrangements from his apartment.

FRIDAY, JULY 2, 1943

MISCELLANEOUS: THE CAROUSEL AT THE GHETTO'S EDGE

Just beyond the outer limit of the ghetto, on Urzędnicza Street at the barbed-wire fence, an amusement park has been set up, as it was last year. The main attraction, the only one visible, is a suspension-type merry-go-round. Every day the children of the ghetto make a pilgrimage to this corner and gaze longingly at the activities on the other side of the fence. It is mostly children too on the other side, who are romping about and climbing into the small hanging boats of the merry-go-round. A radio amplifier broadcasts phonograph music. The ghetto children have never seen a carrousel and have seldom heard music. They listen and peer at a curious, alien world, where children live in a sort of never-never land. A merry-go-round, almost within reach, only the barbed wire keeps them away. Children are children on either side of the barbed wire—and yet they are not the same.

SATURDAY, JULY 3, 1943

PUBLIC HEALTH

The Figures on Contagious Diseases in the Month of June
The following cases of contagious disease were reported in June: tuberculosis—244, meningitis—1, scarlet fever—3, typhoid fever—26, typhus—1. The mortality in the month of June was as follows:

Tuberculosis	265
Other pulmonary diseases	26

Cardiac ailments	75
Tuberculosis of other organs	26
Diseases of the digestive organs	20
Disorders of the nervous system	5
Kidney diseases	4
Blood diseases	3
Cancer and other tumors	6
Other diseases	2
Typhoid	1
Whooping cough	1
Suicide	1
Total	435

SUNDAY, JULY 4, 1943

FOOD SUPPLY

The meager ration has essentially not changed the situation. At all the shops that are distributing the minute vegetable ration, people are backed up in endless lines. These announcements of the rations are only posted on the signs hung at the shops, and yet people hear immediately if one shop or another has just received a shipment of *botwinki* (beet leaves) or other vegetables. No sooner has the handcart pulled up than people come running from every street to their assigned shops and wait, more or less patiently, for the distribution of the ration. The amount of energy expended in this process is hardly covered by the ration itself. Picking up rations, when they are available, often takes seven hours.

PRICES ON THE BLACK MARKET

Bread, 220 marks; flour, 1.60 marks per 10 g; rye flakes, 1.50 marks per 10 g; oil, 6 marks per 10 g; sugar, 1.60 marks per 10 g; potatoes, 25 marks per kilogram; 1 can of meat (beef), 100 marks; cabbage, 5–7 marks per kilogram.

MONDAY, JULY 5, 1943

NEWS OF THE DAY

Concealed Goods and Valuables
Today, an updated proclamation (No. 399, of July 5, 1943) concerning the goods and valuables left behind or concealed in Litzmannstadt and in the ghetto was issued by the Eldest. The population is asked to report to the head of the Special Department any goods and valuables left behind or concealed in Litzmannstadt or in the ghetto. The proclamation stresses that no legal consequences are to be feared. In this connection, we must point out that, although three years have passed since the closing off of the ghetto, goods and valuables have been discovered and confiscated repeatedly both in the ghetto and in Litzmannstadt. All these objects are turned over to the

ghetto treasury or, if need be, utilized in production. The shortage of goods caused by the war has induced both the authorities and the Eldest to conduct an intensive search for merchandise that can be put to good use.

Packages Delivered

In the past few days food packages have arrived from Prague. Four families resettled here from Prague have each received a 1-kilogram package of bread. This news has caused a sensation throughout the ghetto because, as is well known, there is officially no parcel post into or out of the ghetto.

WEDNESDAY, JULY 7, 1943

NEWS OF THE DAY

Today's sensation is the report that all the women and girls employed at Bałut Market are to be dismissed, by order of the Gestapo. At the moment, no definite information is available about the motives behind this decision. According to one story, the entire female staff is to leave Bałut Market; according to another, the executive staff will remain, including Miss [Dora] Fuchs and the two women in the secretariat, [Mary] Schifflinger and [Bronia] Szwebel, as well as Miss [Estera] Daum. At the Central Workshop Bureau, only the two female executives, Walfisch and Burstin, are to remain. According to another, less credible version, even the above-mentioned women are to leave Bałut Market. Supposedly, women will be forbidden to enter Bałut Market in the future. This measure is to be carried out within ten days. It will be difficult to find replacements for these office workers. The chief possibility would be to recruit from among the men resettled here, but this human resource has become greatly depleted by now.

WOMAN FROM PRAGUE TO LEAVE GHETTO

Mrs. Alma Eisenberger, a woman resettled here from Prague, was ordered to report to the Gestapo in Litzmannstadt the day before yesterday; there she was informed that she had received citizenship in the South American Republic of Paraguay. For this reason, she will in all likelihood be able to leave the ghetto. The young woman had the misfortune of losing a 17-year-old son here.

BOOK COLLECTION IN THE GHETTO: HOW A LIBRARY CAME INTO BEING

On February 8, 1940, the German authorities in Łódź (later Litzmannstadt) ordered the systematic evacuation of the Jews from the city into the ghetto. At the same time, it was announced that all Jewish property was to be considered confiscated. Of their possessions, the Jews were permitted to take along only bedsteads and family pictures (photographs). The order made no mention of books—we are thinking, of course, of age-old family heirlooms: the *sforim* [holy books], such as the Talmud, the *Tanakh* [Bible], the Shulkhan Arukh, and, furthermore, the beloved family albums that mark family events.

The people who were evacuated from the city [to the ghetto] had customarily taken along their bedsteads and the books in question. The beds were used as fuel, victims to the hard winter of 1940/41; the books lay covered with dust in the gloomy apartments. The evacuations [out of the ghetto] from January to April, 1942, put some 44,000 Jews—15,000 families—on the road. One could say that these people had to leave the ghetto without bag or baggage, without their precious family albums and books of sacred instruction.

The books remained behind in the vacated apartments. Now and again, Hebrew and Yiddish books turned up on the market as scrap paper—in the latrines, in the shops, or among merchants and street vendors.

There was an obvious danger that, in the foreseeable future, all these valuable books would be destroyed or ruined in some other way. Thus, the question of how this treasure could be saved arose. The director of the Department of Vital Statistics, [Henryk] Neftalin, the attorney, tackled the problem vigorously. He presented the matter to the ghetto's Department of Economics and urged it to order that all house administrators and superintendents deliver to the Department of Vital Statistics any books left in apartments, cellars, and attics.

That was the first step in a task that is now being carried out. So far, 30,000 books have been rescued and preserved, inspected, and registered. In addition, there were a few dozen Torah scrolls, tfiln [philacteries], taleysim [prayer shawls], etc.

These rescued valuables have been stored in three rooms in the Department of Vital Statistics. Shelves reaching up to the ceiling are filled with books that have been handed down for generations, bequeathed from grandfather to grandson, and preserved religious piety.

The director of the library is Engineer Weinhorn. He watches over his treasure with touching solicitude, nay, paternal love. This book collection in the Department of Vital Statistics is among the most interesting sights in the ghetto. (See the article, "In the Book Collection" by J[ózef] Z[elkowicz], July 5, 1943.)[25]

O[skar] R[osenfeld]

FRIDAY, JULY 9, 1943

THE LOOK OF THE GHETTO, JUNE 1943

Every few hours of the day life's image changes, and with it the ghetto dwellers' moods. In general, one can say that people have grown accustomed to living surrounded by barbed wire and tolerate that state as almost natural, as a thing ordained by fate. For, in comparison with the cares of everyday life, the constant psychic constraints seem less burdensome.

The month of June, in the year 1943, with which the fourth year of the ghetto commences, is distinguished from the previous months of the year by a variety of gay colors, movements, and natural images; by the vacillations in hope and the weather. One may say without exaggeration that the days and hours pass before the spectator's eye like the shapes in a kaleidoscope. And what is normally the very essence of

---

25. The article by Józef Zelkowicz was not incorporated into the *Chronicle*. There is a copy preserved in the Archives of the YIVO Institute for Jewish Research, New York.

June—a blending of spring and summer—has not been granted to the ghetto dwell-ers. A few hours of blue sky and warm air are followed by rain showers.

People whose work depends on the weather—those tending the vegetable plots and the fields—have had their share of daily cares. Since the offices of food supply are unable to provide the 85,000 inhabitants of the ghetto with the fresh vegetables they need, the gardeners are required to surrender a portion of their produce to the population. There is, however, quite enough communal land, that is to say, fields not leased to private individuals but tilled by persons specifically assigned to that pur-pose. In the early morning hours one can see groups of people, with agricultural tools in their hands and on their shoulders, marching through the streets to till the soil—heading out to the vegetable gardens in Marysin, where there is plenty of farmwork to do. No such figures were to be seen previously, just as there were no vegetable and potato beds on the grounds of the ghetto. The ghetto has been restructured; and as a result, we are supplied with vegetables not only by the [German] Ghetto Administra-tion, but also by our own soil. . . .

The afternoon sun shines on the rough, uneven pavement. It lights up the puddles after a tempestuous rainfall so that, a few minutes later, dust is rising again. There is no municipal sanitation service. The janitors keep the sidewalks clean in front of their buildings. That is all. The ghetto in June, 1943, a labor camp with a ten-hour workday, cannot afford the luxury of street cleaning.

At five in the afternoon, when people—children and the very old, middle-aged men and women—have finished their work in the factories and offices, the ghetto looks like a factory town. The doors of the workshops open, and troops of badly nourished and badly dressed people step out into the streets. Nearly all of them carry baskets and pots. They chat, laugh, scurry. . . . Some are off to the cooperatives, that is, the shops that distribute the food rations, others are off to the vegetable or coal markets, but most of them hurry home to prepare an evening meal of soup after their tiring labor.

A proletarian city, one might think. But among the wretched figures in the numbed and care-worn crowd one sees a few well-dressed persons, mostly pretty young girls, their hair styled and waved, their nails manicured, their bodies soft, round, and good-looking—except that most of these privileged creatures have round, protruding bel-lies and thereby lose much of their undeniable grace. Those protruding bellies are no doubt the result of the diet here: there is so much water in the potatoes, beets, and lettuce that even twelve-year-old girls often look like pregnant women.

Jewish physiognomies are seldom encountered here. The Slavic type predomi-nates in both sexes; and the children in particular do not look as though they belong to the children of Israel.

During its first week, the month of June was a good friend to the ghetto dwellers. It brought them the most precious food that can be wished for in the ghetto: potatoes. When the carts appeared in the streets—whether horse-drawn or in handcarts—passersby halted and stared hopefully at the round fruits of the earth. What do the hungry care whether the potatoes are first or second quality—as long as there are potatoes? The streets would come alive, whips cracked, draymen whistled, and boys ran after the wagons to grab the few potatoes that might tumble off. Suddenly, the potato shipments stopped. Potatoes were replaced by vegetables—spinach, lettuce, red beets, carrots, radishes—too little to fill empty stomachs. And since no more potatoes came in during the second half of June and the allocated supplies had already been consumed, hunger and despair loomed on the horizon once again. The end of this month of June is reminiscent of last year's "starvation" June. The workshop soups are thinner than before and contain only 150 grams of potatoes. Nevertheless, the price of soup keeps rising on the black market. A brisk trade can be observed in front of the kitchens. "Do you have a coupon to sell?" ask hungry people left and right, hoping to make up for the lack of potatoes by buying soup.

The first truckloads of green vegetables are now rolling through the streets, causing renewed hope. Just hold out for a few more weeks, and then there will be potatoes again—the fresh young potatoes, not the sort of which half has to be thrown into the trash as unfit for consumption. This thought can be read on the faces in the ghetto. The fashionably attired young girls, who wish to appeal to the bons vivants of the ghetto, and the other girls, in whom the pressures of life have stifled any need for beauty and tenderness, all bear the mark of constant anxiety. Ultimately, no one escapes the nightmare of the ghetto. The June sun trickles down through rain and gloom, the people trot in and out of the workshops, and barefoot children with pale cheeks and wise, precocious eyes sing the street tune "Sakharin originele finf a mark" ("Saccharine, the real thing, five for a mark").

O[skar] R[osenfeld]
July 3, 1943

SUNDAY, JULY 11, 1943

FOOD SUPPLY

Situation more and more critical; consequently, a deteriorating state of health, an increase in cases of hunger edema and typhoid.

PUBLIC HEALTH

Typhus Curve Rising
In connection with the above report it must be noted that the Department of Health has released nearly all tubercular patients from the hospital on Dworska Street, which, because of the increasing number of typhus cases, must be kept ready to receive typhus patients. Since the hospital on Mickiewicz Street has a total of 17 beds for inpatients, not even the most urgent cases of pleuritis, and other such diseases requiring hospitalization, can be admitted at present. Furthermore, the hospital on Dworska Street is being used for workers who have been resettled into the ghetto. In this regard the situation in the ghetto is extremely critical.

TUESDAY, JULY 13, 1943

A DAY OF RUMORS

After a relatively long interval of calm and stability, the ghetto was seized by a palpable attack of fear on July 13. No specific manifestations of this anxiety could be identified, but everyone felt instinctively that even those persons who usually keep themselves under control had lost their equilibrium.

When it was learned on July 7 that the female employees would have to leave Bałut Market and be replaced by male personnel, all sorts of conjectures and vague theories about this fact were bruited about. The conjectures seemed to gain plausibility when one of the executive officers of the [German] Ghetto Administration, Schumburg, was removed from office. But none of these events were sufficient to disquiet the ghetto seriously.

However, all the rumors and circulating stories found fertile ground in the mood produced by the sudden advent of hunger. Because of the shortage of potatoes and other essential foods, people have been counting on a steady allocation of vegetables, chiefly cabbage. But since even this merely stomach-filling "fodder" failed to materialize, and the workshop soups were becoming thinner and thinner, one could read misery, even despair, on thousands of faces. "We have nothing to cook," could be heard on every street corner, in every department, outside every kitchen.

Amid this gloom came the report that Dawid Gertler, the head of the Special Department, had been taken to the city and had not returned, that is, that he had spent the night of July 12 to 13 in the city (Litzmannstadt). Countless versions of the story behind this report, which in itself was entirely true, were invented. At first, fear was expressed that Gertler's surprisingly long absence was linked to measures planned against the ghetto, indeed that the ghetto was in danger. Another rumor circulated that Gertler was in the city on a personal matter—which, however, still implied danger to the ghetto. Supposedly, the prelude to these imminent measures was a complete interruption in the ghetto's food supply. The imagination of the ghetto dwellers, who have indeed experienced enough extraordinary things during the three years that the ghetto has been in existence, began to run riot. The "Gertler Affair" was the sole topic of conversation into the late evening hours. There were even some who claimed to know about an alleged action against the Jewish camp in Sosnowice (Poznań), thus only further increasing the ghetto's agitation. Sober observers of the situation, relying on definite information, could make no headway against the rumors. All faces were marked with worry, despair, terror. And one dreadful fear lurked in every heart: resettlement out of the ghetto!

The day passed with no news to put minds at ease. A day of rumors, terror, nightmare.

O[skar] R[osenfeld]

FRIDAY, JULY 16, 1943

A COMMISSION IN THE GHETTO

Today, a German commission again inspected a few specific factories and plants in the ghetto.

A VISIT TO THE RESEARCH DEPARTMENT

The German commission visited the Research Department this morning in order to inspect the showcases on display there. As we have previously reported [cf. pp. 209–

10], this department ceased operations in early May by order of the Ghetto Admin- istration and was recently disbanded. The folklore material that was assembled and prepared for exhibition still remains on the premises of this department. The visiting body, composed of the two members of the Ghetto Administration and two members of the Wehrmacht, inspected the showcases, especially the recently completed figu- rines of "Ghetto Types" and "Work in the Ghetto." The meaning of these groups was explained by the director, E[manuel] Hirschberg [Hirszberg], who took the oppor- tunity to request that the visitors allow him to complete some 150 figurines with the help of five of the workers who had been dismissed.

The commission showed interest in the Eastern European Jewish figurines and promised to inform Hirschberg of its decision. It is likely that the entire assemblage of figurines will soon find its way to Litzmannstadt and serve propaganda purposes as an "Exhibition of the Manners and Mores of Eastern European Jews".[26]

WEDNESDAY, JULY 21, 1943

THE LEGEND SURROUNDING DAWID GERTLER

More than a week has passed since the arrest of Dawid Gertler, the head of the Special Department. Throughout this time, rumors about the reasons for his disappearance and other gossip about this matter have been circulating. The ghetto has gradually succumbed to a Gertler psychosis. Every day it was predicted that Gertler would arrive in the ghetto "today" or "tomorrow" at such and such a time.

All these conjectures and wild speculations proved to be false. Nonetheless, the guessing continued. Today, the fever of expectation reached a new high point. To- ward 8 P.M., the news spread around Bałut Market that Gertler had "just" returned. Supposedly, a car had brought him from the city into the ghetto. He would be leaving the office of the German authorities on Bałut Market at any moment now and appear- ing on the street.

Passersby stopped and waited to witness this interesting scene. More and more people crowded at the corners of Zawisza and Dworska streets (Inselstrasse and Matrosengasse). It was an extraordinary sight and a stirring one. For a while the Order Service men on duty in this area let the crowd alone; but, finally, they decided to restore order and disperse the groups of pedestrians.

The rumor was triggered by a report from Michał Gertler, head of the Dairy Depart- ment. He had called [Marek] Kligier, administrative director of the Special Depart- ment, and informed him that he personally had seen Dawid Gertler in a carriage. Thereupon, Kligier immediately telephoned the Central Secretariat on Bałut Market to have Miss [Mary] Schifflinger inquire of Amtsleiter Biebow whether this report was accurate. Miss Schifflinger, however, misunderstood the call and erroneously re- ported Gertler's arrival to Biebow.

The rumor of Gertler's return has once again proved to be unfounded. No authentic information has as yet been obtained concerning Gertler's whereabouts.

26. See p. 169, n. 48.

THURSDAY, JULY 22, 1943

PEOPLE ARE SAYING

that Mrs. [Stefania] Dawidowicz, the daughter of the well-known physician Dr. [Fabian] Klozenberg, will be leaving the ghetto for Palestine. The facts of the matter are as follows: Mrs. Dawidowicz's husband, a physician, lives in Palestine and has "put in a request" for his wife.[27] On the basis of an agreement, Mrs. Dawidowicz is now to be exchanged for three German nationals interned in Palestine. Mrs. Dawidowicz has already been notified of these arrangements by the Gestapo.

FRIDAY, JULY 23, 1943

FOOD SUPPLY

The situation has improved somewhat. To be sure, it cannot be said that hunger has been eliminated from the ghetto; on the contrary. Hardly has a potato ration like the last one been distributed when the hungry ghetto dweller pounces on and devours this unusual meal. Besides, early potatoes are a delicacy; and, of course, one can hardly expect starving people to hold to a strict daily rationing. Vegetables are indeed arriving, but not in sufficient quantities. Cabbage leaves are again being sold by the ghetto gardeners, as they were last year; likewise, young red beet leaves, which bring a price of 6.50 marks [a bunch], even though a price ceiling has been imposed.

PEOPLE ARE SAYING

that a special allotment of 3 kilograms of potatoes will be distributed every week. The first allotment is scheduled for the 27th of this month. Furthermore, cabbage will be distributed again in the next few days if the shipments, which have already begun, prove to be adequate.

SATURDAY, JULY 24, 1943

SKETCHES OF GHETTO LIFE[28]

The Ghetto Children's Toys
The so-called Belgian cigarettes have been a disappointment to smokers in the ghet-

27. Her husband, Dr. Maksymilian Dawidowicz, a well-known Łódź physician, made his way, as a Polish officer, to Palestine via Rumania toward the end of the Polish-German war in September, 1939. There he resumed work as a doctor in the Polish Army in the West, which had been formed in France, and he later transferred to England. Certainly no one in the ghetto knew that, while his wife's departure to Palestine was still in the process of being arranged, Dr. Maksymilian Dawidowicz had died. He had died in a hospital in India on September 17, 1942, following an automobile accident in Iraq, where he had been on duty. It is not known whether Stefania Dawidowicz succeeded in leaving the ghetto. In any case, the *Chronicle* does not mention her having left.

28. This is the title of a new heading used almost until the last entry in the *Chronicle*. In the original, i.e., in the German, the title reads: *Kleiner Getto-Spiegel*.

to, even to those who have smoked poor-quality tobacco all their lives. The countless packs with their gaudy colors and equally gaudy names could not alter the devastating judgment that has been passed on the quality of the cigarettes. However, a smoker's passion overrides any reservations. The cigarettes go up in smoke, the cardboard box remains. Since every object in the ghetto, no matter how worthless, acquires some value, even these boxes have come to be cherished. The smoker does not throw them out. He saves them, and makes sure that they do not go to waste. Children's eyes beg for those boxes, children's hands reach out for them.

Outside the ghetto, children receive beautiful and appropriate playthings as presents. There is a great industry for manufacturing them; artists and artisans invent new toys and build little altars for children's hearts out of wood, cardboard, metal, silk, and plaster. . . . A fantastic world emerges, and children go strolling through it. The children of the ghetto, however, are not blessed with such good fortune. They have to create their toys themselves. Still, the Jewish child is talented enough to do without the fantasies of the toy manufacturer. Our children collect empty cigarette boxes. They remove the colorful tops and stack them in a pile, until they have a whole deck of cards. Playing cards.

And they play. They count the cards and deal them out. They arrange them by color and name. Green, orange, yellow, brown, even black. They play games that they invent for themselves, they devise systems, they let their imaginations take over.

Thus, the children too have received their portion of the bad "Belgian cigarettes."

O[skar] R[osenfeld]

SUNDAY, JULY 25, 1943

SKETCHES OF GHETTO LIFE

The first truly hot day of summer is luring people outdoors, especially to Marysin, where there is some greenery and the air is considerably purer. It is hardly surprising that nearly all the "dignitaries" have moved to Marysin for the summer; a small world unto itself, so to speak, has developed there. People there live in villas, some small, some large, but all primitive, almost as if they were at a resort. This is picking time for morello cherries. Everywhere, one sees children up in trees, picking these cherries to eat them on the spot and to carry them home in little baskets. This year there is a large number of heavily laden apple and pear trees, both in Marysin and in the middle of the ghetto. These precious fruits are guarded day and night.

MONDAY, JULY 26, 1943

A SUICIDE

Today, Jeremia Guterbaum,[29] 42 years of age, jumped from the third floor of his apartment house at 18 Franciszkańska Street; he was taken to the hospital, where he succumbed to his injuries.

29. In another copy of the *Chronicle*, this name was spelled Guterman.

NEWS OF THE DAY: THE RESEARCH DEPARTMENT

Today Amtsleiter Biebow, accompanied by A[ron] Jakubowicz, appeared at the Research Department in order to inspect the figurines on display there. The visit lasted
barely half an hour. The head of this department, E[manuel] Hirschberg, presented
information about the work accomplished thus far and asked Biebow for permission
to complete some 200 figurines with the aid of five workers previously employed
there. These workers are said to include the two painters I[zrael] Leizerowicz and
H[ersz] Szylis.

Biebow granted this request; thus, all the displays of Eastern European Jews that
were originally planned will now be completed. This work will require approximately
three months.

O[skar] R[osenfeld]

TUESDAY, JULY 27, 1943

NEWS OF THE DAY

A Death
Mrs. Paulina Gertler, the wife of Michał Gertler, head of the Dairy Department, died on
the 26th of this month.

From the Post Office
By order of the [German] authorities, effective immediately, all use of so-called greeting cards (preprinted) has been terminated. Also, the acceptance of money orders has
been restricted because only sums of 20 marks or more can be confirmed. Likewise, a
change, or rather, restriction, is to be noted in the mailing of packages to relatives in
the Andersdorf [Andreshoff-Jędrzejów] labor camp. Previously, packages could be
forwarded through the Bureau of Labor in the ghetto. From now on, however, such
packages cannot be sent in this manner. An application must be made through the
Bureau of Labor to Bałut Market, where permission will be granted on a case-by-case
basis.

THURSDAY, JULY 29, 1943

NEWS OF THE DAY

A Fugitive in the Ghetto
This evening the Order Service was mobilized and German police patrols searched for
an alleged Polish fugitive who had fled into the ghetto. The man could not be tracked
down inside the ghetto. He had undoubtedly escaped again at some other point on
the border of the ghetto.

FOOD SUPPLY

The situation just before the new ration is again extremely critical. The populace is
kept calm only by the hope that a large potato ration is coming; but, unfortunately,

this is wishful thinking; in reality, the occasional truckloads of potatoes that send people's hopes soaring are far from adequate. Thus, any talk of eight to ten kilograms in the next ration is sheer fantasy. Ten kilograms per person would mean a total of some 800,000 kilograms in storage, and that is out of the question. It will be quite an achievement if the Food Supply Department has even five kilograms [per person] available.

BAKED APPLES FOR THE HOSPITALS

Several hundred apples have been cooked in the bakery on Piwna Street. They were cored, filled with sugar, and oven-baked. These apples, we are told, were donated to the hospital by Mrs. [Dawid] Gertler from her own stock of fruit. Baked apples with sugar—a sensation for the ghetto!

WORKSHOP NEWS: A SHOEMAKERS' STRIKE?

There has been an incident in a division of the Shoe Department. The workers demanded that the management provide supplemental soup to all workers. Since the demand either was not or could not be granted, the staff has refused to accept even the basic soup allotment. The Trade Inspection Section is attending to this matter, which will probably be cleared up promptly.

FRIDAY, JULY 30, 1943

NEWS OF THE DAY

Bridges Closed
Twice this morning the bridges across Zgierska Street were closed to traffic, the first time at 8 A.M., the second time at noon. The reason was troop movement across the bridges. At 8 A.M. it was an infantry division, apparently returning from a drill; the second time it was a grenadier regiment, probably marching from or to a review.

SUNDAY, AUGUST 1, 1943

SKETCHES OF GHETTO LIFE: SUNDAY IN THE GHETTO

I

The word *Sunday* has a different ring in the ghetto than it does outside in the free world. A different ring and a different meaning. Here the word has no connotations of rest, joy, and festivity. The ghetto's Sunday bears the imprint of heavy burdens, as onerous and wearisome as those of any workday. In fact, if they had to choose between Sunday and a regular workday, the workday would seem preferable to many a ghetto dweller. The hand does not waver in writing this down. The hand is guided by a brain that reliably preserves all impressions of the eye and the ear.

For almost three long years, from spring, 1940, until spring, 1943, the ghetto did not know a day of rest. The manifestations of the ghetto are as extraordinary as the institution of the ghetto itself. Let us describe things as simply as possible.

The ghetto had seven workdays every week, and every workday was eight hours long. No Sabbath, no holiday, no non-Jewish Sunday. No allowances were made for the high holy days, respected also by gentiles throughout the world—no concessions. As though there had never been a Torah and a tradition. It must be understood that the ghetto of Litzmannstadt was planned not as a Jewish ghetto, but as a ghetto for Jews. One hundred sixty thousand Jews—the original number—were to live behind fences and barbed wire until . . . the whole world took on a different face. Some of these times have already passed. Today is Sunday, August 1, 1943.[30]

Since the spring of 1943, Sunday has been granted as a day of rest. Instead, the workday was increased from eight to ten hours, so that the laboring population, namely 90 percent of the entire population of the Litzmannstadt ghetto, had to pay for this gift with four additional work hours a week. The ghetto, however, was given very little for its extra labor, since Sunday is, in fact, no day of rest, but something else entirely.

II

By early Sunday morning, the streets are already busier than on workdays. People of all ages go into and out of the various shops where the allocated provisions are distributed: shops for groceries, bread, milk, meat, and sausages! But if we take a closer look we see that what has been obtained barely suffices for a few days, and yet it is supposed to last for two weeks. The misery of the ghetto!

Children carry wood. It sounds so lovely: wood! In reality, what they carry are rotten boards, laths, beams, posts, door and window frames, all riddled with rusty nails—the fortunate few are envied for the small hard scraps of wood they have been provided with by the carpentry workshops.

Thousands of bent backs can be seen, shoulders laden with knapsacks. Little boys pull briquettes behind them in toy wagons, old men carry loaves of bread and cabbages in baskets and shopping nets. People crowd in front of the shops. They shout, gesticulate, laugh with tears in their eyes; the staff of the cooperatives yells at those who push and shove, sometimes even striking them. Children whimper, tumble into the open gutters, which now, at the height of summer, smell like stinking fusel oil. Several hours of Sunday are already gone.

Shoemakers, tailors, and barbers catch up on the work they are doing for their private customers. Through the open doors one can see them sweating and toiling. A day of rest! The housewives have even more chores. The laundry has to be done and tattered clothes mended. Linen has to be aired, scrubbed, and ironed. The bedding has to be carried into the courtyard, into the garden. . . . Everything is covered with bedding—red and red-striped pillows and covers, blankets, dust rags, and tablecloths everywhere. Men's, women's and children's laundry on fences, windows, and garden pickets. At times one glimpses men without shirts, bare-legged women, or the

---

30. No doubt, this is an allusion to good news from the front, which had been delayed in reaching the ghetto and, in particular, concerned the landing and successes of the American troops in southern Italy and the progress of the Red Army in the vicinity of Kursk.

feet of dirty, suntanned children. . . . A few people manage to sleep or doze in the sultry, steamy air. No water anywhere, no little water hole, no river, no brook, no lake! A half-dry well yields a few pails of water! And that's all! Such is ghetto sunbathing and fresh-air therapy! Eighty-five thousand people with parched tongues. . . .

Among these people, though, there are a few who have the spirit to wander into open country, to Marysin, to the district of the privileged, the chosen . . . the small group that spends the summer in a kind of fresh-air spa and is in the ghetto only during working hours. . . . These brave souls, mostly couples, are undaunted by the heat and dust; they wander, singing, with stomachs empty and hearts full, quickly plucking a few blackberries or cherries from people's gardens! The gardens in question are the działki [land parcels] created by the ghetto inhabitants; half the yield of the fruit trees belongs to the cultivators, half to the Community. Soon it will be harvest time. The apples hang heavy on the branches. People by the thousands gaze up at them, their mouths watering.

III

Only for the dying is Sunday a day of rest. They can be seen through the curtainless windows—half of them ill, half of them starving—left alone on their fly-infested bedsteads. Their families are busy fetching food, washing, and cleaning. If one is fortunate enough to be buried on a Sunday, he will still not have the honor of a well-attended funeral. For Sunday in the ghetto is a day of rest only for the dead.

O[skar] R[osonfold]

WEDNESDAY, AUGUST 4, 1943

WORKSHOP NEWS

A Change in Health Care Regulations
An important change will be introduced in the granting of sick leave from the workshops. In the future, a physician's certification of illness, hitherto accepted without exception [and qualifications], will be valid for only two days. After this period, the ailing worker will be removed from the roster of his workshop and will remain under the authority of [Miss Rebeka] Wolk's secretariat[31] for the duration of his illness. When the worker recovers, this office will again place him at the disposal of the Bureau of Labor. Workers will no doubt regard this change as a severe measure.

SKETCHES OF GHETTO LIFE: WHAT JEWELRY IS WORN IN THE GHETTO?

It is well known that Jews in the ghetto possess no jewelry, since all Jewish property must be regarded as confiscated and was supposed to be either submitted [to the office of authorities] or else surrendered directly at Kościelna Street [that is, to the German criminal police] upon summons. Nevertheless, the need for small adornments is understandable. Aside from cheap costume jewelry that they owned previously, women now mostly wear brooches [decorated] with ghetto symbols. For the

31. See above, p. 120, n. 10.

most part, these are miniature bread cards, with the owner's name engraved on them and made of chromium, tin or, in rare cases, of silver. Frequently, too, a first name [shaped from] chromium wire serves as a brooch. Pendants are usually the Star of David, in a variety of styles. Other ghetto motifs, such as the bridge or some other characteristic feature, are likewise frequently worn as clasps or brooches. Men and women wear silver rings with engraved ghetto motifs. Young people frequently wear various emblems on their lapels, most often the Star of David. Cigarette boxes with emblems and symbols of departments or workshops are a popular gift item. Even the old smoker's [ration] cards, bearing the owner's name, are engraved on otherwise smooth boxes. It is astonishing how the art of engraving flourishes in the ghetto and continually produces fresh ideas.

SATURDAY, AUGUST 7, 1943

SKETCHES OF GHETTO LIFE: THE FACE OF JULY, 1943

Midsummer in the ghetto: one uses the word "summer" casually, as if it meant the hot month that city dwellers spend outside the city, in a resort—with all the lovely and intimate associations that go with summer in the country. In the ghetto, July is a month of pains and vexation, a month of long days spent worrying about a morsel of bread, a scrap of food.

The sun is white-hot. The gutters are dry. There is not even a tuft of cloud in the sky. In the streets, the boys cry "Saccharine here!" and "Toffee here!" Nearby, women hawk real onions—small, unprepossessing roots. Onions are a rarity in the ghetto, like so much else.

Cherries hang on the trees. By the end of the month they have disappeared. Who picked them? Who will eat them? One of many enigmas. But the apples still hang on the trees, promising a rich harvest. Who will eat them? Another of the many enigmas.

Potato wagons are few and far between. Yet, we can enjoy the sight of wagons that drive into the ghetto piled high with dry heather. Here and there, in the squares and on the streets, they are unloaded; and soon the heather will reappear as brooms for "housewives" [outside the ghetto]. Even the wagons of straw for the straw-shoe workshops have become less frequent. Occasionally, though, we see wagons of the local dry straw, a kind of hay. The straw suits the summer mood, matches the glowing, cloudless, merciless sky. Just imagine: a city of approximately 85,000 people with no open air and no bodies of water!

Nor do the evenings bring any relief from the heat. Many people make up beds in the courtyards or gardens, where they spend the nights. Night now begins at nine o'clock. An order from the Eldest has reminded the ghetto of the nine o'clock curfew. Not long ago, people were strolling and loitering in the streets on these long, bright evenings, enjoying their *corso*, their public promenade. Those days are gone. No one wants to risk being stopped, or possibly even being arrested, by the Jewish Order Service.

On July 12, the head of the Special Department, Dawid Gertler, was taken from the ghetto. As of today his fate is still unknown, but concern for him has not diminished.

Evening after evening, hundreds of persons gathered around Bałut Market hoping to be present at his (rumored) return and to welcome him back. His popularity increased with the length of his absence. These gatherings are no longer possible, so the ghetto is gradually growing used to the continued absence of a popular figure; indeed, the time does not seem far off when the worrisome burdens of day-to-day life will erase even this from our memories.

Morning and evening exhibit the same picture: people rushing to and from the workshops. Home to the inevitable soup. One can ignore the bulletin boards without missing a thing: [there are] no announcements of cabbage or potato rations! It is a difficult time. Again and again, hunger tempered with hope! In June the word was: July will mean potatoes. In July there was the consoling thought: August will mean vegetables.

But solace alone will not feed the hungry or cure the diseased. Every day, dozens of cases of typhus and tuberculosis are reported. On July 1, there were 84,495 inhabitants of the ghetto; on August 1, only 84,280. During the same period, twelve male and five female children were born, a figure that does not take the terrible infant mortality rate into account!

The question: How much longer can this go on? is gradually becoming irrelevant. Death is flourishing. There are practically no births. The ghetto is liquidating itself. The Litzmannstadt ghetto is true to its image as "death's corner" in Europe.

O[skar] R[osenfeld]

SUNDAY, AUGUST 8, 1943

NEWS OF THE DAY

The main topic of conversation today is Amtsleiter Biebow's surprise visit to Marysin, where he made a call at Rest Home I and also, while in the area, at the apartment of Director Józef Rumkowski. This visit was prompted by a certain unpleasant incident. The workers employed in reaping oats asked [Heinrich] Schwind,[32] an executive of the Ghetto Administration, for an allotment of one loaf of bread. Schwind referred the request to the Eldest, who gave him to understand that provisions were extraordinarily scarce and that he could not provide a special ration. The workers grumbled and pointed out that certain persons were enjoying unusually long stays in the rest home, an allegation that Schwind communicated to the head of the Ghetto Administration [Biebow]. Thereupon, he made his inspection. He found nothing amiss in

---

32. Heinrich Schwind arrived in Łódź, as a sergeant-major in the cavalry, along with other German military units in September, 1939. There he married for a second time and, after his release from the army, assumed a position in the German city administration and later in the Gettoverwaltung, where he acted as the supervisor of vehicles that served the ghetto. To that end, he organized (and supervised) a grazing area in the Marysin section of the ghetto, principally for horses, where the above-mentioned Jewish workers were employed. In 1952, he was sentenced to life in prison by the supreme court in Berlin (Landgericht) for his personal participation in and organizing of the transport of Jews to the death camp in Chełmno (Kulmhof) during the deportation in 1942 and to Chełmno and Auschwitz in 1944. (Justiz und NS-Verbrechen. Sammlung Deutscher Strafurteile wegen Nationalsozialistischer Tötungsverbrechen 1945–1956, X.)

the rest home per se, but he did criticize the fact that a number of high-ranking individuals in the ghetto have two residences. This comment was prompted by his visit to the apartment of Director Józef Rumkowski, whose wife is at present suffering from severe jaundice. Undoubtedly, one result of Biebow's visit to Marysin will be that he will take a hand in internal matters that have until now been the personal province of the Chairman.

TUESDAY, AUGUST 10, 1943

A SUICIDE

Today at 9 A.M., Aleksander Gitla, 24 years old, residing at 20 Dworska Street, committed suicide by jumping from the fifth floor of the building at 6 Jerozolimska Street. The physician who was summoned ascertained that death had occurred instantly.

NEWS OF THE DAY

The ghetto is very depressed. It is unclear whether this is attributable to the state of nutrition or to something else, undefinable, in the air. The Chairman has been more nervous recently. This may chiefly be due to the fact that his sister-in-law, Helena Rumkowska, the wife of Director Józef Rumkowski, is critically ill. After the awkward episode in Marysin, which we reported, Józef Rumkowski decided to give up his summer apartment. He brought his ill wife back to the [ghetto] city in a droshky.

The so-called double apartments are being registered. No order has been issued to vacate these summer homes; nevertheless, the "summer resort vacationers" are understandably nervous.

THURSDAY, AUGUST 12, 1943

NEWS OF THE DAY

The mood in the ghetto is extremely depressed. Now, as before, no one quite knows the cause of this deep depression; various alarming rumors are circulating. The mood is no better in the Chairman's office. Furthermore, there is the hunger situation, which is hardly going to raise anyone's spirits.

COMMISSION AT THE CEMETERY

A [German] commission visited the cemetery along with [Leon] Rozenblat, chief of the Order Service, and [Ignacy] Gutman, director of the Construction Department. Air-raid trenches are supposedly to be dug in the cemetery. It should not be assumed, however, that this project can be carried out; for, on the one hand, such a plan would have no practical value; and on the other, the ghetto does not command sufficient manpower at present.

NO DEMOLITION OF THE MARIAVITE CHURCH

We have learned that, for the time being, the Mariavite[33] Church, at 27 Franciszkańska Street, will not be torn down, since no manpower is available for this work at the moment.

FRIDAY, AUGUST 13, 1943

THE FEATHER AND DOWN WORKSHOP HAS RETURNED

As is well known, the Down Quilt Department was transferred to Dąmbrówka [Dąbrowa] a few months ago. This department was returned yesterday and is being set up in the House of Culture. Machines, material, and personnel have already arrived in the ghetto. By order of Amtsleiter Biebow, Dr. Glaser, the physician (from the Special Department), took charge of this plant. The residential properties adjacent to the House of Culture will be taken over as well. The tenants of these buildings must vacate their apartments within a few hours. Given the desperate housing shortage, this is a severe blow to those affected.

SATURDAY, AUGUST 14, 1943

NEWS OF THE DAY

No change in the situation.

Yesterday around noon, the Order Service cleared the cemetery of visitors because an official commission was announced. People returning from funerals were told to leave the cemetery as quickly as possible. During the afternoon the mood was somewhat better, and it was said that there were no grounds for fear. On the other hand, the rumors of a partial resettlement grew increasingly persistent.

Since the Special Department was on alert, the rumor found appropriate fuel. Apparently, a few persons, supposedly with police records, have indeed been sent to perform manual labor outside the ghetto.

SUNDAY, AUGUST 15, 1943

RESETTLEMENT

On Saturday night, the people designated for manual labor outside the ghetto were called up. Some 250 men in the various precincts were conscripted. The exact number of those resettled is still undetermined. They are to supply the manpower demanded by the authorities for a project not far from Litzmannstadt.

For the most part, the men conscripted have already worked in labor camps

33. See above, p. 146, n. 36.

outside the ghetto and have returned to the ghetto in various groups. The candidates for leaving the ghetto can now expect another screening by a commission. Further conscriptions are in progress because adequate reserves must be created, as is necessary in such cases. The day of departure has not yet been set.

TUESDAY, AUGUST 17, 1943

FROM THE SPECIAL DEPARTMENT

Report on arrests in the month of July and subsequent disposition of cases:

July 1943	Persons	Charge	Decision
2	4 men	theft of cabbage	1 man, 10-mark fine
5	1 man	theft of potatoes	remanded to the court
5	5 men	multiple theft of flour waste	remanded to the court
7	2 men	multiple theft of leather	remanded to the court
7	3 men	multiple theft in [soup] kitchen	remanded to the court
7	1 woman 2 men	illicit commerce in vegetables	100-mark fine each
8	2 men	theft of potatoes	remanded to the court
13	1 man	theft in [soup] kitchen	suspension of proceedings
15	7 men	theft of flour	remanded to the court
17	3 men	irregularities in [soup] kitchen	2 men dismissed and assigned to other occupations
18	2 men	theft of packaging	severe reprimand
19	1 man	theft of potatoes	remanded to the court
21	3 men	irregularities in [soup] kitchen	2 men dismissed and assigned to Carpentry Department, Pucka Street
23	1 man	irregularities in distribution of canned meat	dismissal
26	3 men	irregularities in distribution of potatoes	dismissal
27	2 men	theft of carrots	2 weeks excrement removal duty
29	3 men	theft of cabbage	2 men, 14 days excrement removal duty; all 3 dismissed
30	2 men	theft of potatoes	remanded to the court
30	1 man	theft of flour	five days excrement removal duty

| 31 | 1 man | illicit distribution of soup | dismissal |
| 31 | 1 man | theft of potatoes | 7 days excrement removal duty |

SKETCHES OF GHETTO LIFE: A GHETTO FATE

We reported that last Sunday a man named Szymon Kuper was married, and that the Chairman exempted him from resettlement. Kuper came to the ghetto with his parents and seven brothers and sisters. He himself was sent out to perform manual labor in the camp at Poznań (Stadion) in 1941, and did not return to the ghetto until March, 1943. Meanwhile, his parents and all his brothers and sisters had been removed from the ghetto in the course of various resettlements, so that, upon returning, he found not a single member of his large family. Now that he was about to be married, he was once again threatened with being sent to perform manual labor outside the ghetto. He cited the fact that he was about to get married on Sunday, and he managed to interest the Chairman in his case. Thus, he received a letter of exemption from the Chairman—at the altar, so to speak.

This is only one case among countless unknown similar tragedies.

THURSDAY, AUGUST 19, 1943

AN ACCIDENT AT THE RYBNA STREET GATE

Yesterday, a serious accident took place at the Rybna Street crossing. The policeman on duty allowed an old, feeble Jew through the gate in order to spare him the difficult walk over the bridge. A car driving from the direction of Bałut Market at high speed ran the old man down and injured him severely. He was immediately taken to the hospital.

WORKSHOP NEWS

A Visit to the Tailors' Workshop
Yesterday functionaries from the Ghetto Administration accompanied by two officers visited the tailors' workshop at 36 Łagiewnicka Street.

SKETCHES OF GHETTO LIFE: DAYS OF HUNGER

On Sunday, August 14, the general two-week ration was announced; it included three kilograms of potatoes. Since no potatoes were available in the ghetto, every eligible recipient received a coupon for this quantity. Several days went by. No potatoes; and no vegetables either. Hunger set in. It was impossible to get hold of anything to eat. To be sure, there were all sorts of vegetables in the działkas [parcels], such as botwinki [beet leaves], cabbage, carrots, and other midsummer produce; but the działka owners could not bring themselves to part with anything. The slightest willingness to oblige on their part would have resulted in the total depletion of their gardens. And money, money for food, was no inducement.

Workshop soup became a coveted item. Its price rose from 6.50 to 10 marks, even though this soup, which until August 14 had been rich in nutritional ingredients, recently contained only 130 grams of potatoes, 35 grams of starch, and 200 grams of cabbage.

The special-nutrition meals on Młynarska and Ceglana streets contained babka [cake] on a number of occasions. Even the shops engaged in illicit traffic in food could not find anything to sell. The price of bread rose—as in previous periods of hunger—to 260 marks a loaf. Sugar, flour, and [oat] flakes had become rarities even here. The Meat Clearinghouse was unable to deliver a few grams of meat even to the privileged.

People stood in the streets, on the lookout for wagons carrying the potatoes they longed for. All markets were empty! An occasional handcart with a few hundred kilograms of potatoes or cabbage for the soup kitchens was to be seen. A bleak sight! Anyone carrying a bundle of botwinki leaves under his arm was accosted by dozens of would-be buyers and inundated with offers of extremely high sums of money. To no avail! The traffic in food had dropped to a minimum. There was only demand, no supply. Meanwhile, of course, catastrophe had overtaken those who had already fallen ill as a result of undernourishment. Until now, decalcification of the bones had been treated by a few fortunate persons with Vigantol. But no more Vigantol was to be found, nor any similar remedy. Pure fat or oil, such as physicians prescribe in normal times and normal places, was not coming into the ghetto. Fish oil could be purchased on the black market for 20 marks per 10 grams. Thus, a worker would have to spend two months' salary for 50 grams of oil.

Hunger inflamed all passions. Fruit trees at the edges of fenced-in gardens suffered greatly at the hands of thieves. Vegetable beds had to be guarded day and night. Hunger drove people outdoors like hyenas, into the open, where something to eat might be found.

At the same time, the sun blazed from morning until evening. Brief gusts of wind brought dust instead of cool relief. People asked each other: "Have any potatoes come in?" Potatoes, three kilograms of potatoes, meant salvation to a person, redemption from the torment of hunger.

At last, at last! On the afternoon of August 19, after large potato shipments had been rolling in for twenty-four hours, ration cards were honored. People accepted their rations like gifts from heaven—silently, wordlessly, neither grateful nor grumbling. Hunger had left them incapable of any powerful emotion.

With three kilograms of potatoes at home, a person can live. It is said that many a starving person attacked his ration, which was supposed to last two weeks, and devoured it on the spot, oblivious to any "afterwards" or "later on."

Stave off hunger, fill your stomach, let God take care of the morrow! That was the motto, the unspoken motto of August 19 of the year 1943.

O[skar] R[osenfeld]

SUICIDE OR ACCIDENT

On the 19th of this month, at 12:45 A.M., Icek Raschelbach, 37 years old, born in Łódź and residing at 32 Drewnowska Street, fell from the window of his fourth-floor apartment. Raschelbach was taken to the hospital by the Emergency Service. It could not yet be determined whether this was a suicide attempt or an accident.

SATURDAY, AUGUST 21, 1943

WORKERS FROM KOLUMNA IN GHETTO

On the 19th of this month, sixteen men arrived in the ghetto from the labor camp of Kolumna, near Łask, where they had been working since last year. They are in relatively good condition. As always, the group was lodged in Central Prison; and from there, in all likelihood, it will again be placed at the disposal of the German authorities for labor outside the ghetto. The men themselves were told, when leaving their former work site, that they would be used on construction jobs in western Germany.

SKETCHES OF GHETTO LIFE: A MAN WITH AN ONION

In every street of the ghetto the same scene is played: a visibly ill old man or a frail boy crouches in a doorway holding two or three onion plants in his hand. The young plants, as consumptive as their vendors, have had to give their lives prematurely. A tiny onion, a tender little plant with a narrow root—one cannot really call it an onion; a narrow stalk, wilting in the hand of its hawker, 1.50 for a tiny onion. It could have lived, that tiny onion! But even money has become scarce in the ghetto, and onions are a rare item. The short, emaciated man, the delicate boy in the doorway will not have brilliant careers like the little newsboy in New York, who, perhaps, started with one copy of the newspaper and ended up owning a publishing concern.

MONDAY, AUGUST 23, 1943

SKETCHES OF GHETTO LIFE: SLEEPING IN COURTYARDS

The current unbearable heat wave has placed tenants of the ghetto's cramped apartments in an utterly desperate situation. The struggle against vermin, and particularly bedbugs, is hopeless, given the close quarters and the primitive methods being employed. The vermin multiply in the heat and drive people out of their apartments at night—people already exhausted from a hard day's work. Toward eleven at night, one can observe them fleeing from their apartments with their bedding to set up places to sleep in the courtyards. Around the carpentry workshops, hundreds of persons are bedding down on stacks of boards. Here, under the open sky they can breathe more freely and catch a few hours of undisturbed sleep. However, this is dangerous for many persons who are particularly susceptible to colds because of their undernourishment. Anyone who has iron furniture is to some extent able to control this pest, but those who sleep on wooden beds or plank beds live in hell.

WEDNESDAY, AUGUST 25, 1943

SKETCHES OF GHETTO LIFE: A TOY FOR CHILDREN

For several days now the streets and courtyards of the ghetto have been filled with a noise like the clatter of wooden shoes. The noise is disturbing at first, but one gradually gets used to it and says to oneself: this is as much a part of the ghetto as are cesspools. The observer soon discovers that this "clattering" is produced by boys who have invented a pastime, an entertainment. More precisely, the children of the ghetto have invented a new toy.

All the various amusing toys and noisemakers—harmonicas, hobby horses, rattles, building blocks, decals, etc.—are things our youngsters must, of course, do without. In other ways as well, as ghetto dwellers, they are excluded from all the enchantments of the child's world. And so, on their own, they invent toys to replace all the things that delight children everywhere and are unavailable here.

The ghetto toy in the summer of 1943: Two small slabs of wood—hardwood if possible! One slab is held between the forefinger and the middle finger, the other between the middle finger and the ring finger. The little finger presses against the other fingers, squeezing them so hard that the slabs are rigidly fixed in position and can thus be struck against one another by means of a skillful motion. The resulting noise resembles the clattering of storks or, to use musical terms, the clicking of castanets. The harder the wood, the more piercing and precise the clicking, the more successful the toy, and the greater the enjoyment. Naturally, the artistic talents of the toy carver and performer can be refined to a very high level.

The instrument imposes no limit on the individual's musical ability. There are children who are content to use the primitive clicking of the slabs to produce something like the sounds of a Morse code transmitter. Other children imitate the beating of a drum, improvising marches out of banging sounds as they parade with their playmates like soldiers.

The streets of the Litzmannstadt ghetto are filled with clicking, drumming, banging. . . . Barefoot boys scurry past you, performing their music right under your nose, with great earnestness, as though their lives depended on it. Here the musical instinct of Eastern European Jews is cultivated to the full. An area that has given the world so many musicians, chiefly violinists—just think of Hubermann, Heifetz, Elman, Milstein, Menuhin—now presents a new line of artists.

A conversation with a virtuoso: "We get the wood from the Wood Works Department, but only the hardest wood is good enough."—"What is the toy called?"—"It's called a castanet . . . I don't know why. Never heard the name before. We paint the toy to make it look nicer. That guy over there," he pointed to a barefoot boy who was sitting in the street dust, ragged and dirty, "doesn't know how to do it. You have to swing your whole hand if you want to get a good tune out. Hard wood and a hefty swing—those are the main things." A few boys gathered, clicked their castanets, and all hell let loose. It was the first castanet concert I had ever attended.

The chronicler assumes that the clicker music will vanish "after it's run its course" and be replaced by some other sort of music. But he may be wrong.

O[skar] R[osenfeld]

SATURDAY, AUGUST 28, 1943

FOOD SUPPLY: MORE POTATOES

The event of the day is the increase in the potato ration from three to six kilograms—with the understanding, of course, that this ration is meant to last for two weeks. The

painful shortage of vegetables, however, will hardly encourage the populace to ad-
here to this schedule; many will consume their portions more quickly, hoping that
additional potatoes will be allotted before two weeks are up.

The arrival of provisions encourages people to take this risk. After all, one can see
that large quantities of potatoes are arriving again.

PEOPLE ARE SAYING . . .

It is characteristic of the pace of life in the ghetto that people are no longer talking
about [Dawid] Gertler. He is now a topic of conversation only in the Special Department and among those who are close to him personally. On the whole, the ghetto has
made its peace with the facts of the situation and has gone about its daily business.
Only during the critical hunger of the last two weeks did someone occasionally claim
that the food shortage was attributable to Gertler's no longer influencing this sector.
But this is probably a reflection of the general mood, without any basis in fact.

MONDAY, AUGUST 30, 1943

NEWS OF THE DAY

The day passed in calm. Although there is no special cause for alarm, a certain
restlessness can be felt below the surface of the ghetto. The first of September is
approaching. The memory of what occurred on this day last year—the liquidation of
the hospitals—reopens an old wound. Nothing is happening, and yet people feel that
something is imminent. The ghetto is so high-strung that a mere date can create
anxiety. The first of September, the first day of the war and the beginning of the most
horrible agitation that the ghetto has ever experienced; let us hope that it will be a
date without significance.

NO MORE ALLOCATION OF BONES AND VEINS

Over the course of time the Chairman has continually granted an allocation of bones
and veins to various people—usually one kilogram of bones and one kilogram of veins
per week. The number of those thus privileged was not inconsiderable. But as of
today these allocations have been terminated. This measure can be attributed to the
sharply reduced influx of meat. Reports on the receipt of commodities indicate that
the quantities are not very encouraging.

TUESDAY, AUGUST 31, 1943

BROUGHT TO THE GHETTO

14 July 1943	40 men from Andreshoff [Jędrzejów]
22 July 1943	5 men from Friedrichshagen [Chojny]
28 July 1943	1 man from Andreshoff
1 August 1943	4 men from Litzmannstadt
7 August 1943	39 men from Andreshoff
	6 men from Friedrichshagen

16 August 1943	1 man, at the disposition of the Gestapo
19 August 1943	16 men from Waldhorst [Kolumna][34]
31 August 1943	11 men from Waldhorst
Total:	123 men

TOTAL POPULATION

84,140.

NEWS OF THE DAY

Although the morning was perfectly quiet, by noontime there was good reason to be apprehensive. At first, toward noon, a number of unattached men, as well as those who had recently been resettled into the ghetto from various labor camps, were taken into custody by the Order Service. Immediately, a rumor spread that a large number of men had been ordered for labor outside the ghetto. All persons eligible for such a transport were delivered to Central Prison; on the other hand, the returnees from labor camps were subsequently released. In the evening the agitation in the ghetto increased rapidly. Rumor had it that not only people from Central Prison were to be resettled but also patients from the hospitals on Dworska and Mickiewicz [streets]. Supposedly, the incurably ill were to be removed from the Dworska Street hospital. The ghetto's sensitivity is clearly infallible. It can catch the scent of disaster in the air.

WEDNESDAY, SEPTEMBER 1, 1943

NEWS OF THE DAY

A resettlement action was carried out on the night of August 31. First, Order Service men closed off the two hospitals at 74 Dworska Street and 7a Mickiewicz Street. A medical commission examined the inmates. The result of this examination was that 39 patients were declared fit to be sent to perform manual labor outside the ghetto.

Some of the people selected had clear-cut cases of tuberculosis. A total of 225 people were turned over to the German authorities for transport. They were immediately conveyed in two groups to the Radogoszcz train station. Persons who had come to the ghetto from labor camps and who, because they had gone into hiding, could not be found during this nighttime operation, would be forced to turn themselves in because members of their families had been taken hostage. A few of these hostages actually had to leave with the transport. In the course of the night all 225 persons left the ghetto from Radogoszcz Station. Central Prison still holds some 200 additional persons who are to stand by for a subsequent transport.

One can see what a keen instinct the ghetto has. There can hardly be any other part of the world where people anticipate imminent disaster so vividly.

Naturally, although they occurred at night, these events have disturbed the entire ghetto. Once again, it is the first of September. No wonder that the whole populace

---

34. Jędrzejów, Chojny, and Kolumna are located close to Łódź.

fears the coming days in its very bones. The mood at Bałut Market is one of extreme depression, and even the Chairman is in very low spirits because of these events.

BROUGHT TO THE GHETTO

Today a young Jew from Bełchatów was delivered to the ghetto. For about three years the man had been passing as a Pole, in a village in the Warthegau, and he had even possessed the appropriate documents. He was discovered a few days ago and subsequently committed to Central Prison, where he is a prisoner of the Gestapo.

SKETCHES OF GHETTO LIFE: A RECORD-LOW MORTALITY RATE

On August 31, for the first time since the establishment of the ghetto, a day went by with only one death registered. This is not symptomatic of any essential improvement in the general state of health, since it is to be feared that the present period of hunger will eventually take its toll. At any rate, this day was remarkable.

RESETTLED JEWS

A count of the Jews resettled to this ghetto from Prague in October, 1941, and still here on September 1, 1943, yielded a total of 1,625. If we subtract two deaths on September 1 and the four people resettled the night before last, six people all told, then there are 1,619 Prague Jews in the ghetto. Their original number was 4,999.

THURSDAY, SEPTEMBER 2, 1943

NEWS OF THE DAY: THE RESETTLEMENT ACTION

The resettlement action for labor outside the ghetto continued on the night of September 1. We point out the fact that, contrary to the rumors, no patients in Hospital [No.] 1 (Mickiewicz Street)[35] were summoned for resettlement. Since the operations were carried out without any warning and in the middle of the night, no one commanding a view of the whole episode, a rumor spread through the ghetto that many patients were being enlisted both from the hospital for contagious diseases and from the hospital on Mickiewicz Street. This rumor quickly mobilized the families of patients to attempt to rescue their ailing relatives from the hospital while there was still time. A considerable number of such patients actually succeeded in leaving the hospital on Mickiewicz Street. The situation was similar to that on the same date last year. The patients fled from the hospital without attending to the usual formalities and, when the hospital staff came on duty early in the morning, things at the hospital were in complete confusion. The staff members supplied faulty information to any inquiry since they themselves did not know what had taken place—whether the patients had been picked up or had fled on their own. In point of fact, only one group of patients, consisting of terminal tuberculosis cases and a few mentally ill persons, had been removed, from the hospital for contagious diseases on Dworska Street.

---

35. After the elimination of the hospital at 34/36 Łagiewnicka St., the hospital at 7a Mickiewicz St. was called Hospital No. 1.

And so, after a total of 225 people were resettled by way of Radogoszcz on the night of August 31, a transport of a further 100 persons left Central Prison during the night of September 1.[36]

FRIDAY, SEPTEMBER 3, 1943

NEWS OF THE DAY

The ghetto has returned to complete calm. The aftereffects of the past two nights of agitation can still be felt, but a few levelheaded individuals are successfully combatting the whispered rumors of further resettlements. One detail has been learned in the meantime. The physicians in the hospital on Dworska Street were assigned to register all patients not expected to recover in the foreseeable future, but capable nonetheless of being cared for privately, and prepare them for transfer to home care. A hospital vehicle picked up these patients, but did not bring them to their apartments; instead, it brought them to a gathering point at Central Prison, and from there the entire group was driven to Radogoszcz. It is not known from whom the director of the Department of Health, Czarnabroda, received this order.

WORKSHOP NEWS: LEATHER SOLES FOR WORKERS

It was recently determined that the sewing machines in the tailors' and shoemakers' workshops do not operate with enough precision, that is, do not produce straight seams. Experts in the trade have pinpointed the reason: workers at the pedal-driven sewing machines cannot tell how much pressure they are applying to the pedal because they are wearing wooden clogs. Amtsleiter Biebow has therefore ordered that the shoemakers' workshops are not to do any individual work (private jobs for privileged individuals) until the workers in question have suitable footwear.

WORKSHOP NEWS: OLD SHOES COMING IN

The shoe warehouse is constantly receiving large quantities of old shoes from outside the ghetto. It will take months to sort this material.

SKETCHES OF GHETTO LIFE: DEATH FROM THE STREET

A small, wretched, one-story wooden house on Flisacka [Street]. The door to a small shop stands ajar. No business is being done here now. A bed and the usual pitiful household odds and ends are visible from the street. In front of the doorway stand some twenty people, perhaps more, saying nothing, making no sound. We ask a woman: "What's going on here?" "Our neighbor is dying." They are careful not to block access to the door. In the bed lies an emaciated man in his death throes. Death can enter freely from the street. The neighbors form a guard of honor, as though in awe of death's majesty.

---

36. In the original *Chronicle*, the entire last paragraph was crossed out in ink.

MONDAY, SEPTEMBER 6, 1943

WORKSHOP NEWS

Distribution of Apples
Today the Central Workshop Bureau on Bałut Market distributed one-half kilogram each of apples from the bureau's own gardens to a large number of ailing workers.

Old Shoes
More old shoes have come into the ghetto. Twelve freight cars had been unloaded as of September 5. The old-shoe warehouse will be busy for many months just sorting out this vast quantity. Think for a moment of the various categories that need to be dealt with: (1) leather and other shoes; (2) men's, women's, and children's shoes; (3) right shoes and left shoes; (4) whole shoes and half shoes; (5) black shoes and brown shoes. Finally—and this is the hardest job of all—the matching pairs have to be ferreted out. Considering the mountains of second-hand shoes, one can hardly believe that such a job is possible.[37]

TUESDAY, SEPTEMBER 7, 1943

NEWS OF THE DAY: SOUP STRIKE

Last Saturday there was a minor strike at the shoemakers' plant in Marysin (managers: [Bernard] Iźbicki and Gutreiman). During the distribution of the soup, one worker, in the presence of commissioner Iźbicki, complained about its conspicuously poor quality. Iźbicki responded to this protest with a slap in the face. The shoemakers then decided not to accept soup at all. Iźbicki went to a factory section and asked a shoemaker whether he had accepted the soup. When the worker responded in the negative, the director slapped him as well. But this time he had picked the wrong man, for the worker struck back. Deeply offended by this lèse majesté, Iźbicki rang up Bałut Market and informed them of the strike. The Special Unit was notified and detailed a platoon to Marysin, where five shoemakers in the factory were arrested. The Chairman stepped in immediately and settled the matter peacefully.

One cannot record this episode without taking a stand on the evil ghetto practice of physical abuse. One need not approve the fact that the Chairman frequently strikes people in order to vent his anger or to discipline the unruly; nevertheless, those are disciplinary measures meted out by the head of the ghetto. Within the framework of a patriarchal structure this makes a certain sense. But one cannot censure emphatically enough the fact that every kierownik [manager] or Order Service man, from the commander down to the officers and every last militiaman, has gotten into the habit of administering blows. *Quod licet Jovi, non licet bovi* [What is proper for Jupiter is not proper for the ox]. This method of getting one's way does little honor to the ghetto and proves how poorly these uninhibited imitators understand the situation. Perhaps a blow with a club is indeed a milder punishment than the withholding of soup (for this

37. See p. 272, n. 96.

method of punishment too is not infrequent in the ghetto); nevertheless, it must be said that both forms of punishment are indecent. The former offends the last vestiges of human dignity; the latter endangers life itself. If—like Iźbicki in this case—the one who strikes out is himself given a sound beating, then perhaps this evil practice will stop of its own accord. For the sake of our dignity, this is most desirable.

FRIDAY, SEPTEMBER 10, 1943

NEWS OF THE DAY

Today, the Chairman visited the Carpentry Department at 12 Drukarska Street. He arrived around noon, had the entire staff summoned, and delivered his first public speech in a long time. He appealed to the workers to remain calm at all costs and not let themselves be provoked, whether at work or outside the workshop. He emphasized that working calmly is the most important goal of the day. In regard to food, he said he was very hopeful that the situation would greatly improve. He was always trying, he said, to make the rations as good as possible and was always glad to provide whatever he could. When voicing complaints about the quality of the workshop soup, people should understand that this was not the responsibility of the workshop manager. The possibility existed that irregularities were in fact occurring in the kitchens. To prevent the kitchen staff from acting to the detriment of the hungry workers, he recommended that an inspection commission be elected for the workshop kitchens. In response to an objection that this was the responsibility of the Special Department, the Chairman said that this was true only to the extent that the Special Department was supposed to prevent irregularities in the distribution of soup. The commission to be formed would supervise the soup's quality. (He was referring to the friction between manager Iźbicki and the shoemakers.) The Chairman also promised the workers that they would have sufficient footwear for the winter, namely, both leather and wooden shoes. The Chairman was in very good form, and his speech raised the spirits of the workers, who applauded vigorously.

SATURDAY, SEPTEMBER 11, 1943

FOOD SUPPLY

No change. Ongoing deliveries of potatoes and vegetables, but not enough for an uninterrupted distribution of the potato ration. At the moment, the distribution has been stopped, as was, unfortunately, to be expected.

EXTRA RATIONS

The ghetto was surprised today by the announcement of extra rations; as of Sunday, September 12, the populace is to receive 300 grams of flour and 70 grams of marmalade at the price of 50 pfennigs, and half a can of meat at the price of 1 mark, 50. There will also be a ration of 100 grams of curds per person for Coupon No. 58 of the ration card plus the sum of 40 pfennigs.

The Chairman himself intervened to arrange these rations because, as mentioned above, the potato distribution cannot be accomplished quickly enough, but sufficient flour, at any rate, has been delivered. The Chairman is clearly flexible in matters concerning food.

MONDAY, SEPTEMBER 13, 1943

NEWS OF THE DAY: THE BEKERMAN CASE

Today at 6 P.M., Icek Bekerman, 34 years old, was executed. Bekerman was a worker in the Leather and Saddlery Department, where he had misappropriated some scrap leather in order to make shoe laces. The material was found in his apartment during a search by the Kripo [German criminal police]. According to one version of the story, it was a matter of a few decagrams of this material, which he must have known to be Wehrmacht property; according to another version, it was a few kilograms of leather scraps, including a certain amount of Wehrmacht property. Since, in wartime, the German authorities regard such thefts as sabotage, according to military law, and punish offenders very severely, Bekerman was denied mercy. The execution took place on the field at the corner of Próżna and Przelotna streets, opposite the straw-shoe workshop. The ghetto carpentry shop was required to supply the gallows; and the entire personnel of the leather and saddlery workshop and the shoe workshop was commanded to be present, along with delegations from all other workshops, so that the execution would serve as a deterrent. The offender's wife and two children were also driven to the place of execution to witness the death sentence carried out. The offender was brought to the place of execution in a car. The area itself was encircled by a detachment of German Schutzpolizei and militiamen from Central Prison. A clerk from Central Prison read a statement explaining the execution; and the sentence was then carried out by the hangman of Central Prison, who has already been called upon for previous cases of this kind.

WEDNESDAY, SEPTEMBER 15, 1943

FINANCES: FROM THE LOAN OFFICE [CREDIT BANK]

This institution is now working smoothly, without financial difficulties. It was capitalized as follows:

Endowment by the Chairman	250,000 marks
From liquidated loan offices	83,000
From the Chairman's special fund	25,000
From salary contributions	417,000
Total	775,000 marks

This capital is now available, having been gathered mainly through contributions from the populace; the loan office can thus forego any further collection of these contributions. As of September 1, no more deductions were made from the salaries of clerks, while deductions from the salaries of workers continued only until September 4. In August the loan office processed 3,181 applications and paid out a total of 191,030 marks in loans. The files already contain the names of 20,000 loan recipients. The office has grown considerably and now has a staff of 43 employees.

THURSDAY, [SEPTEMBER] 16, 1943

BREAD

Today the Department of Food Supply issued an announcement concerning distribution which makes it clear that the bread allotment remains unchanged: as before, bread is to be distributed every eight days, not every seven. Nevertheless, a rumor still persists to the effect that, as of next week, bread is to be distributed every seven days. Even the head of the Bread Department, [Mordecai] Lajzerowicz, has confirmed that this new regulation is pending for the near future. On the other hand, the head of the Department of Food Supply, commander [Zygmunt] Reingold, claims that he has not received any such notification. It is interesting that, when the rumor first arose, the price of bread sank from the range of 220–240 marks to 200–220. After announcement of the above-mentioned plan for bread distribution, the price immediately rose to 250–260 marks.

COAL SUPPLIES

The ghetto is alarmed about the fact that, with the cold season approaching, no fuel has been stockpiled or even announced. Since the last allocation, on July 20 for the month of August—8 kilograms of briquettes—no new ration has been made. Because only minimal shipments have arrived, the situation threatens to become very critical, especially since the distribution of sawdust has been halted for the present. Daily prices of firewood have risen from 1 mark to 1 mark, 50 in the center of the ghetto and near the wood workshops. In more remote parts of the ghetto, wood already costs as much as 2 marks per kilogram. Briquettes have risen from 3 marks, 50 per kilogram to 4 marks. The rise in wood prices is particularly attributable to Commissioner [Szoel] Terkeltaub's warning speech, which we have reported.[38]

SUNDAY, SEPTEMBER 19, 1943

FOOD SUPPLY

The situation is rapidly developing into a catastrophe. The meager reserves are even forcing the soup kitchens to lower the amount of potato in soups to 150 grams. People

---

38. The commissioners, Order Service officers, were assigned to individual workshops and departments of the Jewish administration to maintain order and safety and also to supervise the blue- and white-collar workers in the units subordinate to them. In time they formed an entirely separate unit known as the economic police (*Wirtschaftspolizei*). Along with its managers, they were responsible for a given workshop, which frequently caused confusion as to who was actually in charge. This is probably the reason that the *Chronicle* sometimes refers to managers as commissioners and to commissioners as managers. Thus, for example, in the two weeks between the 14th and the 29th of September, 1943, S. Terkeltaub was twice referred to as manager (*Leiter*) and once as commissioner (*Kommissar*). The note about Terkeltaub's cautionary speech mentioned above is found in the *Chronicle* bulletin of Wednesday, September 14. In that speech he said anyone removing wood from a carpentry shop for use as fuel would be very severely punished, something that he repeated more than once.

wander in despair through the streets, trying to find something to eat. On September 17, 18, and 19, a total of only 238,340 kilograms of potatoes arrived here. The kitchens will naturally have first priority, leaving nothing for a potato ration. And when there are no potatoes on hand, naked hunger will reign. In these past three days, various vegetables did arrive (kohlrabi, carrots, radishes, white cabbage, parsley, as well as sauerkraut—the latter only for soup), a total amount of 127,800 kilograms. If the situation does not change very quickly, there is no telling what may happen.

MONDAY, SEPTEMBER 20, 1943

WELFARE: INJECTION DEPARTMENT

Immediately upon the establishment of the Injection Distribution Point, endless lines of people began to form there, lines such as could once be observed at the Special Department. People line up at the crack of dawn in order to receive the few available injections during the morning hours. It is certainly very difficult to administer the injections when the need is so great. But if one has a seriously ill person at home, then it is more than just an imposition on the relatives or, for lack of relatives, the friends or acquaintances to spend hours standing in line in the courtyard [of the distribution point]. This system, as it now stands, must therefore be described as highly unsatisfactory.

TUESDAY, SEPTEMBER 21, 1943

FOOD SUPPLY

The crisis has reached a climax. The populace has not been in so desperate a situation in a long time. There has always been scarcity before each ration, but the way things are now, one can only speak of utterly catastrophic starvation. Ridiculously insignificant shipments of potatoes do not permit even a faint hope of improvement. People were hoping that the ration would at least be issued somewhat in advance; but since no potatoes are available, there will hardly be an early distribution of the ration.

Naturally, the free-market prices are shooting up. Potatoes now cost in the range of 38–40 marks per kilogram, beets 20 marks, kohlrabi 7–8 marks.

In the cooperatives, ersatz coffee is being sold in free trade. People are buying it in order to soak it in water and eat it as mush.

THURSDAY, SEPTEMBER 23, 1943

FOOD SUPPLY: THE NEW RATION

Today, in the evening hours, some information was already available about the new ration. The ration will be issued at 9 A.M. on Friday, [and will contain] 400 grams of flour and 200 grams of rye flakes; everything else remains more or less unchanged. A ration without potatoes. The Department of Food Supply has hesitated to make an announcement until now in the hope that enough potatoes would arrive in the interim. But since this is still not the case, it has no choice but to publish the ration as is. When the announcement is made tomorrow, Friday, and the ration is then immediately distributed, the tiny bit of groceries will not, of course, last very long. The provisions, which normally would have been stretched to cover the whole ration period to some degree, will suffice this time for only a few meals in the first few days; and then hunger will resume.

FOOD SUPPLY: POTATO STORAGE

Despite the desperate situation described above, and although no potatoes are arriving in the ghetto, work on setting up potato stockpiles in Marysin is proceeding apace. The terrain for these mounds will be more extensive than last year. At the moment, the work on Marysińska Street and Jagiellónska Street is being extended as far as the ghetto border. In the next few days a branch track will be laid from the Radogoszcz station to the new potato bins. This will make it possible to route potatoes and vegetables directly to these locations.

HEALTH CARE: MEDICINES AND INJECTIONS

Our reports often include news about the establishment of injection distribution points. It is well known that after the liquidation of the special-service office in the Special Department the Chairman set up a new Injection Distribution Point at 1 Dworska Street. A large segment of the population has been steadily streaming in there, seeking all kinds of injections. Various, often difficult, Latin terms have become household words; every child knows names like calcium, betabion, redoxon, campolon, hepatrate, tonophosphane, transpulnine, strychnine, etc. At the moment, all these medications are arriving in relatively small amounts. The renowned Vigantol has become somewhat cheaper. Today, one pays 35 marks for 10 cubic centimeters. On the other hand, cod-liver oil has become extraordinarily expensive. The high price indicates the great demand for this remedy because of the increase in tuberculosis. Prices have changed as follows: October, 1941—60 marks per liter; July, 1942—120 marks; January, 1943—300 marks; and September, 1943—1,500 marks. Small amounts are available now and then in the few private stores.

FRIDAY, SEPTEMBER 24, 1943

JUDICIAL NEWS: THE CHAIRMAN'S WIFE AS DEFENSE ATTORNEY

It is well known that the Chairman's wife, Regina Rumkowska, was an attorney by profession. A few days ago the Chairman asked St[anisław] Jakobson, the presiding magistrate of the court, whether in principle there would be any objection to his wife's defending a client. Since Mrs. Rumkowska has long been duly registered on the list of defense attorneys at the court of the Eldest of the Jews, the presiding magistrate saw no objection. Mrs. Rumkowska thereupon became co-defender of a man named Ordinanz, who had been accused of rape and been convicted on trial; the Chairman's wife will thus make her debut as a defense attorney in the appeal proceedings. Before the war she was already active as a defense attorney and had been about to establish her own practice.

PEOPLE ARE SAYING

that the Chairman will issue a special ration for the high holidays. This rumor cannot be verified and is based purely on popular knowledge of the Chairman's feelings in this matter.

SATURDAY, SEPTEMBER 25, 1943

FOOD SUPPLY

The New Ration
As soon as the rations were announced, people stormed the distribution shops. The starving populace is pouncing on what little rye flour and rye flakes are available. Potatoes have also gradually begun to arrive, so there is hope of some distribution of potatoes on Monday.

The hunger in the ghetto is terrible.

Prices
Before the distribution of the ration, prices of various food items were very high. After the distribution there was a small drop in prices, on Friday and today; however, after the distribution of the last ration, prices remained much higher than two weeks ago. A survey of prices follows:

Item	Friday morning	Saturday evening
Bread	280–290 marks	240 marks
Flour	180 "	160 "
Rye flakes	240 "	200 "
Potatoes	45 "	40 "
Beets	27 "	22 "
Kohlrabi	12 "	10 "
Sugar	220 "	190 "
Oil per decagram	5.50 "	4.50 "
Workshop soup	12–13 "	11 "

PEOPLE ARE SAYING

that the Chairman plans to entrust direction of all special-nutrition kitchens to the experienced hands of Helena Rumkowska. After a long, serious illness, the latter has recovered sufficiently to assume her new duties. In this connection one hears that the outgoing director of all kitchens, Mrs. Gonik, has suffered a minor political indisposition.

SUNDAY, SEPTEMBER 26, 1943

A SUICIDE ATTEMPT

On September 9, Fajga Pelman, born in Łódź in 1907 and residing at 7 Podrzeczna Street, attempted suicide by ingesting methylated spirits. She was taken to the hospital by the Emergency Service.

NEWS OF THE DAY

On September 1, a man from Bełchatów named Lewi was brought to the ghetto by the Gestapo. He had been discovered in Bełchatów while attempting to retrieve money that he had buried in the cellar of his house. He had been spotted by a German and arrested. In the course of the arrest he was shot in the foot and, in the ghetto, was hospitalized on Mickiewicz Street, a prisoner of the Gestapo. He duly surrendered all his possessions and was therefore no longer in imminent jeopardy. The guard assigned to watch him was then removed.

MONDAY, SEPTEMBER 27, 1943

FOOD SUPPLY

Still no improvement in the general situation. The potato shipments remain catastrophically small. On the 22d, 15,000 kilograms arrived; on the 23d, 20,000 kilograms; and on the 24th, 15,000 kilograms. This trifling quantity does not permit a complete distribution of a three-kilogram ration. As we reported, the distribution began on Sunday instead of Monday; but it had to be discontinued today. After many hours in the pouring rain, the endless lines broke up and people went home with empty bags and knapsacks. It is still doubtful whether a distribution will take place tomorrow, Tuesday, since today's deliveries are also inadequate. Likewise, on the three days in question, only trifling quantities of vegetables came in—mainly parsley and celery, that is, vegetables that are nearly worthless. No meat came in at all on the 23d, while a total of 4,900 kilograms came in on the 22d and the 24th. All other deliveries are normal.

Yesterday, the Meat Clearinghouse received, among other things, so-called *ka-szanka*, a Polish country sausage made solely of liver and groats [actually, of blood and kasha]. The sausage arrived in barrels, together with salted meat.

NEWS OF THE DAY

Yesterday, for Rosh Hashanah, the Chairman dipped into the reserve supply at his disposal to distribute some vegetables to a few individuals and social organizations. It is said that he will also take this occasion to grant a special allotment to a few close members of his staff and to persons of particular merit.

WEDNESDAY, SEPTEMBER 29, 1943

FUEL ALLOTMENTS

Today the Coal Department announced its dismal ration, which can be picked up as of October 3. Three kilograms of wood and 1 kilogram of briquettes per person are being offered for 1 mark, upon presentation of Coupon No. 41 of the vegetable card. This distribution is scheduled to continue until October 22 at the various distribution points. It is clear that the Coal Department is making an effort to alleviate the catastrophic fuel shortage and to at least provide something. Unfortunately, this small allotment will not help very much; in fact, the meagerness of the ration merely intensifies people's fear of the coming winter months.

BIG STORY ABOUT A SMALL STRIKE

The previously noted conflict in the carpentry workshop at 12 Drukarska Street [see pp. 379–80] originated and was resolved in the following manner. After the execution of [Icek] Bekerman, who, as is common knowledge, had to pay with his life for a minor theft from the leather and saddlery workshop, the Chairman made a number of speeches warning workers against the theft of materials. He made one such speech in the carpentry workshop at 12 Drukarska Street. That day the head of the Carpentry Department, [Szoel] Terkeltaub, was absent on account of illness. When he returned to the factory, the new machine room was just beginning to produce munition crates—a Wehrmacht order of crucial importance to the ghetto, and one that had been placed directly by the OKH (Oberkommando des Heeres [High Command of the Army]). Terkeltaub took this opportunity to speak to his workers. He explained to them that discipline would have to be sharply intensified for this order: previously, it had not been a critical matter if a set of office desks was somewhat behind schedule, but the deadlines now for delivery of the munition crates would be observed very strictly. Six hundred crates would have to be produced every day. To meet this quota, it was not enough for the workers to exert themselves to the utmost; they would also have to be very strict in husbanding the raw material: that is, under no circumstances, legal or illegal, could the workers remove any material required, directly or indirectly, for production. The components manufactured for these precision-designed crates were so small that they could easily be carried out in pockets, underclothes, etc. Therefore, the legally distributed wood scraps must not include even a single piece that could be utilized as a component of such a crate.

After this speech to the entire staff of the main production line, Terkeltaub gathered his skilled workers, some one hundred carpenters, and urged them to set a good example for the rank and file. The carpenters, he said, received preferential treatment in every respect, and so he had the right to demand the proper attitude from them in particular. Then, manager [Izak] Gersztonowicz also spoke to the carpenters, explaining that he himself had emerged from their ranks and that he had always shown personal sympathy for his fellow workers and associates. Both men emphasized that they would have to hold the carpenters collectively responsible for any theft or infraction of the rules that affected the manufacture of the munition crates.

A few days later, on September 23, while walking home in the evening from the carpentry workshop, Terkeltaub noticed two of his workers trading in wood in the hallway of a building at Bałut Market, and realized that they were selling wood that came from the carpentry workshop. This wood consisted of regular scraps of the kind normally given out for coupons; however, there was also a small board that could still be used as production material. The infraction per se was not serious. But since Terkeltaub had threatened the carpenters with collective punishment, he felt he had to stick to his guns, and the next day he punished the carpenters by withholding their supplemental soup. The carpenters conferred on that same day and decided to refuse even the regular soup. Some eighty carpenters joined this hunger strike. Terkeltaub expected a delegation from the carpenters; none came. Since the soup was in danger of spoiling, he decided to distribute the eighty bowls of soup to those who performed heavy manual labor. The strikers did not approach him during the day on Saturday either. Finally, on Saturday evening, when the carpenters sent a three-man delegation to the manager, he stipulated that the soup would have to be accepted before any discussion could take place. The carpenters rejected this condition and continued their hunger strike. Since the next day was Sunday, a day off, the matter could not be taken up again until Monday. On Monday, a worker came into the office and Terkeltaub told him once again that he refused to negotiate as long as the hunger strike was on. Finally, the carpenters gave in and accepted the soup. Only then did the manager receive the delegation, which declared that the carpenters objected to being held collectively responsible and that the perpetrators alone ought to answer for any violations. Terkeltaub heard them out, but then explained that, originally, no one had protested collective responsibility; consequently, he had every right to assume that the carpenters were in agreement on this point. The workers demanded retroactively the soup they had missed, but Terkeltaub would not give in on this point. The result was an unofficial reconciliation.

The fact that the Chairman and [Aron] Jakubowicz appeared in the carpentry workshop that same day was pure coincidence. Neither man had been informed of the incident. In the end, since there are, in fact, tolerably good relations between management and workers in this particular factory, the entire matter was settled amicably.

THURSDAY, SEPTEMBER 30, 1943[39]

WEATHER

Daily range: 11–15 degrees; cloudy, occasional periods of rain.

DEATHS

Eight.

BIRTHS

None.

ARRESTS

Miscellaneous, one.

EXPULSIONS

Nine (September 27, out of the ghetto).

TOTAL POPULATION

83,694.

NEWS OF THE DAY

Today, the first day of the New Year holiday, the Chairman was off duty. He received only the closest members of his staff, who brought their best wishes for Rosh

---

39. The *Daily Chronicle Bulletin* for Thursday, September 30, 1943, is given in its entirety here.

Hashanah. It is reported that the Chairman distributed coupons to mark the occasion.

A CELEBRATION IN THE DEPARTMENT OF FOOD SUPPLY

This afternoon a small celebration took place in the Department of Food Supply. The management presented an album from the department to the Chairman and [Zygmunt] Reingold delivered a speech. In his reply, the Chairman revealed that he was expecting a general improvement of the food supply situation within the next few days.

The Chairman visited a few workshops and departments on foot and wished those present a happy New Year.

On *erev*, [the eve of] Rosh Hashanah, an accident took place in a wooden building at 18 Lutomierska Street. The second floor collapsed, and a few persons who happened to be present fell to the ground floor. Since the drop was short, there were no fatalities.

FOOD SUPPLY

Still no essential change in the situation. Potato shipments are improving gradually; there is some basis for hope of a new ration.

Cancellation of the B III and CP Coupons
Last night the Chairman informed the Coupon Department that he intends to suspend all current B III and CP coupons and replace them with special nutrition midday meals (14 per month). During the past ten days the carpentry workshops, metal factories, and straw-shoe factories have already been receiving the kolacje [supplemental evening meals] instead of the current coupons; in the next ten days all other factories are to follow suit. Thus all B III and CP coupons will be done away with by October 20.

Vegetables by Way of Radogoszcz
Today, five freight cars of vegetables, the first in quite a long time, arrived by way of Radogoszcz. The shipment was chiefly carrots, and so a carrot ration is to be expected.

Butter Ration
The event of the day is the distribution of 50 grams of butter per person for the sum of 50 pfennigs with Coupon No. 68 of the ration card. This is the first butter allotment for the populace in months.

WORKSHOP NEWS: MANAGER WINOGRAD ARRESTED

In the woodwork factory on Bazarna [Street] there has been an extremely awkward development. Plant manager [Leon] Winograd was summoned to Bałut Market, where Amtsleiter Biebow had him taken into custody by the Ghetto Administration for four weeks. Winograd was immediately transferred to Central Prison. The reason for this action was that the Ghetto Administration had received various complaints about defective deliveries (from customers as well as from [Nazi] party offices). For example, one office complained about the extremely poor quality of the cribs manufactured here. Furthermore, a German woman supposedly injured her hands on a washboard. It was because Winograd is accountable to Biebow for his plant that this draconian measure was taken. In the hearing at Bałut Market, Winograd accepted full responsibility. He is in Central Prison as Biebow's prisoner. It is hoped that this incident will not have any further serious consequences. Winograd is considered one of the ablest and most reliable workshop managers. Perhaps it was a mistake on his part to assume supervision of the plant's technical operations without being an expert.

SOCIAL AID: NEW REGULATION CONCERNING WORKERS

As we have already reported, the Trade Inspection Section has issued a new regulation on health care for workers. We quoted this announcement verbatim on September 13. Also, on September 21 we reported that the Trade Inspection Section was to meet with the physicians and give them precise instructions. This meeting took place on Friday, September 24. The physicians generally spoke against the new regulation because they too fear a demoralization of the workers. At the meeting, certain guidelines were issued: workshop personnel are to be given leave only in critical cases; in other words, an ailing worker will have a right to the benefits listed in the announcement only if he really is seriously ill and/or bedridden.

In response to our inquiry, a physician from one district informed us that he excuses about ten workers a day in serious cases. If the approximately 100 physicians average the same number of excuses, this comes to 300 per doctor every month or 30,000 excuses a month. Ultimately, this could cause all factories to shut down entirely.

SKETCHES OF GHETTO LIFE: ANIMALS IN THE GHETTO

The idyllic scene on the meadow along Marysińska and Sterling streets has lost its charm. Not only because autumn has extinguished the intense colors and prepared nature for the winter, but mainly because the goats and sheep have vanished. According to reliable sources, these animals were requisitioned by the [German] Ghetto Administration and taken into the city; they are to be slaughtered and the meat made available for consumption.

The fine-looking fat cows have likewise not been seen for several days. It is uncertain whether they have shared the fate of the goats and sheep. In any event, they have lost their right to free pasture.

O[skar] R[osenfeld]

FRIDAY, OCTOBER 1, 1943

POSTAL SERVICE

During the past three days the post office has been swamped with work, delivering some 5,000 New Year's greetings—postcards, letters, and telegrams [from within the ghetto]—1,500 or so for the Chairman alone.

WELFARE: SELF-HELP PROGRAMS

In the past few months a number of workshops have resorted to self-help by organizing their own committees for assisting the ill. The committees that have been operating most effectively are in the workshops of the Linen and Clothing Department (manager, Lejb Glazer), the Paper Department, and the carpentry workshop at 12 Drukarska Street. All of these factory committees have a more or less similar organization. First, the holders of Beirat and B I[40] coupons commit themselves to hand over a specific percentage of their allotments. In addition, the work force itself contributes modest amounts to the committee; for example, one potato from every ration, one spoonful of sugar, and so forth. Altogether this constitutes a standing fund. Through certain channels, other special donations also reach the committees. Moreover, nearly every workshop has its own vegetable gardens from which appropriate quantities are diverted to this purpose. Voluntary cash donations are also collected for the purchase of medicines, especially injections. (Care of the ailing by their own fellow workers has been arranged.) The management also makes available to the committees portions of their quotas of special-nutrition midday meals and supplemental soups. Finally, the committees can have a say in the delegating of workers to the bakeries.[41] These self-help programs have generally been doing such a fine job that practically all departments and workshops are now in the process of creating similar committees.

SUNDAY, OCTOBER 3, 1943

TOTAL POPULATION

83,672.

SUICIDE ATTEMPT

On October 2, Martha Schnuller, born June 18, 1905, in Wattenscheid, and residing at 57 Dworska Street, attempted suicide by ingesting a sleep-inducing drug. The victim was taken to the hospital by the Emergency Service.

NEWS OF THE DAY

No events of any importance in the ghetto.

Marriages
The Chairman married 15 couples today in Marysin, at the rest home on Karol Miarka Street.

Disciplinary Actions in the Order Service
The head of the Order Service has taken action against several men suspected of smuggling. Some were dismissed from the Order Service and will work at excrement removal by way of punishment, while others were disciplined internally and restricted from duty along the barbed-wire fence.

---

40. See above, p. 31, n. 44.

41. To be sent to work in a bakery, where one could consume almost as much bread as one wished, for a period of a week or two was a form of reward and aid for deserving or physically exhausted workers in the workshops or in departments of the Jewish administration. The *Chronicle* will provide further information on this subject later.

A few persons who were involved in the smuggling, mostly building superintendents on Zgierska Street, were brought to the city by the [German] police after the investigation was completed.

Since it was principally a matter of saccharine being smuggled from the city into the ghetto, an activity that must now be regarded as having more or less come to an end, the price of saccharine has risen. It now vacillates between two and three tablets to the mark.

FOOD WITHOUT RATION CARDS

All told, there are now only three families that obtain their food with the special coupons issued personally by the Chairman: the Chairman's own, the [Aron] Jakubowicz [his deputy and head of the Central Workshop Bureau] family, and Miss Dora Fuchs [chief secretary of the Chairman at Bałut Market].

WORK DURING THE NEW YEAR HOLIDAYS

The ghetto worked as usual during the Rosh Hashanah holidays. Nevertheless, in several plants, a number of workers, sometimes entire groups, did not work on these two days. Such persons have made up for the production delay by working today, Sunday, and therefore, overall output has not been affected.

WEDNESDAY, OCTOBER 6, 1943

SUICIDE

On October 5, Chaja Flamholz, born August 23, 1914, in Łódź, and residing at 36 Wolborska [Street], committed suicide by jumping from the fourth floor of her apartment house. The Emergency Service physician pronounced her dead.

NEWS OF THE DAY

The Chairman has announced that there will be no work in the factories, workshops, or departments on Saturday, October 9, which is Yom Kippur. For the first time in the history of the ghetto, Yom Kippur will really be a holiday. Today the Chairman issued a memorandum concerning the distribution of the midday meal on Saturday, October 9. It reads as follows:

Memorandum to all factories, workshops, and departments.
Re: Distribution of the Midday Meal on Saturday, October 9.
Since there will be no work in the factories, workshops, or departments on Saturday, October 9, I call upon the directors to issue midday meal cards to workers and employees one day earlier, that is, on Friday, October 8. The latter will then receive, on Saturday, October 9 only, a special-nutrition midday meal consisting solely of steamed potatoes [tsholnt].

I point out that workers and employees of factories and departments without soup kitchens will have to go to their assigned kitchens, since a midday meal will not be delivered to these factories and departments on this day.

YOM KIPPUR IN THE SPECIAL-NUTRITION KITCHENS

The Chairman has granted permission for recipients to take their meals home from the special-nutrition kitchens on Friday, October 8 (Kol Nidre) only. Juveniles are also being permitted to do so.

SKETCHES OF GHETTO LIFE: THE FIRST DAYS OF OCTOBER, 1943

This being a leap year [on the lunar calendar], the Jewish New Year came late this time. The second day of New Year was October 1, which by all rights ought to be overcast, rainy, even melancholy. But it was a pleasant day for the ghetto inhabitants. After an overcast morning the sun broke through, and an autumn day descended from a sky that was as bright and warm as one could possibly wish for in this part of Poland.

The sunny weather improved the general mood, which would otherwise have been quite bleak. For, once again, naked hunger was near at hand. People were on the lookout for something to eat. The yearning cry, "When will there be potatoes again?" died on the lips of the starving masses.

Finally, Sunday, October 3, came, and with it a seemingly endless procession of potato wagons, rolling one after another toward Bałut Market and from there to the vegetable storage lots. Furthermore, one can see handcarts loaded with potatoes, drawn by human beasts of burden, heading toward the kitchens. A two-fold joy!

Whenever a wagonload of potatoes approaches, it is greeted by eyes smiling in anticipation of the feast, as it were. Barefoot boys scurry behind the wagons to snatch any potatoes that might drop off. Special Department men sit on the wagons, Order Service men walk alongside the wagons, keeping watch, preventing any potato, even a fallen one, from being grabbed in the street. And so, things are—how does the ghetto put it?—"in the best of order." The three-kilogram ration is assured; the responsible parties have discharged their duty.

The tomatoes are ripening in the działkas [land parcels]. The ghetto's potato harvest has begun. Whole rows of leeks are waiting for the hand that will pick them. The fields are green, yellow, brown, even red. The autumn is gracious; it has blessed the ghetto too, especially the vegetable dealers, who will harvest thousands of ghetto marks this season. The shipments from outside [the ghetto] provide no competition. The two-kilogram ration of pumpkins—we haven't seen such huge, lovely specimens for a long time—does not make much of a difference. Potatoes still rank first among the various foods. Pumpkins are more a delicacy, like onions, garlic, leeks, tomatoes.

The fall is beautiful, warm, one of God's wonders. But it brings a presentiment of winter too—the mornings are chill and the nights frosty. Fuel is the great concern of every household. The latest allotment, one kilogram of briquettes and three kilograms of wood, only aggravates that concern. Cold is an even more dreaded fear than hunger. It is still easier to fill an empty stomach than an empty stove.

But let us forget this calamity for a moment. Friday evening, October 8, is the start of Yom Kippur this year. The Chairman has succeeded in having Yom Kippur declared a day off from work—in lieu of the following Sunday. Religious people will take satisfaction in this and have a chance to escape from the atmosphere of the ghetto for at least twenty-four hours of the year.

O[skar] R[osenfeld]

THURSDAY, OCTOBER 7, 1943

NEWS OF THE DAY: THE LARYNGOLOGIST, DR. MAZUR, OUTSIDE THE GHETTO

An as yet unexplained incident occurred today around noon. The well-known specialist Dr. [Abram] Mazur, a laryngologist, whom the Chairman brought to the ghetto from [the ghetto of] Warsaw some time ago, was walking towards Brzezińska Street when two members of the Ghetto Administration and A[ron] Jakubowicz asked Dr. Mazur to get in a car which then immediately drove back to Bałut Market. It was reasonable to assume that the specialist was being taken to some consultation or operation outside the ghetto. This seemed doubtful, though, since Dr. Mazur's arm had become infected when he was treating a boil. All that is certain is that Dr. Mazur was driven to the city.

FRIDAY, OCTOBER 8, 1943

NEWS OF THE DAY

Today, for the Kol Nidre service, the ghetto is in a more solemn and ceremonial mood than it has been in years. All minds are occupied with the thought that tomorrow, Yom Kippur, will be a real holiday. The Chairman has ordered the early closing of all departments and factories. Work will halt almost everywhere in the early afternoon. For the first time, people will be able to worship on Kol Nidre night and tomorrow, on Yom Kippur, with a certain feeling of security.

Soup vouchers are being issued today for tomorrow; there will be tsholnt, which must be picked up at the soup kitchens between ten and one. Even though the ghetto has been fasting excessively for years, most of the populace will fast [voluntarily] on Yom Kippur. Indeed, the ghetto as a whole looks much the same as it usually does. In the past, there was always the hustle and bustle typical of a Jewish town on the high holidays, especially on Kol Nidre evening. Happy people ran up to greet each other, hurried from home to home to wish each other a "Happy New Year" or a *Gmar khsime toyve*. Now they do the same, but the greeting is a bit wearier, quieter, and perhaps for that reason, all the more intimate. Acquaintances stop each other on the street and exchange a silent handshake.

THE DR. MAZUR CASE

Dr. [Abram] Mazur returned from the city late last night. As has been learned from the Department of Health, a disciplinary investigation was being conducted by the Ghetto Administration in connection with the sepsis that Dr. Mazur contracted in the course of an operation. The matter has been resolved satisfactorily.

SATURDAY, OCTOBER 9, 1943

NEWS OF THE DAY

Today, on Yom Kippur, all factories are idle, distribution shops are closed; this scene of perfect peace and quiet is marred to some extent only by the depots busy with incoming shipments of potatoes and vegetables and outgoing shipments of manufactured goods. The streets are not very animated. One sees mainly younger people in holiday attire, insofar as such attire is still possible.

Minyonim have gathered in many homes; sometimes, passing by, one hears the chanting or singing of the worshipers.

The Chairman too has observed Yom Kippur, himself chanting the *musef* [extension of the morning prayer, recited on the Sabbath and on holidays] service at a minyen. He visited several minyonim, where he spoke a few words of solace and encouragement, and also visited the hospital on Mickiewicz Street, where he handed out food coupons to several convalescents. He even found time for Central Prison, where he consented to an improvement of the diet and promised an amnesty. (Note: the Chairman provided [Szaja-Stanisław] Jakobson, the head of the court, with guidelines for an amnesty. Details will follow.)

PEOPLE ARE SAYING

that Dr. [Abram] Mazur was summoned to the city not in a disciplinary matter, but for a consultation involving a prominent patient.

MONDAY, OCTOBER 11, 1943

SKETCHES OF GHETTO LIFE: YOM KIPPUR IN THE GHETTO YEAR, 1943 (5704)

Today, those who may later undertake to write the cultural history of the ghetto of Litzmannstadt will be given certain clues that can perhaps serve them as a cornerstone. Let us assure them that during the years of the ghetto there were a few extraordinary hours to be recorded; not only the thousands of bleak hours, but a few uplifting ones as well. To state it as simply as possible: the day of Yom Kippur, October 8/9, 1943 (5704), has a special place in the history of the ghetto.

Today, the chronicler is attempting to report something under the immediate impact of the events. The eve of Yom Kippur, 1943, was a Friday, that is, a Sabbath eve. Young boys stood in the doorways, at the gates, and in the courtyard entrances, hawking [in Yiddish] "Lekht! Lekht!" [candles]. These are short, thin, homemade tallow candles, which are used for the Sabbath. This time they served a double function: to usher in both the Sabbath and Yom Kippur. They were lit at twilight, their modest glow lighting rooms, the tender little stalks visible behind thin curtains.

Nearby, women and girls were bustling about, preparing the evening meal. The meal was as meager as usual, consisting mostly of potatoes and some vegetable or other, but the thought of Kol Nidre transfigured it.

The three thousand fortunate ones now enjoying their fortnight of *kolacje* [supplemental evening meals] are better off. Normally, the rule is that this meal must be eaten by the worker himself in the communal kitchens; no one is permitted to take any of it home to his family. Today, however, the Chairman has allowed people to pick up the special-nutrition soups (as of two o'clock in the afternoon) and to consume them at home with their families. And since this evening meal consists of a large portion of nourishing soup, a meatball with vegetables, the recipient of such a kolacja has the illusion—or the reality—of a holiday meal.

People rushed out of the workshops at five or even earlier. A flurry of movement. Tension in the faces, and a glimmer of hope. Remembrance of the *Yomim neroim* [Days of Awe, that is, the high holidays] and visions of what is to come. But the deepest feelings were focused on the evening itself, the prayers. For this year's prayers are to encompass all the pain and longing for redemption of past years.

Very few people in the ghetto realize that without the efforts of the Eldest their worship service would have been impossible. It was not easy to obtain permission from the authorities. "The Day of Yom Kippur, the Sabbath of October 9, will be a day off from work. To make up for it, factories will operate on October 10 with a ten-percent increase in the rate of production. . . . This is the condition that was stipulated in the arrangement." The Eldest revealed this at a private gathering. This is entirely reasonable since the ghetto is based on work and can survive only on that basis.

The Yom Kippur Sabbath was marked by dignity and solemnity. People walked silently through the streets in their Sunday best. Anyone able to do so at all wore his better clothing. This was particularly obvious with the children. No treppkis [*trepy*— clogs] were to be seen on the street, and no barefoot youths. The boys wore ironed shirts, the girls wore ironed dresses. And the adults too made a point of presenting a well-groomed appearance. Since the sun burned with summerlike intensity, there was no need of an overcoat.

Once again, families could get together, as they had not been able to do in a long time. Parents took their children by the hand and went strolling; on this day, the work in the various workshops did not keep husband, wife, and child apart. Now and then, one could even see a Jew openly carrying a *seyfer toyre* [Scroll of the Torah], without the slightest inhibition, through the streets of the ghetto to some house where divine service was being held.

The ghetto has become aware of the religious tradition of the Eastern European Jews. One hundred thirty minyonim were registered with the Eldest, not to mention the small groups that gathered spontaneously for a Yom Kippur prayer. Summing up the mood in homes and on the streets, one can say: on Yom Kippur in the year 1943, the ghetto has literally become a shtetl. There was even something like a *yontev* [holiday] dish. This time, instead of the normal soup, the kitchens distributed tsholnt—in High German, they called it Gedämpfte Kartoffeln [steamed potatoes]. So even stomachs shared in this extraordinary Yom Kippur.

On Yom Kippur in the year 1943 thousands of prayers, accompanied by memories and sighs, were directed toward heaven from prayer halls and private apartments. The *mazker* service embraced the memory of the dead who have perished in *Kidush ha-Shem* [Sanctification of God's Name, that is, martyrdom] in the ghetto. The list would have been too long had all these dead been mentioned by name. The past four years must have populated the *gut-ort* [cemetery] in Marysin with the bones of more than 30,000 persons—a figure unlikely to be bettered anywhere in the world. But the Yom Kippur atmosphere has magically evoked a bit of the Jewish beauty that is still alive somewhere outside, among our brothers and sisters.

O[skar] R[osenfeld]

TUESDAY, OCTOBER 12, 1943

A DEATH

Today, a young member of the Archives staff, Szmul Hecht, died at the age of 20. Hecht had been resettled here from Wieluń. Since beginning work at the Archives, he had been sickly and severely undernourished, thus contracting tuberculosis. During the resettlement from Wieluń, he had lost his mother and his sister; his father died two weeks ago here in the ghetto; and so the young man was shattered, spiritually as well as physically. Hecht is the fourth staff member of the Archives to have died. He was an exceedingly likable, quiet, modest man, whose memory we will honor.

SUPPLEMENT TO THE DAILY BULLETIN OF SUNDAY, OCTOBER 17, 1943

Conference of the Chairman with the Pressers on October 17, 1943
The Chairman invited the pressers of the tailors' workshop to a conference that took place on Sunday, October 17. The scene of the conference was the special-nutrition kitchen on Zgierska Street.

The Chairman, unaccompanied, arrived at noon in the dining room of the kitchen, where the invited workers were already gathered. After a mutual greeting, the Chairman made an inspection tour of the kitchen he had instituted; he then returned to the dining room and opened the conference as follows, eliciting stormy reaction from the audience:

"Friends, ghetto workers! I greet you who have appeared in such large numbers, demonstrating that your instincts are sound. I bear no grudge" (smiling) "against those who have not appeared because they were not invited; nor against the ailing workers who, unfortunately, could not come; nor even against those who foolishly let themselves be misled into not coming. . . . Perhaps you are suspicious because I am here alone, without your *kierowniki* [managers]! I wish to speak to you alone, frankly and honestly, as is Rumkowski's habit—to speak clearly, in the simple way that is customary here.

"First, a preliminary remark: it is my principle not to speak before an audience that is hungry—first, a bite to eat, then the discussion. This time, however, it had to be the other way around. It was not my fault, but that of the cauldron. I cannot, however, impose any punishment on a cauldron. The kitchen tells me that the food will be ready soon. We will have a bite and then resume our meeting. Meanwhile, I would like to make one thing clear. I am, God forbid, not your enemy, but your friend; and a friend must, above all, be understood, or at least, trusted."

The signal came from the kitchen that the meal would be ready shortly. The Chairman had a few Order Service men hand out three cigarettes to each guest. He used the interval to receive written petitions from the participants in the conference, reading through some of them on the spot and jotting down a few notes.

The staff began to serve the meal. First, a good, thick, tasty soup; then, so-called knackwurst, with side dishes of potatoes, cabbage, pickles, and radishes; finally, stewed pumpkin and 100 grams of bread. In view of the substantial nature of the meal, the Chairman allowed the workers to take any unconsumed food home, and many of them took advantage of this exceptional opportunity.

After the meal, the Chairman continued: "I know that the pressers do hard manual labor. But I also know that they are hard to deal with. In general, the Jews are a people hard to deal with, but the pressers are the hardest of the hard. The pressers have always considered themselves the elite, as if they were the only craftsmen in their department. This was so in the past. Today, it is no longer the case. In the past, I myself had supervision over the workshops and, if anything went wrong, well—after all, I'm a sly Jew—I simply turned a blind eye. Today, the workshops are not supervised by me, but by a different agency [that is, the Gettoverwaltung]. Every workshop has to turn in a report on its level of production. I am responsible only for seeing to it that the production quotas are filled.

"The fact of the matter is, no one works ten hours a day anymore, but only eight. It was very hard to push this innovation through. But I believe that I have thereby eased the lives of the ghetto workers, thus fulfilling my duties and keeping my promise to the ghetto. The very appearance of sabotage must be avoided, for I need not elaborate on the consequences of such an accusation. You all know that, in the Jewish quarter, I am no liar or speechifier and, therefore, I tell you candidly: I will not permit even the slightest irregularity in the workshops that might be interpreted as sabotage. And in this matter I will do anything I have to do. Your so-called leaders, who talk you into believing that they are your friends, are in reality misleading you, and I will be forced to put them out of business. I am no private entrepreneur intent on exploiting you. This is your enterprise as much as it is mine and that of all Jews in the ghetto, who want to live just as much as the pressers do. In order to sustain the ghetto and protect it from disaster, I will—let me say this openly—show no [special] consideration either for individuals or groups of workers! I will remove the troublemakers and agitators from the ghetto; and not because I tremble for my life, but because I fear for you all. You have to be protected; as for me, my hair is white as snow, I walk with a stoop—my life is already behind me!

"I appeal to you again, brothers! Look upon me not as an entrepreneur, but as a man who is familiar with the details of conditions in the ghetto. I have my finger constantly on the ghetto's pulse, and I will continue to do so. I have guaranteed with my life that the ghetto will work and that order will be maintained. I will be forced to eliminate any persons who stir up trouble. The purpose of our meeting today was for me to tell you this frankly. Further negotiations will not alter my resolve, and I have no time for frivolity or empty talk.

"You are angry with me for doing away with the CP and B III coupons and replacing them with special-nutrition meals. If you took a proper look at the facts of the matter, you would certainly drop your objections. As workers performing heavy physical tasks you were accorded coupons; now, you receive the special-nutrition meals instead. Granted, these are meant only for yourselves, whereas the coupons could be enjoyed by your families as well. But the Jewish principle of community, the Jewish concern for the family is not applicable here. At stake is the fate of the collective, not the fates of individuals. Let me give you an example.

"I gave much thought to the difficulties endured by those with no teeth or very defective teeth, and I created a laboratory for false teeth in order to deal with these problems. Now I am besieged by the entire ghetto; everyone needs dentures. But I don't have anything like the amount of material that would be necessary. I have demonstrated my good will often enough, but when something or other goes wrong, it is in fact your fault and not mine.

"It is possible that I do not have the right people around me, but it is too late to do anything about that.

"Another example, which just occurred before your very eyes: I received a written petition from one of your men, then a second and a third one. I read these requests on the spot and tried to deal with them. Suddenly, however, I was inundated with requests, making it impossible for me to deal with them. So I crammed them into my pockets . . . for later attention. I will certainly do everything I can, but I will not be able to take care of everything and everyone. Please understand this point of view. I appeal to you as human beings and Jews! Please accept the fact that you must show consideration for the ghetto as a whole and subordinate your personal interests to the collective interest. Do not force me to avail myself of methods that I would not care to apply. We have already suffered enough blows, and the wounds were slow in healing. I will therefore not permit unqualified elements to interfere in the administration of the workshops."

After this statement by the Chairman several pressers requested permission to speak. The first to take the floor criticized the special-nutrition meals. The *CP* coupons had, in his opinion, been more valuable, and he requested that the meals, therefore, be substantial enough that recipients could leave the kitchen with their hunger appeased. The second speaker complained about the directors and the instructors, who were more interested in their allotments, he charged, than they were in the workers, and who did not make appropriate allowances for the workers' physical condition.

The presser, so a third speaker explained, was on his feet for eight hours a day, continuously wielding an eight- or ten-kilogram iron. Back when he had received coupons, the presser had been able to bring a bit of sugar and marmalade along to the workshop and had eaten some it for quick energy when he was tired. Now this was no longer possible. . . .

These and similar complaints were also presented by other pressers.

The Chairman made the following reply:

"Life in the ghetto is not easy. There will always be dissatisfied and disappointed people. Today you are demanding special meals; tomorrow it will be the metal workers, carpenters, saddlers, and so forth, making the same demand. My answer is to the point, and not mere rhetoric. In good times, the coupon entitled you to 300 grams of meat; in times that weren't so good, to 200 grams of sausage; for three coupons you could thus get 900 grams of meat or 600 grams of sausage a month. Today, in the special-nutrition kitchens, you receive 100 grams of meat daily for two weeks—a total of 1,400 grams of meat, and corresponding amounts of potatoes and grains. These figures tell the story. I would be happy indeed if I could give equally generous meals to all the Jews in the ghetto. I have conferred with medical experts, who have declared that the special-nutrition meal is truly sufficient to give the workers energy and improve their health. The coupons, which you shared with your families, lasted for only a few days in any case, while now you go empty-handed just for fourteen days out of the month. And as for the children, I always do my best to take care of them separately, as you yourselves well know. Four thousand children have been lodged in special okhronkes [ochronki, that is, institutions for homeless children], where they receive good soup twice a day. I ask you to bear in mind that I am dependent on the unique circumstances of the ghetto, with which I am quite familiar. Once again: we will not get anywhere with demagogic slogans. My actions are limited by the range of my options. I will not introduce a system that grants exceptions to a specific group of workers. I can only promise you that I will do everything within my power for the ghetto, just as I have always done. I also hope that it will be possible for me to provide coal for the ghetto, so that it doesn't freeze. I regret that I cannot extend the special-nutrition meals from only fourteen to twenty-eight days a month. Once the overall situation improves, everyone will benefit, not just the pressers."

With these concluding words, the conference ended at three in the afternoon.

O[skar] R[osenfeld]

MONDAY, OCTOBER 18, 1943

During the past few days many postcards from Terezín [Theresienstadt-Getto] have arrived in the ghetto, with news from relatives of those from Prague who have been resettled here.

FOOD SUPPLY

The situation has stabilized. Varying quantities of potatoes are being delivered. Large amounts of tomatoes are already in or have been announced, so a further tomato ration is in sight. It is conjectured that these green tomatoes come from the Sudetenland because a fragment of the *Leitmeritzer Tageblatt* [Litoměřice Daily News] was found in one carload.

TUESDAY, OCTOBER 19, 1943

SUICIDE ATTEMPT

On October 18, Łaja Krumholz, born in Łódź in 1920 and residing at 9 Wawelska Street, attempted suicide by swallowing a sleep-inducing drug. She was taken to the hospital by the Emergency Service.

MARGARINE RATION

As of Wednesday, October 20, fifty grams of margarine can be obtained for 50 pfennigs with Coupon No. 78 of the ration card. This is the first margarine ration in many months.

WEDNESDAY, OCTOBER 20, 1943

SUICIDE

On October 20, Simcha Michał Parzenczewski, born in Łódź on August 14, 1918, and residing at 9 Drewnowska Street, committed suicide by opening his arteries. He died the same day. According to the medical report, he succumbed not to the suicide [attempt], but to tuberculosis.

NEWS OF THE DAY

On the occasion of this year's Simhat Torah, the Chairman was once again mindful of the so-called adopted-by-decree children and distributed coupons to them. The children each received 250 grams of [rye] flakes, 200 grams of peas, 250 grams of sugar, 100 grams of marmalade, 5 kilograms of potatoes, and a can of meat S[chweinfleisch— pork]. The orphans who have not been adopted also received appropriate allotments.

THURSDAY, OCTOBER 21, 1943

NEWS OF THE DAY

Today, on the eve of Simhat Torah, religious life in the ghetto is somewhat livelier than last year. Minyonim were formed in many homes to celebrate the feast of Torah joy. There are still many sforim [prayer books] left in the ghetto. Young people too have participated in various minyonim on this holiday. One can see that the ghetto is breathing relatively freely, the immediate expression of which is the flourishing religious tradition.

FOOD SUPPLY

Regular shipments: It is gradually becoming apparent that the last potato ration will be exhausted ahead of schedule. If the *Chronicle* has not had to speak of hunger in the past few days, it is because the ten kilograms of potatoes have made the situation somewhat more tolerable. In the absence of any other food, however, many people have not been able to husband the potatoes in accordance with the ration schedule. However, it is hoped that this time the problem will not become so acute, since the regular potato deliveries will allow the Chairman more flexibility in planning.

FRIDAY, OCTOBER 22, 1943

NEWS OF THE DAY

Today, Simhat Torah, there are private minyonim again at various locations in the ghetto.

PUBLIC HEALTH

The contagious diseases reported today: paratyphoid fever, 1; typhus, 1; typhoid fever, 4; tuberculosis, 7.

The causes of today's deaths: pulmonary tuberculosis, 6; [other] lung diseases, 2; prostate hypertrophy, 1; heart failure, 1.

TUESDAY, OCTOBER 26, 1943

WORKSHOP NEWS: BAN ON WOOD DISTRIBUTION

Today, Amtsleiter Biebow visited the wood factory on Bazarna Street, where he discussed the production of children's toys for Christmas with plant manager [Leon] Winograd. The latter pointed out the shortage of the scrap wood necessary for such production. Biebow was extremely annoyed and ordered a total suspension of scrap wood distribution in all wood factories, effective immediately. He remarked that only wood from building demolitions was allowed as fuel for the home, and he added that he would shoot any Jew who carried off scrap wood from the factories. In this connection, yesterday, A[ron] Jakubowicz, director of the Central Workshop Bureau, met with all directors of wood factories to discuss the recent developments. Jakubowicz, for his part, also imposed a strict ban on the distribution of scrap wood, sawdust, and shavings. The already critical situation in the ghetto has been greatly exacerbated by this directive. Wood prices soared immediately; today, wood already costs 4 to 5 marks per kilogram on the open market. Another consequence has been the increased use of the [public] gas-cooking points.

WEDNESDAY, OCTOBER 27, 1943

WORKSHOP NEWS: METAL WORKERS VS. MANAGEMENT

In metal workshop II, 56 Zgierska Street, the following incident occurred:

On October 26, foreman Smulewicz slapped a teen-aged worker for one reason or another. The entire morning shift in the forge and the lathe section protested by stopping work. A delegation went to the management offices to demand an explanation. The delegation was not received. The workers thereupon refused to resume work. The management called the Order Service and had the entire personnel of both sections arrested. When the second shift arrived at three in the afternoon and learned about the incident, it demanded the release of the arrested workers. Since management was adamant, the entire staff refused to work. The workshop management notified the Chairman about the episode, and he arrived on the scene at 5:30 P.M. He promptly ordered the release of the arrested workers and promised to resolve the matter by the next day. At the request of management, the strikers were held responsible for the three hours of work they had missed, and, indeed, they worked until 3 A.M. instead of midnight. In the course of these three late-night hours the Chairman telephone the workshop three times to assure himself that everything was in order.

But in the morning the personnel of the factory branch on Smugowa [Street] declared their solidarity with the workers in the main shop. The Chairman hurried over and demanded that the shift resume work immediately, promising an investigation of the matter during the next few days. When the Chairman arrived in the workshop at 7 A.M., he found no management staff on the premises; when they arrived late, he reproached them vehemently. Then he immediately began an investigation of the affair, giving particular attention to the workers' complaints about various abuses. He promised to set these matters right. The main abuses in question are unfair distributions of the supplementary rations and the kolacje [evening meals], as well as of the current coupons. We can be certain that the Chairman will take vigorous action to establish better relations between management and labor in these important workshops.

FRIDAY, OCTOBER 29, 1943

NEWS OF THE DAY

The mood in the ghetto remains very depressed. The reason is that no improvement in the food situation can be expected and there is scant hope of any significant quantity of fuel arriving; this is having a numbing effect on the ghetto.

The Chairman himself is in very low spirits. He is contemplating inviting some representatives of certain social groups to a conference. The fact that the Chairman, who, since the establishment of the ghetto, has been directing it in an authoritarian manner, is now contemplating such a conference is the best indication of how critical the situation is. Meanwhile, no one in the ghetto believes that such conferences can be of significant practical value. On the one hand, it is impossible to think that the Chairman can, or desires to, share power to any degree, and on the other, it is impossible to suppose that such a council could have any effect. Attention is being paid chiefly to the people who might be named as representatives of the workers. Those people will use a unilateral argument: equal division of the food available and also the elimination of the privileges that have existed so far. If only the Chairman were able to reconcile himself to the elimination of the Beirat rations; that, however, is inadmissible, for it is obvious it will do nothing for the ghetto. We will see whether this conference is held and what it brings.

SATURDAY, OCTOBER 30, 1943

JUDICIAL PROCEEDINGS: COURTROOM—YOM KIPPUR AMNESTY

Only today have we received a summary report of the Chairman's amnesty decree for Yom Kippur. The decree quashes current criminal proceedings and remits sentences. There are 42 cases, mostly of petty larceny: 28 cases of a trifling nature, chiefly theft of potatoes and small quantities of provisions, as well as petty theft of vegetables and wood; a few cases of garden poaching; three cases of fraud; one case of public insult; one case of criminal negligence in office; one case of imprudent purchase; two cases of street hawking.

It is interesting, by the way, to take a closer look at some of the cases, because they give us a picture of ghetto criminality. For instance, amnesty was granted for the theft of a man's shirt (two weeks' arrest), the theft of two pairs of socks (one month imprisonment), fraud to obtain two bowls of soup, theft of a cloth remnant in the tailors' workshop, imprudent purchase of one pair of clogs, theft of a garment in the Clothing Department.

The mitigating factors mentioned in the amnesty petition are characteristic. Vegetable theft: committed under extreme duress, sole support of a large family; criminal negligence in office: advanced age (63 years), serious pulmonary disease; potato theft: committed on account of extraordinarily wretched circumstances, contagious disease and hunger edema afflicting the entire family.

Most of the convicted or accused have no prior records; three are juveniles under 17 years of age. On the whole, it can be said that, aside from one case of public insult, these are all cases of food theft.

MONDAY, NOVEMBER 1, 1943

NEWS OF THE DAY

The Chairman is still not feeling well (a cold in his ears). As we already mentioned on October 28, the Chairman did, in fact, invite several persons for talks; these included [I.] Lubliński, [Emanuel] Woliński and [Izrael] Tabaksblat (FUKR [*Fach-und-Kontroll Referat*—Trade Inspection Section]).[42] There is no precise information about those talks except that those men recommended to the Chairman that he equalize food rations and, in particular, abolish the Beirat allocations. The Chairman responded non-committally to those proposals.

WEDNESDAY, NOVEMBER 3, 1943

SKETCHES OF GHETTO LIFE: FROM THE SOUP MARKET

At the very first signs of an imminent potato shortage, the soup market grew lively.

The soup market is the street trade that takes place around the kitchens that distribute the so-called workshop soups (workshop midday meals). Groups and individuals stand, in a great hubbub, at the entrance to a distribution station. People run up to the distribution window with their bowls, dishes, pitchers, menashkes [*menaszki*, mess kits]. On the way they are approached by others. The routine

42. Those invited to the conference by M. C. Rumkowski were representatives of political parties, which had a semi-legal life in the ghetto: the Labor Zionist party, *Poale Zion* (Emanuel Woliński and Izrael Tabaksblat) and the Bund (Mosze Lederman). A representative of a third political group who also took part in the November 1 conference was not mentioned. The presence of Chil Hirszhorn, there on behalf of the Union Left, is not mentioned until the entry for November 4.

question [asked in Yiddish] is: "Do you have a card to sell?" ("*Ver hot a tsetele?*"). The word "card" refers to the voucher that entitles one to the soup, the workshop midday meal.

The person accosted either keeps on walking without a word or else responds to the prospective buyer. The difference between the offer and the asking price is never more than half a ghetto mark—neither the buyer nor the seller will risk having the deal fall through. But small as this business transaction may be, it is, nevertheless, a vital concern in the ghetto. The half mark more or less is not the point; rather, it is the successful conclusion of the deal that is crucial to both parties. Of such trifles is the unofficial, illicit life of the ghetto composed. In order to get the most out of such dealings, though, it is important to understand and to follow the market. The person who wishes to be successful in the soup trade must be informed about the overall situation: the quality of the goods and the gap between demand and supply.

The experienced soup-card buyer knows precisely which kitchen offers soup containing a good deal of grain; or soup with a good deal of cabbage; or, as they say [in Yiddish]—a *gedakhte* [thick] soup. These are the factors that determine market trends. The prices regulate themselves; the market is extremely sensitive. By tacit agreement, soup prices are the same in front of all kitchens. Minor differences are due to the stubbornness of either party, the buyer or the seller. No one, not even the most conscientious observer, can fathom how the individual markets communicate with one another about the prices. But the fact is that these prices are regulated automatically.

Vouchers for extra soup are particularly desirable when they are not restricted to any specific kitchen or specific day. Such vouchers are more valuable because they can be negotiated more easily. You keep them in your pocket and cash them in at a favorable time.

Certain variants of this basic form of trade are not without interest. Occasionally someone will sell a card, a soup voucher, and then use the money to acquire a different voucher for a different kitchen—if he has learned that this kitchen is today serving a better soup or one more to his liking. In such a case the interested party is willing to invest half a mark or even a whole mark. On the other hand, the able speculator will not miss the opportunity of selling the allegedly more valuable soup for a price higher than that asked for inferior soup at another soup exchange. The difference, the profit, is often spent on cigarettes; the man who paces outside the kitchen for long periods scouting for a buyer, especially on cold days, is forced to while away the time by smoking a few cigarettes. November 3 will be remembered as the day on which all this began to change. It was on this day that a proclamation by the Eldest was posted at all street corners (four hundred such proclamations have appeared since the establishment of the ghetto) to the effect that the soup category is being restructured. First of all, as of Sunday, November 7, no more supplemental soups will be made available: each ghetto dweller will receive only one basic soup daily. Furthermore, this soup will contain only 250 grams of potatoes (gross weight). Finally, the proclamation fixes the weekly potato ration at two kilograms per person.

These are, no doubt, serious encroachments on the soup market. Less soup—fewer potatoes! Impossible now to sell one's supplemental soup. Business, that is, supply, is going to suffer terribly. The question, "Do you have a card to sell?" will become more urgent and less speculative. Nevertheless, on the day of the proclamation, the soup exchange did not panic. The price of soup rose by only one mark.

On "Black Wednesday," November 3, of the ghetto year, 1943, workshop soup cost "only" 9 marks, 50. Supply was adequate for demand, though the market was very brisk. There was no price boom in soup. The buyer will not be intimidated; his faith in the immediate future has not been shaken by the Eldest's proclamation.

The price of soup—the most reliable barometer next to the price of bread—indicates that the ghetto will not be easily intimidated. The ghetto seems to know why the price of soup does not yet reflect the catastrophic food situation.

O[skar] R[osenfeld]

THURSDAY, NOVEMBER 4, 1943

NEWS OF THE DAY

The Chairman held a conference this evening. The same people were invited [again] and included [Emanuel] Woliński, [Mosze] Lederman, [Izrael] Tabaksblat, Bande, [I.] Lubliński and Chil [Hirszhorn]. At the first meeting, Kaufman, the head of the Department of Soup Kitchens, had also been present as an expert in matters relating to soup kitchens. He was not invited to the second conference, whose results are not known.

FRIDAY, NOVEMBER 5, 1943

NEWS OF THE DAY

The Chairman is still intensively engaged in reorganizing the rationing system. He has resolved to discontinue the B allotment. The pertinent proclamation reads as follows:

Proclamation No. 402
Re: Suspension of the B Ration
I hereby announce that, consequent to the reorganization of the rationing system, I am forced to order a temporary suspension of the B allotment as of Wednesday, November 10, 1943.

Litzmannstadt-Getto, November 5, 1943
Ch[aim] Rumkowski.

It is rumored that the Chairman has exempted some fifty persons from this discontinuation of the B cooperatives: a few very important physicians, or at least physicians who seem important to him; also, particularly important managers of workshops or departments and persons of special merit. Evidently, this measure cannot be implemented unconditionally. It also appears to be something of a token gesture, for, as we have already explained, discontinuation of the B allotment will not bring about any significant change in the situation. The reckoning is simple:

Every beneficiary of the B cooperatives has been receiving, for a ten-day period: 200 grams of sugar, 150 grams of marmalade, 200 grams of grain. Counting two thousand *B* allotments, this comes to a total of 400 kilograms of sugar, 300 kilograms of marmalade, 400 kilograms of grain for a ten-day period. If distributed among the entire population, this would come to 5 grams per person—unquestionably not enough to make any significant difference.

SKETCHES OF GHETTO LIFE: MATCHES

There is no point in elaborating psychological or economic theories about a utility item such as matches. True enough, a lot of thinking can go into a match—witness the monopoly trust of the Norwegian Ivar Kreuger, the match king. But the ghetto is always concerned with immediate needs, not reflection, whether about potatoes or shoe soles. Matches are rare in the ghetto and seldom appear in the rations.

Although the October ration did include two boxes, they were soon used up. When several families live together, they can economize on matches. The boxes they manage to save enter the free market and command rigorous prices.

A matchbox contains about fifty matches. Such a box cost two marks at the end of September, and four marks at the end of October. The onset of cold weather requires heating and heat means matches. Since very few families own a cigarette lighter (a weatherproof lighter in good working order costs over fifty marks here), people are dependent on matches. And since either the striking surface or the match itself is poor, the fortunate owner of a box of matches uses up several before he finds one that will ignite properly. Thus, even if a ghetto dweller has little fuel to burn or food to cook, he will soon be out of matches.

In the first week of November, a box of matches is selling for nearly as much as the fourteen-day ration. The market is adjusting itself to the current situation. It has converted from wholesale to retail; individual matches are offered instead of entire boxes. One match is 10 pfennigs; a bundle of ten, 1 mark. This corresponds to the price levels in free trade on the black market.

A match is a precious item in the ghetto. One has to be careful with it. A clumsy housewife can squander a mark in the blink of an eye.

O[skar] R[osenfeld]

SATURDAY, NOVEMBER 6, 1943

NEWS OF THE DAY

The discontinuation of the B cooperatives has made no particular impression on the populace. The level-headed realize that this token gesture will hardly affect the general situation. The announcement was received coolly, even eliciting a number of sarcastic remarks because there are to be exceptions and favoritism will run rampant—so it is said. At the moment, the ghetto is busy wondering who the fifty privileged persons are, or when the number will be raised from fifty to twice or three times that number.

SKETCHES OF GHETTO LIFE: LATE HARVEST

The fortunate owners of działkas [land parcels] have gradually gathered their harvest—every fruit in its season, as the Bible tells us. The gardens are empty and bleak, only the last leaves remain on the trees. The fences are slowly disappearing, especially the wooden ones, so that one garden runs into another. For, at this time of year, there are no more property squabbles. The "estate owners" are home in their apartments, no longer concerned about the fate of their działkas.

Now it is the turn of the intruders. There are great shortages, potatoes are not coming in, the ration has been halved. And vegetables too are extremely scarce.

In these difficult days, one can observe people, equipped with bags and knapsacks, who suddenly appear in the działkas. They are looking for something to eat, for anything that the owner forgot to harvest or did not consider worth harvesting: unappealing leek stalks or unsuccessful onions, small, stunted cabbage or shriveled kohlrabi. . . . The hungry stomach is not fastidious, it wants to be filled. It does not covet lovely, highly nutritious fruits; the late harvest will do, no matter how scant it may be. Even a few beet leaves can keep one alive for an hour or two.

O[skar] R[osenfeld]

SUNDAY, NOVEMBER 7, 1943

AMTSLEITER BIEBOW IN THE DEPARTMENT OF VITAL STATISTICS

Today, Amtsleiter Biebow made an appearance at the Registration Bureau, where H[enryk] Neftalin, the attorney, director of the Department of Vital Statistics, showed him the facilities of the registration system. It seems very likely that a visit by an official commission is expected. Amtsleiter Biebow remained at the Registration Bureau for about half an hour and expressed no interest in seeing other branches of the Department of Vital Statistics.

TUESDAY, NOVEMBER 9, 1943

NEWS OF THE DAY: A COMMISSION ARRIVES IN THE GHETTO

The commission visited the most important workshops, especially the Metal Department and the wood and carpentry factories. The group was composed of visitors from Berlin, apparently members of the SD [*Sicherheitsdienst*—Security Service]. The inspection was satisfactory on every point. The commission was probably supposed to inspect the Registration Bureau as well, but did not have time to do so. [Henryk] Neftalin, the attorney, was summoned to Bałut Market where, in the presence of the Chairman, he supplied the commission members with information about the registration system.

Amtsleiter Biebow's visit to the Registration Bureau and Neftalin's report at Bałut Market have again occasioned disquieting rumors throughout the ghetto, for instance that the drums [metal file containers] of the Registration Bureau have been sealed and that another resettlement is in the offing. None of this is based on fact.

THURSDAY, NOVEMBER 11, 1943

SKETCHES OF GHETTO LIFE

There has been a sudden flurry of activity at the sandlots in the vicinity of the carpentry factories. The ground is being dug up with spades. Droves of people are descending on the few square meters of sandpiles. What do they want with sand? On closer inspection one notices that this is not, in fact, sand that is being dug up and loaded into sacks, but the sawdust that was once collected from the carpentry shops to be used for leveling the public squares. What an abundance of sawdust there used to be! Today spades are removing this half-decomposed material from the ground. The sawdust is dried out at home and suffices to cook soup or a pot of [ersatz] coffee.

FRIDAY, NOVEMBER 12, 1943

SALATKA [SALAD]

The populace is embittered about the quality of the current salatka. As we have already reported, potato peels from the soup kitchens have been turned over for salad production. The quality is predictably inferior: only hunger could induce people to accept such garbage, but even the hungry are rejecting this salad. Furthermore, it is simply indecent to ask the same price for this dubious concoction of potato peels as for the previous high-quality product.

The ghetto claims that the idea of processing the potato peels into this salatka was originally suggested by Mr. Litwin. But the ghetto is quite sure that Mr. Litwin himself has declined the product of his ingenuity. So long as the potato peels reached the pots of the fortunate by way of local favoritism a more or less edible dish was produced, because the people in question had some experience in preparing this refuse product; but as salatka the stuff is just about indigestible.

SUNDAY, NOVEMBER 14, 1943

SKETCHES OF GHETTO LIFE: GRAVES IN RESERVE

There is still brisk activity at the Marysin cemetery.[43] Though the mortality rate is relatively low (an average of four deaths a day), long rows of graves are being prepared in Marysin. Those in charge know what they're doing; they are worried about the below-freezing temperatures to come. The workers in the cemetery would never be able to keep up with demand if the frost were severe. On one bowl of soup a day, they would never be able to dig enough graves for their brethren. The cemetery administration has to plan ahead; it must not be caught short. The consequences of the

---

43. During the ghetto's existence the gate of the Jewish cemetery was moved to the back, on the Marysin side, since the entrance and the street it faced did not fall within the bounds of the ghetto.

current period of hunger will be evident soon enough, unfortunately. The cemetery is building up a reserve of graves. . . .

TUESDAY, NOVEMBER 16, 1943

NEWS OF THE DAY

The talk of the day is still the takeover of food distribution by the Ghetto Administration. Reaction to this news has been anything but uniform. The man in the street is actually anticipating a significant improvement in the situation, while the intelligentsia takes a rather skeptical view of this new development. It is primarily those who are not indifferent to things Jewish who deplore the change as dangerous to the Jews as a whole. They sum up their feelings and thoughts in one sentence: "Ivan should not blow shofer" [that is, a non-Jew should not perform Jewish duties].

The stone has been set rolling, but where it is going we don't yet know.

By yesterday evening the distribution offices were ordered to check their stocks (general inventory). Likewise the vegetable markets, where this operation will be supervised by the Special Unit [Department].

There is talk here about all sorts of serious clashes among the actors in this play. Certainly, there have been heated exchanges between Amtsleiter Biebow and the Chairman, but this would not be the first time.

By no means is it true that the Chairman and [Marek] Kligier had a run-in. On the contrary, the meeting proceeded in a perfectly calm and civil fashion. Incidentally, the matter is reported in various ways by the participants. Some have been claiming that the Chairman offered to work with the [newly established food supply] committee, but was turned down because of Amtsleiter Biebow's guidelines. Others allege that the committee invited the Chairman's cooperation, but that he refused. At bottom, it makes absolutely no difference; for if a struggle took place, it ultimately culminated in conflict between the Amtsleiter and the Chairman. If so, it is obvious that the Chairman would have been the weaker.

The future will show which of the two is right in regard to food management. The Chairman is calm, even though one can tell that he was deeply disturbed by the Amtsleiter's decision.

The committee already had its first meeting yesterday evening. Contrary to all rumors, [Max] Szczęśliwy, co-director of the Department of Food Supply, will remain in office. He is not a member of the Food Supply Committee.

SKETCHES OF GHETTO LIFE: THE LAST DAY OF KOLACJA [EVENING MEAL]

Consumers are jamming into the special-nutrition kitchens. For thousands, Monday is simply their first day of kolacja. The lines are hundreds of meters long. The atmosphere in the kitchens is utterly macabre. The staff members are silent. The people waiting in line are mute. They crowd toward the entrance, fearing that the only meal they are to enjoy in their fourteen-day rotation may be in jeopardy—in the ghetto, anything is possible! People eat quickly, knowing that thousands wait outside. Malicious jokesters cause agitation in the long lines by spreading the word that the kitchen has only enough food for those standing up to the corner of Dworska [Street]. The line grows restless, surging toward the kitchen on Młynarska Street, but soon the excitement is over. With gallows humor, many people approach the clerks and ask all sorts of questions that the clerks can answer only with shrugs. Who knows what will happen tomorrow? Every opinion or wishful thought imaginable spreads through the hall and down the lines into the street: the kitchens are not shutting down altogether, merely interrupting service for two or three days and then resuming as before; no, only one kolacja kitchen will open again; nonsense, two kitchens; and so on. No one can answer the many questions. All that is certain is that everyone is hungry and bitterly disappointed and that, as of tomorrow, the kitchens will be closed. Opinions may differ about the value of the special-nutrition kitchens, but one thing is not in dispute: those who consumed their first and last kolacja yesterday agree that their hopes for a happy fourteen days have been dashed.

WEDNESDAY, NOVEMBER 17, 1943

A COMMISSION IN THE GHETTO

Today, a German commission visited the ghetto. It was a rather large group of high-ranking Wehrmacht and SS officers led by a general. The commission arrived in the ghetto toward two o'clock and began by inspecting the new facilities of Metal Department II. Then it visited the Boot Department, the Leather and Saddlery Department, the Tailoring Department at 34–36 Łagiewnicka Street, and finally, the carpentry shop at 12 Drukarska Street. The commission was visibly impressed by all of these plants. Finally, the commission visited the furniture exhibit, which likewise made a satisfactory impression. It is certain that, above all, the [Nazi] party officers have had to revise their opinions about the productivity of Jews. They could not get over their surprise and astonishment. Their comments and the expressions on their faces were clearly saying the same thing: "And this really was done by Jews?"

FRIDAY, NOVEMBER 19, 1943

NEWS OF THE DAY

The talk of the day is still the upheaval in the food supply system and the new ration, which does indeed show some improvement, but also provides ample grounds for skepticism. Since the ghetto knows that the increased flour ration has nearly emptied the storehouses, it is very concerned about the next few days. However, one must assume that, since the Ghetto Administration has officially taken control, it will do all it can to secure a maximum supply of food.

JUDICIAL PROCEEDINGS: DIVORCE IN THE GHETTO

Since the institution of divorce proceedings in the ghetto, a total of 102 divorce petitions or complaints have been filed with the court of the Eldest of the Jews. Of this number, twenty-five cases have been concluded, with sixteen divorces granted and nine rejected. The defender of wedlock in all these cases was the Chairman's wife, Regina Rumkowska.

WEDNESDAY, NOVEMBER 24, 1943

SKETCHES OF GHETTO LIFE: CULTURAL LIFE IN THE GHETTO

Though life weighs heavily upon people in the ghetto, they refuse to do without cultural life altogether. The closing of the House of Culture has deprived the ghetto of the last vestiges of public cultural life. But with his tenacity and vitality, the ghetto dweller, hardened by countless misfortunes, always seeks new ways to sate his hunger for something of cultural value. The need for music is especially intense, and small centers for the cultivation of music have sprung up over time; to be sure, only for a certain upper stratum. Sometimes it is professional musicians, sometimes amateurs who perform for an intimate group of invited guests. Chamber music is played, and there is singing. Likewise, small, family-like circles form in order to provide spiritual nourishment on a modest level. Poets and prose writers read from their own works. The classics and more recent works of world literature are recited. Thus does the ghetto salvage something of its former spiritual life.

FRIDAY, NOVEMBER 26, 1943

NEWS OF THE DAY

As we have already reported, Amtsleiter Biebow has returned from Berlin. Unfortunately, the high hopes pinned on this trip have not been realized, and nothing has been heard about the projected new regulations. We are thereby reminded that the Amtsleiter, in his last announcement of November 15, stated that "a new plan is now being worked out." This plan has yet to materialize. Apparently he was unable to accomplish much in Berlin, which was in a period of crisis at the time.[44]

WEDNESDAY, DECEMBER 1, 1943

PEOPLE ARE SAYING. . .

Around November 23, the ghetto was buzzing with rumors that Dawid Gertler was about to return. Supposedly, some talks were to take place in the city, after which Gertler would be back in the ghetto. A week has passed, but this rumor has not yet proven true.

---

44. In the original *Chronicle*, the last sentence was crossed out and replaced with the following: "It is not known what he arranged in Berlin, which is now living through a critical time."

TUESDAY, DECEMBER 7, 1943

NEWS OF THE DAY

This evening at 5:50, the scheduled assembly took place at the former House of Culture. Amtsleiter Biebow was the speaker. The Central Workshop Bureau issued invitations to the workshop managers, to certain instructors, and to the department directors. Approximately four hundred persons gathered to hear the Amtsleiter's speech.

First Mr. Aurbach, the representative of the [German] criminal police, appeared. Those present rose from their seats at his entrance. The chief of the Order Service, [Leon] Rozenblat, received Mr. Aurbach and ushered him to his seat in the first row.

Then Amtsleiter Biebow appeared with his staff: Messrs. [Friedrich Wilhelm] Ribbe, [Albert] Meyer, and [Franz] Seifert. They entered through the stage door of the House of Culture. Upon taking the stage, the Amtsleiter immediately invited the representative of the criminal police to be seated on the stage and then began his remarks. He spoke for about an hour and a half.

Despite the severity of his remarks, the basic tone was benevolent. The Amtsleiter acknowledged the meritorious services of the Eldest of the Jews, Chaim Rumkowski, and praised certain factories. He delimited the jurisdictions of the Eldest; of [Aron] Jakubowicz, Director of the Central Workshop Bureau; and of [Marek] Kligier, chief of the Special Department. He touched on a wide variety of topics in no particular order (understandably, given the way things work in the ghetto), censuring certain abuses and praising what seemed in his opinion praiseworthy. Then he addressed the main theme of his speech, the new regulations concerning food allotments.

After a rather graphic description of the difficulties of procuring food, he sketched out his new plan: those who work at least 55 hours a week will be accorded special privileges as "long-shift workers" and recieve the designation L [Langarbeiter] on their work cards. Thereby, explained the Amtsleiter, he has declared war on those in the ghetto who play the role of drones; in the future, only the truly productive will enjoy better rations. He gave the managers strict instructions on the drawing up of the L-lists and threatened the death penalty for any abuse. Finally, he observed that, although the coupon system has definitely been abolished, three offices will nevertheless be entitled to dispense coupons: (1) the Eldest of the Jews; (2) Jakubowicz and Dr. [Wiktor] Miller; and (3) Kligier, chief of the Special Department. He read the text of his announcement of November 7, 1943, and repeated that he had appointed a board composed of Kligier, Dr. Miller, and [Zygmunt] Reingold to handle all problems of food and nutrition.

Since the Amtsleiter prohibited a precise stenographic notation of his speech, no verbatim transcript exists. A reconstruction from memory by a representative of the Archives who was present is appended to today's daily report.

The Amtsleiter's speech is very likely to continue to be the subject of discussion in the coming days, and plant managers will have every reason to pay close attention to the instructions and criticisms that he delivered.

In general it can be said that, above all, the Amtsleiter strengthened the position of the Chairman—which was quite a surprise, given the events of November 7. One awkward point was the Amtsleiter's language in regard to the jurisdiction of the chief of the Order Service. Here we refer the reader to the text of the reconstruction.[45]

A final note: At the close of his remarks, the Amtsleiter announced a special ration consisting of 200 grams of flour, 100 grams of curds, one kilogram of radishes, one kilogram of carrots, four kilograms of turnips, and one can of meat.

THURSDAY, DECEMBER 9, 1943

WORKSHOP NEWS: EMERGENCY HOUSING FOR THE SPEER MINISTRY

As we reported at the time, it was originally planned that the ghetto manufacture complete temporary houses for families left homeless by bombings. Then we were told that the plan had been dropped. Now, however, this project appears to have been revived.[46]

Today, a conference of all ghetto carpentry factories took place in the shop at 12 Dworska Street. The Ghetto Administration intends to manufacture the doors and windows for these temporary houses as well. To deal with the technical problems, the carpentry factories have resolved to work out a production plan and submit it to the Ghetto Administration via [Aron] Jakubowicz's office. It turns out that the wood factories are in fact capable of taking on these projects.

The managers of the carpentry shops agreed that the shop on Urzędnicza Street (Division 2) would manufacture the exterior doors; the wood plant on Pucka Street, the two interior doors; and [Leon] Winograd's plant, the windows.

If this plan is approved, the ghetto could expect an extraordinarily large order, which would guarantee work for many months.

FRIDAY, DECEMBER 10, 1943

SKETCHES OF GHETTO LIFE

It is turnip time in the ghetto. As important as this vegetable may be, and as happy as people are that even this cattle fodder is available, one should nevertheless look this gift horse in the mouth.

---

45. In the reconstruction of Hans Biebow's very long and verbose speech, the "awkward point" actually refers to the fact that the jurisdiction of the chief of the Order Service, Leon Rozenblat, was not discussed separately, as were those of Rumkowski, Jakubowicz, and Kligier, but merely mentioned, without names, as follows: "Finally, the Eldest of the Jews is responsible for maintaining calm and order in the ghetto with the aid of the Order Service."

46. The following is a fragment on the subject of temporary houses from the speech by Hans Biebow: "We will now need five thousand workers for the project that has been assigned to us through the [Albert] Speer ministry. [Speer was Minister of Armaments and chief of the *Organization Todt*.] Our factories will have to manufacture the hecalite panels required for these temporary houses. . . . But it will have to be five thousand healthy and able-bodied workers so that we do not deliver the work-equivalent of only four thousand workers. (In this regard, the Amtsleiter mentioned that the camp of 48,000 Jews at Terezín [Theresienstadt], had utterly failed to carry out the assignment, which could have been completed by 5,000, because of the ineptitude of its Jewish leaders)."

The scenes at the distribution centers are indescribable. People stand in endless lines for hours in the damp and the cold; it takes almost half a day to pick up the twenty-kilogram winter-reserve ration. Unique scenes are enacted at the gates of the vegetable storage yards; naturally, favoritism is in full flower there too. But anyone not fortunate enough to know the Order Service man on special duty can count on having his hat knocked off—at the very least—if he tries to circumvent the line.

It is grotesque and sad to see people dragging along their sacks of turnips—turnips already damaged by frost—because they have no vehicles at their disposal or because their backs can no longer bear the burden of twenty or forty kilograms. Naturally, the rotting sacks will not take such abuse, and everywhere one sees helpless people standing with shredded sacks, their turnips tumbling helter-skelter into the gutter.

Even when a man does have the strength to shoulder his twenty if not forty kilograms, the sack will often burst while he carries it. A fortunate few pull their hard-won booty over the bumpy pavement in retired baby carriages or other small wagons that look more like toys. Even these people need luck in order to get their burdens home in good condition, especially if, as often happens, one person is picking up the rations for an entire family of three, four, maybe five, persons. How to get a hundred kilograms home from the vegetable yard is truly an almost insoluble problem. One is tempted to say: *Timeo Danaos et dona ferentes* ["I fear the Greeks even bearing gifts."]

Dr. O[skar] S[inger]

TUESDAY, DECEMBER 14, 1943

NEWS OF THE DAY

A day of extreme agitation in the ghetto. The ghetto has not known such a grave hour since the days of the curfew [Gehsperre] in September of last year. Toward 11:30 A.M., a rumor spread through the ghetto like wildfire: the Chairman had been taken to the city by members of the Secret State Police [Gestapo]. The incident occurred as follows. Toward 9:30 A.M., an automobile of the Secret State Police arrived at Bałut Market from Poznań. Two men, one plainclothesman, the other in uniform, entered the Chairman's outer office and had themselves announced.

"Are you the Eldest of the Jews? . . . What is your name?"

The Chairman gave them his name, whereupon the men entered his office and said: "Let's talk in private." The two men who happened to be with the Chairman at the time, Mosze Karo and [Eliasz] Tabaksblat, immediately took their leave.

The meeting between the two officers and the Chairman lasted approximately two hours, with interruptions. The men also spent some time at the offices of the Ghetto Administration, and while they were gone Miss [Dora] Fuchs had to prepare certain statistical data. They also demanded population statistics from [Henryk] Neftalin, the attorney. Likewise, inquiries were made at the office of Kinstler ([Department of Food Supply,] Bałut Market). At 11:30 A.M., the Chairman left the ghetto in the direction of the city with the two men from the Secret State Police.

At first the ghetto did not quite grasp the meaning of this episode. It was only when the Chairman had still not returned by 7 P.M. that the ghetto heart began to pound.

Groups formed everywhere; people clustered in the offices, heatedly discussing the events. The ghetto's chief officials gathered at Bałut Market to wait for news. As always, the Chairman's droshky stood at Bałut Market and remained there until late at night, but still there was no report. Many were convinced that the Chairman had been taken to Poznań.

When leaving Bałut Market the Chairman just barely managed to say to Dr. [Wiktor] Miller, who happened to be present: "If anything happens, you should know that this concerns food supply problems, only food supply problems." The Chairman was very composed. In these difficult hours everyone recalled the Gertler affair, but the difference between the two cases was obvious. Gertler had simply been a very popular personality in the ghetto; but this incident, as everyone without exception realized, concerned the father of the ghetto. Fear was in everyone's bones, and never before had people felt so deeply the undeniable fact that "Rumkowski is the ghetto." Those who were particularly anxious foresaw disaster and said that the ghetto was in imminent danger. Hardly anyone slept peacefully tonight. People waited for the Chairman's return until 11 o'clock, but he did not appear. Further alarm was occasioned by the fact that the Amtsleiter was also summoned to the city and that there was no word from him either, even by late evening. Under the circumstances, it is assumed that the Chairman has indeed been taken to Poznań. All one can do is wait.

WEDNESDAY, DECEMBER 15, 1943

NEWS OF THE DAY

The Chairman returned to the ghetto from Litzmannstadt last night at 10:30. He came to Bałut Market by tram. The few people who learned of his arrival spread the news as fast as they could. In some buildings people ran from door to door, knocking and calling to the occupants: "The Chairman's back!" In the morning, when the whole ghetto knew that the Chairman had returned, everyone breathed a sigh of relief.

The Chairman was already at Bałut Market by 7 A.M. [He was] clearly tired and weary—he had, after all, gone to the city [the day before] without breakfast and had not eaten anything until late in the evening. Most of all, he had missed his beloved cigarettes, for he is a heavy smoker. During the morning, friends and associates visited him at Bałut Market to congratulate him on his return.

He refuses to discuss the purpose of the investigation. He only repeated his assurances that it had to do with food supply problems. He did relate a few details. When he was brought before the deputy chief of the [local] Secret State Police, the Chairman promptly identified himself as the Eldest of the Jews in Litzmannstadt. The official replied that since he had been brought in [for questioning], he did not have to identify himself as though he had come voluntarily. Rumkowski answered: "Well, since I *am* here, I have most obediently identified myself." With his characteristic resiliency he succeeded in improving the atmosphere by remarking in jest that this was his first day off from work in years. He was said to have been treated correctly; he was told that he bore full responsibility for everything that went on in the ghetto. Nothing more could be gotten out of the Chairman. Perhaps he was less reticent with

[Aron] Jakubowicz or [Marek] Kligier; others learned nothing about the reason for his summons.

In the course of the day, he received a great many managers.

It is typical of the Chairman's quite amazing vitality that, on his first day back, he intervened in the shoemakers' factory ([manager I.] Zonabend), where a small demonstration of the shoemakers, more or less resembling a strike, had been reported.

In the plant run by Gutreiman there had been an incident during which the latter had had three workers arrested. When Gutreiman entered [manager] Zonabend's factory, the shoemakers demonstrated against him and stopped work. The Chair appeared and, tackling the problem with his usual energy and confidence, gaᵛ shoemakers a few minutes to reconsider, and finally punished them by increasiₙₕ their work hours on that day—until nine in the evening.

A few minutes after the Chairman's intervention, members of the Ghetto Administration arrived at Zonabend's [plant]; by then the incident had already been resolved.

The ghetto has breathed a sigh of relief, particularly on account of the Chairman's reassuring statements. Whether he was simply putting minds at ease or further investigations are, in fact, to follow cannot be determined.[47]

A COMMISSION AT BAŁUT MARKET

The investigating commission that questioned the Chairman in the city arrived at Bałut Market this morning and took Kinstler, director of the purchasing office (Food [Supply Department]), and his ledgers to the city. Kinstler, who also does not know what this is all about, returned to the ghetto two hours later.

Amtsleiter [Biebow] is still at Bałut Market.

THURSDAY, DECEMBER 16, 1943

NEWS OF THE DAY

Although Bałut Market assures us that the incident of the 14th of this month is now settled, the investigation by the German authorities does not seem to be closed as yet. This is evident simply from the fact that Mr. [Henryk] Neftalin, the attorney, has ordered the Registration Bureau to stay on alert and is himself awaiting the arrival of a commission.

---

47. The chroniclers had no way of knowing why M. C. Rumkowski was suddenly summoned to the city, and Rumkowski was either himself unaware of the reason or preferred to keep it a secret, sharing it only with those closest to him. In fact, he was summoned in connection with the plans that the SS-Ostindustrie GmbH (Osti) had for the Łódź ghetto. Whether Eichmann and Horn were present when Rumkowski was questioned is not known. However, together with Bradfisch, the mayor and the chief of the Łódź Gestapo, they visited many workshops during the next two days, the 15th and 16th of December, with the ghetto's Department of Vital Statistics supplying them with information of every sort, as the Chronicle reports at once.

A COMMISSION IN THE GHETTO

Today, another relatively large inspection commission arrived in the ghetto and visited several factories. The popular conjecture that this commission is linked to the events of the past few days is incorrect.

FRIDAY, DECEMBER 17, 1943

NEWS OF THE DAY

It has been learned from Bałut Market that the investigating commission is still occupied with the current food supply question. Bałut Market is expecting the commission's arrival from the city. The Registration Bureau also remains on alert.

The ghetto is completely calm.

The Chairman assures us, as before, that this matter implies no danger whatsoever to the ghetto.

SUNDAY, DECEMBER 19, 1943

SKETCHES OF GHETTO LIFE: THROUGH THE LOOPHOLES OF THE LAW

If the ghetto had a newspaper, and if this newspaper had a column for court proceedings, then that column would be called "Larceny Trials." But since the ghetto must do without this literary diversion, as it does without many things, the daily chronicler is dependent on word of mouth and, if they are available, on the reports of the Order Service or the meager transcripts of the ghetto court.

It is not the official dossiers that arouse our sympathy, nor even the persons involved, the sad heroes of these court proceedings. What distinguishes the various cases beyond the banal category of "theft" is the situation in which the theft takes place. Generally, crime is more than a match for the technical prowess of the authorities, who must track down the facts and prove them with hard evidence. Mere circumstantial evidence, without a *corpus delicti*, carries little weight. In the great metropolises of the world, the police are usually a bit less cunning than the criminal element.

In the ghetto, crime is of a different nature. Here, under the pressure of circumstances, a system has developed that uses no violence, but only dodges, tricks, cunning. Ninety cases out of a hundred involve the theft of food—a crime of hunger. Sometimes these petty larcenies are so primitive that one is amazed at how little respect the thief has for the investigatory ability of the police. And sometimes the offense—making off with fallen potatoes, radishes, or other vegetables—occurs so openly, in full view of the street, that one can only call it indecent public behavior.

The scene of the "crime" is usually a vegetable or potato yard, not to mention the grocery stores, where one employee or another abuses his position by pilfering provisions: sugar, marmalade, etc. Here, no skill is required, merely a certain lack of inhibition.

At the yards, the procedure is different. The legitimate consumer shows up with his knapsack. His connection—a friend, a relative, a professional acquaintance—ensures him privileged treatment. A few extra *buraki* [beets] or kohlrabies, a few dozen extra potatoes, and he strolls off blissfully, after depriving the [vegetable] yards, that is, the ghetto, of this little extra and providing himself with a more generous ration. Even the sharpest supervision is useless, for the guardian of the law is himself the offender, the custodian is himself an accomplice.

More difficult are the cases of deceit or manipulation, which must be considered fraud. An example: a food voucher is received by an employee, and after the goods have been handed over, the voucher is invalidated by crumpling or tearing. What happens if the official inspector fails to invalidate the voucher or, in the press of business, leaves it with the customer by mistake? The customer can use the voucher again—no apparent irregularity, an undetected fraud. Such and similar cases have led to more rigorous inspections on all levels. To make any extra weight impossible, every sack and its contents are weighed a second time before the customer leaves the market; favoritism and swindling are to be stamped out once and for all.

But here, too, the wiliness of the hungry ghetto dweller finds a way. En route from the scale to the exit he removes a potato (or whatever is in that day's ration) from the sack and conceals the item in his pocket. The inspector weighs the sack and notices that it is underweight: must be something wrong with the scale. Amends are then made to the "wronged" individual; the missing amount is replaced. [A useful dodge] until it too is exposed.

Over and over again, the arm of the law collides with the dire needs of the citizens. A petty larceny, a bit of fraud, a minor burglary—symptoms of unspeakable misery and of the mind searching for a way out! But since even the world of the ghetto rests on the foundations of the Torah—law and justice—the poor man must be found guilty. He resigns himself—until the next time.

On a single day, six cases of potato theft were reported by the Special Unit. Six cases, but at bottom, one motive: hunger! The Special Unit treats these cases as administrative matters, without a court of law—a swifter and less offensive procedure. The six suspects have used tricks, manual or mental dexterity, to misappropriate a few potatoes.

A man nearing sixty, sick and weak, his wife and four children victims of the September resettlement . . . an elderly woman, undernourished, feverish, consumptive . . . a widow, obviously suffering from erysipelas, in a ragged dress, looking after a starving child (on the day of her arrest, she and the child had had no hot food aside from the workshop soup) . . . an old man, decrepit, trembling, an image of woe—these four accused go free. No one wants to increase their misery. They are sent home. Aside from them, two young boys, parentless; they have prior records for stealing cabbage. They are sentenced to forty-eight hours detention.

So it goes at the Sonderkommando [Special Unit]. The Court is more severe, more faithful to the letter of the law. But life in the ghetto has no respect for either the police or the court. It makes its own laws, even if they lead to arrest or excrement-removal duty.

O[skar] R[osenfeld]

TUESDAY, DECEMBER 21, 1943

MORE TERRIBLE NEWS

The hospital on Dworska Street is in danger. An epidemic of typhus has broken out in the so-called Kripo Camp in Marysin (Camp for Polish Teen-agers),[48] and the German authorities are planning to send the afflicted children to the hospital for contagious diseases on Dworska Street, which will remain within the ghetto. A commission of German physicians and officials visited the hospital, where they were given a tour of the facilities by the Chairman, accompanied by Dr. [Wiktor] Miller. The commission decided that, as a start, one hundred beds are to be freed without delay for these Polish "Aryan" patients. Jewish physicians are now obliged to combat typhus imported into the ghetto from the camp for Poles. Understandably, the ghetto is in an uproar. By dint of great effort, the medical staff had succeeded in reducing the incidence of at least this one terrible disease to a minimum, and now the ghetto is faced with a virtual mass importation of typhus. Moreover, it is a foregone conclusion that a large number of Jewish patients will have to be discharged from the hospital in disorderly haste.

WEDNESDAY, DECEMBER 22, 1943

THE HOSPITAL ON DWORSKA STREET

Today, [Jewish] patients were discharged from the hospital on Dworska Street to vacate the beds required for the Polish children with typhus. Not all patients were discharged; to start with, only the incurably ill and those who, under the present [dire] circumstances, can be consigned to home care. For both groups, the move is a catastrophe. The severely tubercular were loaded together with other patients on open wagons and driven to their homes. Scantily dressed, many in only shirts and coats, they had to endure the cold and the rough jostling over bumps and bulges in the ghetto streets. Most of them came home to icy apartments, often lacking even a primitive stove or oven. Patients who were on the road to recovery and could look forward to restored health will now have little hope of progress. A few could not even be transferred to home care because their buildings had been demolished and had ended up as firewood at the coal storage yard. For such people, [Miss Rebeka] Wołków's secretariat had to be mobilized, so that this office too was suddenly burdened with new problems. The Department of Housing had to make rooms available for these patients, rooms in which the seriously ill were provisionally bedded on excelsior mattresses on the floor. If the evacuees from the hospital had relatives who could provide them with some care, they were somehow accommodated in their dreary apartments. Unfortunately, patients without families, however, face certain death unless emergency relief is provided. As always in such cases, the Chairman is devoting his full energy to arranging prompt assistance. We understand that he has resolved to adapt the former Rest Home on Gnieźnieńska Street for use as a hospital.

48. Cf. n. 112 above.

This decision will supersede plans to convert the facility into a home for workers without families. Since, of course, the patients were removed from the hospital with nothing more than certificates of release, their relatives are now busy attending to the necessary formalities at the Department of Ration Cards and the Registration Bureau. Most of these relatives are themselves ill and weak and are suffering greatly because of the precipitous evacuation measure.

The first Polish children will, in all likelihood, be transferred to the hospital tomorrow.

THURSDAY, DECEMBER 23, 1943

SKETCHES OF GHETTO LIFE: IT IS WINTER

The fifth winter of war in Poland, the fourth in the ghetto. . . . People exchange reminiscences, punctuating them with the exclamation: "Of course, back then. . . !"

Back then things were different, better. Memory gilds the past. In the ghetto's fourth winter we face the same problems as back then! The main worry: fuel. Most ghetto dwellers say that they would rather starve than freeze. Freezing, they say, is a terrible thing. So people prefer to trade any and all necessities for fuel rather than freeze.

A kilogram of wood costs one mark, a kilogram of briquettes, five marks; coal cannot be found even on the black market. It should be mentioned that the majority of households must make do with a single stove that functions for both cooking and heating. This makes it easier to manage resources.

At all hours, one sees people—men, women, children, the aged—carrying an odd assortment of poles, laths, beams, boards, window frames, broken chairs, or dismantled cabinets in sacks and bundles. All this is wood! The word "wood" is easy to say, but to turn rotting materials from demolished buildings into wood—fuel—is no easy task.

Three kilograms of wood was the ration for the month of December. For the entire ghetto, this amounts to three times 80,000 or roughly 250,000 kilograms of wood. In addition, there is a legacy from the month of November for a few thousand privileged individuals: ten kilograms of roofing paper each. The rotting laths and the tarred roofing paper come from the gabled houses throughout the ghetto that were torn down. But even those houses that are still standing stare up at the bleak winter sky with dark window cavities, their roofs gone.

Poverty devours anything: frozen potatoes, rotting rutabagas, foul-smelling salatka; and the doors, windows, and roofs of entire rows of houses find their way into small iron stoves in the freezing rooms of 80,000 ghetto citizens. . . .

O[skar] R[osenfeld]

SATURDAY, DECEMBER 25, 1943

SKETCHES OF GHETTO LIFE: CHANUKAH IN THE GHETTO, 1943

"The living faith has vanished. . . . All that remains is poetry!" A superficial observer of life in the ghetto might come to more or less the same conclusion about the way religious festivals are celebrated here. The ardor of prayer seems to have yielded to ritual, to a practice that feigns devotion, traces of which have survived only among the old and the pious. As any unbiased Jew will acknowledge, however, the symbols of the festivals remain intact, embedded in tradition, and neither hunger nor cold can claim them.

The difficulty in yielding to the enchantment of religious practice is due, first of all, to a lack of suitable space. The *besmedresh* [prayer and study house] is closed. There are only a very few minyonim holding worship service here and there in a secret shul.

Chanukah, of course, does not require such houses of worship. In the ghetto, Chanukah is a family holiday, as it used to be throughout Eastern Europe before the war. It does not have to be performed on an official stage. A Jew who really wishes to commemorate the Maccabees in traditional fashion stages the festival at home.

In the street, a creature wrapped in rags huddles on dirty steps by a broken door. You can just about make out a face through the rags. The creature is hawking candles [in Yiddish]: "Lekht! Lekht!" Normally, these are the Sabbath candles that are peddled every week on Sabbath eve. This time they are intended for something else, something rarer: candles for the menorah.

Not everyone can afford to allow his menorah its full glory. An additional candle every day, until all eight arms of the menorah are lighted, that means thirty-six candles; counting the candle for lighting the others, the *shames* [sexton], thirty-seven. Or, in terms of money, a minimum of eighteen marks, since each candle costs fifty pfennigs. Indeed, there are families that can even afford to treat themselves to candles of the one-for-a-mark variety, and thus pay thirty-six marks for "mere lighting."

And yet, despite the problems of space and finances, Chanukah was celebrated with dignity this year too.

A great number of families lighted candles. Along with the sforim [religious books], makhzoyrim [prayer books for holidays], sidurim [daily prayer books], taleysim [prayer shawls], and tfiln [phylacteries], the man of the house had brought the menorah from the city—rescued it, smuggled it—into the ghetto. One sees simple menorahs of brass or cast iron, but also copper and nickel menorahs, old ones, new ones, factory-made or hand-crafted, free-standing menorahs, or those that are hung on walls. People invite friends and acquaintances. The guests clamber up dark staircases, through dank courtyards and hallways, into an apartment—usually just one room that doubles as living quarters and "best room" for special occasions.

Many people dress for the holiday. Everyone is in a holiday mood. One privileged person, often the daughter of the house, sings the benediction before the lighting of candles. It often happens that Jews brought here from the [western Polish] provinces and Jews from the German west find themselves together in one such room and share in the festival. The candles are bright. Memories of previous Chanukah evenings pass through the mind. Memories of youth, of student days, of happy years in freedom, images and impressions somehow connected with the festival of the Maccabees.

People assemble "in private," without official ritual, with only a lighted menorah. Children too celebrate Chanukah. There are gatherings in larger apartments. Everyone brings a small, appropriate gift: a toy, a piece of *babka* [cake], a hair ribbon, a couple of brightly colored empty cigarette packages, a plate with a flower pattern, a pair of stockings, a warm cap. Then comes the drawing of lots; and chance decides.

After the candles are lighted, the presents are handed out. Ghetto presents are not valuable, but they are received with deep gratitude. Finally, songs are sung in Yiddish, Hebrew, and Polish, as long as they are suitable for enhancing the holiday mood. A few hours of merrymaking, a few hours of forgetting, a few hours of reverie. . . . Let the Chanukah celebration of 1943 be the last Chanukah of the war, the last Chanukah in the ghetto. This is everyone's hope. This is what people wish each other when they part—without a word, mutely, with only a handshake.

The menorah candles burn down. It grows dark again. People step out into the street. Ghetto life resumes.

Dr. O[skar][49]

SUNDAY, DECEMBER 26, 1943

SKETCHES OF GHETTO LIFE: A BOWL OF SOUP

When something breaks down in the ghetto, it takes a great deal of time and effort to get it working again. "It's a wreck," goes the popular expression. But no one gets too worried about it. The *reboyne sheloylem* [the Almighty] will help us out. . . .

Say there's no water in the pipes. A water shortage exacerbates the misery of being in the ghetto. You do what you have to, you go to the well.

But since all the tenants need water at the same time, as do our dear neighbors, a *kolejka* [line] forms at once.

Meanwhile, specialists are called in to fix the water pump after the janitor's skill has failed.

Two strapping youths arrive. They examine and study the problem, and then tackle it. Soon you hear the snort of the motor, a noise that heralds the approach of water. A deceptive hope! There are a few drops in the pipe—[and then] the dream is over. The boys have left the scene.

This game is repeated for several days. Is the repair work really so difficult, or is there some other reason for the delay?

Then we learn that a workshop soup kitchen nearby uses the same water pipes. Naturally, our "hydraulics experts" are aware of this. And since they always receive a good gedakhte [thick] soup gratis whenever they come to do the repairs, they are not in any hurry. Every day, a bit of fixing; every day, a bowl of soup. . . .

That's the ghetto. People will take a job for a bowl of soup and walk out on it for another bowl of soup.

O[skar] R[osenfeld]

TUESDAY, DECEMBER 28, 1943

HEALTH

Two hundred juvenile patients from the Polish camp in Marysin are already in the hospital on Dworska Street.

---

49. The initials used to sign the essay "Chanukah in the Ghetto, 1943" are not legible. Most likely the letter "O" is followed by an "S"[inger].

There is now one more case of typhus in the ghetto, which makes a total of five cases among Jews.

Among the Polish patients are, of course, all the febrile cases from the Kripo camp; thus, patients with pleurisy and tuberculosis are also present.

The work of setting up the new hospital on Gnieźnieńska Street is proceeding rapidly. The Department of Health hopes that the hospital can open its doors next week.

At the gates of the ghetto.

Deportations into and out of the ghetto, 1941–42. Photographer: M. Grossman.

Deportees passing the ruins of the Old City Synagogue on Wołborska Street.

Deportations into and out of the ghetto, 1941–42. Photographer: M. Grossman.

Deportations into and out of the ghetto, 1941–42. Photographer: M. Grossman.

Deportees from Vienna.

Deportations into and out of the ghetto, 1941–42. Photographer: M. Grossman.

Deportations into and out of the ghetto, 1941–42. Photographer: M. Grossman.

eportation of children during the *Gehsperre* (curfew action) in September, 1942. Photographer: M. Grossman.

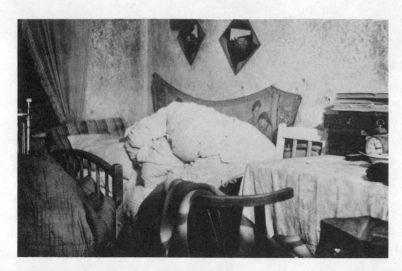

An empty apartment after the deportatio

The Most Blessed Virgin Mary Church,
where down and feathers confiscated from
the deported Jews were sorted and
shipped to Germany. Photographer: M.
Grossman.

Phylacteries sent to the ghetto to be used to make leather accessories. Photographer: M. Grossman.

Bekanntmachung Nr. 429.

Betr.: Verkleinerung des Gettos.

Sämtliche Gebiete des Gettos mit Ausnahme der tieferstehend bezeichneten sind mit sofortiger Wirkung

bis spätestens 25. August 1944, 7 Uhr früh

restlos zu räumen.

Die in den gesperrten Gebieten wohnenden Personen haben ihre Wohnungen bis zum genannten Termin zu verlassen und dürfen die geräumten Gebiete

NICHT MEHR BETRETEN.

Wer dieser Aufforderung nicht Folge leistet und am Freitag, den 25. August 1944, nach 7 Uhr früh, in den gesperrten Gebieten angetroffen wird, wird

mit dem Tode bestraft.

Als Wohngebiet der Juden verbleibt allein das Gebiet begrenzt:

im Westen längs der Hanseatenstrasse von Nr. 1 — Nr. 27 also von der Ecke Sulzfelder—Hanseatenstrasse bis zur Ecke Hanseaten—Matrosengasse

im Norden längs der Matrosengasse von Nr. 1/3 — Nr. 53 also von der Ecke Hanseaten—Matrosengasse bis zur Ecke Matrosen—Siegfriedstrasse

im Osten längs der Siegfriedstrasse von Nr. 8 — Nr. 30 also von der Ecke Sulzfelder—Siegfriedstrasse bis zur Ecke Siegfried—Matrosengasse

im Süden längs der Sulzfelderstrasse von Nr. 2 — Nr. 68 also von der Ecke Hanseaten—Sulzfelderstrasse bis zur Ecke Sulzfelder-Siegfriedstrasse,

Zur besonderen Beachtung:

In den gesperrten Gebieten verbleiben:

1.) die kasernierten Betriebe,
2.) Krankenhäuser,
3.) das Zentralgefängnis,
4.) die IV. 0. 0.-Abteilung in Marysin.

GEHEIME STAATSPOLIZEI.

Litzmannstadt,
d. 23. 8. 1944.

Bekanntmachung Nr. 418.

Betr.: Verlagerung des Gettos.

Da die Betriebe I und II

(Schneiderei, Hanseatenstr. 34/36 und Hanseatenstr. 45)

der Aufforderung Nr. 417 v. 2.8.44. bezgl. Verlagerung des Gettos nicht Folge geleistet haben, wurde mit sofortiger Wirkung folgendes angeordnet:

1.) Die Lebensmittelzuteilungen für die Angehörigen der Schneidereibetriebe I und II werden

mit sofortiger Wirkung gesperrt.

Die Ausgabe der Lebensmittel an die Angehörigen dieser Betriebe erfolgt nur auf dem Bahnhof Radegast.

2.) Wer einen Angehörigen der Schneiderei I und II bei sich beherbergt, versteckt oder verpflegt,

wird mit dem Tode bestraft.

gez.: Der Oberbürgermeister von Litzmannstadt.

Litzmannstadt, den 4. August 1944.

Orders issued by the mayor of the city and the Gestapo during final liquidation of the ghetto of Łódź. They warn that noncompliance is punishable by death

At the ghetto railroad station in Marysin, August, 1944.

PART IV: 1944

SATURDAY, JANUARY 1, 1944

NEWS OF THE DAY

Today at 10 A.M., in the former sanatorium at 55 Łagiewnicka Street, the Chairman celebrated the Bar Mitzvah of his legally adopted son Stanisław Stein. Some thirty persons close to the Chairman were invited. The *bokher* [boy] recited the *haftarah* [concluding portion from the Prophets, recited after the Torah Service] using Sephardic pronunciation. The Chairman had arranged for the boy to receive a complete Jewish education in the course of the year.

Mosze Karo addressed the assembled company at a modest reception. The ladies present were Regina Rumkowska, Mrs. [Aron] Jakubowicz, and Miss [Dora] Fuchs.

The Chairman, gracious as always to his guests, created a warm and intimate atmosphere despite the frugality of the meal.

MONDAY, JANUARY 3, 1944

NEWS OF THE DAY

Today, the ghetto again suffered a severe shock. In the evening a rumor circulated that the Chairman had once again been taken to the city by Gestapo officers. We have learned the following details: between five and six an automobile of the Secret State Police appeared with a Gestapo officer and a member of the Ghetto Administration [at Bałut Market]. The two men proceeded to Amtsleiter Biebow's office, whereupon the Chairman was summoned. The officer asked the Chairman several questions about food distribution and demanded to see records. Accordingly, the Chairman immediately proceeded to the Department of Food Supply and returned with Commander [Zygmunt] Reingold, who brought along all the required documents. Reingold was questioned briefly and then dismissed, with his papers and ledgers. Immediately thereafter the Chairman was driven to the city.

Understandably, the ghetto was in turmoil once again. It was the Chairman's second trip to the Secret State Police within a short period. The matter had to be serious. People recalled certain statements the Chairman had made in his most recent speech, on the 30th of last month. On that occasion he had remarked in a general way that one must be prepared to atone even for the sins of others and that, in a position such as his, one must be ready to sacrifice one's life at any time. In making these remarks, he had perhaps been thinking of the fact that the matter pending has still not been settled. There was conjecture that the Chairman's statements after his first interrogation had all been designed merely to set minds at ease. Indeed, he had offered no specific information at all since, as a matter of principle, he observes a rigorous silence on the subject of negotiations with or interrogations by the authorities. Nothing can be gotten out of him; thus, the ghetto is extremely apprehensive about the outcome of this incident. It is hardly likely that the Chairman will return from Litzmannstadt today. One can only hope that this man, who has never panicked in a difficult hour, will not lose his composure this time either.

TUESDAY, JANUARY 4, 1944

NEWS OF THE DAY

After nearly unbearable suspense and agitation about the Chairman's fate, the ghetto finally learned that the Eldest had returned at four in the afternoon. A police car brought him from the city to Precinct VI, from which he proceeded on foot to Bałut Market.[1] News of his return spread through the ghetto like wildfire. Groups formed everywhere, discussing his safe return; in apartment houses people ran from door to door to spread the good news.

The first person to greet the Chairman upon his arrival was his brother, Józef Rumkowski; the two men immediately proceeded to the Chairman's private apartment. The Chairman received no visitors on this day. The ghetto is happy to have him back.

The Chairman has not disclosed his thoughts even to his closest colleagues. As before, he is maintaining absolute silence about the purpose of the interrogation. He reports that he was treated correctly this time too and that he refused the food that was offered him.

FOOD SUPPLY

The ghetto has received 3,270 onions—the first in a very long time. It is hoped that more onions will be coming in and that the populace will receive a small ration. Also, about 7,000 kilograms of curds have arrived; unfortunately, only 17,660 kilograms of potatoes have come in, but on the other hand, 1,000 kilograms of fat—margarine [—have arrived].

LOTTERIES

The health insurance committees in a number of workshops are resorting to a time-tested prewar method to fill their treasuries: they are raffling off prizes. Ticket vendors from these health insurance committees are showing up in offices everywhere, offering chances for two marks each.

SATURDAY, JANUARY 8, 1944

NEWS OF THE DAY

Yesterday, Dr. Bradfisch, mayor and commander-in-chief of the Gestapo, visited the ghetto. He spent roughly an hour at Bałut Market. Immediately thereafter a new proclamation concerning the mandatory salute was posted. Apparently the mayor had ascertained that people were not saluting cars that drive through the ghetto, as regulation prescribes. The text of the proclamation is as follows:

---

1. Precinct VI of the German police force, assigned to the ghetto, was located across from Bałut Market, at the corner of Limanowski and Zgierska streets, in an enclave separated from the ghetto.

Proclamation No. 406

Re: Obligation to Salute All Uniformed Persons and German Officials (Civilians).

Citing my memorandum of June 3, 1942, and the memorandum, addressed to all departments, workshops, and factories, of June 16, 1942, I again emphatically point out that all ghetto inhabitants (male and female) must unconditionally and unprompted salute all uniformed personnel and all German officials (civilians) in the street as well as in the workshops and factories.

It makes no difference whatsoever whether the uniformed personnel or German civilians are in the ghetto on foot or in an auto.

There thus exists a rigorous obligation to salute. Failure to observe this order will result in extremely severe penalties.

At inspections of departments, workshops, and factories, [by Germans both from outside] and from the Ghetto Administration, everyone must rise from his seat at the command, "Achtung!" [Attention!].

When all the visitors have entered, work will continue, after the same person who called "Achtung!" has ordered, "Weiterarbeiten!" [Continue work!]

The manager of each workshop must delegate a specific individual to call out the above orders, "Achtung" and "Weiterarbeiten," at every inspection or visit.

Litzmannstadt, 6 January 1944
Ch[aim] Rumkowski

Amtsleiter Biebow has still not returned from his winter vacation; this fact has been noted by the populace and is causing uneasiness.

SUNDAY, JANUARY 9, 1944

NEWS OF THE DAY

The Chairman married seven couples in Marysin today.

Incident at the Barbed-Wire Fence

Today, a little before 6:30 P.M., Mojsze Najman, born June 24, 1911, in Bełchatów, was shot and killed beside the barbed-wire fence near the boot workshop. The victim collapsed from two severe bullet wounds about two and a half meters from the fence and died about an hour later. Najman had been evacuated to a labor camp in Germany approximately two years ago and had returned here in June, 1943. Since he had dealt in coal before the war, the Chairman assigned him to work in the Coal Department. The man was very weak, however, and not even the *kolacjas* [evening meals] he was allowed could put him back on his feet. Last year, when the returnees from labor camps were again concentrated in Central Prison, Najman went into hiding for many weeks. Friends collected bread for him. When the [arrest] operation ended, the Chairman obtained his definitive release from Central Prison, to which he had finally reported. Najman seemed utterly apathetic and demoralized, and all efforts by the Coal Department to make him fit to work again were in vain. The Kripo inspected the scene of the shooting, as did [R.] Rybowski, the head of the Jewish [Order Service] section at the Kripo. Recently, Najman had been living at the home for workers without families in Marysin. It is still unclear what he was doing at the fence and how he came to be shot by an officer of the Schupo.

MONDAY, JANUARY 10, 1944

NEWS OF THE DAY

The ghetto is somewhat alarmed by the fact that the Department of Vital Statistics has requested all workshops and departments to immediately provide a list of the workers, male and female, and of the juveniles under fourteen, male and female, whom they employ. A further cause of alarm is the request made by the Trade and Inspection Section that every workshop and department turn in a list of workers who have reported sick since December 27, 1943.

The purpose of the former statistical survey is unknown. It is known only that the order came from the German authorities (Poznań). The deputy of the Amtsleiter [Biebow], Mr. [F. W.] Ribbe, happened to be in the Construction Department when he received a telephone call from Poznań on this matter, which is undoubtedly connected with the new food supply policy.

As for the second statistical survey, concerning the period since December 27, 1943, this is an internal ghetto measure. From all appearances, the Eldest intends to put an end to the excessive granting of sick leave by physicians that now prevails. It is claimed that four physicians have exceeded their authority. Whether the claim is, in fact, true cannot at the moment be established with complete certainty. What is certain, however, is that an influenza epidemic is raging in the ghetto, and that this is undoubtedly why so many persons have been excused from work.

COD-LIVER OIL

The ghetto has received a rather large amount of cod-liver oil, the first such shipment in a long time. Allotments will be made on the basis of a physician's certificate and the requisite approval by the Chairman.

Vigantol today costs 75 marks for 10 cubic centimeters.

TUESDAY, JANUARY 11, 1944

PEOPLE ARE SAYING . . .

It has now been learned in the ghetto that there is a discrepancy of roughly 3000 between the official population figure and the actual number of food cards issued to the populace by the Department of Ration Cards. The discrepancy was caused by the chaotic conditions after the resettlement in September of 1942. The error went undetected until the new cards were issued.

The *Chronicle* refrained from mentioning this fact at the time. But now, after the Chairman has been twice interrogated in the city, the secret, this incongruity in the official population statistics, seems to have leaked; and there is some talk that the ghetto will have to make good the unlawfully obtained food or else suffer cuts in rations until it has compensated for the illegitimate surplus.

It is said that the problem will be resolved by a 7 percent reduction in the food quota for the ghetto; that would entail a 7 percent cut in rations. In any case, it is not yet certain that the authorities are demanding such compensation or that such reductions will actually occur.

WEDNESDAY, JANUARY 12, 1944

NEWS OF THE DAY

The announced SS commission has not arrived. There are now reports that it will not appear until tomorrow, the 13th. A trade commission, however, did arrive here and conducted negotiations at Bałut Market.

Amtsleiter Biebow returned to Litzmannstadt today after a lengthy vacation and communicated with Bałut Market by telephone. Tomorrow he will be back in his office at Bałut Market.

The Registration Bureau and the Ration Card Department, under the supervision of Mr. [Henryk] Neftalin, the attorney, are checking carefully through the files for birth dates in the years 1934 and 1935. Children who have till now been lodged in children's homes, and have reached the age of nine, have been assigned to production in various factories.

THURSDAY, JANUARY 13, 1944

MISCELLANEOUS

On January 12, Josek Sandberg, born October 10, 1896, in Wrzeszczewice, and residing at 36 Franciszkańska Street, committed suicide by jumping from the fifth floor of his apartment house. He was pronounced dead by the Emergency Service physician.

NEWS OF THE DAY

Amtsleiter Biebow arrived in the ghetto today and immediately resumed his duties at the office. He had lengthy conferences with the Chairman and with Aron Jakubowicz, and he instructed the Eldest to provide him immediately with various statistical surveys. The Chairman assigned the preparation of these surveys, which concern production, to the Trade Inspection Section.

A commission of two men has arrived in the ghetto. No information can be obtained about the purpose or nature of this commission. It has been observed only that a certain nervous atmosphere prevails at Bałut Market.

SKETCHES OF GHETTO LIFE: INFLUENZA EPIDEMIC

There is no respite in the sufferings of the ghetto dweller. The summer brought typhoid fever; the fall, tuberculosis—both with fatal results; and now the winter of 1944 has arrived with a flu epidemic.

There is nothing typical of the ghetto in the symptoms of this illness. Basically, influenza is an infection caused by inclement weather. The number of new cases drops when the weather is good. The infective agent has not been isolated bacteriologically in most cases, but it is certain that an influenza bacillus is involved. The first stage of the illness is marked by high fever, up to 40 degrees Celsius; after two days the fever drops, and other symptoms appear, such as weakness, coughing, and lack of appetite. Usually, there is a bronchial catarrh, which is very violent at first but soon disappears.

For the time being, the first week of January, the flu is not, in general, a cause for alarm. Most cases run a normal course and soon clear up completely. Complications are very rare. Often a patient is well again before a physician has had time to examine him and make a diagnosis. Patients recover even under the most unfavorable conditions. Of course, malnutrition, defective footwear, the lack of necessary fuel, unhygienic apartments, and the unavailability of common medications or any sort of nursing always make illnesses in the ghetto a dangerous matter.

The doctors say: Most of the time we prescribe mixtum rectoralis as well as azetynil tablets (a kind of aspirin) for fever, aching limbs, and headache. We have no other drugs.

The pharmacists say: We deal with the flu epidemic by keeping a ready supply of medications for the patients: bottles of expectorant and anti-fever tablets. As for other drugs, insofar as any are available, patients have to wait at least two days because of the mass of prescriptions.

The Department of Health says: We have issued a memorandum to physicians pointing out that the pharmacies are overburdened and their supplies inadequate. At the same time, we have recommended that doctors prescribe only medications which will be of direct aid.

Since the doctors practicing in outpatient clinics cannot make all the house calls necessary, we have delegated a considerable number of workshop physicians to take over many of these calls. Each clinic physician or workshop physician must make up to ten house calls a day. We hope that with this measure we have done everything possible for the care of flu patients and for the successful containment of the epidemic.

The hospital says: The flu epidemic barely affects us, since only severe cases involving pneumonia or other complications are admitted.

Experience says: According to the statistics on cases reported officially, nearly forty percent of the ghetto populace has fallen ill. Not all cases, however, come to the attention of a physician or clinic. Many patients are not bedridden and are going to work.

O[skar] R[osenfeld]

GAS KITCHENS CLOSED

The tragedy is reaching its climax. The Department of Gas Kitchens has been notified that the public facilities for gas cooking are to be shut down immediately.

In view of [today's] suspension of coal distribution and the situation on the private fuel market, this is probably the worst blow that the ghetto populace could suffer right now. The gas kitchen points provided the only possibility of preparing food or beverages (coffee) without having to buy expensive fuel. To cook with gas there for an hour cost thirty pfennigs; and hot [ersatz] coffee and hot water were for sale at ten pfennigs a liter. One can scarcely imagine what the populace will do now. The few turnips still available for cooking have to be boiled twice in order to remove this animal fodder's pungent odor. This was feasible as long as people could do so at a gas kitchen or buy hot water there. Now there will begin a desperate struggle to find ways of cooking the few remaining turnips. The situation is hopeless—utterly catastrophic. No one knows at the moment whether the closing of the gas kitchens is permanent or temporary. The situation seems to indicate a permanent shutdown.

TRAM RIDING PROHIBITED

Jobean news is raining down hard and fast. The Department of Transportation was notified by the Chairman today that an official order now strictly prohibits the use of ghetto trams by private individuals. This means that workers and employees with jobs in Marysin will have to walk there, and that residents of Marysin will likewise have to make the long trip to the ghetto center on foot.

Considering the present thaw, which has partially flooded the streets, and the footgear of ghetto dwellers, which is not equal to even the slightest abuse, this prohibition too is a genuine calamity.

SATURDAY, JANUARY 15, 1944

SKETCHES OF GHETTO LIFE: THE PRIVILEGED CATS

One of the peculiarities of the Litzmannstadt ghetto is the absence of any pets. The horses one encounters in the streets do not support the contention that man and beast constitute a social unity, in the sense of a normal communal existence. Even man's best friend, the dog, is gone. Only sparrows and jackdaws give the ghetto dweller the illusion that there is such a thing as the animal kingdom.

And yet, even in this respect, the ghetto has its "specialty": a very few persons have the right to keep a *cat*. These are the managers of specific grocery shops, the so-called food distribution points.

In these shops the cats pursue their naturally ordained task of destroying mice. The chronicler has neglected to mention that there are mice here in great numbers, chiefly in places where food is stored. They chew up the sacks of flour, [rye] flakes, peas, and so forth; they get into the containers of marmalade, sugar, bread.

To ward off this danger, to destroy the mice—this is the job of the cats. They too have to demonstrate *produktsye* [productivity], like all ghetto residents. In return, they receive their allotment: one kilogram of meat per week—good, fresh, wholesome meat.

The employees in these shops envy the privileged cats, and rightly so. For the past week, since the beginning of January, no meat has been reaching the ghetto, and the residents sorely miss this special-nutrition dish.

But now there is no meat for the good little cats either. Their heads droop, their tails drag sadly. A pitiful sight. The cats accept no other food; they are slowly perishing.

They spurn the ghetto dweller's diet—turnips, radishes, or soup. Truly deplorable. Even they, the privileged creatures, must now know misery and the grim reality of life. In January, 1944, they too must share the fate of the ghetto's masses and starve along with them. All are equal before the law of the ghetto, man and beast. Eating one's fill is not the norm, but the exception. Remember that, O cat in the food shop!

O[skar] R[osenfeld]

MONDAY, JANUARY 17, 1944

NEWS OF THE DAY

The commission is still in the ghetto. The mood here has improved somewhat, but the tension remains.

Obligatory Registration Of Musical Instruments
Today the Eldest of the Jews issued an announcement making it obligatory to register all musical instruments. The text reads as follows:

Public Notice!
Re: Obligatory Registration Of All Musical Instruments.

By order of the authorities, I hereby call upon the populace of the ghetto to surrender all musical instruments in its possession at the secretariat of the Chairman, 1 Dworska Street.

The registration of such musical instruments must take place between Tuesday, January 18 and Friday, January 21, 1944, at the latest. On these days, the above-mentioned secretariat will be open for registration between the hours of 8 A.M. and 8 P.M.

The registration of musical instruments is an unconditional obligation.

Litzmannstadt-Getto, January 17, 1944
Ch[aim] Rumkowski
The Eldest of the Jews in Litzmannstadt

For once, a measure not aimed at the stomach of the ghetto dweller, but no less severe on that account. We have often reported that the culture-starved ghetto maintains a musical life on a modest scale in small private circles. Now this last vestige of that happiness is to vanish. One can readily imagine what it means for a professional musician, a virtuoso, even a dilettante, to be forced to give up his beloved violin; and the ghetto has a number of high-ranking violin virtuosos. We mention here only Miss [Bronisława] Rotsztat and the Prague violinists, [Anton] Kraft and Weinbaum. The few homes still possessing an upright or rickety grand piano, which consecrated them as temples of art, will now be desolate again. Beethoven, Mozart, Chopin, Schumann, will fall silent in the ghetto forever. The street will notice nothing; harsh life will go on; and to the torments of hunger and cold will be added the unappeased craving for music.

THURSDAY, JANUARY 20, 1944

NEWS OF THE DAY

Today, another small commission arrived in the ghetto.

The Chairman is not feeling well, he has a cold; but he is, nevertheless, in his office at Bałut Market.

We have been informed by Bałut Market that three executive members of the Ghetto Administration are leaving office in order to fulfill their military obligations. The men in question are: Deputy Amtsleiter [F. W.] Ribbe, Charnulla, and [Franz] Seifert.

Rumor has it that the Bank of the Eldest on Ciesielska Street is to be liquidated.

The property at 77 Drewnowska Street, where the hospital for contagious diseases was located until the ghetto was sealed off [on May 1, 1940], and where the Low-Voltage Equipment Department now operates, is to be separated from the ghetto and used as a German hospital.

Anna Mandelik, resettled here from Prague, has been missing since Monday, the 17th of this month. Her husband is ill and bedridden. The police are searching for the missing woman. The following has been learned about the matter: some time ago, Manuel Kleinman, director of the Department of Transportation, whose apartment was adjacent to that of Mrs. Mandelik, married and wished to expand his living quarters. It goes without saying that in the case of a ghetto dignitary the neighbors were simply relocated. Mr. and Mrs. Mandelik had to give up their apartment at 18 Berek Joselewicz Street for a squalid apartment at 15 Pieprzowa Street. The wife was so despondent about this that she declared her intention to commit suicide. Nothing is known about her fate. The search is on!

FOOD SUPPLY

The bad situation remains unaltered. The winter supplies of potatoes and partially rotten turnips have been consumed in nearly all households. People are faced with the catastrophe of inevitable starvation.

From The Meat Clearinghouse

Meat consumption by workers and employees, as well as by delegates to this department, has been terminated, effective immediately. One sees how little meat is being imported, if even those who work in the market itself are not receiving allotments.

FRIDAY, JANUARY 21, 1944

A DEATH

Today, Professor Wilhelm Caspari died at the age of 72. He was born in Berlin on February 4, 1872. He had originally studied clinical medicine and became a general practitioner. In the course of his practice, he turned to bacteriological studies, published a series of scholarly papers, and habilitated as a docent at the University of Berlin. Cancer research became his area of specialization. On the basis of his scientific findings, Caspari was offered a chair at the Speyer Clinic in Frankfurt [am Main], where he worked until the summer of 1933. In 1930, as the delegate for Germany, he represented the field of cancer research at the International Congress of Physicians in Madrid, where he was greatly honored as a scholar. In the last years of his scientific activity, he published the results of his bacteriological research in professional journals.

He came to the ghetto in October 1941, with the Frankfurt transport. The Chairman immediately accorded him special status by enabling him to continue his research at the main hospital on Łagiewnicka Street and assigning him a residence at the Rest Home in Marysin. From February, 1942, until December, 1943, Caspari gave talks to the ghetto physicians and other interested persons about nutritional conditions in the ghetto. His wife was resettled in September, 1942. Since the main hospital had recently been shut down to make room for a workshop, the Chairman transferred the scholar to the Department of Vital Statistics, where Caspari occupied himself with compiling tables relating the mortality rate to the caloric and vitamin content of the ghetto diet. That project had advanced quite well.

During the past few months, Professor Caspari showed signs of mental and physical exhaustion. The nearly 72-year-old man was gravely affected by the uncertainty about his wife's fate, compounded by the shortage of food after the Ghetto Administration's elimination of food coupons. The ravages of influenza—this was during the epidemic—were too much for his weakened system. After a brief illness, Caspari succumbed to pneumonia in the hospital on Friday, January 21.

O[skar] R[osenfeld]

EDUCATION

By order of the Chairman, certificates of promotion at the lyceum have been printed in German and in Yiddish. These certificates read as follows:

The Eldest of the Jews in Litzmannstadt
Mordechai Chaim Rumkowski
Certificate

This is to certify that . . . . , born on . . . . in . . . . , attended the first class of the local lyceum during the school year 1940/1941, in the department of . . . . , and was promoted to the second lyceum class in the same department.

Litzmannstadt-Getto, December 1943
The Eldest of the Jews in Litzmannstadt

Serial No. . . . .

SATURDAY, JANUARY 22, 1944

NEWS OF THE DAY

The Chairman is still bedridden. Nevertheless, he intends to perform a wedding ceremony tomorrow in his private apartment.

To its surprise, the Department of Gas Kitchens has received an order to reopen a few of its kitchens. In the course of the next few days, all the other gas cooking points will probably also be reopened. Thus, it appears that the gas kitchens had been closed as a punitive measure for excessive gas consumption. It was the Chairman who persuaded the director to reopen the gas cooking facilities.

The Department of Soup Kitchens has issued regulations to the gas kitchens on the subject of economical gas consumption.

TUESDAY, JANUARY 25, 1944

MRS. AURBACH LEAVES THE GHETTO

At one point we reported that as part of a British-German exchange of internees, accomplished through the Geneva Red Cross, a woman living in the ghetto, Mrs. [Stefania] Dawidowicz, would be leaving for Palestine. We now hear that the Dawidowicz case is not yet officially settled.[2] On the other hand, another case, that of Hanka Aurbach, has been favorably concluded. Her husband, who has been a resident of Palestine for ten years, has succeeded in getting his wife Hanka on the exchange list. Since the necessary formalities have been completed, Mrs. Aurbach may depart. On Monday, January 24, she was turned over to the Special Department [Unit]; and then on Tuesday, January 25, the Secret State Police [Gestapo] in Litzmannstadt took charge of her. Mrs. Aurbach is to be taken to Switzerland by way of Kattowitz [Katowice]. From there the Red Cross will escort her to some neutral port, probably Lisbon, where British authorities will arrange her further transportation.

Hanka Aurbach, née Glücksmann, was resettled from Zduńska Wola and brought here to the ghetto, where she was employed in the hat workshop for over a year. Before the war, she had been living in Palestine; she had come to Zduńska Wola only for a temporary stay, but was stranded there because of the war. Before her departure from the ghetto, the Chairman supplied her with the necessary clothing and directed that her relatives remaining in the ghetto receive one loaf of bread every week in addition to the usual bread ration.

O[skar] R[osenfeld]

THURSDAY, JANUARY 27, 1944

DISTRIBUTION OF MIDDAY MEALS REORGANIZED

The Department of Soup Kitchens has issued Memorandum No. 185, informing the workshops and departments of the new method of soup distribution. The new system will be in effect as of February 1, 1944. The most important points are:

1. All workshops and departments are to supply the Department of Soup Kitchens with an exact roster of individuals entitled to midday meals as of January 22. For each name on the roster, the plant receives a permanent meal card and two control cards bearing the same number.

2. On February 1, 1944, each worker will receive his permanent card at the plant where he is employed. The control cards entitling the bearer to take the meal will be

---

2. Cf. p. 360 and n. 27 above.

handed out as in the past. For each worker reassigned to a new plant after February 1, 1944, the Bureau of Labor will issue the two control cards upon presentation of the permanent card.

3. Soup will be dispensed upon presentation of the permanent card and control cards (the control cards will be collected as before and returned to the worker's plant after the soup has been dispensed).

4. When a worker is dismissed, all of his remaining control cards will be collected at the workplace and retained by the plant. The permanent card, however, must always remain in the owner's possession so that he can present it wherever he may be (hospital, prison, etc.). In case of death, the permanent card and all the other food cards must be surrendered at the registry office.

Finally, the memo explains regulations concerning the distribution of midday meals for the so-called delegates. Point 7 regulates the dispensing of the supplemental midday meals.

The new series of permanent cards has a box marked Z [*Zusatzmittag essen*—supplemental midday meal], which is to be stamped with a small Z-stamp at the workplace. Accordingly, supplemental midday meals will be dispensed only upon presentation of the permanent card.

Point 8 specifies that soup may be taken only on the date when [the control cards] are valid.

The new system was worked out with the Trade Inspection Section. The original copy of the memorandum will be filed in the Archives. Concurrently with Memorandum No. 185, detailed instructions are being issued to the managers of all workshop kitchens. They are also being incorporated into the Archives.

SKETCHES OF GHETTO LIFE: "COULD I TROUBLE YOU FOR A LIGHT?"

Day and night one can observe the following scene in large apartment houses: a person suddenly comes dashing out of some apartment and through the dark hallway holding a burning scrap of paper or pinewood. He has just "borrowed a bit of fire" from a neighbor who happens to be cooking. Even if he still has some matches, to light one would be unforgivably frivolous. It won't be long before some resourceful person in each building starts tending an eternal fire and charging money for a light. There is no flint or touchwood in the ghetto; nevertheless, the Stone Age has returned.

If someone were to stand in the street with a cigarette lighter and, for a fee, light the cigarettes of smokers yearning for a light, he would certainly do a brisk trade. Anyone with a lit cigarette is repeatedly accosted in the street: "Could I trouble you for a light?" This has become a very serious, a vital, question; and if you smoke in the street, you need a great deal of patience and sympathy. Of course, one also sees people without such feelings, who refuse to be detained in their daily rounds. To them, the friendly question " Could I trouble you for a light?" is an annoying imposition.

SUNDAY, JANUARY 30, 1944

FOOD SUPPLY

Today, Sunday, there are absolutely no deliveries of commodities to report. The food situation in the ghetto grows more critical by the hour. People have nothing but their meager grain rations to fall back on. How they are to manage for fourteen days on 800 grams of grain is an enigma. Beyond this, the ration contains only one kilogram of radishes and a half-kilogram of fodder carrots—this is supposed to suffice for fourteen days. What in the world do people cook? In ghetto apartments one sees at best a pot of water with a little bouillon powder and onionseed flour, plus some radishes or carrots—insofar as this ration has even been distributed, for distribution depends on how much has actually been delivered. The only solid food every day is a kind of dough made of a pinch of grain flour, [ersatz] coffee, and onionseed flour which is usually pan-fried without fat. Only a lucky few have some potato peel mush to mix into this splendid dish. If, by pulling strings, someone manages to obtain such potato peels, he adds flour to produce a sort of babka or a tsholnt. The price of a kilogram of potato peels fluctuates between twenty and twenty-five marks.

The authorities have ordered the Meat Clearinghouse to empty the "cinema" warehouse in Radogoszcz of the canned meat there. The approximately 250,000 cans must be transferred to the Meat Clearinghouse at 40 Brzezińska Street by the weekend. For this purpose, the street-front wing of the building at that address is being cleared of all meat reserves, which will be stored elsewhere.

WORKSHOP NEWS: AN INCIDENT IN THE LEATHER AND SADDLERY WORKSHOP

The commissioner of this factory scheduled one of the compulsory air raid and fire drills for the end of a shift. But vehement protests were made by several women who refused to spend another hour in the workshop after ten hours of work. In the excitement, Commissioner [Maksymilian] Seligman struck one of these women, whereupon he was soundly beaten by several men. The Order Service was called, and a squad under the command of Commissioner [Abram] Feldhändler arrived. Having immediately sized up the situation, Feldhändler wisely chose not to intervene. He told the workers that he would not make an issue of the matter if they agreed to calm down. The workers, however, were not satisfied, and they demanded to see the Chairman, who, in fact, arrived on the scene. The Chairman instructed Commissioner Seligman in private that if any workers needed hitting, it would be done by him personally and no one else. The matter was resolved.

On Friday and Saturday, the Chairman visited the jewelry factory at 7 Ciesielska Street, where he held meetings about the imminent relocation.

TUESDAY, FEBRUARY 1, 1944

FOOD SUPPLY

The serious hunger crisis continues, as no alleviation of any sort appears likely. Today 12,750 kilograms of potatoes were delivered to the ghetto and, naturally, allocated to the kitchens. These potatoes are not of the best quality, since the incoming trucks are always "skimmed." The 4,000 kilograms of margarine that arrived today ensure the next margarine ration. The scheduled quotas of rye flour, rapeseed oil, and mustard powder have been delivered.

SKETCHES OF GHETTO LIFE: DON'T WASTE A DROP!

The pail of soup is carried up the two flights to the Loan Fund Office at 17 Zgierska Street. The women carrying it jostle against the edge of a step, and a bit of soup with diced potato is spilled on the staircase. The carriers ignore this minor accident and continue on their way. Behind them, a man is dragging himself up the stairs. He is here to pick up a loan at the office. His tired bones can scarcely support him, he trudges from one step to the next. And then he notices the spilled soup. His eyes fill with tears: soup on the stairs! . . .

The man doesn't even stop to think. He pulls out his spoon—the essential tool that every ghetto dweller always has with him—he sits down on a step and . . . spoons the soup off the filthy stone staircase. The serendipitous "additional soup" is more important to him at this moment than the measly few ghetto marks he is calling for at the office. The few drops of soup won't satisfy his hunger, but he can't help himself. Nor does he care to think that the stairs are filthy and that he might become ill. It's not a problem, he's already immune to typhoid fever.

If a novelist had written this scene for a book about famine in India or China, no one would believe it. But the ghetto can easily compete with India and China.

WEDNESDAY, FEBRUARY 2, 1944

SURRENDER OF VALUABLES

In view of the change in the bank at 7 Ciesielska Street, the Chairman today issued the following:

Proclamation

Re: Surrender of Valuables and Furs at the Special Department. 96 Zgierska Street.

With reference to the earlier proclamation requiring the ghetto populace to surrender its valuables and furs against payment in the bank at 7 Ciesielska Street, the populace is hereby informed that as of Thursday, February 3, 1944, the above-mentioned valuables and furs are to be surrendered against payment *only* at the Special Department at 96 Zgierska Street any day from 9 A.M. until 1:30 P.M.

Litzmannstadt-Getto	Ch[aim] Rumkowski
February 2, 1944	The Eldest of the Jews in Litzmannstadt

SKETCHES OF GHETTO LIFE

Groups of people carrying bags and pots stand patiently outside a kitchen, waiting for potato peels. They don't look like the sort of people who actually *get* potato peels—people with connections don't stand around so timidly. These people were told to come at 9 A.M., then, to come back at 11, finally, to try at 3 P.M. In the afternoon, the manager of the kitchen tells them that no distribution will take place today because the Department of Transportation has a prior claim on the potato peels: it needs them for its horses. The people stand there apathetically, waiting. Maybe the horses will change their minds?

PUBLIC HEALTH

The cases of contagious disease reported today: typhoid fever, one; tuberculosis of the lungs, six; [other] pulmonary diseases, two; heart diseases, two; stomach hemorrhage, one.

SATURDAY, FEBRUARY 5, 1944

NEWS OF THE DAY

Bałut Market
Today, at two in the afternoon, the Chairman was instructed by Amtsleiter Biebow to vacate Bałut Market immediately, so that the premises would be available to the [German] Ghetto Administration by Monday, February 7. The Chairman immediately gave orders to that effect. All furnishings in the offices of the Central Secretariat and in the Chairman's private study have remained; the Chairman has even left the office equipment behind. All he took along was the complete set of files.

The Chairman's new offices (Central Secretariat) will be installed at the Vegetable Distribution Center, which immediately vacated the premises. By Monday morning the Chairman will already be working at the new location.

A Commission in the Ghetto
Another commission arrived in the ghetto today.

Air Raid Defense
The street construction unit of the Department of Special Affairs has been assigned the task of digging air raid defense ditches in the ghetto. The plans for this project have been submitted to the German authorities.

New Gestapo Chiefs
Ghetto Gestapo Chief [Günter] Fuchs has been replaced by Dr. [Maks] Horn and a [Franz] Konrad.[3]

MONDAY, FEBRUARY 7, 1944

NEWS OF THE DAY

Morale in the ghetto is low. People are again whispering about resettlements into and out of the ghetto. As for the former, the rumors are based on advance notice of a rather large shipment of machines from Lublin.[4] They are for a buckle factory that is being

---

3. Incorrect information, as confirmed later by the bulletin of February 7. However, the appearance of those two names—Horn, the head of *Osti* and Konrad, the head of the *Werterfassung*, which dealt with the takeover of property after the liquidation of a ghetto—is symptomatic in the *Chronicle*. Cf. p. 414, n. 46 concerning *Ostindustrie GmbH*.

4. Cf. below, n. 6.

transferred to the ghetto. In this connection, one hears rumors that the staff will also be resettled here.

As for the whispers about a resettlement out of the ghetto, they probably originated several days ago when a fairly large number of metal workers—according to reports, several hundred mechanics and operators of milling machines, grinders, etc.—were requisitioned through the Labor Office in Posen [Poznań]. The Ghetto Administration, however, refused to comply, due to the shortage of such skilled workers in the ghetto itself. Nevertheless, the rumor persists.

A Commission in the Ghetto
Today the ghetto was visited by a relatively large commission consisting of officers from Air Raid Defense. All pertinent facilities in the ghetto were inspected. The air raid defense ditches around the [ghetto] city proved to be unsuitable, since water was reached at a shallow depth, and it is feared that the clay soil could easily collapse.

Amtsleiter Biebow, therefore, ordered the Eldest to have air raid defense ditches dug on the cemetery grounds and to have these ditches buttressed with gravestones. The project was immediately tackled by [Boruch] Praszkier's department.

Horses Drafted
Twenty-eight ghetto horses have been examined and declared fit for military service. No date has been announced for the delivery of these horses.

The Central Secretariat
of the Chairman is already officiating on the premises of the former Research Department. A rapidly completed remodeling has made the new offices quite comfortable for the work of the Central Secretariat.

A Conference with the Chairman
At 2 P.M. this afternoon, a few of the ghetto's prominent figures received invitations from the Chairman to appear at his office at 5 P.M. The purpose of the meeting remains unknown.

The Department of Vegetables
The Department of Vegetables has relocated its headquarters to the vegetable market at 10 Łagiewnicka Street.

The Burglary
at the provisions and bread distribution point [which took place on January 28, 1944] at 4 Młynarska Street is still unsolved. The burglars left no clues.

Anna Mandelik
who disappeared from the ghetto on January 17 of this year, has still not been found. She is originally from Prague.

SKETCHES OF GHETTO LIFE: VANISHING CARROTS

A freightcar of carrots has arrived. Almost nothing else is coming in. The vegetable markets are empty; the ration of one kilogram of radishes and a half-kilogram of carrots was announced a long time ago, but only a fraction of the populace has received anything, since there is nothing to distribute. Only occasionally does any food reach the ghetto. Yesterday, though, a freightcar of carrots did arrive containing all of 4,000 kilograms, quite enough to satisfy about 8,000 consumers. But it will satisfy fewer than 8,000, which comes as no surprise. When such freightcars pull up at the vegetable market, their contents are dumped, and everyone who works there is ready and able—not to work—to eat. These people are so hungry, and have been hungry for so long, that they will eat anything edible raw, especially delicacies such as carrots. All those in the marketplace—the entire crew—pounce on this one carload of carrots and stuff their stomachs. They don't have to eat anything else. Their slices of bread, their soup, everything is left uneaten and carried home, for they have appeased their hunger with the carrots.

Can one blame these people? Some of them can devour three or four kilograms. Those are the champion eaters, but anyone can consume smaller quantities. Who can condemn them for taking home to their families the soup or bread that they have saved in this way!

In the ghetto it is an accepted practice that everyone who works at the vegetable market, in a provision shop, a bakery, etc., consumes food while he is at the work-place; but nothing may be carried away. Thus, the pile of carrots at the vegetable market keeps shrinking significantly. The "Sonder" [Special Department man] is there to keep an eye on things, but he is only human himself, starving like everyone else, and . . . he eats the carrots too!

Now goods are brought from the vegetable market to the distribution centers. The transportation workers who man the handcarts have hearts of stone but good-sized stomachs; they too can devour a tidy amount. And obviously, no carrots are added at the distribution centers; quite the opposite: the supply shrinks visibly. To make up for the underweight, the carrots are doused with water; sand and stones are added. There are various schemes, various dodges for detaining the vegetables at the dis-tribution center and thus gaining time in which to eat them: you can delay distribut-ing the ration for a day or two; you can limit the number of consumers per day— simply to salvage a few carrots for yourself.

So it's no wonder that only maybe 2,000 or 2,500 kilograms are distributed, after all the routes and channels that this small amount of goods has traveled. The rest of it has vanished in transit. The average number of consumers per distribution center is 2,000. When the Department of Vegetables sends the goods for these consumers to the shops, a five-percent margin for error is calculated in for underweight (drying, overweighing, and so on). But after distribution, it usually turns out that not all consumers have received their rations; about five or ten percent is missing. Now the tragedy begins. The manager of the distribution center calls for an additional supply to cover the deficiency. The Department of Food Supply supports him, for the con-sumers must be satisfied. But the Department of Vegetables (though under the same overall management as the distribution centers for provisions and for bread) dis-agrees. The Department of Vegetables says it has sent the required quantity, indeed even more; and thus the matter is settled, as far as the Department of Vegetables is concerned. The Special Department takes the same position. The person who actu-ally suffers is the consumer, who may have to wait for months to get his little share of vegetables; and it is questionable whether he will ever receive it. Some shops repay their debts with food from the next ration when it is delivered. This results in larger and larger deficits, and no one knows how to reduce them. Perhaps with a general bankruptcy, perhaps when the war ends, perhaps . . . who knows. . . .

B[ernard] O[strowski]

TUESDAY, FEBRUARY 8, 1944[5]

THE WEATHER

Eight degrees [in the morning], it is snowing; [at] noon, 6 degrees, sunshine.

DEATHS

Four.

BIRTHS

One.

ARRESTS

Miscellaneous, four; resistance, one.

TOTAL POPULATION

79,777.

NEWS OF THE DAY

Difficult days in the ghetto. It was known already yesterday evening that a new resettlement has been ordered. In accordance with a request by the Labor Office in Posen [Poznań], 1,500 workers must be dispatched from the ghetto.

As we have already reported, [yesterday] at 2 P.M. the Chairman asked several prominent persons to his office. Now we know why. The following men were invited:

Bernard Fuchs	Henryk Neftalin, the attorney
Stanisław Jakobson	Boruch Praszkier
Aron Jakubowicz	Commander Zygmunt Reingold
Mordka [Marek] Kligier	Commander Leon Rozenblat
Dr. Wiktor Miller	Mieczysław Rozenblatt [Trade Inspection Section]
Józef Rumkowski	Kiwa Sienicki and Dr. Oskar Singer

Also present was Miss Dora Fuchs.

The Chairman opened the meeting by announcing that difficult times had again come upon the ghetto and that 1,500 young men had been requisitioned for labor outside the ghetto. This time, however, the situation was aggravated by the condition that neither the workshops nor the coal or transportation departments were to be affected. Therefore, the only possibilities were members of departments of the internal administration. The Chairman reported that he had received the orders through Amtsleiter Biebow on Monday at 2 P.M. While no date had been set, he has been instructed to report back by Tuesday—that is, today, February 8—at 8 A.M. as to whether he could carry out the order.

---

5. The *Daily Chronicle Bulletin* for Tuesday, February 8, 1944, is given in its entirety here.

"You know, my friends," the Chairman said, "how difficult the situation is. A few days ago, when we were asked to make available two groups of approximately twenty-five persons each, we had a hard time forming those groups, and I was apprehensive about what would happen if fifty or even more persons were demanded. We have no human resources, and still we must supply them. If we do not solve the problem ourselves, you know what the practical consequences will be.

"I have invited you here at this hour because I had to attend to certain preliminaries from two to five this afternoon. I have had a list drawn up of the eligible departments. At the moment, I don't know how we are supposed to muster healthy men from these departments. Please give me your advice."

First, M. Kligier cited the order of the head [of the Ghetto Administration] verbatim. Then Miss Fuchs commented on the wording of the requisition—"fifteen hundred men, of sound mind and body, fit for training in a specific line of work, are to be resettled"—which indicates that the present measure is in fact attributable to the severe manpower shortage in the Reich.

The Chairman assigned the attorney, [Henryk] Neftalin, Sienicki, and [Bernard] Fuchs of the Bureau of Labor, to collect the relevant data. He requested that they provide a tabulation of the men being considered, in three age groups: 18–40, 41–45, and 46–50. The attorney, Neftalin, promised that he would have these statistics ready by the early morning hours of the following day.

Finally, it was resolved that the populace should be informed of the state of affairs and given the exact wording of the requisition; this would facilitate its technical implementation. The Chairman expressed grave concern about the latter; in particular, about the danger that, once again, the conscripted persons would not report.

The Chairman instructed Dr. [Wiktor] Miller, director of the Department of Health, to appoint the medical panel; he himself appointed the members of the implementation committee, who received their official letters of appointment on the same day, February 7, 1944. The following men were named and received the letter, which is quoted below:

Henryk Neftalin; Commissioner [Józef] Kohl; Commander [Zygmunt] Reingold; Commander [Leon] Rozenblat; Bernard Fuchs; Akiba [Kiwa] Sienicki; Marek [Mordka] Kligier.

File No. 91/br/44/Pal.   February 7, 1944
Re: Dispatch of 1,500 Workers from the Ghetto.

For the dispatch of the above 1,500 workers, I hereby appoint you to the commission that will oversee this enterprise. Note: Commander Leon Rozenblat has been appointed chairman of the committee.

C[haim] Rumkowski
Eldest of the Jews in Litzm[ann]st[adt]

Also available now is a copy of the memorandum that requires the 1,500 workers through the office of the head [of the Ghetto Administration]. The text is as follows:

Memorandum
of an agreement with Amtsleiter Biebow, February 7, 1944.
Re: Dispatch of 1,500 Workers from the Ghetto.
1,500 healthy workers are to be dispatched from the ghetto.

These men are to be physically and mentally suited to training and instruction for special purposes.

Large pieces of baggage will not be taken along; the workers are to be outfitted only with sound footwear and winter clothing.

The transport should probably proceed in two groups of 750 workers each.

As of Tuesday, February 8, 1944, the Eldest of the Jews will report about if and when it will be possible to dispatch these workers.

The Amtsleiter expressly emphasized that no skilled workers from the factories and no manual laborers are to be sent, since they are needed inside the ghetto itself.

Today, an additional memo was received that exempts three more departments. It reads:

Memorandum

of an agreement with Amtsleiter Biebow, February 8, 1944.

Re: Dispatch of 1,500 Workers from the Ghetto.

In the tabulation to be submitted of manpower available for dispatch from the ghetto, the following departments are not to be drawn upon:

1. Drycleaning and Laundry Facility
2. Gas Department
3. Recycling Department

In the selection of workers, it must first be accurately determined whether they have learned a trade. A list of all craftsmen is to be submitted to me, and I will then decide whether each individual is eligible for a labor assignment outside the ghetto.

signed, Biebow
(Amtsleiter)

The commission met yesterday and immediately issued orders for all the necessary measures.

In the evening, the Chairman conferred with Dr. Miller of the Department of Health, then with the commission at the Bureau of Labor. As of tomorrow, Wednesday, the commission will be working together with the panel of physicians in the outpatient clinic at 40 Lutomierska Street.

The first 300 or so summonses [to appear for medical examination] will be drawn up in the early morning hours, from 4:30 on, so that the men in question will find their notices when they arrive at their jobs. On Wednesday afternoon, another 600 are to report for examination.

Naturally, the ghetto is in a panic again. Even though people know that this is truly a labor transport, they cannot forget the scene of the last resettlement, and certainly not the condition of the few people who returned here after being dispatched to labor outside the ghetto. Since the supply that can be tapped is very small this time, and since only [administrative personnel in] the departments are being considered, the ghetto is in danger of losing the better part of its younger intelligentsia. And it is by no means certain that the ghetto can muster the requisitioned number of 1,500 able-bodied men from this supply. Although initially it was claimed that only 18- to 40-year-olds would be considered, this age group alone will hardly solve the problem.

The Chairman, and the commission, will have to push the age limit up to 50 whether they wish to or not.

We have learned that the Chairman at first tried to stave off this new calamity for the ghetto by informing the Amtsleiter that he did not have enough men of the requisite quality in the departments if coal, transportation, recycling, gas, and drycleaning and laundry were to be exempted. The Amtsleiter is said to have replied that he wished to have this information in writing, so that he could present it to Dr. Bradfisch, the mayor and chief of the Gestapo. What the Amtsleiter was driving at is obvious.

Not even the dreadful famine in the ghetto mitigates the horror of resettlement for labor outside the ghetto. Although many people tell themselves that there is hope of better nourishment at a work site somewhere in the Reich, no one wishes to be separated from his family at this critical time in the war. The next few hours will be extremely difficult. We will not have an overview of the situation until the end of the week, when we will know whether and how many of those conscripted report to be transported out of the ghetto.

A COMMISSION IN THE GHETTO

Today another commission appeared in the ghetto; accompanied by the Amtsleiter it inspected several workshops.

NEW GESTAPO CHIEFS

Command of the Gestapo in the ghetto has been assumed not, as reported, by Dr. [Maks] Horn and a Mr. [Franz] Konrad, but by two other men, one of whom is named Sauter.

FOOD SUPPLY

The situation remains bad. Only a few carrots are arriving.

FOOD ALLOTMENT FOR THE ORDER SERVICE

The latest allotment for Order Service members consists of 1½ kilograms of flour and 200 grams of sugar per month.

For a while, the Order Service men serving at the barbed wire fence were receiving 150 grams of bread and 50 grams of sausage. Then various reapportionments of the sausage allotment within the Order Service reduced the ration to 30 grams. And now these Order Service men receive only bread, without sausage.

DISCIPLINING OF KITCHEN MANAGEMENT

The management of the kitchen at 10 Jakuba [Street] was suspended by the Chairman for dispensing only 0.5 liters [of soup] instead of 0.7, to the detriment of consumers.

POTATO PEELS

The situation in the ghetto is well-typified by the price that potato peels now bring— 60 marks a kilogram. Rutabaga scraps: 20−25 marks.

PUBLIC HEALTH

The cases of contagious disease reported today: typhus, 13; tuberculosis, 9.

The causes of today's deaths: pulmonary tuberculosis, 2; pneumonia, 1; heart failure, 1.

WEDNESDAY, FEBRUARY 9, 1944

A SUICIDE

On February 8, Estera Wasser, born February 22, 1885, in Suwalki and residing at 12 Ceglana Street, committed suicide by hanging herself in her apartment. She was pronounced dead by the Emergency Service physician.

WORKSHOP NEWS

Machines for the Ghetto
Machines from an evacuated buckle factory in the Jewish camp near Lublin (Ponia-towa) have arrived in the ghetto.[6] The machines were brought to the building of the former carpet factory ([manager:] Garfinkel) at 44 Wolborska Street. A new factory will be established there, probably as Metal Department III. The Chairman has appointed [Szmul] Chirurg, from the Meat Clearinghouse, as director of this [new] department.

Solidarity among Juvenile Workers
The juvenile workers of the Electrical Engineering Department have joined together in a sort of self-help program. After soup has been distributed, they gather around a collective pot, and each contributes two spoonfuls of soup and a piece of potato from his own bowl. The ten bowls of soup thus accumulated are then donated to their weak and ailing fellow workers.

In the same workshop, the boys have introduced a timely lottery. Every week they chip in small pieces of their bread rations until they have collected two kilograms. Then lots are drawn, and the lucky winner must eat the entire two kilograms of bread pieces right there in the workshop. This game of lots has been given the telling [Polish] name *raz a dobrze* (once but well).

The Laundry at 68 Zgierska Street
has been shut down temporarily because of defective machinery.

FRIDAY, FEBRUARY 11, 1944

NEWS OF THE DAY

A relatively large commission arrived in the ghetto under the leadership of Dr. Brad-fisch, the mayor [and chief of the Gestapo]. The commission inspected a few work-

6. Poniatowa, one of the largest forced labor camps for Jews in Lublin province. After the liquidation of the ghettos, Jews from the surrounding areas were sent there, as were Jews from Austria and Czechoslovakia and, after the suppression of the uprising in the Warsaw ghetto in April, 1943, Jews from the Warsaw ghetto. The prisoners—who numbered some 14–18,000—were employed in tailoring workshops located in barracks constructed in the woods and also worked at building roads. On November 3, 1943, during the so-called *Sonderbehandlung Aktion* in Lublin province, specially selected Jews, those who were healthy and still fit for work, were sent to a neighboring camp in Majdanek, the rest were executed *en masse* on the spot. Their sewing machines, as the *Chronicle* notes, were sent to the Łódź ghetto. The chroniclers did not know, nor could they, that the machines had been sent to the Łódź ghetto in connection with the planned takeover of the ghetto by the SS and by Police Leader Odilo Globocnik of Lublin province, and its transformation into a concentration camp under his (Globocnik's) leadership.

shops, as well as the Special Department post at Bałut Market; finally, it spent roughly an hour at the main office of the Special Department, where the members of the commission met with M[arek] Kligier.

1,500 Workers
The work of the [recruitment] commission is dragging on. Last night, too, people were pulled out of hiding. Altogether, though, there are hardly more than 350 men at Central Prison; thus, any guarantee of a first transport of 750 men seems out of the question. For that reason, the situation is deteriorating by the hour, and it is feared that the Chairman will resort to extraordinary measures in order to meet the prescribed quota on time.

The Chairman met with the commission for a fairly long time at 40 Lutomierska Street, where the strategy for the next few hours was determined in private session. The first step will be to cancel ration cards. In many cases this has already been done, and the persons involved will not be able to draw their next ration. One will have to wait and see whether this harsh measure will yield the required results. Clearly the Chairman, as well as the commission, is making every effort to ease the heavy burden imposed on the ghetto and to avert more severe action by the [German] authorities in fulfilling the requisition order. It is obvious that the authorities would intervene if the Jewish leadership lost control of the situation. The populace is being assured repeatedly that this is not a resettlement action after the pattern of earlier days of horror, but simply the providing of available manpower, as is customary in the Reich. The very fact that appropriate outfitting has been ordered indicates that this is a case of normal mobilization of labor. But the terrified ghetto dweller's memory of grim experiences cannot be wiped out even with propaganda techniques.

The tally at Central Prison has not increased significantly. Some 400 persons are now concentrated there. As before, very few persons are reporting to the commission. Thus, the next few hours are sure to be highly dramatic.

SUNDAY, FEBRUARY 13, 1944

NEWS OF THE DAY

Today, at 5 p.m., the Chairman spoke to a gathering of the managers of factories and departments. His remarks were as follows:

"Before getting down to the business at hand, I must say a few words about the crucial issue of the day. I must ask you to understand my remarks correctly and to give an undistorted account of them to others. I find it very hard to speak on this subject.

"The issue is the 1,500 men who are to depart for labor outside the ghetto. Now the situation is as follows: we have to hand over 1,500 healthy men, and we are not allowed to touch the factory work force. This time, however, one can say with certainty that these men are in no danger. Well, the order *has* come, and the question is: who will carry it out, I—or another authority?

"I have always maintained that I will need about 4,600 people for new production projects, and that I will have to draw them from the internal administration. But now I am losing 1,500 men who were, so to speak, my labor reserve. When the day I need them comes, I don't quite know how I will solve the problem. At the moment, though, this is not the issue.

"I intended to carry out the entire operation very quietly. But this has not succeeded, because the men have gone into hiding. Now the fact is that, when one is assigned to carry out an order, one must also bear the responsibility. If we do not produce these men, you know very well what might happen. This should be borne in mind by those who are helping others to hide. We are now faced with the dangerous possibility that the authorities will demand that I give them the names of men who have failed to obey the enlistment order. I have called off the arrests for tonight, and tomorrow I will have to report on the present situation. At the moment, I cannot predict what might happen to those who have not reported.

"I warn the managers of factories: I am well aware that people are hiding even in workshops. As for the delinquents themselves, in view of the present situation I cannot say for sure who has acted more sensibly: those who have reported as ordered or those who have gone into hiding. But either way, the authorities will ask me: 'What's the meaning of this? Why haven't these people responded to your order? We'll find ways of flushing them out!' I must point out to you that this is a dangerous game. Of course it is very fine that a family worried about its son or husband is stinting on provisions and soup in order to feed the person in hiding: but such families are also in danger, and I must make this explicit because—hard as it is for me—I have no choice. After all, I cannot endanger the entire ghetto for the sake of 1,500 men who have to be dispatched for external labor. This is no time for mercy. I must avoid creating a precedent under any circumstances. Do not interfere with this regulation! Tell this to your people."

(The Chairman then got down to the business of the day, continuing as follows.)

"Circumstances change daily in the ghetto, and we have to adjust to every new situation. The current problem is that there are too many people in the streets! That is the most serious problem of the day. Commissions can be expected at any time, and we will not always have sufficient advance notice that a commission is coming. A commission might enter the ghetto without first calling at Bałut Market. So, I have decided upon the following measures:

"(1) To begin with, the distribution points will remain closed during working hours, that is, from 7 A.M. to 5 P.M. The same will hold for the outpatient clinics and other institutions and offices that deal with the public.

"(2) The factories will remain hermetically sealed from 7 A.M. to 5 P.M. No one will be permitted to leave his plant. All persons on the official roster of a plant must in fact be there.

"(3) I regret that I, a 67-year-old man, must give the ladies an order concerning cosmetics. But I exhort them: Get rid of your makeup, powder, and lipstick!

"(4) I order those who work at home to remain there and work continuously under all circumstances. Loitering in the street, on whatever pretext, must stop.

"(5) I order a regular inspection of apartments. A campaign against the filth in apartments!

"I know" (the Chairman elaborated) "how hard life is in the ghetto. The father works, and so do the mother and children. Each in a different place, and it isn't easy to manage the housework under these circumstances; but it must be done."

"(6) From now on, no one will be able to leave his job site, factory, or office during working hours without a pass. Every manager will appoint a person to take responsibility for this, along with the gatekeeper, who is to let no one out. The passes will be administered in such a way that it will be easy to check to whom and how often a pass has been issued. Anyone found in the street will have to show his papers. Furthermore, the labor card will indicate the worker's shift. If he works at night, there is no reason why he cannot be outdoors during the day."

(At this point the Chairman touched on various practical issues, mentioned particular cases, and then adjourned the meeting briefly.

Afterwards, he took the floor again and continued as follows.)

"During the recess I caught a few words of the conversations among the managers, and I conclude that you completely misunderstand the situation. Let me assure you that you greatly underestimate the problem. If a commission simply drops in on one of your factories and we haven't been able to notify you in time, then you will see which way the wind is blowing. A random inspection can easily create an extremely dangerous situation. Not only those who are absent but also those in charge will be called to account. I am therefore resolved to implement the measures I have announced here as of tomorrow, Monday. Furthermore, I order that a slate be displayed in each factory with the names of absent workers.

"Now I invite you to ask me questions of a practical nature, and I will answer them immediately, as far as possible. However, I will not permit any discussion of the basic problem."

A few men did, in fact, speak up: Commander Zygmunt Reingold, in regard to the distribution shops and to transportation problems; [Ignacy] Gutman, the engineer (Construction Department), in regard to delegated workers; Szyja Klugman (carpet workshop), in regard to the 3,000 women who work at home for his operation; [Natan] Oberbaum (Department of Tobacco, which consists of both a shop and a manufacturing plant); [Józef] Chimowicz, in regard to juvenile workers.

The Chairman answered all the questions he was asked. In connection with those who work at home, he scheduled a meeting for Monday at 5:15 P.M.

Then M[arek] Kligier made some remarks concerning the dispatch of 1,500 workers for labor outside the ghetto, explaining the gravity of the situation. He also made a few clarifying remarks on the topic of street traffic.

The Chairman concluded the meeting by appealing to the assembled managers to understand the situation in the proper light and to think over the seriousness of the measures to be taken.

(Each participant in the meeting received a slice of bread dripping with fat in exchange for his ticket of admission.)

SKETCHES OF GHETTO LIFE: GHETTO TRAGEDIES

Just as there is a minimum intensity below which no stimulus can be perceived, and a maximum frequency above which no shock reaches the conscious mind, so the heart's capacity for resonating in sympathy with the suffering of others is restricted to a middle register.

There is a Hasidic family consisting of a father, a mother, a daughter, two sons, the young wife of one son, and the girl's fiancé. In the last resettlement, the two sons were separated from their loved ones. One was allowed to return; waiting in Central Prison, he longed to be reunited with his family, especially his young wife, whom he had literally pulled from the railroad car when her parents, Jews from Germany, were being resettled.

Now comes the requisition for 1,500 workers. The man who came home will have to leave again. The daughter's fiancé is also among the chosen. On the day of the latter's conscription, the ailing father dies. The women are now alone. A rough gust of wind has shaken the last leaves from the tree.

P[eter] W[ertheimer]

MONDAY, FEBRUARY 14, 1944

A COMMISSION IN THE GHETTO

Today, a fairly large commission, composed of high-ranking functionaries of the [Nazi] party and the authorities, appeared in the ghetto under the leadership of the mayor [and chief of the Gestapo], Dr. Bradfisch. Among those participating in the inspection was the deputy Gauleiter of Warthegau. The commission inspected a few important factories, including Carpentry Department I, on Drukarska Street, and also the furniture exhibit on the same street. The commission was very favorably impressed by the projects in the carpentry shop and by the exhibit. The latter, in particular, has proved to be an outstanding instrument of ghetto propaganda about Jewish industriousness and productivity. Dr. Bradfisch brought the executive staff and various workers into the discussions.

PEOPLE ARE SAYING . . .

In managerial and ostensibly well-informed circles the conversation always turns to the question of an administrative change in the ghetto. For a long time people have been saying that the ghetto will be removed from the jurisdiction of the mayor and delivered into the hands of the SS. Now a rumor is gaining currency that, since the ghetto falls into the sector of the armaments industry, it will be taken over by the so-called Ostindustrie Gesellschaft [Eastern Industrial Company], a semi-official organization. An SS officer named Dr. [Maks] Horn is reputed to be its representative.

Since the Ostindustrie Gesellschaft naturally maintains close economic relations with all offices that have raw materials at their disposal, it is believed that the ghetto's production capacity would be increased by association with this company. Accordingly, the mood of the above-mentioned circles is not bad, although, on the other hand, an SS regimen of ghetto life is expected to be harsher than the present one.

These conjectures all revolve around the person of Amtsleiter Biebow, who purportedly will either remain as economic head of the ghetto or at least stay in contact with the Ghetto Administration in the event that he assumes some other position.

TUESDAY, FEBRUARY 15, 1944

THE 1,500 WORKERS

The operation is still in progress. Apartments are continually being searched, but the number of persons held at Central Prison is increasing very slowly; [there are] some

600 men there now. How soon the first transport will leave is a question no one can answer. It seems, though, that the Chairman may still have some time. Only if the deadline is postponed will he be able to produce the required number of 1,500—by starving them out. The next bread distribution is scheduled for tomorrow, the 16th. Since the families of men in hiding have had all their ration cards invalidated, they will probably find it difficult to get through the next several days—to feed either themselves or their relatives in hiding. No matter how resourceful family solidarity may be, the problem simply cannot be solved in this way, given the general food situation in the ghetto. Already, men forced from their hiding places by hunger are gradually beginning to report.

Central Prison is holding persons in the T category (*tauglich* [fit for service]) as well as in the *B* I and *B* II categories, that is, Reserve I and Reserve II. They are maintained on a decent daily diet consisting of three bowls of soup, 250 grams of bread, 10 grams of sugar, and a spoonful of paste for spreading on bread, as well as cigarettes. The Chairman is interested in fattening these men up a bit, so that they can hold out under any circumstances.

PHILATELY DEPARTMENT

In November 1943, after six months of inactivity, the Philately Department received a large order from the Ghetto Administration: 20,000 packets containing 50 items apiece. Despite the shortage of material, 6,500 packets were completed by Christmas. At the moment, the department has several small orders to fill for the Ghetto Administration.

THURSDAY, FEBRUARY 17, 1944

NEWS OF THE DAY: THE 1,500 WORKERS

The number of workers to be dispatched was today raised to 1,600. According to reports, the hundred additional men are needed for the same labor detail that was supplied by the last two, smaller resettlement actions. It is claimed that this smaller labor camp is located not far from Litzmannstadt and is under the command of Günter Fuchs, a Gestapo functionary.

The search for men in hiding continues, with extremely meager results. Presumably, the Eldest will have to resort to draconian measures. This coming Sunday, February 20, there is likely to be a total [curfew], similar to the one during the infamous September days of 1942. Police patrols would methodically comb the entire ghetto then in order to round up all the evaders.

Every day a few men who have given up the struggle against cold and hunger report, as ordered—we have described the circumstances. But on the whole, the number of detainees in Central Prison has not risen significantly, especially since certain individuals are being released by the Chairman.

The Care Committee in Central Prison, of which we have already spoken [on February 13, 1944], consists of five women appointed by the Chairman; a few girls have been assigned to assist them. This committee of ladies has the task of monitoring the food and the sanitary conditions, as well as supervising the delivery of money and packages and, furthermore, of arranging communication with relatives and friends of the detainees, so that the latter receive everything they need to have forwarded. Packages and money orders are to be sent through the Postal Department to the Care Committee at 24 Tokarzewski Street.

If a date has been set for the departure of the transport, it has not been announced. Meanwhile, the detainees are being taken in groups to bathing facilities, and a sizable crew of barbers is working steadily at Central Prison.

PEOPLE ARE SAYING . . .

that the ghetto will be reclassified as a labor camp. In the future, the ghetto will supposedly be regarded as a camp for prisoners of war; hence, there are expectations of contact with the outside world and the orderly receipt of food packages. The origin of this rumor cannot be ascertained. At any rate, the entire ghetto is discussing the matter, and the general mood is noticeably brighter. Conducive to the rumor's currency is the fact that packages are now continually being delivered intact to the ghetto and being turned over to the addressees by the Special Department. Packages are arriving from the Reich protectorate of Bohemia and Moravia, and Holland, as well as from neutral countries such as Switzerland and Portugal; also from Rumania. It is perhaps this circumstance that has given rise to the rumor.

FRIDAY, FEBRUARY 18, 1944

NEWS OF THE DAY

Amtsleiter Biebow has been away since yesterday; he is said to be in Berlin, where, allegedly, negotiations are being conducted concerning the takeover of the ghetto by the Ostindustrie Gesellschaft. Insiders claim that he will continue to run the ghetto.

THE 1,600 WORKERS

No essential change in this action. The [curfew] for Sunday, February 20, is now definite.

The manager of the printing office, [Szmul] Rozenstein, was summoned by the Chairman around noon in order to discuss announcement of the curfew. The poster appeared promptly by evening, in German and—for the first time after a long hiatus—also in Yiddish. It reads:

Proclamation No. 411

Re: Total Curfew on Sunday, February 20, 1944.

In connection with the dispatch of 1,600 workers for labor outside the ghetto, a general curfew is hereby ordered for Sunday, February 20, 1944.

The only services functioning on this day will be: hospitals I and II, the pharmacy at 8 Kościelny Square, the pharmacy at 5 Rybna Street, and units of the Emergency Service.

All other departments, as well as factories and workshops, will absolutely be closed all day.

Only firemen and two additional trustworthy individuals, designated for each factory by the manager, may be on the premises on this day.

I must especially point out that the soup kitchens will also remain closed on Sunday, February 20, 1944.

The soup for this Sunday will be distributed to all workers and employees, against control card No. 2, on Saturday, February 19.

Any persons, aside from those designated above, who are found in the plants or departments will be taken into custody immediately. The managers of plants and departments are to issue identification cards with photographs (issued by the Ghetto Labor Office) [Arbeitsamt of the Ghetto Administration] to all male workers (except children and the very old) for Sunday, at the end of work on Saturday, February 19. Should any of the identification cards lack photographs, then photographs are also to be issued to male workers.

Similarly, all persons in question are to be in possession of their permanent kitchen cards on February 20.

The identification cards must be returned at the work place on Monday, February 21. Any male workers unable to produce the aforementioned papers (identification cards and permanent kitchen cards) on Sunday, February 20, will be taken into custody immediately. Any locked attics and cellars must be opened on demand. The appropriate keys are to be in the building superintendent's possession. In any building without a superintendent, the tenants must appoint a person to keep the keys.

To facilitate matters, a notice in clearly legible writing, indicating the name and apartment number of the person holding the keys (to attics and cellars), is to be posted in every building vestibule or on the front door.

The apartments that were sealed off by the Order Service may be opened by the occupants, so that they can be available [for questioning] there.

I again point out that

on Sunday, February 20, every ghetto inhabitant
must be in his apartment.

Street passes will be issued only in emergencies and only by me personally.

To forestall the necessity of punitive measures, I therefore advise every ghetto inhabitant to obey this order scrupulously. Litzmannstadt-Getto.

Ch[aim] Rumkowski

February 18, 1944   The Eldest of the Jews in Litzmannstadt

The Amtsleiter gave the Chairman express permission to publish this proclamation in Yiddish. Thus, this coming Sunday will be reminiscent of the curfew of the September days, with the agreeable difference that this time only the Jewish Order Service will command the streets and no shots will be fired. The proclamation speaks for itself. The only question is what secret instructions the Order Service will receive from the Chairman in regard to detentions and arrests, for the curfew represents only a theoretical solution to the problem. Even with the help of the other uniformed services, such as the Economic [section of Order Service] police and the Fire Department, it is hardly likely that the Order Service will succeed in searching the ghetto thoroughly and combing through all the hiding places in this squalid city in one day. Then, too, the police themselves are tired, and inhibited by their personal relationships with many of the hunted men and, finally, so corrupt that one can only be skeptical about the outcome.

The Chairman himself is said to be counting on only a partial success: the apprehension of some 200 concealed persons. Even this estimate is probably too high.

A DEATH

Adolf Goetz, an engineer, born May 4, 1876, died today. The deceased came to the ghetto in October, 1941, with the Hamburg transport. He was a man of extraordinarily broad education and capabilities; in Germany, he had worked on the problem of the rigid dirigible airship and had taken out a number of patents in this field. In the ghetto, he concerned himself with agricultural questions and, under the aegis of the Department of Economics he founded a research group that concentrated on the cultivation of medicinal herbs.

Remarkably active to the very last, Goetz passed away from pneumonia.

PEOPLE ARE SAYING

that there is a census imminent this coming Sunday.

SUNDAY, FEBRUARY 20, 1944

NEWS OF THE DAY

Early this morning, the persons designated by management took up their positions in the departments and factories. At 7 A.M. the manhunt began, and entire blocks of houses were surrounded and searched. The procedure was relatively swift and was over by 6 P.M. The results were extremely meager relative to the number of those in hiding; all in all, around seventy men were discovered. Nevertheless, some four hundred people were concentrated at the police precincts. Those who could produce a Central Prison pass, namely those who had either been released as unfit or been freed by order of the Chairman, were not bothered. On the other hand, persons who for one reason or another felt that they were in no danger were taken. In order to guarantee the required one hundred additional men, the Chairman ordered that workshop personnel, but only those who are not directly involved in production, be taken into custody.

The Order Service had lists of names. Today's operation has raised the total count in Central Prison to 1,240. Naturally, the physicians' panel will weed out the unfit or, rather, will determine which of the detainees are eligible for labor outside the ghetto.

Today, Sunday, the ghetto seemed like a ghost town. This was the first real day of rest since the ghetto was established. People confined to their houses are, no doubt, using the time to put their living quarters in better order.

MONDAY, FEBRUARY 21, 1944

NEWS OF THE DAY

Last night was quiet. There were no police operations of any sort. From among the approximately 1,240 detainees in Central Prison, a few individuals have been released. Rumor has it that women too are now being considered for labor outside the ghetto.

CHILDREN IN THE WORKSHOPS

The Chairman has issued an order that children born in 1935 are to be integrated into the workshop labor force. This order is to be carried out by the Regroupment Commission by Friday, February 25. [Henryk] Neftalin, the attorney, has received corresponding instructions for executing the administrative work involved; and today, on the basis of the information gathered by Neftalin's department (Department of Vital Statistics), the Reclassification Commission will summon the parents of children in this age group.

SKETCHES OF GHETTO LIFE: THE MEN IN HIDING

The endurance of the men hiding from conscription for outside labor is as great as their fear of being dispatched from the ghetto. They draw no rations because their food cards have been invalidated; and the same holds true for their families. After nearly fourteen days in their hiding places, what are these men living on? If they have connections, they can still obtain soup and other sustenance through intermediaries. If they don't, they try to get through the days on ersatz coffee.

One man who was ferreted out of his hiding place had been living on nothing but ersatz coffee for days and, naturally, was half starved.

Another man was found in a soup kitchen that had been closed down; he was [discovered] in a cauldron, half frozen.

Many others keep changing their hiding places by night, from one district to another, one step ahead of the patrols. Since all parts of the ghetto are interconnected by open courtyards and a labyrinth of passageways, the fugitives can evade the manhunt fairly easily. Their families, though, cannot hold out in the long run; and so every day, emaciated men, in a state of nervous exhaustion, are turning themselves in at Central Prison.

A hunger blockade in the city of hunger. This is hunger to the nth degree.

TUESDAY, FEBRUARY 22, 1944

THE 1,600 WORKERS

The campaign to secure 1,600 workers for labor outside the ghetto is still not completed. The quota has not yet been reached.

Since the authorities have permitted the Eldest to include 235 females, if necessary, among the 1,600 to be dispatched, the selection process will now probably encompass women as well. It is not yet certain how this is to be implemented technically but, in view of the commission's previous experiences with male workers, there will undoubtedly have to be a surprise operation to secure the required number of suitable women. On the other hand, since the ghetto has already learned of the imminent new conscriptions, all the women likely to be considered will, of course, go into hiding, and then the hunt for them will begin.

The Eldest has reassigned a few of the men he exempted from conscription; instead of their previous jobs, mainly in the Department of Food Supply and the Department of Vegetables, they will now do demolition work. The approximately eighteen younger men who are involved received their new assignments in the Demolition Department today.

SURRENDER OF GOLD AND SILVER RINGS AND OTHER JEWELRY

Pursuant to the proclamation of February 12, 1944, No. 408, the Special Department now supervises the surrender of silver and gold objects. Very little, though, has actually been turned in. Very few such objects remain here, except for the last gold wedding bands; after all, practically no one in the ghetto possesses any jewelry, and what was possessed has long since been appropriated by the Kripo [German criminal police].

A DEATH

Today the physician, Dr. Zdzisław Świder, born in 1896, died here in the ghetto. Dr. Świder had been a resident of Warsaw; in the summer of 1941 he moved to the Pabianice ghetto, where he was one of the three practicing physicians until his resettlement to the Litzmannstadt ghetto. In Pabianice, the community was greatly indebted to him for his efforts in the fight against contagious diseases, especially since the sanitary conditions there were extremely poor. Having come to the Litzmannstadt ghetto with the transport of May, 1942, he enjoyed great popularity with other physicians and the populace here on account of his selfless work. He had been stricken by pulmonary tuberculosis, which he probably contracted in the course of his medical practice.

WEDNESDAY, FEBRUARY 23, 1944

NEWS OF THE DAY

Last night the Order Service again went into action, apprehending both men and women. The men were taken to the police precincts and then transferred to the former Special-Nutrition Kitchen on Ceglana Street, while the women were concentrated (in a former Special-Nutrition Kitchen) at 26 Zgierska [Street].

Most of those taken into custody were wives or other family members of fugitives. In addition, single women were apprehended at various departments, predominantly the Department of Food Supply, on the basis of lists.

[Henryk] Neftalin, the attorney, and his staff are checking the family situations of the women listed.

The German authorities (Commissioner Müller of the Gestapo)[7] have put M[arek] Kligier, head of the Special Department, in control of coordinating the actual opera-

---

7. This most likely refers to Hermann Müller, an official not of the Gestapo but of the Labor Office (*Arbeitsamt*) in Łódź who was responsible for recruiting workers within the city to be sent outside to perform manual labor.

tion, so that all other offices are, to this extent, subordinate to him. Commissioner Müller emphasized that Kligier alone would answer to him in duly carrying out the operation. This assignment is extremely disagreeable to Kligier, who has been trying to shirk the entire affair. We have already mentioned that the Chairman appointed the members of the commission in writing—mainly, no doubt, in order to make Kligier one of the responsible parties. Now Kligier must bear sole responsibility. It is too early to tell whether and how this will affect the overall character of the operation. But one thing is certain: the Chairman will judge individual cases from certain perspectives; in particular, from the Jewish and social perspective. Kligier can undoubtedly be expected to behave very correctly, but therefore all the more ruthlessly.

GHETTO ADMINISTRATION TO REMAIN

The authorities that determine the fate of the ghetto—the mayor, the Secret State Police, the Gauleiter, and the office of the Reich province [of Warthegau] in Poznań— have been negotiating with the so-called Ostindustrie Gesellschaft of the SS. But today it is fairly certain that their negotiations have collapsed. As a result, Amtsleiter Biebow will remain in his present capacity. The relations between him and the Chairman are, unfortunately, not satisfactory. Their most acute discord dates back to the well-known period when the Chairman was interrogated in the city. It is to be hoped that relations between these two men will improve in the near future; otherwise, there will inevitably be [dire] consequences for the ghetto.

[Hans Biebow] is still absent; he is reportedly in Berlin. It is rumored, though, that he had an automobile accident on the return trip to Litzmannstadt, and that he and his retinue suffered minor injuries.

CENSUS

A memorandum to all factories, workshops, and departments has ordered a census. Each work place is required to compile a precise tabulation of all persons registered there on February 20, 1944, together with their families. The census was ordered by the German authorities and is to be completed by February 26.

All material will be handed over to the Department of Statistics (Neftalin, the attorney) for further processing.

FOOD SUPPLY

No change. The ghetto continues to starve.

PEOPLE ARE SAYING

that pursuant to the Chairman's order, children born in 1935 are to be integrated into the production process by the Reclassification Commission. Naturally, this has given the ghetto a new basis for unsettling rumors. The parents of younger children are again troubled and confused by the fear that children will be resettled. At the moment, however, no such measure is under discussion. One thing is certain: the mayor [Otto Bradfisch, SS-Sturmbannführer], observing that the ghetto has about 5,000 unemployed persons, inquired how this was possible, since only some 2,000 children remained in the ghetto after the resettlement of September, 1942. The figure of 5,000 is puzzling, since natural population growth cannot account for 3,000 children. Hence the Chairman felt called upon to integrate the children born in 1935 into the labor force; he will probably do the same with even younger children who are physically well-developed.

SKETCHES OF GHETTO LIFE: LOFIX

This is what the ghetto jokingly calls the black pancake that is replacing real food during the current period of hunger: ersatz food made of ersatz coffee, fried in a pan. Lofix pancakes really do resemble the kindling material made of tar and pitch that is distributed at the coal market in lieu of wood. But while the combustible Lofix can ignite a fire, the edible variety cannot spark a person's energy when it is waning. It has no nutritional value; it merely deceives the stomach. Still, it does help to sustain the hope that soon it may again be replaced by potatoes.

P[eter] W[ertheimer]

THURSDAY, FEBRUARY 24, 1944

NEWS OF THE DAY: THE 1,600 WORKERS

The ghetto is still under the sway of the ongoing police action. Last night women were again dragged out of bed and interned at 26 Zgierska [Street]. There is still no exact head count at Central Prison.

Every day an insignificant percent of the fugitives turn themselves in. The committee that qualifies workers for labor outside the ghetto is still in session at Central Prison. It may be assumed that more women will be conscripted tonight. The possibility of dispatching 235 women alleviates the situation in regard to men, who are truly in short supply in the ghetto. But if 235 women are to be selected, according to various criteria (health, family situation, job), then, naturally, the commission must have sufficient reserves. This explains why at least three or four times as many women have to be made available for the selection process. As everyone knows, a date for dispatching the 1,600 workers has undoubtedly been set, but is being kept secret. Meanwhile, the work of outfitting them (work clothes and serviceable footwear) is progressing. The diet of the detainees continues to be good and it is therefore hoped that they can be sent off in relatively good health.

SKETCHES OF GHETTO LIFE: TODAY IS THE CHRONICLER'S BIRTHDAY

I do not mention the fact because it is a historic day in the ghetto or because I am delighted to celebrate another birthday after witnessing so many days of death. In this turbulent ocean of misery, nothing of that sort is even worth mentioning. What I have to say here could just as well be said of someone else, yet my purpose is not to demonstrate a talent for writing fiction—but rather, to trace the features of this day. My birthday was always an occasion for my family and friends to pamper me (already pampered enough) and to chain me even more tightly to the amenities of a proper bourgeois life. And this happened again today, the third birthday that I have been granted after resettlement in the ghetto. I would like to report briefly on how I was pampered on this special day—and not without mentioning that no one knew of the occasion except my family and two elderly ladies who live with us. Like everything in the ghetto, our celebration revolved around the menu. There was a birthday meal for all seven of us, and a special treat for me alone. The table was set with particular ceremony. Since we had not brought any tablecloths along from Prague, each of us got a paper napkin, an inconceivable luxury in the ghetto. The soup consisted of some rye grits into which, to celebrate the occasion, three potatoes had been grated—the best method for thickening a watery soup. A bit of paprika and dried leek added color and flavor. The second course: babka made of potato peels. Something very special indeed. A delicacy such as this is unobtainable without good connections in the public kitchens. And then you have to know which kitchens peel potatoes with a regular knife and which ones with a potato peeler. There's a big difference. If a regular knife is used, then the peels are thick; otherwise, they are nothing but a thin film of vitamins. (There were a few physicians in the ghetto who in all seriousness tried to persuade the Jews that potato peels contain vitamins, and that one ought to eat them in order to prevent softening of the bones.) In any case, my wife managed to get hold of some potato peels, and God only knows what strings she had to pull; or perhaps she bought them at seventy marks a kilogram—the person celebrating his birthday can't ask. The babka was baked so thoroughly in the tsholnt bakery that it actually consisted of sheer crust. This is a great advantage: the teeth have something to dig into, and the palate receives no sensation of flavor. Potato peels ground in the meat grinder, with ersatz coffee and a bit of flour—when done it looks like a deformed briquette. This dark rock on my plate is covered with a cream sauce. How do you make the sauce? Take some sugar, some "coffee powder," and a teaspoon of flour. Mix, while stirring in one cup of water. Simmer the paste, let it cool, and then beat with a whisk. The result is a sweet, dark-brown cream sauce. Just a hair's breadth away from mocha cream—better make it a hair's length, for our taste buds are long since numbed or else have lost their memory. We crush the "rocks" with a few powerful twists of the wrist. Everyone is thrilled, and we gratefully recall the characters in Pearl Buck's novel about China, *The Good Earth* [1931], and the equally innocent coolies who have to eat dirt. We have no right to complain; we ought to remember the real China. After all, we only live in a European imitation. Enough said!

Such was the birthday menu. Then came the presents! My children had saved up a few bowls of soup to sell and had bought a hundred grams of sugar with the proceeds. My sister followed suit with fifty cigarettes, the expensive variety, bought illicitly. They must have cost a small fortune. The two ladies bestowed upon me a tiny case, of unknown content. I was about to make an indignant remark—the case seemed worthy of gold or silver jewelry, and all such objects must now be surrendered. In suspense I unfolded the tiny tissue paper, and out came four flints for my cigarette lighter. I was touched, but I could not suppress a mild reproach for the extravagance. Four flints! Who knows where the ladies unearthed these jewels! They must have been searching for months to collect these four precious stones. And my wife's present—a tear. Well, sometimes one simply loses control of oneself in Shanghai—Litzmannstadt. Can you, who are reading this at some future time, can you calculate how many hours it took her to pick over the potato peels for the babka, my birthday cake?

Dr. O[skar] S[inger]

SATURDAY, FEBRUARY 26, 1944

SKETCHES OF GHETTO LIFE: NIGHT LIFE IN THE GHETTO

Like America, the ghetto of Litzmannstadt is the land of unlimited possibilities. Something that was strictly prohibited yesterday will be the law tomorrow. The ghetto can be turned upside down in a matter of hours. And now this has happened again.

On Monday, February 14, 1944, the ghetto suddenly developed a "night life." Not, however, in bars or at brightly lit café concerts with cheerful, well-dressed people; but rather in the ghetto streets and at the distribution stores.

Last summer, when the days were hot and the evenings warm and lovely, no one was permitted outdoors after 9 P.M. Every tardy pedestrian who wanted to breathe a little fresh air rather than disappear into his room behind blacked-out windows was stopped by Order Service men and asked to show his papers; or, if it was just 9 o'clock, he was admonished in Polish: "Prędko, prędko, iść do domu! Nie spacerować!" [Quick, quick! Go home! Don't dawdle!] But now, it is just the opposite.

Between 8 A.M. at the latest and 5 P.M., during working hours, no one is allowed on the streets—except for people on official errands, with a pass indicating the exact route and hour at which the bearer is entitled to leave his work place. These passes are issued by the management of a factory or department only in the most urgent cases. But that is not all; it is also unlawful to remain in one's apartment unless one works at home or has been certified ill by a physician. You must reckon with the possibility that your apartment may be inspected—if only for hygiene and cleanliness—and that you will have to justify your presence at home exactly as you do on the street.

To be sure, the ghetto dweller has been reduced to very short rations, but he cannot live solely on air and work. Previously, families consisting of several members with different work hours had a chance to pick up their rations during the day, while single persons could leave work for brief periods in order to do the same. In short, things more or less worked. One way or another, you bore the heavy burden of ghetto life. As a consequence, however, there was a constant flow of foot traffic in the streets, and visiting commissions could simply not understand why the streets and shops were crowded with people during working hours.

Now this torrent of tired, hungry workers pours out into the street all at once at 5 P.M., and not before. The schedule is as follows: pick up rations, prepare supper, clean up the apartment—which you left, in most cases, shortly after 6 A.M.; that is, when it was still dark, so that the various "bucket chores," the wood and coal, etcetera, etcetera, are waiting for you when you return. So, everyone wants to get home as fast as possible, picking up rations on the way. Consequently, people rush to the distribution shops to avoid having to be out in the snow, wet, and cold late at night. The commotion outside and inside the shops, which are open from 5 P.M., to midnight, is not only indescribable, but dangerous to life and limb. Take the [most recent] bread day, for instance. Everyone counts on picking up his eight-day, two-kilogram bread [ration] as usual, early in the morning before going to work; hardly anyone has even a slice left. But bread is not distributed until 5 P.M. So nearly all the workers are without bread on this day, and many of them have gone without for several days. No wonder they pounce on the shops like hungry wolves, smashing windows, ripping each other's clothes, punching, arguing, crushing ribs. In many cases it is not so much hunger that drives them, but the fear of getting no bread at all, for bread could be "just out" ("ausfehlen" is the term used here when some item is temporarily out of stock). So a person is very lucky if he can finally leave the store after an hour and a half, maybe even longer, *with* a loaf of bread and with his clothes and limbs intact.

The same is true of the milk shops, meat shops, the coal payment office on Dworska Street, and the coal yard on Spacerowa Street. People stand in line everywhere and shiver in the wet, cold darkness of the night. If the "distribution schedule" does not force you to appear at a specific time, and you choose to go in the late evening, around nine or ten o'clock, then it can sometimes happen that you "march in and out," that is, collect the ration without standing in line. But otherwise you have to *shtupn* [shove].

So you have a choice. You can line up for your rations between 5 and 9 [P.M.], then come home and, if the stove heats nicely and everything goes well, have your evening soup by around 11 o'clock; in the best circumstances, maybe also a black pancake, the so-called Lofix—a "something" made of ersatz coffee that epitomizes the bitterness of ghetto life. Or else you follow the reverse sequence: you cook and eat first, and then you run for your rations when the ghetto's "night life" begins.

A[licja] de B[unom]

MONDAY, FEBRUARY 28, 1944

NEWS OF THE DAY: THE 1,600 WORKERS

Today there is still no change in the situation. No word of a fixed date for dispatching the transport. People are packed like sardines in the limited confines of Central Prison; and although their diet is good, they are suffering from the nearly unbearable living conditions. Families are still sacrificing themselves to sustain their relatives in hiding, and the consequences will not be apparent until next month. Tragedies whose details will not be grasped until later are being enacted.

ADDENDUM TO THE NEWS OF THE DAY: A DEATH

Today, Dr. Abram Jakób Karo died. The physician was born in Łódź on August 14, 1909, and he completed his studies just before the war. In the ghetto he was the first director of the Emergency Service at 13 Lutomierska Street and later the medical director of the outpatient clinic at 40 Lutomierska Street. He enjoyed great popularity in the ghetto. At the age of 35, in the prime of life, he succumbed to tuberculosis, which he had probably contracted in the course of his duties.

TUESDAY, FEBRUARY 29, 1944

NEWS OF THE DAY: THE 1,600 WORKERS

The operation still looms over the ghetto like a thundercloud. The rain of deliverance will not fall. The ghetto is buzzing with all sorts of rumors about a change in the situation: that only a small percent [of detainees] will actually leave; that approximately a thousand persons are to be released tomorrow; that the operation is petering out altogether because the Arbeitsamt [Labor Office] in Poznań has obtained the necessary Jewish manpower elsewhere; that the detainees will be released, but will have to sign a declaration that they will report if conscripted again; and so forth. None of this has been confirmed. Sources close to the Chairman know nothing of any changes in the present German orders.

[GHETTO STAMPS]

The Chairman is planning to issue a ten-pfennig stamp for internal mail service in the ghetto. Two designs have already been submitted; presumably, they will be used one after the other. The Chairman, however, intends to put only a very small number of stamps (barely a thousand) into circulation, and to print only a few thousand altogether. He has received permission from the German authorities to issue these stamps.[8]

THE CHAIRMAN'S APARTMENT

As previously reported [February 15, 1944], the Chairman will have to vacate his apartment at 63 Łagiewnicka Street by March 15, 1944. He has decided to live in Marysin and not occupy a "town apartment."

WEDNESDAY, MARCH 1, 1944

NEWS OF THE DAY: THE 1,600 WORKERS (1,610)

The quota of workers to be dispatched was raised by ten yesterday, so that altogether 1,610 persons are now required for manual labor outside the ghetto. The situation has basically not changed. The detainees are still living in the worst possible overcrowding conditions at Central Prison. An effort has been made to provide them some relief by installing bunks in their quarters, so that they can at least stretch out flat. The normal capacity of Central Prison is approximately 400 persons, so one can gauge roughly what conditions are like now with some 1,200 people there.

Not only are fugitives reporting, but nearly every day there have been volunteers, among them four women from the Feather and Down Department.

---

8. The matter of the ghetto's postage stamp continued for more than two years. On January 30, 1942, the Eldest of the Jews announced, in a proclamation issued especially for that purpose, an open competition for the design of the postage stamp, which was to be used only in internal mail, within the confines of the ghetto. The awarding of three prizes—100, 60, and 40 marks—was scheduled. The announcement of the competition coincided with the deportation action just begun by the Germans, which sent people from the ghetto to the death camp in Chełmno (Kulmhof). After a long while, toward the end of the "peaceful" year, 1943, the question of the ghetto stamp again became a current concern and the ghetto printing shop, in keeping with the three submitted projects (one first prize was won by Pinchas Szwarc [Shaar]), produced sample stamps, among others one with the likeness of Rumkowski on it, and one with emblems of work in the center of a Star of David. As soon as the information that the stamp was ready reached the German authorities, they immediately ordered the stamps already produced to be withdrawn, although, as the *Chronicle* notes, everything until then had been done with their agreement.

THURSDAY, MARCH 2, 1944

SKETCHES OF GHETTO LIFE: VOLUNTEERS STEP FORWARD

Yesterday morning a 48-year-old man reported to Central Prison as a volunteer. He was told to think it over carefully, for it is relatively easy to get into Central Prison, but considerably more complicated to get out; once he entered, he would not be released.

Whereupon the man said that he would pack his satchel and come back. No one expected him to reappear, but that afternoon he indeed marched in whith his satchel. The next day, the volunteer's son appeared at the office of Central Prison and pleaded for his father's release. He said that there had been an argument at home; the father had lost his temper, abandoned the family, and decided to apply for labor outside the ghetto. It is questionable whether the father will succeed in getting out of this venture.

FRIDAY, MARCH 3, 1944

NEWS OF THE DAY: 1,610–1,710 WORKERS

Today the quota of 1,610 workers was raised to 1,710. This makes the situation more complicated for the Chairman, and also for [Marek] Kligier, chief of the Special Department, who is in charge of the operation. Just yesterday Kligier met with the Chairman, and both men entertained hopes that the required number would be reduced. Today's news that the opposite has occurred comes as a great shock. In the evening it was learned that a departure time has been set and that the first group, roughly half the workers, must be ready to be shipped out by 4 A.M. Transportation was still being prepared this afternoon at Radogoszcz Station. Further details about the number of passengers and the destination of the transport are not yet available. All the agencies in the ghetto involved [in this effort] are convinced, however, that the workers can expect an improvement in their situation. During the afternoon, those who had been definitively designated for labor outside the ghetto were segregated at Central Prison. The rest were kept in reserve in a separate area. Last night more workers were conscripted, mostly single men and women, the latter chiefly from the Department of Soup Kitchens. A few from the coal storage yard (*Luftschutz Wart*) [the air defense warden] were likewise brought in.

PUBLIC HEALTH

With reference to reports we have received of the deaths of two physicians, we must observe that the situation of physicians in the ghetto has grown significantly worse. From the beginning, physicians were among the ghetto's privileged inhabitants. Initially, their food allotments were identical to the B[eirat] allotment; furthermore, given the lucrative rates for medical services, doctors were easily able to buy additional food.

Since the suspension of the Beirat [allotments], the situation has changed rapidly. The physicians have lost everything, which was bound to have consequences, considering the truly strenuous duties they must perform in the ghetto. Since the Chairman has absolutely refused to raise the physicians' fee rates, and since the price of food has soared in the interim (as we have reported again and again), physicians can no longer, to any significant extent, obtain additional food with their wages or fees from private practice. Dr. [Wiktor] Miller's repeated attempts to have the L[angar-beiter] allotments approved for physicians (to have them placed in the category of long-shift workers) were thwarted by the German authorities. This situation is, of course, bound to have an impact on the ghetto, for a weary and exhausted physician is hardly willing to make house calls for ten marks if a bowl of soup costs up to 40 marks. The bread and meat allotments granted to most physicians by the Chairman himself do not even come close to compensating for the loss of the previous regular allotments.

SATURDAY, MARCH 4, 1944

NEWS OF THE DAY: 1,710 WORKERS

On the evening of March 3 the following Proclamation, No. 414, was posted:

Warning!
Re: Dispatch of Workers from the Ghetto.

Since various persons have still not reported to Central Prison despite my repeated warnings, I am making a final appeal to them to report without fail to Central Prison immediately after the posting of this proclamation.

Those still in hiding are wrong in believing that the cancellation of ration cards will be rescinded after the transport of workers has been dispatched.

I must expressly point out that this assumption is incorrect, and that after the labor transport has left, the persons in question will have to report to Central Prison along with their entire families.

When applying at Central Prison for reinstatement of ration cards, those who had previously been in hiding will be arrested and detained there; they will be forced to reveal where they have been concealed, who aided them in conceal-ment, and who supported them with any sort of food during this period—so that those people too can be called to account. Ration cards will not be reinstated before this is done.

Those who are still in hiding but who turn themselves in at Central Prison without delay after the posting of this proclamation will be exempted, along with their families, from the measures described above.

Litzmannstadt-Getto   Ch[aim] Rumkowski
March 3, 1944   The Eldest of the Jews in Litzmannstadt

This proclamation was also published in Yiddish. It is obvious that the Eldest is making desperate efforts to flush out those still in hiding. Nevertheless, one must remain skeptical even about this new attempt; knowing how tenacious and fright-ened these people are, one suspects that even such earnest threats will probably not attain their objective.

FIRST GROUP DEPARTS

By yesterday evening insiders knew that the first group of 750 men would leave the ghetto early this morning. The men were alerted at 4 A.M.; and at 5:30 they marched off to Radogoszcz Station, where several freightcars were waiting to move them out.

A representative of the private firm that requisitioned the workers had arrived to take charge of them, and, accompanied by an officer of the Order Service, he led the group to Radogoszcz. En route he conversed with the Order Service officer, remarking that it really wasn't all that far to Częstochowa[9] and that upon arrival the workers would have five days of rest in which to get settled and oriented. They would be working in a metal or textile factory there and would certainly be better off than in the ghetto, since the food situation there was considerably better. As long as they did decent work, they would have nothing to complain about.

He also said that there was a possibility of their establishing contact by mail with their families in the ghetto.

It is not known to what extent this man was in a position to make such a positive prediction. The workers will be living in a camp, and since mail is absolutely prohibited in all Jewish camps in Germany, there is little hope of an exception here.

The first transport group included the physician Dr. Adalbert Löwy (resettled here from Prague) and a few barbers. Dr. Löwy was accommodated very correctly in the official railroad car of the German transport director. This time, the workers were taken into custody and placed in the freightcars in an entirely correct manner. No one was beaten or even roughly treated. The workers' gear was loaded onto the baggage car by the Order Service.

The transport also included Mosze Boms, the so-called V[ertraungsmann—informer] of the Kripo [German criminal police]. And thereby hangs a tale. This Boms was one of the vilest figures in the ghetto. As one of the German criminal police's prime informers he denounced countless Jews in the ghetto. During the search for fugitives from conscription, the Order Service visited his apartment. Boms flaunted his high-level connections in the criminal police; but when the Kripo heard of the matter, it declined [to intervene]; it left it up to the discretion of the Eldest to apprehend Boms and his entire family. The people found in his apartment were also taken in, because they had ignored the Eldest's proclamation that no one was permitted to spend the night in someone else's apartment. Boms's father and the rest of his family are still in Central Prison. Mosze Boms himself did his best to avoid being shipped out, but he was unable to pull any strings. Before leaving with the transport he, of course, had to endure something of a beating from the detainees in Central Prison. It's hardly surprising that the Jews could not pass up a chance to slap and kick this abject scoundrel. Reportedly, Boms tried to maneuver his way out of being sent

9. Częstochowa or, more precisely, the forced labor camp for Jews (Judenlager Hasag) in Częstochowa, was indeed the place where the people were sent who had been seized in the recruitment action that had begun in the ghetto on February 8, 1943. This was probably the first case in which Jews from the Łódź ghetto had been sent out to perform manual labor, not to the Reich or to territories incorporated into the Reich, but to the Generalgouvernement. The Judenlager Hasag employed its prisoners chiefly in armaments factories. The camp was liquidated on January 16, 1945, a few days before the city was taken by the Red Army troops, while the prisoners and those still fit for work were deported to concentration camps in Buchenwald, Gross Rosen, and Ravensbrück.

from the ghetto by opening an artery, but this trick was of no avail. When the workers were loaded onto freightcars, every group refused to take in this ugly customer. Ultimately, the chief informer had to be stowed in the baggage car.

SPECIAL GROUP

The ten persons who were added when the quota of 1,600 was raised to 1,610 formed a special group which left on the same day, but by way of Bałut Market instead of Radogoszcz. It is reported that this group will do agricultural labor. The names of the ten men involved are as follows: Moszek Jakób Cukierman, Chaskiel Cybuch, Zelig Daniel, Całek Działowski, Abram Glanc, Zelman Goldberg, Jankiel Dawid Kordelas, Franz Kraus, Lajb Majsterman, Bencjon Strykowski.

The departing workers received two kilograms of bread, 250 grams of sugar, 100 grams of rendered fat, and 50 cigarettes.

A ROAD BLOCK AT BAŁUT MARKET

A barrier has been erected at the gate on Bałut Market. Its purpose is to isolate Bałut Market from the ghetto in the event of an air raid, so that only those employed at Bałut Market can use the fragmentation-bomb trenches that have just been dug there.

SUNDAY, MARCH 5, 1944

SKETCHES OF GHETTO LIFE: PECULIAR BRAVERY

A woman is standing in the crowd of people waiting outside Central Prison. Her husband is inside waiting to be shipped out of the ghetto. He appears at the second-story window of the building in which his group is quartered. Apparently, he has arranged with her that he will contrive to make himself unfit for labor. He is about to leap out the window; he hesitates. But his wife shouts to him [in Yiddish]: "Hob nisht keyn moyre!" [Don't be afraid!]. She herself goads him to jump. And he actually does jump; he sustains minor injuries and is, in fact, exempted from conscription. The adventure could also have ended more unpleasantly.

MONDAY, MARCH 6, 1944

NEWS OF THE DAY: THE 1,710 WORKERS

The first group, 750 men, has already reached its destination. Although it is physically impossible, people would like to have received messages from the workers in the first transport, which left in the direction of Częstochowa. Naturally, this is quite out of the question.

The roundup continues. Last night was yet another night of terror. Men and women, mostly the latter, were forcibly removed from their apartments—approximately 350 persons, most of them unmarried. The lists were drawn up by the Bureau of Labor and not, as the ghetto grapevine has it, by factory managers.

The Chairman and [Marek] Kligier are clearly making an honest effort to reduce the suffering caused by resettlement as much as possible by selecting only younger, unmarried persons whose departure will not inflict emotional and material hardship on entire families.

Regardless of whether or not their fate has already been determined, the detainees are being taken in groups to bathe at the disinfection facilities.

Today's raid was not, as before, restricted to people employed in the departments; workshop employees were also taken, though only those, of course, whose departure would not impair production in their plants.

MATZOTH

By arrangement between the Chairman and the managers of the bakeries, [Mordecai] Lajzerowicz and [Józef] Gutman, the bakery on Piwna Street will soon begin to produce matzoth. This bakery will have to make do with its own manpower, however, since no additional manpower can be made available. It is clear, of course, that this single bakery cannot produce in any significant quantity; thus the problem of providing matzoth for the coming Peysekh [Passover] holidays has not yet been fully resolved. Perhaps other bakeries will be used during the coming week, but this depends on their ability to muster the required skilled bakers and auxiliary personnel required.

SKETCHES OF GHETTO LIFE: TRAFFIC IN HUMAN FLESH

Not dispassionately—indeed, with sympathy for those involved—the chronicler will now report on the misery caused by the dispatch of 1,710 workers from the ghetto. In many respects the present resettlement recalls the days of September 1942, of cursed memory; and anyone with any memory and any imagination will admit that those days symbolize the essence of the Litzmannstadt ghetto: the mutual reinforcement of terror and hunger!

The roundup laid bare every human passion, the good and the evil. People still remembered the previous labor transports, and so those conscripted for the February transport sought to escape at all costs. They evaded the night roundup by flight, by cunning, by abandoning everything they owned. To little avail. The authority responsible for the labor contingent warned the conscripts, in a series of strikingly sober proclamations, not to ignore their obligation and further underscored the warning by threatening to withhold food from entire families. Nevertheless, the evasion continued. Pursued day and night, the fugitives hid in deserted barracks, in holes, attics, or out-of-the-way spots in the workshops—places unsuitable even for animals to sleep in. The ghetto dwellers assigned to be sent out of the ghetto, the so-called "workers," were hunted like forest game. . . . And this went on for three weeks. Three long anxious weeks.

But even in the depths of misery, a few of the condemned managed to find a way out: they found replacements. Although leaving the ghetto is considered a mortally dangerous venture, they found men who were willing to make this venture in their stead. The price, the fee, was two loaves of bread and one kilogram of sugar, or other food of equal value. In February 1944, in exchange for two loaves of bread and one kilogram of sugar, Jews went forth into bondage, into uncertainty, and perhaps death. . . . The craving to satisfy their hunger was as great as that hunger itself.

"Things can't be worse on the outside," the replacement said to himself, "and now I can at least fill up on bread for a couple of days."

When terror, hunger, and misery exceed all bounds, two loaves of bread and one kilogram of sugar can buy a human life. The ghetto dweller's psychology confronts science with problems never before known.

O[skar] R[osenfeld]

TUESDAY, MARCH 7, 1944

NEWS OF THE DAY

The 1,710 Workers
Last night the Order Service and the Special Department took another 500 persons into custody and brought them to Central Prison. Once again, they were mostly women.

Now word has actually been received from the group that already left the ghetto: having determined that conditions were favorable, the physician Dr. [Adalbert] Löwy[10] has requested that his fiancée, a Miss Haas, be sent out after him. The news spread through the ghetto like wildfire and has, of course, improved the general mood considerably.

Brought to this Ghetto
Perla Rychlewska, born in Bełchatów in 1901 and hitherto residing there, at 14 Adolf-Hitler-Strasse [Piotrkowska Street],[11] was brought to the ghetto today and lodged in the home for persons without families in Marysin. With the aid of forged papers, she had been passing as a Pole.

The Passementerie Plant
Since its opening, this plant has employed a group of four experienced German workers, women and men. Now only two instructors are left. It is interesting to note that before the war the manufacture of passementerie, as a cottage industry, was fairly widespread and even technically advanced among the Jews in Łódź; today, however, there are few skilled workers in this field. In any case, the necessary personnel will be trained here in the course of time, as they have been in all other factories.

GHETTO HUMOR

People here have a saying: There are two Kaufmans [*Kaufmann*: merchant] in the ghetto, one for fire and one for water. (The directors of both the Fire Department and the Department of Soup Kitchens are named Kaufman.)

WEDNESDAY, MARCH 8, 1944

SURRENDER OF MUSICAL INSTRUMENTS

After the Eldest's proclamation concerning the surrender of musical instruments, the owners of such instruments immediately began to register them. This operation was

10. Cf. p. 467.
11. As in every other occupied city in Poland, the main and most elegant street was renamed for Adolf Hitler.

supervised by the conductor Dawid Bajgelman. Well-known as a musician before the war (and not just in Jewish circles), Bajgelman had traveled nearly everywhere in the world and was also an outstanding connoisseur of all kinds of musical instruments.

Soon after their registration the instruments had to be turned in at 32 Łagiewnicka Street. The collection was first inspected by Amtsleiter Biebow, who was accompanied by his deputy Mr. Czarnulla. Then an expert from the city arrived, as well as the general manager of the municipal theater of Litzmannstadt. From among the available instruments the latter two men selected whatever suited their needs, in three categories: A—for the municipal orchestra; B—for the mayor; C—for the music school of the Hitler Youth and for the Reich Chamber of Music.

The expert asked Bajgelman about the value and quality of the instruments, and Bajgelman attempted to explain the special qualities of each item. But [the expert], a young man and probably a mere novice on the organ or some other instrument, showed little comprehension of the various treasures and set prices that sounded like jokes. Two excellent cellos with a prewar market value of approximately 1,000 marks were assessed by him at 120 marks. A trombone with custom-made valves and slide, a curiously constructed instrument of nickel silver with a prewar purchase price of about 500 marks, was assessed at 20 marks; forty-four violins for the Hitler Youth, at a mark each. There was a small accordion, a magnificent work of art that had originally been purchased for about 600 marks; he appraised it at 20 marks and presented it to the mayor. The finest instruments purchased from the Jews went to the Reich's Chamber of Music for the following sums: fifteen master violins, two of them priceless instruments at least 300 years old, for a total of 100 marks (roughly 7 marks apiece); two master saxophones with a prewar value of at least 1,200 marks, for 40 marks.

Four pianos, all of them first-rate makes and nearly new, with a total value of approximately 7,000 marks, were bought from the Jews by the expert for a total of 600 marks.

Splendid mandolins, guitars, zithers, lutes, flutes, clarinets, saxophones, trumpets, cymbals, and so forth, were assigned an average price of 2 or 3 marks apiece. For all the instruments surrendered (a precise list is in the Archives), the Eldest received a total of about 2,400 marks (the present market equivalent of roughly 2,000 saccharine tablets).

SKETCHES OF GHETTO LIFE: BERNSTEIN FINDS A REPLACEMENT

Four loaves of bread, one kilogram of sugar, a half-kilogram of margarine: the deal is concluded in due form, and the replacement reports to Central Prison. While the papers are being processed, he settles down to a good meal. In the course of one day he consumes a loaf of bread and a quarter-kilogram of margarine. He feels fine; he lolls about on the bunk and says that he hasn't been this well off in four years. Nothing can trouble his mood—the news from the Częstochowa camp is reassuring. What could possibly happen? He's simply on the way to a different job with better living conditions.

The next day, the replacement is summoned to the office: "You're working on the excrement removal crew? People like you aren't allowed out. You're staying!" So the deal is off. The replacement was fully aware of this policy, but upon entering Central

Prison he had somehow made the slight *faux pas* of failing to mention the matter. Back to the excrement removal crew he goes, while his partner in the deal has to leave the ghetto. In the courtyard the two of them meet, and you might well imagine that the fellow who has been cheated will go for his "replacement's" throat. The loss of one loaf of bread and a quarter-kilogram of margarine is reason enough. But no, he hasn't lost his composure. He resigns himself to the inevitable and says to the excrement removal man: "Well, you're a shark, but as for the food—enjoy it in good health."

THURSDAY, MARCH 9, 1944

SKETCHES OF GHETTO LIFE: GHETTO MOVIE

Two sisters live in one room together with a cousin. The day before yesterday, the young man was warned that the German police were interested in him and that he might be picked up in the night. He took refuge at the home of friends. To the horror of the sisters, the dreaded visitors did in fact arrive. A civilian with no stars [of David on his clothing], accompanied by a Jewish policeman, appeared at the door and asked for L. When the sisters replied that they had no idea where L. was, he ordered them to turn and face the wall. He demanded to know where they store their own and their cousin's rations. The sisters revealed the location. When they turned around again, the nocturnal visitors were gone, and so was their food. Now the real police will probably have to deal with "the 'politsyanten [policemen]' and the 'German.'"

P[eter] W[ertheimer]

FRIDAY, MARCH 10, 1944

NEWS OF THE DAY: THE 1,700 WORKERS

Early this morning the second group, of 850 workers (men and women), left here to perform manual labor outside the ghetto. Their destination remains unknown. The 100 people remaining in Central Prison are reportedly leaving for agricultural labor on Monday.

TUESDAY, MARCH 21, 1944

NEWS OF THE DAY

Good news is arriving every day from the people resettled to Częstochowa. They are employed in an appliance factory; the work is fairly hard, but the food is relatively good, and all the messages emphasize the excellent reception and the good treatment they have been given. The establishment of mail service between them and the ghetto is reportedly due to the personal efforts of M[arek] Kligier.

SKETCHES OF GHETTO LIFE: A SNATCH OF CONVERSATION IN THE STREET

Two very little boys conduct the following conversation: "Did you drink your lunch already?"

"No, I've only eaten some coffee."

The question and answer characterize the situation in the ghetto. The midday meal consists of a more or less thin soup. The few potatoes hiding at the bottom of the murky liquid offer the teeth little opportunity for exercise. There is really not much to eat, merely something to drink. On the other hand, the Lofix pancakes are made of [ersatz] coffee and roasted until hard in a frying pan; they alone give the teeth a workout.

TUESDAY, MARCH 28, 1944

NEWS OF THE DAY

The reclassification initiated by Amtsleiter Biebow and continued by the Chairman is reaching its conclusion. In the final stage, extra auxiliary workers are to be dismissed from the kitchens. In any event, the tempest has subsided and the ghetto is gradually quieting down again.

FOOD SUPPLY

Today, after a long interruption, the ghetto again received a modicum of potatoes—14,240 kilograms—and 23,000 kilograms of beets. The potatoes are going to the kitchens, of course, while the beets will be sent to the distribution points for a ration that is expected shortly. To be sure, these minimal quantities cannot do much to diminish the prevailing hunger.

MATZOTH

Matzoth are now being produced in a second bakery. Applications for matsoth in place of bread are now being accepted. It will not be possible to bake enough for everyone since that is not technically feasible and, also, because the Amtsleiter has not approved a plan to supply the entire populace. Presumably, the Chairman will reserve part of the matzoth produced for distribution through coupons. By and large, the ghetto anticipates the arrival of rations for the peysekh [Passover] holidays. Hopes are very high, but in view of the short supplies it seems hardly likely that such hopes will be realized. Since the Chairman can freely dispose of only 2 percent of the food supply, we cannot look forward to large allotments. The rumor that the Chairman plans to restore allotments B, B I, B II, and so forth, is without basis. There is even no way to make a good case for such a restoration with the German food supply authorities, who grant special dietary privileges only to manual laborers. Thus, all the Chairman can do is offer coupons from his own reserves.

The ratio of matzoth to bread is one kilogram of matzoth to two kilograms of bread.

Workshop and office employees will be assigned to the bakeries for as long as matzoth is being produced, that is, for ten days.

TUESDAY, APRIL 4, 1944

NEWS OF THE DAY

The Loan Office

The Loan Office, which had been closed, will resume operations very shortly. It will be open to the public from 5 P.M., when the workshops and departments close, until 10 P.M. every day. Loans will be made in the same way as before. The manager of this agency, Dr. Józef Klementynowski, may be given a new function: reportedly, he will be in charge of the office for supplemental ration cards.

The Special Allotments

Who is to receive what coupons from the Chairman for Passover has now been established. The lists are by and large completed; the Chairman has checked and approved them and handed them over to the R-shop. Further lists are in preparation. The categories are as follows:

I. Adopted children: 200 g peas, 150 g matzoth meal, 150 g fat, 200 g marmalade, 100 g sugar, one-half kg matzoth, 100 g cheese, 150 g sauerkraut, 250 g meat.

II. The Hasidim: 200 g peas, 200 g sugar, 250 g sago, 100 g potato groats, 100 g margarine, 1 kg matzoth, 1 kg beets, 250 g onions, one-fourth liter wine, 100 g matzoth meal.

III. The police: 100 g peas, 100 g sugar, 100 g sago, 100 g matsoth meal, 50 g potato groats, 500 g matzoth, one-half kg potatoes, one-half kg beets, 100 g margarine.

IV. The former holders of *B* coupons: 200 g peas, 150 g sugar, 100 g margarine, 150 g marmalade, 200 g cheese, 100 g matzoth meal, 250 g onions, 1 kg potatoes, 1 kg beets, 1 can S[*chwein*—pork] meat.

V. *B* I: 100 g peas, 100 g matzoth meal, 100 g margarine, 100 g marmalade, 100 g sugar, 100 g cheese, 1 kg potatoes, one-half can S-meat.

The Ghetto Loses A District

The Eldest has been ordered by the German authorities to tear down a section of the ghetto from Drewnowska to Podrzeczna streets. This is a hard blow for the ghetto, affecting nearly 2,000 residents for whom apartments will have to be found elsewhere. Reportedly, the Chairman will have to muster a brigade of 500 workers for the project. There are rows of buildings in excellent condition on both Drewnowska and Podrzeczna streets in which a large number of people with special privileges reside (chiefly physicians). It is hoped that the demolition work will proceed at a moderate pace, so that the tenants affected can be relocated with relatively little disruption. The news is, however, casting a pall on the holiday mood, at least of those who were hoping to receive a special allotment from the Chairman.

WEDNESDAY, APRIL 5, 1944

NEWS OF THE DAY: A COMMISSION IN THE GHETTO

A relatively large commission, accompanied by the mayor [and chief of the Gestapo, Otto Bradfisch] of Litzmannstadt, visited the ghetto and, among other locations, the construction site at Radogoszcz.

HOLIDAY ALLOTMENT

The ghetto is entirely under the spell of the Passover coupons. Nothing else is talked about, and the less people know, the more they have to say. Various groups have petitioned the Chairman for allotments. It appears that the Chairman would like to be generous this time, but insiders are baffled by the question of what reserves he can tap. Perhaps he has managed to save adequate provisions from the 2 percent of the food supply at his disposal. It is certain that, in addition to the various coupon categories, there will be special allotments of matzoth—probably mainly for the so-called Hasidim, whom the Chairman has, oddly enough, always favored. The general populace, however, has no great esteem for this particular group.

PEYSEKH SOUP

The Chairman plans to distribute special soup to Jews observing the holidays. The soup will be cooked without flour and will contain only some sauerkraut and potatoes; sago or matzoth meal will be used for thickening. The soup will be distributed from Friday, April 7 to Saturday, April 15.

THURSDAY, APRIL 6, 1944

NEWS OF THE DAY

Passover Coupons
Those so privileged by the Chairman (so far about 3,000) are now picking up their allotments in R-shop I, which is, of course, extremely busy. The first to receive allotments were the adopted children. Their coupons are in Yiddish, which, when translated, reads as follows:

> You are hereby requested to collect a food-coupon allotment as a holiday gift for your adopted child (name . . . .) and your family at R-shop I, 18 Łagiewnicka Street, on Wednesday, April 5, or Thursday, April 6, 1944, from 5 P.M. on.
> I take this occasion to wish you happy holidays.
>
> M[ordecai] Ch[aim] Rumkowski
> The Eldest of the Jews in Litzmannstadt

The wording plainly indicates that this coupon is meant not only for the adopted child, but for the entire family.

Every day, new lists compiled under the Chairman's auspices arrive at R-shop I. Nearly all former beneficiaries of the B-allotment have received coupon IV or V. Coupon III (for the police) was granted only to the regular Order Service, the Fire Department, and the chimney sweeps.

The Special Department is receiving its allotments through its own internal channels. The Chairman has appointed a committee to distribute coupons to Hasidim; the committee consists of the following men: Head Cashier [Salomon] Ser, Boruch Praszkier, Henryk Fein, Perec Blaugrund, and Mendel Rozenmutter.

The Ghetto Printing Plant

has also recently received assignments from the German authorities. It is printing material for both the Ghetto Administration and Precinct VI of the [German] police.

FRIDAY, APRIL 7, 1944

NEWS OF THE DAY

The ghetto is in a holiday spirit for erev peysekh [the eve of Passover]. The meager supplies of matzoth are the only visible sign of a holiday. In all likelihood, there is no real Seder plate in any home. Not even the wine that the Chairman has bestowed upon his Hasidim will contribute much to the festive mood—the wine is made of beet juice. But then no one can give more than he has.

SATURDAY, APRIL 8, 1944

NEWS OF THE DAY

Mayor Dr. Bradfisch's directive concerning the demolition of the ghetto district on Drewnowska and Podrzeczna streets has already officially gone out to the Eldest. A brigade of workers must be deployed immediately; the project must begin without delay. Presumably, the demolition will proceed so that the best buildings are the last to go. The Relocation Division of the Department of Housing is extremely busy making apartments available elsewhere.

WORKSHOP NEWS

The workshops have been notified by the Central Secretariat at Bałut Market that, this year, Easter Sunday and Easter Monday will be days of rest. This is the first time since the establishment of the ghetto that no one will work on these days. Furthermore, work will stop today at 12 noon. The populace is not quite sure how to take this directive. "Timeo Danaos et dona ferentes" [I fear the Greeks even bearing gifts] is the most common attitude. In all likelihood, the members of the Ghetto Administration simply wished to have Easter off this year, so the populace probably has nothing to fear from the directive.

SUNDAY, APRIL 9, 1944

NEWS OF THE DAY

Because of the Peysekh holidays, no weddings took place today.

It is a quiet Sunday; all stores are open. The ghetto [dwellers] walk about in the Easter sun, stomachs growling. There has never been such a hungry Passover, but the benevolent spring sunshine quickens the heart with new hope.

TUESDAY, APRIL 11, 1944

THE PEYSEKH ALLOTMENT

So far, some 13,000 persons have received various allotments, but the program is not over. On the contrary, the Chairman can be expected to issue more food allotments during and even after the holidays.

SKETCHES OF GHETTO LIFE: SHOBEKHTS [POTATO PEELS]

Rifke is happy. By virtue of—shall we say—intervention in high places, she has managed to obtain a kitchen voucher for shobekhts—two kilograms of potato peels every other day. No small thing. A kilogram of potatoes costs 200 marks; a kilogram of peels, 60 marks; so two kilograms are a small fortune. Rifke is, to say it again, happy.

She arrives at the kitchen with a sack. Nothing today, maybe tomorrow; the best time would be the day after tomorrow toward 11 A.M., before the soup distribution rush begins.

Not having a street pass for workshop hours, Rifke is very agitated when she approaches the person in charge of dispensing potato peels to lawful recipients. "Impossible! A commission! Out of the question today. Maybe tomorrow . . . or the day after."

Finally, with God's help, Rifke gets her two kilograms of shobekhts. Well, it's one thing to say potato peels and quite another thing to say high-quality potato peels. The potato peels fed to cattle in the blessed prewar years were lovely, thick, golden potato peels—may all the Children of Israel be so fortunate! Today, however, the peels are razor-thin, full of dirt and dust, some are dried up, some "mere skin and bones," that is, without a trace of potato on them. But so what! As long as you can take home two kilograms of potato peels and fix a tasty meal for the children, depending on the housewife's culinary talent.

Aha, the children! As soon as their mother enters the room they dash to the sack that holds the day's yield, two kilograms of potato peels. Now there's work to be done, so lend a hand.

The peels are thrown into a pail and carried out to the pump in the snow-covered courtyard. . . . Wash them, clean them, remove the dirt and dust. Pick out the pieces that look fit to eat, then back to the pump and wash them again. By now it is late in the evening. The children are tired, they almost fall asleep while working. . . . But there's no stopping, no break. After the cleaning, water is set on the stove. Warm water will rinse off the last remnants of dirt and dust.

It's midnight. Even the housewife is weary. The two kilograms of potato peels have shrunk down to about a half-kilogram. Now into the grinder, as though this were meat.

The next day, the ground potato peels are put to use. One child asks for babka, the second would like *placki* [pancakes], the third prefers *kleyselakh* [potato dumplings]. Mother opts for dumplings—in the soup. The workshop soup, enriched with dumplings, makes a complete meal. The children complain: "The soup doesn't smell so good; it's because of the kleyselakh." But what's the point of such objections? Potato peel dumplings are nutritious—according to physicians and sensible laymen, the ghetto's stomach experts—so it would be sinful to turn up one's nose at such gifts, no matter how laborious it is to achieve an edible result. If only the Lord would provide two kilograms of potato peels every other day. . . . That would be halfway to survival.

O[skar] R[osenfeld]

WEDNESDAY, APRIL 19, 1944

GARDEN PLOTS

The Department of Economics is already allocating plots to private applicants. The ghetto is not pleased with the way this is being administered. The total restructuring of the system, which the Chairman ordered this year, was accomplished somewhat precipitately, and, in this form, cannot possibly satisfy the populace. The proprietors of small parcels, who have gardened for four years, filling only their own needs and never profiteering on surplus produce, have suddenly been robbed of their little patches because some workshop is now expanding there. The system has been criticized for ignoring the individual needs of the little man and following the example of the largely unpopular workshop system. People are all too aware of the way things are usually handled in the workshops, with management's authoritarian, that is, egotistical principles. The garden acreage was intended to be the workshops' communal property, but the managers have bestowed and withheld it entirely at their own discretion. Therefore, the bitterness in the workshops was justified. Only time will tell whether the system will again cause such injustices. The Department of Economics has already begun to distribute seeds to the workshops; needless to say, people with friends in high places have been the first recipients.

SATURDAY, APRIL 22, 1944

SKETCHES OF GHETTO LIFE: GHETTO TREASURE HUNTERS

As recently as a few months ago there were large garbage pits behind the carpentry shop on Drukarska [Street]. All the neighborhood refuse was dumped there, and since the stench polluted the entire area, the Chairman ordered that the nearby sand mounds be used to fill the pits. For several months, especially during the winter, the disgusting garbage of the ghetto (for nowhere else in the world could there be such nauseating garbage, the refuse of refuse) lay forgotten under the beneficent sand. But now something strange is happening there. As you approach the area from Drukarska Street or from the courtyards of Limanowski Street, a choking, pestilential stench assaults your nose. Only a truly God-forsaken ghetto could stink like this. Where was that horrible smell coming from all of a sudden? A swarm of boys, armed with spades and picks, bowls and small sacks, are burrowing into the ground. They dig in like moles, like soldiers taking cover; they dig up the sand until they reach the garbage, and pull something out of the abominable filth. Horrified, I ask a boy: "What are you doing, what are you looking for?" Almost glaring, he replies: "What do you care, it's nothing you'd be interested in." Then, seeing my suit, he comes to the conclusion that I, the prosperous, ever so well-nourished bourgeois, won't offer him any competition: "We're digging for potatoes." I look at these potatoes in horror. Stinking, rotting remains from nearby kitchens, from the ghetto's poor households. And what can a ghetto household really afford to throw out? What is there that a housewife will not attempt to find some use for? Granted, last year potato peels were not yet a treasure; but even back then a housewife peeled potatoes very thriftily, not wasting a single gram. And at the public kitchens too, anything edible in the garbage was taken by someone. Anything consigned to the dump was truly unfit for consumption. And there it was covered with fetid rubbish, excrement, and sweepings; no one would ever have imagined that people would grub in this abyss of misery, undaunted by the obnoxious stench, the ghastly pestilence. And yet every tiny remnant is extracted with the fingers, carefully checked, and collected in a little sack or bowl. This is not simply hunger, this is the frenzy of degenerate animals, for the fruits of these hours of digging, the putrid, paltry dregs, will never compensate for the energy consumed. This is unbridled madness, a shame and a disgrace. This must not be, this cannot be.

Perhaps someone from the Sanitation Section will pass this way, hold his handkerchief to his nose for a moment, then bring some chlorinated lime there and drive these degenerates away—to save them, at least, from death by poisoning.

WEDNESDAY, APRIL 26, 1944

SKETCHES OF GHETTO LIFE: LENDING LIBRARIES

Right after the establishment of the ghetto, before the Jews resettled here from Łódź had even settled into their new quarters, the "people of the Book" evinced a great desire to read. Their need was satisfied by the J. W. Sonnenberg Lending Library, at 19 Zgierska [Street] (that is, Hohensteinerstrasse), which had been in business at that location uninterruptedly since 1931. All the other commercial lending libraries were shut down by the propaganda office of the Warthegau during the first winter of the war in 1939. Initially, Sonenberg had a total of 19 books in Polish, and his customers were from the middle class and [from the poor neighborhood of] Bałut. From April 1940 on, he bought books in all languages, but mainly German and English, from those resettled here from the city of Łódź and elsewhere. By early 1944, the library had grown to 7,500 volumes, of which 800 were in German. Aside from literary works, Sonnenberg also bought schoolbooks, encyclopedias, compendiums of all scholarly and scientific subjects, and textbooks for learning foreign languages. A subscription cost two marks a month, with a required deposit of five marks. After May 1942, readers of German who wished to subscribe had to donate a German book as a subscription fee; thus, the German language section of the library grew very rapidly. By Spring 1944, Sonnenberg's lending library had attracted 4,000 subscribers. Readers of Polish favored (aside from thrillers and detective stories) such classic writers as [Stefan] Żeromski, [Andrzej] Strug, [Eliza] Orzeszkowa, [Henryk] Sienkiewicz, [Bolesław] Prus; and Soviet authors such as [Boris] Pilniak, [Ilya] Ehrenburg, [Maxim] Gorky, and Aldanov [M. A. Landau]. Readers of German favored monographs, historical and philosophical works, and the German classics. Most in demand were [Heinrich]

Heine, [Lion] Feuchtwanger, [Emil] Ludwig, and translations from world literature. The most popular Yiddish authors were I. L. Peretz and [Sholem] Asch.

Besides Sonenberg, another book dealer from Łódź established himself in the ghetto: S. Otelsberg, at 44 Wolborska [Street] (that is, Rauchgasse). He carried 2,000 books and 2,000 subscribers, so all of his books were in circulation continuously.

Lastly, the ghetto has a number of Yiddish lending libraries in private homes, and interested parties can locate them by the notice [in Yiddish] on the gateway: "Akhtung, ikh borg aroys yidishe bikher tsum laynen" [Attention: I lend out Yiddish books for reading].

The [German] authorities tolerated all these libraries, which were, however, prohibited from keeping German books on warfare and any books proscribed in the Reich.

O[skar] R[osenfeld]

THURSDAY, APRIL 27, 1944

NEWS OF THE DAY: COMMISSION IN THE GHETTO

A relatively large commission was expected in the ghetto today. The Order Service had strict instructions to keep pedestrians off the streets, even pedestrians with passes. The commission was expected to arrive during the morning hours, but it never appeared. The only visitors were two men escorted by Amtsleiter Biebow, who inspected the Radogoszcz construction site and Metal Department I.

SKETCHES OF GHETTO LIFE: THE SEASON HAS BEGUN

The ghetto farmers are out in the fields. The last days of April are still quite cold, but the fear of hunger is goading people to work. The "estates" are often only thirty square meters in area. Where a wooden house was standing just a few days ago, then the Coal Department tore it down for firewood, the broken bricks, stones, and rubbish are now being cleared away and the optimistic owner of this działka [parcel] has begun to till the soil with spade and crowbar. There are many wonders in the ghetto, but the saying "Everything is possible in the ghetto" requires some qualification. Actually, the soil of the inner city, especially of the ghetto, is quite sandy; but on the lots where houses once stood, no miracles will occur now; not even paltry *buraki* [beets]—not to mention the nobler vegetables—will grow on rubble and ashes. One hardly knows whether to laugh or to cry at the sight of an emaciated Jew desperately striking his crowbar against the merciless, intractable ground that only recently was covered by a wretched proletarian shack. Yet the Jew wants to live, to impose his will on the earth. Mightn't a miracle happen after all?

MONDAY, MAY 1, 1944

NEWS OF THE DAY

The talk of the day, whether people are affected by the issue or not, is the coupons for the former Beirat. There are two dissatisfied sides; the first, a certain part of the ghetto populace which, although it benefits from the long-shift worker allotments, absolutely begrudges management these same allotments. Some groups are threatening outright strikes. It is mainly the leather and saddlery workshop and Metal [Department] II that are organizing and spreading propaganda. Their strike will, however, be limited to a soup boycott. May 1st is an attractive date for such ventures. The intention is to influence all the other workshops. We will have to wait and see whether there is actual solidarity among all the workshops. While such a move would probably not achieve anything substantial, the consequences could be quite unpleasant. Anyone who knows the Chairman, though, knows that he can cope with the situation.

Another group of malcontents consists of managers who, for their part, feel at a disadvantage because they are not in the top category for these allotments. Since the Chairman has arranged individual allotments, each manager and everyone else involved could draw conclusions from this about his relations with the Chairman. We fully expect that the Chairman will receive quite a number of complaints in this connection.

PUBLIC HEALTH

The cases of contagious disease reported today: tuberculosis, 15.

The causes of today's deaths: pulmonary tuberculosis, 17; tuberculosis of other organs, 2; pneumonia, 2; cardiac diseases, 11; intestinal occlusion, 1; stomach cancer, 1.

TUESDAY, MAY 2, 1944

NEWS OF THE DAY: WORKERS FOR LABOR OUTSIDE THE GHETTO

Again, the ghetto is in a state of nervous anxiety. A notice has been posted on the bridge near the Order Service post: "Wanted: volunteers for labor in Częstochowa." Last night, however, the Order Service pulled a number of people with minor criminal records out of bed and brought them to Central Prison. Reportedly, some 80 workers are needed. This time the Chairman has initiated the operation quietly, and it is expected that the quota will be filled by volunteers—a reasonable expectation, since hunger in the ghetto is now so horrible that no one fears he will worsen his lot by leaving here, especially since the news from Częstochowa has been quite encouraging.

A Soup Strike
has actually materialized in a few workshops. Today Metal [Department] II and the carpenters went on strike, that is, they refused to accept their soup. In the carpentry shop, some of the workers reconsidered at the end of their shift. There have been no disturbances, and the police have had no reason to intervene.

WEDNESDAY, MAY 3, 1944

NEWS OF THE DAY: WORKERS FOR LABOR OUTSIDE THE GHETTO

A group of about 80 people is being assembled without any ado; they are reportedly bound for Częstochowa. Volunteers are coming forward.

A DEATH

Dr. Ernst Neubauer, born July 19, 1880, died here yesterday. Dr. Neubauer came to the ghetto in the second Prague transport, and it was here that he married Mrs. Taussig [a gentile], who had voluntarily followed him in the fourth Prague transport. Dr. Neubauer was highly esteemed not only among his compatriots, but also among the general populace. He was an extremely devoted, conscientious physician. Those resettled to this ghetto from Prague and still living here have lost one of their best people. He succumbed to double pneumonia after six days.

FOOD SUPPLY

Hunger remains terrible. The spinach that was promised is not being delivered to the ghetto. Only a very few people were lucky enough to collect the two-kilogram ration.

A RATION OF LEEKS AND CHIVES

As of Tuesday, May 2, 1944, the following vegetables will be distributed: 300 grams of leeks against coupon No. 52 of the vegetable card, and 50 grams of chives for the sum of 1.50 marks with the appropriate vegetable voucher.

SATURDAY, MAY 6, 1944

NEWS OF THE DAY: THE SOUP STRIKES

A wave of soup strikes is sweeping the ghetto. In nearly all factories, most workers have been refusing the supplemental soup, and in some plants even the basic one. The [strike] organization, led mainly by teenagers, is centered in two plants: the nail factory and the leather and saddlery. From that base of operations these adolescent boys and girls are influencing all the other workshops and supporting one another in every instance. Thus, in one tailoring plant that employs only juveniles, several boys were disciplined or dismissed on account of such activities. Without disrupting production, all the young workers declared a hunger strike and refused to accept the soup in their workshop. There was an immediate expression of solidarity from the youngsters in the neighboring Metal Department, who sent over their own soup in sufficient quantities. The manager of the tailors' central office, D[awid] Warszawski, attempted to break the strike by promising that the young people who had been dismissed would be allowed to return to work; but the strikers replied that they had no faith in his promises, and that they would remain on strike until those who had been disciplined were back at their jobs. Only when their demand was actually met did they notify the Metal Department not to send them any more soup. Naturally, the Chairman is trying not to apply severe measures, which could bring matters to a head. One hopes that such demonstrations will cease; otherwise, they might attract the attention of the [German] authorities.[12]

12. The strikes, called "soup" strikes, were organized by the Union Left, especially by its youth groups. The direct causes for calling the strikes were, by and large: the brutal or particularly mean attitude of management in a given workshop to the men and women working there, the quality and amount of soup, which was not in accordance with the recipe, or simply soup that was very bad.

SUNDAY, MAY 7, 1944

SKETCHES OF GHETTO LIFE: THE GRAVEDIGGERS ARE WEAK

When survival is a constant problem, no one pays much attention to the dead. Particularly now, with tuberculosis on the increase and claiming new victims every day, the consequences of such neglect are all the more tragic. . . . Out in Marysin, the cemetery is one mound after another, grave after freshly dug grave. The work is arduous, and the poor gravediggers are no longer equal to it. For they [suffer] from hunger like all other mortals in the ghetto. They say that they can no longer keep up with the demand for graves, so bodies ready for immediate burial are not buried until a day later, or even several days later.

The cemetery workers are demanding a third bowl of soup a day. Without it, they maintain, they are simply incapable of handling their flourishing business without lengthy delays. So out one goes to Marysin and arranges for the workers' demands to be met.

Boruch Praszkier, one of whose "special assignments" is the care of the cemetery, will procure the third bowl of soup for his men. Without this soup, the living cannot bury the ghetto's dead.

O[skar] R[osenfeld]

MONDAY, MAY 8, 1944

NEWS OF THE DAY: A COMMISSION IN THE GHETTO

Early this morning the streets were closed to pedestrian traffic. No one was allowed outdoors after 7 A.M. A large commission of about forty persons from the Office of Resettlement and Races [Rasse-und Siedlungshauptamt—Race and Resettlement Main Office] arrived in the ghetto toward 7 A.M. and inspected a few of the larger manufacturing plants with Amtsleiter Biebow as their guide. The commission from Berlin had been brought to the ghetto by Dr. [Karl-Wilhelm] Albert, the chief of police in Litzmannstadt.[13] The commission members were mostly SS officers. The results of the inspection in all the factories were satisfactory. Street traffic was permitted to resume when the commission left the ghetto, just before 9 A.M.

SKETCHES OF GHETTO LIFE: GARDEN PLOTS

Just recently there were two wooden houses on Limanowski Street next to the pharmacy. But all earthly things are transitory, and those houses have now been consumed as fuel. The vacant lot on the street has been made available for cultivation in three parcels: 50, 100, and 150 square meters. At around 6 P.M., I passed the ghetto's newest garden, a garden of sand and dust, and I spotted two men in a fierce fight—they were neighbors, neighboring landlords, and none too happy about it. A row of

---

13. SS-Brigadenführer Dr. Karl-Wilhelm Albert, the former chief of police in Oppeln, Upper Silesia, was the chief of police in Łódź (*Polizeipräsident* in Litzmannstadt) from June 30, 1940, until the end of the German occupation in January 1945.

broken bricks marked the border of their properties. I walked over and asked them why they were fighting. The dispute involved a six-centimeter-wide strip along the border; multiplied by its length of five meters the area involved came to three-tenths of a square meter, and for this the neighbors were about to smash each other's heads. It was useless to try to talk to them. They were trampling each other's soil which, fortunately, hadn't yet been sown. The feeble brick wall had collapsed. Well, let them fight it out, maybe they would split the difference in the end. And what's going to grow in that little strip anyway? If farmed right, three heads of cabbage.

TUESDAY, MAY 9, 1944

NEWS OF THE DAY: BAN ON MAIL LIFTED

The major development today is the news that the ban on mail has been lifted. The post office's liaison to [German] police Precinct VI brought word to the ghetto this morning, and everyone learned of it at once. The ghetto will once again be permitted to send and receive mail. It has been almost two and a half years since the ghetto was totally sealed off from the outside world, and now the inmates of this captive city will again be permitted to communicate with their families. First reports were that people would now be able to write anything they wished in letters or cards, to request packages, and to search for relatives. The ghetto is delirious. Of course, many received the news with mixed emotions. The only ghetto residents who have had relatively uninterrupted contact with family members elsewhere are the 250 or 300 people resettled here from Prague, who still receive food packages from the Protectorate of Bohemia and Moravia, primarily from Prague. In the Protectorate, Jews related to Aryans[14] apparently had the good fortune of being permitted to stay in their homeland. Concerned about their relatives in the ghetto, they have been sending packages on the off chance that they might arrive. But to whom should the others write? To family members who at one time fled from Łódź? Who knows whether they are still alive and where they might be? To the fathers, mothers, or children resettled from the ghetto? Who knows whether they have survived and, if so, where they are. Similarly, the people resettled here from the Old Reich and from Vienna have little hope of contacting their relatives since they have no idea of their whereabouts. Indeed, if all the Jews in the Reich, the Protectorate of Bohemia and Moravia, and the Generalgouvernement learn that the mail ban has been lifted, and thereupon write to the ghetto, then perhaps communication could be restored. Many people—alas, too many—fear such communication because the news can only be bad.

The post office at 4 Kościelny Square began to be inundated after 5 o'clock in the evening—primarily by people resettled here eager to contact relatives and friends, and, at last, to receive packages. But the post office is not yet accepting mail; it has no detailed instructions as to what can be written and where. The report that ghetto dwellers will be able to write to the Old Reich, Bohemia and Moravia, the Gener-

14. Cf. p. 40, n. 56 above.

algouvernement, [other] occupied territories, and even to neutral countries, seems obviously exaggerated and overly optimistic.

In any case, the entire ghetto is electrified, and groups of people can be seen discussing this topic at every turn. The post offices are not expected to be mobbed in the next few days, if only because the post office has no postcards or stamps on hand.

At the moment, it appears highly unlikely that letters will be permitted; since, until now, stamps could not even be put on postcards, a sealed letter seems quite out of the question.

Details will not be known until tomorrow.

WEDNESDAY, MAY 10, 1944

NEWS OF THE DAY

Lifting of the Ban on Mail
The new regulations are now explicit. Only postcards will be permitted, and only to the Old Reich, the Protectorate of Bohemia and Moravia, and the Generalgouvernement. Only brief messages to family members are permitted. No food packages may be requested, although the receipt of bread may be confirmed. (The receipt of packages may not be confirmed.) The post office will have a sufficient number of postcards in two or three days. Meanwhile, cards brought to any post office will be held there and submitted to the Jewish censorship. It has been learned from the post office that a German censor will then examine the material. Although this restriction dampens hopes a bit, the joy in the ghetto is undiminished. The feeling that one can again communicate with people outside the ghetto is unquestionably a relief from the heavy burden that had borne on every mind.

Criminal Police Camp Disbanded
The camp for neglected children in Marysin, known in the ghetto as the Kripo, or Polish, Camp [that is, camp for Polish Teenagers],[15] is being closed down today. The ghetto has no idea what provisions have been made for the juvenile inmates.

SKETCHES OF GHETTO LIFE: PERMISSION TO WRITE AGAIN

The lifting of the ban on mail has come as an extraordinary surprise. The ghetto can barely comprehend the news—skepticism [is encountered] here and there, since often enough over the years, so-called positive, agreeable news has turned out to be a rumor, causing painful disappointment. But this time it's real. You can read it in black and white in the post office lobby: mail accepted for relatives in this place and that.

People's first thought is: "Who should I write to? Where is the person I'd want to write to? Is he (or she) even alive? All I can do is wait and see. Maybe my relative will write to me first, and then we'll be in touch."

The main concern of those resettled here from the Protectorate of Bohemia and Moravia is getting something to eat, a food package from that still unexhausted

15. The information is not accurate—the Camp for Polish Teenagers in Marysin existed until the end of the German occupation of Łódź in January, 1945.

country—especially bread—for a few such packages are arriving in the ghetto every day. So then write. . . . Easier said than done. After the thirty-month mail ban people have lost the habit of writing.

Pen and ink are rare possessions here. And so people turn to some acquaintance who may still have them on hand. Or else they knock on apartment doors at random and ask: "Could I write some postcards here? Just a few lines. I'm just trying to find out whether my brother . . . my mother . . . my uncle . . . is still alive. I don't have pen and ink at home. Haven't needed them." And they write a few lines, smiling in anticipation of happiness.

O[skar] R[osenfeld]

THURSDAY, MAY 11, 1944

SKETCHES OF GHETTO LIFE: ON THE BLACK MARKET

"From Mojsze Minz you can get anything your heart and stomach desire," I was told by an expert in ghetto affairs; I had asked him whether ten grams of garlic were available anywhere.

I already knew the name Mojsze Minz as that of a firm. He had originally become popular in the ghetto by selling food, whose existence was now beyond the imagination of a modest ghetto brain; things like pickles, Maggi bouillon cubes, hard cheese, and the like; not to mention items included in the rations, such as sugar, flour, kasha, peas, powdered soup, or seasonal vegetables. The second reason for his popularity was that he would always reward or punish each customer according to his behavior, that is Mojsze would either hand over the items or refuse the deal outright. When Mojsze Minz opened his mouth to grin, revealing a row of gold teeth between his thick, vulgar lips; when his wife, a short, slovenly woman, glared morosely at the customer; or when his son, a bold little lad of about thirteen, took over his father's business for a while, all the customers were bound to acknowledge that the firm of Minz occupied a position of authority in the ghetto. Other members of the black market, like Glücksfeld [Gliksberg] or Tajtelbaum, used the same tricks as Mojsze Minz, but [compared to him] they were definitely second-rate businessmen.

The prices were the same in all these shops. They were regulated automatically, though they never followed the economic principle of supply and demand; actually, they were determined arbitrarily by the shopkeepers. The impossibility of a free market prevented the system from functioning naturally.

"And where did the goods come from?" you ask. Mojsze Minz and his colleagues bought in the same way they sold: from private parties; vegetables mostly from działka [parcel] proprietors who in turn traded their wads of ghetto marks for margarine, bread, flour, sugar, and so forth; [other commodities came] from coupon holders who were not interested in consuming one item or another; and from the man in the street who was forced to sell part of his ration in order to buy medications, tobacco, clothing, medical services. Thus, illicit trade has basically taken the form of barter.

Barter occurred in the ghetto even outside the illicit market. For not everyone was inclined to fight the crowds in places where the goods lay exposed on sticky news-papers spread out on filthy, fly-covered tables and in dusty window niches. The scales were caked with dirt, bits of food, and dead insects. The marketplace itself was nothing but a part of the dealer's living room or kitchen, simply curtained off from the rest of his apartment so that normal appearances could be restored at any moment in case of danger.

Danger?

Certainly. For the Eldest of the Jews has repeatedly outlawed such trade, often shutting down the black-market stores and threatening proprietors with Czarniecki [Street, that is, Central Prison] and excrement removal duty. The shops are closed down and then reopen despite the danger. Bundles of "banknotes" (ghetto marks) have piled up in shopkeepers' closets. One such shopkeeper was the pharmacist Winawer. His distinction was that he carried only the finest and rarest items, mainly spices and remedies such as pepper and iodine, tea and pyramidone, as well as injection ampules—including strychnine, calcium, caffeine, and finally Vigantol, which was in such demand during the ghetto's months of hunger.

Sometimes when out on patrol the Kripo [German criminal police] would also visit the black-marketeers, and either impose large fines (not so much to stop the illicit traffic as to conclude their own dealings successfully) or take valuable drugs and medications. The shopkeeper would be ruined but he would be back on his feet soon enough.

People with "lofty" ethical principles have been up in arms about these "prof-iteers," "usurers," "parasites." But the realities of life have prevailed. People with something to sell or who wanted to buy preferred the neutral territory of a dealer who both bought and sold. In the ghetto, the curse of the black market became a blessing to those who needed or desired goods; and in the process, of course, the illicit merchant made his illicit profit. The ghetto simply has its own particular laws and its own particular morality.

O[skar] R[osenfeld]

MONDAY, MAY 15, 1944

NEWS OF THE DAY: THE CHAIRMAN SPEAKS TO THE YOUNG WORKERS ON STRIKE

Metal Plant [Department] II has had another soup strike. As in the other workshops, it is primarily the juvenile workers, adolescents not burdened by the problems of the ghetto, who strike when the soup doesn't suit them. Do they imagine that anyone else is satisfied by this soup? We have described this scene often enough: the Chairman appears, immediately induces the boys to accept their soup; and only a group of four rebels wishing to prove their heroism at any cost refuse to go along with the others. The Chairman has to discipline them, and he sends them out to do demolition work. He addresses the boys in a calm, forbearing tone, saying: "These soup strikes are senseless; I can't put any more than I have into the soup. Who is this demonstration against? Against me? I'm just a servant of the authorities; I have to bow my head and do as I'm told. No strike of yours can force me to make thicker soup, for I have nothing [to thicken it with]. Do you intend to strike against the [German] Ghetto Administration? Do you believe that they will be intimidated by you? The Jewish authorities are definitely doing everything that can be done. I do what I can, wherever possible. I hope that the situation will improve in the near future."

TUESDAY, MAY 16, 1944

NEWS OF THE DAY

Recruitment in the R-Stores
The Chairman visited all the R-stores and separated out the younger staff members, who were then assigned to the various tailors' workshops, which are constantly short of manpower.

Lifting of the Ban on Mail
The lifting of the ban on mail has not yet gone into effect. Thousands of postcards have been handed in at the counters, but all this material is still at the post office since apparently no precise guidelines for outgoing mail have yet been set. It is mainly those recently resettled in the ghetto, especially those from Prague, who are making concentrated efforts to communicate with their friends and relatives. Their postcards always revolve around a request for food. Since only the receipt of bread may be confirmed, the writers resort to confirming bread that they have not received. Since the mail will probably go to the appropriate German office outside the ghetto by way of police Precinct VI, M[arek] Kligier, head of the Special Department, has instructed the post office to sort all cards according to their post offices of destination and turn all material over to the Special Department. However, the Chairman is extremely displeased with this measure; he rightly points out that the post office is his institution and had been built up by him. Kligier, on the other hand, is concerned with maintaining the flow of packages, and would thus like to avoid overburdening the mail system with superfluous or inadmissible items. For instance, many people are writing to the Judenrat [Jewish Council] in Warsaw or Kielce. The Special Department has definite information that those institutions no longer exist and would consequently like to prevent such mail from leaving the ghetto. Presumably, Kligier's intention is not to encroach on the Chairman's jurisdiction; for better or for worse, he will have to use his own judgment to resolve this issue—the risk being that he might create a new source of conflict between himself and the Chairman.

BROUGHT TO THIS GHETTO FROM LITZMANNSTADT

The person resettled here on the 13th of this month is a 6-year-old girl from Łask who allegedly fled to Litzmannstadt with her parents during the resettlements from Łask.[16] The child had been in hiding with a Polish family. She was detained by the

---

16. I.e. in August, 1942, when the ghetto in Łask, a town southwest of Łódź, was liquidated. About 3,500 people from Łask were at that time deported to the death camp in Chełmno (Kulmhof) while 760 were selected out and resettled to the Łódź ghetto.

German police when she tried to attend a performance of a circus that is currently in Litzmannstadt. Needless to say, the ghetto immediately came to her assistance, and families volunteered to take her in. The dentist J. Karmasin, residing here at 47 Limanowski Street, was informed by a man from Łask that he had seen the child and recognized her as the daughter of Karmasin's brother-in-law [who had lived] in that town. And indeed, Karmasin identified the girl as his niece. Adoption procedures are now in progress. We intend to report further details of this case.

WEDNESDAY, MAY 17, 1944

NEWS OF THE DAY

A Roundup

The ghetto has had another day of agitation. Toward 1 P.M., a total of fifty people were rounded up from Central Prison and two demolition sites, as well as from one workshop (during the shift). They were brought to Bałut Market, and in the afternoon taken out of the ghetto by car.

At 11:30 A.M., M[arek] Kligier was ordered by the Ghetto Administration to provide fifty people by 3 P.M. Kligier attempted to resist this abrupt demand, but the Secret State Police [Gestapo] who were also present, reaffirmed the demand. Finally, Kligier tried to gain time by pointing out that he was not empowered to draft manpower, a fact that the authorities ultimately had to acknowledge. The Ghetto Administration, therefore, transmitted the order to the office of the Eldest, to the attention of Miss [Dora] Fuchs; but the Eldest happened to be ill and in bed. Kligier then went out to Marysin to see the Chairman, who, confined to bed, was unable to intervene. He gave instructions that this unpleasant mission be entrusted to B[ernard] Fuchs, director of the Labor Bureau. For better or worse, Kligier had to take charge of the matter himself and see it through. And indeed, the fifty men were brought to Bałut Market at the appointed time, though of course only by virtue of an outright roundup. The twelve men from Central Prison were brought under escort. Next, a Special Department squad was dispatched to the demolition site, surrounded it, and had the workers form in ranks under the pretense of conscripting them for labor within the ghetto. The men selected were then put aboard a tram, but most of them managed to escape en route, since ghetto residents have extraordinarily well-developed instincts and can smell a rat immediately. Of the thirty conscripted, only three arrived. The round-up had to be started anew. The Special [Department's men] detained a few people who were found outdoors during work hours and could not produce the appropriate papers. The rest were forcibly removed from a workshop. Two cars drove the men away and returned about thirty-five minutes later; the work site is then probably not far from the city. The workers' baggage will be sent after them tomorrow or the next day, with the permission of the Gestapo. Understandably, the agitation this afternoon was very great, and there were repetitions of the scenes common on such occasions. The speed of the operation made it impossible to intercede on behalf of anyone. Each worker was given a loaf of bread and 250 grams of sugar. Furthermore, the Ghetto Administration subsequently ordered that proper gear be supplied to the workers.

The men will still be listed on the ghetto's rolls and be figured into the food supply budget.

THURSDAY, MAY 18, 1944

NEWS OF THE DAY

For Manual Labor Outside the Ghetto
Calm has been restored after the fifty men were sent to perform manual labor outside the ghetto. By now the ghetto is inured to such events, and what today causes the most terrible agitation will be forgotten tomorrow in the stupor of hunger. The authorities have ordered that personal belongings and supplementary gear be sent out to the workers.

SKETCHES OF GHETTO LIFE: WORKERS ON THE OUTSIDE

Twelve men escorted by five policemen march down the middle of Dworska [Street] toward Bałut Market. They carry bags, knapsacks, bundles. Broken figures of men, with blankets and bedding lashed to their backs. Crowds gather on the sidewalks, even though it is 3 P.M. and the workshop day is not over.

People shout, crowding together, gesturing. Many children. A little sunshine. "What's going on?" "People from Czarniecki [Central Prison] on their way to labor outside the ghetto. . . ." Well, not so bad, I say to myself.

Later, a visitor. A Special [Department] man tells me: "Fifty workers are needed. They're grabbing people on the street or taking them from the coal yard. The quota has to be met—the Ghetto Administration insists on it." My neighbor says: "Terrible! Another resettlement!" "You can't really call it a resettlement, it's just work outside the ghetto. . . ." As we chat in my room—it's already 5 o'clock—the street fills with people streaming out of the workshops, the noise increases, and everyone is impatient to find out what new calamity has overtaken the ghetto. It's been a very long time since anyone in the ghetto has expected the news to be good. People have even lost faith in any future potato shipments. A woman cries, sobs, groans. A neighbor supports her, tries to console her. Presumably, one of her relatives was seized on the street and placed in the labor transport. The crowd that has gathered around her is suddenly hushed by the approach of a man whose broad yellow armband inspires confidence. He says something about a loaf of bread that the [departing] workers have "now, just this minute" received. "A loaf of bread?" People shake their heads. "Maybe I ought to . . . Do you think it's true?" The words "a loaf of bread" seem to have a calming effect. The people who have been standing around now continue on their way, thinking about the loaf of bread that brightens the path of bitter sorrows.

A few of the men captured on the street manage to break away and flee. Of the twenty captives, fifteen have escaped; they are pursued, but they have vanished. Nevertheless, fifty men must be delivered immediately, so the hunt continues. Finally, night falls. The chapter is closed. . . .

Eyewitnesses report: A droshky with a few Jewish policemen, senior officers, pulls up at the woodwork workshop. A few seconds later—the men in uniform have meanwhile jumped out—the workshop manager appears on the scene and has a number of workers line up. The Jewish commission reviews the line and separates out those who seem suited to its purposes. Two to the right, five to the left, three to the right, seven to the left. Five men pass inspection. The workers do not understand what's going on. A rumor circulated in the workshop that men were needed to unload potatoes in Marysin, something that is in the ghetto's own interest. As soon as the review was over, the victims were taken by the Jewish policemen to Bałut Market.

A similar incident took place at the demolition site on Brzezińska Street. Anyone with eyes in his head could see that the workers were selected without regard to age or fitness for labor; the police also took the sick, the weak, and the elderly.

The ghetto is virtually paralyzed. Now, after five years of war, just before the end, Jews are being "deported" for labor outside the ghetto. "Deported?" Dragged off somewhere in their work clothes, dirty, tired, their stomachs empty. They were not even permitted to say goodbye to their families—wife, children, parents. This is not how one deals with people whom one requires and expects to work normally.

"They're going for only ten days . . . not far from the city . . . farm work . . ." This rumor alleviates somewhat the pain, the anger, and the sadness of those who remained behind. And late in the afternoon everyone is saying: "Tomorrow's soup will have 10 g of flour, 20 g of peas, 10 g of [rye] flakes, and 100 g of potatoes!" "Yes, but 100 g gross . . ." "They'll rob us blind . . ."

"They" are the kitchen help who serve the soup.

O[skar] R[osenfeld]

FRIDAY, MAY 19, 1944

SKETCHES OF GHETTO LIFE: THE EIGHTH WONDER OF THE WORLD?

Second only to Semiramis and the Hanging Gardens of Babylon, the ghetto deserves credit for inventing the mobile garden. A worker in the tailoring plant who had a small garden last year but lost it because of the new "agriculture policy" quickly resolved to fill an old double baby carriage with soil and plant a few onion bulbs. He now pushes his garden to the workshop every day and parks it in a sunny spot in the courtyard; from the window he can easily guard his "garden plot." The mobile działka [parcel] is quite a conversation piece, and the shrewd farmer has people laughing with him, not at him.

MONDAY, MAY 22, 1944

WORKSHOP NEWS: THE AMTSLEITER VISITS THE LOW VOLTAGE EQUIPMENT DEPARTMENT

Today, Amtsleiter Biebow appeared at the Low Voltage [Equipment] Department and spoke to the workers there, reproaching them for their declining productivity. For the first time, he threatened to assign staff members to excrement removal duty. The workers promised a sharp increase in production. This interlude was probably due to excuses made by Dawidowicz, manager of the plant, who had blamed the decline in productivity on lackadaisical workers rather than on the inferior material.

SKETCHES OF GHETTO LIFE: ONIONS, ONIONS

Onions have been a rarity throughout the ghetto's four years. A very select few—dignitaries and bigwigs of every stripe—could afford to plant onions in their gardens, if they managed to obtain seeds; the ghetto household has always had to do without. Suddenly, there are onions everywhere. Of course, these are not exactly full-grown, juicy onions, but rather a promise of onions. For the first time since the establishment of the ghetto, the Department of Economics has received a supply of bulbs, and now one sees stalks rising everywhere. In some garden beds the onions are arrayed like soldiers; in some, they are more chaotic. But the truly interesting onions are not in gardens at all. Onions are now growing in all the ghetto's windows; everyone has his own pocket-sized działka [parcel]. Quite a few people have hammered some small boards together to make window boxes. What have they planted there? Onions. They may not be conspicuous yet, but there is hardly a window without the tin cans, which are to be found everywhere in the ghetto. In front of some buildings, there is literally no window from the ground to the fifth floor without one, or several, *pushkes* [boxes] from which the stalks poke out at an angle to follow the sun. The onion is the flower of the ghetto. Last year, we recall, there were beets in every window, with an occasional head of lettuce; now onions, onions everywhere. In apartments that once were stores, the tenants now use the display windows as onion plantations. No containers are required. They have simply covered the bottoms of the display windows with soil and planted onions. Elsewhere, anyone without enough cans has resorted to old pots and wash basins. Of course, these indoor onions will prove a bitter disappointment to their cultivators—they will not grow very large. But at least there will be stalks, and as for anyone who was not assigned a garden this time around, well, he has his onion działka on the windowsill. At any rate, the ghetto will see no shortage of onions in the fall; and prices will no doubt be incomparably lower than those of previous years.

O[skar] S[inger]

TUESDAY, MAY 23, 1944

NEWS OF THE DAY: LABOR OUTSIDE THE GHETTO

Today, again there have been volunteers to perform manual labor outside the ghetto. It is reported that eighty persons are to depart on May 30, and that the required number has been raised to a total of one hundred forty. Some thirty men are already awaiting orders.

FROM THE POST OFFICE

The first postcards brought to the post office counters after the lifting of the ban on mail have now gone off. The Special Department has forwarded approximately 3,000 cards to the German authorities, and a decision is expected during the coming week.

It is still unknown whether the cards will be sent directly or by way of the central censorship office in Berlin.

SKETCHES OF GHETTO LIFE: THE VIGANTOL CRAZE

Anyone who reflects on the ghetto's cultural curiosities will not be able to ignore illnesses and their treatment here. The fact that an entire city has been kept for years in an unbroken state of near-starvation is in itself unique in the history of civilized nations. And since there has been no way of combatting hunger, we have attempted to alleviate its consequences, that is, the diseases resulting from it.

Spring 1943: there has been widespread occurrence of softening, or decalcification, of the bones due to vitamin deficiency. Physicians prescribe Vigantol, a synthetic D vitamin. It is available in pharmacies, and it works. Many patients say that, after a dose of ten cubic centimeters, the pain in their bones (the clearest symptom of the disease) has subsided. Some even maintain: "I feel like a new man!"

Vigantol has been effective, and now that its value is recognized, it has become a craze. Pharmacies no longer have enough to go around. The Special Department of the Order Service establishes a medicine distribution office to dispense certain rare medications upon [presentation of a] physician's prescription. Speculators obtain Vigantol and sell it on the black market. In the spring of 1943, a vial of Vigantol already brings thirty-five marks. The high price of the medication stimulates a demand for it even when it is not needed.

Vigantol becomes a miracle drug, a remedy for any and all the consequences of hunger: weakness, fatigue, swelling of the legs . . . The price goes up. Thousands of ghetto dwellers seize upon Vigantol, as though it were their last and only means of salvation. They sell shoes, bread, oil; they sell the most valuable parts of their rations in order to buy Vigantol, the miracle elixir. They stint on food for the table in order to save their loved ones with Vigantol. The price goes up.

Until finally, in May of 1944, Vigantol is absolutely unavailable, even at the price of 300 marks for ten cubic centimeters. Even the black market has dried up. Even Winawer, the star of the illegal market in drugs and spices, is unable to locate any Vigantol.

"Vigantol! Vigantol!" cry ghetto dwellers suffering from vitamin deficiencies. "Get me Vigantol and you'll save my life!"

O[skar] R[osenfeld]

WEDNESDAY, MAY 24, 1944

SKETCHES OF GHETTO LIFE: NO DEALINGS WITH THE DEAD

If someone feels ill and wishes to stay home from the workshop, he needs certification of his illness from a physician. The physician fills out a certificate excusing him from work for a specific number of days. This certificate also entitles the worker to continue receiving the workshop soup. And since soup is his basic nourishment, the physician's excuse is a question of "to be or not to be" for the patient.

"Doctor, could I please have a work excuse (*zwolnienie*) for my brother . . . just for two days."

"I can't do that; yesterday, your brother was dying. Who knows if he's still alive today. . . ."

"He *is* alive, he *is*."

"I'll have to take a look at him," says the physician. The solicitous brother is now embarrassed. If the physician visits his apartment and discovers that his brother is in fact dead, then he can forget those two days of soup. . . . He gives the physician a pleading look, but he is adamant. Rules are rules. Even the naive *Yeke*, the doctor from Western Europe, no longer falls for the soup swindlers' tricks. For a long time, the people receiving extra soup illicitly have made use of physicians' excuses to support the legitimacy of their claims. Thus, the soup of many of the dead found its way into the stomachs of the living. No longer, though. The less there is to eat, the stricter the ghetto laws become. The mass of morality increases as the square of the mass of available food.

O[skar] R[osenfeld]

THURSDAY, MAY 25, 1944

NEWS OF THE DAY: THE CHAIRMAN AIDS ORPHANS

For the holiday of Shabuoth, the Chairman has distributed food coupons to adopted and unadopted orphans: 350 grams flour, 100 grams rye flakes, 100 grams brown sugar, 100 grams bread spread, 50 grams marmalade.

There will be no [special] Shabuoth ration as the populace had hoped. Nor can the majority of coupon recipients look forward to any special ration; the Chairman has in fact distributed such holiday coupons to very few people.

MONDAY, MAY 29, 1944

A SUICIDE

On May 27, 1944, Majer Józefowicz, born in Sieradz in 1907 and residing at 3 Bałut Market, committed suicide by hanging himself. He was pronounced dead by the Emergency Service physician.

SKETCHES OF GHETTO LIFE: ALWAYS THE SAME STORY

One day, someone's son feels so ill that he has to stay in bed. For some time now, his mother says, the twenty-year-old has had pains in his chest. His legs were swollen, his face had an unusual color, and he was often unable to walk. I'll be all right, the boy said, and he dragged himself along for a few more weeks. Then he collapsed.

The doctor comes: "He'll have to be x-rayed. Otherwise I can't make a valid diagnosis." The x-rays show a spot on the lung . . . tuberculosis due to malnutrition. Not much can be done.

The doctor says: "The best thing would be a few weeks of hospital care, then bring him home and feed him well—fat, meat, bread, sugar . . . best of all, cod-liver oil. . . ."

The parents give up some of their rations. The mother becomes weak, bedridden. The elder sister stints on food and works at night in order to draw the L allotment (for long-shift workers). The son's health does not improve. He is not getting enough food, despite the family's sacrifices. They sell off clothing, shoes, portions of their ration, in exchange for more nutritious food.

But now the sister falls ill. Swollen legs—water up to her lungs. The situation is desperate.

The doctor comes. They tell him of their illness and suffering. First the son, and then—after the rest of the family has tried to save him by giving up its precious food— the others have fallen ill. The doctor shakes his head: "The hospital? Too late. The hospital won't accept him in this condition. . . ."

Nevertheless, they attempt the impossible. They try to save the dying man. In the process, the still halfway healthy members of the family travel down the same road. The doctor looks around: "Nothing can be done. Always the same story in the ghetto. One family after another is destroyed. Son, father, mother, sister. Always the same story . . . only the sequence varies. . . ."

O[skar] R[osenfeld]

PUBLIC HEALTH

The cases of contagious disease reported today: none.

The causes of today's deaths: tuberculosis of the lungs, 17; tubercular meningitis, 1; meningitis, 1; heart disease, 11; suicide, 1.

TUESDAY, MAY 30, 1944

NEWS OF THE DAY: LABOR OUTSIDE THE GHETTO

At 8:30 A.M. today, another group of sixty people was sent from Bałut Market to perform manual labor outside the ghetto. Most of them took along their own clothing and linen. Each person received 4 kilograms bread, 125 grams curds, 200 grams salami, 250 grams sugar. In regard to the bread, the difference between 250 grams and 600 grams (which they had received daily at Central Prison) was deducted from the 4 kilograms.

Today, another announcement appeared, reading as follows:

ATTENTION!

Re: Registration of Volunteers for Labor Outside the Ghetto.

Volunteers for labor outside the ghetto may still register at the ghetto Bureau of Labor every day from 5:30 P.M. to 8 P.M.

Litzmannstadt-Getto,   Ch[aim] Rumkowski
30 May 1944   The Eldest of the Jews in Litzmannstadt

This seems not to involve industrial, but, rather, agricultural manpower, which is now required on small farms for the planting season. The workers must be in the immediate vicinity, for the Ghetto Administration has notified the office of the Eldest that these small groups are to remain in the ghetto's food budget. This does not imply, though, that the workers receive no additional provisioning on the outside. Since there have not been any reports, nothing definite can be said about this matter.

SKETCHES OF GHETTO LIFE: A POTATO FOR SHABUOTH

Potatoes are scarce in the ghetto. Occasionally, a potato can be found floating in the miserable workshop soup. A few people, though—you can count them on the fingers of one hand—are managing to prepare a festive Shabuoth meal with a potato. But this is not so simple; it takes energy and requires the extraordinary agility that only young boys have. A potato wagon rattles by, fully loaded, through the bustle of Łagiewnicka Street toward the Vegetable Yard. All eyes pop out of their sockets; people have not seen fully loaded potato wagons for a long time. The wagon is pursued at a trot by a troop of boys. It is not out of the question that the bumpy pavement will "do the trick" on Shabuoth; indeed, a few potatoes actually tumble off the wagon and roll toward the gutter. An Order Service man from the Special Department is up on the wagon. But he cannot jump down after the lost potatoes, for if he left the wagon for a second, its cargo would be doomed. He must let the potatoes roll away. And the boys pounce on the bouncing potatoes before they reach the reeking gutter; then off they trot again behind the wagon. Perhaps God will help; after all, it's Shabuoth! The holiday obligates God and man to partnership. A few more potatoes will drop off by the time the wagon reaches the Vegetable Yard. Will all the boys who breathlessly chase this precious vegetable be lucky?

[Oskar Rosenfeld]

WEDNESDAY, MAY 31, 1944

GHETTO HUMOR: ANALYSIS OF THE WORKSHOP SOUP

The following analysis of the workshop soup (*kolonialka* [starch based]) has been circulating for several days:

Quantity	under 0.7 liters
Color	bluish gray
Aroma	horse stable
Clarity	very murky
Taste	sour to bitter
Protein	none
Sugar	none
Fat	none
Peas	isolated sightings
Groats	traces
Water	80 percent
Soda	15 percent

EFFECT: diuretic.

FRIDAY, JUNE 2, 1944

NEWS OF THE DAY

Today, the Chairman visited the Department of Statistics and conferred at some length about current issues with its chief, Director [Henryk] Neftalin, the attorney; [S.]

Erlich, head of the Statistical Division; and Dr. Oskar Singer, head of the Archives. The Chairman inspected a scrapbook, now in production, concerning welfare assistance in the ghetto, and he heard detailed reports from the three men on all ongoing projects. The Chairman granted an honorarium of thirty bowls of soup a week for outside employees of our bureau.

NEW GUARDS ON DUTY

The ghetto populace has noticed that some of the German guards have been replaced. One no longer sees many familiar faces with which the ghetto dweller had come to be, as it were, on friendly terms. We understand that sixteen of the younger policemen of [German] Precinct VI have left and been replaced by older men.

HEALTH: ENDEMIC TUBERCULOSIS

In a small private circle, Dr. Mosze Feldman recently discussed problems associated with the tuberculosis now endemic in the ghetto. He pointed out that the Department of Health is failing entirely in its fight against tuberculosis and that countermeasures must be devised to combat this scourge. People with tuberculosis are working almost everywhere: in the cooperatives, the kitchens, the bakeries. Every ration, every soup, every loaf of bread brings tuberculosis into homes that may so far have been spared. All complaints to the Department of Health have fallen on deaf ears. Dr. Feldman suggested that [various] social groups in the ghetto might think of possible remedies, and that the Chairman ought to be informed about the matter: only he could take the drastic measures necessary.

Correct as Dr. Feldman's views may well be, they will have few practical consequences. In a city that suffers beyond measure from widespread starvation, it is too late to achieve anything even with comprehensive prophylactic measures.

TUESDAY, JUNE 6, 1944

NEWS OF THE DAY: A COMMISSION IN THE GHETTO

A three-man commission arrived at Central Prison today led by Gestapo chief Müller,[17] who spoke briefly to the reserve squads being considered for labor outside the ghetto. Chief Müller explained that the present group will be used for cutting peat, but will receive considerably better rations than in the ghetto and will be permitted to write to close blood-relatives once a month. He stressed that as little hand luggage as possible should be taken along, since living space is quite limited. Upon completion of this seasonal work, the workers will return to the ghetto. Anyone who does not prove equal to the work will be sent back to the ghetto's Central Prison and be lodged there as a prisoner of the Gestapo.

The quota has been filled chiefly by volunteers. The date of their departure has not been announced.

17. Cf. p. 458, n. 7 above.

On the whole, the ghetto is nervous today, probably because of the various bits of news that have been coming in through the barbed-wire fence.[18]

SOUP STRIKES

There is no end to the soup strikes that are, unfortunately, all too frequent in the ghetto. Such strikes took place at Metal [Department] II yesterday and at the Knitwear Department ([Manager:] Zbar) today. The Chairman arrived immediately and, with watch in hand, ordered the striking youths to accept their soup within five minutes. Before the five minutes were up, soup was in the bowls. In areas that the Chairman had not even entered, the mere fact of his presence in the workshop was enough: everyone ran for his soup. To be sure, the Chairman understands that while he can always end a strike by appearing in person, this by no means solves the problem. This time he resorted to the rather draconian measure of sending a few of the ringleaders, sixteen youths in all, to Central Prison; furthermore, he warned their families that he would suspend their ration cards if there were a repetition of the incident.

One might think that these youths had some unified underground leadership, and that everything was being directed by the so-called "Reds," a legendary party in the ghetto. But it is not so. These are wildcat strikes.[19] Solidarity demonstrations occur only within workshops, or spread from one workshop to another. The Chairman must under all circumstances ensure tranquillity and order in the ghetto; and he must occasionally resort to stringent measures, not only because he is personally responsible for maintaining order but because he is responsible to the Jewish populace for averting the crises that would result from intervention by the German authorities. He cannot indulge in politics; he must maintain tranquillity and do so at all costs.

WEDNESDAY, JUNE 7, 1944

NEWS OF THE DAY

Arrests

The ghetto suffered a severe shock toward six o'clock this evening. The news spread like wildfire that a number of people had been arrested for possessing radios and for distributing transcripts of radio reports. Within a few minutes after the arrest, the entire ghetto knew all the details.[20]

18. "The various bits of news that have been coming in through the barbed wire" on the 6th of June, 1944, were the news about D-Day!

19. The strikes in the ghetto workshops in 1944 were in fact organized by the Union Left. Cf. p. 404, n. 42 and p. 482, n. 12, above.

20. For over four years there had existed in the ghetto a few well-concealed and loosely connected groups of people who listened to the radio. Those groups often consisted only of family members and they used receivers which varied in quality from the very primitive, able to pick up only local German stations, such as the *Litzmannstädter Sender*, to high-quality receivers capable of picking up the BBC and the Polish Radio Station *Świt* (Daybreak), which broadcast from outside London. The information obtained in this manner was discreetly and cautiously circulated through the ghetto, for the most part, by word of mouth, transcripts of radio reports being a rarity. However, on June 6, 1944, the joy at the news of the landing of Allied troops in Normandy was so great that for a moment people seemed to forget themselves and behaved as if the Americans would be in Łódź in a very short while. It was clear to the German authorities (the Gettoverwaltung, Kripo, and Gestapo) that the news of the landing could only have reached the ghetto by means of radio. And as a result of the investigations undertaken in the next two to three days, nearly all those who had been listening to the radio clandestinely were apprehended, as the *Chronicle* itself reports.

First, the [German] criminal police, acting on orders of the Secret State Police [Gestapo], apprehended a man named Altszuler on [38] Wolborska Street. After putting him in the droshky lent them for this purpose by the Department of Food Supply, the criminal police proceeded to 9 Młynarska Street, to the apartment of a man named [Mojżesz] Tafel, who, unluckily, was caught in the very act of listening to the news on the radio and was taken into custody. Altszuler's son, a boy of about sixteen, was also arrested. No radio was found in the Altszuler apartment, but the boy confessed where it was. He also immediately divulged the names of two men who were, so to speak, his father's co-workers, a certain [Szloma] Redlich and Chaim Widawski. Redlich was also arrested immediately, while Widawski went into hiding. The Jewish Order Service received strict instructions from the criminal police to bring Widawski in. Next, the criminal police arrested a man named [Icchak] Lublinski on Niecała Street, and finally, three [brothers] by the name of Weksler [Jakow, Szymon, and Henoch] at 61 Łagiewnicka Street. Furthermore, they raided Tatarka's barber shop on Lutomierska Street, where the [clandestine radio-] newspaper had been available or was read aloud. There, the police found a man named Richard Beer, formerly a newspaper editor in Vienna, who had in his possession transcripts of various political reports. A few other persons in the barber shop at the time were also arrested. They were all taken to the city that same evening. Later it was rumored that the fugitive Widawski had turned himself in, which was not the case. The entire ghetto is extremely agitated, since most of those arrested are well known, quite apart from their function as transmitters of news.

The ghetto, shut off from the world, not permitted even to read the newspapers appearing in the Reich and available just beyond the barbed wire fence, could not, of course, remain hermetically sealed from the outside world forever. Two radio sets were discovered. A closed city of some 150,000 people! Perhaps these were receivers left in the ghetto by Poles, perhaps they were even primitive ghetto contraptions. No one had known whether there were actual radio sets in the ghetto or whether information came in through the barbed wire fence; but one thing is certain: the ghetto has always been filled with all sorts of rumors. Now it turns out that a few persons were daring enough to listen to the news right in the ghetto and to pass on what they had heard.

The ghetto fully understands what danger lies in store for these unfortunates. After all, we know how this harsh law is administered in wartime, outside the ghetto, everywhere in the Reich. Further news of those arrested is awaited with fear and anguish.

THURSDAY, JUNE 8, 1944

NEWS OF THE DAY: THE ARRESTS

The ghetto is still reeling from yesterday's unfortunate arrests. The event is discussed in whispers everywhere, and fear for the lives of these people has a stranglehold on everyone who knew them. The Order Service has not yet found the fugitive Chaim Widawski. It is feared that he will commit suicide rather than turn himself in to the German authorities. Widawski, still a young man, is very well known in the ghetto; his helpful ways and highly developed social sense have made him widely popular. He is a checker in the Coupon Department. Of course, there is little likelihood of his hiding out for very long, since the Secret State Police are demanding emphatically that he be brought in. There is no news about those arrested.

Although a very few copies of the *Litzmannstädter Zeitung* had regularly made their way through the barbed wire before the current arrests, no copy has been seen today. How the paper used to enter the ghetto is unclear. From now on, the law against bringing newspapers into the ghetto will undoubtedly be enforced even more rigorously.

FRIDAY, JUNE 9, 1944

NEWS OF THE DAY: CHAIM WIDAWSKI'S SUICIDE

Today's police report contains a brief, dry notice about Chaim Widawski's suicide. He remained in hiding until today but realized how hopeless his situation was and decided to take his own life. He swallowed a fast-acting poison (probably cyanide) in the gateway of a building on Podrzeczna [Street]. Then he went out to the street and collapsed. An Order Service man hurried over but found him already dead. The body lay there until the criminal police arrived. At first they ordered an autopsy, but later decided it was unnecessary and released the body for burial. Since tomorrow is Saturday, the funeral will most likely be scheduled for Sunday. Widawski left a brief farewell note to his relatives here. The entire ghetto has been shaken by his death.

Reportedly, only five of those arrested are in the city, while the others are being held by the ghetto [German] criminal police. The five are said to be two men named Weksler, the two Altszulers, father and son, and Tafel. This information is probably not quite accurate, though; most likely, all those arrested the day before yesterday are now being held in the city.

SATURDAY, JUNE 10, 1944

NEWS OF THE DAY

The Arrests

An Order Service man on duty at the Kripo [German criminal police] appeared at the Registration Bureau today in order to check on the personal data of six individuals. Yesterday we spoke of five people; the additional person is a man named [Icchak] Lublinski, whose arrest we also reported. Since the criminal police have demanded data on only these six persons, it has been inferred that only these six are being held in the city.

The chief of the Fire Department, [Henryk] Kaufman, was summoned by the Kripo today and taken to the city. There is speculation that the incident is connected with the arrests. Naturally, this development is the talk of the ghetto. Kaufman returned in the evening. It is unclear why his presence was required in the city.

Resettled to this Ghetto

Today's police report mentions two people who have been brought to this ghetto. They are Jewish women, mother and daughter, of Persian nationality. Both had previously been in Litzmannstadt, where they had a business. Both are ill and have therefore been taken to Hospital 1.

SUNDAY, JUNE 11, 1944

NEWS OF THE DAY: A FUNERAL

The funeral of Chaim Widawski took place privately this morning. Only family were present. The burial arrangements were made by Boruch Praszkier since his authority also includes the cemetery.

SKETCHES OF GHETTO LIFE: AT THE POST OFFICE

A tiny, wizened old woman forces her way up to the post office counter. A native of Bałut in the Reich. She wants to buy postcards. Postcards are much sought after now that the ban on mail has been lifted, especially since the people resettled here have been writing to their former homelands with requests for food packages. The post office is out of cards and, moreover, is piled high with postcards that have not been expedited yet. But the tiny woman absolutely insists. The director of the post office, [Mosze] Gumener, walks over to her.

"What can I do for you, my dear lady?"

"I want to buy post cards!"

"To whom do you wish to write, and where?"

"How should I know? I have no one to write to, but everyone else is buying them, so I'm buying them too!"

Thus, postcards have joined the list of items that bring record prices on the black market. Postcards normally costing ten pfennigs apiece at the post office are being offered for sale illicitly for fifteen marks; and people who fail to realize that such huge quantities of mail cannot be expedited are, nevertheless, buying postcards.

MONDAY, JUNE 12, 1944

NEWS OF THE DAY

Yesterday, Sunday, the Chairman entertained the administrative and technical managers of all metal departments at his home in Marysin.

THE ARRESTS

No news has reached the ghetto concerning the Jews arrested and taken to the city. There continues to be extreme anxiety about their fate. The general mood is wretched. People avoid each other, speak only in whispers; and the hackneyed question "What's new?" elicits only a shrug. Distrust is everywhere. Never before has the atmosphere in the ghetto been so poisoned.

FOOD SUPPLY

The situation is unchanged. Incoming shipments are still inadequate.

A few lucky garden proprietors are beginning to harvest their first spinach. These are the few who are able to pull strings and obtain seeds early; otherwise, planting got off to a very late start this year, and the great majority of gardeners still have nothing to bring home from the field. Today, spinach costs forty marks in illicit trade.

The specter of hunger haunts every home, every hearth. The general appearance of people in the ghetto could not be more wretched. A minor exception is the small group of those resettled here from other areas who have been receiving generous packages from their homelands regularly.

SKETCHES OF GHETTO LIFE: THE BOON OF THE LATRINE

The man who installed his działka [parcel] in a baby carriage has found an imaginative successor, a ghetto dweller who was driven to extraordinary lengths by the distress of Spring 1944. Since thousands of persons in the ghetto were not assigned działkas and were thus dependent on the normal vegetable rations, they devised highly original methods of solving the problem. A few of them filled boxes with soil, planted seeds, and placed their artificial gardens in their windows, where the sun did its best to make the crop prosper. Others removed the sidewalk in front of their buildings to make room for a vegetable bed. And one man—for the time being, the only one in the ghetto—covered the long, wide roof of his building's latrine (the open courtyard toilet) with soil and planted radishes and leeks, which are already thriving. . . . Whenever he wishes to water or harvest his crop, he climbs down a short ladder from his apartment window to the latrine roof and sets to work. It's not a long way. You might say that his działka is right under his nose, which catches the smell of both the latrine and the vegetable bed. But why quibble about aesthetics when you are driven by hunger?

O[skar] R[osenfeld]

TUESDAY, JUNE 13, 1944

NEWS OF THE DAY

The Chairman, who felt ill yesterday afternoon, is staying in bed today. He complains of heart trouble.

AIR RAID DEFENSE

There is now much ado about air raid defense in the ghetto. The heads of the air raid wardens, and the workshops, are continually receiving new instructions.

The Ghetto Administration has ordered slit trenches to be dug immediately in all gardens within the ghetto's center. Naturally, this involves a loss of tillage and, in particular, of plots that have already been cultivated and are doing quite nicely.

The number of fire alarm stations is being significantly increased, and a red plaque reading "To Report a Fire" has been placed wherever a telephone is to be found. All fire extinguishing reservoirs in the ghetto are full and regularly inspected. The number of officers in the Air Raid section of the Order Service has been increased.

SKETCHES OF GHETTO LIFE: PACKAGES

The number of people receiving packages continues to grow. Most are from Prague, but food packages are already arriving, even from cities in the Old Reich and from Vienna. Attempts are still being made to solicit small donations from these packages on behalf of resettled people who are going hungry, but progress is very slow. Tight limits are set on inducement of any sort. It is very difficult to deal with this psychological problem. People are stubborn, callous, selfish, inconsiderate; it takes endless effort to convince them, to win them over, one by one. With contributions of 100 grams of bread apiece, a total of only 7.5 kilograms of bread was collected during the period of June 8–10, even though 500 packages are arriving per week. A few people have volunteered to work with the project director. It is to be hoped that the starving people resettled here from Prague, and then those from other areas, will all receive assistance.

FRIDAY, JUNE 16, 1944

NEWS OF THE DAY

Today, the following announcement appeared in German and Yiddish:

Proclámation No. 416
ATTENTION!
Re: Voluntary Registration for Labor Outside the Ghetto.[21]

I hereby announce that men and women (including married people) may register for labor outside the ghetto.

If families have children old enough to work, the children may be registered along with their parents for labor outside the ghetto.

Such people will receive complete outfitting: clothing, shoes, linen, and socks. Fifteen kilograms of luggage per person may be taken along.

I would like especially to point out that mail service has been granted to such workers, who will, therefore, be able to write. Furthermore, it is expressly noted that those who register for labor outside the ghetto will be given the opportunity to collect their rations immediately, without waiting their turn. The above-men-

21. It is not known whether Rumkowski, as the Eldest of the Jews, or someone else in the Jewish administration was aware when issuing Proclamation No. 416 of June 16, 1944, that this time "voluntary registration for labor outside the ghetto" marked the beginning of the action to liquidate the ghetto. It is also not known whether M. C. Rumkowski or someone else in the Jewish administration of the ghetto knew that all the transports that left the ghetto from Radogoszcz station in Marysin between Friday, June 23, and Friday, July 14, 1944, were sent via Kutno to Koło and from there to the death camp in Chełmno (Kulmhof) on the river Ner.

tioned registrations are to take place at the ghetto Bureau of Labor, 13 Lutomierska Street as of Friday, June 16, 1944, every day from 8 A.M. to 9 P.M.

Litzmannstadt-Getto,   Ch[aim] Rumkowski
16 June 1944   The Eldest of the Jews in Litzmannstadt

The proclamation still speaks of voluntary registration. But in the present state of
affairs this formulation is very much out of date; and presumably the entire apparatus
that has always operated in such situations will be set in motion immediately. The
situation is roughly as follows: the planned resettlement is not for some 500 people to
be drawn from the ranks of volunteers. The actual goal is multiple, large-scale shipments of workers outside the ghetto. Reportedly, the first group of about 500 people is
bound for Munich to clear away debris. A further group of about 900 is to leave the
same week, probably on Friday, June 23. Then 3,000 people will leave each week for
the next three weeks, in transports of 1,000. A transport manager, two physicians,
medical personnel, and Order Service men are to be appointed for each transport.
The latter are to be drawn not from the ghetto Order Service, but from the transports
themselves. The destination of these large groups is unknown. The regulations outlined in the above proclamation apply to these large transports as well. Fifteen to
twenty kilograms of luggage may be taken along, but it must be as compact as
possible.

Commissioner [Günter] Fuchs has assured high-ranking ghetto functionaries that
this labor transport is not in any danger, and that what is involved is the clearing away
of debris in cities that have been bombed. This assurance somewhat alleviates the
terror occasioned by every previous resettlement.

AN UNPLEASANT INCIDENT

Towards 5 P.M., an extremely awkward and regrettable incident occurred in the office
of the Eldest. Amtsleiter Biebow suddenly appeared in a highly excited state and
ordered the staff to leave the office immediately and lock it. Then he stormed into
Chairman Rumkowski's office and, in a fit of rage, attacked the Eldest of the Jews. The
Chairman sustained an injury to his face, on the cheekbone. The Amtsleiter himself
was injured by a window pane that he smashed. Czarnulla and [Heinrich] Schwind
rushed in, apparently with the intention of calming the Amtsleiter down, but they did
not succeed in doing so.

After the incident the Chairman was immediately taken to the hospital on Przelotna Street, where Dr. [Michał] Eliasberg administered first aid.

Never before has Amtsleiter Biebow laid hands on the Chairman. In these pages we
have repeatedly hinted at the potentially serious conflict between the two men. No
one imagined that it could lead to such excesses; even to the Amtsleiter, after all,
Chairman Rumkowski is not only the representative of 80,000 working Jews, but also a
man of nearly seventy. Anyone who knows the Amtsleiter knows that this was one of
his fits of rage, which he will most certainly regret later. There is, of course, no way of
learning what exchange of words preceded the violence. No doubt it had something
to do with the mayor [of Litzmannstadt and chief of the Gestapo] Dr. Bradfisch's visit
to the Chairman yesterday. Several sources claim that the Amtsleiter heaped the
Chairman with reproaches for promising the mayor an initial quota of 600 persons
without first consulting him. That supposedly compromised the Amtsleiter, since he

has been maintaining that he is unable to comply with any requisitions of manpower.

Of course, no precise information is available, since the Chairman is hospitalized and in a state of despair. In any case, it is not like him to talk about such matters.

FOR LABOR OUTSIDE THE GHETTO

Every day some forty or fifty people report to Central Prison to volunteer for labor outside the ghetto. At this rate, of course, it will be impossible to meet the quota of 500 or 600 people by Wednesday, the 21st of this month.

A COMMISSION

A commission to solve the technical problems of the forthcoming labor shipments has already been formed. Its members are the head of the court, [Szaja-Stanisław] Jakobson, as chairman, and the following men: [Zygmunt] Blemmer, [Józef] Kohl, [Samuel] Berkowicz (Police Precinct I), Commissioner Wollman (Special Department) and prosecutor Nussbrecher, who is probably in attendance to serve as secretary. The commission is working in close cooperation with the Bureau of Labor. A joint session of the commission with Commander [Leon] Rozenblat, Dawid Warszawski, and [Kiwa] Sienicki will take place tomorrow.

SATURDAY, JUNE 17, 1944

NEWS OF THE DAY

The Chairman is still under medical care in the hospital on Mickiewicz Street. This morning, Amtsleiter Biebow drove to the hospital in his car. It was initially assumed that he intended to pay the Chairman a visit of reconciliation after the incident, but this was not the case. Amtsleiter Biebow was seeking medical treatment for his injured hand, and had x-rays taken. He was found not to have any serious injuries.

The meeting announced yesterday took place today in the Chairman's waiting room. In the afternoon, all the workshop managers and department directors were convened to receive their instructions from the commission. Managers will be required to draw up lists of those people whom the workshops can spare. Factories vital to the war effort will provide less manpower, others more. The carpet plant under [Szyja] Klugman has been closed down, as was the slipper workshop. The Quilt Department was disbanded within the hour. The Amtsleiter had originally intended to solve the problem of manpower requisition in the usual drastic wartime fashion. He had planned to close down the quilt workshop, slipper workshop, carpet workshop, etc. (that is, nonvital factories) and to send their entire crews to perform labor outside the ghetto. That solution was successfully averted. As described above, the managers of departments and workshops will compile quota lists. The application of this procedure has the people who were resettled to this ghetto from other areas extremely worried about their future. The attitude of factory managers toward the nonlocals working under them is very arbitrary and, for the most part, decidedly negative. There is no doubt that this group will be sacrificed first, since it is entirely at the discretion of managers to provide whomever they wish. Nearly all the workshops are organized on a *mishpokhe* [family] basis; that is, the manager has ensured that his own people and in turn their people (in other words, a certain clique of people close to him) are properly provided for, so the managers will naturally first sacrifice workers in whom they have no personal interest. One may therefore assume that, with this resettlement, the prevailing system will cause the last remaining Western European Jews, aside from an occasional special case, to vanish from the ghetto.

The printing shop has been assigned the job of producing 10,000 transport-number sets for the departing workers. This fact also confirms the speculation that, for the time being, some 10,000 people are to leave the ghetto. Sources in touch with the German authorities claim that the latter do not intend to liquidate the ghetto in this way, because business orders are still coming in and there is an interest in maintaining the factories here that are vital to the war effort. Reportedly, 3,000 people are to be dispatched each week for the next three weeks; added to these are the first group of 500 or 600 and the second group of 900—all in all, some 10,000 or 11,000. At any rate, this is what has been learned from the office of the Eldest.

SUNDAY, JUNE 18, 1944

NEWS OF THE DAY: LABOR OUTSIDE THE GHETTO

This afternoon (Sunday) the Post Office delivered the first notices to report at Central Prison. They read as follows:

List . . . .   Number . . . .
DEPARTURE ORDER
[Name] . . . . residing at . . . . is hereby ordered to report to Central Prison at 12 Krawiecka Street on . . . . June 1944 at 9 A.M. for dispatch to perform labor outside the ghetto. Each person is permitted to take along 15 to 20 kilograms of luggage. Such luggage must include a small pillow and a blanket, and must be as compact as possible. Family members may accompany those ordered to report.

. . . . June 1944

Ch[aim] Rumkowski
The Eldest of the Jews in Litzmannstadt

The text of the order is consistent with the directions that the Eldest of the Jews received from the Secret State Police [Gestapo] in regard to these transports. The directions were conveyed orally through Miss [Dora] Fuchs, and, as usual in such cases, a file memorandum was made; it reads as follows:

Transcript

Memorandum:

On Monday, Wednesday, and Friday of each week, a shipment of 1,000 people is to depart for labor outside the ghetto. The first transport is to leave on Wednesday, June 21, 1944 (about 600). The transports are to be numbered (with roman numerals: Transport I, and so forth). Each departing worker is assigned a transport number. The individual is to wear his number, and it is also to be attached to his luggage. Fifteen to twenty kilograms of luggage per person are allowed; it must include a small pillow and a blanket. Food for two to three days must be brought along. In each transport, one person is to be appointed transport manager, and he will have ten people to assist him. In other words: a total of eleven people in each transport.

The transports are to leave at 7 A.M., so loading must begin by 6 A.M. One physician or military paramedic, and two or three medical orderlies must accompany each group of 1,000. The families of these physicians, paramedics, or orderlies may travel along with them.

Baggage is not to be wrapped in a sheet or blanket, but rather, as compactly as possible, so that the individual items may easily be stored in the train and thus are readily transportable.

As to the eleven people: they must wear Order Service caps and armbands.

This memorandum and the previous statement by the mayor [of Litzmannstadt] and chief of the Gestapo, Dr. Bradfisch, to the Chairman have led people to infer that what is involved here is a major deployment of able-bodied Jews. Lists have been drawn up in all the workshops involved, and turned in to Central Prison or the commission. The Post Office immediately began delivering the departure orders. In addition, volunteers are still coming forward.

Central Prison now holds some 400 people. It is assumed that once the orders are issued, the first transport can be formed quickly. As indicated by the memorandum, and as the ghetto knows, the first transport—600 people—is scheduled for Wednesday, the 21st of this month.

Returning to the text of the above memorandum, we should mention that no time limit or numerical limit has been specified, so there is uncertainty in this regard. This has led pessimists to conclude that the true goal is the gradual liquidation of the ghetto. Although the text of the memorandum contains nothing to allay anxiety on this score, one may nevertheless assume that no critical danger is imminent.

The Chairman is still hospitalized. Aside from work-related visits by Miss [Dora] Fuchs and by his secretary, [Mieczysław] Abramowicz, the Chairman is receiving no visitors. His condition gives absolutely no cause for alarm.

We have already mentioned that there is less panic this time than during the other resettlements, large or small. This does not mean, however, that the majority of those affected are quietly resigned to their fate. Such an attitude is to be expected only from the Jews resettled here from other parts who, if for no other reason than because of their upbringing, are not inclined to, or are incapable of, resistance. This element of the populace will probably present the fewest difficulties to the Jewish authorities, for several reasons:

(1) Those resettled from the West are accustomed to obeying official directives without delay. They do not have that environmentally conditioned vitality which is instantly activated by the approach of danger.

(2) They do not have the necessary experience or connections to elude the Order Service for very long, while, to a great extent, the local Jews do.

(3) They are far more weary, and therefore take a more fatalistic attitude.

(4) The German Jews who are still here are toying with the idea that they will

eventually return to the Old Reich, their homeland; thus, they still regard the ghetto milieu as a greater evil than collective-camp life on German soil.

(5) They believe that, toward the end of the war, they can hide more easily in their own country than in the ghetto.

For those resettled here from Prague such arguments have scant validity. First of all, the Prague Jews generally have put down roots in the ghetto more easily; furthermore, they have a significantly better chance of holding out, especially now, because of the frequent arrival of food packages from their homeland. They are not homesick for the Old Reich. Their families are marginally better off in a number of respects. Indeed, there are still a few families intact among those from Prague. One may therefore expect that this element will offer both passive and active resistance in seeking to be exempted from the transports.

The issue of the resettled Jews, however, is only a small factor in the entire picture since, in any case, the largest contingent has to be drawn from the reservoir of local Jews. Thus, thousands of tragedies are in the making.

We will have to wait and see whether the commission can overcome the technical difficulties and prevent German intervention.

MONDAY, JUNE 19, 1944

NEWS OF THE DAY

The Chairman is still in the hospital.

Labor Outside the Ghetto

There has been no essential change in the situation at Central Prison. The first workshop lists have gone into effect, and departure orders have reached those involved. Predictably, some individual workshops have listed nearly a hundred percent of their workers, who had been resettled to this ghetto. Foremost in this respect is Wiśniewski's handmade knitwear workshop, hardly any of whose nonlocal women have been spared. To be sure, this workshop also has the largest number of nonlocal female workers. Consequently, the first petitions to the commission (aside from those by people in Central Prison) were turned in early this morning. This time the commission is proceeding methodically: when it issues the departure order, it simultaneously suspends the worker's ration card and, where applicable, those of the entire family—a result of the problems encountered in the previous operation. As expected, people who were resettled here from the Old Reich reported relatively punctually, while Czech Jews moved heaven and earth to escape fate. Jews from the Old Reich have no agency or influential people they can appeal to in their plight, and they are therefore reporting as ordered. Czech Jews normally turn to Dr. Oskar Singer, and naturally they are doing so again—in droves. It is too early to say whether this unofficial representative of the group will be able to intercede. People who were resettled to this ghetto are fighting with traditional tactics: by night they go into hiding at the apartments of others, hoping thereby to elude the Order Service. As yet, no Order Service operation is scheduled, at least for the next few hours.

The factory managers, who hold the fate of these people in their hands, wield their power according to their various standards of ethical conduct. The factories have been ordered to make available a certain percentage of their workers. Only a few managers are displaying any real sense of responsibility in administering their task. The workers listed fall into two categories: (1) those who know they will be unable to find a way out because they have no connections, or no important ones; (2) and those who, predictably, in one way or another, will find a way out, such as the wives of persons in relatively high places or wives of relatives of Order Service or Special Department members—those close to the ghetto's highest-ranking personalities. The managers will have filled their quotas on paper, so to speak, and the commission at Central Prison can then worry about actually supplying the required contingent; for the nature of things in the ghetto dictates that connections always do the trick. Conscientious managers have used fair criteria. They have listed primarily people without families, whether native or resettled. Today, the first day on which the conscripted are reporting to Central Prison, it is impossible to foresee how the operation will proceed. Word has it that the first dispatch of approximately 600 people will leave not on Wednesday, the 21st of this month, but on Friday the 23d, because the requisitioned freight cars will not be available.

This report has led the ghetto, always susceptible to optimistic rumors, to hope that the entire resettlement action is not yet a certainty.

SKETCHES OF GHETTO LIFE: OUTSIDE THE GHETTO

The Eldest has had announcements posted to the effect that there is work for Jews outside the ghetto and that volunteers are being solicited. Residents of the ghetto, namely some 80,000 Jews, are reacting to this announcement with the formula: "Es shmekt mit 'wysiedlenie' "—"It smells of resettlement!" Great as the temptation may be, the number of volunteers registering for labor is insignificant compared to the actual quota demanded . . . and, finally, volunteering has given way to conscription.

The authorities in charge of the ghetto need around ten thousand people; that number has to be mustered. The machinery is in motion. And soon after the emergence of the first rumors, the printed notices are already fluttering into homes with orders to report to Central Prison, the official staging area for all resettlements or "labor outside the ghetto."

Purpose: Labor Outside the Ghetto
A few thousand Jews are to enjoy the blessing of laboring *outside* the ghetto, of leaving the ghetto, the Jewish residential area, through the barbed wire into golden freedom! What a marvelous prospect! After four hard, torturous years filled with anxiety and distress, they can go out into the world again and see a patch of land that is not surrounded by barbed wire, they can receive food other than ghetto rations. In other words, they can be human beings again. And yet, few people, very few, regard this prospect as a stroke of luck. How deeply must skepticism be ingrained in the souls of the Litzmannstadt ghetto's Jews if they fail to jump at such a chance, if they prefer to remain in the utterly bleak and hopeless conditions of the ghetto. What profound spiritual devastation! They would rather remain in the familiar circumstances of the ghetto with their families and friends than go *outside*. For them the refrain "Outside

the Ghetto" has no attraction. It is true, a few hundred ghetto dwellers have volunteered for labor outside the ghetto (young adventurers, people with nothing to lose) or have voluntarily accompanied their families. But in general the ghetto is immune to temptation. It lives its idiosyncratic life in accordance with the law of inertia, as it were. "Labor Outside the Ghetto" is not what it is waiting for, it waits—if dull fatalism can be called waiting—for a miracle. The miracle of redemption.

O[skar] R[osenfeld]

LABOR OUTSIDE THE GHETTO

The commission at Central Prison is besieged by mobs of people delivering petitions. Aside from a few volunteers and German Jews from the Reich who have obeyed the order without delay, almost every case is being appealed for exemption. Thus, an enormous mass of petitions is piling up, and it is not at all clear how the commission can process them, especially since the members tend to examine every petition conscientiously.

There are plans to close down the hostel for juvenile workers. Since its residents are, without exception, alone in the world, their departure will at least not break up any families. In the present resettlement action, the juvenile element will probably be less protected than before.

Amtsleiter Biebow has made a total of 500,000 marks available for the resettlement. The money is to be used as follows: every worker will receive ten marks upon departure. An appropriate sum will be allocated to the Main Purchasing Agency, which will pay in Reich marks for anything it buys from such workers—up to a maximum of fifty marks. Payment will be in the form of a check made out to Central Prison. The Main Purchasing Agency will agree to buy only upon presentation of a departure order. The idea is to enable the departing workers to convert some of their property into Reich marks. This is the first time in the history of the ghetto that the German authorities have made arrangements for workers to take German currency with them.[22] In earlier resettlements people could sell objects to the Main Purchasing Agency but received only ghetto money.

The current procedure is, understandably, producing positive comment. Mr. Henryk Neftalin, the attorney, has been entrusted with supervision of this financial operation.

The proclamation concerning purchase reads as follows (in German and Yiddish):

No. 417

Re: Furnishings and Belongings of Families Departing for Labor Outside the Ghetto.

I hereby announce that the furnishings and other belongings of families traveling to perform labor outside the ghetto are being purchased by the Main Purchasing Agency, 4 Kościelny Square, Telephone: 72.

At this location, furniture, household utensils, wares, linen, clothing, etc., are appraised by specialists, and the equivalent value is paid out in cash. Families

---

22. This was yet another means of lulling people's vigilance and was supposed to remove all suspicion from ghetto dwellers' minds as to the true nature of the present deportation.

with large pieces of furniture that they cannot bring to the Main Purchasing Agency may arrange there to have specialists visit their apartments to appraise and remove such items.

Those not wishing to sell their belongings can store them at the Main Purchasing Agency and, as the case may be, indicate to whom these articles are to be turned over in the ghetto.

The Main Purchasing Agency is open from 8 A.M. to 7 P.M.

Litzmannstadt-Getto,   Ch[aim] Rumkowski
18 June 1944   The Eldest of the Jews in Litzmannstadt

SKETCHES OF GHETTO LIFE: ESCAPE INTO HELL

The postmen are rushing through town, or rather, they have a rush job to do. But they themselves are trudging through the streets, up and down the stairs. Their bags are full now. When there is a knock at the door, the tenant knows it is neither the milkman nor the baker; and the normally welcome mailman frightens people with his knock in broad daylight as if it were midnight. No sooner are their departure orders in people's hands than they have resolved to resist. They talk themselves into believing that the war, now in its fifth year, is bound to end soon; at this late date they are reluctant to part with their last possessions, to relinquish their beds or cots. No one knows whether it is better at this juncture to be inside the ghetto or outside the barbed wire. No one can tell how the situation in the ghetto might develop if this summer should bring major events. For the fact that such events are imminent is obvious from the preparations the German authorities are making inside the ghetto, the air raid defense measures, and other signs as well. The local populace has its time-tested methods. [Some] people equip themselves for a nightmarish game of hide-and-seek. They move into their hideouts, fix them up, stock them with whatever supplies of food they may have. The "dance" begins. But all the others, the great majority who have no provisions to speak of, will be in mortal jeopardy if they take this route. Nevertheless, they [too] risk it. Their ration cards are suspended; there will be no bread, no soup in the workshops, not even vegetables. The bit of food that formerly kept them from starvation will no longer be available. But instinct drives them, fear hounds them. Whole families are going into hiding. People refuse to leave hell because they have grown accustomed to it.

For the time being, the commission is not expected to take drastic steps. It counts on the suspension of ration cards as an effective measure. Nor will this measure fail. After near-starvation, no one can endure total starvation for two weeks or longer.

O[skar] S[inger]

WEDNESDAY, JUNE 21, 1944

NEWS OF THE DAY

A commission visited the ghetto. It inspected the large church on Kościelny Square. Some claim that this is a matter of air-raid defense, others that the towers were inspected for military reasons.

The Chairman is still in the hospital; his condition is substantially improved.

Air-Raid Alarm
The ghetto has experienced its first serious daytime air-raid alarm. At 11:25 A.M. the sirens began to wail and the air-raid wardens' organization sprang into action.

The Jews working at Bałut Market had to leave their offices immediately for the buildings at 25 and 27 Łagiewnicka Street. The German officials and employees at Bałut Market rushed down to the recently completed bomb shelter on the premises. The ghetto populace remained absolutely calm; in any case, there was no possibility of effective protection, so most people stayed where they were: in apartments, workshops, offices, building entrances, and some, in the so-called slit trenches. In a number of workshops the crews were chased out into the open and had to lie on the ground. Needless to say, gardens were crushed and trampled. From somewhere in the vicinity, a few shots fired by anti-aircraft guns could be heard. A large air squadron, perhaps 300 planes, was observed flying east at an altitude of about 2,000 meters. No bombs were dropped. The all-clear signal came at 12:40.

THURSDAY, JUNE 22, 1944

AN ATTEMPTED SUICIDE

On June 21, 1944, Gerti Sachs, born August 22, 1905, in Brünn [Brno], attempted suicide by swallowing a sleep-inducing drug. She was taken to the hospital by the Emergency Service.

NEWS OF THE DAY

The Chairman is still hospitalized.

Departing Workers
The ghetto is haunted by the imminent bloodletting. People generally suspect that a gradual liquidation of the ghetto is under way, and that shortly after the current transports are completed another resettlement will commence. This assumption is contradicted by the fact that the Ghetto Administration is still accepting orders for the workshops and efforts are being made to prevent the present resettlement from interfering with production in the important workshops.

Removal of More Districts From the Ghetto
Today a meeting took place at Bałut Market between representatives of the Ghetto Administration and a number of Jewish department directors. They discussed under what circumstances certain parts of the ghetto could be severed and incorporated into the city. The districts involved are the residential blocks on Lutomierska, Podrzeczna, Drewnowska, Stary Market, and Wolborska streets. If this area were removed, housing would have to be found elsewhere in the ghetto for approximately 10,000 Jews. Hence [M.] Wolfowicz, head of the Department of Housing, also participated. [Ignacy] Gutman, the engineer, has been assigned to prepare a technical report on the project.

SKETCHES OF GHETTO LIFE: "TOO LATE"

So many things in the ghetto come too late. Patients with edema, decalcified bones, or other ailments try to find more nutritious food, Vigantol, cod-liver oil. Before they do so, they are already beyond hope. "Too late. Nothing can be done now," says the physician, shaking his head. But it is not always the Jews for whom time runs out.

The Kripo [German criminal police] are searching for a family of eleven named Szmulewicz. They knock at the door, shove it open, and question the occupant.

"Does the Szmulewicz family live here?"

"They used to. Now I do, Dawid Botwin. I took over their apartment."

"What about Mordko Szmulewicz?"

"Dead."

"Szaja?"

"Dead."

"Lajzer and Sure Szmulewicz?"

"Resettled."

"Jankel?"

"Jumped out the window. Dead."

"Chawe Szmulewicz?"

"Resettled."

"Mojsze Szmulcwicz, the 15-year-old?"

"Shot to death near the barbed wire."

"The two brothers, Boruch and Hersz?"

"Tried to escape to Warsaw. Didn't make it."

"Boruch's son Józef?"

"No idea. Never came to the ghetto in the first place."

The two officers look around the apartment. A miserable scene. No trace of the Szmulewicz family. Eleven people snuffed out. Nothing to be done now.

The dead will never divulge the location of the little *pekl* [bundle] in question. If the police had come earlier, they might have tracked down some of the Jewish property they intended to confiscate in accordance with the laws of the German Reich.

Too late. Death has thumbed its nose at the authorities. Even the quickest hand is powerless against death.

O[skar] R[osenfeld]

FRIDAY, JUNE 23, 1944

NEWS OF THE DAY

Labor Outside the Ghetto
The first transport of 562 people left Radogoszcz Station this morning at 8 A.M. Before their departure, Gestapo Commissioner [Günter] Fuchs made a few reassuring remarks. He stated that they would be working in the Reich and that decent food would be provided. For lack of passenger cars, they would initially be loaded onto freight cars but be transferred to passenger cars en route. No one had anything to fear.

Naturally, the news of this speech spread through the ghetto like wildfire and had a somewhat calming effect.

The loading of the transport went smoothly, without incident. Families were not broken up. The floors of the freight cars were covered with straw.

A man who was in extreme despair was taken back to Central Prison by Commissioner [Günter] Fuchs.

The travelers did not have to carry their luggage; everything was brought to the station in wagons. Everyone collected his hand luggage at the station, while larger pieces were stowed in separate freight cars. Everything was properly numbered. People were treated correctly.

Fifty People Dispatched via Bałut Market
Today, fifty people left separately for labor outside the ghetto via Bałut Market. Their destination also is unknown, but it is assumed that this small detail will be employed in cutting peat near Litzmannstadt.

Managers' Meeting
The managers of workshops and departments conferred in the offices of Metal Department I, 63 Łagiewnicka Street, at 9 P.M. The meeting was chaired by A[ron] Jakubowicz. The managers were instructed to compile lists of people for dispatch from the workshops and departments and to turn these lists over to the commission at Central Prison.

Reportedly, a total of 25,000 workers has been requisitioned.

The Chairman Still in the Hospital
It is widely regretted that the Chairman is still not back on his feet and, therefore, cannot intercede.

WORKSHOP NEWS

Today, considerable quantities of raw material for the tailoring workshops arrived at Radogoszcz station. The ghetto again concluded (mistakenly) that it will not be liquidated. Of course the two matters are unrelated. After all, the raw material has been en route for some time now and is part of the economic sector, which is managed by other agencies, independent of the political sector.

SATURDAY, JUNE 24, 1944

NEWS OF THE DAY

A Minor Panic
The ghetto is agitated because the railroad cars that carried off yesterday's transport are already back at Radogoszcz station. People infer that the transport traveled only a short distance, and a wave of terror is spreading through the ghetto. People recall the frequent shuttle of transport cars and trains during the period of the great resettlements [of 1942] and the alarming rumors of that time.

Reportedly, a note was found in one freight car indicating that the train went only as far as Kutno [33 miles north of Łódź], where the travelers were transferred to passenger cars. This information has not been confirmed. No one has actually seen the note; so no conclusions can be drawn about the quick return of the cars. Perhaps further transportation is being staged in Kutno. It is hoped that we will soon learn what is happening with these people.

SUNDAY, JUNE 25, 1944

SKETCHES OF GHETTO LIFE: IN EARNEST

Reality has completely stemmed the tide of rumors. Ghetto dwellers are now being shipped out of the ghetto to perform manual labor. One transport has already gone off; the second will leave the ghetto tomorrow. Today is Sunday, June 25. A Sunday of sunshine and drifting clouds, of calm and storm and rain showers. The streets leading to Central Prison are unusually lively. People of various ages and of both sexes, as well as children and the aged, are hauling suitcases, knapsacks and tightly packed bundles on their shoulders. Many valises bear German personal and place names. They belong to the Jews who were resettled to the Litzmannstadt ghetto in the autumn of 1941 and have now received departure orders. There is also a good deal of colorful baggage to be seen: striped pillows and garish blankets—the bedding for future sleeping quarters.

People go their own way. Some pass by holding flowers, hedge blossoms and peonies, jasmine and other June flowers. People chat, stroll. The działkas [parcels] are full of ghetto dwellers at work. Crowds throng outside the stores. Life as usual.

And yet there is a pall over the ghetto. Twenty-five transports have been announced. Everyone knows that the situation is serious, that the existence of the ghetto is in jeopardy. No one can deny that such fears are justified. The argument that not even "this resettlement" can imperil the survival of the ghetto now falls on deaf ears. For nearly every ghetto dweller is affected this time. Everyone is losing a relative, a friend, a roommate, a colleague.

And yet—Jewish faith in a justice that will ultimately triumph does not permit extreme pessimism. People try to console themselves, deceive themselves in some way. But nearly everyone says to himself, and to others:

"God only knows who will be better off: the person who stays here or the person who leaves!"

O[skar] R[osenfeld]

MONDAY, JUNE 26, 1944

NEWS OF THE DAY

Labor outside the Ghetto
Today, Transport II, with 912 persons, left the ghetto (accompanying physician: Dr. Adolf Wittenberg, Berlin). The same train as last time was used under the same circumstances. Once again Gestapo commissioner [Günter] Fuchs said a few words. This transport included a large contingent of young people, several of them volun-

teers, leaving the ghetto in high spirits. On the other hand, there were also a great many feeble and sickly people. Reportedly, the next transport, which is to leave on Wednesday the 28th, will be smaller.

Lists Posted

In accordance with the instructions of the Inter-workshop Committee, which is already operating at full speed, the lists have been posted in all workshops. Inter-workshop Committee is being flooded with intercessions and petitions.

Anyone who plays even a minor role in the ghetto is now besieged by people hoping to pull strings. The workshop corridors are crowded with lines of workers trying to submit their petitions for exemption to the managers. There is a petition for every name on the list. Similar scenes are enacted in physicians' offices. During consultation hours they are mobbed by patients who claim to be sicker than they are and by healthy people who want to be sick at any price. We observe only in passing that doctors are now raking in enormous sums.

Shady deals that involve human lives are negotiated behind the scenes, among the workshop managers. By the time the Inter-workshop Committee completes the clearing procedure, the managers have come to terms. You cross out my Jew and I'll cross out yours; if you list my Jew, then I'll list yours. Personal intrigues and vendettas are rampant.

It's a mystery how the workshops can still function. The streets are teeming with people looking for friends in high places.

Today, the Inter-workshop Committee issued orders to the workshops and departments; they concern mainly the regulation of quotas.

People Are Selling Themselves

Once again people are selling themselves—people who have either nothing to lose or who are reckless or desperate or believe that they are drawing accurate conclusions about the general situation are volunteering as substitutes. They sell themselves. This time the price is fairly uniform: a human being is worth three loaves of bread, a half-kilogram of margarine, one pound of sugar. Plus, perhaps, shoes and other items of clothing.

SKETCHES OF GHETTO LIFE: THE FINAL STAGE

After four years in the ghetto, it turns out that sentiments, predilections, and traditions only fetter those who wish to survive the war and be saved. Cut off all ties, leave the old home without shedding a tear, abandon the furnishings you worked so hard to acquire—these are the slogans of all ghetto dwellers who have received a "departure order."

Money, jewelry, furs, sewing machines, phonographs, musical instruments, stamps, running shoes, bicycles, irons, electrical cooking appliances, carpets, and crystal have all been confiscated. Now the ghetto dweller has to give up the very last of his possessions.

Pillows and blankets and bedding of all sorts lie packed in bales in the courtyard of 4 Kościelny Square, in front of the Main Purchasing Agency's storehouse. Buckets, dishes, and linen are stacked up around the table of the officials in charge of appraising and purchasing such domestic articles. Those about to depart bring their belongings to the purchasing agency in order to raise money for food for the journey: a few grams of sugar or bread or some kind of grain. On the basis of the appraisals, they receive a voucher made out for ghetto marks and Reich marks; the ghetto marks are paid out at the Main Treasury, the Reich marks, at Central Prison.

Thus do people bid farewell to the last of their goods and chattels. No tear is shed, no harsh word spoken. Fatalism prevails. People think: "It's the final stage. Now nothing more can be taken from us. We are as poor as when God created us. The clothes on our bodies and a few remaining necessities—this will suffice until *then.*" *Then* is the moment when fate chooses between life and death.

O[skar] R[osenfeld]

SKETCHES OF GHETTO LIFE: THE LOST BED

In this period of resettlement the courtyard at the Main Purchasing Agency at 4 Kościelny Square is one of the most interesting places in the ghetto. In the middle of the courtyard, a mound of eiderdowns, mostly in their garish red covers, towers up like a coral reef pounded by the surf of a dreary mass of anonymous resettlees. These people have come here to convert their last possessions into cash in order to enhance the first few hours of their totally uncertain future beyond the barbed wire surrounding the ghetto—a barrier that confines but, on the other hand, provides some spiritual protection. These people do not know what awaits them, but who does? They do know what they have lost: there they are in an enormous mound, the last paltry things that they could count on, their own beds.

Thus, the courtyard at the Main Purchasing Agency has become a symbol of these days of anguish.

P[eter] W[ertheimer]

WEDNESDAY, JUNE 28, 1944

NEWS OF THE DAY: LABOR OUTSIDE THE GHETTO

Early this morning Transport III departed with 803 people. The accompanying physician is Dr. Walter Schwerin of Berlin. It is some consolation, at least, that this transport was a bit smaller than the one on the 26th of June.

For the time being, no difficulties worth mentioning have been encountered in the requisition of human resources. The suspension of ration cards has done its share, especially with those who are helpless because they have neither relatives nor influence.

The exemption petitions are still swamping the Inter-workshop Committee, and, needless to say, all the stops have been pulled on the grand organ of "connections." There is all sorts of talk about the commission in Central Prison. Indeed, each of its members has the "proper" experience and credentials for his position.

It is reported with disapproval that entire families are employed there, since various separate food allotments are available.

FRIDAY, JUNE 30, 1944

NEWS OF THE DAY: LABOR OUTSIDE THE GHETTO

In the morning there was some uncertainty whether today's transport would be leaving, since the train was not delivered punctually to Radogoszcz station. But the Reich Railroad [*Deutsche Reichsbahn*] did provide the train toward 9 A.M., whereupon the 700 people could board. This transport included Dr. Elisabeth Singer (Prague) as its physician.

To protect the remainder of the nonlocal intelligentsia from resettlement, Dr. Oskar Singer met with M[arek] Kligier, head of the Special Department, even before the Chairman was back in his office. Kligier was entirely sympathetic with Dr. Singer's viewpoint and ordered protection for several persons. His list was transmitted to the commission in Central Prison.

In regard to protecting the local intelligentsia, especially a certain literary group, S[zmul] Rozenstein, Józef Zelkowicz, and Szaja Szpigel have appealed through [Henryk] Neftalin, the attorney. A separate report on this will follow.

At Central Prison, there is some worry about shortages; presumably raids will be carried out.

As reported, seven hundred people left in today's Transport IV. All told, 2,976 people have left the ghetto, a figure which breaks down as follows:

	Total	Men	Women	Nonlocal men	Nonlocal women
June 23	561	268	293	32	46
June 26	912	361	551	43	71
June 28	803	261	542	32	75
June 30	700	204	496	23	40
	2,976	1,094	1,882	130	232

Contrary to suspicion, the majority of the nonlocal group was not swept away. Of the above total of 2,976 people, 362 are nonlocals from the Old Reich and from the Protectorate of Bohemia and Moravia. These figures are calculated on the basis of transport lists whereby the nonlocals could be identified only on the basis of names. We will supply precise data later.

SATURDAY, JULY 1, 1944

NEWS OF THE DAY: LABOR OUTSIDE THE GHETTO

The commission is now beginning to encounter difficulties in supplying the human resources required for the next transport. Recurrent rumors that the operation will be terminated are providing many with added inducement to go into hiding.

Accustomed to hunger and deprivation, these people are now bearing up under even greater torments. Families endure enormous deprivations in order to protect a father, a brother, a sister from resettlement and to feed the endangered person in the meantime.

The agencies involved are aware of how dangerous it would be to fall behind in supplying the quotas required.

To prevent any possible storage of food, the Chairman has decided to distribute rations for only one week this time, instead of for two. This ration is supposed to be distributed today.

In regard to today's population total, it is worth noting that the figure of 73,234 ghetto residents breaks down as follows:

Ethnic Germans	1
Poles	16
Jews	73,217

The German woman and the Poles are relatives of Jews.

SUNDAY, JULY 2, 1944

SUICIDE ATTEMPTS

On June 30, 1944, Resa Adler, born September 19, 1925, in Łódź, attempted suicide by jumping from the fourth story of her apartment house at 30 Dworska Street. She was taken to the hospital.

On July 2, 1944, Malka Gimpclewicz, born in 1914 in Łódź and residing at 31 Łagiewnicka Street, attempted suicide by jumping from the fourth story of the building at 24 Limanowski Street. She was taken to the hospital by the Emergency Service.

NEWS OF THE DAY: LABOR OUTSIDE THE GHETTO

Tomorrow's Transport V has already been filled.

The ghetto still has no idea where the transports are headed. Since the train is always back on schedule for the next dispatch, it must be shuttling. The transports are no doubt going only as far as Kutno, where the human resources are reportedly screened. Rumor is that healthy, able-bodied persons are then placed at the disposal of farmers. Naturally, no confirmation of this rumor is available.

Although Transport I left on June 23, nine days ago, the ghetto has not yet received any reliable news about the deportees.

SKETCHES OF GHETTO LIFE: MANAGERS TRADE IN HUMAN LIVES

There is a flourishing clearance sale in human beings. A workshop manager now has his best opportunity to rid himself of disagreeable individuals. This is usually done by telephone.

The manager of Laundry I calls up the Textile Factory:

"You've got a man named X working for you. Is he on the list?"

"No."

"Do you need him urgently?"

"Yes."

"Too bad!"

"Why?"

"I was hoping to put his wife on the list."

The manager of the Textile Factory has an idea: "If you agree not to put Mrs. Y on the list, then I'll put X on my revised list. That way you can list his wife."

The deal is made.

If a manager dislikes someone, that person's fate is sealed.

But X uses his pleytses [here: connections]; he gets himself off. By now, though, his wife is on the list, and the struggle begins anew. The deal can't be canceled because Mrs. Y has been listed in exchange for Mrs. X. These matters may be a bit complicated for the astonished reader in the future. We Jews, however, do know how to do business—why not with human lives? It is difficult to describe all the nuances, all the possibilities, all the vile acts that thrive in this slough. A merciful veil covers most of the tragedies caused by arbitrary dealings.

MONDAY, JULY 3, 1944

NEWS OF THE DAY: LABOR OUTSIDE THE GHETTO

Early this morning Transport V left Radogoszcz station with 700 people. The accompanying physician was Dr. Fritz Heine (Berlin).

There remained in Central Prison only a slight reserve for the next transport, to be dispatched on Wednesday.

In the ghetto people are whispering about a new demand for 3,000 able-bodied men, but official sources know nothing of the matter. Nevertheless, the ghetto is even more agitated than before.

SKETCHES OF GHETTO LIFE: "OFF TO CZARNIECKI [STREET]"

The slogan is: "Off to Czarniecki Street [that is, Central Prison]!" Every transport has a quota of 700 people. And since this quota is difficult to fill in the normal way, a stern hand must assist. If the bread basket is hung higher, a person simply starts yearning for the soup on Czarniecki [Street]. And if you actually manage to resist this yearning, then a stern hand will pull you out of bed at night and drag you off to the staging area.

One should sketch for all time the figures that could be seen in the ghetto's streets on their way to Central Prison during the days of the five transports: figures with bundles on their bent backs, suitcases and handbags on their feeble shoulders, children and the aged trotting side by side, drenched with sweat . . . figures like those depicted by Dostoevsky and other Russian writers. But, amid all these people, behind them, since she cannot keep pace, there is a woman: loose strands of gray hair partly concealed under a brightly colored kerchief fall over her temples down to her shoulders; instead of a dress, a tattered fur vest to which a girl's short skirt of coarse linen is attached; feet so swollen that they can barely squeeze into the almost heelless shoes; bundles large and small in her hands; on the left shoulder a patchwork knapsack; a soup bowl and a *menaschka* [mess kit] dangling around the thighs. The old woman's back is so bent that her weathered face and toothless mouth become visible only when she supports herself against a building wall. She stumbles more than walks. The ghetto pavement doesn't permit an even stride. This old woman too is a candidate for "labor outside the ghetto." She too will work on a reconstruction project somewhere on the outside. She too must go. For she is all alone. People without families are favored for the transports. She has lost her husband, children, and close relatives and is by herself. A lonely woman hobbles toward Czarniecki Street. . . . The day is lovely, warm. The misfortune of being alone is rewarded with the good fortune of being allowed to depart for labor outside the ghetto.

O[skar] R[osenfeld]

FRIDAY, JULY 7, 1944

NEWS OF THE DAY: LABOR OUTSIDE THE GHETTO

Early this morning Transport VII left the ghetto with 700 people. The accompanying physician was Dr. Hugo Natannsen, originally from Hamburg but resettled to this ghetto from Prague. His wife and daughter left with him.

At the same time, twenty selected men were dispatched by Bałut Market to cut peat, replacing the workers who returned yesterday.

There is a persistent rumor that 2,000 men apart from the currently resettled are required in Cracow. Officials have no such information. Someone has probably added two zeroes to the twenty men sent to cut peat. There are still people to whom the ghetto's panic does not seem great enough.

SKETCHES OF GHETTO LIFE: A FAMILY DRAMA

R. M., 46 years of age, volunteered for labor outside the ghetto in May, 1944. He had no idea he was headed for the peat bogs—heavy labor. He was glad to hear that the food rations were much better on the outside and even heavy labor was therefore relatively easy to bear. All this he gathered from rumors, which are the sole source of information in the ghetto.

Hunger drove him to abandon his wife and 17-year-old son, and seek his fortune beyond the barbed wire; the only fortune that he could think of desiring was to eat his fill just once.

Then came the new resettlement in June. His wife and boy are not on any list for the moment. They're deluged with offers. After all, a substitute receives three loaves of bread, making a total of six [in their case]. The thought of such wealth makes their heads spin. Inconceivable that one might eat one's fill again. Margarine, sugar, perhaps marmalade, and God knows what else. The sheer thought of such food allays the terrors of resettlement. Furthermore, the father is no longer here anyway, and there is little hope of ever seeing him again in the ghetto.

The temptation is too great. The two go and volunteer. They report on the morning of July 6 and receive the ransom in the form of bread, margarine, sugar, and other things.

They go on a food binge in Central Prison. Oh, to eat your fill! The stomach doesn't accept very much, it's soon full. And once the stomach is full, the mind sobers up. You get to thinking: What have you done? But no retrospective wondering can help you. It's easy to get into Central Prison, but you can't get back out.

Suddenly, fourteen men are brought in. They come from Gąbin [Warsaw province] where they've been cutting peat. They look wretched; you don't recognize them. Nevertheless, the wife and son do recognize one of the returning men. The father is back, and the wife and son have volunteered as substitutes. A desperate situation. The commission's grasp is firm; it doesn't release people very easily, people whom it needs, and especially volunteers, who pose no problems.

Now the hunt is on for friends in high places. They move heaven and earth, for the wife wishes to remain with the son.

Not too much of the bread has been eaten; they'll replace it somehow. Release is practically out of the question. Where are the committee members who can sympathize with their situation and grant a delay? How will the drama end? Life writes more cruelly than the most cold-blooded playwright.

We can only follow the case. Let us see what develops.

SATURDAY, JULY 8, 1944

NEWS OF THE DAY

Labor outside the Ghetto

The commission at Central Prison is coping with its precarious situation by means of nighttime raids. More and more people are in hiding. There are almost no volunteers now. A completely unsubstantiated rumor, namely that the entire operation will be terminated in the next few hours, continues to be fed by God knows what sources.

Nighttime roundups are always the same. We have described them often enough.

Metal factories I and II, wood factories I, II, and IV, and drycleaning and laundry facility I have been exempted from compiling lists. These plants continue to receive a steady stream of relatively large assignments from the military.

Relocation

Tenants of the residential block from 2 Podrzeczna Street to 14 Stodolniana Street, as well as those of 18–28 Drewnowska Street, began to be evicted yesterday. As of today, these properties are at the disposal of the Demolition Department. The area must be cleared of occupants by tomorrow.

Order Service Precinct II has been instructed to search the blocks about to be demolished, to clean them out if necessary, and to have the ghetto fence moved to the new borders without delay.

SKETCHES OF GHETTO LIFE: A FAMILY DRAMA

After returning to a cheerless reunion with his wife and son, the father has taken to his bed in the hospital on Dworska Street. The Chairman provides for such totally run-down people. He visits them and inquires as to their wishes. This man has a wish too: "I've got a son in Central Prison." He doesn't admit that his son volunteered as a substitute and was remunerated. But then, why should he admit it? Under the circumstances, the bargain that was struck can no longer be considered valid, since it was made on completely different premises. The Chairman makes a note of the case and, indeed, the boy is placed on reserve. A lanky 17-year-old, an obvious candidate for tuberculosis. So, for the time being, he remains in Central Prison; the mother is released, leaving her son behind as a hostage.

Everything will depend on how much longer the transports must continue. But now there is a glimmer of hope. Perhaps the family will stay together.

MONDAY, JULY 10, 1944

NEWS OF THE DAY

Labor outside the Ghetto
Today, Transport VIII, under the leadership of the physician Dr. Felix Proskauer (Berlin), left the ghetto with 700 people. The dispatch took place as usual, without incident.

Today's transport was composed of 202 men and 498 women, a very small percentage of them resettled from Western Europe.

PEOPLE ARE SAYING

that the food supply will improve substantially in the next few days. In particular, it is said that about fifty freight cars of potatoes will be coming in. The Department of Vegetables confirms that fairly large quantities of potatoes have been promised, but it is very skeptical about actual delivery; [and] that relatively large quantities of fresh vegetables are also expected to arrive here. This rumor is probably based on natural circumstances. The season is well advanced by now, so why shouldn't sizable quantities of vegetables be arriving? Besides, whenever the ghetto is made to suffer severely from resettlements, the food supply improves.

WEDNESDAY, JULY 12, 1944

NEWS OF THE DAY

Labor outside the Ghetto
This morning Transport IX left the ghetto. No physician accompanied it. The designated physician, Dr. Grödel of Cologne, was called back at the last minute and will presumably go with the next transport. Again, 700 people have departed, bringing the current total to 6,496.

The situation grows tenser by the minute because the commission is no longer able to supply the required human resources. The Chairman has therefore resolved to take drastic measures. People are being rounded up in nighttime raids. Units of the Order Service receive lists, drag people out of bed, concentrate them in the precinct houses, and then deliver them to the Central Prison during the day.

Efforts By Dr. Singer and Dr. Bondy
This morning Dr. [Oskar] Singer summoned the people who had been recommended for exemption and were to see the Chairman later. Dr. Singer prepared them for their forthcoming screening by the Chairman. At 6 P.M. the approximately seventy people arrived at the Bureau of Labor.

The Chairman began with a brief talk and explained that he is in a difficult situation. "I am battered by two hammers," he said, "one on my heart, the other on my brain. My heart refuses to grant what my mind demands, and yet the difficult problem must be resolved. I realize that I must show some special consideration, and I will do so to the best of my ability."

Then the Chairman interviewed each person on the list and dealt with each case on an individual basis. He granted exemptions in all cases but one: a woman who had concealed the fact that she had been called up several days ago. Two of the cases were urgent, since the individuals involved were already at Central Prison. The Chairman settled both cases personally by phoning Central Prison during the afternoon.

The Chairman thus showed full sympathy for the few remaining resettled of particular merit, or of whom certain achievements can be expected in the future.

Although the initiative came from Dr. Oskar Singer, the enterprise was primarily carried out by [Henryk] Neftalin, the attorney, and Commander [Zygmunt] Reingold.

SKETCHES OF GHETTO LIFE: A FAMILY DRAMA (continued)

Meanwhile, the boy has been stuffing himself to capacity. After all, he did volunteer, and he is fully entitled to the purchase price. He hopes to leave Central Prison invigorated and completely recovered. But the excessive eating seems not to have agreed with him; he falls ill. He is released from Central Prison and his mother nurses him at home. Now he is in bed, utterly exhausted and with a high fever. He is alone; his mother rushes from one physician to another, trying to pull strings wherever she can. There is a suspicion of typhoid fever . . .

The father is still in the hospital. Let us hope, let us hope . . .

O[skar] S[inger]

THURSDAY, JULY 13, 1944

NEWS OF THE DAY

A Commission in the Ghetto
An SS commission is now visiting some factories in the ghetto.

A Midday Raid
There is now a new method for catching people who failed to report. Experience teaches that the [resettlement] dodgers hide out only by night; during the day they actually go to work and move about the streets. How do you apprehend such people? It's as simple as can be. Order Service men patrol a street, suddenly cordon it off, and all the people they can lay their hands on are herded together at a given point. These people have to produce their papers. But no one questions them on the spot. The formalities can be attended to only at the precinct house. Occasionally, someone manages to get released fairly quickly if he has good connections; otherwise, the

procedure lasts until late in the evening. The yield is very meager. Those who are truly endangered have gotten wind of this development and keep to their hideouts by day as well.

A shameful, shocking street scene. Jews hunting other Jews like game. A real Jew-hunt, organized by Jews. But what is to be done; there is no choice. Anyone who is called up must report. If he is then exempted, all well and good. If he is not exempted, then he has to go. Such is the harsh law of the hour.

SKETCHES OF GHETTO LIFE: TERROR IN THE STREETS

Whenever an operation *in* the ghetto has the purpose of dispatching people *out of* the ghetto, the result is tension, conflict, tragedy. The ghetto's appearance changes; even the streets look different.

The transports of July, 1944, grew more and more frequent. People refused to report, vaguely hoping that the whole affair would "soon come to an end"—to report to Central Prison was viewed as sheer frivolity.

Then came the 13th of July, the Thursday before the Friday on which a new transport was scheduled. As always, people were trudging through the streets to the kitchens, to the workshops and departments, when—as if out of nowhere—Order Service men burst in on them from right and left, herding together everyone who happened to be present.

"Close the gateway!" shouted several of the Order Service men, clutching the gate that led to a [soup] kitchen. The crowd was jammed in behind the passage.

"What's wrong? Let us out! We have to carry our soup home!" screamed the women in disorderly chorus. They received no answer.

The hunt went on. Anyone out in the streets was in danger of falling into the pursuers' clutches.

Everyone was scared to death. People were herded together. Guarded in front and in back by policemen, they were marched to the precinct houses and screened. Weary hours passed, until it became late afternoon.

"Don't go out in the street. You'll be caught!" one person warned the next.

The ghetto was paralyzed. Limbs went slack; throats were tight with relentless panic. The ghetto had never experienced a raid like that in the four years it has been in existence.

The agitation subsided only toward 5 P.M., when the workshop doors opened, spewing people out into the street.

July 13, 1944, was a day of terror. The catch was meager. Fewer than fifty persons were captured for the transports.

"We have learned something from our guards after all," said a ghetto philosopher: "How to hunt human beings."

O[skar] R[osenfeld]

FRIDAY, JULY 14, 1944

NEWS OF THE DAY

Labor outside the Ghetto
This morning Transport X left the ghetto with another 700 people. The accompanying physician was Dr. Grödel (of Cologne).

Last night, the raids in search of resettlement dodgers continued, for the reserve at Central Prison is very small.

With today's transport, the ghetto has so far yielded a total of 7,196 persons. The difficulties increase with every passing day. The workshops maintain a tight grip on their good personnel, and the departments refuse to surrender their resources of young people because they cannot function with older people. The Chairman has been drumming it into the managers that, in the present situation, they must surrender even skilled workers—indeed, instructors as well—but he is getting nowhere. Moreover, every stop has been pulled on the grand organ of favoritism. The ghetto faces some extremely difficult hours, for this resettlement now strikes at its heart, so to speak: at its best and most valuable human resources. It cannot be repeated often enough that, of course, with the current method of allowing one person to dispatch another, only those are sacrificed who cannot fend for themselves, who do not belong to so-called society, though very many of them, naturally, are valuable individuals. But the same rule applies in the ghetto as on the outside: the strong devour the weak. Someone has to go: 700 people in each transport. Those at the helm are not going to send out their own flesh and blood; so here too, fate depends on the market. This is the naked fact of the matter.

Whether those who leave or those who stay here have drawn the better lot is not the issue here. But we may note marginally that the consensus of opinion is that the travelers are not headed for any dire fate; they are definitely expected to be employed as laborers and treated humanely. That is why the Chairman demands that only the truly healthy and able-bodied be dispatched.

SATURDAY, JULY 15, 1944

NEWS OF THE DAY

Joy in the Ghetto
Never has the ghetto been so happy. Today toward noon, the Eldest was instructed to halt the resettlement.[23] The Chairman himself immediately telephoned the [Department of Ration] Cards office and ordered a reinstatement of all ration cards. Then he raced through town in his droshky, from workshop to workshop and to Central Prison.

People embraced in the streets, kissed in the workshops and departments: "The resettlement's over!"

No one gave a second thought to whether this was only a brief interruption of or a final halt to the transports. One thing is certain: no transport is being readied for Monday. The ghetto has lost the habit of thinking more than a few hours ahead. At first, people refused to believe the news. After so much sorrow, one is reluctant to believe good tidings. Gradually, however, the ghetto is gaining confidence that the

23. This was only an interruption in the action to liquidate the Łódź ghetto. The reason was the sudden dissolution of the death camp in Chełmno (Kulmhof) on July 14, 1944, done out of fear that the camp might fall into the hands of the Red Army as a result of its rapid progress during the summer offensive which was bringing it closer to the borders of the Generalgouvernement.

situation is as reported, and one can imagine people's sense of relief. By afternoon, one saw the first group to be released from Central Prison and the staging areas moving through the streets with their baggage, returning to their apartments. Most of these apartments, though, are just four bare walls, for all belongings were sold off as fast as possible. No beds, no chairs, no cabinets. They'll have to sleep on the floor, but once again they'll manage. The ghetto dweller is like a cat, he always lands on his feet; he can cope with anything. The Main Purchasing Agency will probably return everything. The Chairman will undoubtedly see to it that those returning from Central Prison and the staging areas receive assistance.

The commission in Central Prison and the Inter-workshop Committee have nothing left to do but their final accounting. In Central Prison there are probably some who regret the sudden termination. After all, they were living it up, eating their fill on the misfortunes of others. But the ghetto ignores the disappointment of these few persons. All in all, a day of joy such as the ghetto has never known.

Toward 6:30 A.M. traffic was blocked at the two gates of Łagiewnicka Street. At 7 A.M. a procession of approximately 1,000 Russian prisoners of war who are employed in some prison camp near Litzmannstadt marched down Łagiewnicka Street. Toward 2:30 the same procession returned in the opposite direction.

MONDAY, JULY 17, 1944

A FIRE

At 1:10 P.M. on July 16, 1944, the Fire Department was called to 18 Tokarzewski Street, where a short circuit caused by lightning set a telephone installation ablaze. The fire was extinguished.

A SHOOTING AT THE BARBED WIRE

On July 17, 1944, Mindla Zarzewska, born June 22, 1910, and residing at 15 Podrzeczna Street, was shot and killed between 6:30 and 7 A.M. at the barbed-wire fence near the corner of Drewnowska Street and Hermann Göringstrasse [Stodolniana, Zachodnia, and Kościuszki, interconnected streets renamed for the Nazi marshall] outside the ghetto.

NEWS OF THE DAY

A Death

Last night, the well-known and respected nerve specialist, Dr. Fabian Klozenberg, 68, died of paratyphoid fever after a long illness.

After completing his medical studies in Warsaw in 1899, Dr. Klozenberg settled in Łódź as a neurologist. Immediately upon the establishment of the ghetto, the Chairman appointed him medical superintendent and chief surgeon of Hospital No. 1; and he simultaneously served as consultant to Hospitals No. 2, 3, and 4. Later, he also worked at Outpatient Clinics III and VI.

Because of his extraordinary position as a physician and in society, the Chairman appointed him to the Council of the Department of Health.

Dr. Klozenberg was practicing as a nerve specialist right up to the time of his illness. All efforts to save him after the serious infection that led to paratyphoid fever proved futile. Attendance at the funeral was commensurate with his popularity and therefore extremely large. Eulogies were delivered by the Chairman, the deputy chief of the Department of Health, Dr. [Ignacy] Weinberg, and Dr. [Ludwig] Falk. In addition to medical colleagues, the congregation included representatives of the workshops, headed by A[ron] Jakubowicz as director of all workshops, and Dr. [Wiktor] Miller as representative of the Department of Health.

The deceased leaves a wife, a daughter, and a granddaughter.

O[skar] R[osenfeld]

NEWS OF THE DAY

A Meeting At Bałut Market: Panic Again

[Henryk] Neftalin, the attorney, was summoned to Bałut Market where, after a brief discussion with A[ron] Jakubowicz, he was ordered by Amtsleiter Biebow to draw up a statistical survey of the ghetto population according to sex and age and to submit it by noon on Wednesday the 19th of this month. Biebow also asked Neftalin for data on [non]able-bodied workers by year of birth. Since Neftalin has no records from which to prepare such data, he was unable to fulfill the Amtsleiter's request. Biebow acknowledged this with a remark that he would obtain the data from the Department of Health. It is unlikely, though, that even the Department of Health can provide reliable statistical data on this matter, for it does not keep records of persons unfit for labor.

In his meeting with Neftalin, Biebow emphasized that the data was requested by the Secret State Police [Gestapo], and he, therefore, emphasized the deadline for submission.

The mere fact that Neftalin was summoned by the Amtsleiter and that a discussion of population statistics reportedly took place has once again terrified the ghetto, which is teeming with rumors about the purpose of the required statistical information.

SKETCHES OF GHETTO LIFE: A CRASH ON THE BLACK MARKET

The halting of the resettlement action has totally upset food prices in illicit trade. In the critical days, bread (the ghetto's hard currency) cost 1,400 marks a loaf, soup (the small change), 30 to 38 marks, botwinki [beet leaves], 70 marks a kilogram, etc. Aside from food, nothing else could be marketed except for travel gear such as knapsacks and suitcases. But the termination of the transports has changed everything with a single stroke. Bread is now offered for sale at 700 marks; soup costs 15 marks and less, botwinki go for 45 to 50 marks a kilogram. The reason for this plunge in prices is obvious: those scheduled for resettlement are no longer forced to dispose of their last belongings at any price, which, in any case, they could take with them; and people whose ration cards were suspended are no longer forced to sell the shirts off their backs in order to save their skins. The shepherds have once again shorn the lambs, and many wallets are hidden away, swollen with ghetto marks.

P[eter] W[ertheimer]

TUESDAY, JULY 18, 1944

NEWS OF THE DAY

The Chairman continues to reorganize the factories, and today he reviewed the remaining workers of the hat workshop. Tomorrow he will probably deal with the slipper workshop.

The registration and statistics departments are working on Amtsleiter Biebow's request for a population survey by age and sex. The information will be submitted to him on schedule. It is not yet known whether the Department of Health can supply figures on persons unfit for labor.

Amtsleiter Biebow at the Special Department

Toward 7 P.M., Amtsleiter Biebow appeared in his car at the Special Department just as the distribution of packages was about to begin. He had a long discussion with M[arek] Kligier, the subject of which is not known.

Those who had gathered in the troop room to receive their packages were sent home. The packages will be handed out tomorrow.

The Mood in the Ghetto

The request for statistical data and the Amtsleiter's meeting today with [Marek] Kligier are the subject of lively discussion in the ghetto. Guesswork and anxiety are rife. Ghetto officials believe that there are no grounds for grave concern; presumably Biebow merely wishes to have precise data about the ghetto population on hand. Others who are more pessimistically inclined believe that certain preliminaries are under way for a future resettlement action. But here, too, one may apply the *bon mot* by Commissioner Sutter of the Kripo, which is much quoted in the ghetto: "Rumkowski won't fill your belly, and the Germans give you a belly full."

Actually, such data has always been available in the Department of Statistics and had merely to be updated after the resettlements of the past few days; but given the constant nervous anxiety of the ghetto populace, it is understandable that the work now being done in the Statistics Department gives rise to the most diverse rumors. People talk of lists that are being compiled; and no sooner do they hear the word "list" than they jump to the conclusion that workshops must also submit new lists. There is not a word of truth in any of this.

SKETCHES OF GHETTO LIFE: A BIZARRE SUICIDE [*SELBSTMORD DURCH PFLICHTMORD*]
(See our report of July 17, 1944)

Over the years, those weary of life have used the latest in technology in order to have done with their lives. Probably the most modern way of doing this is to let oneself be shot by someone duty-bound to do so. We have already recorded such suicides in the ghetto; they're called simply "suicides at the barbed wire." In the ghetto you don't have to hang yourself or jump to the pavement from a fourth-floor window, cut your wrists, or poison yourself with large doses of a sleep-inducing drug. You can't drown yourself, because there is no deep water in the ghetto. The easiest and most painless method is to force the policeman on duty to do the job. In the first days of the ghetto this was very simple. All you had to do was approach the barbed wire and look as if you were about to cross it—and immediately, the liberating shot was fired.

In the current instance, however, Mindla Zarzewska, who was tired of life, encountered some difficulties. She came within sight of the policeman nearest the fence at the corner of Drewnowska Street and Hermann Göringstrasse and showed that she intended to climb over the barbed-wire fence. The Schupo [Schutzpolizei man] hurried over and tried to reprimand her. A mature, sensible reserve policeman, and by no means trigger-happy, he tried to reason with her, make her understand the danger she was in. But she refused to be turned back. At that moment, an inspecting officer of the police force happened to appear. But he couldn't deter the woman either; she climbed across the fence. The regulation is strict: "Anyone who crosses the barbed wire will be shot to death!" And so the shot rang out. A woman weary of life had been granted her wish.

Is this murder, cruelty? No; perhaps the appropriate term is "murder in the line of duty."

O[skar] S[inger]

WEDNESDAY, JULY 19, 1944

NEWS OF THE DAY

The ghetto continues to be nervous. People can't keep their minds off the statistical survey that is to be submitted today, and the public is not kept informed of what is demanded and submitted. There is still talk of registrations and lists.

The agitation increased around noon, when Miss [Dora] Fuchs drove up to 4 Kościelny Square in the Amtsleiter's car in order to pick up [Henryk] Neftalin, the attorney. Two sensational developments at once: Miss Fuchs to fetch Neftalin—and in Biebow's car. What was going on?

The Amtsleiter was about to drive to the city on urgent business, but first he demanded a change in the statistical report that had already been handed in, a change pertaining to the number of people unfit for labor, estimated at 7,000. Since a droshky would not have been fast enough, Biebow sent Miss Fuchs on the errand by car.

Neftalin proceeded to Bałut Market, took care of the matter, and that was all.

Furthermore, Biebow ordered Neftalin to present the figures on children nine years of age and under according to year of birth rather than in one category.

FRIDAY, JULY 21, 1944

SUICIDES

On July 20, 1944, Łaja Dimant, 63 Drewnowska Street, born May 27, 1921, in Łódź, committed suicide by jumping from the fourth story.

On July 21, 1944, Chaja Sura Klajn, born April 9, 1922, in Łask, and residing at 21

Tokarzewski Street, attempted suicide by jumping from the second story. She was taken to the hospital.

NEWS OF THE DAY

The day passed calmly despite the many rumors now circulating, especially about the outside world.

The Chairman continued his work today by visiting various factories and reviewing the personnel.

In connection with the reduction of internal departments, several food distribution points were supposed to be liquidated. Considering the probable insignificance of the yield, however, the Chairman has decided to let things stand as they are for the time being.

Pharmacy Inspector Perelmutter Removed from Office
By order of the German authorities, Perelmutter has been removed from his position as inspector of pharmacies. S. Kon has been appointed commissioner of the Medicine Depot. Kon is the former owner and present manager of the pharmacy on Kościelny Square.

The Chairman has ordered circulation of the already minted 20-mark coins. The proclamation reads as follows:

Proclamation
Re: Introduction of Specie Currency (Twenty-Mark Coins).

The ghetto populace is hereby informed that as of today, July 21, 1944, coins in the denomination of twenty marks are being put into circulation.

The old twenty-mark bills will retain their validity along with the new twenty-mark coins.

Litzmannstadt-Getto,   Ch[aim] Rumkowski
21 July 1944   The Eldest of the Jews in Litzmannstadt

SATURDAY, JULY 22, 1944

NEWS OF THE DAY

The problem of restructuring has been shelved, as it were, because of the general situation. Apparently, the restructuring cannot be carried out as radically as the Chairman intended. Also, it seems that the problem of those who work at home will not be resolved as radically as the Chairman announced in his last speech. In other words, one can note a certain relaxation, which is caused, no doubt, by the general world situation.

At this point, the chronicler cannot possibly ignore the events that ultimately concern the entire world and that, of course, are not without influence on the ghetto. Now and then, newspapers and other sources of information do penetrate into the ghetto. The times are certainly critical, and ghetto dwellers await the coming hours with mixed feelings.[24] All thoughts, considerations, hopes, and fears ultimately culminate in one main question: "Will we be left in peace?"

WORKSHOP NEWS

The workshops are all functioning normally. Production may even be increased. The Chairman's policy in these critical days is not to allow discipline to slacken under any circumstances, in order to avert danger for the ghetto.

Carpentry [workshop] I has received an assignment from the Ghetto Administration: to produce as fast as possible a large number of so-called Nat crates. These are supposedly freight crates for the employees of the Ghetto Administration at Bałut Market.

Hand Knitwear

This factory is once more giving out work to be done at home. The job in question again consists of making net bags from pulp yarn. These bags serve as containers for disinfecting the linen of soldiers.

SUNDAY, JULY 23, 1944

NEWS OF THE DAY

The day passed in calm. The populace takes every opportunity to enjoy the open air in Marysin, where the dignitaries have once again established their summer residences.

The mood in the ghetto is rosy. Everyone is hopeful of a speedy end to the war. Nevertheless, people are calm; and we hope they remain so.

SKETCHES OF GHETTO LIFE: "CABBAGE, CABBAGE!"

"No vegetables delivered for weeks, not to mention potatoes!" You could hear these words throughout the ghetto. Almost no one could escape such thoughts . . . until people suddenly started whispering: "Cabbage is due in; 'white cabbage' is the official term—large quantities. We're going to eat. There'll be something to put in our pots again and to fill our stomachs with . . ."

And sure enough, cabbage came in. Wagons and trucks filled with cabbage rolled through the streets from Bałut Market to the vegetable storage lots, and from there to the cooperatives. Cabbage arrived continually from the city. The pale green heads gleamed in the summer sun. Whenever you walked through the ghetto, you saw the wagons rolling through the streets: in front the driver with his expressionless face, in back the Order Service man, oppressed by his great responsibility as a guard.

"Still more cabbage being delivered . . ."

"I've counted ten wagons already . . ."

24. This is an obvious allusion to the events on the Eastern front and in particular to the Soviet-backed Polish government (The Polish Committee of National Liberation) which was formed on July 21, 1944, in the USSR, and was concurrent with the liberation of the city of Chelm Lubelski the next day by the Red Army.

"At least 200,000 kilograms by now . . ."

"A nice ration!"

"So far, it's for the public kitchens. There'll be cabbage soup in the kitchens for the next few weeks."

"A change! Thank God!"

Cabbage soup—every day. Some people had cabbage soup three times every day. Cabbage soup became the chief food for 60,000 people. And there were also the cabbage rations: one kilogram cabbage, five kilograms, [then] five kilograms [again]; cabbage, cabbage, cabbage! People made cabbage soup at home, too. The ghetto wallowed in cabbage. The ghetto reeked of cabbage.

Eventually, people grew sick of cabbage. The price of cabbage soup dropped from twenty-five to five marks. People longed for the grain soup, the so-called *kley* soup, which is made of flour and groats. A yearning unsatisfied! Cabbage kept rolling into the ghetto. Water-bloated bellies expanded. Stomachs revolted. Nor were the intestines any better off. Diarrhea set in. Nausea was a common symptom. Every second ghetto dweller suffered in some way from overindulgence in cabbage. People drank the cabbage soup by day and passed it spasmodically by night. It was hard to get a night's sleep.

Finally, we heard that potatoes were about to arrive, large quantities of potatoes, enough to supply the [soup] kitchens, when suddenly—cabbage came rolling into the ghetto again. Naturally, everyone was sick of cabbage; even the little man began selling his cabbage rations. And then, all at once, a mood arose that cannot be put into words because it cannot be traced back to any tangible event. Be that as it may, the last week of July, 1944, proves that psychological factors can override any physical ill. The last week of July in the ghetto year, 1944, was dominated by the hope that the Eternal, Praised be His Name, would liberate the ghetto from cabbage soup, *mehayro veyomaynu* [soon, in our days] . . .

O[skar] R[osenfeld]

MONDAY, JULY 24, 1944

NEWS OF THE DAY

Commander [Leon] Rozenblat was ordered by the Kripo to make 200 Order Service men available. This squad is to be presented at Marysin cemetery tomorrow at 4 A.M. Rozenblat was assured that the men would be returned to his authority by 8 A.M. The purpose of the squad is not known.

PUBLIC HEALTH

The cases of contagious disease reported today: tuberculosis, 33.

The causes of today's deaths: Tuberculosis of the lungs, 21; infiltration of the lungs, 1; heart diseases, 10; colitis, 1; cirrhosis of the kidney, 1; cerebral contusion (accident), 1; stillbirth, 1.

TUESDAY JULY 25, 1944

NEWS OF THE DAY

This afternoon the Chairman visited the registration and statistics departments, where he held a rather long meeting with chief director [Henryk] Neftalin, the attorney, [S.] Erlich, director of the Statistics Department, and Dr. O[skar] Singer, director of the Archives. The Chairman inspected current projects, in particular, an ambitious and handsomely mounted exhibit on social welfare, under the auspices of the Statistics Department.

Suitcases for the [German] Criminal Police
Today the criminal police removed several empty suitcases from the Main Purchasing Agency.

A Permanent Blackout
From now on the blackout will be constant, regardless of whether there is an air raid. Early warnings have been transmitted almost daily for the past few days. So far, Litzmannstadt has never experienced a real air-raid alarm.

GLAD TIDINGS FOR THE GHETTO: POSTCARDS FROM LEIPZIG

The ghetto has received its first messages from people who left to perform manual labor outside the ghetto in the recent resettlement. Thirty-one postcards have arrived, all of them postmarked July 19, 1944. Fortunately, it is apparent from these cards that people are faring well and, what is more, that families have stayed together. Here and there, a card mentions good rations. One card addressed to a kitchen manager says in plain Yiddish: "Mir lakhn fun ayre zupn!" [We laugh at your soups!][25]

The ghetto is elated and hopes that similar reports will soon be arriving from all the other resettled workers. It appears to be confirmed that labor brigades are truly required in the Old Reich.

It should be recalled that before the departure of Transport I there was mention of Munich as its destination. One group may well have gone there too.

It is also worth noting that the postcards indicate that our people are housed in comfortable barracks.

THURSDAY, JULY 27, 1944

WORKSHOP NEWS

The Corset and Brassiere Sewing Workshop
([Manager:] Gonik) has been ordered to prepare all as yet unfinished goods for shipment. The German originator of the order is moving his ghetto stocks back into the Reich.

---

25. All these "postcards from Leipzig," as well as the "news" from those deported to Munich "to perform manual labor" were either the result of coercion or were outright fakes.

The Clothing and Linen Department

has furthermore been ordered to place all special machinery that is not ghetto property at the disposal of clients. These machines too are being shipped out.

The Boot Department

has also been ordered to return all special machinery not owned by the ghetto.

SKETCHES OF GHETTO LIFE: A FAMILY DRAMA
(See our report of July 8, 1944 [cf. p. 522])

We had assumed that the story of the family was concluded. Fortune was gracious to these three people: the resettlement was interrupted; the father returned from the hospital. The ghetto seemed to have made its peace with them. They had been through a great deal, and we believed that they were safe. But the ghetto is cruel; it grips its victims in its rotting teeth.

The [son, an] unusually tall, intellectually gifted boy, died in the hospital today. Despite an operation, he succumbed to a festering intestinal blockage. His purchase price, which he must have devoured ravenously in the first few days, was what killed him. His frail organism could no longer endure such a large quantity of additional food. One promising life less, one unhappy pair of parents more.

The father had returned, only to find his wife and child in Central Prison, about to be resettled. He remained; the son departed, taking a different and longer road, from which there is no turning back. He has chosen the wrong road in the ghetto!

O[skar] S[inger]

SUNDAY, JULY 30, 1944[26]

WEATHER

Temperature range: 22–38 degrees; sunny, hot.

DEATHS

One.

BIRTHS

None.

ARRESTS

Miscellaneous, two.

---

26. The *Daily Chronicle Bulletin* for Sunday, July 30, 1944, which is given in its entirety here, is the last *Chronicle* entry to have been preserved and was most likely, in fact, the final entry. On the next day, Monday, it was already known that the fate of the Łódź ghetto had been sealed. The final *Daily Chronicle Bulletin*, that of July 30, 1944, listed 68,561 inhabitants in the ghetto of Łódź. They were deported to Auschwitz-Birkenau, with the exception of about 700 people whom the Gettoverwaltung selected to clean the ghetto after the deportations and some 200 who successfully avoided the deportation action by hiding, as well as about 500 men and women sent to Sachsenhausen-Oranienburg and Ravensbrück. The Jewish community of Łódź was brought to an end.

BROUGHT TO THE GHETTO

One (man from outside the ghetto).

TOTAL POPULATION
68,561.

NEWS OF THE DAY

Today, Sunday, also passed very calmly.

The Chairman held various meetings. But all in all, the ghetto is peaceful and orderly.

Łagiewnicka Street now has a different look. Traffic is extraordinarily lively. One can see the war gradually approaching Litzmannstadt. The ghetto dweller peers curiously at the motor vehicles of various service branches as they speed through; for him, though, the crucial question remains: "What is there to eat?"

FOOD SUPPLY

Today, Sunday, only 7,160 kilograms of potatoes, 46,210 kilograms of white cabbage, and 13,790 kilograms of kohlrabi arrived in the ghetto. No other food was delivered.

If no flour arrives tomorrow, Monday, then the situation will be extremely critical. It is claimed that flour supplies in the ghetto will suffice for barely two or three more days.

Potato Ration
As of today, one kilogram of early potatoes will be distributed at the food distribution points.

PUBLIC HEALTH

The cases of contagious disease reported today: none.
The cause of today's death: suicide, one.

APPENDIX. POLISH AND GERMAN STREET NAMES

Bałucki Rynek (Bałut Market)	Baluter Ring
Bartnicza	Imkerstrasse
Bazarowa	Basargasse
Berek Joselewicz	Brunnenstrasse
Bracka	Ewaldstrasse
Brudziński	Edmundstrasse
Brzezińska	Sulzfelderstrasse
Ceglana	Steinmetzgasse
Chłodna	Kühle Gasse
Chopina	Müllerstrasse
Ciemna	Dunkle Gasse
Ciesielska	Bleicheweg
Czarniecki	Czarniecki
Czarnkowska	Lutzowstrasse
Dekerta	Oskarstrasse
Dolna	Talweg
Drewnowska	Holzstrasse
Drukarska	Zimmerstrasse
Dworska	Matrosengasse
Dzika	Stolpergasse
Emilii Plater	Maxstrasse
Flisacka	Hausierergasse
Franciszkańska	Franzstrasse
Garbarska	Gerberstrasse
Generalska	Adm. Scheer
Gęsia	Gänsestrasse
Gibalski	Hilderbrandstrasse
Głowacki	Konradstrasse
Gnieźnieńska	Gnesenerstrasse
Goplańska	Buchbinderstrasse
Grabinka	Mehlstrasse
Hoża	Frohe Gasse
Hutnicza	Hüttenwinkel
Inflancka	Gärtnerstrasse
Jagiellońska	Bertholdstrasse
Jauresa	Wilhelmstrasse

Jerozolimska	Rubensstrasse
Jonscher	Bertramstrasse
Dr. Kaufman	Elisabetsstrasse
Kościelna	Kirchgasse
Koszykowa	Korngasse
Kowalska	Schmüdegasse
Dr. Koziołkiewicz	Idastrasse
Krawiecka	Schneidergasse
Krótka	Kurze Gasse
Krótko-Lwowska	Sackgasse
Krzyżowa	Kreuzstrasse
Lekarska	Krämergasse
Leśna	Waldstrasse
Lewa-Kielma	Ackerweg
Limanowski	Alexanderhofstrasse
Lotnicza	Blattbindergasse
Lutomierska	Hamburgerstrasse
Lwowska	Braune Gasse
Łagiewnicka	Hanseatenstrasse
Majowa	Maienstrasse
Malarska	Malerstrasse
Marynarska	Kelmstrasse
Marysińska	Siegfriedstrasse
Masarska	Storchengasse
Mianowski	Bleigasse
Mickiewicz	Richterstrasse
Miernicza	Glöcknergasse
Miodowa	Honigweg
Młynarska	Mühlgasse
Modra	Blaue Gasse
Moskulska	Paulstrasse
Mostowski	Roderichstrasse
Mroczna	Nebengasse
Nad Łódką	Tizianstrasse
Niecała	Halbe Gasse
Niemojewski	Waldemarstrasse
Nowomiejska	Neustadtstrasse
Oblęgorska	Leiblstrasse
Oficerska	Fähnrichstrasse
Okopowa	Buchdruckergasse
Oszmiańska	Isoldenstrasse
Otylia	Ottilienstrasse
Pasterska	Hirtenweg
Pawia	Plauerstrasse
Pieprzowa	Pfeffergasse
Piłsudski	Oststrasse
Piwna	Bierstrasse
Plac Kościelny (Kościelny Square)	Kirchplatz
Podrzeczna	Am Bach
Podwórzowa	Hofgasse

Północna	Nordstrasse
Próżna	Leere Gasse
Przelotna	Richardstrasse
Przemysłowa	Gewerbestrasse
Pucka	Putzigerstrasse
Rawicka	Tirpitzstrasse
Roberta	Robertstrasse
Rozwadowski	Udostrasse
Rybna	Fischstrasse
Rymarska	Riemerstrasse
Smugowa	Veit-Stoss-Strasse
Sołtysówka	Schutzenstrasse
Spacerowa	Reigergasse
Starosikawska	Krimhildstrasse
Stary Rynek (Old Market)	Alt Markt
Staszic	Hertastrasse
Stefana	Wirkergasse
Dr. Sterling	Robert-Koch-Strasse
Stodolniana	Scheunenstrasse
Sukiennicza	Kachlergasse
Szeroka	Breite Gasse
Szklana	Trödlergasse
Ślusarska	Schlosserstrasse
Środkowa	Winfriedstrasse
Św. Jakuba (Saint Jacob)	Rembrandtstrasse
Św. Wincentego (Saint Vincent)	Runde Gasse
Tokarzewski	Goldschmiedegasse
Towiański	Blechgasse
Urzędnicza	Reiterstrasse
Wawelska	Sattergasse
Wesoła	Lustige Gasse
Widok	Rungestrasse
Wolborska	Rauchgasse
Wróbla	Sperlinggasse
Wrocławska	Sudetenstrasse
Wrześnieńska	Königsbergerstrasse
Zagajnikowa	Bernhardstrasse
Zawisza Czarny	Inselstrasse
Zbożowa	Bretgasse
Zgierska	Hohensteinerstrasse
Zielna	Krautergasse
Zofii	Sophienstrasse
Źródłowa	Am Quell
Żabia	Froschweg
Żurawia	Kranichweg
Żydowska (Jewish)	Cranachstrasse
Żytnia	Korngasse

INDEX